American Foreign Policy

FOURTH EDITION

American Foreign Policy

Pattern and Process

FOURTH EDITION

Charles W. Kegley, Jr.
University of South Carolina

Eugene R. Wittkopf
Louisiana State University

St. Martin's Press, New York

Senior editor: Don Reisman
Project management: Gene Crofts
Text design: Gene Crofts
Graphics: Jeane E. Norton
Cover design: Electric Pencil Studio

Library of Congress Catalog Card Number: 89-63944

Manufactured in the United States of America.

5 4   3   2   1
f e d c b a

For information, write:

St. Martin's Press, Inc.
175 Fifth Avenue
New York, NY 10010

ISBN: 0-312-03656-6

British Library of Congress Cataloguing in Publication Data
Kegley, Charles W. *1944–*
    American foreign policy : pattern and process.-4th. ed.
    1. United States. Foreign relations, history
    I. Title   II. Wittkopf, Eugene R. *1943–*
327.73

    ISBN 0-333-55550-3

Permissions Acknowledgments

Passages reprinted by permission of Atheneum Publisher, an imprint of Macmillan Publishing Company, from ROOTS OF WAR: THE MEN AND INTITUTIONS BEHIND U.S. FOREIGN POLICY by Richard J. Barnet. Copyright © 1972 by Richard J. Barnet.

Passages reprinted from Charles William Maynes' "America Without the Cold War," FOREIGN POLICY 78 (Spring 1990). Copyright © 1990 by Carnegie Endowment for International Peace, and used with permission.

Passages reprinted from James N. Rosenau's THE SCIENTIFIC STUDY OF FOREIGN POLICY. Copyright © 1980 by Nicholas Publishing Co., and used with permission.

Passages reprinted from John G. Stoessinger's CRUSADERS AND PRAGMATISTS: MOVERS OF MODERN AMERICAN FOREIGN POLICY. Copyright © 1985 by W. W. Norton & Company, Inc., and used with permission. Published by permission of Transaction Publishers from THE VIETNAM TRAUMA IN AMERICAN FOREIGN POLICY 1945–1975, by Paul Kattenburg. Copyright © 1980 by Transaction Publishers.

For Lisa and Barbara

Preface

Has American foreign policy changed since 1945? If so, how, and with what consequences? What are the sources of American foreign policy? Do these influences promote policy change or inhibit it? These are the principal questions we seek to answer in *American Foreign Policy: Pattern and Process.*

The years since publication of the first edition of this book in 1979 have been turbulent ones for the United States, and none more so than 1989 and 1990, when dramatic changes in the Soviet Union, in Europe, and in the relations between the United States and its Cold War adversary challenged the very premises on which American foreign policy has been based for nearly half a century and generated heated debate about how to respond to the new circumstances. Still, the conceptions that have guided American foreign policy for so long have proved to be remarkably durable as the legacy of the past continues to shape thinking about the future and the role of the United States in a post-Cold War world.

Because American foreign policy continues to exhibit remarkable continuity, the thesis of previous editions of this book—that both the ends of American foreign and the means through which policy makers have pursued them have become deeply entrenched patterns—remains a compelling interpretation. Indeed, time continues to deal generously with it, as the Carter, Reagan, and now Bush administrations have each reaffirmed the tenets underlying the pattern of post-World War II American foreign policy.

How does one account for such policy continuity? To probe this question, we continue in this edition of *American Foreign Policy: Pattern and Process* to utilize the pre-theoretical framework of the previous editions, which maintains that five factors—international, societal, governmental, role, and individual—collectively influence decisions about foreign policy objectives and the means chosen to realize them. The framework organizes examination of both the international and domestic sources of American action abroad, in order to probe the linkages between political institutions and decision-making processes, on the one hand, and policy outcomes on the other. The framework thus facilitates examination of the determinants of America's postwar diplomatic conduct and provides a basis for anticipating the future—a task more compelling today than ever.

Although the thematic thrust of the earlier editions has been preserved, numerous changes have been made in this edition. Readers familiar with previous editions of the book will quickly notice that the material in Chapters 4 and 5 has been rearranged to clearly distinguish military from the non-military instruments of foreign policy. We have also repositioned other topics and expanded or abridged our treatment of them, as necessary, to bring greater clarity to the presentation.

Substantively, the evidence has been thoroughly updated to account for developments and new scholarly insights. We have been particularly sensitive to the need to incorporate into our discussion of policy patterns and processes the changed and changing global environment of the 1990s and the efforts of the Bush administration to adjust America's external goals and instruments to a post–Cold War world. Although persistence and continuity continue to characterize American foreign policy, that theme should not blind us from recognizing that remedial adjustments have taken place. The invasion of Kuwait by Iraq in the summer of 1990 seems to have sidetracked the prospects that more fundamental reorientations in American foreign policy might occur, but throughout the book we have sought to be sensitive to those developments that work in favor of basic change as well as those that militate against it.

Many people have contributed to the development of this book as it has evolved from the late 1970s to the early 1990s. Special thanks for their contributions to the technical tasks associated with the production of this edition go to Gene Crofts, Steven W. Hook, Christina Payne, and Jonathan T. Wittkopf. We also express our appreciation to Don Reisman, our editor at St. Martin's Press, for his continued enthusiasm for our work and his constructive criticism of the book; and to our valued colleagues—Linda P. Brady, Dan Caldwell, Joe D. Hagan, and an anonymous referee—who reviewed the third edition of the book and made countless suggestions, large and small, for improvements in the fourth. We profited from their insights, even if we did not always heed their advice. Others who have made contributions to the various iterations of the book now number in the dozens. We thank you collectively. Our appreciation is in no way diminished by this general, albeit impersonal, expression of our gratitude.

Contents

Part VIII Pattern and Process in American Foreign Policy

15 The Sources of Continuity and Change in American
Foreign Policy: A Synthesis and Interpretation   527

16 Toward the Year 2000: The Bush Administration and
the Future of American Foreign Policy   544

References   561

Appendix   A Chronology of Selected Diplomatic Events,
1945–1990   593

Index   625

PART I

Analytical Perspectives on American Foreign Policy

CHAPTER 1

Continuity and Change in American Foreign Policy: A Thematic Introduction

I know of no change in policy, only of circumstances.
SECRETARY OF STATE JOHN QUINCY ADAMS, 1823

It is quite true that the central themes of American foreign policy are more or less constant. They derive from the kind of people we are . . . and from the shape of the world situation.
FORMER SECRETARY OF STATE DEAN RUSK, 1983

Throughout history, major wars have led to transformations of the international political system and to changes in the position of states within it. World War II, by far the most destructive and far-reaching global war in all of history, was no exception. The United States emerged from it with unparalleled capabilities. Shortly after the war British author Harold J. Laski described the new circumstances in world politics:

> America bestrides the world like a colossus; neither Rome at the height of its power nor Great Britain in the period of its economic supremacy enjoyed an influence so direct, so profound, or so pervasive. It has half the wealth of the world today in its hands, it has rather more than half of the world's productive capacity, and it exports more than twice as much as it imports. Today literally hundreds of millions of Europeans and Asiatics know that both the quality and the rhythm of their lives depend upon decisions made in Washington. On the wisdom of those decisions hangs the fate of the next generation. (Laski, 1947: 641)

From this advantageous position the leaders of the United States forged a new vision for the U.S. role in world affairs, predicated on assumptions about international politics derived from their experience in world war. A new foreign policy cloaked in internationalism emerged as the United States confidently approached the world with a clarity of vision and consistency of purpose.

Nearly fifty years have now elapsed since these assumptions were embraced. Global circumstances have changed substantially, culminating in 1989 in the most dramatic geopolitical changes in world order in the previous half-century. With the collapse of communism and erosion of the Soviet

3

Union's power, the postwar environment has been fundamentally altered. In addition, the supremacy of the United States also has been challenged. Its ability to influence others politically and militarily has eroded as new centers of power have emerged, and its position in and command over the international political economy have deteriorated.

But while the world has changed, the basic tenets of American foreign policy have not. On the contrary, perhaps the most distinctive feature of America's postwar approach to the world has been its remarkable continuity. Adaptations to changing international and domestic circumstances are discernible, but the same guiding principles and policy goals that were endorsed in the immediate aftermath of World War II have endured.

The theme of continuity pervades this entire book. It derives from our definition of foreign policy as the goals that U.S. officials[1] seek to attain abroad, the values that give rise to those objectives, and the means or instruments through which they are pursued. We will examine why continuity has characterized American goals and values since World War II, and why policy discontinuity (or, perhaps preferably, adaptation) has been largely confined to the tactics used to achieve these consistent goals. In other words, we posit that the goals or ends of American foreign policy have remained relatively constant compared with the more variable means employed to realize them. In order to achieve certain continuing goals in a changing environment, it has been necessary for the United States to modify methods. Tactics have changed; objectives have not.

Clearly, it would be misleading to exaggerate the contrast between an invariant foreign policy "vision" and changing policy instruments. More often than not, the means to policy ends have evolved slowly in response to changes in domestic and international circumstances rather than occurring in the absence of debate about its ends. Questioning of the conventional vision has been continual and consensus about ends and means fragile. Thus we cannot safely ascribe to American leaders universal agreement about the policies they engineered. Yet, despite their differences, it is useful to think of American foreign policy in terms of persistent goals and somewhat more variable tactics. To evaluate the response of the United States to unfolding global developments, an analytical perspective focusing on recurrent behavior rather than transient events is required.

PATTERNS IN AMERICAN FOREIGN POLICY

To the extent that consistencies over time are evident in foreign policy objectives, characteristic *patterns* in American foreign policy behavior may be found to exist. A policy pattern is a way of generalizing about and describing the over-

---

1. Although important, the transnational activities of U.S. nongovernmental actors abroad (for example, businesspeople) will not constitute a primary focus of our inquiry.

all thrust and direction of foreign policy. Such generalizations, however, do not necessarily describe accurately every foreign policy decision and the reasons behind it. Thus, when we make generalizations, we risk distorting history and committing occasional errors of interpretation. But what is gained by generalization is the ability to differentiate the common and perpetual from the infrequent and ephemeral.

To contend that American foreign policy has been "patterned" since 1945 does not require adoption of a deterministic logic that either denies the possibility of policy change or sees policy as necessarily paralyzed by the past. As we have suggested, American foreign policy *has* exhibited in important ways a capacity for adaptation to changing conditions. Consider, for example, the goal of the containment of the Soviet Union and the strategies used to achieve it. Containment has been one of the most enduring themes in postwar American foreign policy, yet even here we find variations in the ways it has been pursued. Under Harry S Truman, containment sought to inhibit the Soviet Union's participation and power in world affairs, while under Dwight D. Eisenhower brinkmanship or the threat of escalation to the brink of nuclear war was emphasized. "Competitive coexistence" was practiced under John F. Kennedy and Lyndon B. Johnson, who, as Soviet military capabilities increased, shifted to a strategy of deterrence known as *assured destruction*. Under Richard M. Nixon, Gerald R. Ford, and Jimmy Carter, détente became the watchword, with containment pursued by a "linkage" strategy tying rewards to cooperative Soviet behavior rather than through coercive diplomacy. Throughout most of his term in office, Ronald Reagan practiced a militantly confrontational approach toward the long-standing goal of containing Soviet expansionism, although a discernible move toward greater cooperation was evident during the latter part of his second term. Most recently, George Bush professed a desire to "move beyond containment," but he moved cautiously and with restraint without ever abandoning the goal of containing the Soviet Union's influence in world affairs. Thus, while the containment policy has evolved over time, its basic tenets and the centrality of its purpose have endured. To be sure, various metamorphoses have occurred, but the containment of the Soviet Union has remained one of the primary objectives of American foreign policy through nine successive administrations, despite extraordinary changes in the nation's foreign and domestic environments.

Today the external environment is undergoing the most dramatic changes of the postwar era. These changes—symbolized by the extraordinary transformations inside the Soviet Union, in Eastern Europe, and in Germany—pose a challenge to the abiding wisdom and relevance of the containment strategy; they raise important questions about the nation's ability to chart new directions that depart from previous policy thinking now that the Soviet threat has receded—or vanished. The continuing grip of the assumptions underlying containment on contemporary American foreign policy making and their resilience in the face of turbulent global changes underscores how resistent to change postwar thinking has become and remains.

The hypothesis that the basic underlying objectives and values of postwar American foreign policy have remained fundamentally unaltered, despite some significant evolutionary challenges and adaptations, prompts consideration of the reasons why. A new occupant of the Oval Office often seems to perceive himself, at least initially, to be devising an innovative policy leading to a new era in American foreign relations. In fact, though, meaningful departures from the established direction of policy have been rare. When they have occurred, they have seldom proved permanent. More typically, intermittent, sudden shifts have eventually given way to a resumption of prevailing assumptions with only modest deviations from ongoing courses of action. Why? What is it about the American foreign policy-making process that promotes continuity with the past rather than changes in response to new challenges and opportunities?

As we will see in the chapters that follow, a number of explanations of policy continuity are worthy of examination. Consider, for example, the view of Joseph A. Califano, once a member of Jimmy Carter's cabinet:

> Presidents since Roosevelt have pursued essentially similar foreign policy objectives on the major issues that face this nation abroad. Where change has come . . . it has often been dramatically expressed. But it has invariably evolved through broad, bipartisan consensus. . . . The . . . international policies of most administrations are founded in a more substantial and nonpartisan ideological consensus than the rhetorical idiosyncrasies and disparate styles and means most presidents tend to reveal. . . . To some extent, a president is a prisoner of historical forces that will demand his attention whatever his preference in policy objectives. . . . Every president is a victim as well as molder of events. (Califano, 1975: 238; 245)

From this perspective the president's ability to change foreign policy is greatly constrained by domestic and historical forces. Likewise, continuity is reinforced by the tendency of presidents to value consistency for its own sake, for there is both logic and reward in the stable pursuit of a continuous set of policy preferences: "Serious nations do not redefine their national interests every few years. . . . Foreign accomplishments generally come about because a nation has been able to sustain a course of action over a long period of time" (Destler, Gelb, and Lake, 1984). "A consistent and dependable national course must have a base broader than the particular beliefs of those who from time to time hold office," Secretary of State John Foster Dulles argued. This inclination to retain, not revise, existing national objectives is illustrated as well by Harry S Truman's advice to his successor, Dwight D. Eisenhower: "What I've always had in mind was and is a continuing foreign policy." Policy continuity may be in the national interest because nations become enmeshed in friendships, enmities, and obligations over time that cannot be radically overturned at a moment's notice without jeopardizing their security and prosperity.

But modifications in policy do occur, and this requires other types of continuities to be recognized. Continuity in postwar American foreign policy also may be characterized, not as the absence of change, but as movement forward that occurs only *incrementally*, that is, by piecemeal accommodation to emergent realities. Roger Hilsman (1967), a principal foreign policy adviser in the Kennedy and Johnson administrations, describes incrementalism as a means of policy modification in the following way: "Rather than through grand decisions on grand alternatives, policy changes seem to come through a series of slight modifications of existing policy, with the new policy emerging slowly and haltingly by small and usually tentative steps, a process of trial and error in which policy zigs and zags, reverses itself, and then moves forward in a series of incremental steps." Thus, because leaders must continually respond to new demands, changes in policy may occur; but because these modifications involve not so much reorientations as piecemeal readjustments, the basic policy direction remains intact. Consequently, the historical pattern of foreign policy behavior, while occasionally appearing on the surface to change, is marked by a preference for gradual adaptation rather than fundamental reorientation. Over the long run, policy responses to disparate events have seldom amounted to more than slight fluctuations around a persistent trend.

INFERRING PATTERNED CONSISTENCY IN FOREIGN POLICY

To some the proposition that American foreign policy has been governed by persistence and continuity may be disquieting.[2] To the casual observer of international events, change in American foreign policy appears endemic, almost constant. Headlines routinely proclaim bold new initiatives in American foreign policy, new approaches to world problems, and rejection by the current administration (whichever it might be) of the tired policies of its predecessor for imaginative new programs. The labels often attached to the policies of an administration (for example, Kennedy's New Frontier and Nixon's Generation of Peace) reinforce this image of imminent change. In fact, continuities in policy are often obscured by the publicity requirements of presidential campaigns, in which every four years presidential aspirants are motivated to capture the headlines by striking a pose that emphasizes the need for policy change and their pragmatic ability to produce it. Even incumbents seem to emphasize the changes and improvements they have made and will continue to make as reasons for reelecting them. The resulting political rhetoric gives the public the impression that change is automatically forthcoming. The appearance of major foreign policy change is made the more pervasive because the electoral process

---

2. Moreover, that interpretation is open to dispute, because continuities in the external behavior of the United States will not be found unless the analyst searches for them, and different analysts can readily reach different conclusions about the common threads that most incisively define the content of postwar American policy. The title of a former policymaker's memoirs, *The Past Has Another Pattern* (Ball, 1982), illustrates that different observers may discern different patterns that define American foreign policy. Cecil V. Carbb's *Policy Makers and Critics: Conflicting Theories of American Foreign Policy* (1986) provides a useful review of these divergent interpretations.

tends to focus voters' discussion of foreign policy on the new initiatives and policy pronouncements of different presidents and secretaries of state.

The record, however, suggests how mistaken exaggerated attention to high-sounding political rhetoric and transient departures in action can be. More often than not, when viewed from a long-term perspective, what initially looked like a turning point was instead another point at which the United States failed to turn. Existing policies were retained. Each administration failed (perhaps deliberately) to recognize the echo of previous policy statements in its own words. The historically minded observer tends to experience a sensation of *déjà vu* when he or she compares current rhetoric and performance with those of the past, because what is sold as an innovation turns out to be at most a shift in emphasis from prior policies, clothed in new labels.

By looking only at current events, we risk failing to see the overall pattern and thus confuse temporary fluctuations with enduring change. An infatuation with current events diminishes our ability to see long-term and ultimately more significant trends and to identify turning points instituting new trends. Former Under Secretary of State George W. Ball lucidly warned of this danger by observing:

> Unhappily, the way we live, including dependence on television and visual impressions, reinforces the short attention span of most Americans. Our current foreign policy practices focus public concern on only one problem at a time, . . . *yet in the episodic and visual comprehension of our foreign policy, there is serious danger that the larger significance of developments will be lost in a kaleidoscope of unrelated events. Continuities will be obscured, causal factors unidentified.* . . . Because we do not have a sense of where things started or why they are leading where they are, we are surprised by events that should have been predictable. We are so often impressed by the symbols of policy—two political leaders shaking hands or drinking toasts together—that we fail to recognize those symbols as mere reflections that have meaning only as part of a process within a larger context. (Ball, 1976: 323–324; emphasis added)

An analogy with the stock market might clarify this idea. On any one day the stock market, as indexed, for example, by the Dow Jones Industrial Average, may go up or down, with exactly the opposite happening the next day. What is the meaning of such day-to-day fluctuations? The significance is difficult to determine unless we view the changes over a period of a week, a month, or even a year. Then we might begin to see a trend characteristic of a bull market (advancing stock values and prices) or a bear market (declining values and prices). In fact, we might even be able to go back to the daily stock market quotations and identify the point at which the old market trend was broken and a new pattern set into motion. In and of themselves, however, the daily quotations often are quite meaningless—and in fact random for most of our purposes. It is only through a retrospective analysis that one is able to discern major shifts in direction, or at least fix a date on which the trend truly began.

The stock market analogy also helps clarify how change may occur in American foreign policy. Just as the trends in the stock market may shift as a consequence of the daily activities of large numbers of investors, so new patterns in American foreign policy may emerge as the nation's policymakers set new priorities and devise new means to deal with changing global conditions. Although we suspect that such adaptations will more often be incremental and marginal than comprehensive and revolutionary, over the long run, gradual adaptations can accumulate so as to culminate in some basic reorientations. It bears emphasizing, however, that we can only reach conclusions about change and continuity in American foreign policy if we view it as a dynamic historical process, as a phenomenon that proceeds through the continued interaction of long-term and short-term forces. Thus we need to take a long-term perspective to distinguish the overall trends often obscured by day-to-day variations and by the discordant details of current events. Viewed in this way, the postwar record reveals an overriding pattern of persistence and continuity.

FROM DESCRIPTION TO POLICY ANALYSIS AND EVALUATION

The thesis that the goals (and, to a lesser extent, the instruments or methods) of American foreign policy have been highly patterned needs to be documented and clarified. This is the purpose of Chapters 3, 4, and 5, in which we identify and examine the major assumptions that have guided American foreign policy since 1945 and the means used to achieve them. Additionally, the description given there of the pattern of American foreign policy invites evaluative questions: What are the *consequences* of the continuity that is revealed? What is the national interest? Has it been served, or harmed, by the maintenance of a consistent vision? Has the pattern remained stable because the assumptions on which it has been based have, on the whole, been warranted? Or instead, have those assumptions been mistaken or rendered questionable by unfolding global developments? If so, does their continued maintenance in the face of global change spell eventual difficulties? Will the United States become a victim of its own orthodoxy? Has it already?

   At issue in evaluating the themes in these chapters is how a nation can best reconcile the conflicting needs for stability and for adaptive change. A critical question for the 1990s and beyond is whether the United States will constructively adapt its policies to step-level changes in the international system. What do changes in the Soviet Union and Europe, the international political economy, and the global ecology portend for the United States, for example? How might the emergence of Western Europe and the Pacific Rim as powerful independent political or economic actors on the world stage influence the definition and pursuit of U.S. interests and objectives? How does recurrent violence in the Middle East exert prospects for new approaches to peacekeeping? What are the obstacles to redefinition and redirection? We will return to these questions at the conclusion of the book, when the prospects for revision or "restructuring" (Steinbruner, 1989) of American foreign policy will be considered.

The patterned consistency of postwar American foreign policy suggests that the inclination to look to the future with a vision inspired by the past, and to postpone the task of developing a comprehensive, long-term strategy for responding to the new realities, is deeply ingrained. But even though the temptation to temporize is powerful, exceptional opportunities for policy revision in the 1990s have emerged. Also at issue, therefore, is whether the American foreign policy-making process is structured in a way that permits these opportunities to be seized.

Reasons for the marked resistance of American foreign policy goals to change must be sought in the social, political, and institutional milieu within which foreign policy decisions are made. For if continuity has characterized the postwar *pattern* of American foreign policy, understanding the forces and factors from which it derives requires an analysis of the *process* of policy formulation and of the sources that coalesce to create those persisting patterns. What accounts for the pronounced continuity in American foreign policy goals? Why has American foreign policy been so immutable when the world itself appears so mutable? American foreign policymakers have adhered to a consistent vision of the major characteristics of the international environment, with the result that the decisions made in the aftermath of World War II largely presaged the next half-century of American policy. Has the vision become so institutionalized in the vast structure of federal agencies that service American policies toward the outside world that precedent, habitual ways of thinking, and bureaucratic inertia stifle consideration of radical policy alternatives and reconsideration of long-range goals? Is the decision-making process that promotes policy continuity deficient, making the United States, in the title of an insightful book on the subject, "our own worst enemy" (Destler, Gelb, and Lake, 1984)? Alternatively, if a turning point in American policy is to occur, what are the forces that might contribute to it? Chapter 2 provides an analytic framework with which to explore this set of questions.

SUGGESTIONS FOR FURTHER READING

Allison, Graham T., and William L. Ury, with Bruce J. Allyn (eds.). (1989) *Windows of Opportunity: From Cold War to Peaceful Competition in U.S.-Soviet Relations.* New York: Harper & Row.

Boyd, Gavin, and Gerald W. Hopple (eds.). (1987) *Political Change and Foreign Policies.* London: Pinter.

Brown, Seyom. (1983) *The Faces of Power: Constancy and Change in United States Foreign Policy from Truman to Reagan.* New York: Columbia University Press.

Destler, I. M., Leslie H. Gelb, and Anthony Lake. (1984) *Our Own Worst Enemy: The Unmaking of American Foreign Policy.* New York: Simon & Schuster.

Goldmann, Kjell. (1988) *Change and Stability in Foreign Policy.* Princeton, N.J.: Princeton University Press.

Kegley, Charles W., Jr., and Eugene R. Wittkopf (eds.). (1983) *Perspectives on American Foreign Policy.* New York: St. Martin's.

Newsom, David D. (1988) *Diplomacy and the American Democracy.* Bloomington: Indiana University Press.

Plischke, Elmer. (1988) *Foreign Relations: Analysis of Its Anatomy.* Westport, Conn.: Greenwood Press.

Rizopoulos, Nicholas X. (ed.). (1990) *Sea-Changes: American Foreign Policy in a World Transformed.* New York: Council on Foreign Relations Press.

Steinbruner, John D. (ed.). (1989) *Restructuring American Foreign Policy.* Washington, D.C.: Brookings Institution.

CHAPTER 2

The Analysis of American Foreign Policy: The Many Faces of Causation

Americans have come to recognize that we . . . face . . . a spectrum of often ambiguous challenges, of uncertain possibilities, of . . . new political developments [that] will outstrip old approaches unless we identify what is happening and deal more flexibly with the difficulties involved.

SECRETARY OF STATE GEORGE SHULTZ, 1988

Unlike the last forty years, the task before us is . . . more complex, and it is more nuanced. It has become less susceptible to the giant gesture, the single solution, or the overarching doctrine.

SECRETARY OF STATE JAMES BAKER, 1989

How can we organize our thinking and collect evidence to explain continuity and change in the response of the United States to the world around it? The answer to such seemingly simple questions as What drives American foreign policy?, and What forces promote or inhibit changes in it? requires that we think systematically. To facilitate that process we will employ a framework first proposed by political scientist James N. Rosenau (1966, 1980), that classifies all the potential forces influencing a nation's foreign policy into five major categories: the *external* (global) environment, the *societal* environment of the nation, the *governmental* setting, the *roles* played by policymakers, and the *individual* characteristics of foreign policy-making elites. Each of these *source categories* encompasses a large cluster of variables that, collectively and simultaneously with clusters belonging to other source categories, operate to shape the course of American conduct abroad. Thus to construct explanations of *why* American foreign policy has undergone—or failed to undergo—change over time, we must first identify and isolate the multiple factors affecting the U.S. response. The framework has demonstrated its ability to perform this task admirably. Furthermore, it suggests guidelines for assessing the relative importance of the multiple factors that account for the evolving performance of the United States in the postwar era and for determining the conditions under

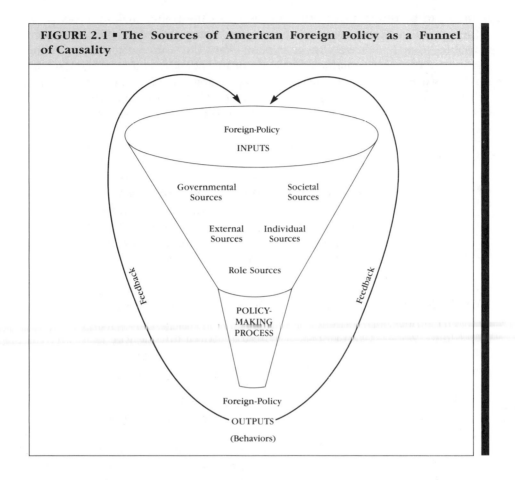

FIGURE 2.1 ▪ The Sources of American Foreign Policy as a Funnel of Causality

which continuity or change may predominate in America's policy in the aftermath of the Cold War.

THE SOURCES OF AMERICAN FOREIGN POLICY

The premise underlying the analytical framework is that each source category can be treated as a causative agent, and that those agents act in conjunction with one another to determine how the United States behaves internationally. In other words, the framework stipulates a theoretical "funnel of causality" (Campbell et al., 1960), as illustrated in Figure 2.1.

The figure depicts the "inputs" in the foreign policy-making process as the external, societal, governmental, role, and individual source categories of the analytical framework. Those inputs are policy "sources" because they give shape and direction to the kinds of behavior the United States pursues abroad, which can be thought of as the "outputs" of the policy-making process. In other words, the behavior of the United States abroad is the dependent variable—that which we wish to explain—and the source categories and the clusters of variables contained within them are the independent variables—the variables used to explain American behavior abroad. Thus the terms *inputs*, *source categories*, and *independent variables* all refer to the forces that exert a causal impact on or determine the evolutionary path of American foreign policy. That policy, in turn, is captured in the terms *output(s)* and *dependent variable*. In most instances, the dependent variable will be multifaceted, but we shall confine attention to those recurring *patterns* of behavior that define continuities in American leaders' assumptions about how the United States should cope with international developments and problems.

Note, however, that whether one is attempting to explain a single foreign policy event or a whole sequence of related behaviors, no single source category fully determines outputs. Rather, the source categories are interrelated and *collectively* determine foreign policy decisions, and hence foreign policy outputs. They do so in two ways: (1) by generating the necessity for foreign policy decisions and, ultimately, action abroad; and (2) by influencing the policy-making process—the procedures through which decisions are reached—that converts inputs into outputs.[1]

In the policy-making process, where decisions are made by those responsible for the formulation of American foreign policy, inputs are transformed into foreign policy outputs. The process is complex because of its many participants and because policy-making procedures cannot be divorced from all of the interdependent sources that shape decision makers' responses to situations demanding action. Conceptually, then, we can think of the foreign policy-making process as an intervening variable linking foreign policy inputs to outputs. In practice, however, we frequently will find it nearly impossible to separate the inputs themselves from the policy-making process that converts them into outputs. But once that conversion has been made (that is, once decisions are reached by those in authority), external action commences—in the form of policy pronouncements and declarations, for example, or in the sending of troops abroad and the granting of foreign aid. By monitoring these outcomes of the policy-making process, we can describe the pattern of American foreign policy.

It should be clear from this brief discussion that the model depicted in Figure 2.1 is explanatory. Each policy decision is viewed as the result of the multiple prior causal events taking place in the funnel. Thus the model stipulates the conditions that precede and promote policy decisions (bearing in

---

1. Linda P. Brady (1978) describes these ideas by observing that "in making foreign policy, decision makers continuously respond to situations created by stimuli. . . . Characteristics of these situations influence both the process by which foreign policy is made and the substance of foreign policy behavior." The "characteristics of . . . situations" referred to are those precipitating factors and preconditions that give rise to or cause specific foreign policy acts to be undertaken by policymakers.

mind that it is frequently difficult to distinguish decision making itself from its prior conditions—the source categories). Policy outcomes depend on the prior conditions occurring in the funnel and are explained by the combined impact of the source categories on the decisions made in the policy-making process.

The diagram also suggests a temporal sequence to the transition from inputs to outputs via the policy-making process. That is, changes in the sources of American foreign policy occurring at time (t) influence decisions at a later time ($t + 1$), which lead to policy outcomes at a still later time ($t + 2$). Moreover, these policy outcomes have consequences for the source categories themselves at a later time ($t + 3$) (because they exert ''feedback'' on the independent variables), so that foreign policy actions alter the source conditions that influence subsequent ($t + 4$) policy making. For instance, a variety of internal and external factors at some point (t) led the United States to make decisions ($t + 1$) to send troops to Vietnam ($t + 2$); but this action exerted a ''feedback'' influence on domestic opinion in American society ($t + 3$), ultimately altering internal conditions in such a way as to promote a revision ($t + 4$) of that original policy outcome. Stated differently, this sequential perspective suggests that the original decision to draft large numbers of Americans into military service and send them into battle overseas provoked demonstrations and riots at home, and those conditions eventually stimulated a reconsideration of the original policy.

Thus the model postulated here is dynamic. It can be used to account for past policy pronouncements and behaviors and for the effects of those outcomes on subsequent policy decisions. This feature of the model enables us to explain theoretically the historical evolution of American foreign policy because the model is not tied analytically to a single time period. The entire record of American foreign conduct since 1945 therefore can be explained. Moreover, because policy outcomes affect the relative importance of the determinants at a later point in time, different outcomes may be better explained by different sets of source categories at different times.

EXPLAINING POLICY PATTERNS

The foregoing discussion implies something about the meaning of *explanation* and *cause* as they are used in this book. These terms require elaboration because their meaning is intimately linked to the book's analytical approach and its level of abstraction.

There are many types of explanations and many competing notions of what it means ''to explain'' phenomena. The *nomological* mode of explanation is appropriate for our purposes.[2] Nomological explanations use lawlike statements (*nomos* is Greek for ''law'') to explain a particular event or a class of events. Usually such statements explain events by reference to generaliza-

---

2. For a discussion of this and other types of explanation, see Raymond (1975) and Isaak (1985).

tions or covering laws, which attach cause to effect. "Civil unrest leads to foreign aggression" is an example of a generalized, lawlike statement relating cause to effect. Foreign aggression is, of course, the effect, and civil unrest is the cause, because our lawlike statement implies that civil unrest occurs prior to foreign aggression. In other words, *cause* implies a sequence in time between event *A* and event *B*. Thus civil unrest is an antecedent, much as the source categories of American foreign policy depicted in Figure 2.1 are antecedents to foreign policy decisions.

Most lawlike statements in social science are hypotheses linking independent variables (causes) to dependent variables (effects) in terms of a tendency or probability.[3] Thus we cannot say with certainty that civil unrest will lead to foreign aggression, only that there is a tendency for this sequence to occur, or that the probability is high that it will happen. The following is a pertinent illustration of this mode of explanatory logic:

> An example of a general explanatory sentence, confirmed to some degree . . . might be that, of the national states that have a differentiated foreign affairs establishment [where decision-making power and authority are dispersed among several centers, not concentrated in any one], 90 percent also manifest continuity in their foreign policy behavior. This is a statistical law in the form, if A, the probability of B is [90 percent]. If someone asks why changes in administration from the Democratic to Republican parties and back again in the United States have not greatly affected the nature of American foreign policy, we could refer to our "law" for an explanation. Our generalization states that 90 percent of the states that belong to the class of states that have differentiated foreign policy bureaucracies also are members of the class of states that show continuity in foreign policy. Thus, because the United States has a differentiated foreign policy establishment, it is a member of the first class and very likely, but not certainly, a member of the second class; it is for this reason that changes in political leadership seem to have no effect. (McGowan, 1975: 64)

In this example the lack of radical change in the pattern of American foreign policy for almost fifty years is explained by reference to a general law positing that bureaucratic differentiation in foreign affairs establishments (in terms of the number of independent units that share responsibility for policy formulation and execution) is directly related to foreign policy continuity. The more differentiated the foreign affairs machinery, the more stable the foreign policy. This particular example of explanatory logic thus suggests how observable patterns of American foreign behavior can be explained by institutional features of the governmental machinery responsible for the making and implementation of foreign policy decisions.

The example also illustrates the interdependence of description (what) and explanation (why) and the fact that explanation requires thinking in causal terms about classes of phenomena rather than about discrete events. In this

---

3. Since hypotheses are, in effect, only expectations, they must be confirmed through empirical testing before confidence can be placed in their validity as generalizations. That is, hypothesis verification requires that substantiating data be supplied.

book the class of phenomena we seek to describe is the pattern of American foreign policy (the dependent variable), which we will then seek to explain using the explanatory classes (the independent variables) labeled external, societal, governmental, role, and individual sources. Reference to these multiple sources implicitly rejects the widespread impulse to search for a single cause of American foreign policy.

To reject out of hand single-factor explanations of American foreign policy is to reject what is intuitively most satisfying—simplicity. To understand complex social phenomena and deal with an inherently ambiguous reality, people often resort to concepts that artificially bring order out of chaos. Similarly, efforts to understand the sources of American foreign policy are often reduced to simple and therefore psychologically satisfying single-factor explanations. For instance, some analysts have interpreted American foreign policy as essentially the product of a capitalist economic system. Others have viewed American action abroad as stemming exclusively from the conspiratorial efforts of invisible but all-powerful pressure groups. Both of these "explanations" of American foreign policy may contain kernels of truth (in part because these factors influence other sources); in addition, under certain circumstances they may explain fairly adequately certain aspects of policy. However, because each relies so completely on a single-factor explanation in the face of a broad array of other equally plausible contributing factors whose explanatory impact cannot be dismissed, neither can be taken seriously as the sole explanation. Foreign policy actions almost invariably result from multiple sources; therefore we are well advised—if we are to avoid oversimplification and capture the complexity of reality—to think in terms of multiple causes.

Our rejection of single-factor explanations of American foreign policy is based in part on empirical observation and in part on the logic underlying the analytical framework we employ. Let us turn, therefore, to a fuller explication of the source categories that organize the subsequent explanatory analysis.

AN OVERVIEW OF THE SOURCE CATEGORIES

Recall that the proposed analytic framework clusters the factors that collectively influence continuity and change in postwar American foreign policy into five source categories. The external, societal, governmental, role, and individual categories are assumed to be exhaustive (every potential source of American foreign policy is embraced by them) and to be mutually exclusive (nonoverlapping). Let us examine in more detail what each encompasses.

External Sources

The external category refers to the attributes of the international system and to the characteristics and behaviors of the actors comprising it. It includes all "aspects of America's external environment or any actions occurring abroad that condition or otherwise influence the choices made by its officials," of which "geographical 'realities' and ideological challenges from potential aggressors" that shape the decisions of foreign policy officials are obvious examples (Rosenau, 1980). Another way of defining this category is to say that external variables refer broadly to the impact of the state of the world on the United States. Thus it draws attention to the kinds of behavior other nations direct toward the United States and other actors and explores how these foreign policy acts influence the response of the United States. Similarly, the external source category draws attention to the attributes of other societies and leads us to focus on how the kinds of nations with which the United States deals shape its foreign policy and behavior.

Because the external source category consists of so many variables (entailing *all* characteristics common to the global arena and changes in it), the questions derived from it are innumerable.[4] What types of governments populate the global system? Are they allies or antagonists? How many formal alliances and other military coalitions exist in the system? Do they have sufficient military might and internal cohesion to deter attack from outsiders? What kinds of issues populate the global agenda, and who among the many other states assume a position toward them similar to the posture maintained by the United States? Are there many or few international organizations? Do they enjoy authority and legitimacy independent of their national members? Does the international legal system effectively prohibit certain kinds of behavior while encouraging others? The answers to these questions and many others are assumed to influence significantly the kind of behavior the United States (or, for that matter, any nation) is likely to adopt. Thus the external environment is a theoretically powerful and multifaceted source of American foreign policy, and changes in it may be hypothesized to stimulate changes in American external conduct. By the same token, of course, changes in American behavior may affect the external environment.

Examples abound supporting the hypothesis that changes in the international environment stimulate changes in American foreign policy. The Bush administration's 1989 pledge to "move beyond containment" was doubtless prompted by the desperate plight and dramatic initiatives of Mikhail Gorbachev, the collapse of European communism, and the denouement of the Warsaw Pact. Similarly, the American-Canadian agreement to create a North American trade zone free of import restrictions was arguably motivated by the European Community's plan to create a unified market by 1992, which may adversely affect the U.S. and Canadian economies.

---

4. In practice, it is useful to distinguish between "systemic" sources of foreign policy and "external" sources. The former are aggregate or general attributes of the international environment (for example, the amount of alliance or war) that are shared by all states—not just the United States. The latter are relationships between particular states (for example, interactions between the United States and the Soviet Union). In the context of this distinction, the subsequent elaboration of the external source category (Chapters 6 and 7) will emphasize primarily external rather than systemic explanations of American foreign policy. Readers should be alert to the possibility that the external source category can be treated in alternative ways.

There is nothing new about the idea that a nation's foreign policy is conditioned by factors external to it. Indeed, the analytic tradition that emphasizes the causal relationship between the international system and American foreign policy making enjoys a wide following. "Political realists" in particular argue that the distribution of power in the international system, more than anything else, influences how its nation-members act. Nations, in turn, are motivated to shape the distribution of power to their own advantage. Because all states are assumed to be motivated by the same drives, the principal way to understand international politics and foreign policy is to follow the interactions of states in the international arena or, in other words, to focus on the external source category (see Waltz, 1979, and the discussion of political realism in Chapter 3).

To argue that American foreign policy is shaped at least partially by external forces and foreign conditions is to recognize that a nation's actions abroad are necessarily affected by what others do and by changes in what the international environment renders practicable. External variables help define the limits of the possible; they preclude certain choices and reduce the utility of others. In this way the international system imposes constraints on U.S. decision makers and limits their freedom to take policy initiatives. In other words, it promotes policy continuity by narrowing the range of viable options. But the external environment can also stimulate policy change. For example, the so-called decline of the United States (and the Soviet Union) relative to other rapidly growing industrialized states, such as Japan (Kennedy 1987), arguably exerts enormous pressure for adaptive changes in American foreign policy in the 1990s.

As important as the external environment is, it would be wrong to think that it alone can dictate foreign policy. It is more accurate to argue that

> factors external to the actor can become determinants only as they affect the mind, the heart, and the will of the decision-maker. A human decision to act in a specific way . . . necessarily represents the last link in the chain of antecedents of any act of policy. A geographical set of conditions, for instance, can affect the behavior of a nation only as specific persons perceive and interpret these conditions. (Wolfers, 1962: 42)

Thus external factors do not alone determine how the United States acts. But they do influence how decision makers may choose to act, and to that degree they serve as a source of foreign policy. We will focus on external factors as a source of American foreign policy in Chapters 6 and 7.

Societal Sources

Societal sources are "those nongovernmental aspects of a political system that influence its external behavior. Its major value orientations, its degree of national unity, and the extent of its industrialization are but a few of the societal variables which can contribute to the contents of a nation's external aspirations and policies" (Rosenau, 1980). This category draws attention to the fact that general features of American society shape its relations with other nations.

Forces within the societal category traditionally have been stressed by those who see the domestic climate shaping American foreign policy more strongly than external conditions. Robert Dallek's *The American Style of Foreign Policy: Cultural Politics and Foreign Affairs* (1983) and Loren Baritz's *Backfire: A History of How American Culture Led Us into Vietnam and Made Us Fight the Way We Did* (1985) are illustrations of interpretations of American foreign policy that rest on societal explanations. Neo-Marxist critics of American foreign policy, who see the nation's capitalist economic system and the need to safeguard foreign markets for American economic exploitation as its driving forces, also rely on societal variables. Similarly, if we recall how American territorial expansion and imperialism in the nineteenth century were often rationalized by references to "manifest destiny" and the belief that Americans were a "chosen people" with a divine right to expand, we find many accounts that argue that American ideological preferences influenced American policies toward peoples outside the nation's territorial jurisdiction.

Other explanations of postwar American diplomatic conduct also rely heavily on societal characteristics. Some analysts maintain that the vast natural resources and territorial size of the United States made its globalist aspirations inevitable. Others interpret American foreign policy as a product of the pressures exerted by special interest groups. Ethnic interest groups in particular are sometimes credited with an ability to "control" the content and conduct of American policy toward particular countries, such as Israel and the Arab states. Similarly, the often overtly military orientation of postwar American foreign policy is sometimes attributed to various "ruling elite" theories, such as the one associated with President Dwight D. Eisenhower's warning in 1961 that a "military-industrial complex" could acquire unwarranted influence over policy making.

Because American foreign policy clearly is rooted in domestic sources, the impact of societal forces would appear to be strong. As one analyst pointedly argued, "To change [America's] foreign policy, its internal structure must change" (Isaak, 1977). The impact of societal variables will be explored more fully in Chapters 8 and 9.

Governmental Sources

Richard M. Nixon once noted "If we were to establish a new foreign policy for the era to come, we had to begin with a basic restructuring of the process by which policy is made." Jimmy Carter echoed this theme repeatedly in his 1976 presidential campaign by maintaining that to change policy one must first change the machinery that produces it. Offering a variation on this same theme, Ronald Reagan argued in 1980 that the greatest policy failures in the past could be traced to the "excessive growth and unnecessary size of government" and pledged to implement more successful foreign policies by making government work more efficiently.

he nation's leaders choose. The category tells more about why certain
s are selected to satisfy particular objectives (and about the ways those
ions are reached and implemented in policy institutions) than it does
t why the objectives are selected in the first place. Yet means become
ortant reflections of ends. And they often reinforce the continued, almost
bitual choice of the same ends, as will be shown in Chapters 10, 11, and 12.

Role Sources

Governmental factors are closely associated with role factors as sources of and
influences on American foreign policy. As a source category, roles refer to the
impact of the nature of the office on the behavior of its occupant. Roles are
important because decision makers indisputably are influenced by the socially
prescribed behaviors and legally sanctioned norms attached to the positions
they occupy. Because the positions policymakers hold substantially affect their
behavior, policy outcomes can be more influenced by the roles existing in the
policy-making arena than by the particular individuals who happen to be in
authority at any given moment.

Role theory goes far in explaining why, for example, American presidents
have acted, once in office, so much like their predecessors, and why each has
come to view American interests and goals in terms so similar to the images
maintained by previous occupants of the Oval Office. The view that "the office
makes the man" has been expressed thus:

> If we accept the proposition . . . that certain fundamentals stand at the core of
> American foreign policy, we could argue that any president is bound, even dic-
> tated to, by those basic beliefs and needs. In other words, he has little freedom to
> make choices wherein his distinctive style, personality, experience, and intellect
> shape America's role and position in international relations in a way that is
> uniquely his. It might be suggested that a person's behavior is a function not of his
> individual traits but rather of the office that he holds and that the office is circum-
> scribed by the larger demands of the national interest, rendering individuality
> inconsequential. (Paterson, 1979: 93)

Correspondingly, this reasoning suggests that merely changing the person sitting behind the desk in the Oval Office will not bring about fundamental
change in the nation's policies. Roles, it would seem, determine behavior more
than do the qualities of individuals. Perhaps this explains why Jimmy Carter
proved to be a less liberal president than many Democrats had expected, and
why Ronald Reagan was not as conservative a president as many Republicans
had hoped.

Role theory is also useful in explaining the kinds of policy decisions
habitually made by and within the large bureaucratic organizations that bear
responsibility for implementing foreign policy—that is, for explaining not
individual behavior, but group behavior. Role pressures may lead, for instance,
to attitudinal conformity within bureaucracies and to deference to the ortho-

The Analysi~

22

Analytic

goals
mear
decis
abo
im
ha

Underlying these viewpoints is the assu
between the way the U.S. government is organ
decisions, on the one hand, and the substance of .
This is the core notion of a governmental influe
governmental source category, in turn, refers "to t.
ment's structure that limit or enhance the foreign
decision-makers" (Rosenau, 1980).

Various facets of the structure of the American gover.
what the United States does—and does not—do abroac
American foreign policy is shaped by: (1) the Constitutior
institutional responsibility for the making and implementa.
policy among the three branches of government; (2) the rise
dominance in foreign policy making, culminating in what has beer.
"imperial presidencies" of Lyndon B. Johnson and Richard M. N
lowed, in turn, by a reassertion of congressional authority; (3) the r.
administrative structures in the United States, wherein a widening a.
government agencies and organizations compete for control over policy .
ing; and (4) growth in the sheer size of government, which may contribute
a fractionalized and inefficient decision-making structure.[5]

Governmental variables undoubtedly constrain what the United States
can do abroad and the speed with which it can do it. Its size and the degree of
bureaucratization, for example, militate against policy reversals. Those factors
combine with the constitutional division of power between the executive and
legislative branches of government to promote policy compromise and
incrementalism over policy innovation and revision. Thus governmental factors in general and democratic institutions in particular certainly inhibit the
nation's ability to change rapidly its course in world affairs. As the French political sociologist Alexis de Tocqueville (1969) observed in 1835, "Foreign
politics demand scarcely any of those qualities which a democracy possesses;
and they require, on the contrary, the perfect use of almost all those faculties
in which it is deficient."

In some instances, however, elements of the governmental machinery
have facilitated, rather than diminished, rapid shifts in policy. State Department
formulation in 1947 of the Marshall Plan for European economic recovery and
White House initiatives in 1971 that altered the role of the dollar in the global
political economy, stand out as cases in point. In most instances, however,
governmental factors tend to inhibit rather than promote policy change.

Although the structure of American government is an intrinsically important influence on the country's foreign policy, we should not rely too heavily
on the governmental source category as an explanation of American foreign
policy, for this category fails to explain much about the kinds of foreign policy

---

5. According to one of Parkinson's (1972–1973) laws, "The useful results of diplomacy are
usually in reverse proportion to the number of diplomatists."

dox views within an agency. As John Kenneth Galbraith (1970–1971) argues, there is a "tendency for any bureaucracy, military or civilian, in the absence of the strongest leadership, to continue to do whatever it is doing. This is a matter of the highest importance, one that explains the most basic tendencies of our foreign policy." Such tendencies are clearly more conducive to continuity than to innovation in policy. The "system" places a premium on behavioral consistency and constrains the capacity of individuals to make a policy impact. It is therefore difficult for individual policymakers to escape their roles by challenging conventional thinking.

In addition, role factors help account for the inability of presidents to get policies implemented by established bureaucratic agencies who typically view the national interest not as the president does but instead (as role theory suggests they will) in terms of their own parochial needs and institutional preferences. Moreover, because bureaucratic agencies are inclined to compete with one another for influence over policy outcomes, decision making tends to be highly politicized and emerges from a bargaining process. Accordingly, the ability of a president to engineer policy change is severely compromised, just as the capacity of a nation managed by fragmented bureaucracies to change policy directions is limited. Thus the resistence of postwar American foreign policy to change can be accounted for quite substantially by role restraints on policy innovation.

Conversely, of course, adaptations in American policy can also be explained in part by changes in role definitions. Policy-making roles may be interpreted differently, and this is one of the ways in which role variables change. For example, occupants of the role of U.S. Ambassador to the United Nations (such as Adlai Stevenson, Daniel P. Moynihan, Andrew Young, Jeane J. Kirkpatrick, and Thomas Pickering) have defined this role quite differently, with corresponding changes in the behavior exhibited. Thus, because part of the definition or expectation of some roles in the U.S. government is the product of leadership and the occupant's choice, changes in role definitions may be sources of policy discontinuity, just as the maintenance of established definitions is a source of policy continuity. Hence role and individual sources interact: what cannot be explained by the role sources might be explained by individual sources, and vice versa.

The impact roles exert on the processes through which foreign policy decisions are made will be examined more fully in Chapter 13.

Individual Sources

Finally, our explanatory framework identifies as the fifth policy source the individual characteristics of decision makers. Individual sources include "all those aspects of a decision-maker—his values, talents, and prior experiences—that distinguish his foreign policy choices or behavior from those of every other decision maker" (Rosenau, 1980). Former Secretary of State John Foster Dulles's pious diplomacy stemming from his moralistic Presbyterian upbringing illustrates how the conduct of American diplomacy may be influenced by personal traits (see Holsti, 1962).

The premise that attributes of individual decision makers may serve as a source of American foreign policy rests on the assumption that decision makers possess unique personal qualities resistant to molding and modification by role variables. The thesis that every individual is unique is not difficult to accept, and the assumption that idiosyncratic qualities can make a difference in the kinds of decisions reached is plausible. Consider the following:

- Why did the United States persist in bombing North Vietnam for so long in the face of overwhelming evidence that the policy of "bombing the North Vietnamese into submission" was failing and, if anything, was hardening their resolve to continue fighting? Could the answer be that President Lyndon B. Johnson was unable to admit failure, that he had a psychological need to preserve his positive self-image by "being right"?

- Why did the United States act so boldly in forcing the Soviet Union to remove its missiles from Cuban soil during the 1962 Cuban missile crisis? (President John F. Kennedy estimated the odds of nuclear annihilation were "between one in three and even.") Kennedy had been, by his own confession, out-bargained and humiliated by Soviet Premier Nikita Khrushchev at their 1961 summit meeting in Vienna. Could it be that Kennedy's pride prompted him to teach Khrushchev a lesson, to show him his composure under pressure and his toughness? ("We stood eyeball to eyeball, and *he* was the first to blink.")

- Why did Secretary of State Dulles publicly insult Chou En-Lai of Communist China by refusing to shake Chou's extended hand at the 1954 Geneva Conference? Could it be that Dulles viewed the Chinese leader as a symbol of an atheistic doctrine so abhorrent to his own values that he chose to scorn the friendly gesture?

- Would the United States have embarked on a moralistic campaign for human rights in the late 1970s had the country not been led by a president, Jimmy Carter, who was inspired by the moral tenets of his evangelical faith?

- Would the Bush administration have been as timid toward Chinese political repression following the Tiananmen Square crackdown in June 1989 if President George Bush had not previously served as the U.S. representative to the People's Republic of China, leaving him with numerous personal relationships with Chinese leaders?

Theories emphasizing the personal characteristics of political leaders enjoy considerable popularity. This is partly because democratic theory leads us to expect that individuals elected to high public office will be able either to sustain or to change public policy in accordance with popular preferences, and because the electoral system compels aspirants for office to emphasize how their regime will be different from that of their opponents. The habit of naming American policies after their presidential proponents (for example, the Monroe Doctrine, the Reagan Doctrine) contributes to the image that individuals do, in fact, matter. It is an image further reinforced by the widespread tendency in American politics to think of presidents as "great men," sometimes even as heroes.

For the same reason that other single-factor explanations of American foreign policy are suspect, however, we must be wary of ascribing too much importance to the impact of individuals. Individuals may matter, and in some instances they clearly do matter, but the mechanisms through which individuals influence foreign policy outcomes are likely to be much more subtle than popular impressions would have us believe.

As suggested above, one way individual variables become important is through the interpretations different individuals attach to the roles they occupy. Roles are generally constraining forces that mold people's behavior regardless of their personal preferences or predispositions. But the boundaries of those constraints are not immutable. Instead, most roles, particularly those associated with the highest levels of the governmental structure, permit a range of interpretation. How the role is interpreted is thus a matter of idiosyncratic choice. One person may see his or her role as permitting considerable latitude in choosing among policy options; another occupant of the same role may see little room for maneuver.

Then, too, the type of person holding office may affect the style if not the content of policy. This is especially obvious in the presidency. Harry S Truman and Dwight D. Eisenhower espoused very similar policies, but the manner in which the two men pursued those policies bears the imprint of their respective backgrounds and personalities. The same contrast might be drawn between the policy-making styles of Ronald Reagan and George Bush, even though the latter served the former as vice president unobtrusively for eight years. Hence no explanation of American foreign policy would be complete without a consideration of the characteristics unique to those who make that policy. This is the subject of Chapter 14.

PUTTING THE PIECES TOGETHER: THE MULTIPLE SOURCES OF AMERICAN FOREIGN POLICY

What is especially inviting about the approach to explanation offered by our analytical framework of five categories is that it encourages an explicitly multicausal perspective. It begins with the premise that we must look in different places if we want to find the origins of American foreign policy. And it tells us where to look, thus providing a helpful guide to understanding policy and how it is made. Rosenau provides an excellent illustration of the utility—and necessity—of explaining American foreign policy decisions by reference to multiple factors by asking us to consider the influences underlying the U.S. invasion of Cuba at the Bay of Pigs in 1961, which was devised to "liberate" the island from its nascent communist regime.

To what extent was that external behavior a function of the individual characteristics of John F. Kennedy . . . ? Were his youth, his commitments to action, his
affiliations with the Democratic Party, his self-confidence, his close election
victory—and so on through an endless list—relevant to the launching of the invasion and, if so, to what extent? Would any President have undertaken to oust the
Castro regime upon assuming office in 1961? If so, how much potency should be
attributed to such role-derived variables? Suppose everything else about the
circumstances of April 1961 were unchanged except that Warren Harding or
Richard Nixon occupied the White House; would the invasion have occurred? Or
hold everything constant but the form of government. Stretch the imagination
and conceive of the U.S. as having a cabinet system of government with Kennedy
as prime minister; would the action toward Cuba have been any different? Did
legislative pressure derived from a decentralized policymaking system generate an
impulse to "do something" about Castro, and, if so, to what extent did these
governmental variables contribute to the external behavior? Similarly, . . . assume
once more a presidential form of government. Place Kennedy in office a few
months after a narrow election victory, and imagine the Cuban situation as arising
in 1921, 1931, or 1951; would the America of the roaring twenties, the depression, or the McCarthy era have "permitted," "encouraged," or otherwise become
involved in a refugee-mounted invasion? . . . Lastly, hold the individual, role,
governmental, and societal variables constant in the imagination, and posit Cuba
as 9,000 rather than 90 miles off the Florida coast; would the invasion have
nevertheless been launched? If it is estimated that no effort would have been made
to span such a distance, does this mean that systemic variables should always be
treated as over-riding, or is their potency diminished under certain conditions?
(Rosenau, 1980: 130–131)

Regardless of how one might respond to these questions, the simple act of
posing them facilitates appreciation of the numerous forces shaping foreign
policy. Furthermore, it also helps to define the factors that presumably have
contributed to the persistence of the view held by decision makers that Cuba is
a "problem" and to explain variations in the way different administrations have
responded to that problem. In the particular case of the Bay of Pigs episode,
American behavior clearly stemmed from more than one factor, and it can
be explained only by reference to several variables. No single-factor explanation is adequate.

Similarly, long-term patterns in American foreign policy goals and instruments are amenable to, and require, explanation by reference to competing
sources. Take, for instance, the dominant theme of American foreign policy
since World War II: the containment of the Soviet Union. As we will demonstrate in Chapter 3, every administration in the postwar era has voiced opposition to Soviet communism and pronounced its determination to contain its
expansion. Why has this basic orientation of post–World War II American foreign policy remained so constant? Why has change, when it has occurred, been
so gradual, so incremental?

To answer these questions, we must look in a variety of places. At the
level of the international system, for instance, it can be argued that the advent

of nuclear weapons and the subsequent fear of destruction from a Soviet nuclear attack promoted a status quo American policy designed primarily to deal with this paramount fear. Would the United States have acted differently over the past fifty years had international circumstances been different? What if the Soviet Union had failed to achieve superpower status? Would that circumstance have removed the restraining fear that a war between the United States and the Soviet Union would devastate both? Or what if the retreat of Soviet power and rejection of communism had occurred much sooner? Perhaps it was the persistence of the Soviet threat that so colored international circumstances for decades that stimulated and perpetuated the anti-Soviet goal dominating postwar American foreign policy.

But consider whether the entrenched preoccupation with Soviet communism would have endured for so long had nationalistic sentiments within American society eroded. Or if a mobilized American public unfearful of external enemies had revolted against high levels of peacetime military expenditures. And ask as well whether American foreign policy might have shifted in the 1950s were it not for the anticommunist, witch-hunting tactics Senator Joseph McCarthy initiated shortly after communist forces came to power in China in 1949, in what many Americans viewed as a Soviet gain at America's expense.

Or turn instead to the governmental sector. Would American foreign policy have changed more rapidly had foreign policy making not become dominated by the office of the presidency—if instead the balance between the executive and legislative branches fostered by the Constitution had been preserved throughout the 1960s? Indeed, would American foreign policy have been different and more flexible if "cold warriors" had not populated the innermost circle of presidential advisers in the 1950s and 1960s and if career professionals within the foreign affairs bureaucracy had challenged their singular outlook?

And then consider whether American foreign policy might not have escaped some of the rigidity of its prolonged anticommunist posture if ideological orthodoxy had been reduced by fewer role pressures for conformity. Would the decisions reached after 1947 have been different had decision-making roles been less institutionalized and more flexible, and encouraged advocacy of more diverse opinions? Might American policymakers have more energetically sought to move beyond the Cold War prior to the late 1980s had policy-making roles been defined so as to allow more long-range planning and less timidity in responding to new opportunities?

And, finally, consider the hypothetical prospects for change in American policy had other individuals risen to positions of power during this period. Would the cornerstone of American postwar policy have been so virulently anticommunist if Franklin D. Roosevelt had lived out his fourth term in office; if Adlai Stevenson and his choice of a secretary of state, and not Eisenhower and Dulles, had been responsible for American policy throughout the 1950s; if Kennedy's attempt to improve relations with the Soviets had not been terminated by an assassin's bullet; if Hubert Humphrey had managed to obtain the

400,000 extra votes in 1968 necessary to make him, and not Nixon, president; if George McGovern's call for America to "come home" had gained him the presidency; if Henry "Scoop" Jackson, and not Jimmy Carter, had replaced Gerald Ford in 1976; or if Ronald Reagan's bid to turn Jimmy Carter out of office in 1980 had met with failure? What coloration would American foreign policy have assumed had the 1988 election placed the responsibilities of the presidency in the hands of Michael Dukakis instead of George Bush?

To ask these rhetorical questions is to question whether the presence of different officials with different kinds of personalities, psychological needs, and political preferences might have made a difference in the ability of the United States to frame new policies toward the Soviet Union. Would other individuals have produced a different outcome? Or would the cross-pressures inherent in the multiple responsibilities of their respective offices have undermined any individual's ability to alter the course of the policy?

"What if" questions are often impossible to answer. Asking them, however, provokes awareness of the problem of tracing causation, since they force consideration of different influences and possibilities. Thus to answer even partially the question Why has the United States acted the way it has in its external relations?, we need to examine each of the major sources of its foreign policy. Collectively, these identify the many constraints and stimuli facing American decision makers, thereby providing insight into the factors that promote continuity and change in American conduct abroad.

Recognizing that each source category places some constraint on decision makers' latitude, our exploration will be presented in descending order of the "spatial magnitude" of each explanatory category. Following description and interpretation of postwar policy output patterns (Part II), the discussion will examine the external environment (Part III), which is clearly the most comprehensive of the categories influencing decision makers. We will turn next to societal sources (Part IV), then proceed to the way in which the American political system is organized for foreign policy making (Part V), and from there shift focus again to role sources (Part VI), which partly flow from, and are closely associated with, the governmental setting. Finally, we will consider the importance of individual personalities, preferences, and predispositions in explaining foreign policy outcomes (Part VII).

This organization provides readers with the opportunity to weigh the relative explanatory power of each of the source categories. By looking at external, societal, governmental, role, and individual sources of American policy independently, we can examine the causal impact *each* category independently exerts on America's external behavior. Completion of the survey should enable the various pieces or causes to be compared, so some conclusions can be reached about the relative potencies of the five categories in accounting for the patterned consistencies and changes in postwar American foreign policy. This will prepare us to probe more incisively the dynamics of foreign policy continuity and change by looking (in Part VIII) at how the interacting sources are related, and finally at how those relationships affect the probable future of American foreign policy.

SUGGESTIONS FOR FURTHER READING

Clark, Michael, and Brian White (eds.). (1989) *Understanding Foreign Policy: The Foreign Policy Systems Approach*. Brookfield, Vt.: Gower.

East, Maurice A., Stephen A. Salmore, and Charles F. Hermann (eds.). (1978) *Why Nations Act· Theoretical Perspectives for Comparative Foreign Policy Studies*. Beverly Hills, Calif.: Sage.

Hermann, Charles F. (1990) "Changing Course: When Governments Choose to Redirect Foreign Policy," *International Studies Quarterly* 34 (March): 3–21.

Hermann, Charles F., Charles W. Kegley, Jr., and James N. Rosenau (eds.). (1987) *New Directions in the Study of Foreign Policy*. Boston: Allen & Unwin.

Holsti, K. J. (1982) *Why Nations Realign: Foreign Policy Restructuring in the Post War World*. Boston: Allen & Unwin.

Isaak, Alan C. (1985) *Scope and Methods of Political Science*, 4th ed. Chicago: Dorsey.

Jensen, Lloyd. (1982) *Explaining Foreign Policy*. Englewood Cliffs, N.J.: Prentice-Hall.

McGowan, Patrick J. (1975) "Meaningful Comparisons in the Study of Foreign Policy: A Methodological Discussion of Objectives, Techniques, and Research Designs," pp. 52–87 in Charles W. Kegley, Jr., et al., eds., *International Events and the Comparative Analysis of Foreign Policy*. Columbia: University of South Carolina Press.

Rosenau, James N. (1980) "Pre-theories and Theories of Foreign Policy," pp. 115–169 in *The Scientific Study of Foreign Policy*, rev. ed. New York: Nichols.

Wilkenfeld, Jonathan, Gerald W. Hopple, Paul J. Rossa, and Stephen J. Andriole. (1980) *Foreign Policy Behavior*. Beverly Hills, Calif.: Sage.

PART II

The Pattern of Postwar American Foreign Policy

CHAPTER 3

The Goals of American Foreign Policy: The Postwar Pattern

The period after World War II marks the first era of truly global foreign policy.
SPECIAL ASSISTANT FOR NATIONAL SECURITY AFFAIRS HENRY A. KISSINGER, 1969

A long-term consistency of behavior is bound to burden American democracy when the country rises to the stature of a great power.
ALEXIS DE TOCQUEVILLE, 1835

On the surface, America's daily foreign policy actions may appear erratic. But behind the ostensible inconsistencies, a pattern can be discerned. Since World War II, American policymakers have consistently adhered to certain fundamental assumptions about the world and the appropriate role of the United States in it. This chapter describes these foreign policy goals and the postulates and perceptions upon which they have been based for nearly five decades.

The guiding policy premises discussed here have rested on a consensual foundation, but that consensus has not been without its critics. Indeed, although general agreement about the priorities that ought to anchor foreign policy has endured, American policymakers have sometimes defined its essential character somewhat differently, and some have vociferously challenged the validity of those assumptions. Nevertheless, most postwar leaders responsible for the formulation and implementation of American foreign policy have embraced a remarkably similar and consistent outlook.

What is that orthodox outlook? U.S. policy pronouncements and external actions since World War II suggest that three tenets have been uppermost in the minds of American policymakers:

1. The United States must reject isolationism permanently and substitute for it an active responsibility for the direction of international affairs.
2. Communism represents a dangerous ideological force in the world, and the United States should combat its spread.
3. Because the Soviet Union is the spearhead of the communist challenge, American foreign policy must contain Soviet expansionism and influence.

To be sure, other convictions about America's foreign priorities have been expressed as well. Nevertheless, the three tenets delineate core beliefs that have given postwar American foreign policy its shape and direction, even if their continuing validity is being tested by revolutionary changes in the global circumstances of the 1990s. Let us examine each in more detail.

GLOBALISM

The history of American diplomacy from the birth of the Republic in 1776 until World War II can largely be written in terms of a debate between two opposed traditions—isolationism and internationalism.

Isolationism

On the one hand, a preference for withdrawal from world affairs has periodically surfaced. The reasoning behind the isolationist impulse was expressed well in George Washington's Farewell Address, in which he warned to "steer clear of permanent alliances with any portion of the foreign world." His concern was that participation in balance-of-power politics with untrustworthy and despotic European governments would lead to danger abroad and the loss of democratic freedoms at home. If the country interacted with corrupt governments it would become like them: lie down with dogs, get up with fleas. Secretary of State John Quincy Adams later extended this interpretation in an often-quoted speech, delivered on July 4, 1821, in which he prescribed America's appropriate role in world affairs.

> Wherever the standard of freedom and independence has been or shall be unfurled, there will [America's] heart, her benedictions, and her prayers be. But she goes not abroad in search of monsters to destroy. She is the well-wisher to the freedom and independence of all. She is the champion and vindicator of her own. She will recommend the general cause by the countenance of her voice, and by the benignant sympathy of her example. . . . [Otherwise] she might become the dictatress of the world. She would no longer be the ruler of her own spirit.

The belief that international involvement should be passive underlies the isolationist sentiment. The tradition maintains that the United States should act as an example, "a beacon of light on liberty," demonstrating to the world how a free society could run its affairs, and holding itself as a model for others to emulate if they chose. But the United States would *not* assume responsibility for the world, even in the name of freedom. It would *not* be an agent of international reform, seeking to impose on others its way of life. Moreover, it would *not* intervene in others' internal affairs (even if by word it might preach to them about the virtues of liberty). Instead of attempting to manage world affairs, the United States would participate only to defend itself against others' predatory actions. To advocates of isolationism, global involvement would subvert democratic freedom at home. From this viewpoint, avoiding a globalist foreign policy is deemed consistent with the national interest. Isolationist sentiments reigned supreme during much of the nineteenth century, and in the twentieth they have typically been resurgent in response to American war experiences. George McGovern's 1972 presidential campaign theme "Come Home America" during the Vietnam War is exemplary.

Internationalism

On the other hand, American history also has witnessed periods in which the penchant for active internationalism has been dominant. When the pendulum has swung in that direction, American leaders have energetically sought to expand U.S. influence by actively playing the game of power politics. Like other great powers in history, the United States has viewed the world's problems as its own, perceived its interests threatened by every international development, and accepted the responsibilities of involvement willingly.

The internationalist tradition entails diverse practices, including not only the exercise of power, but also intervention in the political affairs of others, the economic penetration of foreign markets through investment and trade, maintenance of a high diplomatic profile, the quest for preponderant military and diplomatic status, sensitivity to threats to the nation's honor, active promotion of American values abroad, and a corresponding effort to transplant American institutions.

At the extreme, the globalist tradition places the United States in the category of an imperial republic, or what George Washington termed a "nascent empire." Expansionist diplomacy has sought to spread American values internationally and "export the American revolution" (Fossedal, 1989), as exemplified by the purchases of the Louisiana Territory, Florida, and Alaska; the annexation of Texas; the acquisition by military force of the Philippines, Puerto Rico, and Guam; and the assumption, with the Monroe Doctrine, of sphere-of-influence responsibilities throughout the Western Hemisphere. The treatment of native Americans was reflective of yet another form of expansionism. Here "manifest destiny" was little more than a crude euphemism for, and rationalization of, a policy of expulsion and extermination of American Indians who were, in contemporary terminology, "nonstate nations." The expansionist spirit that animated these episodes is reflected in the policy rhetoric of their proponents. For instance, in 1846 William H. Seward, who later became secretary of state, pledged, "I will engage to give you the possession of the American continent and the control of the world." Similarly, Senator Albert Beveridge, speaking in 1898, referred to Americans as "a conquering race." "We must obey our blood," he urged, "and occupy new markets and if necessary new lands."

In practice, those sentiments reflected less an American desire to acquire others' territory and resources than an underlying attitude about the country's unique place in the world. From that ethnocentric view it has often been but a short step to messianic crusading; self-righteously presuming its innate virtue and innocence, the United States on occasion has operated from a belief in the nation's global *mission*. This moralistic outlook has pictured the world as a legitimate target for reform, and, during periods in which such thinking has been dominant, the urge to practice a globalist foreign policy has proven irresistible. "The assumption is that we are the anointed custodians of the rules of international behavior," Arthur Schlesinger (1984) writes, "and that the function of United States policy is to mark other states up or down, according to their obedience to our rules." But these periods have not persisted throughout American history without interruption.

Globalism versus Retrenchment: Cyclical Patterns

Because American policymakers historically have been unable to reconcile the advantages of withdrawing from the world with the benefits of reforming it, the nation's global posture has alternated between periods of "introversion" and "extroversion," that is, between periods of isolationist withdrawal and global involvement. Debates among policymakers as to which role best serves the national interest have never been conclusively resolved. Instead, one conception has dominated at one time only to be replaced later by the other (for example, an internationalist phase prior to World War I and an isolationist one following it). In fact, America's vacillation between isolationist withdrawal and global involvement appears to have fluctuated in *cycles* (Klingberg, 1983, 1990; Lundestad, 1988). Each introvert phase in the cycle has taken twenty-five to thirty years to run its course before a new extrovert phase of approximately the same duration has arisen. Frank Klingberg (1983) suggests that the cyclical pattern has unfolded as follows.

Introversion	*Extroversion*
1776–1798	1798–1824
1824–1844	1844–1871
1871–1891	1891–1919
1919–1940	1940–1966
1967–1986	1986–2014

The legacies of introversion and extroversion provide American leaders with very different traditions to which they can refer, when the need arises, to justify whatever policy orientation they wish to pursue. By emphasizing either tradition and the values they symbolize, adaptive adjustments to changing perceptions of U.S. interests have been made each quarter-century. Since World War II, however, internationalist practices and sentiment have been particularly dominant.

Globalist Internationalism in the Postwar Era

"Every war in American history," writes Arthur Schlesinger (1986), "has been followed in due course by skeptical reassessments of supposedly sacred assumptions." World War II, more than any other, served such a purpose. It was a seminal event that both crystallized a mood and acted as a catalyst for it; it resolved contradictions and helped clarify values; and it produced a consensus about America's world role. The post–World War I isolationist mood (symbolized by the Neutrality Acts of the 1930s) had made American entry into World War II both reluctant and late. But with participation in that war the United States shifted course and emerged a superpower with a new sense of global responsibility. The isolationist heritage was pushed aside as the nation's leaders enthusiastically plunged into the task of shaping the world to American preferences. Most American leaders came to believe that the United States should not, and could not, retreat from world affairs as it had after World War I. A new epoch in American diplomacy commenced as the isolationist tradition was jettisoned.

In 1947 President Harry S Truman set the tone of American postwar policy in the doctrine that bears his name: "The free peoples of the world look to us for support in maintaining their freedoms. . . . If we falter in our leadership, we may endanger the peace of the world—and we shall surely endanger the welfare of our own nation." Policy pronouncements thereafter prescribed the American mission—to make the world a better place in which to live. "Other nations have interests," declared Secretary of State Dean Rusk in 1967; "the United States has responsibilities." "Our nation," John F. Kennedy asserted in 1962, was "commissioned by history to be either an observer of freedom's failure or the cause of its success." The United States became a global actor; it made "a covenant with power" (Gardner, 1984).

Consistent with its new sense of global responsibility, the United States actively sought to orchestrate nearly every significant global initiative. It was a primary sponsor and supporter of the United Nations. It engineered creation of regional institutions, such as the Organization of American States, and promoted American hegemony in areas regarded as American spheres of influence. It pushed hard for the expansion of foreign trade and the development of new markets for American business abroad. It launched an ambitious foreign aid program. And it built a vast array of military alliances, both formal and informal. Its pursuit of these ambitious foreign policy objectives created a vast American "empire" circling the globe. The indicators in Focus 3.1 describe the scope of America's postwar commitments and involvements abroad, and suggest that for decades following World War II "empire" had indeed become "a way of life" (Williams, 1980).

Not only does the postwar record demonstrate American involvement worldwide, but equally conspicuous is the consistency with which the premises of globalism have been reiterated by every president since Truman. Consider the policy pronouncements in Focus 3.2, which affirm several persistent assumptions: (1) the United States has global obligations; (2) it is an international guardian of freedom and morality; (3) the future of the world depends on its willingness and readiness to act abroad for the good of the world; and (4) the United States should be a world leader. Given the postwar American diplomatic record, the phrase "the first global society" used by Zbigniew Brzezinski, President Carter's national security assistant, to describe the United States, is

---

FOCUS 3.1 ▪ The Scope of U.S. Involvements Abroad

Nonmilitary Involvements

- In 1989 the United States maintained diplomatic relations with 160 governments and was a member of over fifty international organizations.
- In 1988 U.S. direct investment abroad exceeded $325 billion, an amount more than triple the level in 1971.
- In 1989 the value of U.S. exports reached $360 billion, a figure more than eight times greater than in 1970; imports in 1989 totaled $470 billion compared with less than $40 billion in 1970.
- In 1988 U.S. economic aid to more than eighty countries exceeded $8.5 billion.
- In 1987 the U.S. Agency for International Development implemented 1,750 projects in eighty-three developing countries.
- In the late 1980s the U.S. government, through U.S. broadcasting services, promoted its world view in forty-eight languages with more than two thousand hours of broadcasting each week.

Military Involvements

- The United States is committed through bilateral and multilateral treaties, executive agreements, and policy declarations to the defense of over forty nations.
- By the late 1980s military involvements resulting from treaties, executive agreements, arms sales, the stationing of troops, and various kinds of military assistance linked the United States to over one hundred different countries. The estimated 1990 cost of these commitments in Europe exceeded $150 billion, and those associated with Operation Desert Shield in the Persian Gulf were expected to top $1.25 billion per month.
- In 1989 U.S. military sales the world over amounted to $10.9 billion.
- Between 1975 and 1988 the value of U.S. military deliveries to less developed countries exceeded $106 billion. By 1988 the amount of foreign military sales and military aid extended to other countries since World War II stood at $289 billion.
- The U.S. policy of "global containment" as manifested in the Korean and Vietnam wars is estimated to have cost $190 billion.
- In 1989 541,000 U.S. military personnel (plus 450,000 civilian employees) were stationed overseas at 375 major bases in thirty-five different countries.
- The U.S. has nearly forty-five hundred nuclear weapons deployed with its forces in foreign countries.
- In fiscal 1991 the U.S. budgeted $320.9 billion for military preparedness—a figure that exceeds the gross national product of all but a handful of the members of the United Nations.

fitting. Similarly, President George Bush's contention that world peace depends on American leadership because no "other country can pick up the mantle" suggests that globalist aspirations continue to animate American foreign policy. Indeed, no aspirant to the White House is likely to risk challenging the appropriateness of an active leadership role for the United States—for to do so would be to attack a widely accepted image the country holds of itself that both led to and is sustained by the extensive external involvements and ties it has accumulated since its entry into World War II.

However relentlessly pursued, America's postwar globalist vision has not gone without challenge. Consistent with the hypothesized quarter-century cycle, in the mid-1960s enthusiasm for globalism began to wane. The tragedy of the Vietnam War coincided with popular pleas for a U.S. retreat from world affairs. President Nixon's declaration in 1970 that "America cannot—and will not—conceive all the plans, design all the programs, execute all the decisions, and undertake all the defense of the free nations of the world" took cognizance of a resurgent isolationist mood. This confession, part and parcel of the Nixon Doctrine, signaled acceptance of the proposition that American interests could be served by contracting its global involvement. America's superpower status was questioned, and throughout the 1970s the eagle appeared "entangled" in a web of constraints on its global power (see Oye, Rothchild, and Lieber, 1979).

The Carter administration acknowledged these growing limits and attempted to reduce them. The Reagan administration also rejected the rhetoric of restraint. Thus the lack of enthusiasm for active global involvement in the 1970s was a temporary pause that did little to signal an end to the internationalist thrust of American foreign policy characteristic since World War II. "We hear it said that we live in an era of limits to our powers. Well, there are [also] limits to our patience," proclaimed President Reagan in a viewpoint that underscored his commitment to restoring global activism, combating neo-isolationism, and once more making the eagle "defiant" (Oye, Lieber, and Rothchild, 1983). The role of world policeman was reaffirmed and extended, along with the burdens it entailed. Reagan's policies and words come close to repudiating the Nixon Doctrine, which claimed that the cost of protecting international security would have to be shared with others. As Secretary of State George Shultz asserted in 1985, the United States would not allow itself to become "just observers; we are participants, and we are engaged. America is again in a position to have a major influence over the trend of events." That the United States might be "overcommitted," with its obligations abroad exceeding its resources in a classic symptom of imperial "overstretch" (Kennedy, 1987), was denied. Instead, American policymakers in the 1980s and early 1990s preached a "can do" approach. "We're going to affect the future substantially," asserted Secretary of State James Baker in April 1989. "We can . . . be a force for freedom and peaceful change unlike any country in the world." He added in March 1990 that "There is no substitute for American leadership."

"American foreign policy makers," it has been said (van den Haag, 1985), "appear to share a naive belief that American ideals and ideas can and should

---

FOCUS 3.2 ▪ Globalism since 1945: Forty-Five Years of Internationalist Policy Pronouncements

Harry S Truman, 1945	[The United States should] take the lead in running the world in the way that the world ought to be run.
Dwight D. Eisenhower, 1960	Free men everywhere look to us.
John F. Kennedy, 1961	Let every nation know, whether it wishes us well or ill, that we shall pay any price, bear any burden, meet any hardship, support any friend, oppose any foe to assure the survival and success of liberty. This much we pledge—and more.
Richard M. Nixon, 1963	I say that it is time for us proudly to declare that our ideas are for export. We need not apologize for taking this position.
Lyndon B. Johnson, 1965	History and our own achievements have thrust upon us the principal responsibility for protecting freedom on earth.
Gerald R. Ford, 1976	America has had a unique role in the world . . . [and] ever since the end of World War II we have borne successfully a heavy responsibility for insuring a stable world order.
Jimmy Carter, 1977	There is only one nation in the world which is capable of true leadership among the community of nations and that is the United States of America.
Ronald Reagan, 1980	We in this country, in this generation, are, by destiny rather than choice, the watchmen on the walls of world freedom.
George Bush, 1989	Around the globe, we must continue to be freedom's best friend.

---

solve all the problems of the world and that it is their mission to actively apply these ideals abroad.'' Is the belief warranted? In asking this question, we should consider whether a readjustment in orientation is required to restore a balance between globalism and isolationism, between moralistic crusading and escapist withdrawal, between overextension and paralysis.

In probing this question, the link between globalism and another pillar of postwar America foreign policy—anticommunism—must be illuminated. In assuming a globalist policy, has the United States—Secretary of State Adams's warning notwithstanding—gone abroad in search of monsters to destroy?

THE AMERICAN CHALLENGE TO INTERNATIONAL COMMUNISM

Fear of communism (and an unequivocal rejection of it) comprises another recurrent theme and defining attribute of postwar American foreign policy. The fear played a major part in shaping the way the United States perceived the world during much of the postwar period. To most Americans, communism was viewed as a doctrinaire belief system diametrically opposed to the "American way of life." Combating this threatening, adversarial ideology became almost an obsession—to the point, some argued, that American foreign policy itself may have become ideological (Commager, 1983; Parenti, 1969).

The Perceived Threat of Communism

Anticommunism has been premised on the conviction that ideas have consequences, and that Marxist-Leninist doctrine comprises alien ideas that posed a threat to the United States and to the world at large. That conviction, in turn, influenced substantially the goals the United States pursued abroad. For decades the United States defined its mission in terms of the beliefs it opposed; its words and deeds suggested that the United States stood less *for* something (other than the classic goals of self-preservation and national enrichment) than *against* something: communist ideology.

The varied reasons for American preoccupation with and fear of communism, which developed in the formative decade following World War II, rested on a set of corollary assumptions about the nature of "the beast." Included was the assumption that communism was an expansionist, crusading force intent on converting the entire world to its beliefs, and that, however evil, its doctrines might command widespread appeal (see Almond, 1954). For decades communism also was viewed as a cohesive monolith to which all adherents were bound in united solidarity. In addition, because communism was seen as inherently totalitarian, antidemocratic, and anticapitalist, it was perceived as a real threat to freedom, liberty, and prosperity throughout the world.

The passage of time has steadily reduced the cogency of these assumptions. Communism revealed itself to be more polycentric than monolithic; Communist party leaders became increasingly vocal about their own divisions and disagreements concerning communism's fundamental beliefs; and it became clear that the greatest fear that some communist states had were the motives of other communist states. The Sino-Soviet split, which dates back to the 1950s, warfare in the 1980s among Vietnamese, Chinese, Cambodian, and Laotian communists, and the divisions between the Soviet Union and East European leaders in the late 1980s are preeminent cases in point. Moreover, the experimentation of communist leaders nearly everywhere in the late 1980s with free enterprise, capitalist incentives, and democratic reforms—and their citizens' abrupt rejection of Communist party rule in favor of democratic capitalism—demonstrated unambiguously that the stereotypic image of a unified communist bloc cemented by ideological consensus was too simple. Disputes between the communist states themselves were grounded in nationalism, not ideology, and the internal reforms their leaders undertook were motivated by the conviction that communism could not provide a viable program with which to organize the politics and economics of their societies. Moreover, even if communism was in spirit an expansionist movement, it proved to be more flexible than initially assumed, with no timetable for the conversion of non-believers. But whatever the appeal its message once commanded, by the 1990s it had dissipated. Its principles were simply no longer convincing even in countries led by pro-Marxist rulers, as it was repudiated time and again as a model for progress.

But the impact of the assumptions made for decades about communism in the American policy-making community was enormous nevertheless. Successful opposition to communism was defined as one of America's most important interests. This world view has not altogether collapsed, even in today's atmosphere in which the victory of democratic capitalism over communism and socialism is widely assumed and has even been declared by American policymakers themselves (Fukuyama, 1989). The thrust of anticommunism in American foreign policy continues.

Anticommunism: Past and Present

Even as it persists, the historical impact of anticommunism should be neither minimized nor forgotten. The premise of communism's challenge contributed in part to the rise of the Cold War and influenced its perpetuation for four decades. From this perspective, rivalry between the United States and the Soviet Union did not center on conflicts of interests between them but on a contest between their belief systems. Such contests allow no room for compromise because they pit right against wrong, good against evil. Diametrically opposed belief systems require victory. When adherents are animated by a belief in the righteousness of their cause, the world tends to be seen as an arena for a religious war—a battle for the allegiance of people's minds. Under these circumstances the use of any means to proselytize is acceptable; the end justifies the means. Thus, on occasion, American policy rhetoric—like that employed to justify religious wars and religious persecutions in the past—advocated "sleepless hostility to Communism—even preventive war" (Commager, 1965). In short, the world came to be viewed by both adversaries in zero-sum terms: when one side won converts the other side necessarily lost them. Such an outlook almost guarantees pure conflict by recognizing no virtue in conciliation or cooperation with an ideological foe and by offering little tolerance of competing beliefs (Schlesinger, 1986).

Throughout much of the postwar era, official pronouncements about America's global objectives routinely stressed that communist doctrine represented a real menace to America. ''The actions resulting from the Communist philosophy,'' charged Harry S Truman in 1949, ''are a threat.'' ''We face a hostile ideology—global in scope, atheistic in character, ruthless in purpose, and insidious in method. Unhappily the danger it poses promises to be of indefinite duration,'' warned President Eisenhower. Related to those convictions was the assumption that communism was endowed with powers and appeals that made its continued spread likely. The so-called domino theory, a popular metaphor in the 1960s, was coined to suggest that the fall to communism in one country would invite the fall of countries adjacent to it, so that like a stack of falling dominoes an endless and unstoppable chain reaction would unfold, bringing increasing proportions of the world's population under the domination of communist governments. The metaphor warned that this process would continue unabated unless checked by American resistance. ''Communism is on the move. It is out to win. It is playing an offensive game,'' warned Richard Nixon in 1963, who earlier in his political career chastised Truman's secretary of state as the ''dean of the cowardly college of Communist containment'' and recommended ''dealing with this great Communist offensive'' by pushing back the Iron Curtain with force.

The goal of anticommunism became institutionalized following World War II. For nearly two decades thereafter, until the United States became mired in the Vietnam War, few in the American foreign policy establishment challenged the assumption that communism was a cohesive and powerful conspiratorial movement that had to be opposed. Few challenged the belief that the Cold War was rooted in ideological causes. Policy debate was concerned largely with how the anticommunist drive was to be implemented, not with whether communism posed a threat. Some of the ideological fervor of American foreign policy rhetoric later receded with the Nixon-Kissinger program to limit communist influence through a strategy of détente. References in policy statements to communism itself as a force in world politics declined thereafter. President Carter went so far as to declare in May 1977 that ''we are now free of that inordinate fear of communism which once led us to embrace any dictator who joined us in our fear.'' But the anticommunist underpinnings of American foreign policy did not vanish.

The theme of ''communism as the principal danger'' gained renewed emphasis under Ronald Reagan, whose Manichean world view (see Glad, 1983) pictured the world as a place where the forces of the noncommunist world, led by the United States, were arrayed in continuous battle against communist Russia, which he described as ''the focus of evil in the modern world.'' ''We've made it very plain,'' he explained in 1983. ''We don't like [the Soviet Union's] system.''

By the end of the 1980s, however, things began to change. The demonstrable failure of communism and the desertion of communist leaders to other political and economic philosophies reduced the need for strident opposition to communism. Instead, the ideology was dismissed and sometimes ignored. Richard Schifter, an assistant secretary of state in the Bush administration, declared that ''communism has proven itself to be a false god.'' Rejected gods do not need to be condemned. But this did not mean that the anticommunist mentality was dead, or that U.S. dedication to extirpate its (waning) influence had lessened. The "inordinate fear" may have become dormant, but clearly a Cold War perspective continues to color the U.S. interpretation of international events, and the Bush administration's emphasis on the worldwide transition to democracy is inspired by the desire to remove the cursed influence of communist ideology from the globe. American opposition to communism is unlikely to be buried with the loss of the communist movement's momentum. The extinction of communism remains a primary objective of the United States, and the premises on which that goal is based continue to exert their influence on policy planning.

THE CONTAINMENT OF SOVIET INFLUENCE

As the physically strongest and the most vocal Marxist state, the Soviet Union historically was considered the cutting edge of the communist challenge. As a consequence, postwar American diplomacy rested on the following corollary beliefs: (1) the Soviet Union is an expansionist nation intent on maximizing communist power through military conquest and "exported" revolutions; (2) the Soviet goal of world domination is permanent and will succeed unless blocked by vigorous counteraction; (3) as the leader of the "free world," the United States is the only nation in a position to repel Soviet aggression and restore the balance of power; (4) accordingly, the United States must increase its military power relative to the Soviet Union in order to better contain Soviet expansion; (5) appeasement will not work—to stop Soviet expansion, force must be met with force; and (6) the fate of the world is determined by super-power relations; relations with less powerful nations are secondary, as a pyramid of priorities requires that the United States place competition with the Soviet Union above all else. A Soviet-centric foreign policy followed from this interrelated set of beliefs.

To understand what brought about these durable assumptions and the containment strategy derived from them into play, it is important to trace the circumstances that led to the Cold War. The task is difficult because the historical evidence is subject to differing interpretations, as attested to by the continuing debate between orthodox (Spanier, 1988; Ulam, 1985) and revisionist (Kolko, 1968; Yergin, 1978) accounts of the origins of the Cold War (for discussions of rival theories, see Gaddis, 1972, 1982; Melanson, 1983; Schlesinger, 1986). Despite these obstacles, the origins of the Cold War should be examined to prepare the way for a consideration of the evolutionary course of American interactions with the Soviet Union from the inception of the containment policy to the present. A chronological survey of American behavior toward the Soviet Union allows us to detect patterns in the relationship, and provides a basis from which to evaluate whether the containment strategy has proved consistent with American interests.

The Origins of the Cold War: Contending Hypotheses

One view of the causes of the Cold War maintains that the United States and the Soviet Union were destined by fate and historical circumstance to become rivals. In 1835 Alexis de Tocqueville predicted the eventual rivalry, arguing that "there are today two great peoples which, starting out from different points of departure, advance toward the same goal—the Americans and the Russians. . . . Each of them will one day hold in its hands the destinies of half of mankind."

Tocqueville's prophecy was based on his appreciation of the two countries' great natural resources and territorial size. He did not, or could not, foresee the advent of Marxism or the possibility that ideological differences would contribute to the dispute he regarded as inevitable. Instead, he saw the two countries as natural enemies. Why? Because the predicted ascent of the United States and Russia to top international status guaranteed that they would see each other as a threat and compete for supremacy. Preponderance assured conflict, because throughout history great powers have always clashed (Morgenthau, 1985). Rivals have always perceived assertive actions by others as initial steps toward "aggrandizement" and strived to prevent them.

According to a second interpretation, the Cold War was simply an extension of the two powers' mutual animosity since the Russian Revolution, which brought a Marxist philosophy into practice in 1919 in a society Marx himself felt was infertile soil for a communist experiment, and which thereafter strained U.S. relations with the Soviet state. From a long-term perspective, the Cold War was a product of the two states' traditional repugnance for each other's professed way of life. Their incompatible ideologies ruled out compromise or coexistence. What is ironic is that each power's ideology and messianic world view closely resembled the other's (Jönsson, 1982b).

A third thesis holds that the Cold War originated in the experiences of the United States and the Soviet Union as wartime allies. Recall that Hitler's plan for world conquest had drawn the United States and the Soviet Union together in a united, antifascist coalition. Circumstances required their collaboration, for each needed the other to assure defeat of the common Axis enemy. Was the Grand Alliance simply a marriage of convenience or, instead, were the Allies sincere in their wartime proclamations of mutual respect? Even while cooperating in the wartime alliance, did the two countries fail to dispel their latent suspicions about each other's real expansionist intentions? There is much to suggest that their troubled wartime experience nourished the Cold War, as we will describe later.

Roosevelt's and Stalin's wartime pronouncements indicated that their professions of goodwill and trust were not necessarily illusory or mere propaganda. To be sure, differences between the Allies inevitably surfaced as they negotiated wartime strategy, but the dominant mood was not, on the whole, distrustful. In their official discourse American and Soviet leaders proclaimed their desire to cooperate. In fact, as World War II was drawing to a victorious conclusion, policies aimed at continued Soviet-American collaboration were devised, and resumption of great power rivalry looked neither preordained nor inevitable. (Collaboration, in turn, revealed the capacity of the superpowers to subordinate their ideological beliefs to national interests.) A positive spirit of common endeavor was exhibited in the Allies' negotiations about the shape of the postwar world. Franklin Roosevelt clearly expected that Allied wartime collaboration would persist in the aftermath of war. As his adviser Harry Hopkins stated, ''The Russians had proved that they could be reasonable and farseeing and there wasn't any doubt in the minds of the President or any of us that we could live with them and get along with them peacefully for as far into the future as any of us could imagine.''

Roosevelt's optimism stemmed from his conviction that continued friendship could be underpinned by negotiated agreements that permitted both countries to enjoy the benefits of power, but each within its own sphere of influence. The great powers had informally agreed that each would enjoy dominant influence and freedom in specified areas of the globe (see Morgenthau, 1969; Schlesinger, 1986). John Foster Dulles, later President Eisenhower's secretary of state, noted in January 1945 that ''the three great powers which at Moscow agreed upon the closest cooperation about European questions have shifted to a practice of separate, regional responsibility.'' Also implicit was the agreement not to oppose each other in areas vital to national security, as reflected in the Yalta agreement (Ulam, 1983). Symbolic, too, were the mutually agreed-on rules written into the United Nations Charter governing the Security Council that obliged the United States and the Soviet Union to share responsibility for the preservation of world peace.

Why did such ostensibly cordial relations and accommodative aspirations collapse? Perhaps the hope for postwar superpower goodwill died with President Roosevelt; upon assuming power, Truman promptly substituted a confrontational policy and responded to perceived Soviet provocation belligerently. ''If the Russians did not wish to join us they could go to hell'' typified his attitude and approach (Tugwell, 1971). Perhaps adherence to Roosevelt's flexible policies and sensitive approach would have prevented the Soviet-American relationship from freezing into a Cold War (see Theoharis, 1970).

A fourth, perhaps more convincing explanation, interprets the Cold War as rooted in psychological factors, particularly the superpowers' *misperceptions* of each other's motives, not conflicting interests (Larson, 1985). Hence the origins of the Cold War may be found in the propensity of the mistrustful parties to see in their own actions only virtue and in those of the adversary only malice.

To the extent that such *mirror images* existed, as they probably did, cooperation was precluded and hostility made inevitable (Bronfenbrenner, 1961). As perceptions of the adversary's evil intentions became accepted as dogma, the prophecies that were made became self-fulfilling.[1] A month before

---

1. Prophecies are sometimes self-fulfilling because the future can be affected by the way it is anticipated. How predictions can make themselves come true in international relations is illustrated by the tendency of those who predict others' hostility to arm fearfully for defense and provocatively challenge those who they feel are threatening; they then produce enemies whom they have alarmed.

Roosevelt died, he expressed to Stalin his desire, above all, to prevent "mutual distrust." Yet events at the onset of the Cold War indicate that an escalating spiral of threat, misperception, and mistrust were its very foundations. Stalin was as wary of the Americans as they were of him. Hostility and threats by one power were responded to in kind by the other. The Soviet and American perceptions of events during this epochal period contributed heavily to the Cold War. Consider their competing images.

>   *The Soviet Image.* To the Soviets, reasons for doubting American intentions were abundant. The Soviets lived with the memory of American participation in the 1918–1919 Allied military intervention in Russia, which turned from its initial mission of keeping arms from falling into the hands of Germany into an anti-Bolshevik undertaking. They were sensitive to the fact that the United States failed to recognize the Soviet Union diplomatically until 1933—in the midst of a depression perceived to be a sign of capitalism's weakness and the beginning of its ultimate collapse. Moreover, the wartime experience had done little to reduce Soviet suspicions. The Soviets recalled U.S. procrastination before entering the war against the fascists; the American refusal to inform the Soviets of the Manhattan Project to develop the atomic bomb; the delay in sending the Soviets promised Lend-Lease supplies; the failure to open up the second front (leading Stalin to suspect that American policy was to let the Russians and Germans destroy each other so that the United States could then pick up the pieces from among the rubble[2]); the American failure to inform the Soviets of wartime strategy to the extent that it informed Great Britain; and the use of the atomic bomb against Japan, perhaps perceived as a maneuver to prevent Russian involvement in the Pacific peace settlement (see Alperovitz, 1985, 1989; in contrast, see Alsop and Joravsky, 1980; Bundy, 1988). Those suspicions were later reinforced by the willingness of the United States to support previous Nazi collaborators in American-occupied countries, notably Italy, and by its pressure on the Soviet Union to abide by its promise to allow free elections in areas vital to Soviet national security, notably Poland. The Soviets were also resentful of the abrupt U.S. cancellation of promised Lend-Lease assistance that Stalin had counted on to facilitate the postwar recovery of the Soviet Union. (The United States later framed the European

---

2. Stalin's suspicions may not have been completely unfounded. While still a senator, for example, Harry S Truman (*New York Times*, July 24, 1941) expressed the hope that following Hitler's invasion of Russia the Nazis and communists would destroy each other. He stated flatly, "If we see that Germany is winning we ought to help Russia and if Russia is winning we ought to help Germany, and in that way let them kill as many as possible, although I don't want to see Hitler victorious under any circumstances." Although Truman was not speaking for President Roosevelt or the U.S. government, such sentiments expressed publicly by a member of Congress were unlikely to be ignored. Those views resurfaced in the aftermath of World War II when, in a speech before the United Nations (April 26, 1945), Soviet Foreign Minister V. M. Molotov accused the Western powers of complicity with Hitler.

economic recovery program known as the Marshall Plan in such a way as to virtually guarantee Soviet nonparticipation.) Thus Soviet distrust of American intentions stemmed in part from fears of American encirclement that were exacerbated by America's past hostility.[3]

The U.S. Image. To the United States, distrust of the Soviet Union was warranted by numerous indications of growing Soviet belligerence: Stalin's announcement in February 1946 that the Soviet Union was not going to demilitarize its armed forces, at the very time that the United States was engaged in the largest demobilization by a victorious power in world history; Russian unwillingness to permit democratic elections in the territories they liberated from the Nazis; their refusal to assist in postwar reconstruction in regions outside Soviet control; their removal of supplies and infrastructure from Soviet-occupied areas; their selfish and often obstructive behavior in the fledgling new international organizations; their occasional opportunistic disregard for international law and violation of agreements and treaties; their infiltration of Western labor movements; and, perhaps most unacceptable, their anti-American propaganda and espousal of an alien ideology that promised to destroy the American type of economic and political system. The implied threats provoked fears that greatly intensified as a result of the Soviet unwillingness to withdraw the Red Army from Eastern and Central Europe and Iran. The Soviet Union came to be perceived as a military rival straining at the leash to invade Western Europe and to acquire new satellites. Thus, whereas Roosevelt had argued before the American people that postwar peace depended on Soviet-American collaboration, Stalin's actions and anti-American rhetoric led increasingly to the perception that the Soviet Union itself posed the greatest threat to the security of the United States and to world peace.

The two countries' leaders thus operated from very different images. They imposed on events different definitions of reality and became captives of those visions. Expectations shaped the way developments were interpreted: what they looked for is what they got. Hence, even though each power saw its adversary in remarkably similar terms, the misperceptions involved became a source of conflict. George F. Kennan, the American ambassador to the Soviet Union in 1952, noted that misread signals were common to both sides.

The Marshall Plan, the preparations for the setting up of a West German government, and the first moves toward the establishment of NATO were taken in Moscow as the beginnings of a campaign to deprive the Soviet Union of the fruits

---

3. Secretary of Commerce Henry A. Wallace, in a 1946 memorandum to the president, asked how American actions since V-J Day—especially American weapons production—looked to other nations. "These facts," Wallace concluded, "make it appear either (1) that we are preparing ourselves to win the war which we regard as inevitable or (2) that we are trying to build up a predominance of force to intimidate the rest of mankind. How would it look to us if Russia had the atomic bomb and we did not, if Russia had ten thousand mile bombers and air bases within one thousand miles of our coastline, and we did not?"

of its victory over Germany. The Soviet crackdown on Czechoslovakia (1948) and the mounting of the Berlin blockade, both essentially defensive . . . reactions to these Western moves, were then similarly misread on the Western side. Shortly thereafter there came the crisis of the Korean War, where the Soviet attempt to employ a satellite military force in civil combat to its own advantage, by way of reaction to the American decision to establish a permanent military presence in Japan, was read in Washington as the beginning of the final Soviet push for world conquest; whereas the active American military response, provoked by this move, appeared in Moscow . . . as a threat to the Soviet position in both Manchuria and in eastern Siberia. (Kennan, 1976: 683–684)

If the Cold War is correctly interpreted as originating in mutual misperceptions, it is also plausible to see it as a missed opportunity for cooperation. Given each power's insensitivity to the impact of its actions on the other's fears, it is difficult to assign blame for the decay of Soviet-American relations. Both were responsible because both were victims of their images and expectations. The Cold War was not simply an American response to communist aggression, which is the orthodox American view; nor was it simply a product of postwar American assertiveness, as revisionist historians have argued (see Schlesinger, 1906). Both of the great powers felt threatened, and each had legitimate reasons to regard the other with suspicion. Thus the Cold War may be seen as a conflict over reciprocal anxieties bred by the way officials on both sides interpreted the other's actions. Like a bad marriage that gets increasingly tense through constant bickering and mutual mistrust of motives, the Cold War may have arisen from the unwillingness of both the United States and the Soviet Union to take initiatives to alleviate suspicions.

Because theories that explain the origins of the Cold War exclusively in terms of perceptual variables account for some aspects of Soviet-American rivalry but not all, they are only partially valid. An accurate picture must reference a variety of additional contributing factors: the emergence of "power vacuums" that invited confrontation, the pressures exerted on foreign policies by interest groups and changes in the climate of domestic opinion within each society, innovations in weapons technology and the shifts in strategic balances they introduced, and the role that military planners in each country played in fomenting the conflict (Sherry, 1977).

Regardless of the reasons for its eruption, the Cold War ultimately became *the* central issue in American foreign policy, whose shadow stretches across the entire spectrum of the postwar American response to its world environment.

To understand better the assumptions and actions that shaped America's Soviet policy, we must go beyond inquiry into the origins of the Cold War and examine, first, the immediate circumstances that gave rise to America's containment strategy, and, second, how the containment policy has evolved in response to changing circumstances and the way different administrations have sought to implement it. This can be accomplished by charting the course of containment since its birth in 1947.

America's Containment Strategies: Evolutionary Phases

The history of postwar American foreign policy can largely be written in terms of how the containment doctrine has been interpreted and applied to guide American initiatives toward the Soviet Union and its sometime allies. Although containment remains a defining element of American foreign policy even under President Bush, who has voiced the intention to "move beyond" it, the doctrine, as Bush's pledge attests, has undergone continual adaptation as circumstances have changed.

Consider the quantitative evidence in Figure 3.1. It shows at least three characteristics of Soviet-American interactions since 1948. First, a high level of superpower conflict has prevailed. Second, periods of intense conflict have alternated cyclically with periods of relative cooperation. A trend toward relaxed tensions and growing accommodation was evident between the mid-1960s and the mid-1970s; during the late 1970s and 1980s hostility resumed; and on the eve of the 1990s renewed accommodation is once more evident. Third, reciprocal, action-reaction relations are also clearly evident: periods when the United States directed friendly initiatives toward the Soviets have also been periods when the Soviets have acted with friendliness toward the United States; similarly, periods of American belligerence have been periods of Soviet belligerence.

For analytical purposes the postwar history of America's containment policy can be divided into five chronologically ordered phases as depicted in Figure 3.1 (for an alternative periodization, see Nincic, 1989).

Cold War Confrontation, 1947–1962   The birth of containment in 1947[4] was preceded by a brief period of wary friendship between the wartime allies, colored by American apprehension about Soviet intentions. This ambivalent interlude was punctuated by growing pessimism about continued amity and diminished acceptance of the Soviet Union as an ally. The interlude was short-lived but formative, as all pretense of collaboration with the Soviets ceased and the containment strategy was given birth. The Cold War had begun.

In February 1946 Stalin gave a speech in which he spoke of "the inevitability of conflict with the capitalist powers. He urged the Soviet people not to be deluded that the end of the war meant that the nation could relax. Rather, intensified efforts were needed to strengthen and defend the homeland" (Lovell, 1970). Shortly thereafter, George F. Kennan, then a diplomat in the American embassy in Moscow, sent to Washington his famous "long telegram" assessing the sources of Soviet conduct. Kennan's conclusions were ominous: "In summary, we have here a political force committed fanatically to the belief that with [the] U.S. there can be no permanent modus vivendi, that it is desirable and necessary that the internal harmony of our society be disrupted, our traditional way of life be destroyed, the international authority of our state be broken, if Soviet power is to be secure."

Kennan's ideas were widely circulated in Washington through the publication of his views in the influential journal *Foreign Affairs* (1947), which he

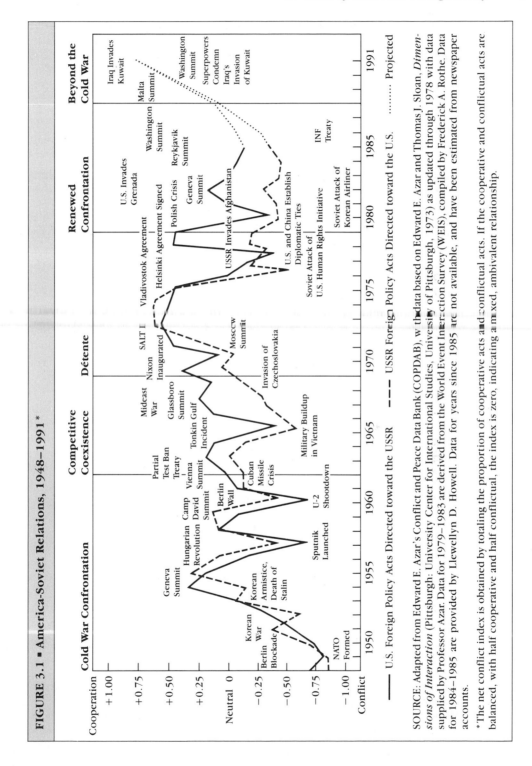

FIGURE 3.1 ■ America-Soviet Relations, 1948–1991*

SOURCE: Adapted from Edward E. Azar's Conflict and Peace Data Bank (COPDAB), with data based on Edward E. Azar and Thomas J. Sloan, *Dimensions of Interaction* (Pittsburgh: University Center for International Studies, University of Pittsburgh, 1973) as updated through 1978 with data supplied by Professor Azar. Data for 1979–1983 are derived from the World Event Interaction Survey (WEIS), compiled by Frederick A. Rothe. Data for 1984–1985 are provided by Llewellyn D. Howell. Data for years since 1985 are not available, and have been estimated from newspaper accounts.

*The net conflict index is obtained by totaling the proportion of cooperative acts and conflictual acts. If the cooperative and conflictual acts are balanced, with half cooperative and half conflictual, the index is zero, indicating a mixed, ambivalent relationship.

signed "X" instead of identifying himself as its author. In it Kennan argued that Soviet leaders would forever feel insecure about their political ability to maintain power against forces both within Soviet society itself and in the outside world. Their insecurity would lead to an activist—and perhaps aggressive— Soviet foreign policy. Yet it was within the power of the United States to increase the strains under which the Soviet leadership would have to operate, perhaps thus leading to a gradual mellowing or eventual end of Soviet power. Hence Kennan concluded: "In these circumstances it is clear that the main element of any United States policy toward the Soviet Union must be that of a long-term, patient but firm and vigilant *containment* of Russian expansive tendencies" (Kennan, 1947, emphasis added).

Not long thereafter, Harry S Truman made this prescription the cornerstone of American postwar policy. Provoked in part by domestic turmoil in Turkey and civil war in Greece, which he and others believed to be communist inspired, Truman declared, "I believe that it must be the policy of the United States to support free peoples who are resisting attempted subjugation by armed minorities or by outside pressures."

Truman's pronouncement, eventually known as the Truman Doctrine, viewed international politics as a contest for world domination, with the Soviet Union as an imperial power bent on world conquest. An American policy crystallized around a commitment to engage fully in this contest to contain the Soviet Union's global designs. This was made the axiom that rationalized a "grand crusade":

> Whenever and wherever an anti-Communist government was threatened, by indigenous insurgents, foreign invasion, or even diplomatic pressure (as with Turkey), the United States would supply political, economic, and, most of all, military aid. The Truman Doctrine came close to shutting the door against any revolution, since the terms "free peoples" and "anti-Communist" were thought to be synonymous. All . . . any dictatorship had to do to get American aid was to claim that its opponents were Communist. (Ambrose, 1988: 85)

With the Truman Doctrine, containment became *the* foreign policy of the United States—a national obsession coloring much of its subsequent thinking and demanding many of the nation's resources.

Whether the policy of containment was appropriate, even at the time of its initial promulgation, remains controversial. Kennan himself became alarmed at the way he felt his celebrated statement was taken out of context and misinterpreted, so that "containment" became an "indestructible myth," a doctrine "which was then identified with the foreign policy of the Truman administration."

> I . . . naturally went to great lengths to disclaim the view, imputed to me by implication . . . that containment was a matter of stationing military forces around the Soviet borders and preventing any outbreak of Soviet military aggressiveness. I protested . . . against the implication that the Russians were aspiring to

invade other areas and that the task of American policy was to prevent them from doing so. "The Russians don't want," I insisted, "to invade anyone. It is not in their tradition. They tried it once in Finland and got their fingers burned. They don't want war of any kind. Above all, they don't want the open responsibility that official invasion brings with it." (Kennan, 1967: 361)

As Kennan later lamented, "the image of a Stalinist Russia poised and yearning to attack the West, and deterred only by our possession of atomic weapons, was largely a creation of the Western imagination." Kennan therefore recommended a political rather than military approach to the containment of Soviet influence, and "cautioned against demonizing the adversary, overestimating enemy strength and overmilitarizing the Western response" (Talbott, 1990b). But his disclaimers notwithstanding, the "containment myth," as Kennan (1967) termed the view that defeating Soviet communism required a militantly confrontational approach, "never fully lost its spell." It became the guiding premise behind postwar American foreign policy.

The emergence of this world view and its attendant policy prescriptions helped heighten the American tendency to regard instability anywhere as resulting from Soviet conspiracy. It was not only the insurgency in Greece and the domestic strife in Turkey that were interpreted as part of a Soviet offensive, nearly all other crises were attributed to Soviet mischief as well.

Central to the superpowers' propensity to interpret crisis situations as the product of the other's aggressive efforts at global domination was their inability to maintain the sphere-of-influence posture tacitly agreed to earlier. When the Soviets moved into portions of Eastern Europe, this was interpreted by the United States as a manifestation of Soviet ambitions for world conquest. Yet the Soviet Union perhaps had reason to think that the Americans would readily accede to Soviet domination in Eastern Europe. In 1945, for example, Secretary of State James Byrnes had commented that the "Soviet Union has a right to friendly governments along its borders," and Under Secretary of State Dean Acheson had spoken of "a Monroe Doctrine for Eastern Europe." Moreover, during the waning days of the fight against Nazi Germany, General Eisenhower refused to let the American army advance to Berlin and the eastern portion of Germany; instead, the Soviet army was permitted to liberate those areas as a prize for the sacrifices the Soviet Union had made in the war against the Nazis. To some this decision reflected the American government's naiveté regarding the postwar structure of international politics in Europe that was being built because of the way the war against Germany was terminated. But to the Soviet Union it may have reinforced the view that the Western powers would accept legitimate Soviet security needs, particularly the need for a buffer zone in Eastern Europe, which had been the common invasion route into Russia for over three centuries. Hence, when the American government began to challenge Soviet supremacy in East Germany and elsewhere in Eastern Europe, the Soviet Union may have felt that previous understandings had been violated and that the West harbored "imperialist designs."

Partly as a consequence of this view, a seemingly unending series of incidents were interpreted as Cold War crises, including the Soviet refusal to withdraw troops from Iran, the communist coup d'état in Czechoslovakia, the Berlin blockade, the formation of NATO in 1949 and the Warsaw Pact in 1955, and, most important, the communist acquisition of power on the Chinese mainland and the Korean War and Taiwan Straits crises that followed. Hence the relationship between the two states was not simply "cold"; it became an embittered and hostile quarrel that continually threatened to erupt into open warfare. In 1952, for example, President Truman twice considered all-out war against the Soviet Union and China (*New York Times*, August 3, 1980).

To be sure, in the chill of this competition temporary efforts at conciliation sometime occurred. Exemplary were the lifting of the Berlin blockade and the Soviet offer in 1952 to hold free elections to unite a neutralized Germany. More characteristic, however, was a continued pattern of hostility. Both superpowers practiced confrontational power politics, and both pursued the same goal: curtailing the global influence of the other and preventing its hegemonic quest for world conquest. Some communication necessarily occurred, but its effect was to carry on the contest, not to end it. The contest remained zero-sum.

Containment took on a somewhat different coloration in the 1950s. Until 1949 the United States enjoyed clear military superiority, for it alone possessed "the winning weapon" and the means to deliver it. This exerted a powerful impact on American policy making (Herken, 1982). But in 1949 the Soviets broke the American atomic monopoly. Thereafter the Soviet quest for military equality and the superpowers' eventual relative strategic parity influenced the entire range of their relations.

As the 1950s wore on the United States talked as if war were imminent,[5] but in practice (especially with the termination of the Korean War) the United States acted cautiously. President Eisenhower and Secretary of State John Foster Dulles promised a "rollback" of the iron curtain and the "liberation" of the "captive nations" of Eastern Europe. They criticized Truman's allegedly "soft" and "reactive" containment doctrine and claimed to substitute for containment an ambitious "winning" strategy that would end the confrontation with godless communism for good. But communism was not rolled back in Eastern Europe, and containment was not replaced by a bolder foreign policy, as Eisenhower and Dulles followed the same basic foreign policy as Truman and Acheson. "'We can never rest [until communism is defeated],' Ike had said, but rest they did, except in their speeches" (Ambrose, 1988).

Thus, despite America's threatening posture, more was promised than delivered. "Massive retaliation" with nuclear weapons was threatened to stop the advance of Soviet communism, and in 1954 Eisenhower and Dulles actively

---

5. For assessments arguing that expectations of another general war were largely a figment of policymakers' imaginations and that nuclear deterrence was therefore largely unnecessary to prevent its outbreak, see Mueller (1991) and Vasquez (1991).

considered the use of the atomic bomb against the Chinese communists (*New York Times*, June 8, 1984). But the threat was not carried out. And significantly, as harsh words continued to be exchanged and the threat of war appeared ever-present, behavior began to change. At the Geneva summit in 1955 a first, tentative step at communication was taken when the two rivals set a precedent for mutual discussion of world problems. With hindsight it is clear that Geneva represented more a pause in hostilities than a fundamental policy change; brinkmanship and massive retaliation were more symptomatic of the strategies through which the United States hoped to force the Soviets into submission. But Geneva was a start. Although this period was punctuated with a series of Cold War crises and confrontations (as in Hungary, Cuba, and Egypt over the Suez, and over such issues as the downing of an American U-2 spy plane deep over Soviet territory), none of these threats to peace resulted in war, and steps toward improved relations (such as the Camp David meeting of 1959) occurred in their midst.

Competitive Coexistence, 1962–1969   The surreptitious placement of Soviet missiles in Cuba in 1962, the onset of the Vietnam War shortly thereafter, and the beginning of a seemingly unrestrained arms race in the 1960s cast a shadow over the possibility of superpower coexistence. The most serious test of their ability to manage confrontation peacefully was the 1962 Cuban missile crisis—a "catalytic" event that transformed thinking about how the Cold War could be waged and expanded awareness of the suicidal consequences of a nuclear war. The superpowers stood eyeball to eyeball. Fortunately, one blinked.

Amidst recurrent episodes in the ongoing Cold War contest, the superpowers searched for ways to coexist, and their efforts laid the basis for détente.[6] The incipient phase was tied to the growing parity of American and Soviet military capabilities. Coexistence or nonexistence were the alternatives. Competitive coexistence resulted, which placed emphasis on bargaining and what McGeorge Bundy termed "existential deterrence." This alleviated the danger posed by some issues and paved the way for new initiatives in other areas. For example, the precedent for summit diplomacy established at Geneva and later at the 1959 Camp David meeting was followed by the installation of the "hot line" in 1963 linking the White House and the Kremlin with a direct communication system, the 1967 Glassboro summit, and a number of negotiated agreements, including the 1963 Partial Test Ban Treaty, the 1967 Outer Space Treaty, and the 1968 Nuclear Nonproliferation Treaty. In addition, the United States tacitly accepted a divided Germany and Soviet hegemony in Eastern Europe, as illustrated by its failure to respond to the Soviet invasion of Czechoslovakia in 1968.

---

6. Kennan (1976) suggests that what later became known officially as détente actually could have commenced as early as 1965, had it not been victimized by (1) Soviet action in Czechoslovakia in 1968 and (2) American action in Vietnam: "It was not until the first could be forgotten, and the second brought into process of liquidation in the early 1970s, that prospects again opened up for further progress along the lines pioneered by Messrs. Johnson and Rusk some four to six years earlier."

At the American University commencement exercises in 1963, President Kennedy explained why tension reduction was imperative and war could not be risked:

> Among the many traits the people of [the United States and the Soviet Union] have in common, none is stronger than our mutual abhorrence of war. Almost unique among the major world powers, we have never been at war with each other. . . .
>
> Today, should total war ever break out again—no matter how—our two countries would become the primary targets. It is an ironical but accurate fact that the two strongest powers are the two in the most danger of devastation. . . . We are both caught up in a vicious and dangerous cycle in which suspicion on one side breeds suspicion on the other and new weapons beget counterweapons.
>
> In short, both the United States and its allies, and the Soviet Union and its allies, have a mutually deep interest in a just and genuine peace and in halting the arms race. . . .
>
> So let us not be blind to our differences, but let us also direct attention to our common interests and to the means by which those differences can be resolved. And if we cannot end now our differences, at least we can help make the world safe for diversity.

Kennedy signaled in this landmark speech a shift in how the United States hoped to deal with its adversary. The Soviet Union by this time had also begun to temper its rhetoric. In particular, it began to emphasize (in a propagandistic fashion?) the necessity for the "peaceful coexistence" of capitalism and socialism, a view far different from the revolutionary thrust of doctrinaire Marxism-Leninism. The Kennedy administration was in many respects as resolutely anti-Soviet as its predecessors, but in style and tone it began to depart from the confrontational tactics of the past. Competition for advantage and influence continued, but the preservation of the status quo was tacitly accepted. Neither side was willing to give ground ("For us," Leonid Brezhnev declared in August 1968, "the results of World War II are inviolable and we will defend them even at the cost of risking a new war.") Neither side proved willing, however, to launch a new war to secure new geostrategic gains.

Détente, 1969–1979   With the inauguration of Nixon and the installation of Henry Kissinger as his national security adviser, a new approach was initiated, officially labeled, for the first time, *détente*: a policy and process designed to relax tensions between the superpowers.

Détente sought to create "a vested interest in cooperation and restraint," wherein "competitors can regulate and restrain their differences and ultimately move from competition to cooperation" (Kissinger, 1974b). The strategy for moving toward permanent Soviet-American accommodation was based on a "linkage" theory: that the development of economic and political ties, equally rewarding to both nations, would bind the two in a common fate and thereby remove the incentives for conflict or war. It was averred that Soviet global aspirations could be mollified because Soviet peace and prosperity would depend on the continuation of peaceful links with the United States. Linkage, in Kissinger's words, was "based on a balance between the carrot and the stick." It offered trade and technology in return for Soviet restraint in international affairs. Enticed by the promise of economic subsidies and of Western pledges of nonaggression, the Soviets, it was reasoned, would behave according to American standards of international conduct and perhaps even engage in liberalization by relaxing their totalitarian grip at home. Furthermore, linkage was designed to make the entire range of Soviet-American relations interdependent so that concessions in any one problem area would be compensated for by equivalent concessions in others. For instance, negotiated arms control agreements were linked to acceptance of rules prohibiting military intervention outside the regions defining the superpowers' traditional security interests. Cooperation in one policy area was made contingent on acceptable conduct in other areas.

Détente was predicated on policymakers' growing awareness that the Soviet Union was vulnerable but no longer militarily inferior to the United States. The central U.S. challenge, given this predicament, was "to evolve détente into a new form of containment of the Soviet Union—or, better still, self-containment on the part of the Russians" (Gelb, 1976). In the Nixon administration's conception, détente was thus an attempt to devise "new means to the old ends of containment." "Détente did not mean global reconciliation with the Soviet Union.... Instead, détente implied the selective continuation of containment by economic and political inducement and at the price of accommodation through concessions that were more or less balanced" (Serfaty, 1978). When in a position of superiority, the United States had practiced containment by coercion and force; from a new position of parity, containment was now to be practiced by seduction and cooperation. Détente was "part of the Cold War, not an alternative to it" (Goodman, 1975).

The cooperation evident between the superpowers during the period of détente demonstrated that easing global tensions was possible. For the first time in several decades, the expectation of superpower war receded and cooperative interaction became commonplace (see Figure 3.1). Visits, cultural exchanges, trade agreements, and collaborative technological ventures replaced threats and tests of resolve.

The changes that transpired in this period can be accounted for by each superpower's recognition of the probability that a nuclear attack by either side would be mutually suicidal, by their growing sensitivity to and empathy for the security needs of the other, by their tacit revival of the sphere-of-influence concept and the advantages it could confer on crisis stability, and by their shared concern for an increasingly powerful and independent China. The escalating costs of a continued arms race may also have contributed to the advent of détente. Moreover, the erosion of the hegemonic position of the United States in the world and its growing awareness of the constraints placed on its ability to act as a global policeman (as evidenced by the Nixon Doctrine) encouraged a new approach to the control of the Soviet menace.

At the center of the dialogue of détente was the issue of arms control. The Strategic Arms Limitation Talks (SALT) became the test of détente's viability.

Initiated in 1969, the SALT negotiations attempted to restrain the threatening, expensive, and spiraling arms race. Two agreements were eventually concluded, the first in 1972 (SALT I) and the second in 1979 (SALT II). With their signing, each of the superpowers appeared to have gained the principal objective it had sought in détente. The Soviet Union gained recognition of its status as a coequal of the United States, and the United States appeared to gain a commitment to moderation of what it perceived as the Soviet Union's quest for preeminent power in the world.

But the difficulties encountered in bringing the SALT II agreement to fruition (it was signed but never ratified by the United States) underscored the substantial differences that still separated the superpowers. By the end of the 1970s, détente had lost nearly all of its momentum and much of the expectation associated with it only a few years earlier. During the SALT II treaty ratification hearings, the Senate focused on continued high levels of Soviet military spending, Soviet "adventurism" in Africa and elsewhere, and the presence of Soviet military forces in Cuba—all of which spoke to the persistence of the deep-seated American distrust of the Soviet Union and its understandable concern for its overt behavior.

Renewed Confrontation, 1979–1988   The Soviet invasion of Afghanistan in 1979 put an end to the Senate's consideration of SALT II—and détente. "Soviet aggression in Afghanistan—unless checked—confronts all the world with the most serious strategic challenge since the Cold War began," declared President Carter. In response, the United States initiated a series of countermoves, including enunciation of the Carter Doctrine declaring the willingness of the United States to use military force to protect its interests in the Persian Gulf, an effort to organize a worldwide boycott of the 1980 Olympic Games in Moscow, suspension of American grain exports to the Soviet Union, and other trade restrictions. Thus antagonism and hostility once more dominated superpower relations.

Détente had provided the United States a respite in which to attend to other foreign policy concerns. Carter's "trilateral" emphasis on better economic and political relations with Japan and Western Europe, his concern for alleviating the plight of Third World[7] nations in an effort to elicit goodwill toward the United States, and his concern for human rights worldwide were among the reorientations his administration had envisioned. The Carter administration also sought for a time to cut arms sales and the burden of

---

7. *Third World* refers to the (economically) developing or less developed countries (LDCs) of Asia, Africa, and Latin America. (A few European countries, such as Greece, Portugal, and Yugoslavia, are also sometimes included.) Although we will use this term throughout the book, it is important to note that wide differences exist among developing nations. For example, the Third World includes the oil-rich nations of the Middle East, the dozen fast-growing developing nations known as the newly industrialized countries (NICs), and the thirty-one nations considered by the United Nations to be the "least developed" (LLDCs) of the developing nations (Kegley and Wittkopf, 1989). Nations falling into the latter category are sometimes referred to as the Fourth World.

defense spending, and it successfully orchestrated a peace treaty between Israel and Egypt as part of what it hoped would be a settlement of the long-simmering Middle East conflict.

But with respect to the Soviet Union, the decade-long U.S. effort to carefully nurture détente as a permanent alternative to more militant forms of containment proved ephemeral (on the reasons for détente's collapse, see Breslauer, 1983; Hoffmann, 1984). Thus by the time Ronald Reagan became president in 1981 the United States had resumed a confrontational approach to the Soviet Union reminiscent of that which had prevailed when the containment doctrine was first enunciated. The tough talk of Eisenhower, the competitiveness of Kennedy, and even the belligerence of Truman were rekindled. Reagan viewed the Soviets as incorrigibly hostile (Leng, 1984), asserted that the Soviet Union "underlies all the unrest that is going on," and accused it of willingness "to commit any crime, to lie, to cheat" to attain world communism. "It's time to stop pretending that détente with the Soviet Union is still alive," Reagan proclaimed. Richard Pipes, a member of Reagan's National Security Council staff, declared in 1981 that the Soviets would have to choose either "peacefully changing their Communist system . . . or going to war."

Tough words were sometimes matched by equally tough diplomatic deeds. Economically, politically, and, most of all, militarily, the United States sought to put the Soviet Union on the defensive. The superpower contest was given preeminence over all other goals, as a "grave new world" (Ledeen, 1985) at the brink of superpower war emerged. Events that punctuated the renewal of conflict included the Soviet destruction of Korean Airlines flight 007 in 1983, the U.S. invasion of Grenada shortly thereafter, the rupture of arms control talks, the Soviet boycott of the 1984 Olympic Games in Los Angeles, and the U.S. support of insurgents in Afghanistan, Angola, and Nicaragua—euphemistically described as "freedom fighters"—who sought the overthrow of Soviet-supported governments. Mikhail Gorbachev summarized the alarming state of Soviet-American relations by fretting in the fall of 1985 that "the situation is very complex, very tense. I would even go so far as to say it is explosive."

But the situation did not explode. Instead, the diplomatic dialogue was renewed, and the basis for a new phase of Soviet-American relations came into being.

Beyond the Cold War, 1988–?   Prospects for a more constructive phase improved greatly in 1986 following Gorbachev's rise to power in the Soviet Union. Although his values were difficult to read, it soon became clear that Gorbachev felt the Soviet Union could not win the war with capitalism and that the Soviet Union's deteriorating economy and international circumstances, in his words, "dictated" "the need for a fundamental break with many customary approaches to foreign policy." Shortly thereafter, he promised daring new steps to relax superpower tensions. Soviet spokesperson Georgi Arbatov went so far as to declare to the United States that "we are going to do a terrible thing to you—we are going to deprive you of an enemy."

Promoting what he termed *new thinking*, Gorbachev abrogated the long-standing Soviet ideological commitment to assist national liberation movements struggling to overthrow capitalism when, in 1986, he declared "it is inadmissible and futile to encourage revolution from abroad." Gorbachev also for the first time embraced the concept of *mutual security* when he proclaimed that national security would be diminished, not increased, by reducing the security of one's adversary.[8]

To reduce the financial burdens of defense and the dangers of an escalating strategic arms race, arms *reduction* was proposed. "We understand," Gorbachev lamented, "that the arms race . . . serves objectives whose essence is to exhaust the Soviet Union economically." The pledge to bring the arms race under control, and the offer to make concessions to achieve this purpose, represented a break with past Soviet policy. No longer could the Soviet Union afford to simultaneously pursue guns *and* butter.

Acknowledging that Soviet economic growth had ceased and its global power had eroded, Gorbachev proclaimed his desire to end the Cold War contest. "We realize that we are divided by profound historical, ideological, socioeconomic and cultural differences," Gorbachev noted during his first visit to the United States in 1987. "But the wisdom of politics today lies in not using those differences as a pretext for confrontation, enmity and the arms race."

The premises underlying the U.S. policy of containment appeared increasingly irrelevant in the context of these promising pronouncements and the opportunities for relaxed tensions they appeared to open. As one observer put it, "Gorbachev's initiatives . . . made containment sound like such an anachronism that the need to move beyond it is self-evident" (Talbott, 1990b).

But the past record of Soviet-American relations, with its periodic swings between intensified tension and efforts to relax it, suggested that these propitious developments could prove temporary, and that a resurgence of rivalry and confrontation could resume, especially if Gorbachev—the man whom one influential former American policymaker (Bundy, 1990) gives primary credit for ending the Cold War—should fall from power. It was this fear that was uppermost in the mind of President Bush, who sensed the fragility of the hopeful new stability and was hesitant to act decisively in response to it (see Focus 3.3). His reluctance, particularly in his first year in office, to accelerate the onset of the new post–Cold War era with concessions was reinforced by his fear that Soviet promises might prove insincere. "The Soviet Union," he warned in May 1989, had "promised a more cooperative relationship before—only to reverse course and return to militarism." The logic of containment thus played heavily on Bush's thinking. Even while claiming the desire to move beyond the Cold War, the Bush administration did *not* abandon containment. Instead, the

---

8. As former Secretary of State Cyrus Vance observed, "The Soviets have made a major change in both rhetoric and doctrine under Gorbachev by adopting mutual security. It runs counter to Leninist doctrine, which was that one had to achieve superiority and threaten others in order to be safe."

FOCUS 3.3 ▪ Ending the Cold War: The Bush Administration's Path to "Moving beyond Containment"

There are reasons to be hopeful. But realism requires us to be prudent. The jury is still out on whether the process of [Gorbachev's] reform will succeed. While there is every reason to look to the future, it would be a serious mistake to assume that continued progress is assured.
Secretary of State James Baker, February 1989

You don't turn a great nation like the U.S. around quickly. We're talking about modifications in direction.
National Security Adviser Brent Scowcroft, May 1989

Forty years of perseverance have brought us a precocious opportunity. And now it's time to move beyond containment, to a new policy for the 1990s, one that recognizes the full scope of change taking place around the world, and in the Soviet Union itself. . . . The United States has as its goal much more than simply containing Soviet expansionism. We seek the integration of the Soviet Union into the community of nations. . . . We will match their steps with steps of our own.
President George Bush, May 1989

It is clear that Soviet "new thinking" has not yet totally overcome the old. I believe in a deliberate, step-by-step approach.
President George Bush, May 1989

To those who question our prudent pace, they must understand that a time of historic change is no time for recklessness. . . . In a new Europe, the American role may change in form but not in fundamentals.
President George Bush, November 1989

We recognize that the Soviet military threat . . . is diminishing, but we see little change in Soviet strategic modernization.
President George Bush, January 1990

I am pleased that [the United States and the Soviet Union] are working together to build a new relationship. . . . Clearly, no longer can a dictator count on East-West confrontation to stymie concerted U.N. action against aggression. A new partnership of nations has begun.
President George Bush, September 1990

---

strategy of linkage was resurrected (Greenberger, 1989), and a "show me" reactive approach was adopted.

Nonetheless, to some, Gorbachev's policies had "already been locked into position by circumstances to such an extent that any complete reversal would scarcely be possible" (McCartney, 1990a). George F. Kennan is among those to whom this view has been attributed. In that expectation a real break from the Cold War strategy of containment may be possible.

Part of what will determine whether containment is discarded in favor of a new grand strategy will depend on how American policymakers view the causes of communism's collapse.

To most observers the arguments that Kennan (1947) advanced in his famous "X" article appeared prophetic. "The United States has it in its power," he wrote, "to increase enormously the strains under which Soviet policy must operate, to force upon the Kremlin a far greater degree of moderation and circumspection than it has had to observe in recent years, and in this way to promote tendencies which must eventually find their outlet in either the breakup of or the gradual mellowing of Soviet power." That was precisely what *did* happen—over forty years later. Left unsettled, however, were the causes of this "victory" over communism. Did *militant* containment work to force the Soviet Union into submission, as conservatives (Perle, 1991) claimed? Or instead, did the Soviet leaders succumb to the inherent *political* weaknesses of their system, which left them unable to conduct an imperial policy abroad or retain communist control at home, as Kennan maintained? What, in other words, made the Soviets more accommodating—intimidating American military strength, or internal economic and political pressures?

Determining what forces contributed most to the end of the Cold War will doubtless intrigue historians for decades to come, just as determining the causes for its onset has done. The debate promises to be important, for it will shape thinking about the principles that should guide a post–Cold War American foreign policy and will figure prominently in American domestic politics for some time to come (Ornstein and Schmitt, 1990). As the United States positions itself for a post–Cold War era, the "squeezers" who "oppose any relaxation of competitive pressure on the Soviet Union" will be pitted against the "dealers" in the U.S. policy-making system who seek "to overcome right-wing attachment to the militantly anti-Soviet stance" that has prevailed for decades (Horelick, 1990).

George Bush did not publicly embrace either position unreservedly, although the cautiousness—prudence, as he put it—that marked his response to the Soviet Union and to the dramatic breakup of the Soviet external empire in Eastern Europe revealed a firm commitment not to jettison the capacity to "squeeze" the Soviet Union in order to contain a potential resurgence of its influence and expansionism. His reliance on vigilance and the logic of containment did not waver, as he remained skeptical (like others; see "Z," 1990) of Soviet motives and capabilities. As Bush warned in May 1989, "a new relationship cannot simply be declared by Moscow." Still, change can sometimes come swiftly. As 1989 came to an end, the pace of change accelerated with dizzying speed. The Cold War—which began in Europe and had centered on Europe for forty years—was ending there. Hungary, Poland, East Germany, Czechoslovakia, Romania, and other communist states permitted democratic elections in which communist party candidates routinely lost and jettisoned socialism in favor of capitalist free-market principles. The Berlin Wall came tumbling down, and unification of the two Germanies and dissolution of the Warsaw Pact proceeded apace.

The Bush administration reacted to these developments with a mixture of astonishment, relief, enthusiasm, and trepidation. It was caught in an unfamiliar position, without a clear vision as to how to respond. "Someone asked me, 'Weren't you surprised?,'" Secretary of State Baker acknowledged November 10, 1989, after the Berlin Wall crumbled overnight; "I said, 'You're darn right, and so was everybody else.'" Paul H. Nitze, who drafted the Truman administration's plan for a military approach to the containment of the Soviet Union (in a document known as NSC 68) and helped establish NATO and the Marshall Plan, summarized the uncertainty that faced the United States: "Standing up to the Russians in Europe, establishing NATO and creating the Cold War [unlike forty years ago] is not called for. We have come out on top. The situation in Europe is going our way, and our task is to simply be helpful to that evolution. Events are going on right now with results that cannot be foreseen. We know things are going to be different, but we are not certain how much better. So maybe we should keep our powder dry."

If in this uncertain environment the United States added a new wrinkle to an old objective, it was a determination to bring the global contest to a (victorious) conclusion. As the president proclaimed during the 1990 Washington summit, "We may not agree on everything but we agree on one great truth: the world has waited long enough, the Cold War must end." But the United States found itself without a grand strategy to replace containment because "the fading of the Cold War [did] not provide a road map or a compass for the post–Cold War era" (Talbott, 1990b). "The task before us," President Bush explained, "is to consolidate the fruits of the peaceful revolution and provide the architecture for continued peaceful change." A historical watershed had been crossed, but a vision of the best path to follow was not articulated, and "new rationales [were] concocted for old arrangements" (Talbott, 1990b). John Lewis Gaddis (1990) explained the "apparent paradox" facing the United States in these radically transformed circumstances: "now that [the United States has] won the Cold War, [its] chief interest may lie in the survival and successful rehabilitation of the nation that was [its] principal adversary throughout that conflict."

How the United States ultimately responds to the constraints and opportunities it now faces—and will continue to face—in its relations with the Soviet Union cannot be predicted with certainty. For the pattern of American foreign policy is the product of a multitude of interacting forces, as we shall demonstrate in the chapters that follow. Our understanding of the possible direction it will take can be broadened by our understanding of these forces. Thus, after completing our examination of them, we will return in Chapter 16 to the question of the future of Soviet-American relations.

THE POSTWAR PATTERN OF AMERICAN FOREIGN POLICY: ALTERNATIVE CHARACTERIZATIONS OF GUIDING PREMISES

It would be misleading to suggest that globalism, anticommunism, and containment adequately capture all of the assumptions on which postwar American foreign policy has been founded, even if they depict what has been most characteristic about U.S. thinking for nearly five decades. In varying degrees, other assumptions also have prevailed as guideposts and have contributed to the postwar persistence of the three core premises examined above. Four of these secondary attributes warrant brief examination: the theses that American foreign policy is (1) antirevolutionary; (2) imperialistic; (3) moralistic; and (4) "realistic."

The United States: An Antirevolutionary, Status Quo Power in a Revolutionary Age?

Students of American foreign policy have observed that, in playing the role of great power on a global scale, the United States has shown a marked preference for the prevention of social revolutions in other countries: American leaders have sought preservation of the status quo and have taken repeated actions to guard against potentially disruptive revolutions. To these critics, the United States has been a counterrevolutionary nation in a revolutionary age; it has prostituted its own democratic ideals, thereby raising the question of whether "a democratic superpower [is] a contradiction in terms" (Isaak, 1977).

Given America's own revolutionary heritage, a fear of the overthrow of repressive regimes is ironic. Senator J. William Fulbright in 1965 summarized this view: "We are not, as we like to claim in Fourth of July speeches, the most truly revolutionary nation on earth; we are, on the contrary, much closer to being the most unrevolutionary nation on earth."

Why? Often it is argued that America's fear of communism led the United States to equate revolution with communism and therefore to dismiss the possibility that some upheavals were merely local revolts against the oppression of totalitarian governments (left or right) that denied freedom to their own people. As a consequence, the United States became an opponent of social and political change. "The convenient 'Communism' label, carrying a connotation of incarnate evil," Neal Houghton (1968) observed, "facilitated Washington's . . . efforts to prevent or destroy all unwelcome basic social revolutions, everywhere on earth." Or, as Hans J. Morgenthau (1985) put it: "In the contest between the colonial powers of Europe and their colonies, the United States took the side of the former, not because it was in favor of colonialism, but because it was afraid that Communism might be the alternative to colonialism. The champion of freedom became the defender and restorer of the colonial status quo."

The symptoms of this counterrevolutionary penchant are numerous. Consider the following:

- For a time during the Truman administration, the Declaration of Independence (defending the right of peoples everywhere to rebel against an unjust government) was removed from American overseas libraries. The principles expressed in the declaration were apparently considered too inflammatory for other people—it might give them ideas.
- On more than one occasion, the United States has suppressed democratic elections. As noted above, a case in point occurred in Germany following World War II when the Russians, against their self-interest, proposed holding elections in which their allies could not possibly win. But the United States resisted, unnecessarily fearing that the communists somehow might gain control through the ballot. Another case occurred in 1956, when the United States prevented United Nations–supervised elections in Vietnam, as called for by the 1954 Geneva Accords on Indochina. The reason? The democratic electoral process risked an unacceptable outcome—the election of communists. President Eisenhower (1963) reported in his memoirs: "I have never talked or corresponded with a person knowledgeable in Indo-Chinese affairs who did not agree that had elections been held . . . possibly 80 percent of the populace would have voted for the Communist Ho Chi Minh as their leader."
- Throughout the postwar era the United States typically chose to play it safe by siding with the existing governing elite, no matter how antidemocratic, rather than side with the forces of social change. That led the U.S. to support "governments throughout the world whose political philosophy and practice were completely at odds with what goes by the name of American principles of government" (Morgenthau, 1985). Consider the list of countries supported by the United States when they were ruled by dictators: Argentina, Brazil, Cuba, the Dominican Republic, Guatemala, Greece, Haiti, Iran, Nicaragua, Paraguay, the Philippines, Portugal, South Korea, South Vietnam, Spain, and Taiwan. In these and other cases, the United States armed and otherwise supported some of the most ruthless tyrannies in the modern world. Such dictatorships shared a common characteristic, however: they were anticommunist.

President Kennedy perhaps as well as anyone helped to explain this antirevolutionary instinct when he commented on the situation faced by the United States in the Dominican Republic following the assassination of Dominican dictator Rafael Trujillo:

> There are three possibilities in descending order of preference: a decent democratic regime, a continuation of the Trujillo regime [a dictatorship] or a Castro regime [a communist government]. We ought to aim at the first, but we really can't renounce the second until we are sure that we can avoid the third.

It was that perceived dilemma that led the United States in Cuba to support Fulgencio Batista and end up with Fidel Castro; in Vietnam to support Ngo

Dinh Diem and Nguyen Van Thieu and get Ho Chi Minh as their successor; in Iran to support the Shah and find itself opposed by the Ayatollah Khomeini. By taking a militant, antirevolutionary position, the United States has repeatedly found itself on the side of the oppressors and against the people, or, in other words, against local nationalism.

In recent years democracy has replaced authoritarianism in many of the countries cited above. The United States has appointed itself the champion of democracy in these countries as elsewhere, but it is by no means certain that the new governments will be able to cope with the enormous problems that they face. The United States will thus continue to confront the issue of how best to support social change in a world rife with economic, nationalistic, political, religious, and social antagonisms. The record of the ability to understand and cope with such divisions and the often revolutionary changes they portend is not good. More than four decades ago, in 1947, Henry Wallace, who ran for the presidency against Harry S Truman as a third-party candidate, warned of the dilemma that the United States still faces: "Once America stands for opposition to change, we are lost. America will become the most hated nation in the world."

An Imperial Foreign Policy?

According to revisionist historians,[9] the primary motive of postwar American foreign policy has been financial profit—American foreign policy serves the interests of investment bankers, actions are taken abroad to address economic problems at home, and a globalist foreign policy is supported by economic interest groups for their own financial benefit. American foreign policy is thus seen as responding to the needs of capitalism as an extension of domestic policy. (It is self-evident, from this perspective, that American foreign policy must necessarily be virulently anticommunist as well.)

Interpretations that focus on motives are difficult to substantiate because intentions cannot be inferred easily from capabilities or behavior. Yet, as evidence, "imperialist" accounts (for example, Magdoff, 1969; Williams 1972, 1980) point to numerous cases where American foreign policy clearly can be traced to economic sources and commercial goals. American foreign aid, trade, tax, and loan policies have been affected significantly by the desire to serve American overseas business interests or, less frequently, to safeguard domestic markets from foreign penetration. The flag often has followed trade;

---

9. Economic revisionism, which is referred to here, is not to be confused with other revisionist accounts that address the expansionist tendencies of the United States (recall the discussion on the origins of the Cold War earlier in this chapter). Economic revisionists see the United States expanding in search of world markets for the surpluses of capitalism, whereas the diplomatic revisionist school sees the creation of an American imperium as the product of the American pursuit of national power or of its quest to impose its political system on others. For discussions of empire as a component of America's efforts to achieve political, not economic, preeminence, see Blachman and Puchala (1991), Hoffmann (1978), and Liska (1978).

policymakers have taken actions to protect foreign investments and expand the global reach of American enterprises (not to enhance strategic interests); and "dollar diplomacy" has been a recurrent motif. The title *Empire as a Way of Life* (Williams, 1980) conveys this ascribed attribute of American diplomacy, and *The Price of Empire* (Fulbright with Tillman, 1989) captures its potential consequences.

Moral Idealism

The history of American diplomacy may be written in terms of the influence of two divergent schools of thought, *idealism* and *realism* (see Osgood, 1953). When Secretary of State Henry Kissinger spoke of America's major foreign policy problem as how to avoid "oscillations between excessive moralism and excessive pragmatism, with excessive concern with power and total rejection of power," he underscored the pronounced impact these incompatible outlooks have periodically exerted on U.S. policy making and how they influence the cyclical alternation of American policy between its isolationist and internationalist phases.

As a world view, the idealist tradition views human nature as essentially "good" and people therefore capable of altruism and cooperation. It posits that human progress is possible; wicked behavior is the product not of bad people, but of bad institutions that breed such behavior. Consequently, the worst properties of international politics (such as war) can be contained and, with appropriate reforms of domestic and international institutions, possibly eliminated.

To universalize those humanitarian ideals and moral principles to which the country has traditionally aspired (see Kegley, 1989; Kober, 1990; Nichols and Loescher, 1989), idealists have prescribed American support for international organizations, international law, arms control and disarmament, free trade to produce goodwill among nations as well as prosperity within them, respect for human rights, and, above all others perhaps, democratic governance. From these goals idealists perceive the possibility of creating a more secure, prosperous, and just world order.

"An absolute national morality," contends Louis Hartz (1955), "is inspired either to withdraw from 'alien' things or to transform them: it cannot live in comfort constantly by their side." Moral idealism prescribes either isolationism or internationalism, for such thinking invites either a withdrawal from an immoral world or a quest to reform it. Consequently, idealism may contribute to the cyclical swings between disengagement and globalism evident in America's diplomatic history.

The years between World War I and World War II are often said to have been the "heyday" of idealist logic, and Woodrow Wilson's ideas about foreign policy the expression *par excellence* of moral idealism.[10] Fighting "a war to end

---

10. "Legalism" is often treated with moral idealism as characteristic of the American world view (Kennan, 1951). The tendency of American leaders to justify foreign policy actions by citing legal

all wars," pursuing a diplomacy of "open covenants, openly arrived at," "making the world safe for democracy," creating a powerful international organization (the League of Nations) to safeguard peace, and advocating the substitution of collective security for interlocking alliance systems and the balance of power system that they lubricate were among the most significant foreign policy initiatives indicative of Wilson's idealism.

Policy pronouncements routinely reveal the grip that this world view continues to exert on American foreign policy thinking even today. The human rights initiative of the Carter administration—captured in President Carter's statement in 1977 that "human rights is the soul of our foreign policy"—is but one of the recent manifestations. So, too, was Project Democracy, a 1983 Reagan administration initiative to "foster the infrastructure of democracy" and to preach and spread the gospel of democracy's benefits throughout the world. The Bush administration's affirmation of this goal as a foreign policy priority in the post–Cold War 1990s reflected the continuing importance of this ideal. As Secretary of State James Baker put it in March 1990, "Beyond containment lies democracy . . . that is why President Bush has defined our new mission to be the promotion and consolidation of democracy."

As described earlier in this chapter, the United States has often engaged in global missionary activity to spread American values worldwide. Yet, critics point out, a foreign policy rooted in messianic idealism can be dangerous, as moral absolutes rationalize the harshest punishment of international sinners, without limit or restraint, to the detriment of American interests (Kennan, 1951). Arthur Schlesinger, Jr. (1977), a Kennedy adviser, observed worriedly, "All nations succumb to fantasies of innate superiority. When they act on those fantasies . . . they tend to become international menaces." Similarly, John F. Kennedy himself admonished in 1962 that "we must reject over-simplified theories of international life—the theory . . . that the American mission is to remake the world in the American image." "The hardest thing for the American people to understand," lamented Jimmy Carter in 1978, "is that we are not better than other people."

These concerns underscore the need to evaluate critically the consequences that may result from a moralistic approach, and to consider the alternative world view with which it is often contrasted.

---

precedents, to assume that disputes necessarily involve legal principles, and to seek legal remedies for conflicts are its manifestations. Some proponents of this view trace the reverence for law to the fact that many of those who have made postwar American foreign policy have had legal training and related professional experiences that have encouraged political and military controversies to be seen in terms of their legal and contractual implications. Thus, when confronted with a policy predicament, American policymakers have been prone to ask not "What alternative best serves the national interest?," but instead, "What is the legal thing to do?" Other proponents argue that the United States has sought to transpose its domestic legal institutions to the international arena and relied on legal reasoning to define the limits of permissible behavior for states.

Political Realism

The heritage of *political realism* is a legacy that has dominated American policymakers' thinking especially since World War II. Adherents of *realpolitik* base their views of world politics and America's global role on the following assumptions:

1. History reveals a grim reality: humanity is by nature sinful and wicked.
2. Of all human beings' evil ways, no sin is more prevalent or dangerous than their instinctive lust for power, their desire to dominate others.
3. Progress is impossible because this instinct for power is inexorable and therefore ineradicable.
4. Under such conditions, international politics is a struggle for power, a war of all against all.
5. The primary obligation of every state in this environment—the goal to which all other national objectives should be subordinate—is to promote the national self-interest by pursuing power.
6. National self-interest is best served by doing whatever is necessary to ensure self preservation.
7. States cannot rely on international organizations or international law for protection; there is no alternative to self-help.
8. The national interest necessitates acquiring military capabilities sufficient to deter attack by potential enemies.
9. The capacity for self-defense might also be augmented by acquiring allies, providing their promises to provide help are not relied on for protection.
10. If all states search for power, peace and stability will result through the operation of a balance of power propelled by self-interest and lubricated by fluid alliance systems.

The pronouncements of postwar American leaders suggest that they have customarily embraced the assumptions identified above, as illustrated by Ronald Reagan's slogan ''trust, but verify.'' Many presidents have even referred to themselves at one time or another as ''realists,'' and nearly all have rationalized their decisions in the vocabulary of realism.

As a world view and theory,[11] realism has retained its popularity in part because many postwar international events seemed to confirm its assumptions. Its view fit many of the needs of a pessimistic era, in which the Cold War, the balance of terror, an arms race unprecedented in scale, terrorist activities, and militant, coercive diplomacy have appeared to be the system's defining features. Nations *have* seemed to pursue only their own self-interest, to the

---

11. The classic statements of realism as an explicit theory can be found in Carr (1939), Kennan (1954), Morgenthau (1985), Niebuhr (1947), and Thompson (1960). For critical discussions, see Keohane (1986), Mansbach and Vasquez (1981), Smith (1987), Vasquez (1983), and Waltz (1979).

exclusion of other values and at others' expense; the world *has* often appeared to be an arena characterized more by competitive struggle for national self-advantage than by collaborative pursuits for mutual gain.

Under such conditions, those urging the United States to "act realistically" by seeking power and pursuing only its self-interest have attracted a large following. The American preoccupation with the East-West conflict, the balance of power, the sphere-of-influence logic of geopolitics, and strategic calculus can be traced to that outlook. The equation of national power with military might also stems from the assumptions of *realpolitik*. Correspondingly, debates about military preparedness, alliance networks, containment of Soviet influence, and the like routinely have been cloaked in the language of realism. Illustrative is the conviction expressed by Ronald Reagan: "The lesson of history is that among the great nations only those with the strength to protect their interests survive." The intellectual tradition of political realism rejects the relevance of moral reasoning in foreign policy and assumes instead that the promotion of American interests above all else is the only acceptable moral obligation of the nation and its leaders.

This orientation has served to promote and perpetuate America's postwar globalist containment strategy. To assume that international conflict is normal and peace unsustainable is to rationalize vigilant preparation for war. Likewise, to assume that an adversary like the Soviet Union is motivated exclusively by its desire to expand its power at others' expense is to promote containment to prevent realization of that objective.

Realism and idealism are *both* continuous traditions in American diplomatic history. They compete with each other as conceptions of how the United States ought to define its foreign policy objectives, yet they coexist with one another in sometimes uncomfortable ways. While one tradition may predominate over the other at any single point in time (as the former has since 1945), neither has obliterated the influence of the other.

Thus the American foreign policy tradition encompasses both moral idealism and raw self-interest. Both survive, Robert E. Osgood (1953) suggests, because they recognize two needs: to stand for ideals worthy of emulation, and to protect adaptively the nation from threats to its self-preservation in a hostile world. The duality they engender accounts for the willingness of the United States at times to sacrifice its cherished ideals for an expedient action, even while reaffirming its ideals and promoting their maintenance.

SUGGESTIONS FOR FURTHER READING

Ambrose, Stephen E. (1988) *Rise to Globalism: American Foreign Policy since 1938*, 5th ed. New York: Penguin.

Bundy, McGeorge. (1989–1990) "From Cold War to Trusting Peace," *Foreign Affairs* 69 (No. 1): 197–212.

Fulbright, J. William, with Seth P. Tillman. (1989) *The Price of Empire*. New York: Pantheon.

Gaddis, John Lewis. (1982) *Strategies of Containment: A Critical Appraisal of Postwar American National Security Policy.* New York: Oxford University Press.

Hamilton, Edward K. (ed.). (1989) *America's Global Interests: A New Agenda.* New York: Norton.

Hyland, William G. (1990) *The Cold War Is Over.* New York: Times Books.

Kegley, Charles W., Jr. (ed.). (1991) *The Long Postwar Peace.* New York: HarperCollins.

Kirkpatrick, Jeane J. (1989–1990) "Beyond the Cold War," *Foreign Affairs* 69 (No. 1): 1–16.

Nincic, Miroslav. (1989) *Anatomy of Hostility: The U.S.-Soviet Rivalry in Perspective.* San Diego: Harcourt Brace Jovanovich.

Nye, Joseph S., Jr. (1990) *Bound to Lead: The Changing Nature of American Power.* New York: Basic Books.

Schlesinger, Arthur M., Jr. (1986) *The Cycles of American History.* Boston: Houghton Mifflin.

Spanier, John. (1991) *American Foreign Policy Since World War II*, 12th ed. Washington, D.C.: Congressional Quarterly Press.

CHAPTER 4

The Instruments of Global Influence: Military Might and Interventionism

Prudence . . . dictates that we maintain our defenses while we wait and see if Soviet capabilities to threaten our security are brought into line with their stated benign intentions.

U.S. DEPARTMENT OF DEFENSE, 1989

Our nuclear strategy is still under the curse of Joseph Stalin. Few realize the extent to which the design and purpose of our nuclear armaments, doctrine, and war plans date from the same old mindset that since 1947 shaped and governed the bulk of our conventional forces.

FORMER UNDER SECRETARY OF DEFENSE FOR POLICY
FRED CHARLES IKLÉ, 1990

America's postwar push for global power and presence, guided by its quest to contain communism and Soviet influence, demanded the development of resources and techniques by which those goals could be effectively pursued. The demand was fed by the need to deal with the threat of the growing strategic capability of the Soviet Union, which necessitated the creation of a retaliatory nuclear force sufficient to deter any aggressive Soviet designs. That threat, understandably, became a fixation. With it, and with America's own global aspirations, there emerged in the aftermath of World War II a foreign policy highly dependent on the possession of powerful military, paramilitary, and related instruments through which its fundamental objectives could be pursued. As Under Secretary of State Lawrence S. Eagleburger stressed in March 1984, the first principle shaping American foreign policy is that "military power is an essential part of diplomacy."

Whether these instruments remain appropriate to the threats the United States faces in the post–Cold War world has been questioned by some. As the United States approaches the millennium it faces a multitude of novel challenges. They include a high instance of drug abuse sustained by international trafficking in illegal narcotics; global warming caused by worldwide deforestation and the burning of fossil fuels; and an influx of political and ecological refugees and other illegal immigrants in search of political freedom and

72

economic opportunity. Terrorist and other threats to American citizens as they travel and work abroad and military threats to the interests of the nation, as demonstrated by Iraq's aggression against Kuwait, also continue. In such an environment what constitutes the primary threat to the national security is no longer self-evident. What is clear is that America's relatively enduring globalist, anticommunist, and containment foreign policy goals continue to animate policymakers' definition of the national interest, with the result that a martial spirit and an urge to shape the world to American interests remain central premises of American foreign policy.

Our purpose in this chapter and the next is to examine the *policy instruments* captured in the themes of military might and interventionism. These embrace the *means* used to achieve the political objectives of foreign policy. They include the threatened use of force, war or other forms of military intervention, propaganda, clandestine operations, military aid, the sale of arms, and economic assistance. Each has played a prominent role in American foreign policy since 1945; all derive from the assumptions of *realpolitik* that informed American foreign policymakers' perceptions of the nation's security needs and guided their choice of the military and other interventionist approaches toward the realization of American foreign policy objectives.

In Chapter 5, we will examine the use of intelligence operations, public diplomacy, and economic and military assistance programs as they relate to the persistent goals of American foreign policy. Here our primary concern is the role that the actual and threatened use of military force, conventional and nuclear, have played as instruments of both compellence and deterrence designed to defend the physical security and survival of the United States and its allies against external attack. Inasmuch as *foreign policy* refers to the totality of objectives and programs whereby the government seeks to cope with its external environment, our attention will be on that subset of foreign policy known as *national security policy*—the weapons and strategies on which the U.S. government has relied to ensure security and survival in an uncertain, dangerous, and often hostile global environment.

MILITARY GLOBALISM

The logic of *realpolitik* is said to encourage the practice of coercive behavior abroad. The possible domination of military thinking in foreign policy planning is one symptom of that instinct. Some critics maintain that American foreign policy became militarized following World War II, in the sense that the nation's policymakers routinely defined international political problems in terms of military solutions. Former Assistant Secretary of Defense Adam Yarmolinsky (1970–1971) argues, for instance, that for at least a quarter-century following the war, American foreign policy was based on a battle-ground conception in which communist forces were pitted against those of the United States and the "free world." Policymakers assumed that any success experienced by the communists or their sympathizers contributed to Soviet strength and correspondingly diminished that of the United States. One consequence of such military thinking was to avoid estimating the adversary's intentions and instead to emphasize capabilities, assuming that the adversary would do "whatever mischief he can." The second consequence was "to emphasize readiness for the worst contingency that might arise," particularly as the Soviet Union began to develop a nuclear strike potential. In the European context the result was a preoccupation with the idea that the Soviet Union would launch a massive surprise attack against Western Europe, an obsession that precluded any realistic test of Soviet willingness to arrive at a European diplomatic settlement. And in other areas bordering the communist world outside Europe, American diplomacy concentrated on building up a ready military force to the exclusion of almost all other political or economic considerations.

A primary reason for the alleged militarization of American foreign policy may be found not in the policy-making roles played by professional military leaders, but in the tendency of civilians to adopt military ways of approaching political problems (see also Chapter 11).[1] It was not until the painful Vietnam experience was digested that many Americans began to suspect that military firepower and political influence are not synonymous.

The rhetoric of American leaders has consistently emphasized the martial[2] outlook derived from the assumptions of political realism. The premise that security and influence are functions of military might has been embraced by American decision makers over the entire postwar period (see Focus 4.1). Indeed, the premise has been reiterated so often that it has become dogma.

The unexpectedly rapid and extraordinary changes in Eastern Europe and the Soviet Union that have taken place since 1989 have called the military premises of American foreign policy into question, although the invasion of

---

1. The observation that civilian policymakers came to adopt military ways of thinking is important, for, as Richard J. Walton (cited in Donovan, 1974) astutely observes, "civilian control versus military control is a distinction without a difference if the civilians think the same way the military does." For additional observations on this point as it applied to the decision to use the atomic bomb against Japan and to other decisions during the Cold War, see Alperovitz (1985), Ambrose (1988), Bundy (1988), Feis (1966), Horowitz (1965), LaFeber (1976), and Sherwin (1973).

2. The diplomatic heritage of American foreign policy is shot through with inconsistent ideas regarding the American use of military instruments and force. Americans are said to display "a peculiar ambivalence toward war. They have traditionally perceived themselves as a peaceful, unmilitarized people, and yet have hardly been unwarlike" (Millett and Maslowski, 1984). Legend maintains that the United States is both peace loving and unbeatable in war; that it opposes the maintenance of standing armies but concurrently keeps an effective and sizable militia; that it enters wars only reluctantly, and always for moral purposes, but then wages them enthusiastically and concludes them victoriously; that it stands opposed to the use of force to get its way internationally, but that it is prone to intervene militarily in the affairs of others "if necessary" to protect its global interests; and that it stands in awe of military power, seeks to acquire it, but fears to use it. Those often incompatible images reveal a kind of love-hate attitude in America's approach to war and preparations for it. The nation is believed to be at once proud of both its peaceful ideals and a martial tradition that commands respect worldwide and includes an enviable record of performance on the battlefield as well as innovation in military tactics and technology.

FOCUS 4.1 ▪ The Militarization of American Foreign Policy: Forty-Five Years of Policy Pronouncements

Harry S Truman, 1945 — We must continue to be a military nation if we are to maintain leadership among other nations.

Dwight D. Eisenhower, 1953 — Regardless of the consequences, the nation's military security will take first priority in my calculations.

John F. Kennedy, 1961 — Only when our arms are sufficient beyond doubt can we be certain beyond doubt that they shall never be employed.

Lyndon B. Johnson, 1964 — United States military strength now exceeds the combined military might of all nations in history, stronger than any adversary or combination of adversaries. . . . Against such force the combined destructive power of every battle ever fought by man is like a firecracker thrown against the sun.

Richard M. Nixon, 1970 — Peace requires strength. So long as there are those who would threaten our vital interests and those of our allies with military force, we must be strong. American weakness could tempt would-be aggressors to make dangerous miscalculations.

Gerald R. Ford, 1976 — Our military forces are capable and ready. Our military power is without equal. And I intend to keep it that way.

Jimmy Carter, 1979 — In the dangerous and uncertain world of today, the keystone of our national security is still military strength—strength that is clearly recognized by Americans, by our Allies, and by any potential adversary.

Ronald Reagan, 1984 — Peace through strength is not a slogan; it's a fact of life—and we will not return to the days of hand wringing, defeatism, decline and despair.

George Bush, 1989 — When it comes to national defense finishing second means finishing last. . . . Let us never forget that our strong national defense policies have helped us gain the peace. We need a strong defense today to maintain that peace.

Kuwait by Iraq, and the U.S. response, have muted the debate noticeably. To understand how extensive and central a role those premises have played historically and how difficult it may be to alter their continuing preeminence in the thinking and actions of policymakers, it is important to examine the nature of the enormous peacetime military establishment the nation has maintained and the actual instances where military forces have been employed for essentially political purposes.

Force Projection: Forward Bases and Conventional Weapons

The network of more than four hundred overseas military bases and the stationing of more than a half million soldiers and sailors abroad are two visible manifestations of the nation's perception of its responsibilities and of its commitment to the containment of communism. European and Asian bases were especially important in the 1950s in enhancing the credibility of the nuclear weapons strategy of massive retaliation, for they provided the forward bases from which American strategic bombers could strike at the heartland of the communist monolith. With the advent of the intercontinental missile, the strictly strategic importance of such bases waned, but they continued to play a role in the nation's overall national security strategy, particularly as a way of demonstrating commitments to allies. That remains the case today, as the United States maintains military facilities in such widely separated countries as Spain and Korea, Turkey and the Philippines. In many instances the continued presence of these bases in the host countries has become a contentious political issue, but the United States has sought to retain them as much for symbolic as strategic reasons.

The importance of U.S. troops has nowhere been more evident than in Europe. Since the 1950s the United States has maintained several hundreds of thousands of troops there as part of the bulwark against possible Soviet encroachment against Western Europe. At one time the troops served a trip-wire function. In the event of an attack by Warsaw Pact forces against Western Europe, the mere presence of American troops virtually assured that some would be killed. In this way the "wire" assuring an American retaliation would be "tripped"—and by the other side—because American policymakers would have "no choice" but to respond. The trip wire was an integral element of the Eisenhower-Dulles national security strategy.

The logic supporting the presence of American troops in Western Europe since that time has taken on various colorations, but the essential function remains the same—to enhance deterrence by making credible the commitment of the United States to come to the defense of Western Europe. "Major war deterrence" was used by the Nixon and Ford administrations to describe concern for conventional military threats to the United States and its allies in Europe and elsewhere and to rationalize the deployment of military troops and hardware overseas. The strategy of *flexible response*, devised during the Kennedy and Johnson years and adopted as the official NATO defense posture in 1967, became the means for coping with conventional war threats. Flexible response remains the official strategy for deterring nonnuclear war, particularly in the European theater. It holds that the United States and its allies should possess the capabilities (and will) to respond to an attack by hostile forces at whatever level may be appropriate, ranging from conventional to nuclear weapons. Indeed, the NATO alliance reserves the right of "first use" of nuclear weapons if necessary.

Preventing all-out nuclear war is the purpose of strategic deterrence. Deterring war at something less than the global level, as in Europe or Asia, and using something less than strategic nuclear weapons, such as tactical nuclear weapons or conventional means, is called *major* or *general war deterrence*. U.S. General Purpose Forces, which constitute the largest program expenditure in the defense budget, are the instruments of general war deterrence. Those forces link the United States to its allies by providing the primarily conventional military capabilities necessary to fulfill the many foreign commitments the nation has accumulated since World War II. The United States also maintains what are sometimes called Theater Nuclear Forces (forward-based systems, primarily in Europe but also in Asia), but the label is misleading because their purpose is to provide a link between U.S. conventional and strategic nuclear forces, thus tying American nuclear capabilities to the defense of its allies. The term itself suggests the possibility of theaterwide (for example, on the order of World War II) conflict involving tactical nuclear weapons without an escalation to global conflagration involving strategic weapons.

The capabilities the United States currently maintains at the less-than-strategic level to ensure its own national security and to contribute to that of its allies are formidable. Included are many thousands of tactical nuclear weapons as well as a vast arsenal of conventional weapons. Also included is a massive peacetime military establishment spread worldwide. In 1989 2.1 million men and women served in the armed forces, about 320,000 of whom were stationed in Europe, with another 21,000 on ships in the Atlantic and Mediterranean. In Asia and the western Pacific the number of land-based forces consisted of 110,000 personnel, with another 25,000 at sea in the Pacific and Indian Oceans. Sea and airborne power projection capabilities were drawn from a six-hundred-ship naval force and some three dozen air force tactical fighter wings (each consisting of seventy-two combat aircraft) with deployable battle forces of diverse types and awesome capabilities. Land forces were organized at the time into eighteen army and three Marine Corps divisions.

As noted, flexible response implies that the United States recognizes that the use of nuclear weapons might be necessary, but as originally conceived the concept primarily sought to increase conventional war capabilities as a substitute for reliance on massive (nuclear) retaliation. In 1962 the capacity to wage "2½ wars" at once was embraced as the official strategy. Apart from a nuclear war, the 2½ wars were to include simultaneously a conventional war in Europe with the Soviet Union, an Asian war, and a lesser engagement (half a war?) elsewhere. With the hindsight of Vietnam, which shook the notion of American military invincibility to its very foundations, the 2½ war strategy appears preposterous. At the time, however, it was not so perceived, a fact that led one observer to view the strategy as a "military expression of the U.S. national policy goals that reached out for Pax Americana [worldwide peace imposed by the United States] and 'world hegemony'" (Melman, 1974).

President Nixon reduced the 2½ war strategy to 1½ wars, with general purpose forces maintained for concurrently meeting a major communist attack in either Europe or Asia and contending with a lesser contingency elsewhere. That move was part of the reordering of the nation's role in world affairs envisioned in the Nixon Doctrine, which called for a lower U.S. profile in the post-Vietnam era and for greater participation by U.S. allies in their own defense.

The Carter administration pursued essentially the same strategy, but events in Afghanistan and the Persian Gulf in 1979 and 1980 spurred plans already in the works to develop a Rapid Deployment Force (RDF) capable of intervening militarily in world trouble spots to defend American interests. The Carter Doctrine, enunciated in the president's 1980 State of the Union address, reaffirmed the determination of the United States to intervene militarily abroad if necessary to safeguard American security interests. As during the Kennedy administration, the emphasis placed on conventional capabilities in an environment characterized by nuclear parity with the Soviet Union underscored the conviction that neither the United States nor the Soviet Union could conceivably win a nuclear war.

In the European theater the long-standing U.S. drive to get its NATO allies to pay a greater share of the costs of North Atlantic defense intensified.[3] Simultaneously, the United States committed itself to the force modernization necessary to enable NATO, as described by Defense Secretary Harold Brown, "to respond appropriately to any level of potential attack and to pose the risk of escalation to higher levels of conflict." Included in that commitment was the controversial decision to deploy a new-generation of nuclear weapons in the European theater. The decision was a direct response to the Soviet Union's growing medium-range capability (specifically the SS-20 missile and the Backfire bomber), which was beyond the strategic weapons framework of the SALT negotiations on limiting strategic arms that had been underway since the late 1960s (see Chapter 3 and below). It was also tied to a pledge to seek negotiations with the Soviet Union on limiting theater nuclear forces—later known as intermediate-range nuclear forces (INF)—an issue of particular salience to many Western European countries. The Carter administration thus reaffirmed the principle of flexible response, but the INF issue became increasingly con-

---

3. The principle that each member of the NATO alliance must do its part to assume a fair share of the cost of the common defense of the North Atlantic area is referred to as *burdensharing*. It is a controversial principle because there is no single formula with which to measure each country's fair contribution. If defense expenditures as a percent of gross national product is used as the measure, which is commonplace, it is clear there are wide differences among the NATO allies, ranging (in 1987) from less than 1 percent of GNP for Luxembourg to 6.5 percent for the United States (U.S. Arms Control and Disarmament Agency. 1989: 34 ff).

troversial after the Reagan administration assumed the reigns of power and a "peace movement" emerged on both sides of the Atlantic whose purpose was to block deployment of the INF weapons and otherwise reverse the nuclear arms race.

The Reagan administration accepted some of the Carter administration's policies, but it adopted a more assertive posture toward the nation's global aspirations than Carter had articulated. It jettisoned the assumption that any conventional war with the Soviet Union would be of short duration and either settled by negotiation or escalate to a nuclear confrontation. Instead, plans and preparations were predicated on the assumption that such a war would be protracted, with fighting occurring in numerous locations around the globe and without any necessary escalation to nuclear confrontation. Greater attention was also given to preparations for "low intensity" conflicts, such as guerrilla wars and terrorist attacks, with counterinsurgency capabilities given priority in a manner similar to the Kennedy administration's emphasis two decades earlier. The assumption was that Third World instability provided the Soviet Union "targets of opportunity" and thus posed a threat that might be dealt with militarily.

The Reagan administration also determined that the earlier decision to modernize NATO's intermediate-range nuclear forces should proceed as planned, but that proved controversial not only from the perspective of the Soviet Union but also U.S. allies in Europe, where the changed political climate in Europe made force modernization no longer attractive. The political potency of the emergent peace movement was fueled in part by the administration's hawkish rhetoric and Reagan's own prediction that a nuclear war centered on Europe, with the United States standing aside, might be possible. It was in this environment of renewed Soviet-American hostility that the Soviet Union chose to boycott both the INF and START (Strategic Arms Reduction Talks, which replaced SALT in the early 1980s) negotiations with the United States. Eventually, however, the two sides renewed their dialogue, and during the 1987 Washington summit the two superpowers made a historic agreement to eliminate INF forces from Europe. The accord was unprecedented for a number of reasons, including the commitment of the United States and the Soviet Union to the elimination of a complete class of weapons from their respective arsenals (the first such disarmament agreement implemented by nations other than those victorious in war) and the agreement of both to verification methods previously unthinkable. The agreement thus became a model and a catalyst for a broad range of arms reduction proposals in the years that followed. Those involving conventional forces in Europe and chemical weapons are especially noteworthy.

The Balance of Conventional Forces in Europe   In a December 1988 United Nations speech, Mikhail Gorbachev announced large-scale unilateral reductions in Soviet military forces, including force reductions in Eastern Europe and in the wider Atlantic-to-the-Urals area that went far beyond what

Western military planners only a short time earlier had dreamed possible. This dramatic announcement, which was followed by voluntary unilateral cuts by other Warsaw Pact nations, set the stage for new negotiations between NATO and the Warsaw Pact nations on Conventional Armed Forces in Europe (CFE). The new Atlantic-to-the-Urals conventional force talks replaced the Mutual and Balanced Force Reduction Talks (MBFR), which were concluded in 1989 after more than a decade of fruitless "bloc-to-bloc" (NATO–Warsaw Pact) efforts to reach agreement on a reduction of European conventional forces to equal and significantly lower levels. In addition, a somewhat larger group consisting of thirty-five nations began a new round of negotiations aimed at enhancing confidence and security building measures (CSBMs), whose purpose is to make military activities in Europe more predictable and transparent. The CFE and the CSBM negotiations both took place under the umbrella of the Conference on Security and Cooperation in Europe (CSCE).

The CSCE concluded its first session in Helsinki, Finland, in 1975. At that time the participants agreed to what was widely regarded as a de facto ratification of the European status quo, a kind of European peace treaty that formalized the division of Europe between East and West in the way that the never-concluded peace treaty ending World War II might have done. That interpretation has always been in dispute, but, regardless, the Helsinki accords accomplished other tasks, among which was a commitment by the Soviet Union and its Eastern European allies to respect a wide range of fundamental human rights and to permit a greater flow of people and ideas between East and West. That effort was supplemented by the Conference on Disarmament in Europe (CDE), consisting of the thirty-five Helsinki participants, which in 1986 adopted an important agreement on confidence and security building measures. The agreement included such CSBMs as advanced notice of military activities, the mandatory right to send military observers to watch large military exercises in any state in Europe, and aerial inspections of suspicious military activities not previously announced. The participants in the new round of CSCE negotiations hoped to extend these measures agreed to in 1986 in new directions.

The United States maintains that whereas confidence building measures can significantly alter perceptions of the intentions of adversaries, the critical questions turn on capabilities. As a result, the CFE negotiations have been more important.

The predecessor of the CFE negotiations, the Mutual and Balanced Force Reduction Talks (MBFR), failed because the two sides could not agree on the base from which to count. As the principle of flexible response—with its concomitant threat to use nuclear weapons—implies, the United States and its NATO allies believed they were at a disadvantage vis-à-vis the Soviet Union and its Warsaw Pact allies. In part this was simply a matter of their differing geostrategic situations—the Soviet Union, an essentially European power, would be able to strike with its allies against Western Europe more quickly and potentially more decisively than the United States and its allies would be able to respond. Beyond such obvious geostrategic asymmetries, the two sides differed fundamentally about how to interpret estimates of relative strength and capabilities, including especially the questionable reliability of some national units. Thus an impasse developed over such key concepts as equal reductions and equal levels.

The CFE negotiations embraced more countries, territories, troops, and equipment than were covered by the MBFR talks. Furthermore, the unilateral troop reductions announced by the Soviet Union suggested a willingness on its part to agree to significantly larger cuts in its own forces and those of the other Warsaw Pact nations than it sought for the United States and its NATO allies (the INF agreement set a precedent in this respect). Thus both sides agreed that tanks, artillery, armored vehicles, and helicopters should be reduced to equal levels some 10 to 15 percent below current NATO levels. Eventually, in October 1990, the United States and the Soviet Union reached an agreement in principle that would require the removal from Europe of tens of thousands of tanks, heavy artillery, armored vehicles, and aircraft. Virtually all of those would have to be removed or destroyed by the Soviet Union and its Warsaw Pact allies; the United States and its allies would have to remove only a few thousand tanks. Although the U.S.-Soviet agreement did not specifically call for troop reductions, these were expected to follow. Unclear was whether the United States and the Soviet Union had resolved long-standing differences on how to treat "dual capable" systems, that is, those that can deliver both conventional and nuclear munitions. It appeared nonetheless that the agreement in principle paved the way for a new treaty on Conventional Armed Forces in Europe which, if ratified by the U.S. Congress and the other participating states, would solidify the end of the Cold War in Europe.

Chemical Weapons   Earlier, at the June 1990 summit, the two superpowers agreed to stop production and significantly reduce their stockpiles of chemical weapons. The United States and the Soviet Union had engaged in bilateral negotiations to ban the production, stockpiling, and use of chemical weapons during the Carter administration. The negotiations shifted to the multilateral Conference on Disarmament following Reagan's election in 1981. They took a significant positive turn in 1987 when the Soviet Union announced its willingness to cease production of chemical weapons, acknowledged previously undisclosed information about its chemical weapons stockpiles, and acceded to U.S. demands regarding inspections. President Bush gave further impetus to an agreement in 1989 when, in a speech before the United Nations, he committed the United States to the eventual destruction of its existing chemical weapons stockpile. Less than a year later, the two sides decided in what Secretary of State James A. Baker called a "trailblazing agreement" to cease all production of poisonous gas and to reduce significantly their stockpiles of chemical weapons.[4] Each pledged further reductions once a multilateral agreement banning chemical weapons was reached.

---

4. The agreement called for each side to reduce their respective stockpiles to five thousand tons. The Soviet Union had previously announced that it held a stockpile of fifty thousand chemical agents; the United States is believed to have between twenty-five thousand and forty thousand tons. Even before the agreement, however, current law in the United States had required the destruction of 90 percent of the U.S. stockpile (most of which had been deemed militarily useless) by 1997.

The Defense Debate   Reaching negotiated arms reduction agreements between the United States and the Soviet Union has always proved difficult, and that is nowhere more evident than at the level of conventional arms where questions of counting and verification are even less tractable than with strategic weapons. Inferring intentions of the adversary is an elusive quest, and drawing inferences from capabilities is sometimes easiest but always suspect.

As long-standing differences between East and West are ameliorated, significant reductions in the overall size of the U.S. military establishment and the resources required to sustain it became possible. The Bush administration early in 1990 projected an annual rate of reduction of 2 percent over five years, which would add up to $200 billion. Critics of the administration's proposed "balanced downsizing" called for much larger cuts, but the administration maintained a posture of prudence on the issue. As General Colin L. Powell, chairman of the joint chiefs of staff, observed shortly before the June 1990 Bush-Gorbachev summit, "I've seen no particular Soviet capability disappear; I've seen no part of the world where we have an interest go off the map." The invasion of Kuwait by Iraq in August 1990 further eroded the position of those seeking larger defense reductions. At the very time of the invasion Bush was about to make a speech about the need to keep the United States strong militarily so as to enable it to respond to terrorism, hostage taking, and "renegade regimes and unpredictable rulers." He quickly seized on Iraq's "brutal aggression" to drive home the point that "threats can arise suddenly, unpredictably, and from unexpected quarters."

Prior to the unexpected threat from the Middle East, the cautious viewpoint regarding the Soviet Union was affirmed in the Bush administration's update of the Defense Planning Guidance prepared under the direction of Defense Secretary Dick Cheney and released in early 1990. The purpose of the document is to provide guidance to the military services about the kind of military strategy necessary to cope with the threats the nation will face in the 1992–1997 period. In it the Pentagon warned that superpower rivalry would continue in the 1990s, as "fundamental Soviet objectives in the Third World do not appear to have changed" (cited in Tyler, 1990). The classified document itself "describes an active U.S. strategy to thwart what are described as aggressive, long-term Soviet military objectives to obtain more overseas bases and to recruit 'subservient regimes'" (Tyler, 1990). It affirms the Reagan Doctrine's pledge to assistant "freedom fighters" and pledges the United States "will use military power to attack the 'root causes of instability' in less developed regions." Furthermore, it goes beyond the Reagan administration's views regarding protracted nuclear war.

> Where the Reagan defense guidance spoke of the need to be able to prevail in a protracted nuclear war, the new guidance states: "Should the war become global, the United States must be prepared for an extended conflict involving the survival of the nation." U.S. tactical and strategic nuclear forces would be used to "deny Soviet war aims" and "hold at risk those assets that the Soviet leadership would

need to prevail in a nuclear conflict and to dominate a postnuclear world," including its "leadership" and "war-supporting industry." (Tyler, 1990: 31; see also Ball and Toth, 1990)

That such thinking should prevail in the Pentagon is no surprise. And while it explained Cheney's go-slow approach toward reshaping the nation's defense posture, it opened the administration to the criticism that it was blind to the opportunities now available. Illustrative is the charge made by Representative Les Aspin, chair of the powerful House Armed Services Committee, that "there are new realities in the world but no new thinking at home to match them" (see also Iklé, 1990).

The defense planning document did recognize that the security environment in Europe was less threatening because of the revolutionary changes that had occurred in Eastern Europe. The continued presence of American troops in Europe will therefore figure prominently in what promises to be a prolonged defense debate. The Bush administration sought an agreement with the Soviet Union to reduce each superpower's armed forces in the "central zone" of Europe to 195,000, but it pledged a continued American presence in Europe to protect its own interests and those of its allies. The need for troops has always been predicated on the presence of a credible military threat to the West. Many contend that threat no longer exists, a viewpoint reinforced by the projected treaty on conventional forces in Europe (which, however, will still remain heavily armed even after the agreement enters into force). It is not so much that the Soviet Union no longer possesses the military capability to strike at the West; instead, because of the profound and perhaps irrevocable political changes that have taken place in the other Warsaw Pact countries, the Kremlin can no longer count on their support. Without it, as NATO planners confidently admit, there is virtually no chance that a conventional Soviet attack on the West could be mounted. But it is to guard against the possibility of precisely such an attack that NATO exists. In the absence of a credible threat to the West, the reason for keeping U.S. troops in Europe becomes problematic. The same is true of the continued existence of NATO as a collective self-defense arrangement. Secretary of State Baker called for a more political role for the alliance, but it is by no means certain NATO can continue without the Soviet and Warsaw Pact threats as its raison d'être (see also Mueller, 1990).

Military Force and Political Purposes

The discussion here and later in this chapter of both major war and strategic doctrinal shifts suggests that the purpose of American military might has been primarily preventive: to deter politically the use of military force by someone else, notably the Soviet Union.

In addition to prevention, American military forces have been used for the purpose of *changing* the behavior of others. As shown in Figure 4.1, there has been a total of 286 instances, traceable across the four decades from 1946

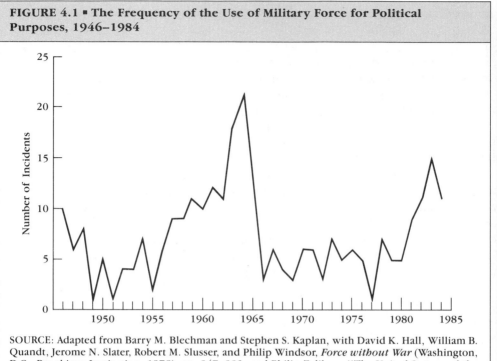

FIGURE 4.1 ▪ The Frequency of the Use of Military Force for Political Purposes, 1946–1984

SOURCE: Adapted from Barry M. Blechman and Stephen S. Kaplan, with David K. Hall, William B. Quandt, Jerome N. Slater, Robert M. Slusser, and Philip Windsor, *Force without War* (Washington, D.C.: Brookings Institution, 1978), pp. 547–553; and Philip Zelikow, "The United States and the Use of Force: A Historical Summary," in George K. Osborn, Asa A. Clark IV, Daniel J. Kaufman, and Douglas E. Lute (eds.), *Democracy, Strategy, and Vietnam* (Lexington, Mass.: Lexington Books, 1987), pp. 34–36.

to 1984, in which the United States has threatened to unleash some of its military might to influence, indirectly, the decisions of other states; that is, force has been used to cause the target either not to do something or to do something that it would not otherwise do.[5]

Figure 4.1 suggests two peaks in postwar American "gunboat diplomacy," the periods from 1957 to 1965 and from 1981 to 1984. In the first the average annual frequency of events in which American force was used as a political instrument was 12.6, compared with the average frequency of 7.3 incidents per year across the entire period since 1945. In the second, which coincides with President Reagan's first term in office, the average was 11.5 incidents. It is also clear that reliance on military forces for the achievement of political ends

---

5. Military forces can also be used to attain desired ends directly. Blechman and Kaplan et al. (1978) and Zelikow's (1987) inventories are concerned only with those instances where the force itself does not obtain the objective, but rather affects the perceptions of others, thereby influencing their decision(s).

has been a recurrent theme in the exercise of global influence sought by virtually every administration since World War II.

Several examples of U.S. reliance on this particular instrument of influence illustrate the modern tactic of gunboat diplomacy. One was the joint air exercises the United States undertook with Egypt and the augmentation of its Indian Ocean naval patrols as a signal to the Soviet Union not to extend its invasion of Afghanistan westward; another was the stationing of a carrier task force in the Mediterranean in 1983 to dissuade Libyan dictator Muammar Qaddafi from launching an attack on Sudan. Others include the staging of naval maneuvers on both sides of the Honduran isthmus in 1983 in an effort to intimidate leftist guerrillas active in Central America and to deter Cuba, Nicaragua, and the Soviet Union from supporting them; and the augmentation of U.S. forces in Panama with an additional 1,900 troops in May 1989 following General Manuel Noriega's disregard of the results of the Panamanian election. Clearly, on these and many other occasions, the practice of gunboat diplomacy was designed for purposes other than protecting the immediate physical security of the nation.

Systematic evidence on the use of force without war since 1984 is not available, but it appears that the Reagan administration relied on this instrument more frequently than any previous administration except Kennedy's. The contrast between it and the Carter administration is especially striking and is consistent with the resurgence of public support for an assertive America many believe to have occurred in the 1980s. For perhaps a decade following the peak of American involvement in Vietnam, the attitudes of many Americans, both inside and outside of government, suggested that there would be considerable restraint on the use of military force abroad in the future. But the Reagan administration arrived in Washington determined to free the nation from the shackles of the Vietnam syndrome. Its determination to do so played itself out in a variety of ways, as we will note again later in this chapter and elsewhere. Early moves indicative of its temperament toward military involvement included the dispatch of several dozen American military advisers to El Salvador in 1981 and of a peace-keeping force of eight hundred marines (with more to follow) to Lebanon in 1982. Overt military intervention in Grenada in 1983, the formation of a vast naval armada in the Persian Gulf in 1987, and, during the Bush administration, the invasion of Panama in 1989 and the dispatch of a massive number of troops to Saudi Arabia in 1990, reaffirmed the view that military force once more occupied a central role propelling active American involvement in world affairs.

The Bush administration's intervention into the Middle East to protect Saudi Arabia and to deter further Iraqi aggression following its invasion of Kuwait in 1990 is the most dramatic exercise of military power by the United States since its withdrawal from Vietnam. Nine weeks into Operation Desert Shield nearly two hundred thousand U.S. troops had been dispatched to the Persian Gulf region, with the ultimate size of the force still in doubt. It is noteworthy, however, that U.S. forces were not immediately engaged in military combat. That fact plus the change in Iraqi behavior sought by the Bush administration, which included the withdrawal of Iraq from Kuwait and the restoration of the legitimate government of Kuwait, characterize the operation as an instance of the use of force short of war to accomplish political objectives, not the application of force itself to realize those objectives. Still, the magnitude of the operation and the danger that actual fighting might erupt gave the operation the appearance of a direct military intervention.

Military Intervention

The maintenance of a high military profile abroad and displays of force comprise two elements of the interventionist thrust of America's globalist foreign policy posture. Outright military intervention is another. Here, too, there has been a striking consistency in the willingness of postwar administrations to intervene in the affairs of others. On six conspicuous occasions—in Korea (1950), Lebanon (1958), Vietnam (1955, 1961, or 1965, depending on one's definition), the Dominican Republic (1965), Grenada (1983), and Panama (1989)—the United States openly and directly used its combat capabilities in another country in order to accomplish its foreign policy objectives. Although ten other instances of less visible overt U.S. military interventions between 1945 and 1985 (Tillema, 1989: 184) might be cited (such as the U.S. attacks on Cambodia in 1970 and 1975 and the hostage rescue operation in Iran in 1980), those six cases, perhaps more than anything else, have pinned the interventionist label on postwar American foreign policy.

Measured in terms of size, Grenada was the smallest operation, involving only 1,900 American assault troops in an operation that met opposition from a local military force of only 1,200 troops plus roughly 700 armed Cuban construction workers. Lebanon was next in size, involving 14,000 American troops in what was essentially a bloodless intervention. The Dominican intervention ranks third in size, with 22,000 troops and some combat activity on the part of American forces. Then comes Panama, with an invasion force of 24,000 who met some resistance but suffered few casualties. Korea and Vietnam were, of course, much larger. In casualties alone, the Korean War outstripped the number of troops involved in the Dominican affair by 11,000. And in the case of Vietnam, where at one point nearly 550,000 troops were engaged, the Vietnam Veterans Memorial on the Mall in the nation's capital commemorates the 58,132 Americans who lost their lives in an intervention that spanned two Republican and two Democratic administrations.

Despite the recurrent nature of American interventionism, the interventionist label may be questioned. How does one explain the far-larger number of instances in which the United States did not intervene when its interests were threatened, as in the decision not to bail the French out of Indochina when they faced defeat at Dien Bien Phu in 1954 or the unwillingness to use overt military force to remove the leftist Sandinista regime from power in Nicaragua in the 1980s? Those cases and the unwillingness of the United States, with the single exception of Lebanon in 1958, to become directly involved in military combat in the Middle East's turmoil, stand out as glaring examples of nonintervention. How do we reconcile those facts with the interventionist stigma?

Herbert K. Tillema (1973) addresses that question in an examination of the only 4 instances of intervention among the nearly 150 postwar conflict situations in which the United States might have become involved between 1945 and 1970. The contrast between the few and the many indicates that American intervention was resisted whenever one or more of several different inhibiting factors were present. Among them were the perceived need to use nuclear weapons, the prior presence of Soviet troops, the absence of armed conflict, the absence of a specific request for intervention, or the willingness of the president to let some other component of the decision-making structure (such as Congress) veto an intervention decision. But "on those occasions when a Communist threat was thought to exist and when none of the other restraints was operative, intervention . . . followed." This view of overt military intervention thus holds that it occurs if, and only if, a communist takeover appears likely in another country, and none of the above-mentioned types of restraints to an armed intervention is present.

This perspective on the pattern of American action during the 1950s and 1960s indicates that, despite changes in the policy-making personnel involved in the decisions to intervene militarily, and despite some obvious differences in the situations they faced, each new case was treated in the same manner as previous ones. "Whatever differences there may have been in the purposes that different policymakers have seen in the use of force," writes Tillema, "all have used it in the same way. The continuing restraints upon intervention have shaped its use to the same mold" (see also Tillema and Van Wingen, 1982).

Interestingly, the Reagan administration's decision to intervene in Grenada followed very much the pattern of American action in the 1950s, the 1960s, and (implicitly) the 1970s. The event that precipitated the invasion was the overthrow of the Marxist-oriented government of Prime Minister Maurice Bishop and his subsequent execution by what President Reagan called "a brutal gang of leftist thugs." The administration provided three primary reasons for choosing military action. The first was to rescue Americans on the island (primarily medical-school students) whose safety was threatened. Fear of "another Iran," referring to the incarceration of American diplomats in Teheran for 444 days beginning in late 1979, reportedly weighed heavily on the president's mind. The second was the invitation of Grenada's neighbors in the Organization of Eastern Caribbean States to support a collective defense effort against external aggression. The final argument, and doubtless the strongest one, was fear that Grenada might become another Cuba from which subversive and other threats to U.S. national security might be launched. The logic was strikingly similar to that used by the Johnson administration to intervene in the Dominican Republic nearly twenty years earlier. That intervention was first rationalized by the need to protect American lives in a chaotic civil circumstance that threatened to bring a leftist regime to power, but President Johnson later admitted that fear of "another Cuba" was a greater concern.

The invasion of Panama in 1989 deviated from the other instances of overt military involvement in that it was motivated neither by an overt communist threat nor the fear that Panama might become another Cuba. But it fit the mold of previous interventions in other ways, as the official rationale closely paralleled the previous cases. The intervention was defended on grounds that it was an exercise of the inherent right of self-defense under international law, specifically Article 51 of the United Nations Charter, in response to armed attacks by Panamanian military forces under the direction of Manuel Noriega. Thomas R. Pickering, U.S. ambassador to the United Nations, explained to the Security Council that the goals of the United States were "to safeguard the lives of Americans, to defend democracy in Panama, to combat drug trafficking, and to protect the integrity of the Panama Canal Treaty." Thus the alleged purpose of Operation Just Cause was to rectify a situation in Panama that had become "intolerable." "The root cause of the crisis in Panama," Pickering continued, "has been the struggle between Noriega and his thugs and the people of Panama."

The fact that Noriega had declared shortly before the U.S. invasion that a state of war existed between the United States and Panama and that attacks had been made on Americans in the country were the precipitating events. But the failure of previous diplomatic efforts and the application of economic sanctions to bring about Noriega's downfall (Weeks and Zimbalist, 1989) doubtless contributed to the belief that the military option remained the only alternative for dealing with him. Moreover, the circumstances surrounding Noriega's rise to power as a "trusted asset" of the CIA and the U.S. government generally cast a shadow over the means finally chosen to remove a former ally. And while the intervention was initially popular in both the United States and Panama, it once more provoked resentment of the "Colossus of the North" in Latin America and criticism of U.S. militarism elsewhere. Critics charged that the invasion was only "the latest in a series of U.S. armed interventions in the Caribbean and Central America that have violated U.S. treaty commitments and the very tenets of international law the United States itself was instrumental in introducing" (Maechling, 1990). Notable in this respect is that neither the United Nations nor the Organization of American States supported the American invasion. In this way, too, the intervention followed the mold that ensued from previous interventions by contributing to antagonism toward the United States (see Kwitny, 1985).

As noted earlier, the U.S. intervention in the Middle East in 1990 is best conceptualized as an application of force short of war, but it was widely interpreted elsewhere as the first U.S. military action in a new, post–Cold War world. Democratic Senator David Boren worried that the outcome of the showdown in the Persian Gulf "could very well determine the extent of American influence in the post–Cold War world," and Secretary of State Baker warned apocalyptically of "a new dark age" if Iraqi aggression went unpunished. President Bush himself appealed to the presumed lessons of a bygone era in disrepute in the United States since the Vietnam War when he asserted "if history teaches us anything, it is that we must resist aggression or it will destroy our freedoms. Appeasement does not work. As was the case in the 1930s, we see in Saddam Hussein an aggressive dictator threatening his neighbors."

Like Panama, the absence of an explicit Soviet or communist threat helped to differentiate this action from other interventionist episodes—indeed, the Soviet Union backed the U.S. initiative, as did the United Nations Security Council. But the fact that the United States was so clearly motivated by concern for assuring access at reasonable prices to the Middle Eastern oil riches vital to the economic well-being of the United States and its Western allies tainted the administration's bold assertion that principle was the primary issue at stake. Furthermore, the prospect of a long-term commitment of U.S. troops to the Middle East raised the specter of fuelling hostility among Arabs sensitive to the presence of non-Moslem soldiers in Islamic holy lands. Thus the first intervention of the post–Cold War era threatened to become a test of U.S. resolve in a region where anti-American feelings run high.

Conventional military intervention comprises one element of American national security policy. Another centers on the place that strategic weapons occupy in protecting the nation's physical security and promoting its objectives abroad. It is to a consideration of those twin purposes that we now turn.

THE EVOLUTION OF STRATEGIC DOCTRINE: THE ROLE OF NUCLEAR WEAPONS AS INSTRUMENTS OF COMPELLENCE AND DETERRENCE

The detonation of atomic bombs on two Japanese cities in the waning days of World War II is the single most important event distinguishing prewar from postwar international politics. The clocks of Hiroshima stopped 8:15 on the morning of August 6, 1945, when, in the blinding flash of a single weapon and the shadow of its mushroom cloud, the international arena was transformed from a balance-of-power to a balance-of-terror system. Ever since, the central questions of American national security policy have turned on what to do *with* nuclear weapons and what to do *about* them. Should they be used, and, if so, how? Also, how can the United States prevent their use by others against itself? Every postwar administration has defined the dangers (or to some the opportunities) such weapons of mass destruction pose as a priority issue, but consensus on the answers to the questions they raise has never been achieved. Thinking about strategic doctrine has evolved in response to changing perceptions of global realities. Accordingly, the postures the United States has assumed toward the use of nuclear weapons display continuities *and* discontinuities.

For analytic convenience, American strategy can be broken into three periods: first, the period of America's atomic monopoly, 1945 to 1949; second, the period of American superiority in strategic weapons, 1949 until roughly

1960; and third, the subsequent period of rough nuclear parity, during which the United States has no longer stood alone in its capacity to annihilate another nation.

The Period of America's Atomic Monopoly

The seeds of the atomic age were planted in 1939 when the Manhattan Project was launched in an effort to construct a superweapon that could be success-fully used in war. As atomic physicist J. Robert Oppenheimer of the Manhattan Project noted, "We always assumed if [atomic bombs] were needed they would be used." Thus the rationale was established for a strategy based on, and backed by, the desire to possess extraordinary means of destruction with which to deal with enemies. President Truman's decision to drop the A-bomb on Japan was the culmination of that thinking.

Why did the United States use the bomb, which demolished two Japanese cities and took over one hundred thousand lives? (For a description of the human and physical damage, see Schell, 1982). The official explanation emphasized that the bomb was dropped "in order to end the war in the shortest possible time and to avoid the enormous losses of human life which otherwise confronted us" (Stimson and Bundy, 1947). Whether the bomb was necessary for ending the war, however, remains in dispute.[6] Revisionist historians (espe-cially Alperovitz, 1985) contend that the bomb's use was motivated not by a desire to save American lives but to prevent expansion of the Soviet Union's postwar influence in the Far East. A parallel interpretation contends that the bomb was used to impress Soviet leaders with its power and the willingness of the United States to exploit its advantages.

Regardless of its true purposes, the use of atomic weapons against Japan departed from traditional military strategy. Prior to the availability of such means of mass destruction, weapons had been seen largely as the means to short-range military ends. Now, however, they were also viewed as instruments for diplomatic bargaining and for the preservation of peace. The shift was pro-found; it marked the beginning of an era in which the instruments of war could be employed for the psychological purpose of molding others' behavior (including allies of the moment—in this instance the Soviet Union). During the period of America's atomic monopoly, the concept *compellence* (Schelling, 1966) described the new American view of nuclear weapons as instruments of influence, used not for fighting but to get others to do what they might not otherwise do. Nuclear weapons were seen as synonymous with strategy itself (Summers, 1989), the ultimate method of coercive diplomacy.

---

6. In retrospect, it is clear that Japan desperately wanted to surrender to the United States on acceptable terms. Tokyo was already in ruins; Japan's fate was certain. As the U.S. Strategic Bomb-ing Survey concluded, "certainly prior to 31 December 1945 Japan would have surrendered even if the atomic bombs had not been dropped." The United States knew through diplomatic channels a month before the bomb was actually dropped that the Japanese government wished to sue for peace (Alperovitz, 1985, 1989; Miles, 1985; for rebuttals, see Alsop and Joravsky, 1980, and Bundy, 1988).

President Truman and Secretary of War Henry L. Stimson counted on the new weapon to elicit Soviet acceptance of American terms for settling outstanding war issues, particularly in Eastern and Central Europe (Alperovitz, 1985). Truman could confidently advocate "winning through intimidation" and facing "Russia with an iron fist and strong language" because the United States alone possessed the greatest intimidator of them all, the bomb. Although he reversed his position shortly thereafter, Stimson was initially persuaded that the United States should "use the bomb to pry the Soviets out of Eastern Europe" (cited in LaFeber, 1976). But his advice suggested the direction that American strategic thinking took during this formative period, which was crystallized in a document (NSC 68) written by Truman's National Security Council in 1950, that rationalized "increasing American military and allied military capabilities across the board both in nuclear and conventional weapons [and] making it clear that whenever threats to the international balance of power manifested themselves, the United States could respond" (Gaddis, 1987–1988). In particular, the bomb was considered a tool that could be used. Nonetheless, the Truman administration's practice of atomic diplomacy in the years following World War II was restricted to bargaining, not warfare.

The Period of Superiority

The United States has never used atomic weapons since those two fateful days in August 1945, but it has sought to gain bargaining leverage by relying heavily on nuclear force as an instrument of strategic defense (that is, defense of U.S. territory) and as a means "to defend its interests wherever they existed" (Gaddis, 1987–1988), which implied its willingness not only to threaten but actually to use nuclear weapons. The monopoly on atomic weapons that the United States once enjoyed gave way to superiority in 1949, when the Soviet Union also acquired the bomb. Nonetheless, the assumption that America's adversaries could be made to bend to American wishes through atomic blackmail became a cornerstone of the Eisenhower containment strategy, particularly as it was conceived by its chief architect, Secretary of State John Foster Dulles. He devised an interpretation of the containment strategy built around three concepts, all of which made clear how important nuclear weapons had come to be perceived as instruments of coercive diplomacy: rollback, brinkmanship, and massive retaliation.

Rollback identified the goal the United States was to pursue: reject passive containment of the spread of communist influence and instead "roll back" the iron curtain by liberating communist-dominated areas. "We can never rest," Eisenhower swore in the 1952 presidential campaign, "until the enslaved nations of the world have in the fullness of freedom the right to choose their own path." Dulles pledged that the United States would practice rollback—and not merely promise it—by employing "all means necessary to secure the liberation of Eastern Europe."

American strategic superiority was assumed to make *brinkmanship* practicable. Dulles explained how nuclear power could be harnessed for bargaining purposes in his explication of brinkmanship:

> You have to take chances for peace, just as you must take chances in war. Some say that we were brought to the verge of war. Of course we were brought to the verge of war. The ability to get to the verge without getting into the war is the necessary art. . . . If you try to run away from it, if you are scared to go to the brink, you are lost. We've had to look at it square in the face. . . . We walked to the brink and we looked it in the face. We took strong action. (Dulles, 1952: 146)

Brinkmanship, in short, was a strategy for dealing with the Soviets by backing them into the corner with the threat of nuclear annihilation. Soviet leaders would then be compelled to comply with American demands, Dulles believed, because the overwhelming U.S. strategic advantage gave it capabilities the Soviet Union could neither match nor counter.

To be effective, brinkmanship had to be backed by a credible threat. To convince its adversary that the United States was willing to carry out its threats, the doctrine of *massive retaliation* was proclaimed (labeled the "New Look" to distinguish it from Truman's strategy). Massive retaliation was a *countervalue* nuclear weapons strategy that sought to provide "the maximum deterrent at bearable cost" by threatening mass destruction of the things the Soviet leaders were perceived to value most—their population and industrial centers. Massive retaliation grew out of the Eisenhower administration's simultaneous impulses to save money and to challenge the perception that American foreign policy had become largely a reflexive reaction to communist initiatives. No longer was containment restricted to retaliation against localized communist initiatives; instead, it would target the very center of communist power. Hence massive retaliation pledged a willingness to use nuclear weapons to accomplish foreign policy objectives. In a confrontation, Dulles explained, atomic weapons "would come into use because, as I say, they are becoming more and more conventional and replacing what used to be called conventional weapons."

Despite the assertiveness implied by such bold posturing, the actual record indicates that the Eisenhower administration (like Truman's) was for the most part cautious. As noted in Chapter 3, few of the threats enunciated in its tough talk, such as the promise to supply military aid to those revolting against Soviet rule in Hungary in 1956, were actually carried out. The United States did threaten to use nuclear weapons for purposes of coercive diplomacy on at least nine occasions between 1948 and 1962,[7] but it never carried through on them. Nevertheless, the concepts of rollback, brinkmanship, and massive retaliation

---

7. The instances occurred in 1948, 1959, and 1961, when the Soviet Union was the target and Berlin the issue; in 1950 and 1953, when China was the target and Korea was the issue; in 1955 and 1958, when China was again the target and the offshore islands of Quemoy and Matsu were the issue; in 1958 when the Soviet Union was the target and Lebanon the issue; and in 1962, when the Soviet Union was again the target and Cuba the issue (Russett, 1989: 180).

built around weapons of mass destruction and the threat of nuclear force had long-lasting consequences. They became the origins of faith in the belief that nuclear force could be used for political purposes, and that sufficient strategic force could be relied on for defense and possible victory, as the United States continued the compellence strategy Truman had initiated.

From Superiority to Parity

A shift away from compellence toward what would come to be called a strategy of *deterrence* began in the late 1950s and became readily discernible with the Kennedy administration in 1961. One reason for the shift was the Soviet Union's growing strategic strength; another was growing appreciation among American policymakers of U.S. vulnerability to nuclear attack and the limited policy purposes to which weapons of mass destruction could safely be put. "On the day the Soviets acquired [the bomb as] an instrument and the means to deliver it," George Ball (1984) observes, "the bomb lost its military utility and became merely a means of mutual suicide . . . [for] there are no political objectives commensurate with the costs of an all-out nuclear exchange." The development of intercontinental ballistic missiles (ICDMs) further undermined the assumption that nuclear arsenals could actually be used in warfare, because now the United States itself was vulnerable to Soviet attack.

President Kennedy felt it necessary to educate the world to the new reality; in a 1961 speech to the United Nations General Assembly he warned:

> Today, every inhabitant of this planet must contemplate the day when this planet may no longer be habitable. Every man, woman and child lives under a nuclear sword of Damocles, hanging by the slenderest of threads, capable of being cut at any moment by accident or miscalculation or by madness. The weapons of war must be abolished before they abolish us.
>
> Men no longer debate whether armaments are a symptom or cause of tension. The mere existence of modern weapons—ten million times more powerful than any that the world has ever seen, and only minutes away from any target on earth—is a source of horror, and discord and distrust.

And later, in the aftermath of his willingness to go to the brink of a nuclear war with the Soviets following their installation of offensive missiles in Cuba in 1962, which elevated America's growing sense of vulnerability, Kennedy expressed a related viewpoint that implied a new policy direction when he spoke of "the living envying the dead" in the event of a nuclear exchange and cautioned that we should "never fear to negotiate." The decline of American strategic superiority commanded a new strategy that took cognizance of the suicidal perils of nuclear weapons. Weapons of mass destruction ceased to be thought of as instruments for compellence in diplomatic bargaining; hereafter, they were seen as performing primarily a deterrent function. They would be relied on to prevent wars waged against the United States and, secondarily, its allies. Every president since Kennedy has pointed to the risks of viewing the bomb as merely another weapon that can be used offensively to induce concessions or combat aggression. Instead, strategic nuclear weapons have been assigned primarily a defensive purpose, even though the United States did threaten to use nuclear weapons on four identifiable occasions in the years following the Cuban missile crisis.[8]

Deterrence means discouraging an adversary from using force by convincing him that the costs of such action would outweigh the potential gain. To ensure that such costs can be imposed, a *second-strike* capacity is necessary. That is, American offensive strategic forces must be able to withstand an initial strike by an adversary and retain the capacity to respond with a devastating second blow. In this way the adversary will be assured of destruction, thus deterring the initial preemptive attack. Hence strategic deterrence implies sensitivity to the survivability of American strategic forces. In practice, the United States has sought that objective through the maintenance of a triad of strategic weapons consisting of piloted bombers and land- and sea-based intercontinental ballistic missiles.

The Kennedy administration's doctrine of strategic deterrence rested on the principle of *assured destruction*—a condition realized if a country can survive an aggressor's worst possible attack with sufficient firepower to inflict unacceptable damage on the attacker in retaliation. It differed from massive retaliation in that the earlier principle presupposed U.S. strategic superiority, which enabled the United States to choose the time and place where nuclear weapons might be used in response to an act of Soviet aggression (as defined by the United States). In contrast, the principle of assured destruction pledged that a direct Soviet attack against the United States (or perhaps its allies) would automatically result in a devastating American retaliatory nuclear strike. Therefore the initiative would be given to the Soviet Union, under the assumption that it would not attack first if convinced that a first strike against the United States (or perhaps its NATO allies) would assure its own destruction.[9] Noteworthy is that this strategy of survival through nuclear attack avoidance depends critically on the rational behavior of the Soviet leaders.

Because the shift from massive retaliation to strategic deterrence based on the principle of assured destruction was stimulated by changing perceptions of Soviet military capabilities, American strategic doctrine increasingly stressed that what held for American deterrence of Soviet aggression also held for Soviet deterrence of American aggression. From this, *mutual deterrence*, based

---

8. The instances occurred in 1969, when North Vietnam was the target and South Vietnam the issue; in 1973, when the Soviet Union was the target and Israel the issue; in 1975, when North Korea was the target and South Korea the issue; and in 1980, when the Soviet Union was the target and the Persian Gulf the issue (Russett, 1989: 180).

9. American leaders have built their strategies on the premise that "deterrence rests on a perilous paradox. What is perceived as an impossible war has to be perceived as possible if it is to be impossible. On the one hand, a nuclear war entails an unacceptable holocaust for all parties. It is assumed to act as a deterrent from aggression and to render impossible any and every military use of nuclear weapons. On the other hand, deterrence is not credible if these weapons cannot be used" (Tunander, 1989).

on the principle of *mutual assured destruction*, evolved as both a condition characterizing superpower relations and a policy goal. That is, each side now had the capacity to assure the destruction of the other (note the ironic acronym for mutual assured destruction: MAD). The term "balance of terror" accurately describes the essential military stalemate that emerged between the superpowers, for mutual assured destruction is based on the military potential for, and psychological expectations of, widespread death and destruction for both combatants in the event of a nuclear exchange. The preservation of this condition became a preferred policy goal: because the price of an attack by one state on its adversary would be its own destruction, stability and war avoidance are the expected results. In this sense nuclear deterrence "is like a gun with two barrels, of which one points ahead and the other points back at the gun's holder," writes Jonathan Schell (1984). "If a burglar should enter your house, it might make sense to threaten him with this gun, but it could never make sense to fire it."

The Nixon Administration   The Nixon administration echoed Secretary of Defense Robert S. McNamara's thesis that it was dangerous for the United States to recapture superiority and made mutual assured destruction the premise of its national security strategy. But Nixon also extolled the value of sufficiency or parity. Termed *realistic deterrence*, the modified strategic doctrine stressed military strength, a defense burden shared with U.S. allies, and a willingness to negotiate with adversaries. In point of fact, it recognized that the strategic edge over the Soviet Union had disappeared, that the Soviets had an arsenal roughly equivalent to that of the United States, and that if a military exchange occurred the Soviet Union now possessed the capacity to respond to the United States in kind.

At the same time that the Soviet Union narrowed the capability gap separating it from the United States, American policymakers began to confront gnawing questions about the utility of attempting to enhance destructive power. As Henry Kissinger, Nixon's national security adviser and later secretary of state, observed:

> The paradox of contemporary military strength is that a gargantuan increase in power has eroded its relationship to policy. . . . The capacity to destroy is difficult to translate into a plausible threat even against countries with no capacity for retaliation. . . . Other nations have an unprecedented scope for autonomous action . . . [and military] power no longer translates automatically into influence. (Kissinger, 1974a: 59–60)

Cognizance of the new realities set the stage for other refinements in American policymakers' strategic thinking. Three premises were central: (1) a full-scale nuclear war could not be won and must not be fought; (2) there is no alternative to deterrence; (3) deterrence requires approximate equality in the superpowers' force capabilities so that neither will perceive a preemptive first strike advantageous.

The logic of these tenets has been challenged from time to time (see Jervis, 1984). During the early phase of the Reagan administration, for instance, a number of strategists advocated a departure from these principles by supporting a policy of nuclear blackmail for political purposes to coerce compliance from adversaries, and they advanced the view that it might be possible to fight, survive, and even win a nuclear war (see Gray and Payne, 1980). In 1980 George Bush asserted "you can have a winner" if "you have a survivability of command and control, survivability of industrial potential, protection of a percentage of your citizens, and you have a capacity that inflicts more damage on the opposition than it can inflict on you." But the orthodox view, that a "prevailing" (Gray, 1984) strategy is unrealistic, has endured. In fact, it has been widely reaffirmed even as the threat of a Soviet nuclear attack has diminished in the 1990s (Warnke, 1991). The purpose of nuclear weapons therefore is to prevent nuclear war, not to wage it.

The "retaliation-only" corollary derives from this principle governing the uses of nuclear weapons. As stated in 1983 by former Secretary of Defense McNamara, "nuclear weapons serve no military purpose whatsoever. They are totally useless—except only to deter one's opponent from using them." This principle was reaffirmed in the statement Ronald Reagan and Mikhail Gorbachev endorsed at their 1987 summit meeting, which declared that "a nuclear war cannot be won and must not be fought." It implied support for the reasoning behind the "no first use" declaratory policy advocated in the mid-1980s (Bundy, et al. 1982), even though no first use runs counter to NATO doctrine, which maintains that nuclear weapons are to be used should NATO conventional forces face defeat on the battlefield.

There is a third premise of contemporary American national security policy related to changes in U.S. thinking about nuclear weapons: that peace requires maintenance of the superpowers' *relative* strategic capabilities. Most adjustments in U.S. force structures and doctrines have been geared toward enhancing *crisis stability*; that is, changes in the levels of arms capabilities and the kinds of doctrines controlling their use are designed so that, in the event of a crisis, the incentives for selecting a preemptive first strike are minimized. In the 1950s, when the United States enjoyed measurable strategic advantages, it could threaten "escalation dominance" by permitting the tension level to rise to a point where the adversary would not dare respond (and would therefore have no choice but to submit). But with the Soviet achievement of essential nuclear equivalence, that strategy became too risky.

Alongside these developments still other adjustments were made in an effort to keep thinking about the design and potential use of the U.S. nuclear arsenal abreast of changes in weapons technologies and force ratios. Recall that the Eisenhower administration's doctrine of massive retaliation embraced a countervalue targeting strategy that held population and industrial centers hostage. As early as 1962 Secretary of Defense McNamara suggested that the United States ought instead to adopt a *counterforce* strategy that targeted American destructive capacity on the enemy's military forces and weapons rather than its population centers. In 1974 James Schlesinger, then secretary of defense in the Ford administration, publicly announced that the United States would pursue a counterforce capability that would enable U.S. strategic forces to attack heavily protected Soviet military targets. Such a nuclear option requires a weapons technology providing improved accuracy in nuclear delivery systems and increased "hard-target kill"[10] warhead yield capacity. It also presumably requires a multitude of types of nuclear weapons so as to make a "limited" nuclear strike feasible. In his pronouncement Schlesinger criticized the principle of assured destruction as "insufficiently flexible and selective to allow the President to order a less than all-out nuclear attack."

The Carter Administration   The counterforce option became the official strategic doctrine of the United States in 1980, when President Carter signed Presidential Directive (PD) 59. Known in official circles as the *countervailing* or "war fighting" strategy, the new posture, which in fact was little more than an extension of ideas advanced earlier by the Ford administration, was designed to enhance deterrence by targeting *both* military forces and weapons *and* industrial centers in the Soviet Union. As Secretary of Defense Harold Brown explained in 1981, "The essence of the countervailing strategy is to convince the Soviets that they will be successfully opposed at any level of aggression they choose, and that no plausible outcome at any level of conflict could represent 'success' for them by any reasonable definition of success." The change was presumably incorporated into the top-secret master plan for waging nuclear war known as the Single Integrated Operational Plan (SIOP), which operationalizes strategic doctrine by targeting Soviet military and nonmilitary sites that would be attacked in the event of war (see Ball and Toth, 1990).

The doctrinal shift embodied in PD 59 represented, at least symbolically, a possible tactical use of nuclear weapons beyond their orthodox deterrent function. Understandably, therefore, the countervailing strategy it articulated came under criticism. Some questioned the premise that an enhanced counterforce capability and an expressed willingness to use nuclear weapons would increase deterrence and thus lessen the possibility of all-out nuclear war. Because an effective counterforce strategy could eliminate the Soviets' ability to mount an effective second strike, critics argued, it might be interpreted as a U.S. move to achieve overwhelming offensive strategic superiority and a corresponding first-strike capability. They worried that the countervailing strategy offered "an illusion of victory that [made] nuclear war seem less unthinkable and thus more likely" (Barnet, 1981). That is, the actual use of nuclear weapons in a conflict might now be considered a viable option. If so, the strategy would conceivably undermine the fragile balance of terror, thereby hastening rather than preventing a nuclear holocaust.

---

10. Hard-target kill capacity refers to the destructive capacity of weapons directed against an opponent's land-based ICBM forces. For both superpowers, those ICBM forces are vital to the second-strike capability which, in turn, is widely assumed to be necessary for effective deterrence.

The Reagan Administration   Even while the United States modified its plans for coping with the Soviet threat, the Soviet Union continued a strategy of massive military spending in the 1960s and 1970s that enabled it to substantially enlarge and modernize its strategic forces. As a result, the Soviets achieved advantages in terms of numbers of missiles, missile warheads, and missile throw-weight (one measure of the payload a ballistic missile can lift from the ground and propel toward its targets). This expansion and force modernization alarmed Ronald Reagan who, upon his election in 1980, promised to "make America stand tall" and do whatever was necessary to enable the United States "to prevail." "Our ability to deter war and protect our security declined dangerously during the 1970s," Reagan claimed. Indeed, the proposition that the 1970s had been a "decade of neglect" for the security interests of the United States became a cornerstone of Reagan's policies. Thus the administration embarked upon the largest peacetime military buildup in history, which saw defense spending double between 1980 and 1988 in an effort to enhance military strength and the ability of the nation's strategic forces to deter and compel.

Even as the Reagan administration embarked on an ambitious force modernization program, defense analysts agreed that the weapons in the U.S. arsenal were far more sophisticated technologically than those in the Soviet arsenal, and that Soviet strategic systems, being heavily concentrated in land-based missiles (over 70 percent of Soviet warheads are on ICBMs), are far more vulnerable to destruction than American systems, where reliance on submarine-launched ballistic missiles (SLBM) in particular gives the United States a comparatively invulnerable force (see Train, 1990). The administration was nevertheless concerned about what it perceived as the growing vulnerability to a Soviet attack on the land-based leg of the strategic triad.

Fearing in particular that Soviet technological developments had rendered the Minuteman missile force vulnerable to a devastating first strike (which would undermine the second-strike capability but not eliminate it because of the SLBM forces), and convinced that the Soviet Union could no longer be deterred simply with the threat of assured destruction, the Reagan administration pledged to develop capabilities sufficient not only to ensure the survivability of U.S. strategic forces in the event of a first strike (so that a devastating second strike could be launched), but also to deter a second strike by threatening a third.

To some, the real purpose of the initiative was to move U.S. strategy from deterrence toward a preemptive capacity. Talk of striking the Soviet Union with a devastating first blow (so destructive that it could not mount a retaliatory strike) fed the speculation. So, too, did talk of the "winnability" of a nuclear exchange and, in the event deterrence should fail, of "damage limitation," that is, minimizing destruction of the United States and its allies by destroying a portion of the Soviet strategic forces before they could be launched. (Civil defense and other defensive measures also fall under the rubric of damage limitation.) These pronouncements and preparations suggested that Reagan sought to develop a nuclear war-fighting capacity and believed it possible to fight a protracted nuclear war (Craig and Jungerman, 1986), because his statements implied that he did not believe that any use of nuclear weapons would necessarily escalate to an unmanageable, all-out nuclear exchange. By making nuclear weapons more usable, Reagan administration officials claimed, deterrence would be enhanced by making the nuclear threat more credible.

To many strategists, however, the outbreak of nuclear war was believed certain to end in nuclear catastrophe. Given the probability of technical or human error, they found it difficult to envision a scenario in which a protracted nuclear war could be waged in such a manner that it would not escalate out of control. These critics often pointed in particular to the vulnerability of the nation's command, control, communications, and intelligence (C^3I) capability. A Soviet attack by a comparatively small number of weapons would effectively "decapitate" the nation by killing its political leaders and destroyingthe communication links necessary to ensure a coordinated and coherent U.S. retaliation (Schneider, 1989; Ball, 1989). These dangers, it was argued, undermined the feasibility of conducting a limited nuclear war. Hence many concluded that a strategy premised on the usability of nuclear weapons in war would in fact make war more likely, not less, and thereby diminish the weapons' deterrent capability.

If there was a novel twist in Reagan's policies regarding strategic weapons, it was his dramatic call in 1983 for a new high-tech ballistic missile defense (BMD) system designed to render nuclear missiles "impotent and obsolete." As a complement (or substitute?) to his "prevailing" strategy, the Strategic Defense Initiative (SDI)—popularly known as "Star Wars"—sought to create a "defense dominant" strategy. Foreshadowing a distant future in which the United States might be able to neutralize Soviet offensive weapons launched in fear or anger, Reagan pledged to inaugurate a profound shift in nuclear strategy away from reliance on offensive missiles to deter an attack; that is, away from dependence on mutual assured destruction, which President Reagan deemed "morally unacceptable." Instead, SDI promised a substitute that would lessen the probability of nuclear war and reduce, even eliminate, damage to the United States should it occur.

The Strategic Defense Initiative was the object of criticism from the very beginning. Official statements about the program raised expectations that many experts felt could not be met technologically until well into the next century, if ever. Conceptually, SDI initially envisioned a "layered" defensive system in which threatening Soviet missiles and warheads would be destroyed at some point between launch and impact. The curvature of the earth, the short time span for decision, and the inherent advantages of the offense (including deliberate deceptions during attack) all render a defensive posture unimaginably complex.[11] The billions of virtually instantaneous computer calculations

---

11. The tragedy that befell the space shuttle *Challenger* and its seven-member crew in 1986 reinforced the uncertainty surrounding SDI by raising serious questions about the limits of extraordinarily complex machines and of humans' capacity to command and control such technology.

such a system would require could not be met until the next generation of computers come on-line in the late 1990s or later.

Furthermore, many critics warned that if SDI were pursued the Soviets would undoubtedly increase their nuclear arsenal to ensure their ability to overwhelm U.S. defenses, while at the same time proceeding with development of their own defensive system. SDI could thus incite a rapid and extremely expensive escalation of the arms race, the outcome of which might well further impair both superpowers' security (Carnesale, 1985). Still, advocates of a "defense-dominant" strategy maintain that "defending through active defense is preferable to defending through terrorism—the ultimate mechanism by which deterrence through threat of retaliation operates" (Congressional Research Service, 1989). In some respects, SDI symbolizes an elusive American quest for invulnerability or "absolute security" whose roots can be traced to the early years of the Republic (Chace and Carr, 1988).

Arms Control, the Military Balance, and Deterrence

Even while the United States has continued to press forward in the development of strategic weapons, it has pursued a "dual track" approach to the goal of mutual deterrence, wherein efforts to preserve an acceptable deterrent capacity and strategic balance with the Soviet Union have relied on both weapons acquisitions and on arms control negotiations. As Secretary of State George Shultz explained, "the arms control process has always had as a main goal to ensure deterrence by enhancing stability and balance in the strategic relationship." Thus arms control negotiations are viewed not as a substitute for national security policy but a component of it. As President Reagan's Commission of Strategic Forces (the Scowcroft Commission) observed, "Stability should be the primary objective both of our strategic forces and our arms control programs. . . . [Both] should work together to permit us, and encourage the Soviets, to move in directions that reduce or eliminate the advantage of aggression and also reduce the risk of war by accident or miscalculation." "The main goal of arms control," Secretary of State James Baker echoed in 1989, "is to reduce the risk of war. . . . Stability requires military forces and policies such that no one can gain by striking first even in the worst crisis."

The SALT Process   The Strategic Arms Limitation Talks (SALT) agreements of 1972 can be interpreted as a joint effort by both sides to prevent the collapse of the fragile balance of terror that supports mutual assured destruction. The SALT negotiations attempted to guarantee each superpower's second-strike capability and thereby preserve the fear of retaliation on which stable deterrence presumably rests.

Agreement was not easy. Principal among the difficulties was how to compare the superpowers' strategic forces. The problem was compounded by the fact that the United States enjoyed a substantial lead in MIRV technology (multiple independently targetable reentry vehicles—in other words, more than one independently targetable warhead on a single missile). This enabled it to opt for a force posture built on a large number of comparatively small weapons, whereas the Soviet Union relied on fewer but larger weapons, which required a larger number of delivery vehicles. But in a sense the different force postures balanced one another. Thus there was "parity" in the two sides' strategic forces, recognition of which enabled the superpowers to move, however modestly, to place a limit on what threatened to become an unlimited arms race.

SALT I consisted of (1) a treaty that restricted the deployment of antiballistic missile defense (ABM) systems by the United States and the Soviet Union to equal and very low levels, and (2) a five-year interim accord on strategic offensive arms that restricted the number of ICBM and SLBM launchers that each side was permitted to have. The latter agreement was essentially a confidence-building "stopgap" step toward a more comprehensive longer-term treaty limiting strategic weapons.

The SALT II agreement of 1979 (though never ratified) sought that objective by substantially revising the quantitative restrictions of SALT I and by placing certain qualitative constraints on the superpowers' strategic arsenals. It placed a ceiling on the overall number of strategic launchers (including bombers, which were not covered in SALT I) each side was permitted. Within this overall ceiling, several subceilings specified additional restrictions on particular types of nuclear systems, most notably the numbers of missiles that could be equipped with MIRVs.

At the time that SALT II was signed these limitations were expected to dampen dramatically the momentum of the superpowers' arms race. And while they may have kept the total number of strategic weapons below what would have been produced in the absence of the SALT process, the evidence summarized in Figure 4.2 demonstrates that the spiral of weapons production—notably deliverable warheads—has continued largely unabated. The destructive capacity of these weapons deserves some emphasis.

When World War II ended, there was but one atomic bomb still in existence. By 1990 the United States and the Soviet Union each had stockpiled nearly 12,000 strategic nuclear weapons. In addition, each is estimated to possess between 11,000 and 13,000 tactical nuclear weapons (those designed for the direct support of combat operations.) The rate of growth in nuclear weaponry averaged three additional bombs a day in the 1980s (Sivard, 1989). The 57,000 warheads in existence globally in 1989 represented an explosive force some 1,600 times greater than the eleven megatons of explosive power used in World War II and the wars in Korea and Vietnam combined, in which some forty-four million people were killed (Sivard, 1989: 15, 14). The warheads carried aboard only one U.S. submarine are estimated to contain the force equivalent to nearly 18,000 Hiroshima explosions; those on U.S. ICBMs another 27,000 Hiroshimas; and those on U.S. bombers still another 33,400 Hiroshimas. And as unimaginable as it may seem, Soviet strategic nuclear forces are capable of even greater destruction, with the megatonnage necessary for some 115,600 Hiroshima-equivalent explosions (Harris and Markusen, 1986: 25–26). It is

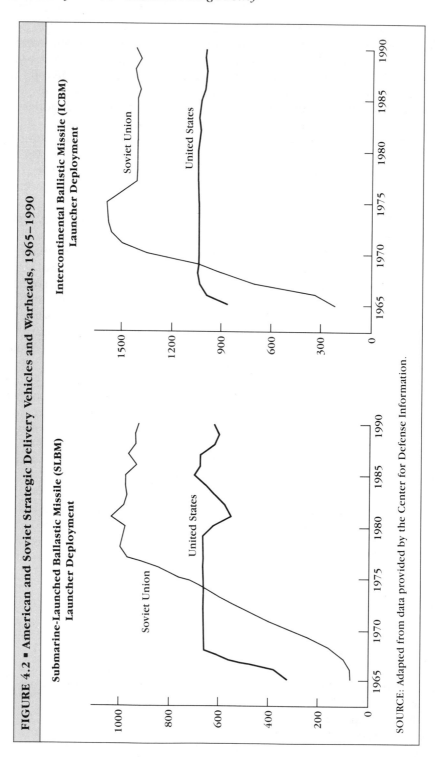

FIGURE 4.2 ■ American and Soviet Strategic Delivery Vehicles and Warheads, 1965–1990

Submarine-Launched Ballastic Missile (SLBM) Launcher Deployment

Intercontinental Ballistic Missile (ICBM) Launcher Deployment

SOURCE: Adapted from data provided by the Center for Defense Information.

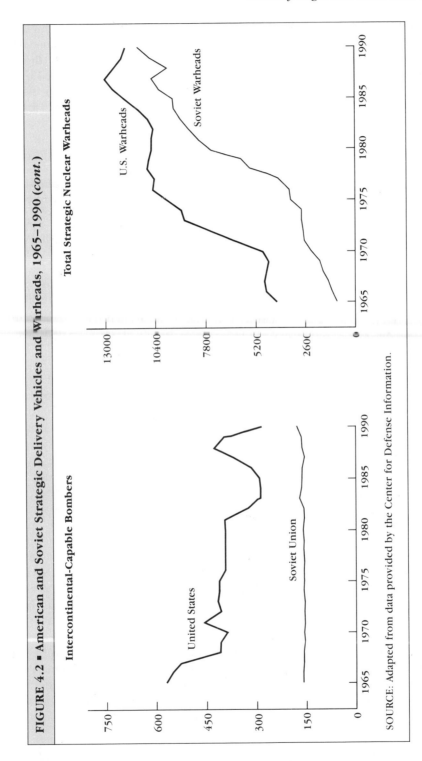

FIGURE 4.2 ▪ American and Soviet Strategic Delivery Vehicles and Warheads, 1965–1990 (cont.)

SOURCE: Adapted from data provided by the Center for Defense Information.

obvious that the use of such weapons in large numbers would threaten the destruction not only of entire cities and countries but possibly, when radiation effects and potentially catastrophic changes in the global climate through a "nuclear winter" are considered, of the entire world population (see Ehrlich et al., 1983 and 1985; Sagan, 1983–1984; Robock, 1990). The threat is vividly captured in Albert Einstein's famous remark that, although he did not know what the weapons of a third world war would be, in a fourth they would be "sticks and stones."

It is against the backdrop of weapons of such incredible destructive force that the United States has sought simultaneously to ensure the physical survival of the nation and its allies while seeking to reduce the threat that the existence of the weapons themselves pose. Thus motivated by fear that the other side might achieve a technological "break out," the United States has pursued negotiated arms control agreements while also pursuing research and development on the most sophisticated generation of weapons. The combination is a curious yet persistent mixture that stretches across the entire record of postwar American foreign policy. It reflects a preference for military might in pursuit of globalism, anticommunism, and containment, on the one hand, and a concern for what weapons of mass destruction and an unrestrained arms race might ultimately portend for the survival of the nation and its ideals, on the other.

The START Process   The Reagan administration followed the "dual track" of its predecessors by pursuing arms limitation talks and a military buildup simultaneously. Early in the first Reagan term there was little willingness to discuss arms limitations, but a combination of domestic and international pressure gave impetus to two sets of negotiations, the Strategic Arms Reduction Talks (START) aimed at reducing the superpowers' strategic forces, and the intermediate-range nuclear force (INF) talks directed toward reducing tactical nuclear force weapons in Europe. The administration's intransigence on the issue of SDI, which the Soviet Union saw as highly threatening, was the major stumbling block in the START negotiations. In the case of the INF talks, the Soviet objective was to prevent NATO deployment of its new Euromissiles consisting of ground-launched cruise missiles and Pershing II intermediate-range ballistic missiles. When that failed, the Soviets abruptly ended the INF talks in November 1983 and the START negotiations shortly thereafter. It was as frigid a point in Soviet-American relations as at any time since the height of the Cold War in the 1950s and 1960s.

The debates surrounding the NATO force modernization decision of the late 1970s and the later INF negotiations had centered on the credibility of the American commitment to defend Europe from a Soviet attack, which is captured in the concept *extended deterrence*. American policy applies deterrence not just to the nation's homeland, but also continues to promise *horizontal escalation* by applying deterrence to the enemy's remote and vulnerable outposts in retaliation for Soviet adventures elsewhere.[12] NATO's force modernization program was motivated by a concern for the credibility of this commitment. Was the United States, its European allies worried, truly willing to risk its own destruction in the event of a war with the Soviet Union to prevent an attack not only on the United States but also on its Western European allies? The decision to build and deploy a new generation of intermediate-range nuclear weapons was conceived as a way to guarantee that U.S. strategic forces remained "coupled" to the defense of Western Europe. The fear that the United States might stand aside in the event of a nuclear war in Europe was heightened by President Reagan, who startled European leaders with the statement shortly after his election that he "could see where you could have an exchange of tactical weapons against troops in the field without it bringing either one of the major powers to pushing buttons." Such rhetoric heightened the fear of war that already accompanied the renewed hostility between the United States and the Soviet Union in the early 1980s and thus provided incentives for renewed arms control efforts as a way of confronting the larger security problem that Europe as well as the United States faced.

As noted earlier, the superpowers reached a historic agreement on these issues in 1987 when they signed a treaty that banned INF forces from Europe. Although the accord required dismantling less than 5 percent of the world's nuclear arsenals (the U.S. pledged to destroy about nine hundred missiles and the Soviet Union roughly twice that number), it set the stage, as British Foreign Secretary Sir Geoffrey Howe put it, for "the beginning of the beginning of the whole arms control process."

On the strategic front the superpowers agreed at the 1985 Geneva summit that "deep cuts" in their strategic forces were in order. They differed substantially in how those cuts should be accomplished, however. Again the issue turned essentially on how to deal with the differences in the two sides' force composition. As a traditional land power, the Soviet Union has placed heavy reliance on land-based missiles, as noted before. The United States sought to reduce their number, viewing them as the gravest threat to U.S. land-based forces. Conversely, the Soviets, facing an American strategic force more widely dispersed among the three legs of the strategic triad, sought cutbacks that would directly offset U.S. areas of superiority. The Soviets also expressed deep apprehension about SDI, but the Reagan administration remained determined to forge ahead on the plan.

Both sides offered a number of proposals and counterproposals in the months that followed the Geneva summit. Although wide differences remained, the dialogue between the United States and the Soviet Union suggested there was room for bargaining. The INF accord added momentum to the process, as the superpowers also agreed during the 1987 Washington summit

---

12. Because horizontal escalation globalized deterrence by spreading it worldwide, it has also been called *geographical escalation* and a *war-widening strategy* (Epstein, 1983).

that each should cut its arsenal of strategic nuclear warheads by half (to approximately six thousand). Thereafter, effecting "deep cuts" became the mutually accepted goal of the superpowers' arms control process.

Strategic Defense in the 1990s

George Bush pledged in his presidential campaign to pursue negotiated arms control agreements with the Soviet Union, but his embrace of prudence dictated moving slowly and verifying Soviet concessions before placing trust in them. The Bush administration had hoped that a new START agreement could be reached by June 1990, when the Soviet and American presidents met in Washington. That goal was not realized, but the two sides did agree on a statement of fundamental principles in which they pledged to cut sea- and air-launched offensive ballistic missiles by a third by 1997. The statement of principles also opened the way to reducing overall long-range arsenals, and it set the stage for discussing the more difficult issue: how to cut the newer, more important sea- and air-launched cruise missiles that figure so prominently in both superpowers' modernization plans. It also set the stage for breaking the impasse over slashing conventional troops and weapons in Europe.

Alongside these promising changes, however, continuities are evident. Despite the Kremlin's moderate new tone, "the threat itself, in terms of military power, is still there," Secretary of State Baker cautioned in November 1989. Secretary of Defense Cheney warned at the same time, "By the late 1990s, even if you have a START agreement, the Soviets will have phased out, completely replaced and modernized every single leg of the triad." Given these expectations, America's continuing reliance on nuclear deterrence appeared certain to remain the cornerstone of its national security policy. As Secretary Baker asserted in October 1989, "We are not on the verge of a perpetual peace in which war is no longer possible. We cannot disinvent nuclear weapons nor the need for continued deterrence." Hence fears still appeared to dominate hopes even as the Cold War waned.

Although it was not explicit about its strategic assumptions, the Bush administration quietly pursued the goal of developing a nuclear war-fighting capability and the planned use of strategic weapons in a military conflict, while publicly stressing that America's nuclear weapons were primarily for deterrence. Bush affirmed his faith in the defensive uses of strategic weapons but, as in the case of conventional force planning, he undertook drastic revisions of SIOP that would expand American capabilities for fighting a nuclear war by paralyzing the Soviets' war-making abilities in the opening hours of a war. The strategy was redesigned to "penetrate the [Soviets'] deepest underground bunkers and 'decapitate' the entire Soviet leadership" (Toth, 1989). Whether these costly plans to blitz Soviet leaders at the beginning of hostilities would increase or decrease the risk of a nuclear holocaust was questioned by many, who averred that Bush's revised SIOP took "war fighting to dangerous extremes" (Ball and Toth, 1990).

The fact that these changes were made at the very time that the Soviet threat was diminishing gave testimony to the persistence of old ways of thinking about matters of national security and strategy. As one defense expert noted in 1990:

> Even now the nightmare of a Soviet nuclear attack continues to darken the waking hours of Western military leaders and the theoreticians who advise them. The Bush administration remains committed to an expensive, redundant and provocative array of new strategic nuclear weapons—the MX and Midgetman intercontinental missiles, the B-1 and B-2 (Stealth) bombers and the Trident II submarine-launched missile. These programs are monuments to old thinking. They are throwbacks to the days when the strategists accepted, as an article of their dark faith, the vulnerability of the U.S. to Kremlin crapshooters. (Talbott, 1990b: 68)

The Reagan administration's Strategic Defense Initiative can be added to Talbott's list. Confidence in SDI has steadily declined since it was first advanced. The very concept of the system has also been revised continually as the obstacles to an impenetrable system capable of destroying all of an attacker's incoming warheads have been identified and the politically difficult task of managing a coordinated, safe transition to a defense-dominated strategy has become understood (Glaser, 1989, Goldberg, 1989). Still, President Bush remained a fervent supporter of SDI and continued to push a reluctant Congress for the funds necessary to continue research and development of the costly system (estimated at between $55 and $69 billion)—and despite the fact that the perception of a Soviet threat to the physical security of the United States faded (Seib, 1990). "Even as we work to reduce arsenals and reduce tensions," Bush argued, "we understand the continuing crucial role of strategic defense." By 2000 some twenty different countries will be able to fire ballistic missiles in anger. Perhaps the purpose of a BMD system will be to intercept one of those missiles, not a Soviet one.

To be sure, vigilance is always a treasured value, and danger resides in relaxing defense capabilities. Nonetheless, some worried that America's strategic posture may have become obsolete. As one critic put it, because "the threat of deliberate Soviet attack on Western Europe has dropped to the vanishing point for the foreseeable future . . . it is hard now to imagine what it is that nuclear weapons must deter" (Russett, 1991). Fred Charles Iklé, under secretary of defense in the Reagan administration, elaborated:

> What, now, are the threats against which the [United States] should prepare? How should America's strategy and military forces, indeed its overall foreign policy, be changed to take account of the transformed environment? [During 1989] things have changed in the center of Europe—and indeed, in Moscow. Nonetheless, Washington's national security establishment continues to see the world in terms of the 1947 mindset. By regarding the basic strategy as an unchanging core, it recognizes improvement only at the edges. . . . The obsolete dogma that our nuclear retaliation must be prompt is responsible for the Pentagon's insistence that one must maintain a large force of land-based missiles, with all the difficulty

and expense this entails. More dangerously, it perpetuates a vulnerable and hence hair-triggered deterrent of thousands of missiles, both American and Soviet, sitting there like a thousand Chernobyls—till something, someday, goes terribly wrong. . . . Perhaps the time has come to pay some attention to Soviet criticism of our nuclear deterrence doctrine. Gorbachev called mutual deterrence a source of tension. (Iklé, 1990: 13, 14, 20)

New times are said to call for new thinking. Yet, responding to the new security requirements of a post–Cold War world proved difficult. The Bush administration followed the path blazed by its predecessors by stressing military preparedness while seeking to reduce arms through negotiated agreements. Bush declared in 1989 that "our aim is nothing less than removing war as an option," and he proposed the next year the complete elimination of the dangerous land-based missiles topped with multiple warheads (MIRVs) each superpower maintained. At the same time, as Rear Admiral Eugene Carroll noted in May 1990, "the United States still gives first priority to creating the military means to dominate the Soviet Union—despite the political and military changes there and in Eastern Europe."

POWER AND PURPOSE: IN PURSUIT OF THE NATIONAL INTEREST

The Bush administration's approach to the twin questions regarding nuclear weapons that have haunted American foreign policymakers for over four decades—what to do with nuclear weapons, and what to do about them—has displayed the same curious approach-avoidance mixture that has characterized the policies of its predecessors. Its strategies have rested on the pillars of nuclear strength, efforts to stabilize or reduce strategic arsenals through negotiated arms control agreements, and preservation of deterrence and crisis stability. The ultimate product sought remains protection of American national security through an unwavering reliance of the acquisition of military might. "The American eagle holds arrows in one hand and the olive branch in the other," George Shultz observed in 1985, "and his eyes look toward the olive branch. Our goal is peace, and, therefore, we are always ready for serious dialogue with our adversaries on ways to control and reduce weapons."

President Kennedy observed that "it is an unfortunate fact that we can only secure peace by preparing for war." That simple proposition has never been seriously questioned, although increasingly the strength of a nation seems more accurately measured in terms of economic output than in numbers of missiles and warheads. Moreover, the ability to use weapons as instruments of influence has eroded as their destructive capability has increased. The suicidal nature of nuclear weapons in particular may have inhibited their use (for critiques of this thesis, see Mueller, 1991; Vasquez, 1991). Many believe nuclear arsenals no longer have a purpose other than to prevent their use by others, while other strategists maintain that their deterrent value is also bankrupt (Summers, 1989).

In the post–Cold War world, protective measures may be required to guard the United States against nonmilitary threats to its security, but a fundamental reordering of priorities and resource commitments is not evident. "American policy-makers have not changed the basic strategies and commitments that were first made in the late 1940s. . . . [While] tactics have changed, basic strategies and commitments have not" (Krasner, 1989).

The decline in the Soviet threat and the surge in democratic governance evident around the globe present new opportunities and perhaps portend new risks for American foreign policy as it moves beyond containment and the Cold War. A measured response to the declining Soviet military threat is in order. As Charles William Maynes (1990), editor of *Foreign Policy*, has observed, "Even though the Cold War is over, history and prudence dictate that at least in its early stages the coming retrenchment not be too sweeping. Just as individuals prudently purchase insurance, so should nations." Furthermore, it is important to remember that the long peace that has characterized world politics since 1945 has depended to a large extent on a credible U.S. military capability in the context of great power competition. "We need to make sure as we put the Cold War behind us that we do not also jettison those principles and procedures that allowed it to evolve into the longest period of great-power rivalry without war in the modern era. If a long peace was in fact the offspring of the Cold War, then the last thing we should want to do, in tossing the parent onto the ash heap of history, is to toss the child as well" (Gaddis, 1990).

Still, as the defense debate over the meaning of "prudence" and "measured response" proceeds, adjustments in the nation's dependence on military might and interventionism can be expected. One scenario envisions selective disengagement.

> A foreign policy of strict national interest could . . . permit a drastic retrenchment of the U.S. military presence in the world. Over half of the American defense budget is designed to defend against a Soviet attack on Western Europe—the probability of which has never been high and is now effectively zero. From the standpoint of strict national interest, the American army could be slashed back to an expeditionary force designed to meet the modest military requirements involved in protecting American lives abroad, combatting terrorism, and maintaining a deterrent force suitable for emergency deployment. As a hedge against Soviet recidivism, the United States might reach agreement with key European states for pre-positioning of U.S. equipment on European soil. It could cooperate with its allies in providing sea and air support for Europe's defense. And perhaps even a token U.S. army presence could remain on European soil. But virtually all the American troops on European soil could be brought home and disbanded.
>
> The same point applies to Japan. Again for reasons of prudence, the United States might maintain a military alliance with Japan. . . . But most of the bases could be closed and the troops brought home.
>
> The country's nuclear forces could be pared back to a minimum deterrent since no other country's nuclear force now threatens the survival of the United States as a political entity. (Maynes, 1990: 11–12)

There is another scenario that envisions reorientation, not disengagement. As the Soviet threat diminishes, anticommunism as a pattern of American foreign policy may lose some of its ideological appeal. In its place may emerge a new crusade on behalf of democracy—an orientation that hinges on high levels of defense spending to hedge against a possible resurgence of Soviet imperialism. "For most of this school of thought, the American invasion of Grenada or Panama, covert operations to overthrow undemocratic governments, or direct subsidies to opposition parties in other countries are all appropriate tools in a new crusade to plant democracy's flag around the world" (Maynes, 1990). The bipolar power configuration of the Cold War era, which reflected the concentration of political and military power in the hands of the United States and the Soviet Union, induced caution and restraint in the behavior of *both* nations (Gaddis, 1991; Mearsheimer, 1990). As the Soviet threat diminishes, external restraints on U.S. global activism will also recede. Internal restraints in the form of resource shortages may multiply, but they are unlikely to be so great as to prevent the promotion of democratization through interventionist means.

The application of military force against other societies is the most obvious form of interventionism, but the practice of American foreign policy in pursuit of its persistent goals of globalism, anticommunism, and containment has also given rise to less obvious forms of involvement in the affairs of other nations. It is to an examination of these other policy instruments that we now turn.

SUGGESTIONS FOR FURTHER READING

Arms Control Association. (1989) *Arms Control and National Security.* Washington, D.C.: Arms Control Association.

Blechman, Barry M., and Stephen S. Kaplan, with David K. Hall, William B. Quandt, Jerome N. Slater, Robert M. Slusser, and Philip Windsor. (1978) *Force without War.* Washington, D.C.: Brookings Institution.

Cohen, Eliot A. (1984) "Constraints on America's Conduct of Small Wars." *International Security* 9 (Fall): 151–181.

Freeman, Lawrence. (1989) *The Evolution of Nuclear Strategy*, 2nd ed. New York: St. Martin's.

Jervis, Robert. (1989) *The Meaning of Nuclear Revolution: Statecraft and the Prospect of Armageddon.* Ithaca, N.Y.: Cornell University Press.

Kegley, Charles W., Jr., and Kenneth L. Schwab (eds.). (1991) *After the Cold War: Questioning the Morality of Nuclear Deterrence.* Boulder, Colo.: Westview Press.

Kegley, Charles W., Jr., and Eugene R. Wittkopf (eds.). (1989) *The Nuclear Reader: Strategy, Weapons, War*, 2nd ed. New York: St. Martin's.

Maynes, Charles William. (1990) "America without the Cold War," *Foreign Policy* 78 (Spring): 3–25.

Nolan, Janne E. (1989) *Guardians of the Arsenal: The Politics of Nuclear Strategy.* New York: Basic Books.

Schraeder, Peter J. (ed.). (1989) *Intervention in the 1980s: U.S. Foreign Policy in the Third World*. Boulder, Colo.: Lynne Rienner.

Treverton, Gregory F. (1989–1990) "The Defense Debate," *Foreign Affairs* 69 (No. 1): 183–196.

CHAPTER 5

The Instruments of Global Influence: Covert Activities, Public Diplomacy, and Foreign Aid

For decades we have justified spending tens of billions of dollars in security assistance to contain communism. Our rationale for and structure of foreign aid is outdated and no longer serves American interests.

SENATOR PATRICK J. LEAHY, 1990

I don't see why we need to stand by and watch a country go Communist due to the irresponsibility of its own people.

SPECIAL ASSISTANT FOR NATIONAL SECURITY AFFAIRS HENRY KISSINGER, 1970

On June 5, 1947, at a Harvard University commencement, Secretary of State George C. Marshall delivered an address in which he set forth the commitment of the United States to assist in the reconstruction of war-torn Europe as a basic principle of American foreign policy. The plan was sold to a skeptical Congress and the American people on the basis of strategic arguments and as an instrument of anticommunism in the emerging Cold War struggle with the Soviet Union. Two years later President Truman called in Point Four of his inaugural address for "a bold new program for making the benefits of our scientific advances and industrial progress available for the improvement and growth of underdeveloped areas." Some American foreign aid programs had existed prior to this time, but with the Marshall Plan and Point Four they became, and have remained, primary instruments of American foreign policy.

The National Security Act, which created the Central Intelligence Agency (CIA) and the Department of Defense, was also passed in 1947. Two years later, in 1949, the Soviet Union successfully tested an atomic bomb. That event had a profound impact on the Truman administration's thinking about how best to pursue the containment of the Soviet Union. A governmentwide reevaluation of American foreign policy ensued, and in April 1950 the National Security Council (NSC), a top-level interagency body that advises the president on foreign policy matters, issued its famous, top-secret memorandum, NSC 68, which set in motion the militarization of American foreign policy and the containment strategy that would persist for many years. U.S. foreign aid programs were shaped to serve that approach to containment, and the CIA became actively involved as one of its primary instruments.

COVERT ACTIVITY AND INTELLIGENCE OPERATIONS

Perhaps even more than with overt military involvement, the persistent covert involvement of the United States in the affairs of other nations has contributed measurably to the interventionist label so frequently attached to postwar American foreign policy. American defense policy and its related interventionist posture developed in an atmosphere in which decision makers held widely shared perceptions about the nature of communism and Soviet expansionism. NSC 68 spelled out the connection between the containment of communism and military preparedness. A decisive sentence in NSC 68 asserted that "without superior aggregate military strength, in being and readily mobilizable, a policy of 'containment'—which is in effect a policy of calculated and gradual coercion—is no more than a policy of bluff." NSC 68 also called for a nonmilitary counteroffensive against the Soviet Union, which included covert economic, political, and psychological warfare designed to foment unrest and revolt in Soviet bloc countries. By as early as November 1951, at least some in Washington recognized that such broad and comprehensive undertakings could be accomplished only by the establishment of a worldwide structure for covert operations (*Final Report of the Select Committee to Study Governmental Operations with Respect to Intelligence Activities*, Vol. 4, 1976; hereafter cited as *Final Report*, 1–4, 1976).

In the ensuing years the CIA became infamous worldwide as the arm of the U.S. government that was responsible for perhaps otherwise inexplicable political events in other countries. "The CIA has been accused of interfering in the internal political affairs of nations ranging from Iran to Chile, from Tibet to Guatemala, from Libya to Laos, from Greece to Indonesia. Assassinations, coups d'état, vote buying, economic warfare—all have been laid at the doorstep of the CIA," observed a Senate committee that during the mid-1970s investigated American intelligence activities. "Few political crises take place in the world today in which CIA involvement is not alleged" (*Final Report*, 1, 1976). The accuracy of that picture is open to dispute, but enough information is available to indicate it is not farfetched.

The Nature and Role of Intelligence

Intelligence collection per se provokes little concern or criticism. Because foreign policy decision makers are expected to protect the physical security and general welfare of the population, they require detailed information necessary for understanding the varied military, economic, political, scientific, domestic, and foreign issues and events requisite to sound policy making. Providing such information is the task of the intelligence community (described in Chapter

11). More specifically, its task is to produce "finished intelligence," defined as "data collected from all sources—secret, official, and open—which has been carefully collated and analyzed by substantive experts specifically to meet the needs of the national leadership" (Marchetti and Marks, 1974). Much of what constitutes raw intelligence (the uncollated and unanalyzed data) is not acquired through mysterious cloak-and-dagger escapades, but rather comes from readily available public sources, such as the reports of journalists, professional diplomats, and information and cultural officers, and the publications of governmental agencies, private businesses, and scholars. Data from such public sources are supplemented by so-called hard intelligence derived from code breaking and reconnaissance satellites.

Covert operations, on the other hand, are secret activities typically undertaken abroad against foreign governments, installations, or individuals with the expressed purpose of directly influencing the outcome of political events. The term *covert operation* is itself often used interchangeably with the terms *covert action* and *clandestine political operation*. Covert operations are conceptually distinct from the clandestine collection of intelligence, otherwise known as espionage (the illegal collection of intelligence through agent networks), in that covert action attempts to influence events directly whereas clandestine intelligence collection does not.

Many have argued that certain clandestine intelligence activities are necessary, particularly because access is universally denied to important information relevant to sound policy making, such as that relating to the military capabilities and intentions of potential adversaries. Informed and responsible decisions about the appropriate U.S. position in the SALT talks, for example, would not have been possible without information gained from satellite reconnaissance and other technical sources. Yet efforts to obtain information on the capabilities and intentions of other nations have themselves often resulted in significant foreign policy ramifications. Perhaps the most celebrated example occurred in 1960, when the CIA U-2 spy plane piloted by Francis Gary Powers was shot down deep within Soviet territory on the very eve of the Paris summit between President Eisenhower and Soviet Premier Khrushchev. The summit was never held, and American-Soviet relations became as frigid as at any point during the Cold War. Another example occurred in 1968 when the North Koreans captured the ELINT (electronic intelligence) spy ship *Pueblo*, operated by the navy and the National Security Agency, near the coast of North Korea. The crewmen were eventually returned, but the ship was not, which doubtless contributed to Soviet knowledge of U.S. ELINT capabilities.

Both of those incidents illustrate the kinds of embarrassments and complications that can arise out of an otherwise legitimate need for policy-making information. More questionable in the eyes of critics are the many instances of covert actions undertaken by intelligence agencies in an effort not simply to gather information but actually to carry out plans and programs designed to accomplish specific political ends. Among the more notorious cases that have come to public light are the CIA-engineered coups in Iran and Guatemala in the 1950s and Vietnam in the 1960s; the CIA-trained, -financed, and -directed armies that sought to overthrow Cuba's Castro and that conducted a "secret" war in Laos in the 1960s; the CIA-supported political action programs designed to prevent Marxist-oriented President Salvador Allende from winning and then exercising political power in Chile in the 1970s; and the covert war directed against the Nicaraguan government in the 1980s.[1]

Cold War Confrontation, Competitive Coexistence, and Covert Actions

If the initial impetus toward covert operations was provided by the increasingly hostile international political environment of the late 1940s and early 1950s, the perceived success attributed to the CIA in carrying them out contributed to its status as an instrument of policy. By as early as 1953 the CIA had gained a reputation for its political action and paramilitary warfare. It was reinforced by what were widely regarded as two of its boldest and most spectacular operations—the overthrow of Premier Mohammed Mossadegh in Iran in 1953 and the coup that ousted President Jacobo Arbenz of Guatemala in 1954 (see Gasiorowski, 1987; Immerman, 1982; Treverton, 1987). By those quick and virtually bloodless operations two allegedly procommunist leaders were replaced with pro-Western officials. Out of such early acclaimed achievements both the agency and Washington policymakers acquired a sense of confidence in the CIA's capacity for operational success.

Throughout the 1950s the CIA was directed by Allen Dulles. Master spy of the OSS (Office of Strategic Services—forerunner of the CIA) operations in Switzerland during World War II and brother of Secretary of State John Foster Dulles, Allen Dulles was personally interested in the intrigue of clandestine operations. Under his tutelage the CIA moved from being the servant of other government agencies to being the initiator in defining the ways in which covert operations could enhance foreign policy goals and in determining how specific operations could enhance particular policy objectives. Thus it achieved the enviable bureaucratic position of not only defining foreign policy programs for top-level decision makers, but also of providing the information on which they would base their decisions and then implementing them once they were made. The invasion of Cuba at the Bay of Pigs in 1961 by a band of CIA-trained and -financed Cuban exiles, which combined in one agency the roles of information collection, policy formulation, and program implementation, stands out as a classic case of CIA prominence in policy making.

The Bay of Pigs operation was to be the CIA's method of eliminating the problem posed by Castro. Although it was engineered along the lines of the successful 1954 Guatemalan operation, the defeat suffered by the Cuban exiles

---

1. Other, less famous CIA operations disclosed in Senate investigations strain the imagination. For instance, it was revealed that in 1959 CIA agents tested LSD on a houseful of unwitting people in San Francisco who thought they had been invited to a party. Those same hearings revealed that the CIA once tried to humiliate Fidel Castro by dusting the Cuban leader's shoes with a substance that would make his hair fall out; less humorously, the investigation reported that Castro had survived at least eight CIA-sponsored assassination plots.

tarnished the agency's reputation—and cost Allen Dulles his job. But covert operations nevertheless continued to be seen as an acceptable policy option. Operation Mongoose was one manifestation of that perspective. Mongoose consisted of paramilitary, sabotage, and political propaganda activities directed against Castro's Cuba between October 1961 and October 1962. Paramilitary operations were also initiated in Laos, where over thirty thousand tribesmen were organized into a kind of private CIA army. However, as the 1960s wore on, the Vietnam issue came to dominate the CIA, as it did other government agencies. In one CIA operation there, known as Phoenix, over twenty thousand suspected Vietcong were killed over a period of less than four years (Lewy, 1978: 281; also Marchetti and Marks, 1974).

The catalog of both proven and alleged CIA involvement in the internal affairs of other nations could be broadened extensively. Not unlike the preference for military solutions to political problems, covert operations became commonplace because the assets were available to foreign policy decision makers. "To these officials, including the President, covert intervention may seem to be an easier solution to a particular problem than to allow events to follow their natural course or to seek a tortuous diplomatic settlement," write Victor Marchetti and John Marks (1974). "The temptation to interfere in another country's internal affairs can be almost irresistible, when the means are at hand." "Every administration ultimately turns to the use of covert operations" is the way a former deputy director of central intelligence put it in 1982 (see Chapter 11).

One cannot understand the reliance on either covert or military forms of intervention without recognizing the extent to which fear of communism and the drive to contain it have motivated postwar American foreign policy. The war might have been cold, but it was war nevertheless. Hence it was deemed appropriate to use the same tools as the other side, no matter how repugnant they might be. Questions of morality and legality were seen as irrelevant; a higher purpose—the "national security"—was being served.

Covert Actions in the 1970s and 1980s

During the 1970s domestic criticism of known intelligence abuses led both the president and Congress to impose restraints on the foreign and domestic activities of the intelligence community. By then the justification for covert operations changed sharply compared with previous decades, when their purpose was framed in terms of opposition to international communism. Now covert actions were described simply as those secret activities designed to further American policies and programs abroad. American involvement in Chile in the early 1970s illustrates the change.[2]

---

2. The meanings and motivations underlying some of the facts surrounding the events in Chile between 1970 and 1973 are as controversial as the actual events themselves. For relevant discussions see Fagen (1975), Farnsworth (1974), Petras and LaPorte (1972), and Sigmund (1974a, 1974b).

A concerted governmentwide effort was mounted in Chile in the 1950s to prevent the Marxist-oriented Salvador Allende from gaining and then exercising political power in Chile. By the 1970s it included not only covert activities but also a close working relationship between the U.S. government and giant U.S.-based multinational corporations doing business in Chile, whose corporate interests were threatened, and pressure on multilateral lending institutions to do America's bidding. Anticommunist thinking was involved in U.S. efforts to contribute to the eventual overthrow of the Allende government, but the story also illustrated the U.S. willingness to use a range of instruments to oppose those willing to experiment in leftist domestic political programs. The lesson played out in the various efforts of the Reagan administration to subvert and overthrow the leftist Sandinista regime that came to power in Nicaragua in 1979.

The Reagan administration's commitment to exorcise the ghost of Vietnam was nowhere more apparent than in its drive to "unleash" the CIA. Its capacity for covert actions in terms of staff and budget was greatly reenergized under William Casey, who was appointed director of the CIA by Reagan upon his election in 1980 and reportedly given wide latitude to conduct secret wars against U.S. enemies (see Emerson, 1988). Among the missions Casey pursued were covert support for Iranian exile groups seeking to overthrow the Ayatollah Khomeini and the provision of arms and financial assistance to military forces in Angola, Chad, Cambodia, Ethiopia, Liberia, and the Sudan. The intention of the United States to support anticommunist movements worldwide was underscored in the Reagan Doctrine, enunciated by the president in 1985 when he declared: "We must not break faith with those who are risking their lives on every continent from Afghanistan to Nicaragua to defy Soviet supported aggression and secure rights which have been ours from birth . . . . Support for freedom fighters is self-defense." A year later Angola, Cambodia, and Ethiopia were added to the list of countries in which the president pledged to "support with material assistance your right not just to fight and die for freedom, but to fight and win freedom."

Afghanistan and Nicaragua became the most celebrated applications of the newly enunciated Reagan Doctrine proclaiming unashamed American support for anticommunist revolution under the "radical" supposition that "support for democratic rebels is 'self-defense' and sanctioned by international law" (Krauthammer, 1985). Using Pakistan as a gateway, the CIA provided the anti-Marxist *mujaheddin*, the Moslem guerrillas challenging Soviet troops and the pro-Soviet regime in Afghanistan, with guns, ammunition, and other support at a cost that by 1986 exceeded $500 million annually. The United States also decided in 1986 to supply the *mujaheddin* with weapons made in the United States, the most important of which was a shoulder-fired antiaircraft missile known as the Stinger. The decision broke a cardinal rule of covert operations, which is to avoid sending weapons made in America so as to maintain a façade of noninvolvement, but the weapon proved enormously successful in the hands of the insurgents and may have played a critical role in the decision of the Soviet Union to withdraw from Afghanistan.

In Nicaragua the CIA supported the *contras* (so-called counterrevolution-aries who were themselves largely a creation of the agency) by participating in the planning and execution of naval blockades, air strikes, espionage, and propaganda operations. Its activities were of such magnitude as to spark charges that it had once more gotten out of hand. (As in Afghanistan, knowledge of U.S. support for the insurgents was an open secret, which again does not conform to the usual pattern in the case of covert activities.) Its role in producing a manual that called for "neutralization" (read assassination) of Nicaraguan officials and in mining Nicaraguan harbors led some to challenge the legality of its acts under both domestic law and international law.[3] More generally, the actions of the *contras* against their own people as part of their war against the Sandinistas raised widespread dissatisfaction in the United States about the direction of American policy. Eventually, the U.S. role in Nicaragua became part of the so-called Iran-*contra* affair, a domestic scandal of multiple dimensions that rekindled fears of an abuse of power in the name of national security not unlike those Watergate had raised.[4] A central issue raised by the scandal was whether funds diverted from the sale of arms to Iran in a secret arms-for-hostages deal violated a legal prohibition against continued CIA support of the *contras'* activities.

We will have more to say about the Iran-*contra* affair in subsequent chapters as we discuss its relevance to various facets of the legality and control of intelligence activities in a democratic society (see Focus 5.1). Suffice it here to underscore how unambiguously it demonstrated a resurgence during the 1980s of the role of the CIA and covert activities as agents of American foreign policy. As Fred Charles Iklé, under secretary of defense for policy during the Reagan administration, put it in reference to covert war, "The [Reagan] administration . . . tried to reduce the asymmetry, the extent to which the Soviet Union

---

3. Harvard law professor Abram Chayes, who earlier laid the legal foundations for the Kennedy administration's naval quarantine of Cuba during the 1962 missile crisis with the Soviet Union, elected to represent Nicaragua in its suit against the United States in the World Court, in which it challenged the legality of U.S. operations, overt and covert, designed to undermine the Nicaraguan government. Believing that the Nicaraguan leaders were acting "to uphold the rule of law in international affairs," Chayes stated that he thought it appropriate for the United States, which "purports to be bound by the rule of law," to be judged under "appropriate international procedures" (*New York Times*, April 11, 1983). In the summer of 1986 the World Court ruled that U.S. actions in support of the *contras* were indeed a violation of international law. The United States chose to ignore the ruling.

4. Concern for domestic "dissidents" and unrest at the time of the Vietnam War led the Nixon administration to create a special intelligence group within the White House known as "the Plumbers," whose ostensible purpose was to fix news "leaks" and "flush" dissident opinion out of the American political system. Creation of the Plumbers was prompted by Dr. Daniel Ellsberg's release of the *Pentagon Papers*, which contained national-security-related classified information. The group was responsible—in the name of national security—for the burglary of the office of Dr. Ellsberg's psychiatrist. It was also responsible somewhat later for the surreptitious entry of Democratic National Headquarters in the Watergate Hotel complex in the summer of 1972, an action that precipitated the infamous Watergate affair and the eventual resignation of the presidency by Richard Nixon. Nixon defended his action on grounds that national security was being served.

FOCUS 5.1 ▪ On the Nature and Control of Covert Actions: Contrasting Viewpoints from the Iran-*Contra* Affair

I misled the Congress. . . . And . . . I participated in preparation of documents for the Congress that were erroneous, misleading, evasive and wrong, and I did it again here when I appeared before [the members of the House Intelligence Committee] convened in the White House Situation Room. . . . I [denied the elected representatives the facts upon which they needed to make a decision] because we have had incredible leaks from discussions with closed committees of the Congress.

Lt. Col. Oliver L. North, 1987

This is a dangerous world, we live at risk and . . . this Nation is at risk in a dangerous world. . . . By their very nature covert operations or special activities are a lie. There is great deceit, deception practiced in the conduct of covert operations.

They are at essence a lie.

We make every effort to deceive the enemy as to our intent, our conduct, and to deny the association of the United States with those activities.

Lt. Col. Oliver L. North, 1987

The hearings [on the Iran-*contra* affair] have been about how the United States . . . runs its foreign policy. . . . Some believe that a decision-making process that calls for shared powers and public debate just will not work in a dangerous world. They argue that sometimes bypassing normal checks and balances through procedural shortcuts and secrecy are necessary to protect our freedom. They argue that the President, and those who work for him, must be given near-total power. . . . But . . . shortcuts in the democratic process and excessive secrecy in the conduct of government are a sure road to policy failure. . . .

Covert actions . . . can be an important instrument of policy. . . . To be effective . . . they must be used to supplement policy, not become the policy itself; and they must meet a standard of acceptability. That standard includes consistency with public policies and a reasonable assurance that the American people would support a covert action if they knew about it.

Representative Lee H. Hamilton, 1987

---

can use all means—terrorist, covert, arms shipments, what have you—to topple governments or support governments that are opposed by the people, while the United States would be left with the choice between vacating the field, abandoning the friends of democracy, or getting into an all-out conflict." In this sense the strategies and tactics of the United States and the Soviet Union often resembled one another, for the Reagan Doctrine mirrored the doctrine put forward by the Soviet Union in 1960, which said it would support "wars of national liberation" in the Third World. The result was a resurgence of the kinds of covert activities abroad that gave the CIA its notoriety in an earlier stage of the East-West conflict. There is no way of knowing how pervasive such thinking remains in the councils of government, but the evidence from the Iran-*contra* affair demonstrates it is always there if not always visible. Moreover, even as the Cold War fades, the need for intelligence to monitor global developments persists.[5]

INFORMAL PENETRATION

The overt and covert interventions the United States has embarked on through its military and intelligence apparatus in the postwar era are, on the surface, qualitatively different from the extensive "public diplomacy" initiatives it has also undertaken in the same period. Yet they derive from the same globalist and anticommunist orientations, and they have become persistent and prominent instruments defining the American approach to the external world. Moreover, they form part of a nexus of informal penetrations of other societies that may contribute to the kinds of covert and overt interventions discussed previously. In the sense that a fine line distinguishes involvement from intervention, therefore, they are also part of that interventionist strategy.

Public Diplomacy

Public diplomacy is a polite term for what many would regard as straightforward propaganda (the methodical spreading of information to influence public opinion). The United States Information Agency (USIA) is in charge of American public diplomacy efforts aimed at winning support around the world for America and its foreign policy.[6] Its instruments are cultural and informational activities directed overseas at both masses and elites that have essentially two functions: (1) the projection, interpretation, and advocacy of current U.S. foreign policy, and (2) the portrayal of American society as a "complex, pluralistic, tolerant and democratic community" (*Commission on the Organization of the Government for the Conduct of Foreign Policy*, 1975).

The United States Information Agency carries out its tasks through a worldwide network of overseas offices using a variety of media, including

---

5. In the face of jockeying among U.S. intelligence agencies for increased funds and staff, Democratic Senator David Boren of the Senate Intelligence Committee commented in April 1990: "As the arms race is winding down, the spy race is heating up."

6. Public diplomacy is normally thought to target foreign audiences, but during the Reagan administration the American public became the target of sustained efforts by the administration to build support for its Central American policies, particularly aid to the *contras*. The efforts were carried out by the White House Office of Public Liaison and the State Department Office of Public Diplomacy. The latter eventually came under fire from Congress, which cut off funds for its operation. See Parry and Kornbluh (1988) for a critical view of the State Department's operation and the letters to the editor in the Winter 1988–1989 issue of *Foreign Policy* for a rejoinder.

radio, television, films, libraries, and exhibitions. Among the most well known are the Voice of America, which broadcasts news, political journalism, music, and cultural programs in over forty languages to many parts of the globe, and Radio Free Europe and Radio Liberty, which broadcast respectively to Eastern Europe and to the Soviet Union. The Reagan administration added Radio Marti, which broadcasts to Cuba, to USIA's broadcasting network, and TV Marti was later launched on an experimental basis. USIA also administers a variety of cultural exchange programs that support travel abroad by American athletes, artists, dramatists, musicians, and scholars, and travel to the United States by foreign political leaders, students, and educators for study tours or other educational purposes.

Information and cultural programs are undertaken in the expectation that specialized communications can be used to make world opinion toward the United States more favorable. However, opinion varies widely regarding the propriety and effectiveness of public diplomacy as a policy instrument. Should such efforts be designed only to provide information? Should public diplomacy aggressively promote American culture and its values, as was the explicit purpose behind the Reagan administration's Project Democracy initiative in the early 1980s? Or should it be linked intimately to the political contests in which the United States becomes engaged, the most notably historically being the struggle against communism?

In practice, each role has been dominant at one time or another. During the 1950s, for example, USIA was heavily involved in supporting the anti-communist containment policy, and during the Vietnam conflict emphasis was placed on justifying American intervention. During the Carter administration the emphasis shifted to cultural exchange programs, which "evoke more cooperative sentiments" when compared to information activities that have "the image of a more confrontational posture" (Adelman, 1981). Under the Reagan administration the shift was clearly toward confrontation, as USIA sought vigorously to promote U.S. policies abroad and to engage in the "war of ideas" with the nation's adversaries. Public diplomacy thus once more became an active instrument of the containment foreign policy strategy as the policy-oriented activities of USIA gained prominence. Indeed, in its efforts to sell U.S. policies abroad, critics (see, for example, Nichols, 1984) suggested that there was a tendency to view these propaganda efforts in essentially *military* terms. In the words of President Reagan's USIA Director Charles Z. Wick, "The only war the United States has fought in the past four years has been the propaganda war." Still others, including members of Congress, wondered whether such a bold approach to "telling America's story to the world," USIA's motto, would politicize the agency's exchange programs, suggesting an inherent tension between its policy-oriented and non-policy-oriented activities (Malone, 1985). The issue surfaced again as the budgetary stringency faced by the Bush administration renewed concern about how most expeditiously to promote America's ideas and ideals using the broadcast media (Elliott, 1989–1990).

A related concern was USIA's inability to redirect its programming to encourage the process of democratic change sweeping Eastern Europe. "Our opportunities are blossoming, not only in Eastern Europe, but around the world," exclaimed President Bush's USIA director Bruce S. Gelb. "But our resources are shrinking." Critics asked, however, whether it was not instead a matter of bureaucratic inertia that prevented the United States from using its public diplomacy capabilities more aggressively in the face of changing opportunities, and whether an unwillingness to abandon traditional Cold War views might not have prevented it from taking advantage of opportunities to promote democracy in areas long dominated by communist governments (McCartney, 1990b).

Even if it were possible to agree on the nature and role of public diplomacy, evaluating its impact is difficult. During the Polish labor turmoil of 1980, the Soviet Union criticized American broadcasts beamed at Poland as being "provocative and instigatory" and as "aimed at generating among the Polish population unfriendly sentiments with regard to the Soviet Union" (cited in Adelman, 1981).[7] Were American interests served in Poland by such broadcasts, because authorities in Poland complained of them? Or instead, were American interests, defined as preventing the deterioration of relations with the Soviet Union, damaged by them? If that situation seems ambiguous, an earlier, analogous one does not. In 1956 revolutionaries seeking to rid Hungary of Soviet domination received messages from Radio Free Europe implying that American assistance was on its way. It never came.

Even the exchange programs that are a part of public diplomacy seem to yield ambiguous results. Although more than 60,000 American scholars and 111,000 foreign students, teachers, and scholars have participated in the well-known Fulbright Program,[8] some of the most vociferous foreign critics of the United States have been able to visit the country under the sponsorship of the American government. It would seem, then, that advocates of public diplomacy must necessarily view it "as a long-term foreign policy asset, one designed to present foreigners with a mosaic impression of America's mosaic society and to incline them favorably toward American values" (Adelman, 1981). But in the short run, public diplomacy can also be expected to encounter criticism, particularly when it offers to other societies ideas and values that may not always be welcome and in a manner that may sometimes breed resentment.

---

7. Some of these verged on the ludicrous, including production of "a worldwide television extravaganza called *Let Poland Be Poland*, which featured Frank Sinatra crooning *Ever Homeward* in pidgin Polish. The show drew howls of ridicule" (*Time*, September 9, 1985, p. 33).

8. The data cover the period from 1949 through 1988 and are based on a personal communication with the Fulbright Alumni Office in Washington, D.C.

Military Assistance

Giving aid and lending money are other ways the United States has sought to influence other nations. Of the two forms of foreign aid, military and economic, the former has been more clearly related to the military orientation of postwar American policy. Indeed, it has been a favored foreign policy instrument ever since the Korean War. Coming out of that conflict was the Mutual Security Act, which provided the legislative umbrella under which all foreign aid was distributed until it was replaced by the Foreign Assistance Act of 1961.[9] The view that military aid is an essential element of defense and security planning has been reaffirmed many times. In testimony before Congress on the fiscal 1990 security assistance program, for instance, H. Allen Holmes, Assistant Secretary of State for Politico-Military Affairs, recited the mutually reinforcing goals that security assistance attempts to serve as an instrument of American foreign policy:

- Enhancing the ability of U.S. security partners to deter and defend against aggression and instability
- Maintaining the cohesion and strength of our alliances
- Developing sound military-to-military relations that support our diplomatic strategy and enhance U.S. influence and prestige
- Promoting regional stability
- Contributing to our access to military bases and facilities abroad, thereby maintaining the strategic mobility of U.S. forces
- Strengthening the economies of key countries that are attempting to adjust to heavy debt, depressed commodity export prices, and startling changes in the global economic environment
- Providing support for emerging democracies while defending existing democratic institutions and values in other countries

As shown in Table 5.1, the total dollar amount of American military aid to other nations since the onset of the Korean War (including commercial sales) approached $300 billion by 1989. Even that is likely to be a conservative estimate, because it is based on unclassified information and does not include the value of "outdated" military hardware the United States at one time routinely gave away.[10]

Historically, the Military Assistance Program (MAP) served as the principal mechanism through which recipient countries were provided defense articles,

---

9. Foreign military sales (discussed later in this chapter) are now governed by the Arms Export Control Act, first passed in 1968. The Foreign Assistance Act continues to govern other military aid programs; economic assistance is authorized by both statutes.

10. The accumulated acquisition cost of outdated military equipment distributed under the Excess Defense Articles Program between fiscal 1950 and fiscal 1982 was $6.4 billion (*Foreign Military Sales, Foreign Military Construction Sales and Military Assistance Facts*, 1989: 80). No distributions under this program have been made since.

TABLE 5.1 ▪ American Military Assistance and Foreign Military Sales in the Postwar Era (millions of dollars)

Military Assistance Program (MAP)	$ 54,950
International Military Education and Training Program	2,397
Foreign Military Sales (FMS) and FMS Construction Agreements	182,741
Commercial Exports	45,897
	$285,985

SOURCE: Adapted from *Foreign Military Sales, Foreign Military Construction Sales and Military Assistance Facts* (Washington, DC: Defense Security Assistance Agency, 1989), pp. 3ff.

Note: Data are for fiscal years 1950 through 1989.

services, and training. All assistance was grant aid, requiring no repayment on the part of recipients. Beginning in fiscal 1976 training of foreign military personnel has been provided under the International Military Education and Training Program. Between 1950 and 1989, over 550,000 were trained either under MAP or its successor. In early 1990 the secretary of defense described the program in his annual report to Congress as "one of the most cost-effective tools of the U.S. government. Investing in the military education and training of military personnel from friendly countries greatly enhances the capability of those countries to defend themselves, at a low cost to the American taxpayer."

Today foreign military sales (FMS) are the most important component of U.S. military assistance links with other nations. They accounted for nearly three-quarters of the $135 billion in military assistance and sales provided other nations during the eight years of Reagan's presidency and the first year of Bush's. Although most government-to-government sales are on a straight cash basis, the Defense Department provided more than $40 billion in credits toward foreign military purchases between 1981 and 1989, and increasingly these debts have been waived. By 1989 virtually all of the Defense Department's financing was on a grant basis, as foreign military sales financing effectively replaced MAP assistance. Egypt and Israel together accounted for 73 percent of these credits.

Israel and Egypt have received the lion's share of Defense Department foreign military sales credits and other forms of U.S. foreign assistance as part of the 1978 Camp David Middle East peace process, during which the United States committed itself to substantial financial rewards and security guarantees. Beyond Israel and Egypt, a large proportion of foreign military sales have been to Saudi Arabia and, prior to the 1979 revolution that toppled the Shah, to Iran, both of whom were major suppliers of oil to the United States in the 1970s, and for whom the United States became a major arms supplier. In the decade following the Iranian revolution, Saudi Arabia continued to purchase an average of $2 billion in military equipment annually which helped to transform the desert kingdom into a formidable military power.

A Historical Sketch of the Ebb and Flow of Military Assistance   As suggested by the title Mutual Security, U.S. military assistance programs were conceived historically in terms of the Cold War competition with the Soviet Union. The rationale underlying the distribution of aid was therefore linked closely to the policy of containment. Military assistance was justified on grounds that it augmented the capabilities of American allies to resist Soviet and Soviet-backed expansionism. Special attention was therefore given to the members of the NATO and SEATO (Southeast Asia Treaty Organization) alliances, plus other nations bordering on the communist world, some of which were covered by bilateral defensive arrangements with the United States. Another manifestation of the Cold War motivation was the use of military aid for "rental" of base rights in countries such as Spain and the Philippines and for landing rights for ships and planes elsewhere.

The emphasis shifted in response to changing international circumstances in the decade between 1966 and 1975. The aid program became targeted not only toward "allies" but now embraced "friends and allies" (Semmel, 1983). Substantially greater emphasis was given to developing nations, which in turn reflected the more self-reliant economic capabilities of Western European nations. Whereas NATO nations received 53 percent of the U.S. military aid pie between 1950 and 1965, their share dropped to only 20 percent in the 1966–1975 period.

It was during this period that the United States became involved in a major land war in Southeast Asia, and the allocation of U.S. military assistance reflected its involvement in the region. During the decade the amount of military aid received by South Vietnam, Cambodia, Laos, Pakistan, South Korea, and Taiwan, all of whom bordered on the communist world and were bound to the United States in multilateral or bilateral defensive arrangements, more than doubled, and together they accounted for half of all U.S. military aid granted between 1965 and 1975. (Similar attention characterized the economic aid program, as noted later in the chapter.) The shift in emphasis away from Europe and toward the Asian developing world is noteworthy, but the persistent anticommunist security motivation of the military assistance program is apparent across the two regions and time periods.

The most dramatic reflection of the changing international situation manifested itself in the tremendous increase in arms purchases by Middle Eastern nations beginning in the early 1970s. The flow of arms to those nations, which achieved massive proportions during the Nixon and Ford administrations, grew in part out of the persistence of the Arab-Israeli conflict and in part out of the tremendous surge in world oil prices in 1973–1974, which gave the oil-exporting countries substantial financial resources with which to purchase arms.

From the American viewpoint the shift in arms assistance policy from grants to sales during the Nixon administration was a direct consequence of the

Nixon Doctrine—the pledge that the United States would provide military and economic assistance to its friends and allies, but that those nations would be responsible for protecting their own security. The emphasis in American policy on Iran and Saudi Arabia was consistent with that viewpoint, as they were to become the twin pillars of U.S. Persian Gulf policy designed to promote stability and prevent the spread of communism in the region.

The shift from grants to sales during this period also reflected a subtle shift in emphasis away from anticommunism and the benefits assumed to accrue to the United States from stable, anticommunist regimes overseas. The overriding motivation remained an overtly political one—to enhance the ability of the United States to influence others so as to realize its own foreign policy objectives. But some of the presumed benefits of foreign military sales were economic in nature, including maintenance of the defense industry and a reduction in the per unit cost of defense articles in addition to balance-of-payments considerations.

The foreign military sales program itself goes back to the early days of the Kennedy administration, which began to experiment with foreign military sales as an alternative to grant assistance.[11] The reasons for doing so were opposition to outright grants emanating from Congress, the continuing adverse balance of payments the nation suffered, and a growing concern for the lack of an integrated logistical system among the NATO nations (Louscher, 1977). The same forces served to sustain the program once it was started. Over time FMS became a multipurpose instrument of policy designed to symbolize American resolve, to project American credibility, and to strengthen American allies generally. In the case of Europe it also became a vehicle to encourage greater logistical cooperation and spread the financial burdens of the collective defense, and among developing nations it was viewed as a means of generating regional power balances, controlling arms races, maintaining American influence, and selectively modifying recipients' human rights policies.

Proponents of the FMS program argued that the United States could not curb or control the desire of other nations in an intensely nationalistic world to acquire arms, and they pointed out that other Western nations, as well as the Soviet Union and its allies, were both able and willing to provide military hardware to nations seeking them. Still, some critics worried that grants of advanced military technology to countries and regions where the incidence of conflict was high, as in the Middle East, might actually contribute to the likelihood of local aggression. They noted the frequency with which the United States had armed both (or all) parties in Third World regional conflicts, many of which erupted into violence, as in the conflicts between India and Pakistan (1971), Israel and Jordan (1973), and Greece and Turkey (1974). They also

---

11. As David Louscher (1977) notes in his survey of the development of FMS, the search for an alternative to outright grant assistance actually goes back to the Eisenhower years. At that time the emphasis in economic aid programs shifted from grants to loans and sales of foreign agricultural surpluses as forms of aid. See also Semmel (1983).

observed that today's allies have a way of becoming tomorrow's enemies, especially among Third World nations, where the incidence of political instability is high. Time and again, those in need of American arms to protect themselves from Soviet penetration later became Soviet clients. Ethiopia and Yemen were examples in the late 1970s, Nicaragua in the early 1980s. Finally, the Iranian revolution of 1979 demonstrated that old friends need not become Soviet allies to become new enemies. Despite pumping billions of dollars worth of arms into Iran, the United States not only failed to build the regional power that it had sought but it also came to face a population bitter with resentment.

Jimmy Carter raised concerns during the 1976 presidential election about the consistency between massive arms sales and the nation's avowed goal of seeking world peace. Upon assuming office, he announced a new policy of "restraint" designed to curb the explosive arms trade, but the policy was fraught with contradictions from the start and eventually abandoned.

Ongoing commitments and interests in the Middle East became the occasion to revert to arms sales as the acceptable rather than exceptional policy instrument. Carter asked Congress early in his administration to approve sales of sophisticated airborne warning and control system aircraft (AWACS) to Iran and, later, F-15 fighter planes, the most advanced in the U.S. arsenal, to Saudi Arabia as part of a massive arms package involving Egypt and Israel as well (see also Chapter 12). And in 1980 he approved development of a new fighter aircraft solely for the export market. Meanwhile, conventional arms transfer talks initiated with the Soviet Union ended in stalemate, and Soviet, French, and British trade in arms captured an increased share of the overseas market. Collectively, those factors sounded the death knell for the policy of restraint. Thus the only serious attempt to curb what became during the 1970s the growing trade in sophisticated American weapons of war ended in failure.

The Reagan administration cast aside all pretense of restraint as it declared, in the words of national security adviser Richard V. Allen, that "the U.S. views the transfer of conventional arms and other defense articles as an indispensable component of its foreign policy." Thus arms sales remain an integral element of the U.S. military assistance program, even as the number of arms suppliers has grown to include not only other industrial states but also a growing number of Third World countries (Klare, 1990a, 1990b).

Foreign military sales and other forms of military aid are part of a broader category known as *security assistance*. It includes funds known as security supporting assistance which, while related to the nation's security needs, are not strictly military aid. During the Reagan administration's first term the proportion of security assistance in the overall mix of U.S. military and economic aid increased. As before, anticommunism and the perceived security threats to the nation dictated the flow of funds. Central America then became the focus of attention.

In 1984 the National Bipartisan Commission on Central America, popularly known as the Kissinger Commission, issued a report that emphasized the need to increase to $6 billion the amount of foreign aid sent to the region by the end of the decade. Implementation of the recommendation, which later became part of the Reagan Doctrine, involved substantial amounts of security assistance as well as economic aid. Although the Reagan administration never received all of the Central American aid it sought (and in particular military and other aid for the *contras*), aid levels overall did grow dramatically, to the point that on a per capita basis Central American nations became among the most heavily funded of all U.S. aid recipients. Elsewhere, Pakistan received several hundreds of millions of dollars in security supporting assistance and other forms of aid to facilitate (and reward) its support of anti-Marxist guerrillas fighting in Afghanistan. There, as in Central America, the result conformed to a well-established pattern in which a symbiotic relationship between anticommunism and security concerns guided a redirection of U.S. security assistance toward the latest trouble spot.

Historically the Philippines has also received sizeable amounts of security supporting assistance and other aid, and it continued to do so during the 1980s as the United States sought to shore up the government of Corazon Aquino. At stake here was the maintenance of two large U.S. military bases, Clark Air Base and the naval facility at Subic Bay. Their presence remains a sensitive issue in Philippine domestic politics, and aid is a means of making them more palatable.

U.S. bases are also sensitive issues in other countries that host U.S. forces, and the United States is finding that many of them are asking for more foreign aid as compensation for basing rights. The United States, in turn, is sensitive to the charge that it is paying rent to the host governments. As the secretary of defense explained in a report to Congress early in the Bush administration, "the United States does not view foreign assistance as 'rent' or compensation for base access, but rather as one element of U.S. participation in mutual defense efforts with its allies."

The flexibility of the Defense Department to deal with the demands of sometimes stubborn allies has been diminished by the determination of Congress to "earmark" foreign aid expenditures for particular countries. Overall military assistance funding decreased from about $6.5 billion to roughly $4.5 billion between fiscal years 1984 and 1989; simultaneously, the proportion earmarked for particular countries grew from less than half to more than 90 percent (Cheney, 1990: 8). Israel and Egypt have been favorite targets of congressional earmarks, as have others we have mentioned, namely Pakistan, the Philippines, and four Central American countries (Costa Rica, El Salvador, Guatemala, Honduras). In fiscal 1988 Congress earmarked 90 percent of the $3.2 billion it provided in economic support funds, which includes security supporting assistance, for these eight countries. When other earmarks are added, only $99 million was left for discretionary use among dozens of other countries throughout the world (Goshko, 1988: 32). The message is that having a friend in Congress will count as the United States downsizes its military establishment at the same time that demands from abroad multiply and resources at home dwindle.

The Uncertain Utility of Military Assistance   Although military aid and sales have contributed measurably to the pattern of globalism in American foreign policy, their utility as instruments of policy has often been challenged. On the one hand, by helping to secure access to military bases abroad, security assistance enhances U.S. power projection capabilities at a comparatively minor cost (Koch, 1986). On the other hand, the linkages forged by aid and sales result in quasi-commitments by the donor nation to support the recipient nation—if for no reason other than to "protect" the donor's "investment." Transfers of high-technology weapons systems, for example, often require the influx of large numbers of technicians and military advisers into recipient countries. When combined with the stationing of troops abroad and formal guarantees via treaties and executive agreements, the result, as noted in Chapter 3, has been a commitment by the United States to over one hundred different nations throughout the world.

Since the mid-1980s the world has witnessed a surge toward democratic governance in virtually every region of the globe. Authoritarian regimes of one sort or another were more characteristic before then, and many of these enjoyed U.S. security commitments after World War II that military assistance helped to solidify. In the mid-1970s, for example, it was determined that more than half of the recipients of U.S. arms were dictatorships (*Defense Monitor*, August 1975).

Of concern is whether American military ties with recipient countries might not also have retarded the growth of democratic governments throughout the world. One study of this question (Rowe, 1974) has suggested that regardless of the intentions of American military aid programs, the consequences include an increased probability that military groups within recipient countries will intervene in the politics of those societies. Although most developing nations in the postwar era have not been under the control of their military, arms transfers have contributed to the militarization of foreign governments (see Luckham, 1984), and, when these governments become recipients of military aid in the form of money, equipment, and training, the probability also increases that they will experience political instability in the form of successful and abortive military coups (see Weede, 1978). Similarly, when the military is already in control, the evidence suggests that the receipt of military aid has increased even further the military's entrenched hold. "In short, U.S. military assistance appears to be a contributing factor in undermining civilian elements and increasing the incidence of praetorianism in the less developed areas of the world" (Rowe, 1974).

In those instances where military control of Third World governments remains, U.S. equipment may sometimes be used to "terrorize the public at large" and enable the governments to practice "state terrorism" against their own citizens; the use of U.S. supplied arms for this purpose by the governments of El Salvador, Haiti, and Guatemala in the mid-1980s attests to the potential dangers (see Klare, 1988–1989). In the long run, warns one observer, foreign-supplied arms can imbue "dissidents and insurgent forces with an abiding resentment of the suppliers of such hardware. This was clearly the case in Iran and Nicaragua. . . . Furthermore, . . . these exports help to ensure that such dissent will ultimately take violent forms—often to the detriment of U.S. interests" (Klare, 1984).

In a related vein, the security threats that most recipients of U.S. military assistance face today are not threats from other nations, for which military equipment is normally sought. Instead, the threats are from *within* in the form of "economic failings" and "social inequities which grind away at the internal stability of the nation" (Koch, 1986).

> In instances where the government holds power by controlling the military— not unusual in the Third World—the military's price for being controllable includes hardware. Tanks, trucks, guns, aircraft—these have totemic values which may not always be well understood by outsiders, but should not be underestimated. The cost of this hardware, purchased in the name of security, helps to maintain economic deprivation, which is conducive to chronic insecurity. (Koch, 1986: 54)

In short, U.S. military assistance programs have produced mixed results. They have in some cases strengthened anticommunist governments but may at the same time have inhibited the transition to democracy. Moreover, military aid to Third World conflicts has demonstrably accelerated the tempo of global violence (Klare, 1988–1989) while creating a climate of diffused military capabilities with which Third World wars have been fought. Whether American national interests have been served by aggressive American competition in the global arms trade therefore promises to be questioned in the post–Cold War era.

Economic Assistance

Questions about the purposes sought and the political character of the regimes being assisted with American aid have plagued economic assistance programs much as they have military assistance programs. That should not be surprising, of course. The same international circumstances and corresponding rationales gave rise to both programs. The importance of economic aid as an instrument of policy is demonstrated in Table 5.2, which shows the aggregate distribution of economic aid over the four major periods of the American aid-giving effort.

Currently, the major American economic assistance programs are carried on under the aegis of the Agency for International Development (AID), the Food for Peace Program, subscriptions to international lending organizations, and refugee assistance. Of the two largest programs, AID commitments refer to loans and grants, including technical assistance grants and economic support funds; Food for Peace commitments refer to sales of agricultural commodities on credit

---

TABLE 5.2 ▪ Commitments of Economic and Technical Assistance Distributed by the United States in the Postwar Era (millions of dollars by fiscal year)

Postwar Relief Period (1946–1948)	$ 12,482
Marshall Plan Period (1949–1952)	18,634
Mutual Security Act Period (1953–1961)	24,053
Foreign Assistance Act Period (1962–1988)	164,455
Gross total	$212,480

SOURCE: Adapted from *U.S. Overseas Loans and Grants and Assistance from International Organizations, Obligations and Loan Authorizations, July 1, 1945–September 30, 1988* (Washington, DC: Agency for International Development, 1989), p. 4.

Note: Numbers do not add up because of different reporting concepts in the pre- and post-1955 periods. Data include security supporting assistance totaling $55,584 billion between 1949 and 1988.

---

terms that are repayable in dollars[12] and to grants for providing emergency relief, promoting economic development, or assisting voluntary relief agencies.[13]

Economic Assistance Trends: A Historical Sketch   At noted earlier, the first major peacetime effort to utilize foreign aid as an instrument of foreign policy was the remarkably successful Marshall Plan—or European Recovery Program, as it was formally known. Directed toward Western European countries ravaged by world war, the Marshall Plan was designed to use American capital to rebuild the economic, social, and political infrastructures (basic facilities and systems) of European societies in the hopes of rebuilding a market for American products and enhancing Europe's ability to resist communist subversion. During the Korean War the emphasis shifted from recovery to containment, and from Europe to Asia. As shown in Figure 5.1, Europe received 78 percent of the U.S. aid dollars in 1950; by 1960 two-thirds was going to the Middle (Near) East and the Far East (Asia). The overwhelming concern of the United

---

12. Prior to fiscal year 1977 some sales were also made payable in local currencies (the currency of the purchasing country), which were then used for local purposes, such as maintenance of U.S. government facilities in the purchasing country.

13. Food for Peace expenditures, perhaps more widely known as PL 480 expenditures in reference to the Agricultural Trade Development and Assistance Act of 1954, which created the program, account for $39.7 billion of the $212.5 billion in economic aid. Of this amount 57 percent has been in the form of sales for dollars or local currencies, 16 percent in emergency relief or economic development grants, and 27 percent in donations to voluntary relief agencies. Interestingly, PL 480 contributed to the legitimacy of the idea, in Congress in particular, that commodity sales constitute a form of aid, making possible the subsequent emphasis on military arms sales as a way of assisting other nations (Louscher, 1977).

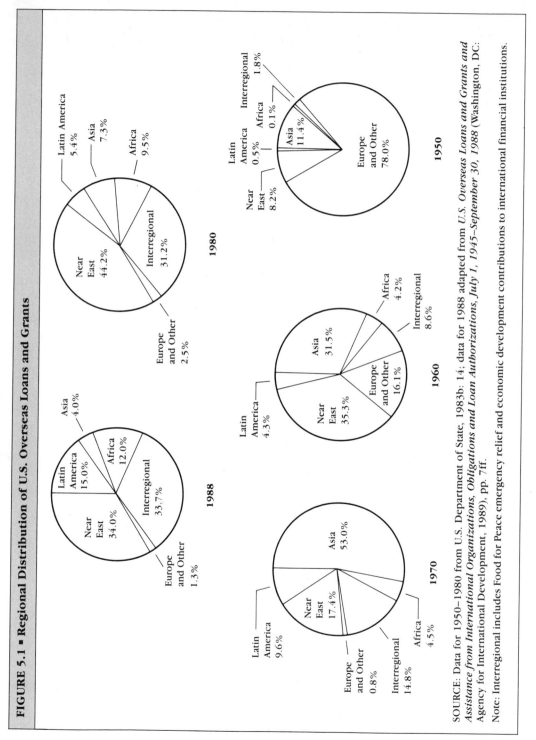

FIGURE 5.1 ▪ Regional Distribution of U.S. Overseas Loans and Grants

1950

Latin America 0.5%
Africa 0.1%
Asia 11.4%
Interregional 1.8%
Near East 8.2%
Europe and Other 78.0%

1960

Latin America 4.3%
Asia 31.5%
Near East 35.3%
Europe and Other 16.1%
Africa 4.2%
Interregional 8.6%

1970

Latin America 9.6%
Asia 53.0%
Near East 17.4%
Europe and Other 0.8%
Interregional 14.8%
Africa 4.5%

1980

Latin America 5.4%
Asia 7.3%
Africa 9.5%
Interregional 31.2%
Near East 44.2%
Europe and Other 2.5%

1988

Asia 4.0%
Latin America 15.0%
Africa 12.0%
Interregional 33.7%
Near East 34.0%
Europe and Other 1.3%

SOURCE: Data for 1950–1980 from U.S. Department of State, 1983b: 14; data for 1988 adapted from *U.S. Overseas Loans and Grants and Assistance from International Organizations, Obligations and Loan Authorizations, July 1, 1945–September 30, 1988* (Washington, DC: Agency for International Development, 1989), pp. 7ff.

Note: Interregional includes Food for Peace emergency relief and economic development contributions to international financial institutions.

States during the post–Marshall Plan period was reflected in the title of the governing legislation—the Mutual Security Act.

By the 1960s it had become apparent that economic and social progress was the dominant concern of many of the newly emerging Third World nations, not the Cold War that had been the primary motivating force behind aid until that point. Castro's rise to power in Cuba demonstrated that security and economic and social progress were not necessarily incompatible concerns, but the degree of emphasis and the appropriate means became problematic.

The U.S. response to the rising challenge presented by developing nations was the Foreign Assistance Act of 1961, which replaced the Mutual Security Act as the legislation governing economic and military aid programs. AID was created by executive order as the administering agency for economic assistance; greater emphasis was placed on development capital and technical assistance relative to defense support aid. The Alliance for Progress was launched in an attack on incipient revolution and communism in the Western Hemisphere.

Specific factors related to the allocation of economic aid under the Foreign Assistance Act can be categorized roughly into clusters reflecting (1) the political importance of aid recipients to the United States, (2) Cold War considerations, (3) recipients' need and performance, and (4) the availability of alternative sources of assistance. These, in turn, track underlying motivations with respect to national security, humanitarianism, the promotion of economic gains, and diplomatic leverage (Frank and Baird, 1975), all of which have parallels in the military aid programs of the United States as well as the aid programs of other Western foreign aid donors.

Although those motivations are multifaceted, security concerns related to the anticommunist thrust of American foreign policy have predominated. In both the Mutual Security Act period (1953–1961) and the Foreign Assistance Act period (through 1975), nations formally aligned with the United States received roughly 60 percent of the total bilateral-aid pie. Similarly, Third World nations formally aligned with the United States received 41 and 45 percent of the share in the two periods, respectively, and nonaligned nations bordering on the communist world received roughly 20 percent in each. The security concern is particularly evident in the overwhelming attention given Asia during the Vietnam War era (see Figure 5.1). Once more, the parallel between military and economic aid is evident.

A significant new thrust in thinking about foreign aid occurred in the 1970s, when the concern shifted toward meeting basic human needs as a way of alleviating the deprivation in which literally hundreds of millions of people live throughout the world. Thus the emphasis of development assistance shifted from social infrastructure projects to projects directly helping the poorest in developing societies. In part that decision was related to growing concern in Congress with linking aid allocations to the human rights practices of Third World countries. After the "new directions" legislation passed by Congress in 1973, meeting "basic human needs" became a dominant goal of aid-granting countries and international institutions. The underlying belief was that it was just as important to improve the distribution of income and basic services to the very poorest people as it was to promote capital-intensive projects designed to stimulate economic "takeoff." Today, strategies directed toward basic needs and toward growth are commonly viewed as reinforcing: "developing countries cannot sustain improvements in basic human needs without broad-based economic growth.... But neither can these countries sustain economic growth without the increasing participation of healthier, better educated, better fed, and more involved workers" (Callison, 1990).

The basic needs perspective is closely identified with the efforts of Robert McNamara, the former Defense Department secretary who served as president of the World Bank during the 1970s. McNamara sought to focus attention on the plight of the poorest of the poor in what amounted to a critique of previous theories of economic development, particularly those that argued that the benefits of economic growth would "trickle down" to the needy. Because that seldom happened—more typical was "dualism" in developing societies: one modern, growing sector and one traditional, stagnant sector—meeting basic human needs came to be perceived as necessary. The new approach also enjoyed the political advantage of linking the plight of the world's poor directly to Third World countries themselves. Leaders of Third World countries often prefer to lay the blame elsewhere; in the context of the North-South debate (see Chapter 6), many have asserted that their problems are the result of the inherent inequality between the world's rich and poor nations, which the hierarchical structure of the international system perpetuates. In contrast, the human needs perspective generally places blame at home.

National security considerations, as we might expect, remain a predominant justification for foreign economic assistance. But even here the overlapping concerns at the base of the aid program are apparent. During the 1960s in particular, the argument advanced was not that aid would result in direct political benefits to the United States but rather that aid would contribute to recipients' economic development. Economic development was expected to be accompanied in turn by the emergence of stable democratic governments, the existence of which would ensure peaceful and cooperative relations among countries. This complicated reasoning was used not only to rationalize the aid program but also to guide the actual allocation of aid dollars, with emphasis placed on economic efficiency criteria (for example, the ability of recipients to generate savings out of current income or to increase gross national product growth rates), rather than overt political considerations.

In practice, aid has often been allocated on the basis of short-run political considerations. The financial rewards to which the United States committed itself as part of the Egyptian-Israeli peace treaty, noted earlier, stands out, as do the payments made for basing rights for U.S. military forces abroad. Similarly, the Reagan administration sought (unsuccessfully) to link U.S. foreign aid allocations to the voting behavior of Third World countries in the United Nations.[14] Strategic considerations also motivated the ambitious Caribbean Basin Initiative (CBI). Launched in 1984, the program of tariff reductions and tax incentives seeks to promote the growth of industry and trade in Central America and the Caribbean in hopes of thwarting the economic conditions on which Marxist revolutionaries thrive.

The market-oriented approach to political problems embodied in the CBI came increasingly to characterize the U.S. aid effort in the 1980s. Meeting basic human needs through programs such as "rural health delivery systems, population, primary education, small-scale agriculture, labor-intensive construction of secondary roads, and community development" (Preeg, 1989b) continues to figure predominantly in the aid program, but an increasing proportion of aid has gone to provide direct, quick-disbursing balance-of-payments support to recipient countries in return for their making domestic reforms designed to make their economies more market-oriented. The approach is similar to that pursued by international lending institutions in their efforts to assist Third World nations in coping with the crushing debt burden many of them suffer (see Chapter 7). Finally, the aid program has also been used to deal with narcotics control in **drug producing and drug-trafficking** countries.

The Utility of Economic Assistance   As in the case of military aid, Congress has earmarked substantial proportions of AID's expenditures, which limits its ability to use foreign aid in particular ways among different countries in pursuit of varied foreign policy goals. In part this congressional maneuver reflects an ongoing struggle between Congress and the executive branch over who should direct American foreign policy (see Chapter 12). But it also reflects a lack of consensus on how aid is best used to achieve those objectives. In Central America, for example, the Reagan administration sought to use aid to stabilize the economies of the recipients as part of a larger strategy to cope with leftist insurgencies in the region. Critics argued that that focus was misdirected, that aid should have been used to push for basic social and political reform that would improve the lot of the least fortunate in the region as a means of stemming the appeal of leftist political forces (Sullivan, 1989). The differences of opinion on these issues are fundamental. They relate to differences about the relationship between economics and politics and between economic development and political development. And they relate to differences about the causes of conflict not only in the particular case of Central America but in world politics generally (see Kegley and Wittkopf, 1989). Often these become

---

14. The mandate, written into law in 1986, sought to deny aid to countries "engaged in a consistent pattern of opposition to the foreign policy of the United States." See Kegley and Hook (1990) for an analysis that concludes the policy "produced neither an immediate nor a longer-term impact on the relationship between assistance and voting agreement." Earlier examinations of this relationship can be found in Wittkopf (1973) and Rai (1980). Moon (1985) provides a useful critique of the conceptual orientation underlying such approaches to understanding the foreign policy behavior of Third World countries.

partisan and ideological disputes, as there is little convincing evidence to demonstrate one argument is right and the other wrong.

Although foreign aid has been made to serve multiple political purposes, for example, there is little evidence that the relatively modest inflows of external capital have contributed significantly to economic growth. Part of the reason is that economic policies pursued by some developing nations have led to inefficient use of external capital. It is also a consequence of the enormous needs of developing nations. A gap between expectations and performance is perhaps inevitable, therefore—a gap that has opened the aid program to much criticism. Among other things, the lack of a clear and strong connection between foreign aid and economic growth has undermined the national security justification for aid. For reasons not unlike those discussed earlier regarding foreign military assistance, critics have argued that aid is detrimental to security, for it involves the United States in countries in which it initially has little real interest. According to this reasoning, "foreign aid is the 'slippery slope' that leads eventually to an over-extension of commitments and to a greater likelihood of military involvement" (Frank and Baird, 1975). It was a viewpoint that permeated the decade-long debate about the Reagan administration's Central American policies, among others (see Chapter 12).

The foreign aid program has been scrutinized repeatedly (see, for example, Woods, 1989, and the comments on recent reviews in Callison, 1990, and Thompson, 1990). The absence of evidence as to its effects on recipients and the absence of sustained domestic political support for its maintenance explain the persistent introspection. Despite this, the program persists, and the focus during the Bush administration asked *how* (and by how much), not *whether*, to continue it. Specifically, the debate turned on how best to support the emergence of democratic regimes in Nicaragua and Panama and in Eastern Europe in fulfillment of long-standing American foreign policy objectives and ideals. In the words of Secretary of State James Baker, "The time of sweeping away the old dictators is passing fast; the time of building up the new democracies has arrived. . . . The promotion and consolidation of democracy . . . is a task that fulfills both American ideals and American interests."

As long as Congress earmarks funds for particular recipients and purposes, fledgling democratic societies can only be funded with new resources. But those are not readily available, which increases pressure for downsizing the defense budget and spending the "peace dividend" on foreign aid. But no agreement exists on the size of the dividend, because there is no consensus on whether and by how much traditional threats to the national security may have diminished. A tradeoff between guns and butter (between national defense and domestic welfare) has always existed. Now, it appears, policymakers face a tradeoff between defense and democracy.

Still, we must be careful not to exaggerate the magnitude of the resources at stake. There was some growth but no dramatic increase in the amount of economic aid between the 1970s and 1980s, but since the mid-1980s the amount declined by about a third, from $12.3 billion in 1985 to $8.7 billion in

1989. The conservative ideology of the Reagan administration, reinforced by the nation's mounting debt burden, persistent federal government budget deficits, and a trade imbalance of enormous proportions with the rest of the world were among the many factors (to which "donor fatigue" and the widespread belief that foreign aid is a massive "giveaway" might be added[15]) that contributed to the decline and refusal to expand substantially the level of U.S. economic aid. From the viewpoint of recipient nations, which experienced tremendous population increases in the postwar period, per capita aid receipts thus actually declined.

From the viewpoint of donors, whose economies have grown enormously in both real and inflated dollars, the volume and value of aid given also have actually declined. Measured in comparable dollars, American foreign aid in the decade ending in 1955 was nearly double the amount allocated in the decade ending in 1985. Put differently, the $40 billion spent on postwar relief and reconstruction between 1946 and 1952 would today amount to more than $150 billion (U.S. Department of State, 1983: 12–13). Thus the "burden" is comparatively small (which may account for the Bush administration's efforts to increase assistance to deal with the increasingly salient economic problems of a post–Cold War world). Still, when measured against gross national product (GNP), the aid effort of the United States has been among the least burdensome of all Western industrialized nations, as indicated by the fact that its official development aid in 1985 stood at less than .25 percent of its GNP, and has dropped since then. The United States ranks *lowest* of seventeen Western foreign aid donors in the percentage of GNP given in aid to other nations, and far below the internationally agreed on target of .7 percent.[16]

THE ELUSIVE QUEST FOR NATIONAL SECURITY

"If the fundamental truths of development remain the same," a recent report on the foreign aid program observed (Woods, 1989), "the face of America, and the world, is changing faster than ever before." Against this background the

---

15. The popular conception that foreign aid is a massive "giveaway" program is wrong for several reasons, but including the fact that much of it is tied to purchases in the United States. As former Secretary of State George P. Shultz explained:

> About 70% of our bilateral foreign assistance funds is spent in the United States. Virtually all of our military financing, both grant and loan, is spent in the United States on U.S.-produced equipment. Our PL 480 program supports U.S. agricultural exports. Thus, our assistance programs, essential instruments of U.S. foreign policy, help to generate increased economic activity in the United States, which, in turn, helps boost trade and economic prospects in developing countries.

Moreover, a primary goal of the aid program is promotion of economic growth in recipient societies so as to create larger markets for American goods. See also Preeg (1989b).

16. Keep in mind that public (that is, official) foreign aid differs from private assistance, in which the American people have been extraordinarily generous historically in their efforts to alleviate human suffering abroad (see Woods, 1989).

contribution that foreign aid can make to realization of the national interest and at the same time "to be in harmony with good neighborliness" is not easily determined. As we noted at the outset of Chapter 4, in part this is because many of the challenges that the United States now faces no longer fit easily into the prism of globalism, anticommunism, and containment that for so long has rationalized and guided the behavior of the United States abroad. Here the concern is not so much with arms and armies as with the threats emanating from narcotics, demographic trends, and environmental degradation (Brown et al, 1990; Ehrlich and Ehrlich, 1990; Foster, 1989). Military resources and foreign aid can profitably be used to deal with some of the transnational aspects of these issues, but in other ways they are likely to call for a fundamental reordering of priorities in such a way that old solutions will no longer fit and new means to new policy ends will have to be devised (Barnet et al., 1989). At the same time, of course, we can expect that many traditional challenges will persist, as will those instruments that have over the postwar period become staples in the American approach to the world.

The national interests that American policymakers elect to make priorities will depend, ultimately, on the kind of post–Cold War environment that emerges in the 1990s. Thus trends and transformations in world politics will give direction to the external environment that the United States is likely to face in the twilight of the twentieth century, just as the behavior of the United States will help to shape them. It is to a description of these and the interaction of American foreign policy with them that our attention now turns.

SUGGESTIONS FOR FURTHER READING

Eberstadt, Nicholas. (1988) *Foreign Aid and American Purpose.* Washington, D.C.: American Enterprise Institute for Public Research.

Elliott, Kim Andrew. (1990) "Too Many Voices of America," *Foreign Policy* 77(Winter):113–131.

Emerson, Steven. (1988) *Secret Warriors: Inside the Covert Military Operations of the Reagan Era.* New York: Putnam.

Hyland, William G. (1990) "America's New Course," *Foreign Affairs* 69 (Spring): 1–12.

Klare, Michael. (1989) "Subterranean Alliances: America's Global Proxy Network," *Journal of International Affairs* 43 (Summer/Fall): 97–118.

———. (1984) *American Arms Supermarket.* Austin: University of Texas Press.

Laufer, Leopold Yehuda.(1989) "Changing Perspectives in Redistribution of U.S. Foreign Aid," *The Jerusalem Journal of International Relations* 11(September):26–39.

Sorensen, Theodore C. (1990) "Rethinking National Security," *Foreign Affairs* 69 (Summer): 1–18.

Treverton, Gregory F. (1987) *Covert Action: The Limits of Intervention in the Postwar World.* New York: Basic Books.

Weiner, Tim. (1990) *Blank Check: The Pentagon's Black Budget.* New York: Warner Books.

Woods, Alan. (1989) *Development and the National Interest: U.S. Economic Assistance into the 21st Century.* Washington, D.C.: Agency for International Development.

CHAPTER 6

The International Political System in Transition

We are living in an era of transition. The postwar system is being transformed, and a new environment is emerging.

SECRETARY OF STATE JAMES A. BAKER, 1989

At no time in our peacetime history has the state of the Nation depended more heavily on the state of the world; and seldom, if ever, has the state of the world depended more heavily on the state of our Nation.

PRESIDENT GERALD R. FORD, 1975

The state of the American nation and the state of the world are inextricably inter-dependent. The price of gasoline at American service stations is influenced by events in distant lands. The availability of automobiles, televisions, and other consumer products is governed not simply by internal market forces but also by agreements between Washington, on one hand, and Tokyo, Taipei, and Seoul, on the other. And decisions reached in the Kremlin substantially determine the level at which Americans are taxed and how federal revenues are spent. In short, developments abroad and conditions at home are perhaps more closely linked now than at any time in American history. As Secretary of State George Shultz stressed in 1984, "our well-being as a country depends . . . on the structural con-ditions of the international system that help determine whether we are fun-damentally secure, whether the world economy is sound."

Changes in the international system's condition act as catalysts to reassess-ments of America's vital interests and the kinds of opportunities that exist for the realization of its foreign policy objectives. How, or even whether, a change is perceived is as important as the actual circumstances that precede the way policy priorities are finally defined. Hence the external environment is properly conceived as a cluster of variables that shapes the international cli-mate in which the United States competes and that creates opportunities for and constraints on the attainment of foreign policy goals. Yet we cannot assume that changing international realities will necessarily result in corresponding policy accommodations, as the constraining forces of other potential explana-tions may inhibit policy adaptations.

141

We will assess the impact of the international environment on American foreign policy in Chapters 6 and 7. We begin by focusing on three changing characteristics of the postwar international political system: the distribution of world power; the postwar emancipation of colonial peoples and the consequent emergence of the Third World; and the rise in the importance of nonstate actors. These global political developments and forces have significantly influenced the way America's foreign policy agenda since 1945 has been defined, and they promise to shape American policy thinking in the future.

In Chapter 7 we continue this investigation by examining postwar changes in the global political economy. There we will explore more deeply global interdependence and how changes at the intersection of international politics and economics have influenced American perceptions of its national interests. Specifically, we will examine the changing role of the United States in the transforming international monetary and trade systems.

SHIFTS IN THE DISTRIBUTION OF POWER

The international political system of which the United States has been a member for over two hundred years is distinguished by two continuing attributes. The first is its *decentralized* structure. The system's principal actors—sovereign nations—monopolize power in the absence of a central institution, such as a world government. No authority exists above the nation-state to enforce order. Consequently, independent countries must rely primarily on bargaining and self-help to ensure their own national security. A decentralized, competitive system places a premium on the quest for power as a means of defense and influence. In such a politically primitive system, arms races and a high incidence of international violence become readily understandable.

Decentralization is related to the system's second basic attribute—its highly *stratified* structure. Nations are equal in law but not in influence. Power is distributed very unevenly. A few political and economic giants near the hierarchical apex possess a vast proportion of power, whereas many others near the bottom of this metaphorical pyramid are relatively powerless. The ascribed status of states and the distribution of resources are also very uneven.

But this decentralized, stratified political system has profoundly changed since 1945. Let us examine the most significant changes in postwar political circumstances and the responses of the United States to them.

Hegemonic Dominance: A Unipolar World

The postwar period began with the United States emerging as the only major industrial power unscathed by the ravages of World War II. In fact, that war transformed the American economy. The gross national product (GNP) rose 72 percent between 1941 and 1944; agricultural production increased by 25 percent; and civilian consumption of goods and services rose by 20 percent

(Lovell, 1970: 93). In contrast, the Soviet economy had suffered enormous devastation. Its industrial, agricultural, and transportation systems had either been destroyed or severely damaged, and an estimated twenty million Soviet soldiers and civilians perished in the war. Although the United States had suffered some 292,000 casualties, the ratio of Soviet to American war deaths was about seventy to one.

The Soviet Union had, of course, secured control over vast areas of Eastern Europe following the war, and it was over this issue that American-Soviet conflict centered. On balance, however, the United States was clearly in the superior position—a true hegemonic power. In 1947 the United States alone accounted for nearly half the world's total GNP. And the nation's monopoly of the atomic bomb gave it military predominance.

It is against this background that we can begin to see how fundamental the shifts in the international distribution of power have been during the past five decades. The postwar era began with the United States possessing the capability—if not the will—to exercise greater control over world affairs than perhaps any nation had previously. It alone possessed the military and economic might to defend unilaterally its security and sovereignty; its position of strength relative to other states was unchallenged (recall Sir Harold Laski's description in Chapter 1).

The unparalleled supremacy of the United States may, without risk of exaggeration, permit the system during this interlude to be termed a *unipolar* one, for power was concentrated within the hands of a single state. So unchallenged was American dominance at the time that some observers, such as Henry Luce, editor of *Time* and *Life* magazines, spoke hopefully of "the American century"—of a prolonged period in which American power would enable it to shape the world to its interests.

That situation began to change almost as soon as it was recognized, however, when the atomic monopoly was cracked with the successful Soviet atomic test in 1949. Then in 1953 the Soviet Union exploded a thermonuclear device less than a year after the United States had done so. And in 1957 it shocked the Western world by being the first nation to orbit a space satellite—a feat that proved as well its capability to deliver a nuclear warhead. Thereafter the two superpowers competed for global influence, and their race for advantage in arms accelerated.

The Bipolar System

The term *bipolarity* describes the concentration of effective world power in the hands of the United States and the Soviet Union from the late 1940s until the 1962 Cuban missile crisis. The less powerful nations looked to one or the other superpower for protection, and the two world leaders energetically competed for their allegiance. Each superpower recruited allies to give it forward bases from which to carry on the competition with the other, and each promised to extend deterrence to its allies to bolster their sense of security. The

North Atlantic Treaty Organization (NATO), linking the United States to the defense of Western Europe, and the Warsaw Pact, linking the Soviet Union in a formal alliance to its Eastern European satellites, were the two major products of this early competition.

The bipolar distribution of power contributed to a crisis-ridden postwar atmosphere. By grouping the nations of the system into two blocs, each led by a superpower with the capacity to "veto" instantaneously the existence of entire nations (Kaplan, 1957), the bipolar structure bred insecurity throughout the system (Spanier, 1990). Each superpower perceived the balance to be constantly at stake; what one side gained was seen as a loss for the other. Utmost importance was therefore attached to recruiting new friends and allies, while fear that an old ally might desert the fold was ever-present. The bipolar structure provided little room for compromise. Every maneuver appeared to be a new initiative toward world conquest; hence every act was perceived to be hostile and was to be met by a retaliatory act of hostility. Because conciliation was perceived as unrealistic, only momentary pauses in the exchange of threats, tests of resolve, and challenges to the territorial status quo were expected. This period was fraught with repeated great power interventions in the Third World and recurrent crises at the brink of great power war (see Brecher and Wilkenfeld, 1991).

Nonetheless, the bipolar period did not experience system-wide war. One of the ironic characteristics of the bipolar system was that, amidst endemic threats, major war between the great powers did *not* occur. Paradoxically, the perpetual competition and enormous destructive power in the hands of the contestants produced caution and stability rather than recklessness and war (see Waltz, 1964; Gaddis, 1991).

The Bipolycentric System

The rigid bipolar structure began to fragment in the wake of the Cuban missile crisis. The gradual loosening of the major Cold War alliances associated with bipolarity was symptomatic of the impending disintegration of tight bloc structures and the growing assertion of independence by other states. As bipolarity eroded in the 1960s, a *bipolycentric* (Spanier, 1990) system emerged to replace it.

Bipolycentrism aptly described the continued military superiority of the United States and the Soviet Union and the continuing reliance of the weaker alliance partners on their respective superpower patrons for security. At the same time, the new system permitted measurably greater room to maneuver on the part of weaker members; hence the term *polycentrism*, connoting the possibility of many centers of power and diverse relationships among the nations subordinate to the superpowers. In the tiered, polycentric system, each superpower became committed to developing links with the secondary powers formally aligned with its adversary (such as those that were once nurtured between the United States and Romania and between France and the Soviet

Union). At the same time, the secondary powers exploited those ties and sought to establish relationships among themselves (for example, between Poland and West Germany) that transcended the boundaries of the Cold War coalitions in order to enhance their bargaining position within their own alliance. While the superpowers remained dominant militarily, greater diplomatic fluidity than in a strictly bipolar system became evident. New foreign policy roles for states (other than simply *aligned* or *nonaligned*) were created in this less rigid system.

Rapid technological advances in the superpowers' major weapon systems were principal catalysts of change in the system's increasingly fluid polarity structure. In particular, intercontinental ballistic missiles (ICBMs) decreased the need for forward bases from which to strike the adversary[1] and the necessity of maintaining cohesive alliances composed of reliable defense partners. In addition, the diminishing gap between Soviet and American military capabilities accelerated the breakdown of trust in the superpowers' commitments and belief in their willingness to sacrifice their own security for their allies' defense.

The polycentric tendencies that first emerged in the 1960s intensified steadily. Symbols of the changes that were occurring included the superpowers' acceptance of the view that strategic stability required the preservation of nuclear parity (as signaled by the Strategic Arms Limitations Talks [SALT] agreements); their intermittent pledges to avert resort to nuclear weapons to settle their differences; a shift from reliance on others to self-defense; and a growing conviction that the destructiveness of modern weapons reduced the utility of defensive alliances. Collectively, these ideas accelerated the polycentric divisions already evident.[2] Increasingly, political leaders asked what purposes were served by alliances that could not guarantee their members' security. Did membership diminish rather than increase national security by making

---

1. That consideration has always applied more to the United States than the Soviet Union, since the latter had not created forward bases of the sort maintained in Europe and Asia by the United States. Soviet military facilities in Eastern Europe were built as ''buffers'' to cordon the Soviet Union from possible Western European aggression. Soviet efforts to convert Cuba into a forward base comparable to American forward areas in Europe were largely unsuccessful, as witnessed by the abortive attempt to place strategic missiles in Cuba in 1962. The presence of Soviet-bloc military personnel in Afghanistan, Angola, Ethiopia, Laos, and Cambodia in the 1980s exemplified the Soviet Union's emphasis on proxy-states, in contrast to forward bases. The U.S. network of ''subterranean'' alliances evident in its own extensive proxy network should also be mentioned (see Klare, 1989).

2. The unwillingness of some members of NATO to participate in U.S.-initiated sanctions against the Soviet Union for its invasion of Afghanistan in 1979 or to support the American attack on Libya in 1986 illustrates the tensions and differing perceptions inherent in the Western alliance. Other examples include the open disapproval by many European governments of U.S. policy in Vietnam during the 1960s; their refusal of landing rights to American planes resupplying Israel during the 1973 Yom Kippur War; their lukewarm support in 1979 of American efforts to squeeze Iran economically in an effort to secure release of American hostages there; their participation, over American objections, in the Yamberg pipeline project designed to transport natural gas from Siberia to Western European markets; and their criticism of Washington's policies for dealing with domestic turmoil in Central America. Furthermore, Western European opinion during the 1980s swung further toward neutralism and pacifism as it challenged the ''Atlanticist'' orientation that previously had bound the United States and Western Europe together.

the alliance partners certain targets in a superpower nuclear exchange? If so, the presumed benefits of alliance membership warranted reevaluation.

We now turn to examining the meaning of these questions and the changes they portended for the cohesion of the major postwar alliance systems, NATO and the Warsaw Pact.

The Weakened Atlantic Alliance   In a system shaped fundamentally by a "balance of terror," European members of NATO in particular worried increasingly about whether the United States would sacrifice New York city for Paris or Bonn. The credibility of the U.S. threat of massive retaliation was especially questioned, but even the "flexible response" doctrine adopted as official NATO strategy during the Johnson administration as a means to extend through graduated military retaliation the principle of assured destruction of the Soviet Union in the event of a Warsaw Pact attack on Western Europe did not restore the Atlantic community's confidence in American promises. Under what conditions would Washington be willing to risk a nuclear holocaust? Would a U.S. president escalate a local conflict into a global one to protect its allies? For many Europeans, flexible response signaled America's reluctance to expose itself to destruction for the sake of ensuring its allies' security. Mounting uncertainties such as this led to the French decisions in the late 1950s to develop its own nuclear *force de frappe* and, in the mid-1960s, to evict NATO headquarters from French soil and to withdraw from the integrated NATO command.

Despite Washington's assurances about the American commitment to its allies, talk of "decoupling" Europe from American protection undermined trust in its word. "When NATO was founded in 1949," observes Jay Winik (1985), "it was basically a unilateral American nuclear guarantee of European security in the guise of an alliance. This situation has remained largely unchanged. But with the advent of at least strategic parity, the U.S. nuclear commitment to defend Europe has been reduced to a pact of mutual suicide. It has lost much of its credibility, if not sense." The specter of Europe devastated in a limited nuclear exchange, that is, by a nuclear attack confined to the European theater without escalation to general war between the superpowers themselves, inspired the European quest to create a new architecture that would prevent Europe from becoming a nuclear battleground. At the same time, growing linkages between Eastern and Western European countries in the 1970s and 1980s contributed to the pace at which relatively fluid diplomatic relationships were developing.

These stresses and strains gathered strength in the 1990s as the prospect of a European war became increasingly remote. As the East-West confrontation eased, the superpowers' animosity that for decades had cemented their allies' loyalty dissipated. Hence cohesion in the Atlantic alliance dissolved (Rubenstein, 1987) as the "allies in crisis" (Sherwood, 1990) made challenges other than deterrence of a Soviet attack a priority.

The Splintering of the Soviet Bloc   The fragmentation of long-standing alliances has been an Eastern as well as Western phenomenon. The Sino-Soviet split, dating back to the 1950s, was the most visible manifestation of the breakup of what was once seen as a communist monolith. Growing out of ideological differences as well as security concerns befitting two giant neighbors, the dispute was elevated in the 1960s to rivalry for leadership of the world communist movement that opened a new era of Washington-Moscow-Beijing triangular politics.

Tripolarity was sometimes used in the 1960s and 1970s to describe a system comprising three nations with relatively equal power potential vis-à-vis one another as defined by their military (especially nuclear) capabilities (Yalem, 1972; Spanier, 1975). The metaphor was fashioned to interpret the role of China in superpower relationships and its growing independence from Moscow's control. However, the term did not then, nor does it today, apply to strategic realities. Objectively, China cannot be defined as a power rival of either the United States or the Soviet Union. Possession of a second-strike nuclear capacity and the means to deliver it are preconditions for a power to be considered a "pole." China, which does not possess such capabilities and suffers from chronic economic problems, cannot be said, therefore, to comprise a third pole. Yet China's membership in the nuclear club automatically makes it a significant regional if not global power, one perhaps destined, as former President Richard M. Nixon predicted in 1989, to become "an economic and military superpower." As the Chinese continue development of nuclear weapons and a capacity to deliver them, they may some day achieve a limited second-strike capability that will complicate the global roles the United States and the Soviet Union have long played. Deterrence on which the Americans and Soviets have relied would, in a tripolar system, have to be directed not simply at one actor, but two, and in particular toward preventing a military attack by two against one.

Although tripolarity does not currently exist, it nonetheless explains many aspects of American, Soviet, and Chinese interactions since the 1960s, and serves to highlight the growing divisions within the communist bloc.[3] Chinese apprehension about Soviet-American détente; Soviet concern for Sino-American rapprochement; and American support of polycentric tendencies in the communist camp generally, and fear of Soviet-Chinese fence-mending in particular, symbol-

---

3. Nixon's historic visit to China in the winter of 1972 remains the most well-known symbol of triangular diplomacy. The visit was preceded by Henry Kissinger's announcement in February 1970 that the United States "would no longer treat conflict with the U.S.S.R. as automatically involving the People's Republic." To end the isolation of China (which had been the cornerstone of American containment policy in Asia since 1949), the Carter administration established formal diplomatic relations with China and openly spoke of playing the "China card" in an effort to moderate Soviet behavior around the globe. The Reagan administration pursued the same strategy, as illustrated in 1981 when Secretary of Defense Caspar Weinberger threatened to sell arms to China if the Soviet Union intervened militarily in Poland. Later in the year, without any specific reference to Poland or other events, the Reagan administration lifted restrictions on the sale of arms to China. The subsequent decision in April 1984 to permit China to buy civilian nuclear reactors from the United States added a new dimension to the strategic equation, although the Chinese did pledge not to supply nuclear fuel to other nuclear weapons aspirants. Despite China's ruthless crackdown on pro-democracy demonstrations in June 1989, the Bush administration subsequently pursued as energetically as ever political ties with the Chinese.

ized tripolar calculations (see Goldstein and Freeman, 1990). Ronald Reagan's bid to China in early 1984 to "lay aside disputes and cooperate in trade and space," which was followed later in the year by a Sino-Soviet agreement to develop trade and science together over the next twenty-five years, presaged the kind of triangular maneuvering that has continued in the aftermath of the Cold War, as witnessed by the Bush administration's decision in 1990 to renew most-favored-nation trade status for China while refusing to grant it to the Soviet Union.

Polycentrism within the Soviet bloc was not confined to the Sino-Soviet clash. Periodic assertions of Eastern European independence, despite the shadow of the Red Army, also marked the behavior of the East Germans, the Poles, and the Hungarians during the 1950s. During the 1960s the most visible example of polycentric tendencies within the Warsaw Pact occurred in Czechoslovakia, whose democratic experimentation was abruptly terminated by Warsaw Pact military intervention in 1968. The Brezhnev Doctrine justifying that invasion was enunciated as a threat to other satellites tempted to experiment with reform and possible defection from the communist fold.

Despite that threat, East European assertions of independence from "Moscow's line" grew in the 1970s and early 1980s, as illustrated especially by the polycentric deviation exhibited by Romania, Poland, and Hungary. These anticipated the far-reaching domestic reforms and assertions of foreign policy independence that swept Eastern Europe in 1989 and 1990. In 1989, Poland elected a noncommunist prime minister, Hungary declared itself an independent republic, East Germany's communist leadership resigned and their successors tore down the Berlin Wall, and Czechoslovakia permitted free elections and opposition parties. Mikhail Gorbachev's radical reforms under *glasnost* required the application of new thinking in Soviet policy toward its former East European satellites; reform at home licensed reform of communist mismanagement abroad. Freewheeling discussion promptly gave way to criticism of past policies and the push for their revision. "Almost overnight," noted Adam Bromke (in Smolowe, 1989), "all the rivalries and tensions in the bloc that Communist orthodoxy had papered over for decades burst into the open." Hesitant to deny Soviet allies the liberalization he must permit to save his own nation, Gorbachev was forced to accept their defection. Thus Moscow's grip relaxed further, symbolized by Gorbachev's repudiation in October 1989 of the Brezhnev Doctrine. The so-called alliance of communist nations had ceased to speak with a single voice or act in united solidarity, as the members of the Warsaw Pact renounced communist rule and endorsed free market principles. What was left institutionally of "the bloc that failed" (Gati, 1990) drifted de facto into irrelevance.

In the absence of a united communist front, a new era in world politics appeared to be dawning. Bush's national security adviser, Brent Scowcroft, exclaimed in 1989 that the surge of reform "is a really historic set of developments in the postwar era" that has brought about "a fundamental change in the whole international structure."

The Diffusion of Economic Power   Changes in the distribution of economic strength coincided with these geostrategic trends. As fear of a Soviet attack receded in importance in the minds of Western leaders, a broad range of neglected nonmilitary issues (such as trade, European economic integration, fiscal harmonization, and environmental protection) began to replace security as the problems perceived most critical. While America's allies questioned the Reagan administration's narrow focus on the East-West contest, they gave increasing attention to building trade and diplomatic relationships with those in the communist orbit. Such differences are the essence of polycentrism.

Already by the 1960s and 1970s many of America's allies were vibrant economic entities and no longer weak dependents. Their growing capabilities permitted them to become more assertive and independent. This accelerated with the erosion of the ability of the United States to impose its own chosen solutions on nonmilitary questions. By the 1980s the United States was no longer singularly predominant at the apex of power. The "century" of American hegemony predicted by Henry Luce lasted a quarter-century. The United States now had serious rivals in its own camp and could no longer command political compliance from others.

The phenomenal postwar growth of the Japanese and Western European economies largely accounted for the relative decline of America's economic dominance.[4] In 1988 the combined output of the twelve European Community (EC) countries[5] and Japan was over $950 billion greater than U.S. output; thirty years earlier, in 1960, it did not even equal U.S. output (*Handbook of Economic Statistics, 1989*, 1989: 30).

Despite the relative national economic growth of other states, they still do not rival the power of either the United States or the Soviet Union militarily. Both remain dominant in this sphere, as revealed by the facts that each accounted for roughly a quarter of total world military expenditures in each year from 1963 to 1987 and that collectively the two never accounted for less than 55 percent of all military expenditures in the world during those years (U.S. Arms Control and Disarmament Agency, 1975, 1989).

Nevertheless, the now firmly established economic strength of Japan and Europe, notably Germany, permits these states to steer a course independent of the United States—indeed, one that often challenges the United States. Already,

---

4. It is important to emphasize that this decline was *relative*. It was not due to the failure of the U.S. economy to expand, for, indeed, the United States had nearly quadrupled its GNP since 1945. Instead, it was due to the ability of others to grow more rapidly, with the result that the United States was no longer able to command the same *proportion* of world economic product that it once did. Militarily, of course, the United States remained without rival in the Western world, and economically its production greatly exceeded that of its superpower rival (see Nye, 1990).

5. The European Community (EC) is made up of three organizations that, since 1967, have shared common institutions: the European Economic Community (EEC, created in 1957), the European Coal and Steel Community (ECSC, 1952), and the European Atomic Energy Community (Euratom, 1958). The initial members of the EC were Belgium, France, Italy, Luxembourg, the Netherlands, and West Germany. It has since been expanded to include Denmark, Greece, Ireland, Portugal, Spain, and the United Kingdom.

Germany and Japan excel where arguably the real global contest of the future will be fought—on the economic battlefield. With the dispersion of economic power, and with arms increasingly questioned as a measure of political power, has come the end of American hegemony. "Our principal problems," Deputy Secretary of State Lawrence Eagleburger summarized in 1989, "are no longer East-West relations with the Soviet Union; they are West-West relations with allies in Europe and Japan." "The real gut issues of the next decade will rest on the ability to manage trade," national security adviser Scowcroft explained in 1989.

Collectively, the declining cohesion of the Western alliance, the splintering of the communist coalition, and the rise of new economic centers of power point to an emergent external setting in which the place of Europe will be critical.

The New European Landscape   Whether the transition from a Europe divided by Cold War to an altogether new (and as yet undefined) geostrategic subsystem will bring continued peace or set the stage for another global war as occurred twice in this century is problematic.[6] The postwar division of Europe into competing blocs under conditions of both a bipolar and bipolycentric distribution of power introduced a degree of predictability to otherwise fluid diplomatic relationships (Gaddis, 1991; Mearsheimer, 1990a). However threatening it may have been, this clear-cut division of counterpoised alliances covaried with the longest period of great power peace in Europe since the birth of the nation-state system in 1648. But the events in 1989 and 1990 tore apart the post-World War II architecture that had been built on the ashes of the classical European balance-of-power system. At issue, therefore, is whether European stability will persist without the restraining effects of a bipolar distribution of power.

In the absence of a clear Soviet threat, the consistency of outlook and singularity of purpose that once bound NATO members together no longer exists. Moreover, growing economic interdependence within what Gorbachev termed the "common European home" has altered the circumstances of European states on both sides of the Cold War divide. In this rapidly changing world, the urge to break the chains of restraint imposed by the Cold War's alliance obligations has become compelling. To many critics NATO and the Warsaw Pact had become obsolete because they institutionalized antagonisms and perpetuated the Cold War. In the early 1990s the need to replace them with a new security arrangement was widely perceived; but collective defense pacts were also still valued as mechanisms to cement relationships and stabilize the rush of cascading events following the collapse of the Soviet Union's external empire in Eastern Europe and the unification of Germany.

President Bush was a vocal advocate of the continuing need to anchor security in alliances, and he sought to restore the faith of U.S. allies in America's commitments. His pledge in 1989 to keep American troops in Europe alleviated

---

6. The discussion that follows draws on Kegley and Raymond (1990a; 1990b).

fears that the United States might, in a fit of isolationist withdrawal, disengage itself from Europe and abandon its allies, and his promise that the United States would remain the backbone of NATO sought to prevent a return by European states to the balance-of-power politics that preceded the outbreak of war in 1870, 1914, and 1939. New thinking in Soviet foreign policy and democratization in a prostrate Soviet state, he argued, would not end the need for deterrence, which would persist even if deep cuts in troops and weapons systems were achieved through arms control negotiations.

Central to the shape of the future is "the German question." According to Lord Ismay, the first Secretary General of NATO, the purpose of the Atlantic alliance was "to keep the Russians out, the Americans in, and the Germans down." Bush's design sought to keep the Soviets out and the Americans in, but it paved the way for a resurgence of German power. However, even though the Soviet Union feared a "Fourth Reich"—a united, powerful, and potentially revisionist German state—the Soviet Union reversed its longstanding opposition to German unification. Still, that concession was not made without conditions: that unification take place within a European-wide framework, and that it be orchestrated through the active management of *all* the major World War II Allies—the Soviet Union, the United States, Britain, and France. As Soviet Foreign Minister Eduard Shevardnadze repeatedly stressed, the involvement of all the great powers was required to manage the transition to a post-Cold War peace.

The Soviet proposal anticipated creation of a new Concert of Europe like that created in the wake of the Napoleonic Wars in 1815. The remnants of NATO and the Warsaw Pact could productively be preserved, some experts (Mueller, 1990) reasoned, if they were merged in a new confederation—that is, if a new Concert of Europe were built *with* Soviet participation and with the intention not to contain enemies, but to control allies. For that, *all* of the countries in Europe would be required to coordinate their defense policies. In other words, it would require that security decisions within the Atlantic alliance be made in conjunction with the European states who do not presently belong to NATO or the Warsaw Pact.

Whether this prescription is an idea whose time has come remains unclear, but it was widely recognized that peace in Europe requires the agreement of the two superpowers about the rules that will govern a post-Cold War European subsystem, much as they had earlier devised informal rules to govern their behavior toward one another (see George, 1983). For those rules to develop, Moscow needed reassurance that a unified Germany in NATO would not threaten Soviet security. In June 1990 Secretary of State James A. Baker provided that assurance, proclaiming that "The way to build peace is to reassure the Central and Eastern Europeans and the Soviets that they will not be left out of the new Europe." Thus the negotiated settlement of the German problem was based on a recognition that sensitivity to the security interests of all was necessary for its success. In October 1990, when the two Germanies formally merged and began preparations for defense according to the rules to which both of the superpowers gave their approval, a new era commenced.

FOCUS 6.1 ▪ Grave New World? An American Policymaker's View of the Changing Face of the International System

We're in the middle of a transition that will be obvious to historians 100 years from now. Unless we recognize what's taking place and reorganize the West to deal with it, the problems of the next 20 years will eat us alive. . . . If it is true that we have emerged victorious from the Cold War, then we, like the Soviets behind us, have crossed the finish line very much out of breath. . . . Both we and the Soviets are faced with a frankly diminished capacity to influence events and promote our respective interests throughout the world on the scale to which we have become accustomed. . . . What we have to understand is that the bi-polar world of the post-war era, in which the U.S. and the Soviet Union dominated world events and set the agenda for their respective alliances, is over. We are now moving into . . . a world in which power and influence is diffused among a multiplicity of states. . . . We can do nothing to alter the fact that we are no longer going to be able to get our way . . . as we once did. . . . The multipolar world into which we are moving [is not] necessarily going to be a safer place. . . . [The democracies must] renew their commitment to a collective and cooperative approach to the major issues [and this] will require American leadership of the highest order.

Deputy Secretary of State Lawrence Eagleburger, 1989

Beyond the question of Germany, the Bush administration offered "the partnership of the United States" in furthering the process of communist reform and retrenchment. "The Cold War began with the division of Europe," Bush declared in 1989. "It can only end when Europe is whole. . . . As President I will continue to do all I can to help open the closed societies of the East." The U.S. posture toward the historic changes sweeping Europe thus began to crystallize, in Secretary of State Baker's words, "toward a new objective: overcoming the division of Europe by making Europe whole and free. We are seeking to bring a new unity to Europe." The U.S. goal appeared "to be nothing short of a 'rollback' of communism in Eastern Europe. But unlike the belligerent policy that bore that name in the 1950s, this rollback would be peaceful, infiltrating Communist territory not with spies or troops but with Western-oriented economic reforms" (McManus, 1989).

With communism no longer a threat and Europe becoming united, complex questions about the role of the United States in the new Europe remained, all the more so since they take place in a sea of uncharted—and perhaps unsafe—waters (see Focus 6.1). A united Europe would create a far more equal distribution of power than that which existed in the bipolycentric system of the 1970s and 1980s and the bipolar system of the 1950s and 1960s that preceded it.[7] The wave of change could inundate the previous relationships on which prolonged great power peace has rested.

A Multipolar System?

A *multipolar system* similar to the classical European balance-of-power system may best describe the distribution of power that is presently emerging. Such a system would include, say, five actors of relatively equal power and, if the historical analogy holds, the equilibrating mechanisms of the system would be grounded in the logic of *realpolitik*, with ideology a distinctly secondary concern. Such a multipolar system might consist of the United States, the Soviet Union, Japan, perhaps China, and either the united Germany or a united Europe as the major actors.

Historical experience suggests that when power is relatively evenly distributed among a cluster of major players, a fluid set of changing relationships typically results. Each player in the game is assertive, independent, and distrustful of the motives of the others; diplomacy displays a rational, nonideological, chesslike character; alliances and alignments are of short duration; and conflict is intense as each contender for preeminence nervously fears the power accumulation of potential challengers and seeks to protect itself from their domination by struggling for its own supremacy. Historically, periods of multipolar balance-of-power politics have typically ended in global war, which resolves the contest by creating a victorious new world leader.[8] It is this history that has led some observers (Gaddis, 1990; Mearsheimer, 1990b) to warn that we will soon miss the stability of the simpler bipolar Cold War era.

In such a fragmented system of contending centers of power, the challenges of diplomacy will demand more of American leaders than in the simpler bipolar and even bipolycentric periods. A multipolar system will be more complex and turbulent and less orderly; power and influence will be more dispersed, and the ability to distinguish friend and foe on various issues will diminish. With uncertainty will come unprecedented obstacles to defining

---

7. With unity, competition would follow. A merged Western Europe would seriously challenge American power. The European Community is already the world's biggest merchant; in 1990 it accounted for almost a third of all world trade. The European Community's plan to create a unified market that could allow the free flow of products and services by 1992 will certainly expand further its ability to compete with the United States. And with economic weight could follow political might, especially if political integration follows economic integration. "The Community of Twelve," French President François Mitterrand pledged in a 1989 summit, could seek "a new type of relationship between the European Community, which is progressing along the road to unity, and the confines of the other Europe which are transforming themselves."

8. These historical patterns have been revealed by a body of scholarship labelled *long cycle* and *hegemonic stability* theories. Exemplary investigations pertinent to the future security and position of the United States include Gilpin (1981), Goldstein (1988), Modelski (1987), and Thompson (1988); for critiques, see Gaddis (1991) and Levy (1991).

national interests as well as new opportunities. As Deputy Secretary of State Eagleburger elaborated:

> We are leaving the atypical period of a bipolar world in which two superpowers reigned supreme, and are returning to a more traditional and complicated time of multipolarity, with a growing number of countries increasingly able to affect the course of events despite the wishes of the superpowers. Japan and the European Community, although still dependent on the United States for their security, wield great economic power, and will be increasingly important in the years to come . . . while the People's Republic of China (PRC) may slowly be moving toward a more market oriented economy that could lead it to a more influential international role early in the next century. . . .
>
> The issue for the West, then, is how well the United States accomplishes the transition from overwhelming predominance to a position more akin to a ''first among equals'' status, and how well America's partners—Japan and Western Europe—adapt to their new found importance. The change will not be easy for any of the players, as such shifts in power relationships have never been easy. . . . The test will be whether, under these new circumstances, we regress to the bad old days of unilateralism, with each nation intent on achieving its narrow objectives.

The dispersion of power toward a multipolar system does not mean that peace and prosperity are necessarily precluded in the global future. But

> as the world becomes more multipolar—with economic leverage and even political-military power being more widely dispersed among nations—it isn't necessarily becoming a safer, gentler globe. And as nations become more interdependent, they aren't necessarily becoming more cooperative.
>
> [There] is every reason to believe that the world of the 1990s will be less predictable and in many ways more unstable than the world of the last several decades. The need, then, is all the greater for a global leader to protect peace and prosperity.
>
> It is rather basic. So long as there were only two great powers, like two big battleships clumsily and cautiously circling each other, confrontations—or accidents—were easier to avoid. Now, with the global lake more crowded with ships of varying sizes, fueled by different ambitions and piloted with different degrees of navigational skill, the odds of collisions become far greater. (House, 1989: A10)

The picture emerging from the foregoing historical survey of changes in the global distribution of power shows that that distribution has undergone substantial change since Hiroshima. A unipolar system gave way to a bipolar system, followed by the emergence of a bipolycentric world, which may subsequently be replaced by a multipolar configuration of four, five, or more centers of power atop a multitude of weak states on their periphery. The fundamental postwar trend has been toward the dispersion of power globally, which has been due to the erosion of American power. The era of U.S. hegemony has ended. The decline of American power relative to others and the dispersion of power worldwide require policy adjustments.

The deterioration of the U.S. position internationally has placed limits on the country's options and also has stimulated different foreign policy orientations toward these changing external realities. The Nixon, Ford, and Carter administrations sought to accommodate the nation to the growing limits of American military and economic power, while also, in the pessimistic view of Henry Kissinger, seeking to retard the pace of America's future decline. The Reagan administration, on the other hand, denied the existence of these circumstances and attempted to alter perceptions and reassert American influence over external affairs through military spending and hawkish diplomacy. The pursuit of regained stature was designed to reverse the trend toward the global diffusion of power and perhaps to regain the privileges of a unipolar past. Whether the effort succeeded, however, remains uncertain; to some observers, the costly commitments may paradoxically have accelerated the pace of America's decline (see Kennedy, 1987; Mead, 1990).[9]

The efficacy of the Bush administration's orientation toward the dilemmas posed by the diffusion of global power and the erosion of America's position will be tested by subsequent events. In wrestling with those fundamental changes, the United States must also contend with the challenge posed by the burgeoning number of less powerful nations. It is to them we now turn.

AN INTERNATIONAL SYSTEM WITH NEW MEMBERS: THE THIRD WORLD

Another conspicuous feature of the international political system is the enormous increase since 1945 in the number of independent nation-states. By 1990 the membership of the United Nations had increased more than threefold over its original fifty-one. For the most part, this expansion was accomplished by the postwar breakup of the vast British, French, Spanish, Dutch, and Portuguese colonial empires that had been created little more than a century ago. Because from today's perspective we tend to think of the international system as populated by sovereign, independent states spread the world over, we may forget both the magnitude and speed of the decolonization process. In the postwar ebbing of the tidal wave of imperialism that swept the world a century ago, nearly a hundred territories today containing nearly three billion people have been freed from colonial rule. Such a spectacular move toward political emancipation is unparalleled in history.

A Snapshot of Third World Economies

The consequence of the proliferation of new states is the rise of the Third World, most of whose members are found in Latin America, Africa, and Asia. They are often referred to collectively as the South to distinguish them from the advanced industrialized societies of the First World, consisting of the United States, Canada, Western Europe, Japan, Australia, and New Zealand, who make

---

9. Evidence for the decline of American hegemony in recent decades and discussions of its meaning can be found in Gilpin (1987) and Kennedy (1987). Contrasting viewpoints are expressed in Huntington (1988–1989), Nau (1990), Nye (1990), Rosecrance (1990), and Strange (1987).

up the North. (The Soviet Union and its erstwhile Eastern European allies comprise the Second World.) The distinction generally categorizes the nations of the world as either rich or poor, and the conflict between North and South came to overlay the East-West cleavage as one of the dominant features of post–World War II international politics.

A legacy of colonialism is a characteristic shared by many of the Southern states at the periphery of the international system. Most also lack the capabilities shared by the superpowers and the other industrialized nations. Indeed, some would even question the appropriateness of the term nation-state to describe many of them, as they fail most tests of the basic attributes of nationhood. In addition to poorly developed political institutions and a high incidence of civil strife, many are particularly lacking in that combination of population size and economic capability traditionally associated with the "powerful." In 1987, for example, the twenty-seven poorest of the less developed countries had an average annual per capita income of only $650, and over half of them had a population of less than ten million (Woods, 1989: 131, 136–137). These might appropriately be thought of as comprising the Fourth World.

The striking reality of the differences between North and South is captured by the fact that the roughly three-quarters of the world's people who live in the South account for 13 percent of its aggregate gross product, whereas those in the North, making up less than one-quarter of the world's population, account for more than 85 percent of its production (see Figures 6.1 and 6.4). This means that the people living in the advanced industrialized societies generally enjoyed income levels (in 1987) seven times greater than those living in the South—and more than twenty times greater than the poorest twenty-seven countries in the South (Woods, 1989: 129).

Clearly these disparities are striking, but because they are averages they mask important differences. Within Third World countries themselves, for example, a tiny fraction of privileged elites often control most of the wealth, while a majority live in comparative poverty.[10] In fact, the number living in *absolute poverty* has been growing. Robert McNamara used that term when he was president of the World Bank to describe "a condition of life so limited by malnutrition, illiteracy, disease, squalid surroundings, high infant mortality, and low life expectancy as to be beneath any reasonable definition of human decency." In the early 1980s the number estimated to be living in absolute poverty ranged between 700 million and 1 billion; by the end of the decade estimates stood at 1.2 billion, or nearly a quarter of humanity (Durning, 1990: 136, 139). "Grotesque" is the way one analyst described how the differences between the world's rich and poor manifest themselves:

> In 1989, the world had 157 billionaires, perhaps 2 million millionaires, and 100 million homeless. Americans spend $5 billion each year on special diets to lower

---

10. See *World Resources 1988–89* (1988: 242–243) for evidence from the period 1970–1986 on income distribution within various Third World countries.

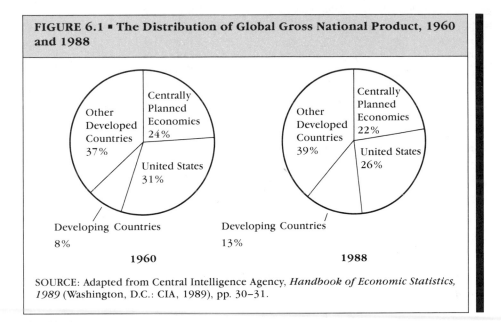

FIGURE 6.1 ▪ The Distribution of Global Gross National Product, 1960 and 1988

SOURCE: Adapted from Central Intelligence Agency, *Handbook of Economic Statistics, 1989* (Washington, D.C.: CIA, 1989), pp. 30–31.

their calorie consumption, while 400 million people around the world are so undernourished their bodies and minds are deteriorating. As water from a single spring in France is bottled and shipped to the prosperous around the globe, nearly 2 billion people drink and bathe in water contaminated with deadly parasites and pathogens. (Durning, 1990: 135)

At the same time that the number living in absolute poverty has grown, the disparities among Third World countries themselves have also widened. The data in Figure 6.1 reveal the interesting fact that developing nations as a whole have increased their share of the global product measurably during the past three decades. But a comparison of economic growth rates among different groups of them indicates widely differing experiences (Figure 6.2). The performance of the nations of East Asia is most striking, as they have consistently demonstrated strong economic performance since the 1960s. Included in the region is a small group known as the *newly industrialized countries* (NICs) consisting of Hong Kong, Singapore, South Korea, and Taiwan[11] who have experienced such remarkable economic growth as to actually narrow the per capita income gap separating them from the world's rich nations.

The experience of East Asia is more the exception than the rule, however. Although the Third World as a whole enjoyed more rapid economic growth than the industrialized nations of the First World during much of the 1960s and 1970s, during the 1980s its fortunes changed as economic conditions in many

---

11. In addition to these, Brazil and Mexico are regarded as NICs, and Spain, Portugal, Yugoslavia, and Greece are sometimes referred to as NICs.

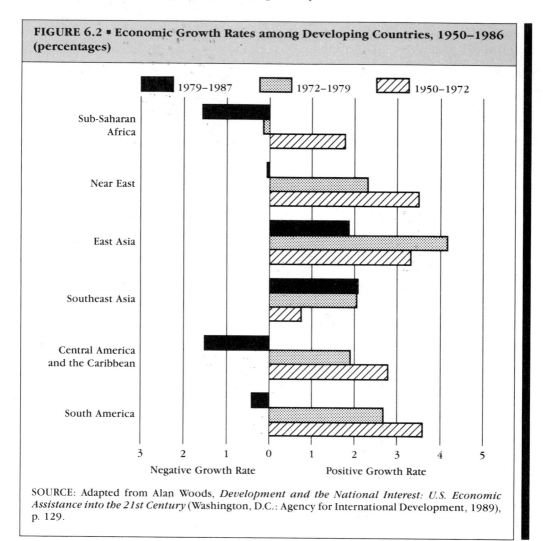

FIGURE 6.2 ▪ Economic Growth Rates among Developing Countries, 1950–1986 (percentages)

SOURCE: Adapted from Alan Woods, *Development and the National Interest: U.S. Economic Assistance into the 21st Century* (Washington, D.C.: Agency for International Development, 1989), p. 129.

developing nations deteriorated rapidly. In Central and South America and especially in Africa, economic growth rates reversed themselves and became "negative" (see Figure 6.2), with the result that living standards actually worsened. "For industrial nations, the decade [of the eighties] was a time of resurgence and recovery after the economic turmoil of the seventies. For the poor, particularly in Africa and Latin America, the eighties were an unmitigated disaster, a time of meager diets and rising death rates" (Durning, 1990). Thus wide disparities exist in the per capita income of different groups of Third World countries, as shown in Figure 6.3, and they have grown more pronounced in the past decade.

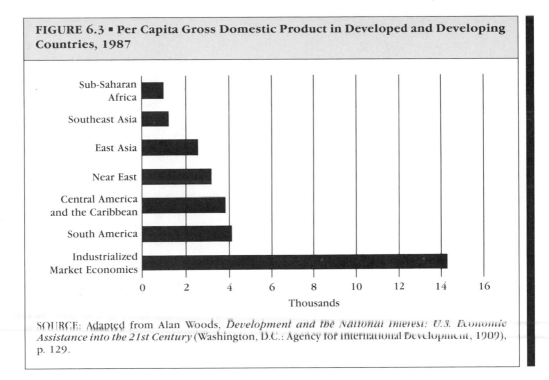

FIGURE 6.3 ■ Per Capita Gross Domestic Product in Developed and Developing Countries, 1987

SOURCE: Adapted from Alan Woods, *Development and the National Interest: U.S. Economic Assistance into the 21st Century* (Washington, D.C.: Agency for International Development, 1989), p. 129.

Figure 6.3 also illustrates how wide the gap is between the world's rich nations and its poor—and that gap has widened, not narrowed. One estimate puts the ratio between incomes in the industrializing societies of Western Europe and the rest of the world in 1850 at roughly two to one (Brown, 1972: 42). By 1950 the gap had opened to ten to one, and by 1960 to nearly fifteen to one. Since 1950 the developed nations have nearly tripled their incomes, but the incomes of those at the periphery have remained largely unchanged (Durning, 1990: 136).

There is no easy explanation of the vastly disparate economic experiences of the world's nations. Differences in history, politics, economics, and culture are intermixed in complex and often poorly understood ways. We will touch on some of these differences and the perceptions that are borne of them in Chapter 7. Here we direct attention to global disparities in population growth as they relate to the economic experiences and potential of developing nations and their consequences for the rest of the world.

Population Growth, Economic Opportunity, and the Global Commons

The rate of population growth worldwide has slowed from about 2 percent per year in the late 1970s to 1.8 percent in 1990, but "the decline has been so gradual that the annual increment grows larger each year. During the 1980s

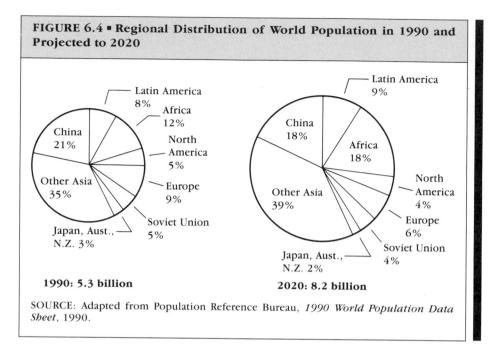

FIGURE 6.4 ▪ Regional Distribution of World Population in 1990 and Projected to 2020

1990: 5.3 billion

China 21%
Other Asia 35%
Japan, Aust., N.Z. 3%
Latin America 8%
Africa 12%
North America 5%
Europe 9%
Soviet Union 5%

2020: 8.2 billion

China 18%
Other Asia 39%
Japan, Aust., N.Z. 2%
Latin America 9%
Africa 18%
North America 4%
Europe 6%
Soviet Union 4%

SOURCE: Adapted from Population Reference Bureau, *1990 World Population Data Sheet*, 1990.

world population increased by 842 million, an average of 84 million each year. During [the 1990s] it is projected to grow by 959 million'' to 6.2 billion (Brown, 1990: 4–5).

Vast differences characterize various world regions, however. The greatest population increases have occurred in developing countries, where the medical and agricultural revolutions have most dramatically affected the incidence of death; population has increased least in the developed countries, where births and deaths have nearly stabilized. Among the developed nations of the North, for example, the rate of natural population increase (births minus deaths) ranges from zero in Denmark to .8 percent in the United States. In the South, on the other hand, the population growth rate ranges from 2.1 percent in Asia and Latin America to an astounding 2.9 percent in Africa (Population Reference Bureau, *1990 World Population Data Sheet*). This means Africa's 661 million people will double in only twenty-four years, growing to 1.48 billion by the year 2020. Figure 6.4 illustrates the differences among the regions of the world today and projects them into the future. It shows that by the year 2020 the nations making up the First and Second Worlds will comprise but 16 percent of the world's population of 8.2 billion people compared with 22 percent of its 1990 population of 5.3 billion; the Third World, on the other hand, will account for nearly 84 percent.

The Domestic Consequences of Population Growth   Although a large population traditionally has been associated with being powerful, for many developing nations today it would appear that their rapidly expanding populations are contributing more to persistent poverty than to the achievement of international prestige and power.[12] Population growth is not the sole cause of poverty and the associated ills of underdevelopment, but it is a major contributing factor that undermines efforts to deal with them and aggravates existing problems.

Hunger is closely associated with poverty and population growth. Nearly two centuries ago the Reverend Thomas Malthus predicted that the world's population would eventually outstrip its capacity to produce enough food to sustain its growing numbers. That has not happened because of tremendous increases in agricultural production, particularly since World War II. Indeed, the growth in food production between 1950 and 1985 was so spectacular that it permitted a 25 percent increase in per capita food supplies and a corresponding increase in meeting minimum nutritional standards (O'Brien, 1988: 395).

The gains from increased food production have not been evenly shared, however. In developed nations, increases in per capita food production since the 1950s have generally moved upward in tandem with increases in total food production, but among developing nations per person food production has generally lagged behind. The difference between total and per capita production of food is what is eaten up in population growth. And in Africa per capita food production has actually declined, as population growth outstripped it during the 1980s. As a result, "more than 5 million infants—one of every five or six children born— . . . died each year in Africa from causes related to hunger" (Ehrlich and Ehrlich, 1990: 80). Moreover, mass hunger often persists even when food supplies are abundant because poor people do not have the money to purchase the food that exists.

A second consequence of rapid population growth is a large number of dependent children relative to the number of working-age adults. This results in a heavy burden on public services, particularly the educational system, and encourages the immediate consumption of economic resources rather than their reinvestment to promote future economic growth. Moreover, as the children mature, the demands for new jobs, housing, and other human needs multiply, but the resources to meet the demands are typically scarce and inadequate.

A number of developing countries, particularly in Asia and Latin America, are now poised for a reduction in their dependency ratios (the number of people under fifteen and over sixty-five). If the experience of Europe, North America, and especially Japan is a guide, this should facilitate the realization of economic gains (Woods, 1989). Ironically, however, the demographic life cycle also portends that the countries that now have the greatest burden of a burgeoning population of young people will also be those with a growing number of older dependents as today's youth grow to maturity and old age fifty years

---

12. See Kegley and Wittkopf (1989: esp. 271–292) for an examination of the causes and consequences of a rapidly expanding world population and of the variations in the population profiles of developed and developing nations.

hence. Demands for social services, particularly expensive health care, will once more multiply.

A third correlate of population growth has been the rapid migration from rural to urban centers. In 1950 less than a third of the world's population lived in cities; by 1990 the proportion had grown to over 40 percent; and by the year 2020 as many as 60 percent will live in urban areas. Urbanization is a global phenomenon, but increasingly the world's largest cities will be in the Third World. London, New York, and Shanghai were the only cities with a population in excess of 10 million people in 1950. By 2000 there will be twenty-three cities of this size or larger, with seven of the top ten in the Third World. In all cases the capacity for effective governance will be taxed severely.

The Transnational Consequences of Population Growth   The social and political stresses associated with population pressures are a prescription for political instability, which frequently spills into the wider international arena (see McNamara, 1984). In the extreme, population pressures and the ever-growing demand for natural resources they generate are often among the contributing factors leading to war (Westing, 1986). Political turmoil and war, in turn, give impetus to international migration by political refugees who move from one country to avoid political persecution or threats to their lives. Others migrate for economic reasons. The United States is a preferred home for many of them, settling each year nearly three-quarters of the estimated 1.1 million international emigrants in search of new homelands (Arnold, 1990: 46). The United States is also the haven for many illegal immigrants (variously estimated to be between 200,000 and 500,000 per year) fleeing their labor-rich, job-poor homes in search of opportunities elsewhere.

Increasingly, many migrants (internal as well as international) can be thought of as "environmental refugees"—people forced to abandon lands no longer fit for human habitation due to environmental degradation. The number is estimated to be at least ten million, which rivals the number traditionally classified as political refugees by various national and international agencies (Jacobson, 1989: 60). Some become environmental refugees due to catastrophic events, such as the explosion of the nuclear power plant at Chernobyl in the Ukraine in 1986; others suffer the consequences of long-term environmental stress, such as excessive land use that results in desertification (a sustained decline in land productivity). Population growth often contributes to such environmental stress.

> Pressed by growing families and deepening poverty, farmers make decisions to increase productivity that, in the long run, prove environmentally and economically disastrous. Cultivating land that should be fallowed, dividing already small plots among family members, bearing numerous children to help with farm chores, cutting ever-scarcer trees for fuel and fodder are all practices that, while they may ensure a meager harvest for tomorrow, make certain that famine is inevitable. (Jacobson, 1989: 61)

Deforestation often accompanies desertification and soil erosion, and the evidence points toward rapid deforestation worldwide (*World Resources 1988–89*, 1988). The destruction of tropical rain forests to make room for farms and ranches, as in the Amazon basin of Brazil and in Indonesia, is a matter of growing international concern, as it contributes markedly to global warming through the "greenhouse" effect. Global warming occurs when carbon dioxide (CO_2) and other gas molecules trap heat that would otherwise be remitted from earth back to the atmosphere. Carbon dioxide is routinely removed from the atmosphere by green plants during photosynthesis. When forests are cut down, the natural processes that remove greenhouse gases are destroyed, and, as the forests decay or are burned, they increase the amount of CO_2 discharged into the atmosphere. This makes deforestation doubly destructive. Yet many governments have failed to stop destruction of forests, which are being depleted at an alarming rate: an area the size of Austria is deforested every year (Mathews, 1989: 165).

Although deforestation contributes heavily to the greenhouse process, the burning of fossil fuels is an even greater culprit, and here it is the advanced industrial societies of the North, not the developing societies of the South, who are primarily at fault, since they consume over 70 percent of the world's energy. Interestingly, however, the greatest increases in the *rate* of energy consumption are now occurring in the South. This also means that the greatest increases in atmospheric pollution due to fossil-fuel combustion will result from Third World policies and economic achievements. If, for example, China were to increase its per capita gross national product to just 15 percent of the U.S. level, it "would have to burn so much fossil fuel that the increase in CO_2 emissions would equal the total CO_2 released from all the coal currently consumed by the United States" (Owen, 1989: 40).

Even without economic growth, the expected doubling of the world's population by the middle of the next century (which will take place almost exclusively in the Third World) will require a tremendous increase in fossil-fuel consumption just to maintain living standards at their current levels. Thus as demographic patterns already in place unfold in the decades ahead, disruptions of the world's climate and delicate ecosystems will continue and probably accelerate. This makes achieving zero population growth worldwide, as has already occurred in much of the North, not a Southern problem but a pressing global one.[13]

The Foreign Policy Strategies of the South

In addition to the factors we have already described, other circumstances common to many if not all Third World nations include (1) economic "dualism" (a rural, impoverished, neglected sector alongside an urban, developing, and

---

13. Against this background it is noteworthy that during the Reagan administration the United States withdrew its funding for the United Nations Fund for Population Activities and that the Bush administration adopted a go-slow approach toward international efforts designed to slow the process of global warming.

modernizing sector); (2) adverse terms of trade due to export concentration on primary products (such as foodstuffs and other basic commodities) and import reliance on relatively more expensive manufactured goods; (3) massive indebtedness, both public and private, often accompanied by runaway inflation; (4) dependence on the economic assistance, trade, loans, technology, security protection, and arms supplied by states from the First and Second Worlds; and (5) penetration by alien cultures and by the omnipresent multinational corporations headquartered in the First World and the international financial institutions these nations control.

These are, understandably, national circumstances Third World leaders do not accept willingly. Not surprisingly, therefore, they have pursued foreign policy strategies that, on the one hand, express a basic dissatisfaction with the existing international system but that also, on the other, demonstrate a pragmatic accommodation to the fundamental character of the exiting international order. Three Third World strategies warrant comment: (1) a drive to reform the global political economy; (2) a determination to steer clear of Cold War political alignments; and (3) a conviction that the acquisition of modern military capabilities is prudent policy.

The New International Economic Order   Third World efforts to reform the global political economy have been pursued in a variety of ways, but none was more visibly nor more vigorously pushed than their drive for a New International Economic Order (NIEO). This became a rallying cry of developing nations during the 1970s as they sought a North-South dialogue on a range of pressing politico-economic issues. The demands for a new order challenged the ''global liberalism'' philosophy championed by the United States in the postwar era. The politics of resentment, of challenge, of attack on the status quo by the Third World was an outgrowth of the perpetuation of a global political economy marked by gross disparities between the rich and the poor. ''Structural conflict'' (Krasner, 1985) between North and South was the consequence.

We will examine the demands embraced by the NIEO and additional reasons underlying them in Chapter 7. Here we can summarize them simply by noting that the net effect of restructuring the existing economic order along the lines once envisaged by the NIEO would have been to direct substantial amounts of the world's wealth away from those who now have it to those who do not. Not surprisingly, therefore, the First World rebuffed the Third World's efforts at reform, and the North-South dialogue gradually degenerated into a dialogue of the deaf.

Nonalignment   A foreign policy strategy of *nonalignment* as it relates to the Cold War competition between the United States and the Soviet Union is one expression of the pragmatic accommodation of Third World nations to the existing international order in the politico-security area. Third World nations could not materially affect the outcome of the Cold War, so they sought a strategy that maximized their own gains while minimizing their costs. The strategy—as preached with firebrand language at the nine summits convened between 1961 and 1989—stimulated keen efforts by the United States and the Soviet Union to woo the uncommitted to its own side while preventing their alignment with the other. In effect, nonalignment enabled developing nations to play one superpower off against the other in order to gain advantage for themselves, while the Cold War competitors, in keeping with the sensitivity each manifested toward the other in the context of the bipolar distribution of power and what was perceived as a zero-sum contest, were willing players in the game.

Foreign aid was a favored instrument used by the United States to prevent defection of the nonaligned to "the other side."[14] As noted in Chapter 5, total U.S. foreign economic and military aid and sales in the period from the end of World War II until the late 1980s stood at nearly $500 billion. The motivations behind these vast sums were not always without regard for the welfare of the recipients, but security concerns and an overriding emphasis on containment of communism were the principal driving forces.

The value of Soviet and Soviet-bloc aid has never rivaled that of the United States, and much of what has been committed has apparently never actually been drawn on by recipient nations. The Central Intelligence Agency (CIA) estimates that total economic aid extended by the Soviet Union to developing nations in the period from 1954 through 1988 was $47.4 billion, of which $20.7 was actually drawn. Eastern Europe and China added another $27.5 billion, of which roughly three-fifths was drawn. The CIA also estimates that communist arms transfers (deliveries) during this same period totaled $243.3 billion, of which 85 percent came from the Soviet Union (*Handbook of Economic Statistics, 1989*, 1989: 174). Still, like the United States, the historic pattern of Soviet bloc aid follows the path of its strategic and geopolitical interests as manifested in other ways, with much of it concentrated in the Middle East and South Asia and with smaller portions going to several African states and a few in the Western Hemisphere (notably Nicaragua).

It should be added that the other nations making up the First World, and also the members of the Organization of Petroleum Exporting Countries (OPEC), are now major contributors of foreign aid to developing nations as well. Their motivations, too, are understandably political and sometimes geared to geostrategic considerations, although in many cases commercial interests and humanitarian concerns figure prominently. Saudi Arabia is the principal donor among OPEC nations, whose total allocations, however, declined markedly as oil prices plummeted during the 1980s—from $9.6 billion in 1980 to only $3.3 billion in 1987 (*World Development Report 1989*, 1989: 201). Among the Western

---

14. The use of foreign aid for political purposes is often perceived as a costly game, but objectively it is not. In absolute terms the United States is the largest foreign aid donor in the world, but in 1986 it spent more than twice as much on tobacco products and nearly four times as much on alcoholic beverages as it did on economic and military aid combined (Sewell and Tucker, 1988: 242).

aid donors, France, West Germany, and Japan figure most prominently. Together they accounted for more than half of the $32.3 billion in official development assistance extended in 1987 by members of the Organization for Economic Cooperation and Development (other than the United States, which gave $8.9 billion) (*World Development Report 1989*, 1989: 200). Here the notable trend is the substantial increase in Japanese foreign aid, which doubled from $3.4 billion in 1983 to $7.5 billion in 1987. The Japanese have committed themselves to further foreign aid increases in the years ahead.

What these data demonstrate is that foreign aid is a common instrument of economic statecraft in contemporary world politics. Nonalignment may have paid dividends for a time, but with the demise of Soviet-American competition "the [nonaligned nations] are facing an identity problem now that they don't really have anybody to be nonaligned with, and the enemy is more likely to be [its] neighbor than a superpower" (Lewis, 1989). Simultaneously, the largesse once used to woo the nonaligned may go elsewhere. As expressed by Prime Minister Mahathir bin Mohamad of Malaysia at the opening of a meeting of fifteen developing-nation representatives of the nonaligned movement in June 1990, Third World nations "have reasons to worry" that the foreign aid and loans once sent by Western nations to developing nations will be redirected toward Eastern Europe (see also Chapters 5 and 12). He also wondered about what would happen to the Third World now that the East and West have begun to put aside their historic antagonisms; would the superpowers present the Third World with a united East-West front to replace the divisions that once allowed the nonaligned nations to play the superpowers off against one another? If so, the Third World risked being "marginalized," that is, ignored (Lyon, 1989; Bissell, 1990).

If Third World nations enjoyed certain benefits as a consequence of Soviet and American efforts to win their allegiance during the Cold War, there were also costs. Frequently they were the battleground on which the superpowers' covert activities, paramilitary operations, and proxy wars were played out. CIA Director William Casey explained the logic leading to interference in the internal affairs of Third World countries when he declared in 1983, "The less developed nations of the world will be the principal U.S.-Soviet battleground for many years to come." If the Soviet Union continues to disengage from support of "wars of national liberation" and otherwise retreat from competition with the United States for Third World allies, then it may be possible to lay the "battleground" conception of the Third World aside. There are reasons to be cautious, however, not least of which is the widespread belief in the United States in the competence of the CIA as an instrument of American foreign policy: "President after president has turned to the CIA precisely because it could get the job done" (Treverton, 1987). Moreover, the Bush administration has continued to support the proxy wars in Afghanistan, Angola, Cambodia, and El Salvador that it inherited from the Carter and Reagan administrations, and it has sought money for the Defense Department that would enhance the ability of the United States to intervene in the Third World, as it did in Panama (Van Evera, 1990).

The historical record on the nature and location of conflict situations since World War II is another reason to be cautious. Almost all civil wars in the post-1945 era have occurred in the Third World, where the number of casualties has run into the tens of millions (Singer, 1991), and in many of them—as in Afghanistan, Angola, Cambodia, and El Salvador—the superpowers themselves have typically become involved in one way or another. Furthermore, of the more than 125 interstate conflicts that have occurred since World War II, all but 2 (in Hungary and the Sino-Soviet border area) have been in the Third World (Sivard, 1989: 23).

The Search for Military Might   The probability that Third World nations will become involved in either domestic or foreign conflict has given them incentives to join the rest of the world in its quest to acquire modern weapons of war. The increasing commitment to the armaments game worldwide is illustrated by the increase in global armament expenditures from about $10 billion at the turn of the century to $1 trillion annually by 1987. The United States and Soviet Union together with their NATO and Warsaw partners continue to account for the bulk of the world's military expenditures. But efforts by Third World leaders to enhance their military capabilities have become one of the most striking manifestations of their intense nationalism, their often equally intense determination to steer an independent course in world politics, and their desire to protect themselves from internal insurrection and foreign attack. As shown in Table 6.1, the expenditures that otherwise resource-poor nations devote to military purposes are substantial and frequently far outstrip public expenditures on education and health. Indeed, the burden of military spending, as measured by the ratio of military expenditures to GNP, bears little relationship to the level of development.[15] More relevant is whether a state is embroiled in a war or is threatened by ethnic, religious, or tribal strife at home.

Most Third World nations acquire their weapons from foreign suppliers. During the 1980s a number of Third World nations developed arms export industries of their own, including, most important, Brazil and China, but also Argentina, Egypt, India, Israel, and North and South Korea. "All the new producers offer reliable, no-nonsense weapons at prices way below those charged by traditional suppliers. And, unlike the usual sellers, the newcomers rarely look for political favors from recipients, such as access to military bases

---

15. As in the advanced industrial societies of the North, military expenditures by Third World countries are sometimes justified on grounds that they promote economic growth. According to this view, "military spending can have positive spinoff effects, such as fostering technological innovation, training personnel who later move into civilian work, providing employment opportunities, building domestic institutions, stimulating a country's tax effort, and promoting more intensive use of existing resources. Furthermore, military industries can be a focus of industrialization activities" (*World Development Report 1988*, 1988). On the other hand, "these positive effects appear to be more than offset by the long-term negative impact of military spending.... The most basic criticism is the high opportunity cost of military spending, that is, the diversion of scarce resources from more productive civilian uses.... Moreover, defense spending often has a high import content.... Payment for such imports can add considerably to balance of payments problems and to the debt burden" (*World Development Report 1988*, 1988).

TABLE 6.1 ▪ Relative Burden of Military Expenditures—1987

ME/GNP*	*GNP PER CAPITA (1987 dollars)*		
(%)	*Under $200*	*$200–499*	*$500–999*
10% and over	Vietnam Cambodia† Laos†	Yemen (Aden)† Afghanistan† Guyana†	Cape Verde† Yemen (Sanaa) Morocco Albania
5–9.99%	Ethiopia Mozambique	Zambia† Pakistan	Zimbabwe El Salvador Thailand Honduras Bolivia Ecuador Botswana Senegal
2–4.99%	Tanzania† Guinea-Bissau Burkina Faso Somalia† Madagascar	China Mauritania India Liberia Chad Togo Sri Lanka Burundi Burma Sudan Mali Kenya Equat. Guinea† Lesotho Benin† Indonesia Can. Afr. Rep.† Rwanda	Ivory Coast Guatemala Papua N. Guin.† Dominican Rep. Swaziland Philippines Jamaica
1–1.99%	Zaire† Bangladesh Malawi The Gambia† Nepal	Haiti Guinea† Uganda†	
Under 1%		Ghana Sao Tome & Prin. Niger† Nigeria Sierra Leone†	

*Countries are listed in descending order of ME/GNP. †Ranking is based on a rough approximation of one or more variables for which 1987 data or reliable estimates are not available.

ME/GNP* (%)	GNP PER CAPITA (1987 dollars)		
	$1,000–2,999	$3,000–9,999	$10,000 and over
10% and over	North Korea Jordan Syria Angola† Mongolia†	Oman Iraq† Israel Saudi Arabia Soviet Union Libya Nicaragua† Bulgaria	Qatar†
5–9.99%	Egypt Lebanon† Cuba† Gabon†	Iran Poland Czechoslovakia Greece Romania Hungary Singapore†	East Germany Un. Arab Emir.† United States Kuwait
2–4.99%	Peru South Korea Congo Turkey South Africa Chile Venezuela Malaysia Tunisia Algeria Suriname Yugoslavia Panama	Taiwan Bahrain Portugal Trinidad & Tob.† Spain	United Kingdom France Norway Netherlands West Germany Belgium Sweden Australia Italy New Zealand Canada Denmark Switzerland
1–1.99%	Cameroon Uruguay† Argentina Fiji† Colombia Paraguay	Ireland† Malta	Finland† Austria Japan
Under 1%	Brazil Costa Rica Mexico Mauritius	Cyprus Barbados†	Luxembourg Iceland

Source: U.S. Arms Control and Disarmament Agency. *World Military Expenditures and Arms Transfers 1988* (Washington, D.C.: U.S. Government Printing Office, 1989), p. 14.

or support for covert paramilitary activities'' (Klare, 1990b). Still, the traditional suppliers, namely, the United States and the Soviet Union and their allies, remain the most important arms exporters, and the Middle East remains the most important recipient region, as illustrated in Figure 6.5.

The arms that enter the global marketplace are increasingly the most sophisticated in the world—and their numbers are staggering.

> Between 1981 and 1988, developing countries spent $345.6 billion (in 1988 dollars) to acquire over 37,000 surface-to-air missiles, 20,000 artillery pieces, 11,000 tanks and self-propelled howitzers, 3,100 supersonic fighter planes, and 540 warships and submarines. . . .
>
> To counter the growing incidence of ethnic conflict and guerrilla insurgency, Third World nations have also ordered vast quantities of small arms, infantry weapons, off-road vehicles, and police hardware. These "low-intensity" wars rarely produce major battles of the sort witnessed in the Persian Gulf [between Iraq and Iran], but they have nevertheless killed hundreds of thousands—perhaps millions—of people in Latin America, Southeast Asia, sub-Saharan Africa, Lebanon, Afghanistan, and the Philippines. Continuing economic problems will only worsen the social tensions that give rise to such conflicts in the [1990s]. (Klare, 1990b: 44–45)

Of special concern to many analysts is the growing number of sophisticated ballistic missiles now in the hands of Third World countries. "Nations that possess ballistic missiles can fire large, destructive warheads deep into one another's territory with assurance that defenses have little likelihood of stopping an attack," the U.S. Arms Control and Disarmament Agency (1989) has noted. "The very presence of these weapons in conflict prone regions of the world aggravates instability." Ironically, these developments come at the same time that the United States and the Soviet Union have negotiated a treaty for the removal of intermediate-range missiles from Europe and have sought to reduce their own stockpile of strategic weapons (those with ranges of three thousand miles or more). There is also concern about stemming the flow of sensitive technology to Third World countries (also coming at a time when Western barriers to the transfer of military-sensitive technology to the Soviet Union are being rapidly dismantled) that might permit Third World countries to develop longer-range missiles and chemical and nuclear weapons.

Already, a number of Third World countries are capable of producing chemical weapons, including Iran, Iraq, Libya, Syria, China, North and South Korea, Taiwan, and perhaps Israel and Egypt (Pine, 1990). The new government of Czechoslovakia also revealed that during the years of Soviet domination, Czechoslovakia provided Libya with a forty-year supply of Semtex, a plastic explosive nearly impossible to detect that was used to blow up Pan American flight 103 over Lockerbie, Scotland, in 1988. Finally, although most Third World nations are signatories of the Nuclear Nonproliferation Treaty, which prevents the transfer of nuclear weapons and nuclear weapons technologies to nonnuclear states, several recalcitrants remain outside the nonproliferation

FIGURE 6.5 ▪ Value of Arms Transfers, Cumulative 1983–1987

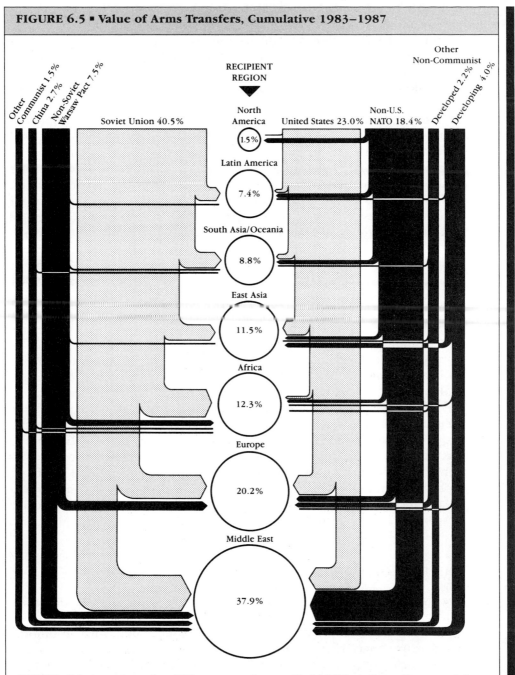

SOURCE: U.S. Arms Control and Disarmament Agency, *World Military Expenditures and Arms Transfers 1988* (Washington, D.C.: U.S. Arms Control and Disarmament Agency, 1989), p. 9.

regime. When the treaty comes up for renewal in 1995, others may deem it wise to join those who remain outside the regime, especially since the treaty is the preeminent example of a multilateral arms control measure that many Third World leaders view as "inherently discriminatory" because it allows "weapons to the North that they deny to the South" (Klare, 1990a).

Another factor that will make it difficult to stem the flow of sophisticated arms to Third World countries through formal arms control agreements is the "colonial legacy," which makes many of them "reluctant to forgo options—such as chemical weapon production and missile delivery systems—that could be useful in resisting future pressure or actual attacks by the developed world." Finally, "the military imbalances that characterize many Third World antagonisms, for example, Israel versus its Arab neighbors, have prompted the weaker and more vulnerable countries to expend much greater resources per capita on armaments. These countries can be expected to resist arms control agreements that would institutionalize their military inferiority or require reductions in the armaments they acquired through economic sacrifice. The more powerful nations, on the other hand, are likely to resist agreements that would appear to create parity between themselves and a less powerful rival" (Klare, 1990a). Meanwhile, the arms exporting countries of the North have their own political and economic incentives to continue selling the weapons of modern warfare to the South, even as they become wary of the growing military might and technological sophistication of many Third World countries.

As the foregoing attests, the rise of a new class of state actors at once poorly developed economically but with a growing capability to engage in prolonged, highly destructive warfare has presented new problems for American foreign policy and has led, almost inevitably, to adaptations in the kinds of policies the United States has pursued abroad. Indeed, many of the doctrinal and behavioral shifts in postwar American foreign policy described not only in this chapter but also in preceding ones have been linked closely to the alteration of the composition of the international *political* system. And it is highly probable that future adaptations in American foreign policy will continue to be linked closely to the changed and changing international *economic* system, as we will show in the next chapter.

THE RISE OF NONSTATE ACTORS

The growth in the number of nation-states and the dispersion of economic and military capabilities among them are twin features of the external environment that have altered the options open to American foreign policymakers. Another noteworthy characteristic of the postwar period is the growth in the number of international institutions and other types of nonstate actors, of which international organizations and multinational corporations are the most ubiquitous. To these must be added another prominent but less benign type: international terrorist groups.

With the obvious exception of terrorists, nonstate actors have provided both forums for international contact and the glue of interdependence. In this sense they are the extragovernmental agents of *international regimes.* "Regimes can be defined as sets of implicit or explicit principles, norms, rules, and decision-making procedures around which actors' expectations converge in a given issue area of international relations" (Krasner, 1982). They are important in understanding the regularized patterns of collaborative and cooperative behavior in international politics. The international political system may appear anarchical, which is a central concept underlying the logic of political realism, but it is nonetheless an ordered anarchy. Regimes help explain that apparent anomaly.

The global monetary and trade systems created during and after World War II are clear examples of international regimes. Both evolved under the leadership of the United States, the hegemonic power in the postwar political economy, and together the two regimes defined the Liberal International Economic Order (LIEO) embracing a combination of principles, rules, norms, and decision-making procedures that limited government intervention in the international economy and otherwise facilitated the free flow of capital and goods across national boundaries. The International Monetary Fund (IMF) and the General Agreement on Tariffs and Trade (GATT) played important institutional roles in the LIEO, but it was the overriding power of the United States that ensured stability and effective operation of the monetary and trade regimes (see Chapter 7 for elaboration). But as American hegemony declined, as was especially apparent during the 1970s, the continuing operation of the trade and monetary regimes helped to preserve order, although the shape of the regimes themselves became a contentious political issue.

Agents of International Interdependence

International Organizations   The IMF and GATT are two of the specialized agencies of the United Nations, which itself is a multiple purpose international organization embracing a broad array of organizations, commissions, institutes, and the like. The distinguishing characteristic of the United Nations family of organizations is that governments are their members. Hence they are known as international intergovernmental organizations (IGOs). There are over three hundred IGOs in existence, and their concerns embrace the entire range of political, economic, social, and cultural affairs that are the responsibilities of modern governments.

In addition to IGOs, more than forty-two hundred international nongovernmental organizations (INGOs) are also in existence (*Yearbook of International Organizations, 1987/88,* 1987: vol. 1, app. 7). The members of these international organizations, such as the International Red Cross, are individuals or societal groups, not governments. INGOs also deal with the entire panoply of transnational activities, and it is useful to think of them as intersocietal organizations that help facilitate the achievement and maintenance of agreements among countries regarding elements of international public policy (Jacobson, 1984). Rule making regarding security at international airports and the treatment of hijackers would not be possible without the cooperation of the International Federation of Air Line Pilots Associations, for instance. As a consequence, INGOs, in turn, have an influence on what those rules are. It is noteworthy in this respect that the greatest growth of INGOs has been among those involved in activities of direct concern to governments—namely, the economy, industry, commerce, finance, the ecology, and technology—and not among those concerned with essentially noneconomic matters, such as sports and religious affairs. And INGOs, we may hypothesize, exert their greatest impact in advanced industrial societies with pluralistic orientations, such as the United States, since those societies are most likely to involve interest groups in the policy-making process. Thus INGOs illustrate how the activities and influence of nonstate transnational actors help to blur the distinction between domestic and foreign policy issues.

INGOs and IGOs alike mirror the same elements of conflict and cooperation that characterize international politics generally. Accordingly, not all are appropriately conceived as agents of interdependence. NATO, for example, is a collective security arrangement; although an international organization, it depends for its existence (at least historically) on the continuing presence of a credible adversary. The cooperation that exists among its members is to a large extent attributable to shared hostility toward its nonmembers. Regional collective security organizations, such as the Organization of American States (OAS), often exhibit similar elements.

The United States was a primary mover behind the creation of NATO, the OAS, the United Nations (UN) and its specialized agencies, and numerous other of the multitude of international institutions now in existence. They became an expression of the international ethos that promoted America's global activism in the postwar era. But as the nature of the international system and of the role of the United States within it has changed, so have American attitudes. That is nowhere more apparent than in the attitudes of the United States toward the United Nations.

American idealism was a motivating force behind creation of the United Nations during the waning days of World War II, with the result that the world organization was shaped by American values and molded after its own political institutions. Almost immediately, however, the Cold War competition between the United States and the Soviet Union began to be mirrored in the United Nations. Thus the United States sought—with considerable success—to utilize its own position as the leader of the dominant Western majority in the UN to pursue its own foreign policy objectives vis-à-vis the Soviet Union. That became more difficult with the passage of time, however, especially as the decolonization process unfolded and the United States found itself on the defensive along with its European allies—most of which had been colonial powers—in the face of a hostile Third World coalition with whom the Soviet bloc typically aligned. In 1975 that coalition succeeded in passing a General Assembly resolution over vigorous U.S. protest that branded Zionism "a form of racism and racial discrimination." The vote outraged the U.S. ambassador to the United Nations at the time, Daniel P. Moynihan, who lashed out vehemently against "the tyranny of the UN's 'new majority.'"

In the years that followed, U.S. attitudes toward the United Nations and many of its affiliated organizations ranged from circumspection to outright hostility. The Carter administration withdrew from the International Labor Organization (ILO) in protest of what it regarded as the organization's anti-Western bias; the Reagan administration followed by withdrawing from the United Nations Educational, Scientific, and Cultural Organization (UNESCO). Disenchantment with multilateralism was also reflected in the Reagan administration's indifference to and attack on the World Court and by its decision to selectively withhold funds for various UN activities, a tactic it had long decried when the Soviet Union chose it to protest UN policies and operations its leaders found inimical to their interests. The United States also became wary of turning to the United Nations to cope with various regional conflict situations, as it had previously.

By the end of the Reagan administration, the once prevalent retreat from multilateralism, often accompanied by a preference for a unilateral, go-it-alone posture toward global issues, began to wane. The decision of the Soviet Union under Gorbachev's leadership to pay its own overdue UN bills and in the wake of its misadventure in Afghanistan to turn (or return) to the UN Security Council to deal with conflict situations, in a manner reminiscent of what the UN's founders had intended, helped to stimulate the reassessment of U.S. policy toward the United Nations. In response, the Reagan administration committed the United States to payment of the money due the UN that it had previously withheld (although the Bush administration found that Congress was reluctant to make good on that pledge).

The warming of superpower attitudes toward the United Nations was given impetus by the growing ability of the world organization to resolve international conflicts. Secretary General Javier Perez de Cueller was credited with brokering an end to the eight-year Iran-Iraq war and the withdrawal of Soviet troops from Afghanistan, and the UN successfully supervised Nicaragua's first free elections as well as those in Namiba. Then, in the wake of Iraq's brutal invasion of Kuwait, it was through the United Nations Security Council that the world community organized a trade embargo against the renegade Iraqi dictator Saddam Hussein and authorized the use of force to enforce it. (This achievement occurred, of course, because the superpowers acted in concert rather than, as had been their custom throughout the Cold War, using their power to veto any action that might benefit their adversary.) As the concept of collective security, which had been the original purpose of the United Nations, was revived through joint U.S.-Soviet action, the UN was freed from paralysis and began to emerge as a peacekeeping force—a development that served American interests and purposes in these cases. Accordingly, U.S. leaders voiced enthusiastic support for the organization they had so harshly condemned in the 1970s and 1980s. Although the Bush administration continued to harbor resentment for the manner in which many Third World nations used the UN as a platform to assail the United States, it found in the world organization a valued instrument with which it could pursue its foreign policy objectives. This represented a radical departure from the attitude American policymakers had held for many years.

Multinational Corporations   Since World War II, multinational corporations (MNCs, business enterprises organized in one society with activities abroad growing out of direct investment, as opposed to portfolio investment through shareholding) have grown enormously in size and influence, thereby changing dramatically patterns of global investment, production, and marketing. In the early 1980s, for example, worldwide about eighteen hundred MNCs controlled assets in two or more countries, and these were estimated to be responsible for marketing roughly four-fifths of the world's trade (excluding that of the Second World) (Clairmonte and Cavanagh, 1982: 149, 152). Moreover, a comparison of nations and MNCs according to the size of their gross economic product shows that over forty of the world's top one hundred economic entities (in 1985) are multinational corporations. Among the top fifty entities, multinationals account for only nine, but in the next fifty they account for thirty-two (Kegley and Wittkopf, 1989: 164–165).

Third World countries have spawned some multinational corporations, but most of them are headquartered in the First World, where the great majority of their activities originate. If the source of foreign direct investment is used as a measure, it is apparent that practically all activity stems from developed market economies, which also absorb more than three-quarters of all investment flows (Commission on Transnational Corporations, 1986: 5). The developing nations' share of direct investment grew in the 1970s, but it plummeted during the debt crisis of the 1980s (see Chapter 7).

Historically, the United States has been the home country for the largest proportion of multinational parent companies, followed by Great Britain and West Germany. Since the 1970s, however, the outward stocks and flows of foreign direct investment from the United States have declined steadily, while the shares of Canada, Japan, Switzerland, and West Germany have grown. On the other hand, the United States received a dramatically increasing proportion of all foreign direct investment in the 1980s compared with previous decades (Centre on Transnational Corporations, 1987). It has taken the form of acquisitions by European and Canadian firms already established in the U.S. market, and of the building of new production facilities by Japan (a trade-replacing form of foreign direct investment) in an effort to establish itself in a market in which it had little previous presence. Japanese investments in banking and real estate, such as hotels and office buildings, have also been substantial (see also Chapter 7).

A related major recent development in the global pattern of foreign direct investment is the emergence of Japan as a major home country. The outward flow of Japanese foreign direct investment increased nearly fourfold between 1975 and 1985, moving from $3.3 billion to $12.2 billion during that period (Centre on Transnational Corporations, 1987: 9). A primary motivation, as noted, has been penetration of the U.S. market. Western Europe has also been the target of Japanese investments, and for similar reasons. Together, Western Europe and North America accounted for three-fifths of Japanese foreign direct investment in 1985 (Centre on Transnational Corporations, 1987: 9). Developing nations accounted for most of the rest. Historically, Japan has invested in Third World nations to secure access to critical raw materials and to take advantage of lower labor costs in developing countries. Japanese transnational banks have also emerged as among the largest in the world.

Although most MNCs are headquartered in the North, they pose little direct threat to the economies or the policy-making institutions in these large, complex societies. Not so in the case of the Third World, where the economic power and reach of multinational firms—typically American—to some extent have enabled them to become a global extension of First World societies, serving as an engine for the transfer of investment, technology, and managerial skills across national boundaries. Although such transfers may prove to be beneficial, Third World countries are also wary of the costs that the economic giants can also impose on host countries. From their perspective, both debits and credits accrue to the impact that MNCs exert on their welfare.

Critics argue, for example, that the Third World has become dependent on technology imported via MNCs from the industrial world, even though that technology may be inappropriate to the local setting and inhibit the development of local technological expertise. A variant of that theme sees the MNC as a vehicle for the export of Western materialistic values and hence an agent of "cultural imperialism." In addition, because MNCs seek to maximize profits, which are then repatriated to shareholders in the industrial world, they may retard rather than promote the economic growth of Third World countries by depriving them of much needed capital. Still another allegation is that multinational firms sometimes engage in unsavory political practices in host countries, although more often they are likely to lobby their governments for policies and programs favorable to their own private interests, as profit is their primary motive, not the alleviation of poverty or the promotion of the interests of a particular state (see Barnet and Müller, 1974).

Perhaps the most notorious instance of a multinational's intervention in the politics of a host state occurred in Chile in the early 1970s. There, International Telephone and Telegraph (ITT) sought to protect its interests in the profitable Chiltelco telephone company by seeking to prevent Marxist-oriented Salvador Allende from being elected president and subsequently by seeking his overthrow. ITT's efforts to undermine Allende included giving monetary support to his political opponents and, once Allende was elected, attempting to induce the American government to launch a program designed to disrupt the Chilean economy (see also Chapter 5).

There are other instances in which MNCs engage in practices that may be embarrassing to home countries—as when the West Germany government found that a German firm had sold mustard-gas manufacturing equipment to Libya—or that seem to defy them—as when the French subsidiary of Dresser Industries of Dallas, Texas, exported energy technology to the Soviet Union in defiance of the Reagan administration. Ultimately, behavior such as this and the ITT case raise the question of whether multinational corporations are beyond the control of governments. In practice, the question has been more salient among developing countries, and most of the efforts at control have evolved nationally rather than internationally (see Spero, 1990). Meanwhile, some corporate visionaries see national borders disappearing as multinational corporations serve a world-class consumer. "There are no longer any national flag carriers," in the words of Kenichi Ohmae, a prominent Japanese management consultant. "Corporations must serve their customers, not governments."

A variant of this view sees a world more secure against war and invasion because of economic interdependence. "If the Japanese enjoy a growing ownership of American assets," according to this logic, "they have a stake in the health of the American economy. A new generation of warlords in Japan, should they ever emerge, would find it harder to sell the idea of bombing Pearl Harbor now that the Japanese own many hotels and office buildings there" (Rowen and Allen, 1989).

International Regimes   During the 1960s and 1970s in particular, multinational corporations became the object of considerable discussion and animosity because of their size and "global reach" (Barnet and Müller, 1974), but today "their existence has become a fact of life. They are now permanent—and influential—players in the international arena" (Spero, 1990). Indeed, it is inconceivable to think how international economics might function without them, just as it is inconceivable to think that international commerce or other forms of interaction could occur in the absence of rules made by governmental bodies. Thus states and nonstate actors coalesce to form regimes that facilitate cooperative international relations. The global oil regime consists of a number of governments and an international organization, OPEC, which attempts to set price and production levels of oil traded in the global marketplace, and multinational corporations, which play a critical role in the actual mining and marketing of the resource. Similarly, the global food regime depends on multinational corporations for marketing and distributing grain worldwide under rules of commerce set by national governments and international agencies (although these rules are less well defined than for industrial products, as we will note in Chapter 7).[16]

---

16. Historically, the most important multinational corporations involved in the oil market were British Petroleum, Exxon, Gulf, Mobil, Royal Dutch Shell, Standard Oil of California, and Texaco, which were often called the "seven sisters" (see Sampson, 1975). The comparable "merchants of grain" (Morgan, 1979) were Cargill, Continental, Louis Dreyfus, Bunge, and André.

These examples suggest that we can think of nonstate actors as helping to build and broaden the foreign policy agendas of national decision makers by serving as "transmission belts of policy sensitivities across national boundaries" (Keohane and Nye, 1975). From that perspective, we can further suggest that transnational interactions have the capacity to influence the international system by (1) *changing attitudes* of policymakers and the public alike by altering their opinions and perceptions of reality through face-to-face contacts with citizens of different states; (2) increasing *international pluralism* by linking national interest groups in transnational structures, usually for the purposes of transnational cooperation; (3) increasing the constraints on states through *dependence and interdependence*, particularly in the areas of international transportation and finance; (4) creating *new instruments of influence* whereby some governments, as a result of the unequal distribution of transnational linkages, may be able to carry out more effectively their wishes regarding other governments; and (5) as already noted, creating new *autonomous international actors* capable of pursuing their interests largely outside the direct control of nation-states while at the same time frequently involving governments in particular problems as a result of their activities (Nye and Keohane, 1971).

International regimes facilitate many of these processes. Ironically, their importance to the system as a whole may increase as the dominant role of the United States in world politics wanes. The United States was instrumental in creating regimes in the postwar environment in that its overriding power provided the stability and order necessary for their birth and effective functioning. In effect, and in contrast to what the logic of *realpolitik* predicts, the United States provided a collective good to other nations that enabled them as well as the hegemon to prosper. Instability might therefore be expected as the power of the United States relative to others declines, but instead the regimes put in place following World War II persist—and these institutionalized rules for the collective management of global problems in a decentralized international system help to maintain order in an environment where chaos might otherwise have been expected. Thus nonstate actors play a critical role in the maintenance of international equilibrium.

International Terrorism and World Politics

Transnational terrorist organizations are an exception. Their objective as nonstate actors is chaos, not equilibrium. Thus they pose a vexing challenge to nation-states generally—and to the United States in particular.

Although terrorism dates to antiquity, it rose as a significant international problem from seeds planted in the 1960s (Kidder, 1990) to epidemic proportions in the 1970s and 1980s (see Figure 6.6). As President Reagan warned in 1985, "In recent years, there has been a steady and escalating pattern of terrorist acts against the United States and our allies and Third World nations friendly toward our interests. . . . The number of bombings alone [in 1984 averaged] almost one a day." Moreover, the prospect that this problem will fade

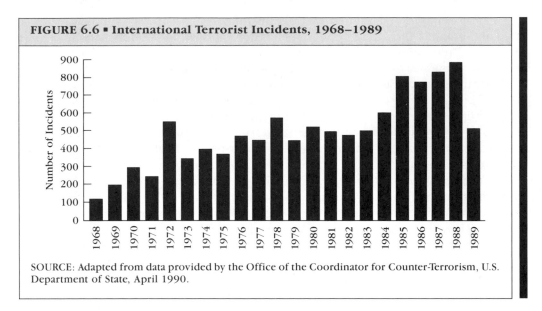

FIGURE 6.6 ▪ International Terrorist Incidents, 1968–1989

SOURCE: Adapted from data provided by the Office of the Coordinator for Counter-Terrorism, U.S. Department of State, April 1990.

appears remote. As Morris D. Busby, President Bush's coordinator for counterterrorism, predicted in 1990, "We cannot expect to completely eradicate terrorism. It is now, and will remain, a persistent international problem."

Terrorist violence has increased because it is a strategy that even the weak can employ. Modern technology may have contributed to its growth, for a crucial part of the terrorists' strength derives from media publicity of their grievances. Indeed, international communication makes almost any terrorist act against prominent figures an instant media event. The terrorist's ability to bring his or her presence into the global spotlight by securing publicity provokes widespread fear—precisely the intended effect (which is why international terrorism has so often been likened to theater). And part of what makes terrorism so terrifying is the message that anyone can become its victim.

International terrorists use a variety of methods in pursuit of their goals. Included are time-honored techniques such as kidnapping, assassination, hijacking, hostage taking, and sabotage. But in response, governments in the 1980s strengthened their capabilities to deter these methods by, for example, providing greater security at airports, guarding likely kidnap victims, training special commandos to deal with hostage situations, and expanding technologies for surveillance. In response to these countermeasures, terrorists adjusted their modes of operation, moving to hit-and-run tactics, bombings with hard-to-detect plastic explosives, and paramilitary attacks using handheld missiles, all of which make detection and deterrence more difficult. Their intensified efforts increased their willingness to become more violent in order to gain attention. As one expert observed, "If terrorism stops terrorizing—if it ceases to have an explosive impact on public opinion—then terrorists have an innate tendency to escalate [the violence] in order to recapture the headlines" (in Kempe, 1983).

Terrorism is a tactic of the powerless against the powerful. Thus it is not surprising that many acts of terrorism are perpetrated by political or social minorities or ethnic movements. Those seeking independence and sovereign statehood, like the Palestinians in the Middle East and the Basques in Spain, typify the kinds of aspirations that animate terrorist activity. In the industrialized world, terrorism often occurs where discrepancies in income are severe and where minority groups are deprived of the political freedoms and privileges enjoyed by the majority. Guerrilla warfare normally associated with rural uprisings is not a viable route to self-assertion in the urbanized areas of the industrialized world, but terrorist tactics are.

Consideration of terrorists' motives underscores the fact that terrorism is not perceived by all to be a disease. One person's terrorist may, to another, be a liberator. In fact, both governments and countergovernment movements claim to seek liberty, and both are labeled terrorists by those they oppose. The difference between a "freedom fighter" and a protector of freedom often lies in the eye of the beholder—a problem that makes determination of a terrorist group not altogether obvious or noncontroversial (see O'Brien, 1990).

Put into a historical context, terrorism can be seen as something more than the effort of relatively powerless movements to upset by threat of violence the established order within and among nations. Although many terrorist groups today are undeniably groups without sovereignty that seek it, a broader definition of terrorism would acknowledge that many terrorist acts are state supported (see Bell, 1990; Crenshaw, 1990). Indeed, some states condone and support the terrorist activities of movements that espouse philosophies they embrace (or challenge the security of states they see as enemies). This *state terrorism* is part of the claim that the United States has leveled at the behaviors of the Soviet Union, Syria, and Libya, among others. In an analogous way, the United States has been accused of sponsoring terrorist activities in Vietnam, Chile, Nicaragua, and elsewhere (see Schlagheck, 1990).

Whatever the origins and composition of terrorist groups, the alarming rate with which international terrorist activity has spread has unquestionably altered the global environment in which American foreign policy must operate. Terrorism poses a serious challenge because Americans frequently have been the targets and victims of this lethal tactic: according to the Department of State, since 1968 U.S. citizens and interests have consistently been the target of about a third of all terrorist attacks worldwide. Global terrorism thus is a particularly American problem. "We are in the midst of an undeclared war" is the way former CIA Director William Casey characterized the threat.

While counterterrorist action begs for a concerted international response, the United States has taken a unilateral approach toward the deterrence of terrorist activity. But disagreement over strategies to combat terrorism has long been evident among American policymakers because the challenge does not lend itself to a compelling and effective solution, and nearly all proposed remedies entail risks that are politically unacceptable and tactics that could easily backfire. This is because a major part of the terrorist's strategy is deliberately to provoke repression and the suspension of civil liberties so as to undermine the legitimacy of the government undertaking the punitive, counterterrorist measures. In this context, consider, for example, Secretary of State George Shultz's push in the 1980s to fight terrorism with violence. Not only would the approach risk innocent lives, but by conducting retaliatory or even preemptive military actions against international terrorism the wrong targets might be struck, thus further legitimizing violence and terror by removing the blurred distinction between terror by states and terror by nonstate actors. Moreover, by practicing counterterrorism by force, critics worried that the United States would become like the perpetrators of the very behavior it sought to extirpate. But even less punitive counterterrorist strategies entail unacceptable costs, and in the end neither approach can promise to eradicate the threat. The problem remains unresolved because most strategies to combat terrorism require tactics that threaten to prostitute the democratic ideals that the retaliatory tactics are designed to defend—the very reaction that anti-American terrorist groups hope to provoke. Thus terrorism as a form of transnational political behavior by nonstate actors remains a dilemma for American policymakers, as it does for much of the international community.

AMERICAN FOREIGN POLICY IN A CHANGING ENVIRONMENT

The trends toward systemic diffusion of economic and military capabilities among the great powers, the emergence of a group of comparatively poor and often antagonistic new states, and the increase in the number of nonstate international actors identified in this chapter are among the most salient changes that have occurred in the postwar international system. Those developments have simultaneously diminished the capacity of the United States to exercise control over events abroad and provoked the necessity for adjustments in its foreign policy.

American foreign policy thus is to some extent molded by both the structures and processes of an evolving international political system. Changes in that system have precipitated pressures for policy adaptation. Over the past five decades the United States has struggled to accommodate its foreign policies to monumental transformations of the international political system in an effort to keep pace with the tempo of global change, and, most important, to encourage the development of a world receptive to American national interests. Often, however, it has met with frustration and failure as the external environment has frequently been inhospitable to those interests.

That was not the case in the immediate post–World War II years. At that time the global system was fraught with opportunity for the United States. From a position of strength, the United States embraced global responsibilities and pursued an assertive posture that shaped a world compatible with the

American vision. It took the lead in forming a variety of new global institutions shaped in its own political image. It sponsored formation of NATO and followed it with involvement in a complex network of peacetime military alliances. It pushed friendly nations to augment their defensive capabilities and assisted them in various ways. It ushered in the nuclear age with its own technological innovations. It embraced the fight against colonialism and pushed the creation of international financial institutions that eventually sought to promote the economic development of the newly emergent nations. It also promoted the multilateral trade regime to encourage free exchange between countries in an effort to avert repetition of the disaster of the Great Depression. And U.S.-based multinational corporations assumed a high profile in the world system. To a large degree, therefore, the nature of the postwar international political system was a product of the policies and programs the United States engineered in the late 1940s, the 1950s, and beyond.

Paradoxically, the United States today finds itself burdened by its responsibilities. The institutions it promoted and once supported without reservation are sometimes the unwelcome symbols of a contemporary international political system that has often proven intractable and inhospitable to American interests.

The American foreign policy response to this fundamentally changed environment has varied somewhat from one time period to the next, depending on the changed and changing nature of the external environment. One response reflects hostility toward and detachment from global involvement, as witnessed in the attitude of the United States toward the United Nations in much of the period since the mid-1970s. Unilateralism sometimes accompanied detachment.

A second response has been reassertion of American control by confronting those challenging America's hegemonic influence. The approach was especially evident in the Reagan administration's combative posture toward the Soviet Union and others believed to be supported by and sympathetic toward the nation's historic adversary.

Debate exists in the United States about the wisdom of these approaches and about how the nation can best balance them so as to promote its security, welfare, and values. The United States finds itself significantly affected by the multiple changes that have swept the international political system since Hiroshima. Taken together, shifts in the distribution of world power, in the composition of the world community, and in the kinds of actors populating it have created an external environment radically different from that existing in 1945. We clearly live in a transitional period, an era, according to former national security adviser Zbigniew Brzezinski, in which "an old world order is coming to an end and the shape of a new world order is yet to be defined." That transformation will stimulate—indeed, it may well necessitate—changes in American conduct abroad, just as past global changes have promoted important adaptations in American foreign policy as the United States continually has sought realization of its persistent foreign policy objectives. The emergence of a new

European landscape and the changing face of Soviet power are particularly pertinent to the challenges and opportunities the United States now faces in the external environment.

SUGGESTIONS FOR FURTHER READING

Brzezinski, Zbigniew. (1990) *The Grand Failure: The Birth and Death of Communism in the Twentieth Century.* New York: Collier Books.

Calleo, David. (1987) *Beyond American Hegemony: The Future of the Western Alliance.* New York: Basic Books.

Ehrlich, Paul R., and Anne H. Ehrlich. (1990) *The Population Explosion.* New York: Simon & Schuster.

Karns, Margaret P., and Karen A. Mingst (eds.). (1990) *The United States and Multilateral Institutions: Patterns of Changing Instrumentality and Influence.* Boston: Unwin Hyman.

Kegley, Charles W., Jr. (ed.). (1990) *International Terrorism: Characteristics, Causes, Controls.* New York: St. Martin's.

Keohane, Robert O., and Joseph S. Nye, Jr. (1989) *Power and Interdependence: World Politics in Transition*, 2nd ed. Glenview, Ill.: Scott, Foresman/Little, Brown.

Klare, Michael. (1990) "Who's Arming Who? The Arms Trade in the 1990s," *Technology Review* 93 (May/June): 45–50.

Mearsheimer, John J. (1990) "Back to the Future: Instability in Europe After the Cold War," *International Security* 15 (Summer): 5–56.

Ruggie, John Gerard. (1989) "International Structure and International Transformation," pp. 21–35 in Ernst-Otto Czempiel and James N. Rosenau (eds.), *Global Changes and International Challenges.* Lexington, Mass.: Lexington Books.

Sabrosky, Alan Ned (ed.). (1985) *Polarity and War: The Changing Structure of International Conflict.* Boulder, Colo.: Westview.

CHAPTER 7

The International Political Economy in Transition

The international economy could continue to grow, or the stresses of competition, trade imbalances, and debt could lead to protectionism; it could lead to rival trading blocs—ultimately to the disadvantage of all of us.

SECRETARY OF STATE JAMES A. BAKER, 1989

Efforts to improve global growth, to ease the burdens of developing countries . . . and to open markets for trade have demonstrated anew that progress is best achieved by facing pressing issues together. This is the lesson that we must carry with us into the 1990s if we are to pass on to future generations a global economy that is strong and resilient . . . .

PRESIDENT GEORGE BUSH, 1989

Interdependence captures the essence of the increasingly interlocked national economies of the world and the corresponding intersection between domestic and international politics. The United States plays a predominate role in this global scene. The nation's gigantic gross national product (GNP), which now stands in excess of $5 trillion, overshadows that of other nations. American output is more than 25 percent of the total produced in the world, about five times its proportion of the world's population. The consequence of the overwhelming size of the U.S. economy is that little can be done in the United States without repercussions abroad. Recession in the United States becomes recession abroad; domestic inflation is shared elsewhere; the general health of the U.S. economy is a worldwide concern. Although it is no longer the case, as thirty years ago, that when the United States sneezes the rest of the world catches pneumonia, it is still true that "when the United States sneezes the rest of the world catches cold" (Cooper, 1988).

Part of the reason for the worldwide importance of the U.S. economy stems from the international position of the dollar, which throughout the postwar period has been a reserve currency for other nations. That means that the dollar has been used as a medium of exchange to settle international accounts. The dollar also has become a "parallel currency" that central banks in other countries either buy or sell in currency exchange markets in order to maintain the value of their own currencies. Mammoth American investments abroad, which in 1988 stood at $327 billion, and the dominant position of the United States (whose 1988 share of world exports was 12 percent) in the world network of trade relationships are two additional factors making the American economy critical to world prosperity.

Normally, we think of economic activities in a democratic capitalistic system as being the concern of private entrepreneurs, largely unencumbered by governmental interference. But the domestic economy of the United States actually comprises a mix of private ownership and government regulation, as does international economic activity. In this setting international economic relations have become part of, and subject to, the way the United States seeks to cope with a loosely organized, interdependent, global environment sensitive to the United States; likewise, the partially regulated American economic system has become closely tied to developments abroad over which the United States often has little control.

In this chapter we explore the changing nature of the link between politics and economics through an examination of selected aspects of U.S. monetary and trade ties with Western industrialized societies, Third World countries, and communist countries.[1] Throughout, we are concerned with the place of the United States within the evolving international political economy and its role in the creation and management of the Liberal International Economic Order (LIEO) in the years following World War II. Underlying the examination is the assumption that both change and continuity in American foreign policy are influenced by an international economic order that has changed markedly during the past five decades.

THE FIRST WORLD: INDUSTRIALIZED NATIONS

As envisioned in the Bretton Woods agreements of 1944, the wartime Allies sought to build a postwar international monetary system characterized by stability, predictability, and orderly growth. The International Monetary Fund (IMF) was created at that time to assist states in dealing with such matters as maintaining balance-of-payments equilibria (that is, stability in the balance between their financial inflows and outflows) and exchange-rate stability (that is, the rate at which one nation's currency is exchanged for another's) and, more generally, to ensure international monetary cooperation and the expansion of trade (see Focus 7.1). Over time the IMF evolved to serve as the most useful and influential of the many new international organizations created

---

1. In the idiom of international diplomacy, these countries are known, respectively, as developed-market economies, developing economies, and centrally planned economies. Collectively, developed-market economies are also often referred to as the First World, communist nations as the Second World, and developing nations as the Third World. The accuracy and utility of these designations are increasingly suspect, but they continue to inform the way national governments and international organizations conceptualize the world.

FOCUS 7.1 ▪ The Bretton Woods Conference and Its Twin Institutions

The International Monetary and Financial Conference of the United and Associated Nations was convened in Bretton Woods, New Hampshire, on July 1, 1944. By the time the conference ended on July 22, 1944, based on substantial preparatory work, it had defined the outlines of the postwar international economic system. The conference also resulted in the creation of the International Monetary Fund (IMF) and the International Bank for Reconstruction and Development (IBRD, or the World Bank)—the Bretton Woods twins.

The World Bank was to assist in reconstruction and development by facilitating the flow and investment of capital for productive purposes. The International Monetary Fund was to facilitate the expansion and balanced growth of international trade and to contribute thereby to the promotion and maintenance of high levels of employment and real income. Also discussed at Bretton Woods were plans for an International Trade Organization (ITO). This institution did not materialize, but some of its proposed functions are performed by the General Agreement on Tariffs and Trade (GATT), which was established in 1947.

The discussions at Bretton Woods took place with the experience of the interwar period as background. In the 1930s every major country sought ways to defend itself against deflationary pressures from abroad—some by exchange depreciation, some by introducing flexible exchange rates or multiple rates, some by direct controls over imports and other international transactions. The disastrous consequences of such policies—economic depression with very high unemployment—are well known. The participants in the Bretton Woods conference were determined to design an international economic system where "beggar thy neighbor" policies, which characterized the international economic community when World War II began, did not recur. There was also a widespread fear that the end of World War II would be followed by a slump, as had the end of World War I.

Thus the central elements of the system outlined at Bretton Woods were the establishment of convertibility of currencies and of fixed but adjustable exchange rates, and the encouragement of international flows of capital for productive purpose. The IMF and the World Bank were to assist in the attainment of these objectives. The economic accomplishments of the postwar period are in part the result of the effectiveness of these institutions.

SOURCE: *World Development Report 1985* (New York: Oxford University Press for the World Bank, 1985), p. 15.

during and immediately after World War II. During the period known as the Bretton Woods system (1946–1971), the IMF helped member states to maintain fixed rates of exchange for their currencies (as required by the Bretton Woods agreements). This gave the IMF considerable influence in getting member states

(especially the economically less powerful ones) to undertake the often difficult domestic tasks of coping with the causes of balance-of-payments disequi-
libria. More recently, the IMF assisted nations' adjustment to the two surges in
worldwide oil prices (1973–1974 and 1979–1980) induced by the Organization of Petroleum Exporting Countries (OPEC) cartel, and helped to ease the
crushing external debt burden that plagued many nations in the wake of the
OPEC oil-price squeezes. More generally, the IMF has served as both a catalyst
to, and forum for, negotiations among the world's monetary powers on how to
organize the international monetary system.

In the immediate postwar years, however, the IMF and the World Bank (the
International Bank for Reconstruction and Development, IBRD, also created at
Bretton Woods) proved insufficient for the task of managing postwar economic
recovery. Those institutions were simply given too little authority and too few
resources to cope with the enormous economic devastation suffered by Western
European nations during the war. The United States stepped into the breach.

The Role of the United States in Managing the International Monetary System

The Early Years   The dollar became the key to the American managerial
role.[2] Backed by a vigorous and healthy economy, a fixed relationship between
gold and the dollar ($35 per ounce of gold), and a commitment by the U.S.
government to exchange gold for dollars (known as *dollar convertibility*), the
dollar in effect became as good as gold. Indeed, it was preferable to gold. Dollars earned interest, which gold did not; they did not require storage and insurance costs; and they were needed to buy imports necessary for survival and
postwar reconstruction.

The problem in the immediate postwar years was how to get American
dollars into the hands of those who needed them. One mechanism was the
Marshall Plan, which provided Western European nations with resources to
buy the American goods necessary to rebuild their war-torn economies. Eventually, $17 billion in Marshall Plan assistance was channeled to Western Europe.
International liquidity (reserve assets used to settle international accounts) in
the form of dollars was also provided by deliberate encouragement by the
United States of deficits in its own balance of payments, partially accomplished
through massive outflows of foreign aid and expenditures to maintain burgeoning American overseas military commitments. In addition to providing international liquidity, the United States supported European and Japanese trade competitiveness, as well as protectionism (for example, Japanese restrictions on
American exports) and discrimination against the dollar (for example, the
European Payments Union, a multilateral European group that promoted intra-
European trade at the expense of trade with the United States). Those short-run
costs were incurred on the basis of the long-run assumption that a rejuvenated

---

2. The subsequent discussion of the role of the United States in the management of the international monetary system draws on Spero (1990). See also Blake and Walters (1987).

Europe and Japan would provide widening markets for American exports. The perceived political benefits of strengthening the Western world against the threat of world communism were also considerable.

"The system worked well. Europe and Japan recovered and then expanded. The U.S. economy prospered partly because of the dollar outflow, which led to the purchase of U.S. goods and services" (Spero, 1990). Furthermore, the "top currency" role of the dollar facilitated America's globalist foreign policy posture. The foreign economic and military aid programs and the growing military presence of the United States overseas were made possible by acceptance of the dollar as the means of paying for them. Business interests could readily expand abroad because American foreign investments were often considered desirable, and American tourist dollars could be spent with few restrictions. In effect, the United States operated as the world's banker. Other nations were required to balance their financial inflows and outflows. In contrast, the United States enjoyed the advantages of operating internationally without the constraints of limited finances. The political and economic clout of the United States, and the global ubiquity of the dollar, also meant that developments within the nation significantly affected the monetary (and political) affairs of other nations.

Yet costs were associated with this condition: just as the United States was able to exert influence over others, it became tied to others' circumstances and policies. Massive private investments overseas to promote domestic prosperity heightened fears of potential nationalization. The vast number of dollars held by others also made the American domestic economy vulnerable to financial disruptions abroad. Decision makers therefore sought to insulate the American economy from these shocks, but the task was made more difficult because some tools available to others were proscribed by the status of the dollar as a reserve currency.

For most countries an imbalance between financial inflows and outflows could be corrected most readily by changing the rate of exchange of its currency, that is, the value of one nation's currency in relation to that of other nations. A country with an adverse balance of trade (one that imports more from other nations than it exports to them) could devalue its currency. That would give it a trade advantage by reducing the price of its exports in order to make them more attractive to foreign buyers (because the exports would become less costly in relation to the goods of other countries). At the same time, imports from other countries would become relatively less attractive to domestic consumers. The consequent improvement in the balance of trade—caused by promoting exports and curtailing imports by redirecting domestic demand from foreign to domestically produced products—would contribute ultimately to a favorable balance-of-payments position by increasing financial inflows and reducing outflows. Reducing domestic unemployment by promoting exports would be an additional benefit realized, in principle, by devaluing one's currency.

But this simple mechanism—devaluation (and revaluation) of currency exchange rates, which lies at the heart of international financial adjustments—was especially burdensome for the United States because of the pivotal role of the dollar. Devaluation, for example, would affect adversely political friends and military allies who had chosen to hold large amounts of dollars—an impact to be avoided under conditions in which competition with Soviet communism was a priority. Furthermore, because of the importance of the dollar in other countries' reserve assets, a devaluation of the dollar by the United States could easily be offset by a subsequent devaluation of the currency of the country adversely affected by American action—which effectively would restore the status quo.

The Demise of Bretton Woods   By as early as 1960 it was apparent that the status of the dollar as the "top currency" was on the wane. Thereafter, the dollar-based international monetary system unilaterally managed by the United States became a multilaterally managed system under American leadership. Several factors explain the dollar's declining position.

If a dollar shortage was the problem in the immediate postwar years, by the 1960s the problem had become a glut, which eroded the willingness of others to hold the dollar as a reserve currency. Indeed, the costs of overseas military activities, foreign economic and military aid, and massive private investments produced increasing balance-of-payments deficits, which earlier had been encouraged but were now out of control. Furthermore, U.S. gold holdings in relation to the growing number of foreign-held dollars declined precipitously. Given those circumstances, the possibility that the United States might devalue the dollar led to a loss of confidence by others and hence an unwillingness to continue to hold dollars as reserve currency. The French under President Charles de Gaulle even insisted on exchanging dollars for gold, albeit in part for reasons related more to French nationalism than the value of the dollar.

At the same time that a dollar glut came to characterize the international liquidity situation during the 1960s, massive transnational movements of capital accelerated monetary interdependence. The internationalization of banking, the internationalization of production (via multinational corporations), and the development of a *Eurocurrency* market (Eurocurrencies are dollars and other currencies held in Europe as bank deposits and lent and borrowed abroad, primarily in Europe) outside direct state control were all catalysts to interdependence. The result was an increasingly complex connection between economic policies engineered in one country and their effects on another. This in turn spawned a variety of less formal groupings of the central bankers and finance ministers of the leading economic powers[3] who sought various solutions to their common problems.[4]

---

3. One such group, established in 1962 to discuss monetary issues, is known as the Group of Ten. Its members are the finance ministers and central bank governors of the United States, Belgium, Canada, France, Great Britain, Italy, Japan, the Netherlands, Sweden, and Germany. A number of subgroups of the Group of Ten also now operate on a more or less continuing basis. These are known as the Group of Three (the United States, Japan, and Germany), the Group of Five (the Group of three plus France and Britain), and the Group of Seven (the Group of Five plus Canada and Italy).

Although the United States typically gave the most support to the various remedial efforts devised in the 1960s to assure monetary stability, it found them of little help when crises affected the dollar in the late 1960s and early 1970s—crises that were products of unfolding political and economic changes in the international system. By the 1960s, European and Japanese economic recovery from the war was complete, which meant that American monetary dominance and the privileged position of the dollar were no longer palatable. The Europeans and Japanese came especially to resent the prerogatives the United States derived from its position as the world's banker and from its ability to determine the level of international liquidity through its balance-of-payments deficits. Not only did those prerogatives place the economies of Europe and Japan at a disadvantage; they also gave the United States the ability to pursue policies that came to be less and less acceptable to others.

Among the U.S. pursuits with which many European nations disagreed was the Vietnam War. And among the economic conditions that they came to share was inflation, which in the United States was stimulated by the Johnson administration's unwillingness to raise taxes to finance either the Great Society programs or the Vietnam War. In a sense, Europe was "forced" to pay for American foreign policy adventures about which they had strong reservations. Soviet-American détente also entered the picture; as fear of the Soviet threat declined, the willingness of U.S. allies to defer to American leadership eroded.

The declining leadership position of the United States accelerated as domestic inflation contributed to a relative loss in competitiveness of U.S. exports. In response, the Nixon administration in 1971 abruptly announced that the United States would no longer exchange dollars for gold, and it imposed a surcharge on imports into the United States as part of a strategy designed to force a realignment of others' currency exchange rates. These startling and unexpected decisions presaged the end of the Bretton Woods system. In its place a system of free-floating exchange rates emerged, one in which currency values were to be determined primarily by market forces rather than by government intervention. What was not foreseen was that the system would introduce an unparalleled degree of uncertainty and unpredictability into international economic relations.

American concern for the competitiveness of the United States in international trade surrounded the decision to terminate Bretton Woods. In 1971 the United States for the first time in the twentieth century ran a trade deficit. Although modest by later standards (it was only $2 billion), it contributed to growing demands in the United States by industrial, labor, and agricultural interests for protectionist measures designed to insulate them from foreign

---

4. Among these solutions was an ad hoc agreement to swap currencies to cope with exchange crises. Another was the creation of a form of "paper gold" in the IMF, known as Special Drawing Rights (SDRs), whose purpose was to facilitate the growth of international liquidity by means other than increasing the outflow of dollars. SDRs remain as a form of liquidity, but they have never assumed a central role in international finance.

economic competition (particularly from Germany and Japan, whose share of world trade was increasing at the same time that the U.S. share was declining[5]).

Although the U.S. share of world trade declined, trade as a proportion of the nation's gross national product increased sharply during the 1970s (and has remained high ever since).[6] The trend signaled growing U.S. involvement in the interdependent global political economy and its increased sensitivity and vulnerability to developments abroad that it could not control. In this sense the United States was becoming a more "ordinary" power. Correspondingly, its willingness (and capacity) to exercise leadership waned. Yet American leadership was one of the important political foundations on which the successful operation of the Bretton Woods system had rested. Thus the political bases on which the system had been built lay in ruins. American leadership was no longer willingly accepted by others nor exercised willingly by the United States. Power, once concentrated in the hands of a small number of Western nations, had come to be more widely dispersed; and the interests that once bound them together, including a commitment to the precepts of liberal economic thought and fear of communism, had dissipated.

The "OPEC Decade" and Its Aftermath   Formal negotiations on reform of the international monetary system commenced in 1972, but before anything could be decided the world economy had to cope with two oil shocks administered by the Organization of Petroleum Exporting Countries. The first came in 1973–1974 shortly after the 1973 Yom Kippur War in the Middle East, when the price of oil increased fourfold; the second occurred in 1979–1980 in the wake of the revolution in Iran and resulted in an even more dramatic jump in the world price of oil. The oil shocks were especially important to the United States, the world's largest energy consumer, as they coincided with a decline in domestic energy production and a rise in consumption. A dramatic increase in U.S. dependence on foreign sources of energy to fuel its advanced industrial economy and a sharp rise in the overall cost of U.S. imports resulted.

As dollars flowed abroad to purchase energy resources (a record $40 billion in 1977 and $74 billion in 1980), other nations began to worry about the value of the dollar—which contributed to its marked decline on foreign exchange markets in the late 1970s and early 1980s (see Figure 7.1). Demand for oil worldwide and in the United States softened in the early 1980s as a consequence of conservation measures, economic recession, and a shift to

---

5. The U.S. share of total world exports declined by a third between the 1950s and 1970s, from 16.7 percent in 1955 to 11.7 percent in 1971. By way of contrast, the member countries of the European Economic Community, later known simply as the European Community, increased their share from just over 30 percent in 1955 to 41 percent in 1971; and Japan increased its share from 2.1 percent in 1955 to 6.4 percent in 1971.

6. *Trade turnover* (exports plus imports) as a proportion of GNP grew from 6.7 percent in 1960 to 8.1 in 1970, 12.8 in 1975, and 17.4 in 1980. Reflecting the value of the high-flying dollar in the mid-1980s, discussed below, the proportion slipped to 13.8 percent in 1985 but was back up to 15.7 percent by 1988.

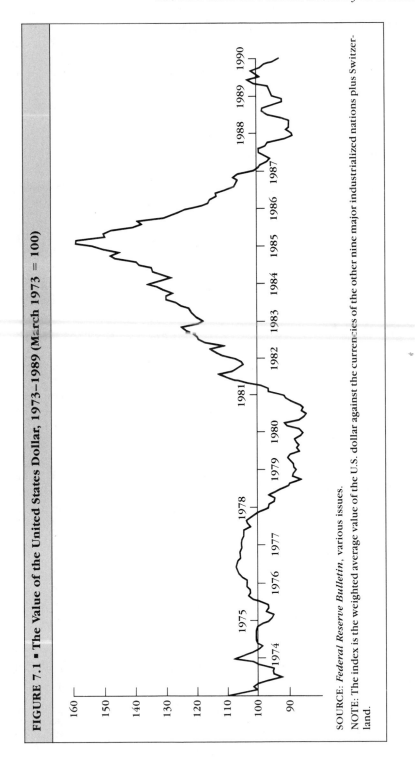

FIGURE 7.1 ▪ The Value of the United States Dollar, 1973–1989 (March 1973 = 100)

SOURCE: *Federal Reserve Bulletin*, various issues.

NOTE: The index is the weighted average value of the U.S. dollar against the currencies of the other nine major industrialized nations plus Switzer-land.

alternative sources of energy. Oil prices also began to ease as a result and then plummeted in 1986 due largely to a worldwide oil glut resulting from the decision of key members of OPEC to increase their output in an effort to regain market shares that had been lost to others. The decline in the price of oil helped to keep inflation in check and contributed to economic growth in the United States. Simultaneously, the dollar experienced a dramatic surge from its previously depressed levels.

Each oil shock was followed by global economic recession. The close relationship between the changing fortunes of the dollar and the price of oil was in part due to the way in which the leading industrial powers sought to cope with the recessions.[7] In response to the first, they chose conventional fiscal and monetary expansion to stimulate their economies so as to avoid politically unacceptable levels of unemployment. In response to the second, which proved to be the longest and most severe economic downturn since the Great Depression of the 1930s, they shifted their priority to controlling inflation through strict monetarist policies (that is, policies designed to reduce the money supply in the economy). Large fiscal deficits and sharply higher interest rates resulted, both of which were particularly apparent in the United States. The industrialized powers also experienced higher levels of unemployment than they had been willing to tolerate previously.

In an era of complex interdependence, none could escape the consequences of these developments, including Third World nations. In response to the two oil shocks, many Third World countries borrowed extensively from abroad to pay for the increased cost of energy rather than curtail domestic economic activity. Borrowing was made possible by the billions of ''petrodollars'' that flowed to the oil-producing states and that private banks and various multilateral institutions helped to recycle. In the process, however, the debt burden of many nations assumed ominous proportions, particularly as interest rates climbed following the second oil shock. The threat of massive defaults by countries unable to service their debts pushed the international monetary order to the brink of crisis in the early 1980s, thereby challenging in yet another way the viability of the established global political economy. (The threat to the political economy has receded, but the debt problem persists, as we will note when we shift attention to the Third World.)

High interest rates in the United States relative to others not only contributed to the debt burden of Third World states; they also contributed measurably to the changing fortunes of the U.S. dollar as increased demand for dollars drove up the exchange rate. Renewed economic growth in the United States, a sharp reduction in inflation, and the perception that the United States was a safe haven for financial investments in a world otherwise marked by political instability and violence also contributed to a restoration of faith in the dollar. Foreigners therefore rushed to acquire the dollars necessary to take

---

7. See Weatherford (1988) for an examination of the policy constraints and opportunities posed by the 1973 oil shock and earlier crises involving the international monetary system.

advantage of profitable investment opportunities in the United States. This situation contrasted sharply with the 1970s, when the overwhelming foreign indebtedness of the United States, often called the *dollar overhang*, was a principal fear.

For the United States, the appreciation of the dollar was a mixed blessing. On the one hand, it reduced the cost of imported oil. On the other hand, it increased the cost of U.S. exports to foreign buyers, thereby reducing the competitiveness of American products in overseas markets. This meant the loss of tens of thousands of jobs in American industries that produced for export. It also meant a series of record trade deficits—$122 billion in 1985, $145 billion in 1986, and $160 billion in 1987—as imports from abroad became relatively cheaper and hence more attractive to American consumers. Simultaneously, the United States became for the first time in more than a half-century a debtor nation as it moved in five years from being the world's biggest creditor to being its largest debtor. At the end of 1989 U.S. overseas assets stood at $1.4 trillion while foreign holdings in the United States stood at $2.1 trillion, for a net debt to foreigners of $663.7 billion. Borrowing from others does not necessarily mean problems today, but it does mean that money spent tomorrow to pay today's bills will not be available to meet future problems or finance future growth. A decline in the unusually high standard of living Americans have come to enjoy is the likely consequence.

The basis for that prediction stems in part from the impact of foreign direct investment in the United States, alongside the nation's status as the world's largest debtor at a time when the position of the United States in the international political economy has receded. Foreign direct investments[8] in the United States have grown dramatically in recent years, with investments in the United States actually surpassing U.S. investments abroad for the first time beginning in 1988 (see Figure 7.2). Western Europe, Canada, and Japan accounted for nearly 85 percent of foreign direct investment in the United States in 1988 (Scholl, 1989: 48). The apparently rapid and extensive ''selling of America'' has resulted in a contentious public debate as politicians, academicians, and journalists have tried to come to grips with the meaning of this unprecedented development (see Aho and Levinson, 1988; Bergsten, 1988; Burgess, 1988; and Omestad, 1989). A principal fear is that the American economy will come under foreign influence. Congress has been particularly concerned about foreign investments that may impair national security. Analysts are by no means united in their assessments of the consequences of the rapid growth of foreign ownership of U.S. assets, but they are generally agreed that the tipping of the balance in favor of greater foreign ownership of U.S. assets

---

8. *Foreign direct investment* ''implies that a person in one country has a lasting interest in and a degree of influence over the management of a business enterprise in another country.'' In the United States, ''ownership or control of 10 percent or more of an enterprise's voting securities is considered evidence of a lasting interest in or a degree of influence over management sufficient to constitute direct investment'' (Quijano, 1990).

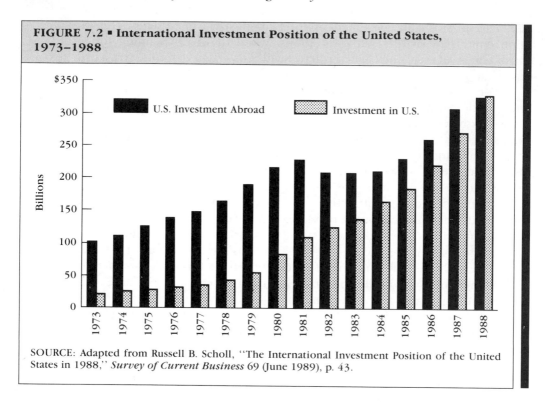

FIGURE 7.2 ▪ International Investment Position of the United States, 1973–1988

SOURCE: Adapted from Russell B. Scholl, "The International Investment Position of the United States in 1988," *Survey of Current Business* 69 (June 1989), p. 43.

compared with U.S. ownership of foreign assets is a consequence of the nation's growing dependence on foreign financing caused by the trade deficit and persistent federal budget deficits, which reached record levels of more than $200 billion annually in the mid-1980s.

In a normally functioning market, the combination of a strong dollar and severe trade imbalance would set in motion self-corrective processes that would return the dollar to its equilibrium value. Growing American imports, for example, though beneficial to United States trade partners in generating jobs and thus stimulating their return to economic growth, should create upward pressure on the value of others' currencies. Conversely, a drop in American exports should ease the demand for dollars, thereby reducing the dollar's value in exchange markets. Most analysts agree that in the early to mid-1980s these mechanisms did not work as they should have because of the persistently high interest rates in the United States. These were sustained in large measure by the federal government's "spend and borrow" policy that contributed to the huge federal deficits and the service costs they entailed. (Interest costs to service the national debt doubled during the Reagan administration and now comprise the third largest item in the federal budget.)

Eventually, the twin U.S. deficits were deemed the culprits underlying a long decline in the value of the dollar from the lofty heights it had achieved in the mid-1980s. A renewed sense of global economic uncertainty plagued decision makers in the advanced industrial societies, whose economic fates had become increasingly intertwined. That point was dramatized in October 1987, when stock prices in markets throughout the world plunged dramatically, resulting in billions of dollars in lost equity worldwide. Just as the multinational corporation earlier had propelled development of a global system of production, these events demonstrated the existence of a global market. And the dollar played a key role in the health of the market as experienced in such widely separated financial centers as London and Tokyo, Bonn and Hong Kong, Sydney and New York.[9]

The International Monetary System and Macroeconomic Policy Coordination: Toward the 1990s   Historically, the United States had been loath to intervene in the international marketplace to affect the value of the dollar. In 1978 the Carter administration broke with tradition when, in an unprecedented step, it instituted a new restrictive monetary policy in an effort to shore up the sagging dollar. This departed from the customary practice of keeping domestic and international monetary policy concerns on separate tracks. Maintenance of that separation was an article of faith during the Reagan administration at least for a time. Despite the obvious and ubiquitous interconnectedness of the national and world economies, Reagan's policies at home disregarded their impact abroad (Garten, 1985).

By 1985, however, the erosion of American trade competitiveness in overseas markets due to the overvalued dollar had become unpalatable domestically (Destler and Henning, 1989). In response, the Group of Five (the United States, Britain, France, Japan, and West Germany) met secretly in the Plaza Hotel in New York and decided to coordinate efforts to bring down the overvalued dollar. The agreement was important not only because it signaled an end to the benign neglect toward the consequences of interdependence that the United States had hitherto demonstrated, but because it also committed the major economic powers to a coordinated effort to manage exchange rates internationally and interest rates domestically. It also signaled the emergence of Japan as a full partner in international monetary management (Spero, 1990). But the Plaza agreement did not result in all that had been intended (see Funabashi, 1988). As a result, the financial ministers of the world's economic powers reconvened in Paris at the Louvre in 1987 to discuss exchange rate stabilization and management of the international monetary system.

As before, the Louvre summit promised more than was delivered. An important result was that Japan moved away from its export-led economic strategy toward one designed to stimulate domestic demand (see Balassa and Noland, 1988), but progress in macroeconomic policy coordination among the industrialized nations proved elusive (see Mead, 1988–1989, 1989). The inabil-

---

9. See Soros (1988) and Spero (1988–1989) for discussions of the rise of a global financial market, the role the dollar played in the events leading up to the stock market crash, and policy issues raised by both.

ity of the United States to devise a politically acceptable budget-deficit reduction strategy was a critical factor. It was in this environment of failed domestic policy and the disintegration of macroeconomic policy coordination among the industrialized nations that the 1987 stock market crash occurred (Spero, 1990). That event stimulated a renewed effort among the Group of Seven (the Group of Five plus Canada and Italy) to coordinate their domestic and international efforts to stabilize the dollar internationally. A degree of success was finally achieved, aided in part by some reductions in the twin U.S. deficits (see Figure 7.1).[10] "However, the long-term success of international monetary cooperation of the Group of Seven continued to depend on the ability of the key monetary actor, the United States, to pursue policies that would reduce its twin deficits" (Spero, 1990). That prospect remained dim as the Bush administration assumed the reigns of power and the United States moved into the 1990s seemingly still lacking the political will required to put its own house in order.

The dollar remains preeminent in the global political economy, as does the U.S. economy generally, but movements afoot portend the possible emergence of a monetary order in which the dollar will play a less pervasive role. Potentially the most important change involves Europe, where the European Community (EC) has launched a European Monetary System (EMS) designed to stabilize the currency values of the EC's member nations against one another and against the dollar. As with other initiatives of the EC, promise and performance of the EMS often have diverged. Nonetheless, the goal of securing a "zone of monetary stability in Europe" has been reached (Spero, 1990).

The commitment of the European Community to the realization of a single, integrated common market by 1992 gives further impetus to the objectives of achieving monetary stability in Europe, stabilizing EC monetary relations with non-EC nations, and moving toward creation of a single European currency unit (ECU). How the disruptions caused by German unification will be managed by the EC and how unification will affect the development of a common currency in Europe remain to be seen. Still, the EMS may contain the seeds of a regionalized international monetary system in which the EC will emerge dominant in Western Europe and in those areas of Africa and the Caribbean linked by treaty to the European Community. Such a scenario may also

---

10. Maintaining a stable dollar exchange rate has required considerable government intervention by the major industrial nations. In 1987, for example, the central banks of Western Europe and Japan spent $150 billion to support the dollar and prevent a free-fall in its value that would have adversely affected their export industries by making their products more expensive in the world marketplace (Berry, 1989b). In the United States the Treasury Department played a key role in moving the Reagan administration away from its policy of benign neglect and toward the coordinated strategies embodied in the Plaza and Louvre agreements (Destler and Henning, 1989). It continued to be the advocate of intervention during the remainder of the decade.

The Federal Reserve, however, which is responsible for monetary (interest rate) policy, often opposed intervention to support the dollar, arguing that "intervention cannot alter the value of a currency for very long if fundamental market forces are pushing it in the other direction" (Berry, 1989a). Moreover, the Federal Reserve has tended to gauge its policies on interest rates to their impact on the domestic economy rather than the value of the dollar. Nowhere are the competing demands of foreign and domestic policy more evident.

depict Japan as dominant in the Far East and Southeast Asia, with the United States remaining dominant elsewhere, notably in the Western Hemisphere (Gilpin, 1987).

As the dominant economic power in the 1990s, as in previous decades, the United States is likely to resist regionalization. But it is no longer unilaterally able to realize its preferences. The United States is necessary for effective management of the system, but it is not sufficiently dominant to fulfill its earlier leadership role. Negotiations with others, notably Germany and Japan, are necessary to manage successfully the competing and sometimes contradictory demands that economic interdependence and the desire for sovereign autonomy impose (see Cooper, 1988, on the desirability of macroeconomic policy coordination). "The danger in this present multilateral system is that with incomplete management, crises may go unregulated, cumulate, and wreak havoc. . . . The leaders of the developed states have time and again stressed the necessity of interdependence and of cooperating to maintain economic prosperity and political stability. Mechanisms for consultation and policy coordination still operate, but what will be done with them remains to be seen" (Spero, 1990).

The Role of the United States in Managing International Trade

The restructuring of America's place in the international monetary system since World War II has been paralleled by its changing position in the network of international trade relations. The United States still retains its preeminent position in the global political economy, though in monetary affairs and trade it is no longer as dominant as it once was.[11]

The Early Years   Management responsibilities in the postwar economic system as envisaged during World War II were to be entrusted not only to the IMF and the World Bank but also to an International Trade Organization (ITO), whose purpose was to lower restrictions on trade and set rules of commerce. The hope was that these three organizations could assist in avoiding repetition of the international economic catastrophe that followed World War I. But ITO was stillborn.

The United States was the prime mover behind all three specialized international agencies. ITO failed when the liberal trading system envisioned in its proposed charter, popularly known as the Havana Charter, became so watered down by demands from other countries for exemptions from the generalized rules that the U.S. government deemed the document worthless. In its place,

---

11. Evidence for the decline of American hegemony in recent decades and discussions of its meaning can be found in Gilpin (1987) and Kennedy (1987). Contrasting viewpoints are expressed in Huntington (1988–1989), Nau (1990), Nye (1990), Rosecrance (1990), and Strange (1987).

the United States sponsored the General Agreement on Tariffs and Trade (GATT). In a sense, GATT, which is now an established international agency, became the cornerstone of the liberalized trading scheme originally embodied in the ITO.

The mechanism of free and unfettered international trade, of which the United States has been a strong advocate throughout most of the postwar period, was the most-favored-nation (MFN) principle. According to this principle, the tariff preferences granted to one nation must be granted to all other nations exporting the same product; that is, the principle ensures equality in a nation's treatment of its trade partners as opposed to preferential treatment for some of them. Under the aegis of GATT and the most-favored-nation principle, a series of multilateral trade negotiations aimed at reducing tariffs (and resolving related issues) was conducted. The eighth and most recent session, the Uruguay Round of multilateral trade negotiations, was launched at a special session of GATT at Punta del Este in 1986 and scheduled for completion in late 1990. Prior to the Uruguay Round, the last major international effort to address global trade issues was the Tokyo Round, which was concluded in 1979 after six years of intensive negotiations.

Domestically, four major statutes (as amended) have governed the American approach to international trade issues: the Reciprocal Trade Agreements Act of 1934; the Trade Expansion Act of 1962; the Trade Act of 1974; and the Omnibus Trade and Competitiveness Act of 1988. Under each, Congress authorized the president to engage in international negotiations on trade issues, often with specific grants of authority to lower American tariff barriers if other nations would do the same. The Trade Expansion Act of 1962 and the Trade Act of 1974 set the stage for the Kennedy and Tokyo rounds of negotiations, respectively. Another statute, the Trade Agreements Act of 1979, implemented rules agreed on during the Tokyo Round. The 1988 Omnibus Trade and Competitiveness Act was passed while the Uruguay Round was in progress, but it still contained provisions relating to the conduct of the negotiations, and it established *fast track procedures* for congressional consideration of the agreements expected to be reached.[12]

The intimate tie between domestic trade legislation and the onset of major new international efforts to reach multilateral trade agreements attests to the continuing importance of the United States in the postwar international trade regime. This derives from the size of the U.S. economy, the high proportion of international trade for which the nation accounts, and the fact that it is the principal supplier of many products traded in the world marketplace. More

---

12. The *fast track procedures* were first spelled out in the 1974 Trade Act to augment congressional implementation of agreements reached by the president. They help explain the unusual swiftness with which the Trade Agreements Act of 1979 sailed through Congress. The procedures themselves do not guarantee congressional approval, but they ensure that Congress will consider the agreements on an expedited, nonamendable basis, which makes it more likely that they will survive congressional scrutiny. See Nivola (1990) for a discussion of Congress's role in devising trade policy.

important, the United States has been the principal actor in the postwar negotiating sessions and, throughout the 1940s and 1950s in particular, was willing to accept fewer immediate benefits than its trading partners in anticipation of the longer-term benefits of freer international trade. In effect, the United States was the locomotive of expanding production and trade worldwide. By stimulating its own growth, the United States was an attractive market for the exports of others, and the outflow of U.S. dollars stimulated the economic growth of other nations in the "American train." Evidence supporting the link between trade liberalization and export growth is found in the fact that as the average duty levied on imports to the United States was reduced by more than half between the late 1940s and the early 1960s, world exports nearly tripled.

The high point of the movement toward liberalized trading was reached with the Kennedy Round of negotiations in the mid-1960s, which grew out of the 1962 Trade Expansion Act. The act was motivated in part by concern for maintaining American export markets in the face of the growing economic competition from the European Economic Community (EEC),[13] and it specifically granted the president broad power to negotiate tariff rates with EEC countries in particular. Today, as during most of the past two decades, the EEC (otherwise generally known as the European Community [EC]) rivals Canada as the country's principal trading partner (based on trade turnover, that is, exports plus imports). Each accounts for about a fifth of U.S. trade turnover (see Figure 7.3), for a total of nearly $320 billion in 1989 between them. Similar proportions are evident in U.S. overseas investments. Seventy-five percent of the nation's direct investment abroad in 1988 was in developed nations, with the European Community accounting for over 60 percent of that proportion, followed by Canada with another 25 percent (Scholl, 1989: 46).

Progress was made during the Kennedy Round on industrial tariffs, to the point that by the time of the Tokyo Round the United States and the European Community had reduced tariff rates on industrial products to an average of about 9 percent. But little headway was made on the important question of agricultural commodities, which was of growing importance to the United States. The lack of progress on this issue and subsequent disagreements over it began to raise doubts among American policymakers about the wisdom of expansionist economic policies. The immediate challenge was posed in 1966 by the EEC's Common Agricultural Policy (CAP). Toward others, CAP was a protectionist tariff wall designed to maintain politically acceptable but artificially high prices for farm products produced within the EEC. The effect was to curtail American agricultural exports to the EEC.

Developments in Europe have long figured prominently in American economic policy and promise to continue to do so as the European Com-

---

13. The rhetoric surrounding passage of the act cloaked trade liberalization in the mantle of national security, and the act itself was described as an essential weapon in the Cold War struggle with the Soviet Union (Berkowitz, Bock, and Fuccillo, 1977).

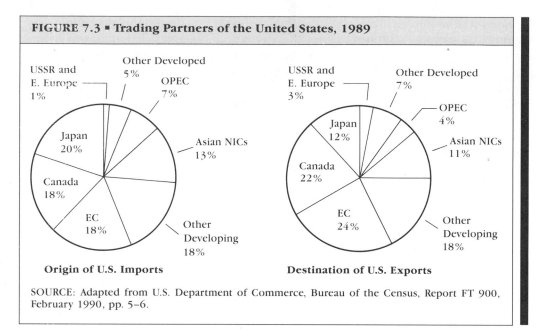

FIGURE 7.3 ▪ Trading Partners of the United States, 1989

Origin of U.S. Imports

Destination of U.S. Exports

SOURCE: Adapted from U.S. Department of Commerce, Bureau of the Census, Report FT 900, February 1990, pp. 5–6.

munity moves toward its 1992 goal of a single market (for an overview of U.S. interests at stake, see Schwartz, 1989). The economic potential of an integrated European market is suggested by the fact that its gross national product ($4.1 trillion) will rival that of the United States and its population (320 million people) will exceed that of the United States. Of special concern to the United States is whether it will be open or closed to non-European nations.

Promoting European economic integration has been a goal of American foreign policy since the 1950s, and officially it remains so. "Our reasoning is simple," observed one State Department official early in the Bush presidency. "An economically integrated Europe promotes political and social integration, and a United Europe—a strong Europe—is a cornerstone of U.S. policy." At the same time, he warned that "if 1992 is implemented in a closed or protectionist manner, it would cast a pall over the future, giving succor to those that would prefer isolation, self-sufficiency, and protection. If 1992 results in an inward-looking European Community, it could prompt others to respond in kind." "Fortress Europe" is a phrase often used to express concern that the 1992 process might cause the community to turn inward. Thus President Bush expressed the conviction that "we must all work hard to ensure that the Europe of 1992 will adopt the lower barriers of the modern international economy, not the high walls and the moats of medieval commerce."

American concern about the challenge of an economically revitalized and politically united Europe was among the factors that marked a change in the postwar multilateral trade system in the 1970s and 1980s. Other concerns that began to erode the foundations of the liberalized trading system included the extension by the European Community of preferential trade treatment to nations in Africa, the Mediterranean, and the Caribbean; the expansion of the community from six members to nine in 1973; the extension of associate status to others; and the feeling by many Western nations that Japan continued to pursue highly protectionist trade policies in contrast to the liberalized trading scheme the others upheld. Generally, the forces undermining the trade structure were the same ones that undermined the international monetary system. (The time line in Figure 7.4 illustrates the interconnectedness of trade and monetary issues and the role of the United States in their management.) The collapse of that system in turn contributed to the lack of forward movement on trade matters. Thus no new trade negotiations were held in the six crisis-prone years between the end of the Kennedy Round and the Tokyo Round.

Challenges to U.S. Leadership and the Rise of Protectionist Sentiment
The president's authority to negotiate trade matters under the Trade Expansion Act of 1962 expired with the end of the Kennedy Round. Thereafter, Presidents Lyndon B. Johnson and Richard M. Nixon fought a rearguard action against increasingly strong domestic protectionist forces that demanded trade restrictions from Congress. The strident posture assumed by the Nixon administration on international monetary issues, which resulted in termination of the Bretton Woods system, carried over into trade issues, while the collapse of the system of fixed exchange rates itself slowed forward movement on trade issues. The shifting political forces within the Western world—and between it and the communist world—were also important. The consequence was a loss of American leadership within the system.

The Nixon administration's bellicose approach to monetary and trade matters dealt a serious blow to the multilateral free-trade scheme. However, the world was spared a spiral of retaliatory, protectionist trade measures similar to that of the 1930s. Instead, once the immediate crisis had receded, the major industrial powers committed themselves to a new round of multilateral trade negotiations. But new obstacles had yet to be surmounted. High inflation and global recession induced by the 1973–1974 oil price shock, both of which encouraged protectionist trade practices, were among them. And in the United States, the Congress was not only attempting to deal with a trade proposal that sought to increase the president's power to negotiate trade matters beyond what previous statutes had accorded him; it was also grappling with an issue that made presidential power appear excessive already—Watergate.

By the time the Tokyo Round commenced, trade negotiators found themselves in a radically different environment from that of the previous GATT sessions. Trade volume had grown exponentially worldwide, economic interdependence among the world's leading industrial powers had reached

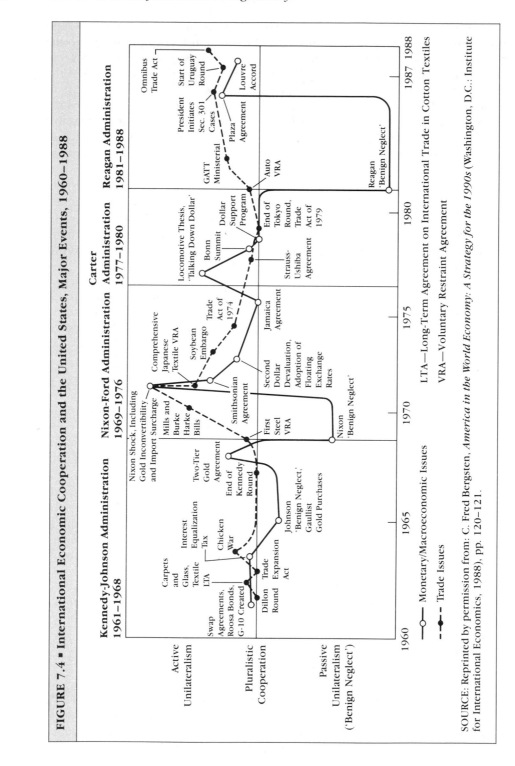

FIGURE 7.4 ■ International Economic Cooperation and the United States, Major Events, 1960–1988

SOURCE: Reprinted by permission from: C. Fred Bergsten, *America in the World Economy: A Strategy for the 1990s* (Washington, D.C.: Institute for International Economics, 1988), pp. 120–121.

unprecedented levels, tariffs were no longer the principal barriers to trade, and the United States was no longer an unfaltering economic giant. In such an environment, increased emphasis was placed on reducing barriers to the free flow of agricultural products and on coping with nontariff barriers to trade.

Nontariff barriers (NTBs) refers to a wide range of government regulations that have the effect of reducing or distorting international trade, including health and safety regulations, restrictions on the quality of goods that may be imported, antidumping regulations (designed to prevent foreign producers from selling their goods for less abroad than they cost domestically), and domestic subsidies. Import and export quotas also have been used to place quantitative restrictions on certain goods traded internationally. The United States, for example, has used types of export quotas known as *orderly market arrangements* (OMAs) and *voluntary restraint agreements* (VRAs) (often called voluntary export restrictions, or VERs), which are negotiated with exporting countries to limit the flow of such products as autos, steel, textiles, and footwear into the United States.[14] In 1986, 22 percent of the $360 billion in goods imported into the United States were under some kind of protection (compared with only 12 percent in 1980) (*U.S. News & World Report*, April 6, 1987, p. 45). More generally, it has been estimated that the restrictive effects of nontariff barriers to trade are three or four times as great as the restrictive effects of tariffs and that NTBs "probably diminished world commerce [in 1987] by about $330 billion" (Hufbauer, 1989–1990: 68).

It is important to note that many of these "behind-the-border" measures occur outside the GATT framework and therefore technically are not transgressions of the liberal trade system it seeks to promote. Still, NTBs comprise one of several *neomercantilist*[15] challenges to the principle of free trade, that have assumed prominence in American foreign economic policy as the economic preeminence of the United States relative to others has declined. The allegation is that the gulf between free trade and fair trade is often very wide.

The principle of *free trade*, based on the theory of comparative advantage, promises that all countries will benefit from international trade when each specializes in the production of those goods in which it enjoys advantages and trades them for goods in which others enjoy advantages. *Fair trade*, on the other hand, draws attention to the role that governments play in *creating* comparative advantages.

Historically, the United States had espoused a laissez-faire attitude toward trade issues, believing that market forces are best able to stimulate entrepre-

---

14. Not all nontariff barriers are designed specifically to limit trade. Health and safety standards, for example, have come to be regarded as necessary and legitimate forms of government regulation. They have no necessary bearing on international trade, though they are sometimes used to limit external competition rather than to safeguard domestic welfare. It is often difficult, however, to distinguish legitimate nontariff barriers from regulations designed primarily to limit foreign competition and to protect domestic industries.

15. *Neomercantilism* refers to "a trade policy whereby a state seeks to maintain a balance-of-trade surplus and to promote domestic production and employment by reducing imports, stimulating home production, and promoting exports" (Blake and Walters, 1987).

neurial initiatives, investment choices, and the like. Increasingly, it has come to believe that "the playing field is tilted"—that American businesspeople are unable to compete on the same basis as others, notably the continental European states, Japan, and less developed countries, where governments routinely intervene actively in their economies and play entrepreneurial and developmental roles directly. Senator Lloyd M. Bentsen, a long-time advocate of free trade, captured the shifting sentiment when he said of free trade, "I think in theory, it's a great theory. But it's not being practiced, and for us to practice free trade in a world where there's much government-directed trade makes as much sense as unilateral disarmament with the Russians." Similarly, Congressperson Richard A. Gephardt lamented in 1988, "Today's policies cannot deal adequately with foreign protectionism, for offending countries will always have an explanation or a new evasion."

Neomercantilism and Challenges to the Liberal International Trade System in the 1990s   It was against the background of a trade system increasingly rife with restrictive barriers, subsidies, invisible import restraints, the setting of standards for domestic products that foreigners can't meet, and other unfair trade practices (see also Anjaria, 1986) that go beyond the principles of GATT that the United States urged a new round of trade negotiations to "level the playing field." By the mid-1980s, however, the United States was part of the problem as well as the solution as its position in the trade system had eroded measurably, with a corresponding chorus of domestic interests seeking increased leverage with the outside world.[16] Compared with the environment when Congress passed the 1974 Trade Act, by the time it enacted the 1988 omnibus trade bill the United States had become the world's largest debtor; its trade deficit, while reduced from the peak in 1987, still exceeded $125 billion annually; and its trade imbalance with particular countries, notably Japan, had burgeoned to seemingly intractable levels. Furthermore, its role as a principal exporter of foodstuffs had eroded, as world food production, fed by high levels of government subsidies, had markedly increased foreign market competition.

Other nations were not quick to accept the analogy of an uneven playing field skewed in their favor that the United States espoused. They were sensitive nonetheless to the need to keep protectionist sentiments in the United States at bay. Because U.S. imports stimulated the economic growth of its trade partners, which enabled the United States to act as the engine of Western economic growth generally, America's trade partners conceded that new trade talks were necessary to cope with issues of special concern to the United States. Conversely, the Reagan administration used the proposed trade talks to thwart growing protectionist sentiments at home, where, at one time during 1985, some three hundred bills were pending before Congress that offered protection

---

16. Although the efforts of domestic interest groups to secure trade protection are well known, less understood is that antiprotection forces also exist among those who depend on international trade and suffer from restrictive measures (see Destler and Odell, 1987).

to one industrial sector or another (including steel, copper, lumber, and automobiles to shoes, textiles, neckties, and waterbeds), and where public support for protective measures had expanded.

In addition to coping with traditional tariff issues and the new protectionism, particularly how to bring VRAs under multilateral management, the United States pushed hard in the Uruguay Round to reduce barriers to trade in services (for example, insurance), intellectual property rights (for example, computer software), and investments—areas that traditionally have been outside the GATT framework but are of special concern to the United States due to its comparative advantages.[17]

Similarly, the Uruguay Round addressed another issue of special importance to the United States, namely, agriculture. World trade in agriculture evolved outside of the main GATT framework and thus has not been subject to the same liberalizing influences that have applied to industrial products (Spero, 1990). The issue is especially controversial because it is deeply enmeshed in the domestic politics of producing states. At the core of differences on agricultural trade are the enormous subsidies that governments of the leading producers in the First World pay farmers to keep them competitive internationally, where prices are often much lower than in Europe or North America. In 1986, for example, the European Community spent over $20 billion, or more than two-thirds of its budget, on agricultural subsidies. The United States, for its part, spent about $30 billion in farm support programs, an amount that exceeded the net income of U.S. farms (Wallis, 1986:2). During the Uruguay Round the United States aggressively proposed to phase out all agricultural subsidies and farm trade protection programs within a decade. It gained the support of some other producing states but was opposed by the EC, which viewed the proposal as unrealistic and sought instead to maintain its own Common Agricultural Policy.

At the same time that the United States pursued resolution of outstanding trade issues via the multilateral GATT mechanism, it also undertook important bilateral and unilateral measures perceived by many to be at variance with the spirit if not the letter of GATT. It concluded free-trade agreements with Israel and Canada which, while rationalized as consistent with GATT, nonetheless raised questions about whether the specific reciprocity each embodied violated the rule of general reciprocity underlying the liberal trade system. The U.S.-Canada Free Trade Agreement, in particular, also raised fear that the United States was moving toward the same kind of regionalized monetary and trade system that it opposed in Europe.

The United States also pursued unilateral remedies in response to what it regarded as unfair trade practices by foreign governments. These were carried

---

17. See Spero (1990) for a discussion of the issues faced in the Uruguay Round, the positions taken by various nations and groups of nations on them, and the factors that enhance or impede agreement on them. Preeg (1989a) usefully summarizes the broader range of issues that challenge the GATT trading system itself.

out under Section 301 of the Trade Act of 1974 and what came to be known commonly—and somewhat ominously—under the 1988 omnibus trade act as "Super 301." According to Super 301, which was a specific remedy to perceived unfair trade imposed by Congress on the president, the executive branch is to identify countries engaged in unfair trade practices with a view toward negotiation to seek remedies or face U.S. retaliation. Japan and the four Asian newly industrialized countries (NICs) (often called the "four tigers"—Hong Kong, Singapore, South Korea, and Taiwan) were generally perceived as the primary targets. The intent was to level the playing field with those in greatest violation of the rules of free (fair?) trade so as to right the overall U.S. imbalance of trade.[18]

The persistent U.S. trade deficit underlies the determination of the United States to take unilateral action against those deemed to play the game unfairly. The causes of the deficit, however, are multifaceted. As noted earlier, the dollar exchange rate is an important factor. As the dollar soared in the first half of the 1980s, the ability of American exporters to compete in the global marketplace plummeted, with the result that thousands who depended on exports lost their jobs. But even as the dollar declined in the latter half of the decade, the deficit, while reduced, persisted as U.S. imports from abroad continued their upward trend. The aggressive strategies of major exporters to the U.S. market, who sought to protect their coveted market shares, partly explained why the trade deficit proved so intractable. Moreover, capital flows now play a more dominant role than trade in the global political economy, with the result that exchange rate fluctuations no longer work solely in tandem with changes in the direction of international trade (Bergsten, 1987; Thurow and Tyson, 1987). Other factors influencing the deficit include the decline in U.S. productivity over many years, resulting in a loss of the technological edge to Japan and others that the United States enjoyed in the 1950s and 1960s. Insufficient domestic savings and insufficient investment in civilian research and development as well as basic education contributed to the erosion of the nation's trade competitiveness (see Hufbauer, 1989–1990; Thurow, 1985).

Japan is often viewed in the United States as the preeminent neomercantilist power, based on the belief that its spectacular export growth since the 1960s resulted from an intimate government-business alliance that tilts the playing field in its favor. The enormous trade imbalance the United States experienced with Japan in recent years reinforces the belief that Japanese neomercantilist policies are inherently disadvantageous to American business. In 1989, for example, U.S. imports from Japan topped $97 billion, but its exports to that island nation were less than $45 billion (see Figure 7.5).

---

18. Despite a trade imbalance with Japan of $49 billion, the Bush administration decided in April 1990 to remove Japan from the list of countries targeted for possible economic retaliation under Super 301. The move surprised and angered members of Congress. "I am thunderstruck," said Senator Robert C. Byrd on the floor of the Senate. "Excuse me, Mr. President, but this boggles the mind. . . . Letting Japan off the hook is a serious mistake." Similarly, Senator Don Riegle, one of the sponsors of Super 301, said, "Our government is not using the tools that are available to correct this continuing hemorrhage of U.S. capital and jobs.

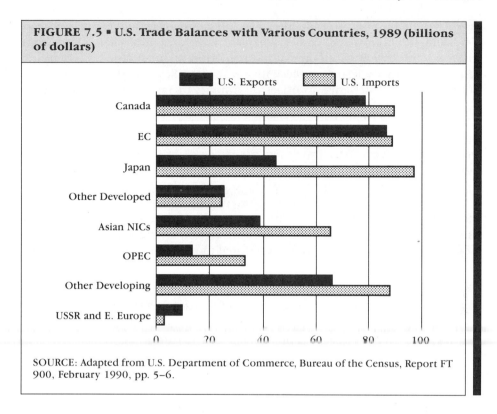

FIGURE 7.5 ▪ U.S. Trade Balances with Various Countries, 1989 (billions of dollars)

SOURCE: Adapted from U.S. Department of Commerce, Bureau of the Census, Report FT 900, February 1990, pp. 5–6.

Beyond the demonstrable preference of millions of Americans for products made in Japan, a broad array of trade restrictions doubtless constrains the ability of American producers to penetrate the Japanese market. Included in addition to traditional tariff barriers are such nontariff restraints as restrictions on license transfers on medical devices and pharmaceuticals, limits on the acceptance of foreign clinical data for medical items and drugs, and product testing of telecommunications equipment. The United States and Japan have engaged in a series of negotiations designed to reduce structural impediments to trade, but penetration of the Japanese market is hampered further by a cultural tradition that views foreign products as ill-suited to the Japanese consumer. Furthermore, the domestic savings rate in Japan is considerably higher than the average savings rate among the other Western industrialized nations.[19] Domestic consumption in Japan, moreover, is low, which also means Japanese industry must look overseas for growth. In other words, the excess of savings

19. In 1988, Japanese savings as a percent of GNP stood at 32.76 percent; in comparison, U.S. savings were at 12.60 percent (Rosecrance, 1990: 100). The impact of this difference is substantial: "Because Japanese save their money at four times the rate Americans save, Japanese firms can borrow money at one-fourth the rate American firms must pay. This gives Japanese corporations a huge advantage in financing long-term investment to extend their global industrial expansion, a process Tokyo coordinates through government ministries" (Rankin, 1989: 16).

over investment, and of production over consumption, finds its way abroad (Feldstein, 1985). As noted earlier, Japan since the mid-1980s has shifted from an economic strategy based on export promotion to one focused on domestic demand, but its trade imbalance with the United States and others persists. Until policies are designed to offset the impact of Japan's high savings rate, Japan will continue to have an important impact on the global political economy generally—and on the American economy in particular, for it has become Japan's most important overseas market (see Rosecrance, 1990). It should be recognized, moreover, that just as the drive to erect protectionist barriers in the United States is a potent political issue, dismantling those barriers is an equally emotional issue on the other side of the Pacific basin.

No easy solutions to the multifaceted problems that plague the multi-lateral trade regime exist. The positions that the United States takes on them will, however, significantly affect the direction and ultimate outcome of these problems. Still, as in the case of international monetary matters, U.S. influence over the outcomes has declined, so that

> the continued vitality of a multilateral liberal system will . . . depend on the development of plurilateral management. Economic power is now more evenly dispersed. The United States as the largest (although no longer the dominant member) will have to continue to provide leadership for the system. This will be possible only if the United States can redress its trade imbalance and revitalize its competitiveness. At the same time, Europe and Japan must define new, more active roles in trade management. Europe will have to find the appropriate balance between looking inward towards the creation of an internal market and its need to look outward to the multilateral trading system. Because of its size and its role in world trade, reestablishing a reasonable balance between Japan and its trading partners, as well as integrating Japan into the management of the international trading system, will be a central challenge for the remainder of the century. (Spero, 1990: 97)

These are demanding challenges. Meeting them will not be made easier by the problems and challenges posed by Third World nations, to which we now turn.

THE THIRD WORLD: THE NORTH-SOUTH DIALOGUE

The international monetary and multilateral trading systems that evolved during the postwar decades did so primarily under the aegis of the Western industrialized nations whose interests and objectives they served. Developing nations on the periphery largely were outside the privileged circle. Many of these nations came to view the existing international economic structure as a cause of their underdog status.

Already by the 1950s the nonaligned nations began efforts to promote their common interests. The strategy was to devise a unified posture toward the superpowers in the context of the Cold War and to press for consideration of their special problems and needs in the context of the global economic structure. But it was not until the 1960s that these efforts produced results. Taking advantage of their growing numbers in the United Nations, developing nations were able to utilize that forum to make repeated demands for a restructuring of the existing international economic order. They were successful in having convened, in 1964, a United Nations Conference on Trade and Development (UNCTAD). In that conference, the Group of 77 (sometimes referred to simply as G-77) was formed as a coalition of the world's poor to press for concessions from the world's rich.

UNCTAD conferences have been held at periodic intervals since 1964. UNCTAD itself has become an autonomous structure within the family of United Nations organizations; as a practical matter the organization has come to be a voice for the interests of the poor. And the Group of 77 (which still goes by that label but now numbers well over one hundred states) continues to operate as an economic negotiating caucus of the world's less fortunate nations.

The G-77 effectively joined the nonaligned movement during the 1973 Algiers summit of nonaligned nations, when issues relating to economic as well as political "liberation" came to the fore. Algeria, then the chair of the non-aligned countries, led the call for what became the Sixth Special Session of the United Nations General Assembly, held in the spring of 1974. Using its superior numbers, the G-77 secured passage of the Declaration on the Establishment of a New International Economic Order (NIEO). It is significant that both the special session and the declaration coincided with the worldwide food and energy crises the world experienced in the mid-1970s, for not until the OPEC cartel successfully raised petroleum prices were the demands of the Third World of the South given serious consideration by the Western industrial nations of the North. OPEC's success also augmented the stridency of developing nations' demands, for whom the phrase *New International Economic Order* became the rallying cry for their drive for a basic restructuring of the existing international political economy.

The Third World's demands challenged the Liberal International Economic Order (LIEO) and the processes that sustained it, which had been created during the 1950s and 1960s under the leadership of the United States. Inspired by the belief that *commodity power* endowed the Third World with the political strength necessary to challenge the advanced industrial nations of the North, developing nations sought through their superior numbers to exercise influence in the United Nations, UNCTAD, the IMF, the World Bank, the Third United Nations Law of the Sea Conference, and various other global and regional forums in which a North-South dialogue was sought. In these institutions the Third World called for more rapid economic development, increased transfers of resources from industrialized to developing nations, and a more favorable distribution of global economic benefits. Other more specific issues addressed included aid, trade, foreign investment, foreign ownership of property, multinational corporations, debt relief, and commodity price stabilization.

Collectively, the demands for a New International Economic Order sought a redistribution of income and wealth from rich nations to poor. In addition to that motivation, at a more fundamental level they sought a transfer of political influence to Third World nations through a substantial alteration of the rules and institutional structures governing the transnational flow of goods, services, capital, and technology. Simply put, the Third World sought *regime change*—a revision of the rules, norms, and procedures of the Liberal International Economic Order to serve the interests of the Third World rather than the industrialized North (Krasner, 1985).

The Third World drive for regime change derived from its belief that the international political economy is structured so as to perpetuate developing nations' underdog status. The feeling is widespread among Third World nations that present international economic institutions, such as the IMF and GATT and the political and economic processes governed by them, are "deeply biased against developing countries in their global distribution of income and influence" (Hansen, 1980). The perception is buttressed by a legacy of colonial exploitation, the continued existence in many Third World countries of levels of poverty and deprivation unheard of in the North, and a conviction that relief from many of the economic and associated political ills of the South can only result from changes in Northern policies, in whose hands responsibility for prevailing conditions and the means to correct them lie.

The North rejects the view that the economic woes of developing nations are a product of the structure of the current international order or of Northern policies; instead, it locates the cause of those problems in the domestic systems of Third World countries themselves. Accordingly, proposals to alter radically existing international economic institutions as well as the more modest elements of the Third World program advanced during the 1970s and 1980s met with resistance and resentment. The United States was especially intransigent, as the Reagan administration approached the Third World primarily from the vantage point of its role in the East-West conflict, with little interest shown in those aspects of Southern objectives related to transformation of the Liberal International Economic Order. Moreover, the incentives for the North to accept such changes were rapidly disappearing. By the time of the UNCTAD VI meeting in 1983, it was apparent that the commodity power with which the South had hoped to force the North to come to terms was a transient phenomenon. The G-77, in turn, began to express greater concern with immediate issues than with the long-term goals of structural reform and regime change that had dominated its agenda earlier. The new mood was summarized in 1983 by Farouk Sobhan of Bangladesh, chairperson of the G-77: "We cannot change institutions overnight. We have to do this gradually with a sense of purpose and pragmatism."

What accounts for the Third World's apparent retreat from its earlier, militant posture toward regime change?

First, the economic climate faced by most Third World nations changed sharply. North and South alike experienced a general and prolonged economic slump in the early 1980s, but for many Third World nations the consequences were especially damaging. Economic growth rates deteriorated in many of them, and in some, particularly in Africa, they actually reflected "negative growth'' (see Chapter 6). The prices of many of the commodities exported by Third World nations fell sharply compared with the prices they had to pay for their imports. Faced with reduced export earnings and higher interest rates, the debt burdens of many Third World nations assumed ominous proportions. Thus acute economic problems at home caused many Third World leaders to focus pragmatically on immediate policy problems rather than ideologically on the longer-term drive for structural reform that had been launched a decade or more earlier.

Second, the erosion of the Third World's bargaining leverage contributed to the softening of its militancy. OPEC's successful cartelization of the oil market in 1973–1974 served as a rallying point for the entire Group of 77 and gave rise to the belief that commodity power could be used to break the North's resistance. But the denouement of the OPEC decade in the face of a worldwide oil glut in the 1980s removed any reason the North might have had to make major concessions to Southern demands.

Third, as the unifying force of commodity power receded and different countries were affected in different ways by the changing economic climate of the 1980s, latent fissures within the Group of 77 became more evident, with the result that the South no longer spoke as a unified group. The differences between the more advanced of the developing nations, on the one hand, of which the NICs stand out, and the less well-off, especially the least developed of the less developed countries—the Fourth World—on the other, became especially pronounced. Others among the more advanced developing nations, particularly in Latin America, were hardest hit by the debt crisis, which also had the effect of dividing the Third World into competing groups rather than uniting them behind a common cause.

Against the background of these changes, the Third World drive for a New International Economic Order might properly be conceived not as the ''beginning of the end'' of the Liberal International Economic Order but ''as the 'end of the beginning,' a period of transition to a more complex order with a different international division of labor and different economic and political prospects for different Third World states. In this sense, the heated North-South conflicts of the 1970s were transitory and not part of a permanent conflict between two unchanging blocs of rich and poor'' (Rothstein, 1988).

The United States has been a major player in the changing North-South game and the issues that have animated it in recent years. It has assumed an active role in international efforts to deal with the Third World debt problem. The United States has also become acutely sensitive to its trade imbalance with the NICs, especially the four Asian tigers that have become important sources of manufactured imports; it is fearful of the loss of traditional markets for American agricultural exports in the face of growing foreign competition, much of it from Third World producers; and it has evinced a marked trend toward increased dependence on foreign energy supplies, particularly OPEC oil. For all of these reasons—plus the fact that the United States maintains continuing strategic interests in a number of Third World countries, such as

Panama, the Philippines, Saudi Arabia, and Turkey—the Third World is salient to American foreign policy. Concomitantly, the Third World has become increasingly sensitive and vulnerable to U.S. fiscal and monetary policies as well as its trade and security policies. *Interdependence* thus increasingly applies to U.S.-Third World linkages, much as it applies to those among the advanced industrial societies of the West.

We will briefly examine the nature of U.S.-Third World interdependence in the context of the contention between North and South by examining several areas in which the interests of the United States and the developing nations intersect, including trade in commodities and manufactures, agricultural policy, and, most especially, the debt crisis.

U.S.-Third World Interdependence: Commodities, Manufactures, and Agricultural Policy

Trade-related issues are at the core of the North-South dispute. The structure of trade relationships between developed and developing nations evolved during the age of imperialism, when colonies presumably existed for the benefit of the colonizers. Frequently, that arrangement meant that the colonies were sources of primary products, such as agricultural commodities and mineral resources, and markets for the finished manufactured goods produced in the mother country. That pattern persists today as a general description of the structure of trade ties between developed and developing nations. As shown in Figure 7.6, in 1987 developing nations as a whole relied on primary products (including fuels and related materials) for 48 percent of their export earnings (the money necessary to buy goods from abroad), while 68 percent of their imports were in the form of manufactures. That pattern is virtually the reverse of developed nations, for whom primary products are comparatively insignificant export products. At the same time, the developed-market economies of the First World are the principal source and destination of the manufactured goods that enter the international marketplace.

Although the patterns described above still mirror those of the bygone imperial era, they are not nearly as striking as even a few years ago. In 1980, for example, following the second oil shock, 80 percent of the developing nations' exports were in the form of primary products and fuels; only 20 percent were manufactured products. Since then global dependence on OPEC oil has lessened, while other Third World nations, notably in East Asia, have become important exporters of manufactured products. But still others, particularly African nations, remain heavily dependent on exports of primary products and imports of manufactured goods. OPEC nations themselves also remain heavily dependent on revenues from oil exports.

A central proposition in developing nations' efforts to restructure the LIEO alleged that their terms of trade (the ratio of export prices to import prices) problems stemmed from their dependence on a narrow range of primary product exports. Many believed that the prices Third World countries

FIGURE 7.6 ▪ The Composition of World Exports and Imports, by Groups of Countries, 1987

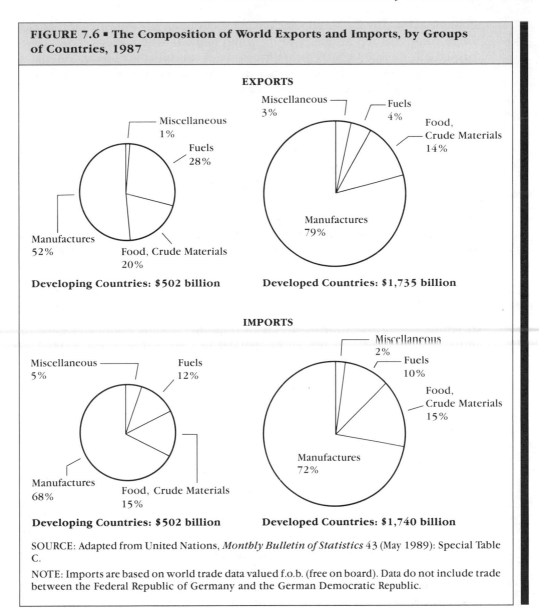

EXPORTS

Developing Countries: $502 billion

Miscellaneous 1%
Fuels 28%
Manufactures 52%
Food, Crude Materials 20%

Developed Countries: $1,735 billion

Miscellaneous 3%
Fuels 4%
Food, Crude Materials 14%
Manufactures 79%

IMPORTS

Developing Countries: $502 billion

Miscellaneous 5%
Fuels 12%
Manufactures 68%
Food, Crude Materials 15%

Developed Countries: $1,740 billion

Miscellaneous 2%
Fuels 10%
Food, Crude Materials 15%
Manufactures 72%

SOURCE: Adapted from United Nations, *Monthly Bulletin of Statistics* 43 (May 1989): Special Table C.

NOTE: Imports are based on world trade data valued f.o.b. (free on board). Data do not include trade between the Federal Republic of Germany and the German Democratic Republic.

received for their exports vary erratically in the short run and deteriorate steadily in the long run, whereas the prices of the manufactured goods that they import increase steadily.

The structural characteristics of the international economic order are among the alleged causes of the deteriorating terms of trade. The South remains critically dependent on the North not only for manufactured goods but also for technology (see Head, 1989). The greater technological sophistication of the North causes natural resources to flow into markets where they can be transformed into finished goods most efficiently. Powerful labor unions and giant corporations institutionalize, through wage and fringe-benefit programs, the comparatively high cost of the technologically sophisticated products produced in the North, the demand for which is sustained by worldwide advertising campaigns. Developing nations are unable to compete on similar terms with the North. The South cannot bid up the prices for the materials produced in developing nations, the argument continues. In a system where those with the most money determine prices, Third World nations find themselves unable to determine the terms of trade for their products.

Commodities   There is no question that developing nations' primary product exports are subject to sharp price fluctuations (see Figure 7.7). As noted earlier, for example, nonfuel commodity prices dropped sharply during the recession induced by the second oil shock. By 1982 they had reached a lower level in real terms (after adjusting for the rise in prices of manufactures imported by developing nations) than at any time since World War II (*World Development Report 1983*, 1983: 11). Whether such fluctuations are a result of a long-term structural deterioration of the terms of trade developing nations face, or of short-term perturbations related to changes in the business cycle, remains a matter of controversy among analysts. In 1985 and again in 1988, for example, nonfuel commodity prices turned sharply upward. They did not regain the ground that had been lost earlier in the decade (Figure 7.7), which may reflect the fact that the industrial economies of the First World have increasingly become uncoupled from the primary product economies of the Third World (Drucker, 1986). Regardless, the policies Third World leaders pursue are influenced by perceptions as well as objective facts. Moreover, whether caused by cyclical or more deep-seated forces, swings in commodity prices have caused serious structural adjustment problems among commodity producing and exporting countries.

Faced with the circumstances described above, diversification of export industries, rather than continued dependence on a few primary products, is a preferred goal of many developing nations. At the same time, they have sought new means of ensuring stable and remunerative prices for the commodities they already export. Such was the goal of the Integrated Programme for Commodities pushed by the G-77 as a central element of its drive for a New International Economic Order (see Finlayson and Zacher, 1988). As originally conceived, the program sought commodity price stabilization through a common fund supported by producing and consuming nations and administered by an international agency. A much less ambitious version was finally agreed on in 1979, but it failed to win approval by the required number of signatories necessary to put it into operation. The United States was among those states that refused to ratify the agreement, even though the Carter administration had earlier signed it. Thus a key item on the NIEO agenda simply fell by the wayside.

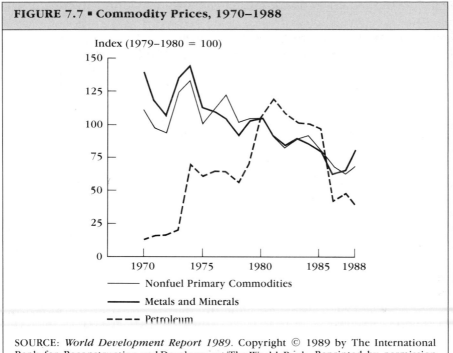

FIGURE 7.7 ■ Commodity Prices, 1970–1988

Index (1979–1980 = 100)

——— Nonfuel Primary Commodities

——— Metals and Minerals

– – – – Petroleum

SOURCE: *World Development Report 1989.* Copyright © 1989 by The International Bank for Reconstruction and Development/The World Bank. Reprinted by permission of Oxford University Press Inc.

NOTE: Real prices are annual average prices in dollars, deflated by the annual change in the manufacturing unit value (MUV) index, a measure of the price of industrial country exports to developing countries. Prices for nonfuel primary commodities are based on a basket of thirty-three commodities.

Third World nations remained concerned with commodity price stabilization during the 1980s, and they tended to adopt more pragmatic policies on the issue than they had a decade earlier. But the industrialized nations became even more strident in their opposition to the notion that structural rigidities caused the plight of the poor, believing instead that deliberate government policies and price changes associated with the business cycle were better explanations. Thus little headway has been made on alleviating the plight of Third World nations heavily dependent on commodity exports. As noted earlier, many of them are in Africa where, as we saw in Chapter 6, economic growth rates during the 1980s were actually negative, with the result that living standards fell markedly.

Oil   The decline of Third World commodity power is nowhere more evident than with oil. As noted previously, world oil prices plunged in the 1980s (see Figure 7.7) as conservation measures, economic recession, a shift to alternative sources of energy, and overproduction undermined the ability of OPEC to extract monopoly prices for its resources. The centrality of OPEC itself diminished as reduced demand for oil combined with the discovery of new oil resources in Alaska, the North Sea, and elsewhere to lessen dependence on OPEC oil. Still, much of the world remained vulnerable to interruptions in oil imported from the politically volatile Persian Gulf region. The United States underscored its own sensitivity on this point when, in 1987, in response to the fear that the continuing war between Iran and Iraq might widen and thereby threaten the continued flow of Middle Eastern oil as well as U.S. security interests in the region, it substantially increased its naval presence in the Persian Gulf region and made the controversial decision to escort Kuwaiti oil tankers through the perilous Strait of Hormuz, where oil tankers had become routine targets in the war. Three years later President Bush responded to Iraq's invasion of Kuwait with a massive military buildup whose avowed purpose was the protection of Saudi Arabia and restoration of Kuwait's sovereignty, but the administration's determination to prevent Iraqi control of Kuwait's rich oil resources, which would also give it a significant voice in determining global oil prices, figured prominently in the decision. (Iraq and Kuwait accounted for about 20 percent of the oil supplied by OPEC countries in 1989; OPEC accounted for half of total global demand.)

For a variety of reasons, including the restructuring of the global oil market in the aftermath the OPEC decade (Morse, 1986), it is unlikely that the world will see a repeat of OPEC's efforts to utilize commodity power for political purposes on the scale sought during the 1970s. Still, even before the 1990 crisis over Kuwait, many analysts warned of a coming crisis in which only a handful of nations that control the vast bulk of known reserves of world oil—all of whom are in the Persian Gulf region—would control the flow of oil to the West, and hence significantly influence its price. The scenario was based on a combination of increased demand and reduced production outside the oil-rich Middle East in the absence of incentives (largely destroyed in the aftermath of the OPEC decade) for devising politically acceptable alternatives to energy derived from fossil fuels (see Kegley and Wittkopf, 1989).

As before, the United States figures prominently in this picture. During the latter half of the 1980s a combination of rising demand for oil and reduced domestic production saw U.S. dependence on foreign sources of oil grow at an alarming rate—and at an increased cost. Projections to the end of the century call for a continuation of these trends. Dependence on imported energy resources is not necessarily bad—Japan, for example, imports virtually all of its oil—but the rising cost of energy is a matter of special concern to the United States because of its already excessive trade imbalance. Even before the dramatic rise in the price of oil that followed Iraq's invasion of Kuwait, for example, U.S. oil import costs alone were expected to exceed $100 billion by the mid-1990s (Schlesinger, 1990: 113). Now, it seems, that may turn out to be a very conservative estimate, as world oil prices more than doubled following the events in the Middle East in the fall of 1990, and could conceivably remain well above pre-crisis levels for many years into the future (World Bank, 1990). Thus growing dependence on oil from the Persian Gulf political cauldron and mounting trade deficits virtually ensure U.S. vulnerability to foreign powers on this vital issue quite apart from any effort by OPEC to renew its cartelization of the global oil regime.

Uncertainty over the behavior of the Soviet Union in the Middle East in the aftermath of the breakup of the Soviet external empire adds further concern. The United States has long enjoyed a local strategic advantage in the Western hemisphere. In the Persian Gulf, other things being equal, the advantage goes to the Soviet Union. To be sure, Soviet leaders supported U.S. efforts to force Iraq to withdraw from Kuwait in what was a clear test of Gorbachev's new foreign policy thinking. But in the long run the ability of the Soviet Union to carve out a new role as a world leader will doubtless depend on devising an independent and distinctly Soviet posture in the Middle East (Dobbs, 1990). Thus the prophetic observations made by James Schlesinger shortly before the crisis over Kuwait remain relevant. As the world has "grown increasingly and perhaps excessively dependent on the Gulf region for its energy resources and for the performance of its economies," he wrote in early 1990, the Middle East "will . . . become the cockpit of contending world forces—and a potential tinder box. If there is a major conflict, the Middle East is likely to be its vortex" (Schlesinger, 1990).

Manufactures   At the same time that the North rebuffed the South's efforts at commodity price reform, it became increasingly disturbed by the growing economic challenge posed by the NICs as well as the growing importance of export markets in the Third World and the need to maintain access to them.

As described earlier, the rise of protectionist sentiment in the United States can be traced to the early 1970s, when domestic inflation began to erode the trade competitiveness of U.S. products abroad. Protectionism was spurred by the economic recession that followed the first oil shock and by subsequent developments at home and abroad that inhibited the process of structural adjustment to the changing world economy. Among those changes was increasing competition from the NICs, particularly Brazil, Mexico, and Asia's four tigers. By the mid-1980s the Asian tigers in particular had become among the most important U.S trade partners in the Third World. Moreover, they have consistently maintained a favorable trade balance with the United States surpassed in magnitude only by Japan's (see Figure 7.5). Thus their economic success and their ability to penetrate the U.S. market have contributed to the view that they, too, have stimulated the export of American jobs and the deindustrialization of the U.S. economy.

Exploiting advantages in the cost of labor and access to advanced technology, the NICs have achieved spectacular economic growth rates since the 1960s compared with other Third World nations by pursuing export-led rather than import-substitution industrialization policies. A successful export-led strategy requires access to First World markets.[20] But the more successful it is, the more it stimulates domestic protectionist sentiments in the importing countries.

---

20. A number of other countries have sought to emulate the NICs' successful economic development strategies, but for a number of reasons, including market access, that may not be possible. See Broad and Cavanagh (1988).

As described in Chapter 5, foreign aid has been a preferred mechanism whereby the United States has sought to assist Third World economic growth and development. But "trade, not aid" has been a persistent plea of many developing nations, which feel they have been denied access to markets in developed countries through tariff and nontariff barriers alike. The Multifiber Arrangement (MFA) is a classic case in point. Designed in the 1950s as a mechanism to protect textile producers in the United States from imports from the Far East, the scheme today is an elaborate market-sharing arrangement among more than three dozen textile-producing countries that effectively denies access to others. Because textiles are among the simplest semimanufactures that Third World nations aspiring to export-led growth might hope to ship abroad, the MFA is a blatantly discriminatory barrier to free trade.

To overcome the obstacles Third World nations face in their drive to gain access to First World markets, developing nations have sought preferential, as opposed to most-favored-nation, trade treatment. The argument is that preferential treatment would enable them to build diversified export industries capable of competing on equal terms with those in the North.

In partial response to that plea, the United States established (by the Trade Act of 1974) a Generalized System of Preferences (GSP), thereby joining most other industrialized nations in creating a system of nonreciprocal and nondiscriminatory tariff preferences for developing nations. The principle of nonreciprocity was extended by the Tokyo Round of GATT trade negotiations, thereby enabling developed nations to grant trade preferences to developing nations without violating GATT's rules regarding most-favored-nation trade treatment. The extension of preferential treatment was a significant departure from the nondiscrimination principle dominant throughout the postwar era.

Despite these apparent Northern concessions, the effects of the concessions have been disputed. For example, some of the countries that have benefited most from the trade preferences, such as Hong Kong and South Korea, have needed them least (Spero, 1990). Moreover, the Tokyo Round failed to grapple with the protectionist sentiments in the North that were often directed at products in which some developing nations already enjoyed comparative advantages, such as clothing, footwear, textiles, and steel. In fact, in 1986, 21 percent of the imports of industrial countries from the Third World were subject to "hard-core" nontariff barriers[21] compared with only 16 percent of the imports from industrial countries (*World Development Report 1987*, 1987: 142). And the proportion is on the rise.

The Tokyo Round not only failed to devise a code to limit the effect of protectionist measures in the North on those nations; following the insistence of the United States, it also included a "graduation clause" stipulating that as

---

21. "Hard-core" NTBs comprise that subset of all NTBs most likely to have significant restrictive effects, including "import prohibitions, quantitative restrictions, voluntary export restraints, variable levies, MFA restrictions, and nonautomatic licensing" (*World Development Report 1987*, 1987).

developing countries reached higher levels of development, they would be given less special treatment and be forced to compete on a more equal footing with Northern states. When the U.S. GSP came up for renewal in 1985 (it was extended to 1993), Congress wrote the graduation principle into law and specified conditions that the United States might use to deny GSP benefits. Congress also for the first time tied the trade preferences to steps by the beneficiaries to open their markets to U.S. exports and to other issues of importance to the United States, such as the protection of intellectual property rights.[22] Both of these moves reflected concern about the operation of the preference scheme and the fact that, in the view of opponents, the majority of GSP benefits went to the NICs who "don't need special treatment anymore." As various labor groups and business interests mobilized to exempt their products from duty-free status, Congressperson Bill Frenzel remarked that "it has often been said facetiously that if Congress had known what GSP was in 1974, it never would have included it in the Trade Act." Eventually, in 1989, the United States removed the Asian NICs from the list of countries entitled to preferential treatment. It was the first time that trade benefits were denied for trade (rather than political) reasons to countries rather than specific products.

Agriculture   Agricultural trade is of special interest to the United States, for the economic well-being of American agriculture depends more heavily on exports than do other sectors of the U.S. economy. Exports generated more than 20 percent of total agricultural receipts in 1987, and in some major crops, such as wheat and soybeans, the proportion was half or more.

American dependence on foreign markets grew dramatically in the 1970s, as favorable agricultural conditions caused a dramatic rise in world agricultural trade and U.S. exports. Because of their massive exports of wheat, corn, and soybeans in particular, the United States and Canada were commonly referred to as both the world's breadbasket and its feedbag. By the mid-1980s, however, the picture had changed dramatically, as the strong dollar, worldwide recession, and increased production by and competition from others eroded the agricultural export supremacy of the United States.

U.S. policy remains committed to a liberal trading system that enhances the export opportunities for U.S. agriculture. In contrast to others among the growing number of exporters of agricultural products (particularly the new, developing country exporters), however, U.S. agricultural policy has been "driven more by the need to protect a major domestic economic, social and political interest than by the need for foreign exchange produced by these exports, no matter how significant those trade earnings may be" (Insel, 1985).

---

22. Textbooks and Apple computers are among the products and technologies some NICs have pirated in violation of international standards and copyright laws designed to protect intellectual property rights. As noted earlier, this is an issue of special concern to the United States in the Uruguay Round of trade negotiations.

As competition has grown among exporters, each seeking to realize its particular policy objectives, international trade in agricultural products (particularly grain) has been affected by aggressive national strategies designed to increase the competitive advantage of one exporter over another, including "a variety of export incentives and subsidies, such as differential export taxes, tax rebates, direct support payments to allow lower export prices, subsidized domestic credits, subsidized export credits and 'food aid'" (Insel, 1985). The widespread use of such tactics—which, incidentally, the United States itself employs in varying degrees—has led to growing political pressure in the United States to fight what are believed to be unfair trade practices in this area. Simultaneously, as noted earlier, the United States proposed in the Uruguay Round a radical departure from existing domestic policies toward agriculture by urging the complete elimination worldwide of agricultural subsidies and farm protection programs by the end of the century. Apart from its own domestic concerns regarding agricultural production and subsidies, the United States was urged to do something on the issues by the "Cairns group," a collection of thirteen agricultural exporting nations, including nine from the Third World, that was organized in 1986 for the specific purpose of pressuring the United States and the European Community on agricultural matters.

Many analysts believe that the decline in U.S. competitiveness in agricultural trade that occurred in the 1980s will be a temporary pause (see, for example, Paarlberg, 1988). Moreover, increased export competition and the increased productivity that makes it possible imply that the goal of enhancing global food resources so as to ensure global and individual food security in the face of a rapidly expanding world population may still be attainable. In fact, however, that remains problematic. As Lester Brown and John Young (1990) of the Worldwatch Institute have noted, "pushing [agricultural] production above consumption [is] a task that is becoming more difficult. Growth in world food output is being slowed by environmental degradation, a worldwide scarcity of cropland and irrigation water, and a diminishing response to the use of additional chemical fertilizer. Meanwhile, the annual addition to our numbers is moving above 90 million people."

Ensuring food security became an item on the North-South agenda during the 1970s when, at about the same time as the first oil shock, the ability of the multitude of nationally based agricultural systems to produce sufficient food for the world's growing billions was severely challenged. World grain reserves, defined in terms of days of worldwide grain consumption, dropped from over a hundred days in 1968 to only forty days in 1974 (Sewell et al., 1980: 178). With that, food prices soared worldwide. Meanwhile, famine struck in Africa, where starvation and death became daily occurrences in broad stretches of the Sahel, ranging from Ethiopia in the East to Chad in the West. The situation was repeated a decade later, when, in Ethiopia in particular, world consciousness was awakened by the tragic specter of tens of thousands suffering from malnutrition and dying of starvation at a time of unprecedented food surpluses worldwide. Indeed, Africa is the one world region where the grim prediction made by the Reverend Thomas Malthus over a century ago—that population growth would outstrip food production—seems to have proved accurate. At the same time, however, the pattern of world trade in grain that evolved during the 1970s and 1980s demonstrated the extent to which food consumption depends on wealth, as most food imports permitted enhancement of both the quality and variety of the importing nations' dietary intake, especially in Europe, Japan, and the Soviet Union.

As suggested earlier, debate persists about the shape of the economic and ecological demands that can be expected to exert pressure on the global food regime as the world moves toward the twenty-first century and what now appears to be the realistic goal of producing enough food for the generations who will live in that century. The United States will play an active role in efforts to achieve that goal. The mechanisms will be found in its own agricultural production, its food aid and agricultural development assistance programs, and its domestically managed system of grain reserves that can be used to cushion year-to-year fluctuations in grain production. It will doubtless also play a critical role in meeting the increased demand for food that rising population and income will inevitably generate. From a near-term perspective, however, the important challenge of foreign agricultural policy will be how to cope with increased foreign competition.[23] As suggested earlier, this is now a contentious issue on the global political agenda that extends beyond North-South relations to include North-North relations and domestic politics in a multitude of different national settings.

The theory of free trade promises benefits to all who specialize in the production of those goods in which they enjoy comparative advantages, trading them for the goods produced by others pursuing their own comparative advantages. On the surface the conclusions of the theory are irrefutable and were recognized as such by policymakers who, contemplating the global economic disaster of the 1930s, determined that the institutional arrangements that were to govern the post–World War II system should encourage the free flow of capital and goods across national boundaries. The political task today is to balance promised benefits against the immediate costs imposed by the structural adjustments that free trade inevitably demands. The task is more difficult when one or more of the partners believes the game is biased, as does the United States. The political economy of North-South trade relations, and of the role of the United States within it, promises to continue to be colored by the inevitable contest between parochial, short-term national interests, on the one hand, and collective, long-term interests on the other. That viewpoint also

---

23. Shlomo Reutlinger (1985) reminds us that "it is important to distinguish between foods that are internationally traded, whose prices and level of supply are largely determined by world prices and the exchange rate, and nontraded foods, whose prices are determined by domestic demand and production. The domestic supply of traded foods can be increased only by deliberate measures to increase imports or restrict exports. The supply of nontraded foods can be increased only by increasing domestic production." Public policies relating to traded and nontraded foods and their effects on different groups within society therefore differ.

applies to the persistent debt crisis that has plagued developing nations for more than a decade and that has colored the entire tapestry of North-South relations from the early 1980s onward.

World Debt and the Challenge of Interdependence

The success of OPEC in cartelizing the global oil regime during the 1970s was important in galvanizing the non-oil-producing developing nations into the belief that commodity power would enable them to "force" the North into replacing the Liberal International Economic Order with a new order more amenable to their interests and objectives. Ironically, however, the two oil shocks of the 1970s created an environment in which many Third World nations deemed it prudent to borrow heavily from abroad, while they simultaneously eroded the economic bases on which repayment of those loans depended. The result was a debt crisis that "dominated—some would say 'consumed'—international economic discussions in the 1980s" in what effectively became the "debt decade" (Nowzad, 1990).

The specific event that triggered the debt crisis was the threat in August 1982 that Mexico would default on its loans. The United States was instrumental in averting the disaster, and it urged at that time that the International Monetary Fund assume a leadership role in securing debt relief for many Third World countries. Its arm's-length if not always hands-off strategy toward the debt crisis continued until mid-decade, when the United States adopted a more active role in devising strategies aimed at a long-term resolution of the problem. Two initiatives named after the secretaries of the treasury who sponsored them symbolize the change: the Baker initiative, announced in 1985, and the Brady initiative, announced in 1989. The first was directed essentially at the crisis for U.S. banks that arose out of the fact that they had lent to too much to Third World nations; the second was aimed at those nations themselves who had borrowed too much (Sachs, 1989).

Averting Disaster, 1982–1985   As it first emerged in the early 1980s, the debt crisis spread to a broad group of countries, ranging from Poland to Brazil, from the Philippines to Nigeria. It grew out of a combination of heavy private and public borrowing from private and public sources during the 1970s that led to an accumulated debt estimated to have been over $600 billion by 1980 and nearly twice that amount seven years later. Many debtor nations found that they needed to borrow more money, not to finance new projects, but to meet the debt service obligations (interest and principal payments) on previous loans. In addition to Mexico, others with the largest debts, including Poland, Argentina, and Brazil, required special treatment to keep them from going into default when they announced they did not have the cash necessary to pay their creditors. Eventually, Third World debtor nations, especially those in Latin America, received the most attention. Although the debt obligations of many Eastern European nations remained perilously high, their improved trade status with the West eased concern about their ability to meet their debt obligations.

The foreign debt accumulation of the 1970s was part of a process that saw private loans and investments and official nonconsessional loans become more important than public foreign aid for all but the poorest of the poor countries (Burki, 1983).[24] Among the many results was a greater sensitivity to the interdependence of North and South as "the financial solvency of a great number of developing and some developed countries became a major preoccupation of the commercial banks and other developed country investors" (Burki, 1983). Governments, in turn, became concerned because many of the world's major private banks had significant exposure in these countries. As a study by the U.S. Federal Reserve Bank would later characterize the situation, "International bankers and policy makers faced a threat of financial disorder on a global scale not seen since the Depression" (cited in Spero, 1990).

The first oil shock gave impetus to the privatization of Third World capital flows. As dollars flowed from oil consumers in the West to oil producers in the Middle East and elsewhere, the latter, unable to invest all of their new-found wealth at home, "recycled" their "petrodollars" by making investments in the West. In the process, the funds available to private banks for lending to others increased substantially.

Many of the non-oil-exporting developing nations became the willing consumers of the private banks' investment funds. The fourfold rise in oil prices effected by the OPEC cartel hit these nations particularly hard. To pay for the sharply increased cost of imported oil along with their other imports, they could either tighten their belts at home so as to curb their economic growth or borrow from abroad so as to sustain that growth and pay for needed imports simultaneously. Many chose the latter, and they often preferred private banks to other governments or multilateral agencies because the banks generally placed fewer restrictions on the use of the borrowed money than did the public sources. Private banks for their part were willing lenders, as *sovereign risk*—the risk that governments might default—was believed to be virtually nonexistent.

Just as the United States was a net borrower from the world when it was building its own economy in the past, countries seeking today to industrialize must often rely on external capital. As long as the exports needed to earn the money to pay back the loans grow at the same rate, the accumulation of further debt is no problem. Moreover, there can be long-run payoffs in that investments made today in development projects, such as roads, hydroelectric dams, and steel plants, may eventually more than make up the cost of the original loans by generating new income, employment, and exports.

---

24. During the 1970s, private financial institutions surpassed not only official aid but also multinational corporations as the principal source of financial capital available to Third World countries. The result in many cases was a condition of "indebted industrialization" (Frieden, 1981) as governmental institutions in state-capitalist regimes became actively involved in promoting industrial growth. A decade later many observers (for example, Kuczynski, 1987) as well as some state-capitalist regimes (such as Mexico) came to the conclusion that disengagement of the state from direct involvement in industrialization activities, often through a process of privatization, was a necessary component of the internal reforms needed to cope effectively with the debt crisis.

Whether developing nations always spent their borrowed money wisely can be questioned. Argentina, for example, is reported to have spent as much as $6 billion on sophisticated military equipment between 1978 and 1982, which it used against Britain during the Falkland Islands (Malvinas) war (*Washington Post*, September 13, 1982, p. A18). Brazil, the largest Third World debtor, used foreign loans to finance a number of "white elephants," including three nuclear power plants built at a cost of over $5 billion—but only one of which works; the world's largest hydroelectric dam—which still was not operational after thirteen years of construction and $15.2 billion of investment; and a never-completed railroad—which cost $1.2 billion (Henry, 1987: 29).

Others argue that the capital flight from debtor nations was in many instances as great or greater than the amount of new loans made to them, with much of the money flowing from unscrupulous political leaders or well-heeled elites into private accounts in the very banks extending the loans to the governments in the first place (Henry, 1986, 1987, 1988). Whether caused by corrupt officials or middle-class entrepreneurs seeking a safe haven for their profits, the outflow of money reduces that available for the investments that create new jobs and new wealth.

At the same time that developing nations' debt grew substantially during the 1970s, however, so did the resources needed to service it. Consequently, the burden of the growing debt was essentially the same in 1980 as it was in 1970. But that situation changed sharply after 1980 as the drop in commodity prices associated with the worldwide recession caused the ratio of Third World debts to exports to rise markedly between 1980 and 1982. Economic growth slowed as the prices of the commodities needed to pay for the debt dropped, and the money needed to pay off the loans simply failed to materialize. The appreciation of the dollar in foreign exchange markets added to the debt burden, as many developing nations' loans are denominated in dollars. Similarly, the strict monetarist policies adopted by the Western industrialized nations as a way of coping with their persistent inflation caused interest rates to rise, with the result that developing nations' debt obligations, which were tied to those rates, also inched upwards. In Brazil, for example, each percentage point increase in interest rates is estimated to have cost the country an additional $700 million annually (*New York Times*, April 12, 1984, p. A27). For developing nations as a whole, the ratio of debt service obligations to export earnings rose sharply, moving from 13 to nearly 20 percent between 1980 and 1982 as a consequence of rising interest rates (International Monetary Fund, 1987: 180). The magnitude of the debt also grew to staggering proportions, increasing from $634 billion, or 82 percent of exports in 1980, to $850 billion, or 120 percent of exports, two years later (International Monetary Fund, 1987: 181, 186). For countries in the Western Hemisphere, like Brazil, the jump in the debt-to-exports ratio was even more dramatic.

Not all of the debtor nations were hit equally hard by the difficulties described above, but many found themselves severely strained and thus sought to *reschedule* their debts, that is, to stretch out the original repayment schedules so as to ease the immediate debt burden. By 1985 record numbers of debts and debtors became involved in debt-rescheduling negotiations.

As noted, the IMF assumed a leadership role in securing debt relief for many Third World countries, but it did so at the cost of imposing strict conditions for domestic reform on individual debtors, including, for example, programs designed to curb inflation, limit imports, restrict public spending, expose protected industries, and the like. It also typically urged those it helped to increase their exports, thus giving rise to the label *export-led adjustment* as a description of the IMF's approach to the debt problem.

The fact that the *conditionality* of IMF's aid adds so clearly to the strains on the political and social fabric of debtor nations led some commentators to ask whether its policies might not have been self-defeating. As one caustically observed, "The I.M.F. is probably the most effective neocolonialist instrument the modern world has yet devised" (Krauthammer, 1983).

Economic austerity caused by demands for drastic economic reforms was blamed for the overthrow of the Sudanese government of President Jaafar Nimeri in 1985, and debt and related financial issues inflamed domestic political conflict in many other of the most heavily indebted nations, including Brazil, Argentina, Mexico, Chile, and Nigeria. Meanwhile, proposals were advanced for creating a "debtors' cartel" that would confront the creditor nations with a unified approach for easing their problems, as political leaders in the debtor nations began adopting a more defiant posture toward the predicament they faced.

The Search for Long-Term Solutions   It was in this emotionally charged atmosphere that the Baker initiative was unveiled in the fall of 1985. The initiative sought new loans (of $20 billion) from private banks and coupled these with renewed efforts to stimulate Third World economic growth via domestic economic reforms in debtor nations. Thus it emphasized a "market approach" to the debt problem that fit well with the Reagan administration's conservative philosophical beliefs that stimulating the world economy was the only viable way out of the problem, and that multilateral approaches through the IMF were no longer appropriate for the long term. Growing noncompliance with IMF conditionality in fact ultimately signaled failure of the IMF strategy and made the World Bank a preferred institutional instrument. Whereas the IMF austerity program pushed vigorously between 1982 and 1985 could claim considerable success from a strictly financial viewpoint (see Amuzegar, 1987), the domestic burdens it sought and the political costs they imposed proved simply too great (Sachs, 1989).

Ultimately, however, the Baker initiative also failed because it failed to deliver the promised new resources. The Reagan administration did signal with the initiative a turn in the direction of U.S. policy, but in the final analysis its "main accomplishment . . . was to skillfully steer incipient—and recurrent—debt crises away from the brink through what amounted to a strategy of containment" (Cohen, 1989).

Two events in 1987 added renewed urgency to the imperative of finding long-term solutions to the debt problem. In February Brazilian President José Sarney announced his country would suspend interest payments on the bulk of its $108 billion debt, declaring, "We cannot pay the debt with our people's hunger"; and in May Citicorp chairperson John Reed astonished the financial world when he announced the giant American bank would take a billion dollar loss to cover its shaky international loans. Other major American banks quickly followed suit. Meanwhile, the debt burden of the most hard-pressed debtors continued to mount, as did bitterness among the debtor nations toward their creditors, who resented being told that the poor should not borrow more than they could repay. Peruvian President Alan Garcia reflected the sentiments when he asserted in 1987, "Each of us has the right . . . to not pay more than what its economy can pay. . . . That is the moral law of the debtors."

The explosive domestic situation that foreign indebtedness exacerbates was underscored again in 1989, when widespread rioting broke out in Venezuela in protest against the government's austerity measures. "In the course of a few days an estimated 300 people died. This was particularly shocking since Venezuela had long been regarded as one of the most stable Latin American democracies" (Sachs, 1989). Yet the occurrence could easily be repeated elsewhere. "The constraints imposed by the debt problem act like a pressure cooker to heat up conflicts of interest among societal forces, eroding the political basis for continuing the acquiescence to creditors. With persistent economic stagnation the domestic political pot could reach the boiling point, raising the specter of disorder or worse" (Cohen, 1989). It is a situation the creditor nations have a stake in averting.

The Brady initiative, announced shortly after George Bush became president in 1989, pursued debt reduction as a strategy to cope with the debt crisis. Specifically, it sought to reduce the debt of all debtors by as much as 20 percent over three years. In focusing on debt relief rather than debt restructuring, the plan signaled that "the foreign policy concerns over the deteriorating situation in the debtor countries finally came to the fore," whereas, previously, concern for the banks had taken precedence (Sachs, 1989). Still, the initiative did not fully break with the Baker plan in that it depended on voluntary actions by creditors to bring about the debt reductions which, for a number of reasons, are difficult to achieve (see Cohen, 1989; Sachs, 1989). In this respect it was an extension of the strategy of containing the debt crisis the Reagan administration had pursued, not an alternative to it (Cohen, 1989).

The debt-reduction approach was not altogether new. It previously won approval with introduction of the menu approach in 1987, which permitted banks to choose among various conversion and buy-back schemes in an effort to avert financial collapse by particular debtor nations. The Brady plan extended the menu approach and added the hope that additional resources from Japan, the IMF, and the World Bank would be forthcoming. Still, critics questioned whether a voluntary scheme and one that continued fundamentally to reflect the interests of the banking community and their backers in Washington, namely the Treasury Department and the Federal Reserve, would work in the long run. "More and more, calls [were] made to accord higher priority to commercial and security considerations. Pressures [had] visibly grown to loosen the close, albeit tacit, bank-government alliances that [had] dominated decision making on [Third World] debt" (Cohen, 1989).

The adverse impact of the debt crisis on the commercial interests of the industrialized nations is underscored by the fact that their exports to Third World nations fell from 30 percent of all exports in 1981 to only 20 percent in 1987. U.S. exports to Latin America and the Caribbean fell by more than a quarter during this same period (Spero, 1990: 198). "By one estimate, every dollar of interest collected by the United States involved a loss of 1 dollar in trade" (Amuzegar, 1987: 146). American agricultural exports were especially hard hit.

Debt reduction doubtless makes a contribution to alleviating the chronic debt problem, but it is insufficient to restore North-South trade from which creditors and debtors alike would benefit should the creditworthiness of Third World nations be reestablished and economic growth rejuvenated. Similarly, debt reduction would defuse the potentially explosive domestic political strife caused by debt-induced economic austerity. An interdependent world binds all in a common fate whose control eludes each—a condition that provides incentives for all collectively to address shared financial problems.

THE SECOND WORLD: THE SOVIET UNION AND EASTERN EUROPE

During World War II, Western planners anticipated the participation of the Soviet Union in the postwar international economic system, just as they originally anticipated Soviet cooperation in maintaining the postwar political order. Trade between Eastern and Western Europe had been extensive before the war, and even though economic ties between the Soviet Union and the West had not been extensive, the war itself, through American Lend-Lease assistance, contributed to closer ties. Furthermore, the Soviet Union had participated in the Bretton Woods negotiations that ultimately led to creation of the IMF and the World Bank.

East-West Commerce and the Cold War

Shortly after the war, however, enthusiasm for establishing closer economic ties between East and West began to wane.[25] The critical year was 1947, when

---

25. Attention is confined in this chapter to U.S. relations with the Soviet Union and Eastern Europe. For a discussion of Soviet relations with its Eastern European allies in the postwar era in which special attention is given to the question of the costs and benefits to the Soviet Union of its hegemony in the region, see Bunce (1985).

President Harry S Truman effectively committed the United States to an anticommunist foreign policy strategy. In June 1947 Secretary of State George Marshall outlined an American commitment to aid in the economic recovery of Europe. American policymakers considered the possibility that the Soviet Union itself might participate. Whether the Soviets were ever serious contenders for Marshall Plan assistance can be doubted, however, as the program was formulated in such a way that the Soviet Union would have had to divulge information about its internal conditions and to permit Western involvement in its reconstruction efforts. Moreover, much of the debate in Congress over the plan was framed in terms of the onslaught of communism, rhetoric that certainly did not endear the recovery program to Soviet policymakers. In any event, the Soviet Union rejected the offer of American aid and also refused to permit Poland and Czechoslovakia, both of which had been offered Marshall Plan assistance, to accept it. Thereafter, East and West developed essentially separate economic systems from which the other was excluded. In the East the Council for Mutual Economic Assistance (Comecon) was organized under Soviet leadership to promote economic integration among the socialist countries. Bipolarity contributed to the mutually perceived necessity of isolation, and economic warfare joined political hostility to create the Cold War.

The economic isolation of East from West continued for a decade or more. Some trade between the United States and the Soviet Union did occur during the mid-1960s, but not until the late 1960s and early 1970s did the Soviets and the Americans begin to shift their views about commercial ties with "the other side." (The countries associated with the erstwhile communist experiment still remain largely outside the international monetary system described above.) As shown earlier in Figure 7.3, American trade with communist countries is still insignificant compared with its trade with other parts of the world. Yet it grew appreciably during the 1970s, with American agricultural exports accounting for a significant share of this growth. Agricultural products remain the most important U.S. export to the Eastern Europe and the Soviet Union, especially the latter.

East-West Commerce during Détente

The shift in American-communist trade relations was both a symptom of and a spur to détente. Trade became part of a series of concrete agreements on a range of issues that would contribute to what Henry Kissinger described while a member of the Nixon administration as a "vested interest in mutual restraint" on the part of the superpowers. The contrast with the Cold War is striking. Going back even before 1951, when Congress stripped communist countries of most-favored-nation tariff treatment, the United States introduced numerous legislative and administrative regulations designed to restrict communist nations' access to American exports, aid, and commercial credits. The United States was particularly sensitive about trade in so-called strategic goods, items that might bolster Soviet military capabilities and thus threaten Western security. Accordingly, the United States sought to embargo the sale of strategic goods to the Soviet Union and its allies, and it sponsored the Coordinating Committee (Cocom) as a mechanism for inducing its own allies to join in the development of a common policy on limiting exports to communist countries.

Over time, the willingness of U.S. allies in the industrialized West to restrict trade with communist countries waned, with the result that they captured the major share of communist trade with the West. By the mid-1970s, for example, other Western industrialized nations benefitted from nearly a third of the communist world's trade, compared with less than 3 percent by the United States (U.S. Department of Commerce, 1978: v). As a result, the commercial advantages that could accrue from greater trade between the United States and the Soviet Union and its allies were added to the overtly political motives for normalizing relations. From the U.S. viewpoint, however, the political motives remained paramount. The vested interest in mutual restraint envisioned as an element of détente sought to give the Soviets "a stake in international equilibrium." Expanded commercial intercourse with the Soviet Union thus became a key element in Kissinger's linkage strategy for the containment of Soviet influence and expansionism.

The desire of Soviet leaders for increased commercial ties with the West was inspired in part by the growing tension between the Soviet Union and China, which placed a premium on the Soviets' establishing relatively stable relations with the West that trade might facilitate. In addition, it was motivated by their perception of the desirability of reducing tensions with the United States, presumably as a way to reduce the prospect of war and the cost of armaments. Moreover, the Soviets saw in trade an opportunity to participate in the entire global economy, rather than remaining confined to trade within their own bloc and with the Third World.

To fly its commercial flag, the Soviet Union had to move from "extensive" economic development ("growth based upon increases in the labor force and the capital stock") to an "intensive" mode ("growth resulting from improved technology leading to higher productivity") (Yergin, 1977). For this, Soviet access to Western technology and the credits necessary to buy it were imperative in order to rejuvenate the sluggish Soviet economy. In addition, grain imports were required to supplement shortfalls in Soviet agricultural production.

The high point of détente was achieved at the 1972 Moscow summit when the two Cold War antagonists initialed the first Strategic Arms Limitation Talks (SALT) agreement. SALT was certainly the cornerstone of détente, but expanded East-West trade was part of the mortar. A joint commercial commission was established at the summit, whose purpose was to pave the way for the granting of most-favored-nation status to the Soviet Union and the extension of U.S. government-backed credits to the Soviet regime.

Shortly thereafter, in part to symbolize to the American public the tangible rewards of détente (Kissinger, 1979), the American government negotiated an agreement providing the Soviet Union with $750 million in credits with which to buy American agricultural products. Unknown to the administration at the time, however, the Soviet Union was facing a catastrophic crop failure and the Soviets desperately needed American grain. Acting as "state capitalists," the Soviet government successfully bargained with private U.S. grain dealers to put together one of the largest commercial transactions in history, one that led to a sharp increase in the world price of grain. Thus, to the chagrin of American policymakers, an initiative designed to produce a positive impact on American public opinion turned into a blunder that cast a shadow over the entire question of expanded East-West trade. Eventually, an agreement providing for the more orderly entry of the Soviet Union into the American grain market was negotiated, but the political damage wrought by the "Great American Grain Robbery" was substantial.

Even more damaging was the fate of most-favored-nation status and increased credits for the Soviet Union. Most-favored-nation treatment was to have been granted by the U.S. Trade Act of 1974, which provided MFN status for the Soviet Union and other communist countries in fulfillment of the 1972 Trade Agreement between the United States and the Soviet Union. Attaining MFN status "had great political significance as a symbol of the end to the Soviet Union's exclusion from the West's international economic system" (Spero, 1990). But a congressional amendment, known as the Jackson-Vanik amendment, made MFN status contingent upon the liberalization of communist policies relating to Jewish emigration.

Although the Soviet Union had tacitly permitted freer emigration of Soviet Jews, early in 1975 it repudiated the 1972 trade agreement in response to what it regarded as an unwarranted intrusion into its domestic affairs. Hungary and Romania were eventually granted most-favored-nation status. However, the grant was subject to annual review by Congress of each country's emigration policy, which became an impediment to better relations (especially with Romania, which finally renounced its MFN status rather than be subject to the Jackson-Vanik conditions).[26] In 1980 the United States played its "China card" and granted MFN status to China in what was a further slap in the Soviets' face.

More significant than symbolic has been the persistent issue of American government-backed credits. Because Soviet and Eastern European currencies are not convertible (that is, they are subject to government controls and therefore are not easily exchanged for Western currencies), and because the exports from which they earn hard (Western) currencies have been relatively limited, the socialist economies have long lacked the foreign exchange necessary to buy the goods from the West that they desire.[27] During the 1970s this situation

---

26. The United States also granted Poland and Yugoslavia most-favored-nation status. In these cases, however, the grants were made before passage of the Trade Act of 1974 and are therefore not subject to annual review by Congress before extension of MFN status by the president.

27. Prior to the economic liberalization that has taken place in Eastern Europe and the Soviet Union since the late 1980s, Comecon countries sought to balance their trade on a bilateral, rather than a multilateral, basis. Thus the Soviet Union sought to balance its trade with each of the Eastern European nations rather than with all of them collectively, as is the case in the Western multilateral trading system. Consistent with this strategy, various forms of barter trades with the

changed as a consequence of heavy borrowing from the West. By 1982 the East's gross debt to the West stood at $100 billion (Spero, 1990: 328), up from only a few billion dollars at the beginning of the 1970s. The debt itself created the need for greatly increased export earnings by the Comecon nations or the extension of government-backed credits by the West, particularly the United States, but these were not forthcoming because of restrictions that Congress placed on government-backed credits extended through the U.S. Export-Import Bank and the blanket prohibitions of the Jackson-Vanik amendment.

Eventually, the Comecon countries reduced their net debt to the West, largely by curtailing imports. However, the Soviet Union substantially increased its own borrowing from the West after Mikhail Gorbachev came to power. The West now seems motivated to support market-oriented reforms in the Soviet Union and in Eastern Europe, but by the early 1990s the industrial world's leading commercial bankers (over the Bush administration's objectives) expressed concern about further private lending and began to look to the Western governments themselves for additional lending. The wisdom of making such loans promises to remain an issue, even though the Soviets themselves seem determined to keep the amounts manageable (Stevenson and Frye, 1989).

East-West Commercial Ties during the Period of Renewed Confrontation

On assuming office, President Jimmy Carter committed himself to détente and normalization of East-West commercial relations. But because of congressional constraints, East-West trade stagnated in the second half of the 1970s. Furthermore, the Carter administration's commitment to a worldwide campaign on behalf of human rights often led to American attacks on the Soviet Union's human rights policies. Commercial relations with the Soviets (particularly their desire to acquire high technology goods from the United States) were seen as a source of leverage to realize American foreign policy objectives with respect to human rights. As Soviet-American relations deteriorated, the administration used economic instruments to counter the continued high levels of military spending by the Soviet Union, its overseas military buildup and arms transfers to the Third World, and its backing of Cuban intervention in Angola, Ethiopia,

---

West could be used to circumvent the constraints of limited availability of hard currencies. Compensation deals were particularly attractive as a means through which Western firms might gain access to the Soviet Union's extensive reserves of raw materials, including oil and natural gas. In return for paybacks in raw materials, the Soviet Union gained access to Western technology, equipment, and managerial skills.

The nonconvertibility of the Soviet ruble continues to plague prospects for its integration into the Western international economic order. Under Gorbachev, joint ventures have been promoted as a way of accelerating Soviet economic engagement with the West. Moscow's much publicized McDonald's fast-food restaurant is a Soviet joint venture with McDonald's of Canada. "Understandably Moscow hopes that the joint ventures it now encourages will concentrate on exports to generate hard currency revenues, but the projected scale of such enterprises remains relatively modest" (Stevenson and Frye, 1989).

and elsewhere in Africa. Additional punitive measures were instituted following the Soviet invasion of Afghanistan in late 1979, including a partial grain embargo. The commercial ties that a decade earlier had been built to cement détente became the victim as well as the instrument of renewed Soviet-American rivalry.

Whereas previous presidents had sought to use trade as an inducement to Soviet leaders to moderate their foreign policy behavior and improve East-West relations, "the Reagan administration . . . sought to use trade as a stick to punish the East for policies such as the invasion of Afghanistan or the imposition of martial law in Poland and generally to deny to the East the Western technology and hard currency that would enhance the Soviet bloc's economic development and military strength" (Spero, 1990). The restrictions earlier placed on the export of energy technology to the Soviet Union were stiffened as the United States sought, first, to punish the Soviets for their presumed complicity in the imposition of martial law in Poland, and, second, to abort the planned Soviet-Western European pipeline to bring natural gas from Soviet Siberia to markets in Western Europe. The administration also pushed in Cocom for more stringent controls on the export of strategic goods to the Soviet Union than American allies were prone to support.

In the important case of grain exports, however, domestic political considerations outweighed the administration's ideological predispositions. Making good on an earlier campaign promise, Ronald Reagan lifted Carter's ban on grain sales to the Soviet Union. Two years later, in 1983, Washington and Moscow concluded a new long-term grain sales agreement. Interestingly, the accord—the first major bilateral pact negotiated since the Soviet invasion of Afghanistan—contained language that effectively pledged that the United States would not interrupt future grain shipments in pursuit of its self-defined foreign or national security goals. A week after the agreement was signed, the Soviet Union shot down a Korean civilian airliner, killing all of its 269 passengers. Despite clamors by some members of Congress to abrogate the new grain agreement in retaliation, it was permitted to stand. Domestic politics again reigned supreme.

As had earlier administrations, the Reagan administration found that U.S. allies did not always share its views on how to deal with the Soviet Union in the economic sphere. The pipeline issue in particular created a serious split in the Atlantic alliance. Administration supporters of a hardline stance on the issue cited Lenin's prophecy that the capitalists would gladly sell the rope with which they would be hung—and contended that the Siberian pipeline was just such a rope because it could provide high-technology equipment needed to feed the Soviet "military machine." Many European allies of the United States simply did not share that view. Nor did they share the belief that completion of the trans-Siberian pipeline would make Western Europe unduly dependent on Soviet sources of energy. Instead, they saw U.S. policy as hypocritical in that it attempted to pressure the Western Europeans into not selling the Soviets energy technology at the same time that the United States sold them grain. Eventually, a face-saving measure was devised that enabled the United States to back away from an unwinnable issue without conceding it had lost.

The pipeline fracas illustrated once more that the United States and its allies approached the issue of commercial ties with the Second World quite differently. Their contrasting viewpoints stem from differing domestic political considerations in Europe compared with the United States, from the geographic proximity of Western Europe to the Soviet Union and its erstwhile Eastern European allies, and from the fact that to Western Europe (and Japan), Second World countries are generally more important trade partners than they are to the United States (see Spero, 1990). Those facts make it likely that the United States and its North Atlantic alliance partners will view the prospects and opportunities for economic advantage with Eastern Europe and the Soviet Union in the 1990s and beyond quite differently.

For the United States, politics has always been more important than economics in dealing with the Soviet Union and its allies. Not surprisingly, therefore, the Reagan administration began to moderate its posture on economics as it moved toward a more accommodative posture on arms control and related issues during the president's second term. The U.S.-Soviet Joint Commercial Commission, moribund since the Carter administration, was reactivated; sanctions imposed on the Soviets at the time of the invasion of Afghanistan were eased; and recommendations were made for easing technology export controls once Soviet troops were withdrawn from Afghanistan. The Bush administration likewise adopted a more liberal policy on Cocom technology-transfer issues.

From the Soviet perspective, integration into the Western Liberal International Economic Order, of which the United States has been a leader since its inception, would facilitate *perestroika* and the goal of domestic economic improvement Soviet leaders have long sought and promised. Moreover, an argument can be made that such a move would be in the security interests of the United States and the other member of the North Atlantic alliance, as "a Soviet Union more engaged in the global economy would be less prone to backsliding in its economic and political evolution. In the phrase of one close observer, Brezhnev wanted foreign investment to avoid reform, Gorbachev wants it to foster reform" (Stevenson and Frye, 1989).

East-West Commercial Ties beyond the Cold War

The United States agreed to grant the Soviets observer status in GATT following conclusion of the Uruguay Round of negotiations, but Soviet participation in the IMF is precluded until the Soviet currency becomes convertible, which is not foreseeable. Even its full participation in the multilateral trade regime presupposes dramatic movement toward market principles and away from the Soviet command economy that may take years to implement. Still, important incremental adaptations in Soviet and East European relations with the West can be expected in the years ahead. In 1988, for example, Comecon requested the establishment of diplomatic relations with the European Community, and a year later the Soviet Union and the EC signed a far-reaching ten-year trade agreement. The EC also announced its willingness to provide aid and credits to Eastern Europe.

The United States likewise sought to promote the democratic process in Eastern Europe and promised various forms of public and private assistance to that end (see also Chapter 5). Because of Eastern Europe's earlier historical and hence more firmly rooted experience with capitalism and market principles, some observers believe the prospects for the integration of Eastern Europe into the Liberal International Economic Order are more promising than those for the Soviet Union (or China).

Clearly, political considerations will continue to color relations with the Soviet Union and the West, especially the United States. In early 1990 the United States and the Soviet Union began discussions on dismantling barriers that long prevented normal trade relations between the two powers. The Jackson-Vanik amendment remained the principle barrier, inasmuch as it prevented most-favored-nation status for the Soviet Union as normally extended to others. The June 1990 Bush-Gorbachev summit had been the target for normalization, but it was missed as political differences between the United States and the Soviet Union continued to affect the prospects of regularized commercial exchanges. Later in the year, however, the Bush administration expressed interest in assisting the Soviet Union financially as a reward to the Gorbachev regime for its support of U.S. policy toward Iraq following Iraq's invasion of Kuwait. Nonetheless, until the United States and the Soviet Union are able definitively to resolve the political and military issues that divide them, their economic interactions will remain relatively inconsequential.

U.S. Relations with China

As noted earlier, the United States granted China MFN trade treatment at the very time it denied the Soviet Union MFN status. Normalization of commercial relations was part of a larger process of normalizing political relations to which the United States and China had been committed since the early 1970s. Moreover, it was commonplace in the context of détente for both the United States and the Soviet Union to utilize the prospect of improved relations with China as a lever against the other superpower. Hence the concept of triangular politics and the strategy of playing the "China card."

By some standards U.S. trade with China is comparatively small, but it has grown appreciably since commercial relations between the two powers were normalized. Bilateral trade increased from about $1 billion in 1978 to over $18 billion in 1989, making China one of the top fifteen U.S. trade partners in the world. (By way of contrast, U.S. trade with the Soviet Union averaged only $2.8 billion per year in the 1980s.)

The bloody massacre by Chinese troops of pro-democracy demonstrators on Tiananmen Square in early June 1989 threatened to reverse a decade of progress toward normalization of U.S.-Chinese relations, of which their growing trade volume was an integral part. The United States and other Western nations imposed a variety of economic sanctions in response to the suppression of the protestors, but they eased perceptibly in a comparatively short time. And most important, the Bush administration decided just before the Tiananmen anniversary to renew unconditionally China's MFN status with United States. Members of Congress, where pro-sanction sentiments had run high in the wake of Tiananmen, protested vigorously that Bush was too accommodating to the Chinese leadership, but the president fell back on the provision of the Jackson-Vanik amendment governing the situation, arguing that China permitted free emigration. Further, he reasoned that the decision was "not a special favor" to Beijing but instead was "the basis of everyday trade." In contrast to U.S. policy toward the Soviet Union, then, the implication was that commercial interests reigned supreme over political objectives. This despite the fact that China remains a highly centralized, socialist society whose actions in June 1989 were as flagrant a violation of human rights as any in the Soviet Union the United States had previously protested.

A STATUS QUO POWER IN A WORLD OF CHANGE

The changing nature of the international political economy combines with the evolving structural characteristics of the international political system described in Chapter 6 to underscore how radically different the world of the 1990s is from the world in which the United States first emerged a superpower. Throughout those decades of evolutionary change, the United States has shown itself capable of adapting to new situations and new circumstances, although often the adaptations have come neither rapidly nor with enthusiasm. Yet in the process of adaptation it is difficult to find evidence that the nation's fundamental goals and objectives have also changed. On the contrary, in both economic and political matters, the same goals have persisted, with the United States seeking in different ways a preferred position, if not dominance, in world politics.

The United States remains the single most important actor in the global political economy, much as it remains preeminent in the military sphere. In the latter case the United States continues to share with few other nations the ultimate decision on the fate of the world. It is less easy to draw a caricature of how United States preponderance plays out in political economy matters, however. What is clear is that a leveling process has occurred; the economic disparity between the United States and other First World nations has steadily narrowed. More than ever before in the postwar era, less distance in "power potential" now separates the United States from its military allies and economic partners (most notably Germany and Japan, who, ironically, were its enemies during World War II). Resurgent nationalism and increasingly widespread polycentrism within the major postwar alliance systems have combined with leveling to make the international system less hierarchically organized than in the past. The stratification between rich and poor is more apparent, however. Although the United States has championed the cause of democracy around the world, it continues to appear ill equipped to direct the forces of change operating in many of the world's less advantaged societies—a failure that suggests that its own revolutionary heritage is largely irrelevant to the underlying social and economic injustices that plague so many nations in the contemporary world.

The neomercantilist challenge to the Liberal International Economic Order embodied in the rise of protectionist sentiment in the United States is in part a response to the nation's loss of control over its own well-being. It reflects a penchant to deal aggressively and unilaterally with the costs of complex interdependence, which, ironically, is the product of the success the United States realized in promoting a LIEO. The complexity of the system is itself a principal reason for the U.S. loss of control over its environment. Today, there are more issues and more actors, and the weak are more assertive; the United States, still the dominant state, continues to have leverage over others, but it has far less leverage over the whole system (Keohane and Nye, 1989). Thus the era of American domination of the international arena has ended. What looked four decades ago like the beginning of the American century, an era of *Pax Americana* in which U.S. dominance of world politics, like that of the British in the nineteenth century, would be the defining feature of the international system, now appears to have been a rather transitory period. No other power has emerged to assume the hegemonic role in politics and economics that the United States played in the global system following World War II—and none is on the horizon—which means the power and policies of the United States will continue to be pivotal. But the determination of outcomes will more likely follow patterns characteristic of a multipolar system than either a unipolar or bipolar configuration. As a consequence, the external environment is henceforth likely to provide even more pronounced stimulants to and constraints on what the United States does abroad.

SUGGESTIONS FOR FURTHER READING

Bergsten, C. Fred. (1990) "The World Economy after the Cold War," *Foreign Affairs* 69 (Summer): 96–112.

Cohen, Benjamin J. (1989) "A Global Chapter 11," *Foreign Policy* 75 (Summer): 109–127.

Drucker, Peter, F. (1986) "The Changed World Economy," *Foreign Affairs* 64 (Spring): 768–791.

Head, Ivan L. (1989) "South-North Dangers," *Foreign Affairs* 68 (Summer): 71–86.

Macchiarola, Frank J. (ed.). (1990) *International Trade: The Changing Role of the United States.* New York: Academy of Political Science.

Schlesinger, James. (1990) "Oil and Power in the Nineties," *National Interest* 19 (Spring): 111–115.

Sewell, John W., and Stuart K. Tucker. (1988) *Growth, Exports, and Jobs in a Changing World Economy: Agenda 1988.* New Brunswick, N.J.: Transaction Books.

Spero, Joan Edelman. (1990) *The Politics of International Economic Relations*, 4th ed. New York: St. Martin's.

Stevenson, Adlai E., and Alton Frye. (1989) "Trading with the Communists," *Foreign Affairs* 68 (Spring): 53–71.

Vernon, Raymond, and Debora L. Spar. (1989) *Beyond Globalism: Remaking American Foreign Economic Policy*. New York: Free Press.

PART IV

Societal Sources of American Foreign Policy

CHAPTER 8

The Impact of National Values: Political Culture, Elitism, and Pluralism

Democracies forego certain [foreign policy] options by the nature of their societies and the whole set of ideals they represent.

FORMER SECRETARY OF DEFENSE JAMES SCHLESINGER, 1985

The government of the United States . . . is a foster child of special interests.

PRESIDENT WOODROW WILSON, 1913

Foreign policy making is often seen as being "above politics." According to this view, domestic interests are subservient to national interests—on international issues Americans lay aside their partisan differences and support their government's policies. Politics, in short, stops at the water's edge.

Is this image realistic? Are foreign policy decisions made to further the nation's international interests, without regard to domestic political consequences? Or are the foreign policy choices of political leaders influenced measurably by their anticipated effect on their popularity and power at home?

Picture for a moment the following scenario: The president's day begins in the Oval Office at 6:45 A.M. with briefings from principal advisers. The chief domestic adviser opens with reports of growing budget deficits, sluggish economic growth, and a worsening balance-of-trade picture; the latest polls indicate that the president's popularity among the American electorate has plummeted; and the president's opponent in the forthcoming election has accused the incumbent of pursuing a "wishy-washy" policy toward the nation's Middle East allies. The national security adviser is next. The adviser warns that Central Intelligence Agency (CIA) reports indicate the Middle East is about to erupt into armed conflict again and strongly urges that immediate action be taken to protect American interests and investments in the region. A strategy session is quickly crammed into the day's agenda, which includes separate consultations with representatives from the American Petroleum Institute and from groups calling themselves "Friends of Israel" and "Citizens for Arab Justice."

What factors will most influence a president confronted by such circumstances? Although we cannot get into a president's mind, the calculations likely   **243** to influence presidential choices can be estimated. When forced to reach a decision, it is likely that the president will ask, What is the likely domestic repercussion of option X or Y? Will it enhance or erode my public standing? Will it undermine the strength of the political party I lead? And might it convert, perhaps overnight, my political backers into antagonists? Countless questions about the likely response of America's allies and adversaries in the region and elsewhere can also be anticipated, but the urge to give priority to the domestic consequences of foreign policy decisions may be irresistible. As a former policymaker concluded, U.S. leaders have shown a

> tendency to make statements and take actions with regard not to their effect on the international scene to which they are ostensibly addressed but rather to their effect on those echelons of American opinion . . . to which the respective [states-persons] are anxious to appeal. The questions, in these circumstances, [become] not: how effective is what I am doing in terms of the impact it makes on our world environment? but rather: how do I look, in the mirror of domestic American opinion, as I do it? Do I look shrewd, determined, defiantly patriotic, imbued with the necessary vigilance before the wiles of foreign governments? If so, this is what I do, even though it may prove meaningless, or even counterproductive, when applied to the realities of the external situation. (Kennan, 1967: 53)

This viewpoint suggests that foreign policy decisions are guided by a concern for the reactions they will provoke at home. Preserving one's power base and the psychological desire to be admired encourage foreign policy decisions designed to elicit favorable domestic responses. At the extreme, theater substitutes for rational policy choice; image management becomes an overriding preoccupation.

The purpose of this and the next chapter is to explore the ways in which American foreign policy is conditioned by America's internal or societal characteristics. From among the vast array of interlocking domestic influences, we will examine in this chapter the impact of political culture (Americans' beliefs about their political system and the way it operates) and elite and special-interest group influences on foreign policy. Then, in Chapter 9, we will explore the functions that public opinion, presidential elections, and the mass media perform in the policy-making process.

The societal sources that conceivably can influence foreign policy are almost infinite. For example, we might ask how the country's economic growth rate, chronic federal budget deficits and national debt, resource scarcities, racial divisions, income inequalities, demographic changes, and other national characteristics affect U.S. foreign policy. To derive propositions about the impact of these, contemplate some of the ideas commonly advanced about the linkage between domestic society and foreign policy. A legalistic mentality is often said to shape American foreign policy (Kennan, 1951; also Chapter 3). Is this because two-thirds of the world's lawyers ply their trade in the United States (*Wall Street Journal*, October 3, 1983, p. 30)? Similarly, the United States suffers from an unusually high level of violent crime compared with other nations. The U.S. government estimates that in 1988 one American was killed every twenty-five minutes (Malcolm, 1989: 14). What are the consequences of recurrent violence? Could it be that American policymakers subconsciously think of violence as normal? If so, does the expectation encourage a militant foreign policy?

To extend this kind of inquiry about the potential domestic sources of American foreign policy, let us consider how national attributes and internal conditions may make the United States different from other countries.

AMERICA IN THE COMMUNITY OF NATIONS:
AN EXCEPTIONAL CASE?

The attributes that make the United States the kind of nation it is shape Americans' self-images and their perceptions of their nation's proper world role. Table 8.1 describes America's salient national attributes compared with other countries. These indicators reveal that the United States is far from a typical society. It is the world's fourth largest country in geographical size and fifth in population, and it is extraordinarily endowed with vast natural resources, wealth, technology, and mobilized military power — a superpower among the advanced industrial states. Relatively speaking, Americans are urbanized, highly educated, literate, and informed by a free and sophisticated media. Moreover, American society is well off materially (even though its rate of economic growth, saving, and investment are relatively low); although Americans comprise less than 6 percent of the world's population, in any given year they produce (and consume) over a fifth of the world's total economic output. Personal wealth is far from equally distributed, but the "average" American is better off than his or her counterpart living in nearly every other country.[1] American society, in short, is in many respects quite unlike any other in the world (cf. Rose, 1989).

It is tempting intuitively to assume that America's enormous capabilities and resources dictate its foreign policy objectives. But direct causal linkages are unwarranted. For example, simplistic, single-factor propositions of the sort

---

1. According to the World Bank, Switzerland, Japan, Iceland, and Norway ranked ahead of the United States (in 1988).

Averages can be misleading, especially in a heterogeneous society like the United States where wealth is not equally shared. "The top 0.5 percent [of the population] own more than 45 percent of the privately held wealth while 90 percent of the American people have little or no net financial assets" (Parenti, 1988: 10). In addition to wealth, income is not distributed evenly and the gap between rich and poor continues to widen: "The wealthiest 20 percent of Americans received 44 percent of aggregate income in 1987, up from 40 percent 20 years earlier. The poorest 20 percent of Americans received 4.6 percent, down from 5.5 percent in 1967" (*Washington Post*, November 23, 1988, p. A19). In addition, many Americans are not strangers to poverty and homelessness. In 1987, 32.5 million Americans lived below the poverty line as defined by the government (U.S. Bureau of the Census, 1989: 453), and anywhere from as "few" as 250,000 to as many as three million are thought to be homeless (Beirne, 1988: 68–69).

TABLE 8.1 ▪ **American Society in the Global Village: The U.S. Rank on the Eve of the 1990s**

National Attribute and Its Indicator	Date of Observation	U.S. Rank among Other Countries
Economic Status		
Gross national product	1988	1
GNP per capita	1988	5
Average annual growth rate of gross domestic product	1980–1987	33
Average annual growth rate of GNP per capita	1965–1987	58
Average annual rate of inflation	1980–1987	86
Average annual growth rate of exports	1980–1987	76
Average annual growth rate of imports	1980–1987	3
Balance-of-payments deficit	1987	1
Gross domestic savings	1980–1987	11
Average annual growth rate of gross domestic investment	1980–1987	20
Gross domestic savings (percent)	1987	64
Military Power		
Military expenditures	1987	1
Military technology	1986	1
Military expenditures (as percentage of GNP)	1986	19
Military expenditures per capita	1987	3
Armed forces	1987	3
Nuclear warheads and bombs	1989	1
Resources		
Territorial size	1990	4
Energy consumption per capita	1987	3
Population	1987	5
Average annual growth rate of energy production	1980–1987	84

(continued)

TABLE 8.1 ▪ *Continued*

National Attribute and Its Indicator	Date of Observation	U.S. Rank among Other Countries
Education		
Public expenditures per capita	1986	5
School age population per teacher	1986	19
Percent of school age population in school	1986	6
Literacy rate	1986	4
Health		
Public expenditures per capita	1986	5
Population per physician	1986	24
Population per hospital bed	1986	38
Infant mortality	1986	17
Life expectancy	1987	13
Percent of infants with low birth weight	1986	31
Percent infants immunized against measles	1986	32
Percent of population with access to sanitation	1986	15
Social		
Index of economic/social standing	1986	4
Average annual growth of population	1980–1987	87
Urban population (as percentage of total population)	1987	22
Governmental		
Central government expenditures (as percentage of GNP)	1987	11

SOURCE: U.S. Arms Control and Disarmament Agency, *World Military Expenditures and Arms Transfers 1988* (Washington, D.C.: U.S. Government Printing Office, 1989), pp. 28–61; World Bank, *World Development Report 1989* (New York: Oxford University Press, 1989), pp. 145–225; Ruth Leger Sivard, *World Military and Social Expenditures 1989* (Washington, D.C.: World Priorities, 1989), pp. 46–55.

NOTE: The number of countries against which the United States is compared varies according to the sources listed above.

asserting that "large, populous countries inevitably are imperialistic," that "educated societies pursue peaceful foreign polices,"[2] or that "militarized countries are necessarily expansionist"[3] cannot be substantiated empirically. Too many counterexamples exist. Moreover, because most societal conditions remain stable over extended periods, they seldom precipitate policy change. More appropriately, national attributes such as size, population, and resources are conceived as background factors that make some foreign policy options possible while limiting the feasibility of others.

Another way to think of the impact of societal factors are as data forming part of decision makers' perceptual maps of the world and their nation's place in it. Policymakers' subjective images of American society may shape foreign policy more strongly than do more tangible conditions (Dallek, 1983). Changes in American society—be they in demography, import dependence, life-style, domestic savings and investments, consumer consumption, public and private indebtedness, or environmental quality—may also shape decision makers' thinking about the country's proper international role and ultimately influence the kinds of policies and programs proposed.

Policymakers' perceptions of American society influence their thinking and behavior, but these images are, in turn, rooted in their prior beliefs and experiences, for they are creatures of the nation's political culture and cannot escape its influence.

POLITICAL CULTURE AND FOREIGN POLICY

The *political culture* of the United States refers to the political values, cognitions, ideas, and ideals about American society and politics widely held by the American people. To the extent that deep-seated values, beliefs, and self-images are shared, as surely they are because most Americans have been socialized by the same cultural influences, the political culture concept taps a potentially important domestic source of American foreign policy.[4] Indeed, it is commonplace to observe that "the United States was founded upon values that were

---

2. Evidence does not show that educated people are necessarily more peaceful or hold more conciliatory attitudes about foreign affairs. A highly educated populace supported the imperialism of Nazi Germany, for instance. Educational level is a poor predictor of foreign policy attitudes because the crucial determinant of such attitudes is not the level of information possessed but the kind of information about war and peace that is propagated in the educational system.

3. It is dangerous to infer intentions from capabilities; countries that allocate large proportions of national income to armaments do not necessarily plan to use them for aggressive purposes.

4. Like its related concept, *national character*, political culture is broad and elastic and must properly be able to differentiate between the beliefs within subcultures or embraced by individuals and the composite attitudes describing American society as a whole. Characteristics that describe the entire nation cannot be safely generalized to all parts of the population. For example, we do not necessarily know the characteristics of a given individual simply by knowing the characteristics of the groups of which he or she is a member. If a nation's foreign policy displays belligerence, for instance, that does not make each citizen or policymaker a warmonger.

different from the rest of the world" (McCormick, 1985). Thus American foreign policy may be uniquely different from the policies of other states because the United States itself is different.

What are the core values widely embraced in American society? On this question opinions vary, not only because the existence of political subcultures and alienated groups makes it difficult to generalize safely about the degree to which some values are universally embraced, but also because the American political tradition emphasizes the need for consensus but simultaneously tolerates disagreement, parochial loyalties, and counterallegiances. The American polity is often torn between competing values and impulses: individualism and community, production and consumption, saving and spending, work and leisure, charity and greed, religiosity and secularism, and the like. America's "loosely bounded culture" (Merelman, 1984) is fluid and pluralistic, allowing the individual citizen freedom to practice his or her own philosophy.

The Liberal Tradition

Despite diversity (and respect for it), certain norms dominate.[5] There are values and principles to which all American politicians appeal in their campaigns for office, irrespective of the particular political philosophy they espouse, and to which the general populace largely responds. Although no single definition adequately captures its essence, the complementary assumptions that comprise "mainstream" American political beliefs may be labeled *liberalism*, whose roots stem from the seventeenth-century political philosophy of the English thinker John Locke. Basic to the liberal legacy is Thomas Jefferson's belief, enshrined in the Declaration of Independence, that the purpose of government is to secure for its citizens their inalienable (natural) rights to life, liberty, and the pursuit of happiness. "Whenever any form of government becomes destructive of those ends," he concluded, "it is the right of the people to alter or abolish it." Abraham Lincoln's espousal of government of, by, and for the people is also fundamental.

In the liberal creed, as Jefferson affirmed, legitimate political power arises only from the consent of the governed, whose participation in decisions affecting public policy and the quality of life is guaranteed. Government's primary duty is the protection of the civil and political rights of individuals, and the people's right to revolution against the government should it violate these rights is fundamental. Many other principles and values embellish the liberal tradition: individual liberty, equality of treatment and opportunity before the law ("all men are created equal"), due process, self-determination, free enterprise, inalienable rights, majority rule and minority rights, freedom of

---

5. A note of caution is in order here. Because characterizations of the dominant American values stem partly from ideology, it is mistaken to put the American political culture into any all-encompassing mold. For discussions of alternate ways of conceiving the American political culture and their implications for public policy, see Dolbeare and Edelman (1985), Elazar (1972), Morgan (1988), and Parenti (1981).

expression, federalism, the separation of powers within government, equal opportunity to participate in public affairs, and legalism ("a government of laws, not of men"). All are consistent with Locke's belief that government should be limited to the protection of the individual's life, liberty, and property through popular consent. The "social contract" among those who created the American experiment, which sought to safeguard these inalienable rights, is sacred.

Together, these tenets form the basis for the concept of *popular sovereignty*, which holds that "the only true source of political authority is the will of those who are ruled, in short the doctrine that all power arises from the people" (Thomas, 1988). Because the American ethos subscribes enthusiastically to these principles, Americans think of themselves as a "free people."

Liberalism is neither immutable nor invariant. Over time, successive reformulations in response to changes in national and international circumstances have placed emphasis on different tenets. An important synergism is the set of beliefs that forges the premises of both classical democratic theory and capitalism into a deeply entrenched ideology of "democratic capitalism" (Greenberg, 1985). "Capitalism and liberalism represent the mainstream because they are the established, enduring, 'orthodox' ideologies that have dominated the thinking of American political and other leaders" (Dolbeare and Dolbeare, 1971). Even those who regard themselves as conservatives politically are in fact "traditional liberals who have kept faith with liberalism as it was propounded two hundred years ago" (Lipsitz and Speak, 1989). Thus American leaders, regardless of their partisan or philosophical labels, routinely reaffirm the convictions basic to the Lockian liberal tradition, as do the documents Americans celebrate on national holidays.

Liberalism and American Foreign Policy Behavior

The interpretation summarized above is widely embraced by others (see Focus 8.1). In a classic treatment by Louis Hartz (1955) called *The Liberal Tradition in America*, the author contends that Lockian liberalism has become so embedded in American life that Americans may be blind to what it really is, namely, ideology. The basis for those ideological beliefs, so the reasoning holds, is the "exceptional American experience," which includes the absence of pronounced class and religious strife at the time of the nation's founding, complemented by the fortuitous blessing of geographic isolation from European political and military turmoil. That ideology has in turn affected the nation's foreign policy behavior.

Strands of the linkages between the Lockian ideological tradition and foreign policy behavior are evident in American diplomacy from the Monroe Doctrine to today. To mobilize public support for U.S. actions abroad and endow policy decisions with moral value, American leaders have often cloaked their actions in the rhetoric of these ideological precepts (see Focus 8.2). Principles such as self-determination and self-preservation have continually been voiced to justify policy action, as "concern with wealth, power, status, moral

FOCUS 8.1 ▪ Does American "Exceptionalism" Influence American Foreign Policy? Three Views

American exceptionalism expresses the conviction that the U.S. has a moral mission which flows out of its identity and which should guide its policies. Our exceptional character, which was originally used to justify disdaining alliances and quarrels of the so-called old world, has often been cited as the grounds to improve the world.

U.S. Ambassador to the United Nations Jeane J. Kirkpatrick, 1984

Our confidence in democracy . . . in our approach to the rest of the world is, of course, a projection of our own national experience. Beyond that, however, it has proven to be an effective force—perhaps the most effective force—in our foreign policy. We emphasize our support for democracy not only because our own experience gives us great sympathy for the democratic aspirations of other people; we have also become convinced through hard experience that our own national interests are best served through the creation and strengthening of functioning pluralistic democracies in other countries.

U.S. Ambassador to the Philippines Stephen W. Bosworth, 1984

America began free; its struggles were never to become free, but to stay free. Moreover, it never, for a single moment, lost its freedom. History, in other words, has made America naive. It has made Americans the luckiest and the least understanding people in the world. Indeed, the happy American experience with freedom may be at the root of the time-honored American inability to find its proper global place. The appeal of American isolationism and the awkwardness of American interventionism—both may be owed to the American unfamiliarity with the political oppression and social injustice that is the common experience of most of the rest of the world. Our natural consciousness of freedom has equipped us badly for the spreading of it. That may be history's bad joke on the American century.

New Republic, April 30, 1984, p. 1

virtue, and the freedom of mankind were successfully transformed into a single set of mutually reinforcing values by the paradigm of Lockian liberalism'' (Weisband, 1973).

The way political development doctrines influenced the American foreign aid program in the postwar era illustrates the relationship between political culture and foreign policy. Four assumptions derived from the exceptional American experience had an impact on the aid program: (1) change and development are easy; (2) all good things go together; (3) radicalism and revolution are bad; and (4) distributing political power is more important than accumulating it (Packenham, 1973). The first two assumptions were reflected in the economic approach of the aid program, which was predicated on the

---

FOCUS 8.2 ▪ Democratic Ideology and Foreign Policy

Our democracy encompasses many freedoms—freedom of speech, of religion, of assembly, and of so many other liberties that we often take for granted. These are rights that should be shared by all mankind. . . . We have an obligation to help [freedom-loving Central Americans]—for our own sake as well as theirs.

President Ronald Reagan, 1983

The survival of democracy at home and abroad is perhaps our most fundamental national interest.

Secretary of State James A. Baker, 1989

---

belief that fantastic results would flow from what in fact was a rather meager effort and that economic development would beget political development and a host of "other good political things." Its anticommunist, Cold War underpinnings were rooted in the third assumption; and the democratic mentality that permeated the program was based on the fourth assumption, which rationalized the export of American political institutions. Together, these assumptions derived from the liberal tradition lend coherence to otherwise disparate and inconsistent American policies.

> Deviations from the patterns of economic and political development as they occurred in the United States—especially radicalism and revolution—are due to "unnatural growths," which the United States then tries to remove "by diplomacy or war." In this fashion the "right" hand of the liberal tradition (as manifested in the Cold War approach) counters what the "left" hand (the economic and explicitly democratic approaches) has helped to create. (Packenham, 1973: 163)

More precise conclusions about the relationship between political culture and foreign policy practice remain elusive—although the logic underlying such a relationship seems unassailable. The premises of democratic capitalism embedded in the American culture certainly help to explain the repulsion the United States has expressed toward socialism and communism. Similarly, anticommunism helps to explain how a country committed to individual rights and liberties could sometimes suppress them in the name of national security. And the postwar ascent of the United States to the status of a global power helps to explain how a nation committed to "limited government" could nonetheless justify the creation and maintenance of a gigantic peacetime military establishment. Remaking the world in America's image is also alleged to have sprung from the nation's cultural traditions. The National Endowment for Democracy (NED), launched by the Reagan administration in 1983, is a recent manifestation of a tradition with a long heritage. Its purpose is to encourage worldwide the development of autonomous political, economic, social, and cultural institutions to serve as the foundations of democracy and the guarantors of individual rights and freedoms. Many other plausible propositions relating foreign policy predispositions to the influence of American values have also been advanced.[6] It seems, then, that the appropriate question is not whether there is a relationship between culture and foreign policy, but how that relationship operates.

A probable link can be posited here. A *law of anticipated reactions* may be operative whereby decision makers screen out certain alternatives because of their anticipation that the options would be adversely received, an anticipation born of their intrinsic image of the American political culture, which helps to define in their minds the range of permissible foreign policy goals and options.[7] Robert Kennedy's argument against using an air strike to destroy the Soviet missiles surreptitiously placed in Cuba in 1962 illustrates the hypothesized screening process:[8]

> Whatever validity the military and political arguments were for an attack in preference to a blockade, America's traditions and history would not permit such a course of action. Whatever military reasons [former Secretary of State Dean Acheson] and others could marshal, they were nevertheless, in the last analysis, advocating a surprise attack by a very large nation against a very small one. This, I said, could not be undertaken by the U.S. If we were to maintain our moral position at home and around the globe. Our struggle against Communism throughout the world was far more than physical survival—it had as its essence our heritage and our ideals, and these we must not destroy. (Kennedy, 1971: 16–17)

Of course, this screening process has at times been rendered inoperative by the sacrifice of ideological ideals to self-interest based on the calculations of *realpolitik*. When principles have clashed with needs, the former at times have been shunted aside. Two examples from the 1980s stand out: U.S. immigration policy and U.S. trade policy. President Ronald Reagan labeled the United States an "island of freedom," a land placed here by "divine Providence" as a "refuge for all those people in the world who yearn to breathe free," and the Statue of Liberty was refurbished as a continuing reminder that America is a beacon of freedom for immigrants from around the world. And yet, American policy officially sought to stem the tide of refugees as the "open door" was closed;

---

6. The case for a cultural explanation of American foreign policy is argued persuasively in Knudsen (1987).

7. In fact, decision makers may not even be conscious of the way in which the political culture shapes their thinking. "Political culture, as such, determines behavior in relatively few situations or in response to relatively few particular issues. Its influence lies in its power to set reasonably fixed limits to political behavior and provide subliminal direction for political action . . . ; limits and direction all the more effective because of their antiquity and subtlety whereby those limited are unaware of the limitations placed upon them" (Elazar, 1970).

8. Although this is the orthodox interpretation of Robert Kennedy's role during the deliberations over the Cuban missiles, recently released transcripts of taped conversations during those meetings suggest that Kennedy was actually a proponent of the invasion option, of which air strikes would obviously be a part (see "White House Tapes and Minutes of the Cuban Missile Crisis," 1985).

approximately 600,000 new immigrants entered in 1988, but immigration as a proportion of the population was less than a fifth of what it was in 1900 and, in absolute numbers, it fell far short of the numbers welcomed to America when its population was but half as large. And with respect to the capitalist principle of free trade, we find that here, too, pressing economic exigencies generated strong pressure for a compromise of this cornerstone of America's cultural heritage; calls for protectionism and neomercantilist programs became intense in the 1980s as the trade balance deteriorated to historically high levels and the federal deficit reached unprecedented proportions (see Chapter 7). Thus core precepts are not always honored—in part because they are elastic and amenable to different interpretations.

Still another potential culture-policy link can be noted. Developments may coalesce over time to generate changes in a political culture's otherwise durable values and beliefs (McClosky and Zaller, 1984). Consider what happened to the 1960s' generation. Raised to believe that the United States was a splendidly virtuous country, young Americans found—through the Bay of Pigs invasion; racial discrimination in Selma, Alabama, and elsewhere; the assassinations of President John F. Kennedy, his brother Robert, and Martin Luther King, Jr.; and then Vietnam—that ideals were prostituted in practice. Outraged, large numbers of alienated Americans protested the abuses that undermined seemingly sacred assumptions. Simultaneously, the faith the American people reposed in their political and other social institutions declined precipitously (see Chapter 9). American culture underwent a substantial alteration as the nation wrestled with the violation of the ideals within its tradition, as reported in the book (and subsequent movie) *Born on the Fourth of July* (Kovic, 1977).

With the political culture in flux, the climate of opinion was conducive to changes in policy. A war ended ignominiously. Two American presidents were toppled, one (Lyndon B. Johnson) in the face of enormous political pressure from domestic as well as international forces, the other (Richard M. Nixon) in disgrace. Legal barriers to racial discrimination were dismantled. New constraints were placed on the use—both overt and covert—of American force abroad, and the range of permissible action was reduced in ways that continue to shape policy thinking today. Thus it appears that changes in the political culture—whether they stem from public disillusionment, policy failure, or whatever—can affect the kinds of policies that are subsequently proposed and the ways in which they are carried out.

The period just described is not unique. Every age reevaluates the past in light of the needs of the present, and the American political culture is therefore constantly undergoing modification. Indeed, the climate of opinion shifted after the turbulent 1960s and the introspective 1970s toward pragmatic *realpolitik* in the 1980s; and there are elements pointing toward a potential resurgence of liberal ideals in the 1990s (Kober, 1990). The fluctuations illustrate the almost cyclical propensity for different values within the American tradition to receive varying degrees of emphasis in different periods and circumstances.

In the final analysis, as the law of anticipated reactions implies, the critical variable linking an altered cultural environment with policy change is the attitudes of leaders. Thus changes in the political culture will not affect foreign policy making unless those who make policy both appreciate the changes and accommodate their policies to them. To understand more fully the domestic sources of American foreign policy, therefore, we must look beyond the causal impact of American political culture and examine how American leaders serve as links between national values and foreign policy and how, by virtue of the things they say and do, they may modify those values.

DEMOCRATIC LIBERALISM IN THEORY AND PRACTICE

According to liberal democratic theory, leaders are chosen to reflect societal values by converting public preferences into policy.[9] By extension, American foreign policy is ultimately an expression of Americans' sentiments; in the words of a former secretary of defense, "Foreign policy does not rest upon a definition of the national interest. It rests on public opinion" (Schlesinger, 1989).

How realistic is that theory? Do elected leaders indeed devise policies that correspond with the majority's general preferences? Or do they, instead, devise policies that cater to a privileged elite from which the leaders themselves are drawn or appeal to specialized interests in American society? How, in short, does liberal democratic theory operate in practice when it comes to the nation's foreign policy? We will seek answers to these questions by examining two competing theories that purport to explain how public preferences may be translated into public policy: the elitist model and the pluralist model.

Does a "Power Elite" Control American Foreign Policy?

The United States is undeniably a democratic society. The complication with that description is that it is also a special-interest society (as well as a bureaucratic society, an information society, a mass consumption society, a technocratic society, and so forth). In particular, when we examine those who make American foreign policy, and ask if those leaders share the convictions and attributes of Americans in general, perplexing findings emerge.

Who Is Chosen to Lead?   In terms of numbers, not many: "Great power in America is concentrated in a handful of people. A few thousand individuals out of 240 million Americans decide about war and peace" (Dye, 1990). It is also quite clear that only certain types of people have for years been recruited into the nation's foreign policy "establishment." Not everyone is eligible; people are

---

9. The meaning of democracy, and the democratic premise, is captured by its Greek root: *demokratia: demos* ("people") and *kratia* ("power").

selectively recruited and those outside the mainstream are denied the opportunity to serve. Furthermore, because some hold advantages in the competition for positions—by virtue of family connections, income, education, gender, and race—top officials are not drawn proportionately from a cross-section of American society. The result is an *elite* not only in the sense that a small minority controls policy-making power but also in the sense that America's postwar foreign policy managers have been drawn largely from an unrepresentative coterie.

The elitist character[10] of foreign policy making becomes apparent when policymakers' backgrounds are inspected. Remarkable similarities characterize America's postwar foreign policy "establishment." Consistent with what is usually meant by the term *elite*, this group is rather small, and its composition very enduring, having changed little in nearly a half-century. In the postwar era the top positions have been filled by people from the upper class who were educated at the nation's best schools. They are, as the title of a prize-winning book put it, "the best and the brightest" (Halberstam, 1972).[11] Furthermore, they have tended to be males from predominantly white, Anglo-Saxon, Protestant (WASP) backgrounds; a disproportionate number have been trained in law; and many have had extensive experience in big business. Indeed, most postwar policymakers' prior careers were spent as managers or owners of major corporations and financial institutions or on the faculty of the nation's elite universities, and more often than not they served in appointed rather than elected positions (Brownstein and Easton, 1983; Burch, 1980). The evidence from 1961 to 1988 on the career experience of executive officials in the "inner cabinet" (the secretaries of State, Defense, and Treasury, and the Attorney General) shows that 81 percent served in the national government previously, 46 percent worked in private business, 62 percent were attorneys, and 27 percent had academic careers (Lowi and Ginsburg, 1990: 268). In essence, the existence of this governing elite makes popular sovereignty fictional—a myth that "served to legitimate the rule not of the people, but of a small and privileged elite. Against populist rhetoric, the few . . . rule the many" (Thomas, 1988).

In effect, those who have made postwar American foreign policy have glided between government and the private sector through a "revolving door,"

---

10. The core idea behind elitism in policy making can be stated thus: "The discovery that in all large-scale societies the decisions are typically in the hands of a small number of people confirms a basic fact: Government is always by the few, whether in the name of the few, the one, or the many" (Lasswell and Lerner, 1952). Even if one accepts the elitist perspective, determining the size and composition of the elite is difficult. One estimate suggested that only fifty-five hundred people control key industrial, banking, communications, and cultural organizations in the United States or hold key federal government jobs (Dye and Pickering, 1974). Profiles of those who make it to the top and elaborations of the elitist perspective can be found in Brownstein and Easton (1983), Burch (1980), Destler, Gelb, and Lake (1984), Domhoff (1984, 1980, 1971), Dye (1990), Dye and Zeigler (1990), and Froman (1984).

11. Education and training are not necessarily guarantees against foolish policy decisions; indeed, one of the main points of Halberstam's book is that intelligent people are capable of making wicked and stupid decisions.

in front of which the line has seldom been very long. The names of Robert Lovett, Robert McNamara, Henry Stimson, Averell Harriman, James F. Byrnes, the Dulles brothers (Allen and John Foster), Dean Acheson, Clark Clifford, Paul Nitze, Nelson Rockefeller, Paul Warnke, the Bundy brothers (William and McGeorge), Dean Rusk, Elliot Richardson, George Ball, Richard M. Nixon, the Rostow brothers (Walt and Eugene), Henry Kissinger, Zbigniew Brzezinski, James Schlesinger, George Bush, Cyrus Vance, George Shultz, Alexander Haig, Dick Cheney, Caspar Weinberger, James A. Baker, Brent Scowcroft, and Larry Eagleburger come readily to mind. Many more fit the pattern. Since 1945 many of the same people, sharing many of the same attitudes, have managed postwar American foreign policy. The homogeneous social and occupational attributes of America's postwar foreign policymakers have been described by a former Kennedy administration adviser thus:

> Between 1940 and 1967, when I stopped counting, all the first- and second-level posts in the huge national security bureaucracy were held by fewer than four hundred individuals who rotate through a variety of key posts. The temporary civilian managers who come to Washington . . . , the national security managers, were so alike one another in occupation, religion, style, and social status that, apart from a few Washington lawyers, Texans, and mavericks, it was possible to locate the offices of all of them within fifteen city blocks in New York, Boston, and Detroit. Most of their biographies in Who's Who read like minor variations on a single theme—wealthy parents, Ivy-League education, leading law firm or bank (or entrepreneur in a war industry), introduction to government in World War II. . . . Seventy of the ninety-one people who have held the very top jobs . . . have all been businessmen, lawyers for businessmen, and investment bankers. (Barnet, 1972: 48–49)

The pattern continues: 90 percent of the Bush administration's cabinet-level appointees held previous government posts and 35 percent previous corporate posts; 40 percent had careers in law; and 50 percent were educated in the Ivy League (Dye and Zeigler, 1990: 18–19).

Commonality of experience has fostered uniformity in foreign policy attitudes; the continuity of postwar American foreign policy can be traced to the shared characteristics of the self-selecting, self-recruiting, and self-perpetuating *governing elite* who have been in charge of that policy. Like-minded individuals have "guarded" American foreign policy by instructing incumbent administrations on similar policy principles (Domhoff, 1984). Every postwar president has found himself dependent on these "Wise Men" and their advice. Perhaps this dependence is what led John F. Kennedy to respond, when urged during his 1960 campaign to hit his critics harder: "That is not a very good idea. I'll need them all to run this country."

The recruitment and advisory roles of the Council on Foreign Relations illuminate the channels whereby the values of corporate and financial elites have often been funneled into the foreign policy-making process. The council has been described as "the most influential policy-planning group in foreign affairs" (Dye, 1990). Its limited membership is drawn from among the most prestigious and best connected of the nation's financial and corporate institutions, universities, foundations, media, and government bodies. And its members (limited by its by-laws to nineteen hundred individuals), past and present, include most of those previously named. "Every person of influence in foreign affairs" (Dye, 1990) has been a member, including presidents. Among them was Jimmy Carter, who as governor of Georgia was appointed to the Council's multinational wing known as the Trilateral Commission.[12] Created to coordinate economic policy among the United States, Western Europe, and Japan, the Trilateral Commission was headed at the time of Carter's appointment by political science professor Zbigniew Brzezinski of Columbia University. Brzezinski subsequently became Carter's national security adviser. In all, nineteen of those who had been among the Trilateral Commission's sixty-five members were appointed to top positions or served as official advisers early in the Carter administration (*Washington Post*, January 16, 1977, pp. A1, A4)

The council's continuing influence is also suggested by the fact that in the 1980s "at least a dozen of [the Reagan administration's top officials] and thirty-one advisors were members of the Council" (Parenti, 1988: 200). Vice President George Bush, Secretary of Defense Caspar Weinberger, Secretary of State George Shultz, Secretary of State Alexander Haig, Secretary of the Treasury Donald Regan, and CIA Director William Casey were all members. Bush later resigned from the Council "to deflect right-wing attacks that he was part of the CFR 'conspiracy' to subvert U.S. interests to an 'international government'" (Dye, 1990).

In the postwar period, recommendations by the Council on Foreign Relations and subsequent U.S. foreign policy actions have been remarkably consistent. For example, the council played a key role in the origination of such policies as containment, the North Atlantic Treaty Organization agreement, the Marshall Plan, the International Monetary Fund, the World Bank, and diplomatic relations with China. The council also advocated major initiatives in American military strategy; for example, it proposed flexible response as a substitute for the doctrine of massive retaliation, and it supported military involvement in Vietnam and, later, withdrawal. The council's influence was dramatized by its 1980s Project which paved the way for a number of the Carter administration's policies:

> The [1980s] project began in 1975, and it [included] (1) an international campaign on behalf of "human rights"; (2) a series of alternative approaches to nuclear stability, including a new strict policy toward nuclear proliferation; (3) an effort to restrict international arms sales; and (4) a study of "North-South global relations" —relations between richer and poorer countries. (Dye, 1978: 318)

---

12. The Trilateral Commission officially disavows any "formal ties" with either the Council on Foreign Relations or the Brookings Institution, although the organization acknowledges that "a considerable number of Commission members are involved in one or more other organizations of this sort," and its coordinator, George S. Franklin, served formerly as executive director of the Council on Foreign Relations.

Similarly, it was the council that called in the late 1970s for a fundamental reevaluation of Soviet-American relations in response to a perceived Soviet military buildup, even before Ronald Reagan took office. Reagan subsequently made massive military spending the centerpiece of his foreign policy. Later, the council "urged a policy obviously at variance with the Reagan administration's" when it "strongly supported a new thaw in U.S.-Soviet relations" (Dye, 1990). The council was intimately involved in the initiation of the Strategic Arms Reduction Talks (START) and the intermediate-range nuclear forces (INF) arms control talks with the Soviet Union and advocated the "no first use" principle regarding nuclear weapons.

The Council on Foreign Relations is the most important private policy-making entity linking the elite in American society to the U.S. government, but it is not alone. The Brookings Institution, the Committee for Economic Development, the Business Roundtable, the American Enterprise Institute, and the Heritage Foundation also seek to exercise influence (see Dye, 1990). In a similar vein, many analysts speculated that Kissinger Associates, Henry Kissinger's international consulting firm, was probably also influential with the Bush administration because two of its former executives, Brent Scowcroft and Lawrence Eagleburger, occupy key positions in the administration (national security adviser and deputy secretary of state, respectively). That view seemed to be confirmed by the role Kissinger played in jump-starting the U.S. relationship with China less than six months after the 1989 Tiananmen Square massacre that had soured it.

Elites have long played a prominent role in foreign policy formulation. That continues to be the case, although the cohesion and perhaps influence of the traditional foreign policy elite waned in the 1980s as it was challenged by new centers of power and wealth (Schulzinger, 1985) and the rise of a "counter establishment" (Blumenthal, 1988). Power dispersed and new factions surfaced, as attested by the emergence in the 1980s of a division between "the newly rich, entrepreneurial Southern and Western *cowboys* and the established, managerial Eastern *yankees*" (Dye, 1990).[13] Moreover, the "establishment" has been challenged by the ascendance of a new class of foreign policy "professionals" whose technocrat outlook differs from the perspective of the traditional elite (Destler, Gelb, and Lake, 1984). And some have discerned the rise to positions of power and prestige of a new American establishment of "inventors and risk takers, innovators and organizational wizards" (Reed, 1988). The effects of these changes in the elites' composition are difficult to predict. But—appearances to the contrary—new fissures within it will fail to

---

13. James R. Kurth (1989) suggests that Northrup, a California-based defense contractor not normally among the prime aerospace military manufacturers, may have received the prime contract award for the B-2 (Stealth) bomber because "the Reagan administration was the first truly Californian administration in U.S. history. At one time (1982–1983), the president, the secretary of defense, the secretary of state, the national security adviser, and the White House chief of staff came from California, and from 1982 to 1987 the first three did so . . . . Consequently, it is not surprising that California aerospace firms might have been given favorable attention."

produce major policy changes as long as the emerging factions continue to operate on the basis of the same assumptions about foreign policy as those maintained by the "old guard" who have served as the gatekeepers.

Elite Attitudes and Behavior   The consistency between government policy and the recommendations of this cadre of policymakers-advisers-financiers outside of government does not necessarily pose a problem for liberal democratic theory, because a democracy encourages the participation of people and the expression of their preferences. But what if we ask the related question: Are the values and outlook of foreign policy-making elites and others with influence different from those of the American people they presumably represent? If leaders are different from those they lead, does a small minority actually control the majority?

Available evidence on these issues is mixed. Elites generally have been "public regarding," perceiving themselves as "guardians of the public good"; moreover, most Americans have generally registered approval of elites' policies. (The exception, of course, was Vietnam, which destroyed much of the credibility and clout of the "Wise Men.") Ironically, however, the attitudes of elites and the general public about the democratic process itself often diverge:

> Democratic values have survived because elites, not masses, govern. Elites in the United States—leaders in government, industry, education, the media, and civic affairs and the well-educated, prestigiously employed, and politically active—give greater support to basic democratic values and "rules of the game" than do the masses. And it is because the American masses respond to the ideas of democratically minded elites that liberal values are preserved. (Dye and Zeigler, 1990: 14)

But elites' commitment to liberal democratic values appears only relatively greater than that of the masses, and that commitment may turn out to be especially fragile during times of crisis. When war threatens, fearful elites tend to

> respond by curtailing freedom and strengthening security. Convincing themselves that they are themselves preserving liberal democratic values, elites may cease tolerating dissent, curtail free speech, jail potential counterelites, and strengthen police and security forces in the name of "national security," or "law and order." Ironically, these steps make society less democratic rather than more so. (Dye and Zeigler, 1990: 16)

Even in routine circumstances elites often frame policies to protect their advantaged positions.[14] The result, argue Thomas R. Dye and Harmon Zeigler (1990), is that "changes and innovations in public policy come about when

---

14. Interestingly, the majority of Americans also see government leaders as driven primarily by their desire to promote their own power. Public opinion surveys reveal that from 1970 to 1985 between 55 and 80 percent of the American public agreed with the statement that the U.S. government is run by a few big interests looking out for themselves, whereas between 20 and 40 percent believed that it is run for the benefit of all (*Public Opinion*, September 1985, p. 21).

elites redefine their own values. However, the general conservatism of elites—that is, their interest in preserving the system—means that changes in public policy will be incremental rather than revolutionary. Public policies are often modified but seldom replaced."

The assertion that American foreign policy is democratic because the foreign policy elite represent the public at large is challenged by those who see elite opinion diverging from that of the general public. Indeed, a "power elite" (Mills, 1956) consisting of a select few is said to govern America[15] without direction from the general public. Thus the American political system gives the public participation (elections, for example) without power, involvement without influence, while a small set of elite participants, acting both openly and behind closed doors, makes the important decisions. Even elected officials might properly be thought of more as "proximate policymakers" whose actions give official sanction "knowingly or unknowingly" to the values of the power elite rather than as conduits through which mass preferences are translated into public policy (Dye, 1990). Thus actual government authority does not reside with the people—the Lockian liberal tradition and the doctrine of popular sovereignty notwithstanding. It rests instead in the hands of a select minority who exercise substantial power over foreign policy making and public policy in general.

This discrepancy between the theory and practice of democratic governance is most visible wherever power is concentrated. This is often alleged to be the case with respect to the military-industrial complex.

Does a Military-Industrial Complex Control American Foreign Policy?

The Theory   President Dwight D. Eisenhower, a highly decorated World War II general, first brought national attention to the existence of a *military-industrial complex* when he warned, in an often quoted passage from his farewell address, given on January 17, 1961:

> This conjunction of an immense military establishment and a large arms industry is new in the American experience. The total influence—economic, political, even spiritual—is felt in every city, every statehouse, every office of the Federal

---

15. "Power elite" as used in the context of foreign policy making is essentially synonymous with the "establishment" described above, which includes those who have access to persons occupying foreign policy decision-making roles and who themselves from time to time assume positions of authority. Note, however, that the "power elite" or the "establishment" is not necessarily synonymous with the governing elite, which refers exclusively to those who occupy positions of authority in the government. Particularly at the top levels of government, of course, there is an overlap between the "establishment" and the governing elite—an overlap that provides an important channel between those inside of government and those on the outside. Although the existence of various interlocks and overlaps among different elites makes it difficult to segment them into discrete, empirically identifiable groups, those same connections among variously defined minorities are among the empirical proof of the veracity of the elitist perspective on public policy making.

Government. We recognize the imperative need for this development. Yet we must not fail to comprehend its grave implications. Our toil, resources, and livelihood are all involved; so is the very structure of our society.

In the councils of government we must guard against the acquisition of unwarranted influence, whether sought or unsought, by the military-industrial complex. The potential for the disastrous rise of misplaced power exists and will persist.

We must never let the weight of this combination endanger our liberties or democratic processes. . . .

Eisenhower's warning preceded Harold D. Lasswell's (1962) prophecy that a "garrison state" governed by "specialists in violence" would arise to dominate policy making and followed C. Wright Mills's (1956) view that a power elite promotes policies designed to serve its own, rather than the nation's, interests. The military-industrial complex was a threat, Eisenhower felt, because its vast power undermined the countervailing forces that would otherwise keep in check the abuse of power. Specifically, the military-industrial partnership is seen as consisting of "(1) the professional soldiers, (2) managers and . . . owners of industries heavily engaged in military supply, (3) top government officials whose careers and interests are tied to military expenditure, and (4) legislators whose districts benefit from defense procurement" (Rosen, 1973). C. Wright Mills described the partnership this way:

> What is called the "Washington military clique" is not composed merely of military men, and it does not prevail merely in Washington. Its members exist all over the country, and it is a coalition of generals in the roles of corporation executives, of politicians masquerading as admirals, of corporation executives acting like politicians, of civil servants who become majors, of vice-admirals who are also the assistants to a cabinet officer, who is himself, by the way, really a member of the managerial elite. (Mills, 1956: 278)

According to Mills, the partnership among these interests is more a natural coalition than a conspiracy. The interests do occasionally join forces to strive for the same self-serving ends, but not necessarily by design, and not frequently through coordinated activities. "The power elite," wrote Mills, "is composed of political, economic, and military men, but this institutionalized elite is frequently in some tension: it comes together only on certain coinciding points and only on certain occasions of 'crisis.'" Members of the elite speak in a cacophony of voices over key issues. Nonetheless, its entrenched (if disorganized) power is believed to derive naturally from a capitalist economic system dependent on foreign involvement for economic benefit. In particular, the postwar arms race and the high level of American military spending are often attributed to the self-aggrandizing activities of the military and industrial sectors which, so the reasoning goes, propagate policies favorable to their interests. As a "peddler of crisis" (Sanders, 1983) which benefits from trouble (Sampson, 1977) through lobbying and mass advertising, the complex justifies its existence by provoking fear of the Soviet menace and capability gaps and promotes through propaganda the need for vigilance in order "to wage a war against cutbacks and not the Soviets" (Thompson, 1990).[16] External dangers have allegedly been exaggerated to rationalize unnecessary weapons programs and ensure that the military budget will continue to grow "regardless of whether there is war or peace" (Parenti, 1988). In addition, the continuation of the Cold War mentality was attributed to elites "too entrenched and too dependent on the continuation of the Cold War for their power to accommodate to a shifting world scene" (Rosenau, 1973).

Adherents to the thesis of a powerful military-industrial complex stress the probability that in combination its various military and industrial components outweigh any countervailing domestic forces. The complex is perceived to dominate all other American interest groups. "Each institutional component of the military-industrial complex has plausible reasons for continuing to exist and expand. Each promotes and protects its own interests and in doing so reinforces the interests of every other. That is what a 'complex' is—a set of integrated institutions that act to maximize their collective power" (Barnet, 1969). As Eisenhower put it,

> The Congressman who seeks a new defense establishment in his district; the company in Los Angeles, Denver, or Baltimore that wants an order for more airplanes, the services which want them, the armies of scientists who want so terribly to test their newest views; put all of these together and you have a lobby.

Like many special-interest groups, the military-industrial complex promotes policies beneficial to itself but possibly detrimental to the nation as a whole. The complex is so influential because it permeates the entire notion: "American society," Marc Pilisuk and Thomas Hayden (1965) concluded, "*is* a military-industrial complex" (emphasis added).

The Evidence   A number of factors have promoted the popularity of the military-industrial complex's hypothesized hold on American foreign policy (Kotz, 1988). The extraordinary level of defense spending during the Cold War, and even after its proclaimed termination, is purportedly explained by the ability of the "iron triangle" (Adams, 1988) that links the armed forces to influential allies in private industry and in Congress to maintain a system of preferential treatment for those it serves. From this viewpoint, the periodic scandals that surround the Pentagon's weapons contracting and procurement processes are also to be expected, leading to the conclusion that the practices exposed— "the revolving door between government and industry, the mutual back-

---

16. Because Cold War tension contributes to the power of both the American and Soviet military-industrial complex, they both had a stake in the preservation of hostilities: "The irony is that the Pentagon and the Soviet Defense Ministry prosper symbiotically. There is no greater racket in the world . . . than generals claiming the other side is ahead in order to get bigger budgets for themselves" (Schlesinger, 1983).

scratching between the military and the companies that build its weapons—
aren't abuses of the system. They *are* the system" (Ignatius, 1988).[17]

The belief that the military-industrial complex has been favored to the
possible detriment of the national interest is based on considerable circumstantial evidence, as described below.[18]

- "In the mid-1980s, at the height of the Reagan administration's planned
  $2.3-trillion defense buildup, the Pentagon was spending an average of
  $28 million an *hour*. . . . By 1990 . . . the total defense-spending boom
  for the Cold War years [would] total $3.7 trillion in constant 1972
  dollars—nearly enough 'to buy everything in the United States except
  the land: every house, factory, train, plane and refrigerator'" (Ignatius,
  1988: 23).

- "One of every 16 American workers relies directly on the military-
  industrial complex for his or her paycheck. Millions more depend on
  those workers . . . as customers" (Thompson, 1990: 10). "More than
  30 percent of mathematicians, 25 percent of physicists, 47 percent of
  aeronautical engineers, and 11 percent of computer programmers work
  in the military-industrial complex" (Lipsitz and Speak, 1989: 290).
  "For every billion dollars that the Pentagon cuts from its arms budget,
  almost 30,000 jobs will be lost by industry" (Reifenberg, 1990: 22).

- Congress often appropriates more money for military spending than
  requested by the president and micromanages the Pentagon's budget in
  ways that treat it as a source of patronage (to protect contractors in their
  districts) but that saddles the Pentagon with extra costs (Fossedal, 1985;
  Mossberg, 1983).

- The list of top fifteen companies receiving prime contract awards from
  the Pentagon has remained remarkably stable since World War II, especially among aerospace manufacturers (McDonnell Douglas, Lockheed,
  Boeing, Rockwell International, General Dynamics, General Motors,
  and United Technologies). "Six of the eight aerospace production lines

---

17. Senator Warren Rudman underscored the symbiotic relationship between Congress and the
military-industrial complex with the observation that "there is not a member of this Senate, or a
member of the House, who does not have some defense facility in their state, some of which are
necessary and some of which are not." Examples of the alleged influence of the military-
industrial complex in Congress are abundant. For instance:

In early 1961 some of the White House people were trying to slow down the arms race. . . .
At that point the United States had 450 missiles; McNamara was asking for 950, and the Joint
Chiefs of Staff were asking for 3,000. The White House people had quietly checked around
and found that in effectiveness . . . the 450 were the same as McNamara's 950. . . .
"What about it, Bob," Kennedy asked.
"Well, they're right," McNamara answered.
"Well, then, why the nine hundred and fifty, Bob?" Kennedy asked.
"Because that's the smallest number we can take up on the Hill without getting mur-
dered," he answered. (Halberstam, 1972: 72)

18. Supporting data and additional information for each of these observations can be found in
Atkinson and Hiatt (1985), Dolbeare and Edelman (1985), Etzioni (1984), Fossedal (1985), Good-
win (1985), Hiatt and Atkinson (1985), Parenti (1988), Pincus (1985a), Proxmire (1970), and
Rosen (1973).

have had a continuous contracting relationship with one military service . . . in most cases back to World War II'' (Kurth, 1989).

- Typically, the prime aerospace contractors receive a new contract as a current production line phases out an existing award according to the "follow-on imperative," which holds that "a large and established aerospace production line is a national resource. . . . The Defense Department would find it risky and even reckless to allow a large production line to wither and die for lack of a large production contract. . . . Further, the disruption of the production line will be least and the efficiency of the product would seem highest if the new contract is structurally similar to the old; that is, it is a follow-on contract. Such a contract renovates both the large and established aerospace corporation that produces the weapons system and the military organization that deploys it—that is, both halves of the military-industrial duplex'' (Kurth, 1989).

- "The imperatives of the industrial structure are reinforced . . . by the imperatives of the political system. Four of the major production lines are located in states that loom large in the Electoral College: California (Rockwell and Lockheed-Missiles and Space), Texas (General Dynamics), and New York (Grumman). Three others are located in states that for many years had a senator who ranked high in the Senate Armed Services Committee or Appropriations Committee: Washington (Boeing; Henry Jackson), Georgia (Lockheed-Georgia; first Richard Russell and then Sam Nunn), and Missouri (McDonnell division of McDonnell Douglas; Stuart Symington). And Texas benefitted both from its weight in the Electoral College and from John Tower's tenure on the Senate Armed Services Committee'' (Kurth, 1989).

- The Pentagon's 20,000 prime contractors and 150,000 subcontractors and vendors "labor" under a noncompetitive "funny form of capitalism" that subsidizes corporate profits and cushions contractors "from the impact of their inefficiency" by a process known as "contract nourishment" (Atkinson and Hiatt, 1985). One study "estimated that virtually all large military contracts have cost overruns from 300 to 700 percent" (Parenti, 1988: 88). According to the Extraordinary Contractual Relief Act (Public Law 85–104), since 1959 the government, at a cost of $1.4 billion, has on more than six thousand occasions given grants to bail out defense contractors in trouble, picked up the costs for "even unsolicited and unsuccessful proposals," and awarded hundreds of millions of dollars in interest-free loans. The government also allows its contractors to defer taxes on their huge profits, sometimes for many years, through a practice known as "The Method"[19] (Hiatt and Atkinson, 1985).

---

19. An examination in the mid-1980s of the nation's largest defense contractors revealed that General Dynamics Corporation had paid no federal taxes since 1972; Lockheed none since 1979; and Boeing none since 1980. It also found that "General Electric, ranked fourth in the defense industry, earned $6.5 billion in profits from 1981 to 1983. Yet it paid no federal income tax and claimed a refund of $283 million" (Atkinson and Hiatt, 1985).

- Fraud, waste, bribery, and corruption have been chronic in military contracting (Magnuson, 1988), as attested by procurement abuses in the 1980s that included "$748 . . . for a pair of $7.61 pliers, a $7,000 coffee pot, and $600 toilet seats" (Meier, 1987: 125). "In 77 cases of shoddy construction work reviewed by Pentagon auditors in 1982, only once was the contractor forced to pay for his mistakes" (Atkinson and Hiatt, 1985). The consequence of poorly built equipment has been the expansion of the Pentagon's staff and budget to manage its operations. In the wake of disclosures in 1984 that the Defense Department was paying $400 each for $8 claw hammers, "the military . . . added 7,000 additional staffers to solve its spare-parts problems" (Reich, 1985: 36).

- Universities now do a substantial amount of the Pentagon's basic research; seduced into partnership, they no longer serve as a countervailing balance to the military-industrial community.[20] "Our job," one MIT researcher noted, "is not to advance knowledge but to advance the military" (cited in Parenti, 1988).

- Numerous private "consulting firms" and "nonprofit" think tanks compete over a share of military "research monies." "Few civilian analysts are to be found" in the employment of these firms; the "beltway bandits," as they are known, are populated with former Pentagon personnel and retired officers (Pincus, 1985). "Studies that challenge higher authority, that deviate much in either tone or color from the represented service's pitch or uniform hue" are few and far between (Brewer and Bracken, 1984).

- Defense spending consistently accounts for a high percentage of federal outlays. Under the Reagan administration the defense budget doubled and "defense production grew at three times the clip of U.S. industry as a whole" (Parenti, 1988: 85). Even under conditions of massive budget deficits, federal debt, and a diminishing Soviet threat, the Bush administration in January 1990 sought a $7 billion increase in military spending for 1991. As a Pentagon budget official wryly noted, "Only over here do we call a $1 billion hike—we wanted a $10 billion hike—a $9 billion cut" (Thompson, 1990: 6D).

These insights provide empirical support for the alleged existence of a complex of military-industrial interests. But the influence of the complex on American foreign policy is easily overestimated. Whereas the military-industrial complex undoubtedly colors much activity abroad and at home—particularly with respect to the structure of defense spending and the corresponding impact on the shape of the nation's military capabilities—foreign

---

20. The absorption of both academic and governmental sectors into the military-industrial complex has enhanced its collective power and correspondingly called for a broadened definition captured by the acronym *MAGIC* (military-academic-governmental-industrial complex).

policy initiatives do not derive solely from the pressures of the faceless complex. The evidence is too contradictory.

Moreover, some components of the theory are either unconvincing or illogical. While it may be true that pressures for increased defense spending are brought to bear by some lobbyists and defense contractors, it does not follow that the complex single-mindedly pursues this objective above all others. The profits of American industry are not contingent exclusively on military sales (Goodwin, 1985). Nor is the theory's conspiratorial version, which sees conniving generals and industrialists collaborating to enrich themselves at the public's expense, convincing; instead, "the problem is not conspiracy or corruption, but unchecked rule" (Galbraith, 1969b). And the proposition that the complex actively promotes foreign adventure and derives pleasure from international instability is not cogent—both war and foreign adventure directly threaten the financial interests of corporate America and the lives (though not the prospects for promotion) of military officers.

Clearly some segments of American society realize benefits from an excessively vigilant or martial foreign policy posture, but where there is interest, there is not necessarily influence. The conclusion reached in a previous examination of the theory of the military-industrial complex remains relevant today:

> Demonstrating that some segment of the military-industrial complex will benefit from a given policy is not tantamount to a proof that the policy was in fact initiated for this purpose. Inevitably, private interests will be served by a [multi-billion dollar] annual procurement, but it does not follow that these interests determine policy. . . . Overall, we may say that C. Wright Mills has been sustained in the essential propositions of his theory, though some of the more simplified conspiratorial versions developed by his most ardent followers must be rejected. (Rosen, 1973: 4, 25)

The Impact of Special-Interest Groups on American Foreign Policy

The "power-elite" thesis and the related theory of an influential military-industrial complex challenge the theoretical tenets of liberal democracy. If in practice an elite indeed rules, and if its behavior is supported by an all-powerful military-industrial complex, then "democratic" policy formation may be little more than a political myth. Foreign policy making under such conditions becomes less an expression of the values and interests of the American people at large and more a reflection of the values and interests of a privileged minority.

Juxtaposed to this conclusion is an alternative view—that individual Americans influence policy by organizing themselves into groups to petition the government on behalf of their shared interests and values. This is the basis of the *pluralist* model of public policy making. It purports to explain how liberal values and democratic institutions are preserved even while democracy in its purest form (direct participation and control by the people) is precluded.

Advocates of the pluralist model acknowledge that the demands of a modern, complex government with global entanglements necessarily concentrate power in the hands of a few. Citizens cannot participate directly in public policy making. Nonetheless, the potential tyranny of elites is prevented, and democracy preserved, because multiple public interests are represented by leaders who themselves are in competition with one another. Public preferences therefore find expression through bargaining among interest group elites who take the public into account not simply because they are sincerely concerned about the public welfare (as elite theory maintains) but also because the public exerts pressure on them through the voluntary associations they represent.

Thus the American people do, after all, have the means of influencing policy; and ultimately public preferences may be translated into policy. The mechanism is interest group competition, with each group pursuing its own particularistic interest; the public interest is served much as Adam Smith theorized it is served in the economic sphere, where the invisible hand of the marketplace supposedly converts the pursuit of private interests into the general welfare. The potential abuse of power is controlled by competition among countervailing centers of power. The product is government for the people if not necessarily of or by them.[21]

So pervasive are the organized interests in American society that the United States has been described as an "interest group society" (Berry, 1984). And the description is supported by the evidence.

> In 1986 the Internal Revenue Service listed 929,415 tax-exempt organizations— an increase of nearly 43,000 in a single year. Among that throng, an observer atop the White House gatepost can count over 19,000 that, national in scope, were formed in part to press their views on the federal Executive and Legislative branches. That is *double* the number that existed in 1970; new ones form at the rate of 1,000 a year. These groups act through 11,000 Washington representatives—who are regular habitués of the White House neighborhood. (Patterson, 1988: 15)

With so many Americans actively organized to promote and protect "the general welfare," pluralism commends itself as an alternative to the elitist model of public policy making.

Types of Interest Groups   The many thousands of organizations that Americans join and support to further their causes range in size from the large, powerful groups representing heterogeneous constituencies (such as the AFL-CIO or the National Chamber of Commerce), to smaller, more homogeneous groups organized around rather specific issues (such as the China Lobby [formally the Committee of One Million] which for over two decades resisted U.S.

---

21. See Lowi (1979) for an examination of the proposition that pluralism has become irrelevant because the immense growth of government has placed control of public policy in the hands of special interests.

recognition of the communist regime on mainland China). The largest proportion of them are concerned primarily with economic issues and seek to promote policies that benefit the particular interests of their members. The AFL-CIO is an example in the area of organized labor, as is the American Farm Bureau in agriculture. Among the smaller proportion of noneconomic groups three types stand out: public-interest groups, single-issue groups, and ideological groups (Patterson, 1990).

Public interest groups differ from the economic interest groups in that they seek to represent the interests of society as a whole and to realize benefits that are often less tangible. Ralph Nader's Public Citizen is perhaps the most visible public interest group, but other prominent examples of this comparatively new breed of interest groups include Common Cause and the League of Women Voters. *Single-issue groups* seek to influence policy in a more narrowly defined area, such as the environment, which is of special concern to the Sierra Club. The United Nations Association of America, for whom U.S. policy toward the United Nations is the special concern, is an example in the foreign policy domain. Various ethnic interest groups for whom foreign policy is a special concern, as we will note below, are also properly regarded as single-issue groups. *Ideological groups,* on the other hand, are concerned with a broad array of policies but from a particular philosophical viewpoint. Americans for Democratic Action, for example, generally supports liberal positions in foreign and other policy arenas, and the Heritage Foundation conservative positions.

In another sense, three other types of actors should be regarded as interest groups broadly defined. First are foreign governments who hire lobbyists in an effort to influence the decisions of American foreign policymakers and members of Congress on issues of importance to them (by law, nondiplomatic representatives of other nations are required to register as lobbyists). The potential influence of foreign powers' lobbyists should not be underestimated; approximately one thousand registered agents represent foreign countries' interests (Schlozman and Tierney, 1986: 54), whose $150 million in 1984 for lobbying greatly exceeded "the $42 million reportedly spent by the 7,200 domestic lobbyists registered by Congress" (*U.S. News & World Report*, June 17, 1985, p. 35).

Second, agencies of the U.S. government act much like interest groups; they have their own conceptions of appropriate policy and take steps to ensure their conceptions are represented in decision-making circles. The Pentagon, for example, historically has employed (using taxpayers' dollars, of course) hundreds of "congressional liaisons" whose purpose is to secure legislation favorable to itself. As discussed in Chapter 13, the size and complexity of the U.S. government has expanded the lobbying role of bureaucratic agencies, whose activities occur largely outside the public eye. The formation of "iron triangles" consisting of the interlocking expertise, specialization, and coordinated activities of lobbies pushing for their own interests, bureaucrats in charge of the administration of policy with respect to those special interests, and the congressional subcommittees dealing with them, are a noteworthy phenomenon. These triangles comprise a powerful layer of governance that dominates some areas of public policy making. Because there are literally dozens of such iron triangles in operation, it is sometimes fashionable to conceive them as "issue networks" (Perry, 1989).

And third, both state and city governments conduct their own foreign economic policies, and their activities (and competition with one another), especially in the solicitation of foreign direct investment, resemble in many ways the practices of special-interest groups (Kline, 1983; Tolchin and Tolchin, 1988).

Interest Groups and Foreign Policy   However reassuring to democratic theory the pluralist interpretation may be, in the foreign policy arena, where the questions at issue are often technical and remote from the daily lives of Americans, the presence of organized interests raises the specter of policy domination by narrow vested interests. Because interest group activities are not always visible or attended by the press, interest groups are often assumed to be working secretly behind the scenes to devise policies that serve private interests, not the national interest. Indeed, many people are apparently persuaded that foreign policy is necessarily determined by interest groups—and their beliefs are reinforced by some dramatic evidence. For instance, the American Israel Public Affairs Committee (AIPAC), a principal component of the so-called "Jewish" or "Israeli Lobby," is often suspected of controlling America's Middle East policy (see Bard, 1988; Tivnan, 1987). U.S. recognition of Israel only eleven minutes after it declared its independence; congressional passage of the Jackson-Vanik amendment denying the Soviet Union promised trade benefits pending changes in its policies regarding the emigration of Soviet Jews; and U.S. support to the tune of $12,350 (in 1987) in military aid per Israeli soldier (*Harper's*, October 1987, p. 15) lend credence to these perhaps exaggerated impressions.

Ethnic interest groups—representing, in addition to Jewish Americans, Arab-Americans, Greek-Americans, Irish-Americans, Americans of Armenian decent, and those with ancestry in what was once referred to as the Captive European Nations, among others—have long played an active role in seeking to shape American foreign policy, understandably so as the United States is a nation of immigrants. Yet one long-time senator, Charles McC. Mathias (1981), has worried that the effects of ethnic group lobbying may be more harmful than beneficial: "Ethnic politics, carried as they often have been to excess, have proven harmful to the national interest. . . . They have generated both unnecessary animosities and illusions of common interest where little or none exists. There are also baneful domestic effects: fueled as they are by passion and strong feelings about justice and rectitude, debates relating to the interplay of the national interest with the specific policies favored by organized ethnic groups generate fractious controversy and bitter recrimination."

Ethnic interest groups lobby Congress and the administration on matters that are of immediate concern to their members. Trade is another policy arena that has evoked considerable interest group activity, again because of the tangible interests—such as jobs and profits—that are at stake. Congress is often the focal point of organized activities designed to affect trade policy. The economic pressure groups involved historically have included such well-known multiple purpose organizations as the Chamber of Commerce and the AFL-CIO as well as a veritable cacophony of more specialized groups whose numbers have grown in recent years, ranging from the California Walnut Growers Association to the United Auto Workers; from the International Association of Ice Cream Manufacturers to the National Association of Stevedores; and from the Sugar Workers Council of America to the Semiconductor Industry Association (see Bauer, Pool, and Dexter, 1972; Destler, 1986; Destler and Odell, 1987).

Despite the ubiquity of ethnic interest groups and those involved in trade policy, which to a large extent is more domestic in nature than most foreign policy matters, the interest groups involved in other foreign policy questions historically have not (with some notable exceptions, such as the China Lobby) figured prominently in efforts to influence American foreign policy. Defense policy questions have emerged as an important exception in recent years, as did U.S. policy toward Central America during the Reagan administration. In both cases, special interest groups sought to influence policy using the same tactics normally associated with domestic interest group activity, including testifying at congressional hearings, initiating letter-writing campaigns, meeting with members of the media, publicizing the voting records of candidates for office, contributing work to electoral campaigns, engaging in protests and demonstrations, and the like.

During the early phases of détente, for example, a number of well-known lobbying groups were active proponents of U.S. efforts to relax tensions with the Soviet Union, such as the Arms Control Association, the Center for Defense Information, the Council for a Liveable World, Committee for a Sane Nuclear Policy, the United Nations Association, and the Women's Strike for Peace, among others. They were opposed in their efforts by an equally prominent set of organized groups, which included the AFL-CIO, the American Legion, the American Enterprise Institute, the American Security Council, the Heritage Foundation, the National Conservative Political Action Coalition (NCPAC), the Veterans of Foreign Wars, and various ethnic interest groups (Cox, 1976). Eventually, the Committee on the Present Danger emerged as an especially visible and vocal critic of détente and in particular the SALT II treaty signed by President Carter and Soviet President Leonid Brezhnev in 1979. It doubtless played a critical role in creating a domestic political environment inhospitable to its ratification (see Sanders, 1983).

In the case of Central America, the Reagan administration confronted a broad array of organized opponents of its policies in which various church groups figured prominently, but it also enjoyed the support of a countercoalition of groups that at one time numbered more than fifty (Arnson and Brenner, 1990: 16). On balance, however, it appears as though the opponents enjoyed the upper hand, especially in Congress—where the administration's policies toward Nicaragua were never popular (see Chapter 12)—as witnessed by the fact that the administration organized its own efforts both in the White House and in the State Department to build public support for its policies.

The decision of the Reagan administration to launch its own domestic "public diplomacy" efforts on behalf of its Central American policies implies that organized interest groups do indeed have the ability to affect foreign policy. Reagan lent further credence to that view when, six weeks prior to leaving the presidency, he complained that an "iron triangle" in a "Washington colony" composed of the Congress, the news media, and special-interest groups was "attempting to rule the nation according to its interests and desires more than the nation's."

How Influential Are Special-Interest Groups?   How effective are the lobbying efforts of interest groups, particularly in the area of foreign policy? Is it true that special-interest groups operating both openly and behind the scenes to pressure the government for certain policy positions in essence control public policy? Are private interests, but not the national interest, being served as a result?

Studies of the linkage between domestic interest groups and policy making, with particular reference to foreign policy decisions, may be summarized as follows:

- As a general rule, interest groups exert a far greater impact on domestic than on foreign policy issues because the requirements of national security give policymakers relative immunity from domestic pressures.
- Interest group activity operates as an ever-present, if limited, constraint on policy making. But the impact *varies with the issue*; in particular, "the less the importance of the issue, the greater the likelihood of group influence" (Milbrath, 1967).
- Similarly, the occasions when interest groups are most influential are rare. Interest group influences are greatest when the issue is not in the public spotlight, attended by the mass media, and when only a small segment of the populace is affected.
- Crises tend to stimulate interest; as the crisis level increases, the interests of more groups are likely to be at stake, and groups are likely to try to exert more influence. But "as the crisis level increases further, and especially as decision time shortens, there is relatively little opportunity for group interests to be taken into account [and] the President has enormous power to shape public opinion and receives little effective challenge from interest groups" (Milbrath, 1967).
- Influence between the government and interest groups is reciprocal, but it is more probable that government officials manipulate interest groups than that interest groups exercise influence over government policy.

- The capacity of interest groups to mold opinion on foreign affairs is very limited; mass attitudes are not amenable to manipulation by interest group efforts (even though many groups concentrate their efforts on attempts to influence public opinion rather than policy itself).
- Single-issue interest groups have more influence than large, national, general-purpose organizations.[22]
- Interest groups sometimes seek inaction from government and maintenance of the status quo; such efforts are generally more successful than efforts to bring about policy change. For this reason interest groups are generally regarded as agents of policy stability.
- Interest group influence tends to expand during election years, when candidates for office are most prone to open channels of communication and to give interest groups access.
- Interest groups exercise power over policy most effectively through Congress; correspondingly, when congressional interest in a foreign policy issue mounts, interest group activity and influence increase.
- The ability of a special-interest group to exert influence on foreign policy increases in those situations—such as national security—where "symbols" can be created that are unlikely to be opposed by other groups with material interests in that symbol.
- Interest groups will tend to exert their greatest influence on nonsecurity issues that entail economic considerations commanding attention over a long period of time (Cohen, 1983).

The foregoing characteristics of interest group efforts to direct foreign policy suggest that the mere presence of such groups, and the mere fact they are organized with the intent of persuasion, does not guarantee their penetration of the policy-formation process.

Special-Interest Groups and American Foreign Policy Continuity

Several reasons can be offered for the failure of interest groups to shape American foreign policy, except in the most episodic circumstances relating to discrete policy decisions and specific issues. The most important is that the ability of any one interest group to exert influence is offset by the tendency for *countervailing powers* to materialize over the disposition of an issue. That is, as one group emerges and begins to be powerful, other groups tend to spring up to balance it. When an interest group seeks vigorously to push policy in one direc-

---

22. But the influence of single-issue groups is limited largely to their special policy interest. For instance, "commodity groups have no effect on foreign policy beyond whatever arrangements they are able to make respecting the treatment of their particular commodities in international trade or a foreign aid program. Ethnic groups have no influence on policy with respect to areas of the world other than those to which they have a direct connection" (Cohen, 1959).

tion, other groups or coalitions of groups—aroused that their interests are being threatened—are stimulated to push policy in the opposite direction.

A classic illustration of countervailing processes was the threat during the Industrial Revolution that Big Business would gain control of American society. But Big Business was balanced by the emergence of Big Labor, which, once it grew in disproportionate influence, was balanced in turn by Big Government. Contemporary illustrations include the resistance to the nuclear energy lobby mounted by those concerned with safety and environmental threats posed by nuclear power, the opposition to abortion posed by the right-to-life movement, or the manner in which the advocacy of the Equal Rights Amendment generated a countermovement dedicated to the defeat of that proposal. With respect to foreign policy, the effort of the Committee on the Present Danger and its allies to defeat the SALT II treaty can be interpreted as a response to the emergence of pro-détente lobbyists earlier in the decade.[23] Similarly, the success of the Israeli lobby has led to the creation of the National Association of Arab-Americans, patterned after AIPAC, whose purpose is to take advantage of the American political process in the way AIPAC has to promote a more "balanced" U.S. Middle East policy.

Issues related to Soviet-American relations or the Middle East are seldom settled. No side can ever claim permanent victory, for each decision that takes policy in one direction merely sets the stage for the next round of the contest, with the possibility that the losers of the moment will be winners tomorrow. The result with respect to fundamental foreign policy issues is usually a kind of unstable equilibrium, with no permanent resolution of the struggle. Even in the icy period of the Reagan administration's confrontational stance toward the Soviet Union, the debate about the merits of differing approaches toward the containment of Soviet global influence continued. Nor did those debates abate as the Cold War thawed in the 1990s.

More discrete foreign policy issues, such as those entailing single decisions, also have the capacity to arouse interest groups counterpoised against each other. President Carter's decision in 1977 not to deploy the B-1 bomber, for instance, was influenced by a coalition of three dozen opponents that included Clergy and Laity Concerned, the American Friends Service Committee, the National Taxpayers Union, the Federation of American Scientists, the Women's International League of Peace and Freedom, and Common Cause (Ornstein and Elder, 1978). Of course, the pressure exerted by proponents of the B-1 (which included the Department of the Air Force), was enormous, too. Perhaps these counterpoised pressures led President Carter to characterize his choice as "one of the most difficult decisions that I have made since I have been in office."

---

23. Domestic support for the Reagan administration's massive increases in military spending was provided by many of the same anti-détente groups, including, in addition to the Committee on the Present Danger, the American Security Council, the Coalition for Peace through Strength, the Emergency Coalition against Unilateral Disarmament, the American Conservative Union, the National Conservative Political Action Committee, the Conservative Caucus, and the Committee for Survival of a Free Congress.

The presence of countervailing forces suggests another reason for the relative impotence of interest group influence on American foreign policy: interest groups maintain crisscrossing relationships with one another and have overlapping memberships. This tendency creates *cross-pressures* within and among the multiplicity of groups operating within the domestic political setting. Because of the number and diversity of groups striving for influence, the predominance of any one is precluded. Bargaining and competition among the various groups prevent any one group from gaining advantage over others and establishing preeminent power over foreign policy. Cross-pressures pull individuals in opposing directions, thereby reducing their capacity to concentrate on any single set of interests and diminishing their dedication to a single cause. Thus it is the fragmentation of power within a pluralistic domestic environment that prevents any one organized interest from dominating the foreign policy process.

Counterbalancing interest groups comprise a constant in the otherwise turbulent game of foreign policy making. The nature of the game has been modified, however, by the emergence of single-issue group politics and of political action committees (PACs).

The two developments are symbiotically related. Committed to but one cause (to the exclusion of others), single issue groups strive to pursue their single objective with singular dedication. The number of such groups rose spectacularly in the 1980s, as did their financial resources and fanaticism. As a result of "give no quarter politics," policymakers' freedom has been reduced and an "impassioned, dogmatic style of antagonistic politics created" (Elshtain, 1990). Because a zealous interest group is intolerant of compromise, it will accept no decision that promises anything less than complete agreement with its cause. In a policy-making arena dominated by such groups, the bargaining that in a pluralist system is supposed to produce an equitable agreement or compromise solutions does not occur.

To reduce the influence of single-issue groups, Congress passed election reform legislation in the 1970s to limit individuals' financial donations to candidates for political office. Inadvertently, Congress thereby compounded the problem because these laws encouraged political action committees to solicit voluntary contributions which they could channel to particular candidates to support particular causes. The number of PACs rose from about five-hundred in 1974 to more than four-thousand by 1988, of which more than two-fifths were associated with corporations (Patterson, 1990: 330, 332). In 1988, PACs contributed more than $172 million to candidates for federal office, most of it going to congressional incumbents. The largest contributor was the National Security Political Action Committee (NSPAC) whose controversial fund-raising activities led the Bush campaign to disavow its support (Morin, 1989a). PACs formed by foreign countries had contributed $2.4 million to congressional candidates in 1986 (*Harper's*, March 1988, p. 15), and PAC contributions in 1989 increased 24 percent from 1987, the previous nonelection year (Abramson and Jackson, 1990: A20). The campaign-support role played by PACs is now so extensive as to warrant calling them the "new political parties" (Dye and Zeigler, 1990).

PACs were particularly visible in their support of the "New Right" during the 1980s.[24] Pro-Israeli PACs were also highly active, spending over $4 million in 1984 alone. "The highest concentration [of contributions] was on races involving members of the Senate and House committees with Middle East juris-dictions and on opposition to five senators who supported the sale of AWACS aircraft to Saudi Arabia [in 1981]" (Uslaner, 1986). Senator Charles Percy of Illinois, chairperson of the Senate Foreign Relations Committee, was a target of Jewish PAC efforts and lost reelection to Paul Simon, his ardent pro-Israeli rival.

Even with the rise of single-issue politics and PACs, however, countervail-ing power persists; no particular interest group dominates foreign policy mak-ing and no particular PAC or coalition of PACs reigns supreme. The plurality of interest group activity nevertheless affects the style with which policy is for-mulated. Interacting interest groups ensure that the policy-making process is governed by bargaining among different groups, ensuring that policy is made through negotiated compromise among contending special interests. Foreign policy making resembles a taffy pull: every group attempts to pull policy in its own direction while resisting the pulls of others, with the result that policy fails to move in any discernible direction. The struggle encourages middle-of-the-road solutions and maintenance of the status quo. Thus postwar American foreign policy has been resistant to change in part because of the effects of a plurality of competing interest groups petitioning the government for favors:

> When almost everybody is organized, society reaches a point where almost noth-ing can be done. Groups with limited power usually find it easier to veto someone else's proposal than to push through any positive policy of their own. When this happens, politics becomes negative, and interest groups turn into veto groups. Even where positive policies are possible, any substantial proposal has to be cleared with every relevant interest group. And the larger the number of organized groups, the more of them that must be consulted, the longer are the resulting delays, and the harder it becomes to turn any idea into action. (Deutsch, 1974: 61)

Political action committees reinforce that view; "most PACs have no positive agenda; they are in business to kill bills that might harm their constituents.... The result is grid lock" (Bennett, 1989).

Is it any wonder given these circumstances that postwar American foreign policy has manifested such continuity in the midst of often rapidly changing

---

24. PACs may be differentiated from the *think tanks* that service them. Examples of think tanks that support the political Right include the Hoover Institution at Stanford University, the Institute for Contemporary Studies, the Heritage Foundation, and the Center for Strategic and International Studies (Easterbrook, 1986; Bodenheimer and Gould, 1989). Examples of think tanks on the Left include the Center for Defense Information, the Institute for Policy Studies, the World Policy Insti-tute, and the Center for National Security Studies. Many of these think tanks are also appropriately regarded as interest groups.

international circumstances? Ironically, even the elitist perspective on policy making reinforces this viewpoint, as it too implies the prevalence of continuity over change in American foreign policy. Countervailing powers may not be operative, but the result is the same nonetheless. Powerful military-industrial interests combined with a homogeneous policy-making elite promote the continuation of existing policy, as their interlocking interests have remained fairly constant since World War II. Their interests have constrained policy innovation by posing obstacles to redirections. To revise foreign policy would be to challenge entrenched and vested interests that support it. Because many influential Americans benefit from military spending, for example, and also because external threats inspire insecurity, America has steadfastly pursued military preparedness as a primary instrument of American foreign policy. The resistance of the Pentagon to reductions in defense spending, even in the era of relaxed relations, attests to the power of the interests promoting the maintenance of those expenditures when, arguably, they are no longer required.

POLITICAL CULTURE, INTEREST GROUPS, AND AMERICAN FOREIGN POLICY

The elitist and pluralist models may result in essentially the same policies, but is one a better description of the impact of societal forces on the foreign policy process than the other? Although inconclusive, the balance of evidence is weighted somewhat in favor of the elitist model and lends credence to Richard J. Barnet's (1972) telling observation that American foreign policy is "an elite preserve . . . made for the benefit of that elite." "The flaw in the pluralist heaven," writes E. E. Schattschneider (1960) in his classic study, *The Semisovereign People*, "is that the heavenly chorus sings with a strong upper-class bias." In fact, the elitist and pluralist accounts both depict a process in which the ordinary citizen matters very little when it comes to foreign policy making (a point we will expand on in the next chapter).

At the same time, however, the evidence strongly suggests that the substance and direction of American foreign policy are subject to societal influences. Societal changes may stimulate foreign policy adaptations (recall the policy changes that followed changes in the post-Vietnam and Watergate political culture), but they also constrain policy revision, as seen, for example, in the domestic influences on continued defense spending. Such constraints help explain why policy change, when it does occur, usually comes in incremental steps rather than as bold revisions.

To understand more fully how the societal source category influences foreign policy—and in particular why "foreign policy is essentially politics-driven," with greater attention often given to poll results than to policy effectiveness (Schneider, 1990)—other societal forces must yet be worked into the equation. It is to these we now turn.

SUGGESTIONS FOR FURTHER READING

Dallek, Robert. (1983) *The American Style of Foreign Policy: Cultural Politics and Foreign Affairs.* New York: Knopf.

Dye, Thomas R. (1990) *Who's Running America? The Bush Era*, 5th ed. Englewood Cliffs, N.J.: Prentice-Hall.

Hunt, Michael H. (1990) *Ideology and U.S. Foreign Policy.* New Haven: Yale University Press.

Knudsen, Baard B. (1987) "The Paramount Importance of Cultural Sources: American Foreign Policy and Comparative Foreign Policy Research Reconsidered," *Cooperation and Conflict* 22(No. 2): 81–113.

Kotz, Nick. (1988) *Wild Blue Yonder.* Princeton, N.J.: Princeton University Press.

Kurth, James R. (1989) "The Military-Industrial Complex Revisited," pp. 195–215 in Joseph Kruzel (ed.), *American Defense Annual, 1989–1990.* Lexington, Mass.: Lexington Books.

McCormick, James M. (1985) *American Foreign Policy and American Values.* Itasca, Ill.: Peacock.

Milbrath, Lester W. (1967) "Interest Groups and Foreign Policy," pp. 231–252 in James N. Rosenau (ed.), *Domestic Sources of Foreign Policy.* New York: Free Press.

Parenti, Michael. (1988) *Democracy for the Few*, 5th ed. New York: St. Martin's Press.

Rosen, Steven (ed.). (1973) *Testing the Theory of the Military-Industrial Complex.* Lexington, Mass.: Heath.

CHAPTER 9

The Impact of Public Opinion, Presidential Elections, and the Mass Media

Nobody can know what it means for a President to be sitting in that White House working late at night and to have hundreds of thousands of demonstrators charging through the streets. Not even earplugs could block the noise.

PRESIDENT RICHARD M. NIXON, 1977

The biggest advantage a modern president has is the six o'clock news. Presidents can be on the news every night if they want to—and usually they want to. They can easily make themselves the focus of every major news report, because the president of the United States is the most powerful individual in the world.

PRESIDENT RONALD REAGAN, 1984

Continuity in post–World War II American foreign policy is evident in the fundamental assumptions that American leaders have made about the nature of international realities and the corresponding role of the United States in world affairs. Change is also apparent when we move beyond the broad patterns of postwar objectives and inquire into the more variable tactics that different presidents have chosen to achieve them. Not surprisingly, therefore, public attitudes also contain elements of both continuity and change—as well as contradictions and inconsistencies.

Public attitudes toward the nation's world role over the course of its history have alternated rhythmically between periods of introversion and extroversion, between isolationist withdrawal and global activism (see Chapter 3). The latter has dominated since World War II, as the vast majority of Americans has supported an active world role for the nation. The nature of internationalism has undergone fundamental changes, however, especially during and since the Vietnam War, as we will note in more detail later in this chapter. Moreover, the American people espouse goals whose pursuit requires the embrace of sometimes competing objectives. They favor active internationalism but oppose sending economic and military aid to other nations. They yearn for peace through strength but are wary of international institutions, fear nuclear weapons, and oppose the use of force abroad. Still, they back presidents when they choose force of arms and prefer military victory to limited war. And they fear communism and distrust Soviet leaders (at least until recently; see Hinckley, 1989) but support efforts to reach negotiated agreements between the United States and the Soviet Union. Little wonder that the role public opinion plays in shaping the nation's conduct is poorly understood and often suspect, and why policymakers sometimes disparage it. President John F. Kennedy's view, as described by his aide Theodore C. Sorensen, is perhaps representative of leaders' views:

> Public opinion is often erratic, inconsistent, arbitrary, and unreasonable—with a compulsion to make mistakes. . . . It rarely considers the needs of the next generation or the history of the last . . . . It is frequently hampered by myths and misinformation, by stereotypes and shibboleths, and by an innate resistance to innovation. (Sorensen, 1963: 45–46)

Still, the presumed importance of public opinion is almost axiomatic in today's world. As one observer put it, "Politicians court it; statesmen appeal to it; philosophers extol or condemn it; merchants cater to it; military leaders fear it; sociologists analyze it; statisticians measure it; and constitution-makers try to make it sovereign" (Childs, 1965).

In Chapter 8 we suggested several ways in which American foreign policy making is colored by domestic considerations and how the attributes of American society define the bounds of leaders' permissible policy choice. In this chapter we consider how public opinion affects the nation's conduct beyond its borders and the role that presidential elections play in the translation of public preferences in the policy process. We also examine the impact that the mass media, notably the press and television, exert. Throughout, we are concerned with how these societal forces constrain leaders' foreign policy behavior (thereby contributing to policy persistence) and also with whether and under what circumstances they promote the possibility of policy change.

PERSPECTIVES ON PUBLIC OPINION AS A SOCIETAL SOURCE

Democratic theory presupposes that citizens will make informed choices about the issues of the day and ultimately about who will best represent their beliefs in the councils of government. The American people, in turn, expect their attitudes and opinions to be considered when policies are promulgated by leaders, because leaders are chosen to represent and serve the interests of their constituents. The Constitution affirms the centrality of American citizens by beginning with the words *we the people*.

The theory that public policy is conditioned by mass opinion is appealing, but it raises troublesome questions. Do public preferences lead American foreign policy, as democratic theory would have us believe, or is the relationship more subtle and complicated? Are changes in foreign policy a function of shifts in American public attitudes? Or is the relationship one of policy first and opinion second? Indeed, are the American people capable of exercising the tasks expected of them?

The Nature of American Public Opinion

The premise on which democratic theory depends does not hold up well under scrutiny. That most Americans fail to possess even the most elementary knowledge about their own political system, much less international affairs, is an inescapable fact. Moreover, peoples' "information" is often so inaccurate that it might better be labeled "misinformation." The following reveal the often startling levels of ignorance:

- In 1964, only 58 percent of the American public thought that the United States was a member of NATO; almost two-fifths believed the Soviet Union was a member (Free and Cantril, 1968: 60).
- In 1979, only 23 percent of the adult population knew the two countries involved in the SALT negotiations (Erikson, Luttbeg, and Tedin, 1988: 42).
- In 1985, 45 percent of the American people thought the United States supported the Sandinista government in Nicaragua, not the *contras*, a nearly identical number indicated they had not heard or read about the fighting between the Sandinistas and the rebels (Sobel, 1989: 120).
- In 1985, 28 percent of those surveyed thought that the Soviet Union and the United States fought each other in World War II; 44 percent did not know the two were allies at that time (Clymer, 1985b: 48).
- In 1985, only 63 percent of the public knew that the United States supported South Vietnam in the Vietnam War, which cost fifty-eight thousand Americans their lives (Clymer, 1985a: 1).
- In January 1989, less than 20 percent of the American people could name even one member of the President George Bush's choice for the cabinet; an even smaller proportion could correctly identify James A. Baker as the new secretary of state (Morin, 1989b: 37).

Evidence demonstrating the extent of political misunderstanding and ignorance about basic issues could be greatly expanded, but it would only reinforce the picture of a citizenry ill informed about major issues of public policy and ill equipped to evaluate government policy making. Noteworthy is that the issues about which the public is persistently ignorant are not "flash-in-the-pan" current events but typically ones that have long figured prominently on the national political agenda.

The absence of basic knowledge about foreign affairs does not stem from deficiencies in U.S. educational institutions. It stems from disinterest. Public ignorance is a function of public inattention, for people are knowledgeable about what is important to them. And more Americans are concerned about the outcome of major sporting events than with the shape of the political system. Again, consider some evidence:

- *Inattention to public issues.* In 1986, less than half of the American public indicated they were "very interested" in reading articles either dealing with national news or news about the relations between the United States and other countries. The proportion of those closely following specific foreign policy issues was even lower (Rielly, 1987: 8).
- *Apathy and voter turnout.* In comparison with turnout rates in other democratic countries, American voters are apathetic. The percentage of eligible voters who voted in presidential elections has ranged from 51 percent (1948) to 63 percent (1960) in the eleven presidential contests since World War II. If, in 1980 and again in 1988, the number of "no shows" is added to those who voted against them, Ronald Reagan and George Bush were both elected president by only a third of the eligible electorate.
- *Other forms of political nonparticipation.* The proportion of Americans who profess to have worked for a political party or candidate never exceeded 7 percent between 1952 and 1984 (Conway, 1985: 7). In 1978, only 23 percent of the public indicated they had written or spoken to a public official about some political issue in the preceding three or four years; of these only 18 percent—4 percent of the entire population—had written or spoken to a public official about an issue concerning foreign affairs (Rielly, 1979: 30).

In short, even though the United States purports to have a mass democratic system of government, few are deeply involved in politics and most lack the interest and motivation to become involved.[1] Moreover, most Americans seem more interested in domestic than in foreign policy (although concern is low in both categories). This fact led Gabriel A. Almond (1960) in his classic study, *The American People and Foreign Policy*, to conclude that public opinion toward foreign policy is best thought of as "moods" that "undergo frequent alteration in response to changes in events." Instead of resting on some kind of "intellectual structure," he argued, "the characteristic response to questions of foreign policy is one of indifference. A foreign policy crisis, short of the immediate threat of war, may transform indifference to vague apprehension, to fatalism, to anger; but the reaction is still a mood, a superficial and fluctuating response."

Are Interest and Information Important?

That conclusion has long been regarded as conventional wisdom (cf. Caspary, 1970), but there are important reasons to question it. The public may be uninformed about and seemingly indifferent to the details of policy, but is is able to discriminate among issues and to identify those that are salient. Foreign and

---

1. Such findings invite a negative estimate of the intelligence of the American people and their importance in the political system by suggesting, as Friedrich Nietzsche concluded, that "the masses are asses." It also invites the conclusion that leaders should ignore the opinions of the masses, along the lines akin to Oscar Wilde's famous adage that "those who try to lead the people can only do so by following the mob." Although some may be attracted to these viewpoints, neither conclusion is warranted by the evidence, as we shall demonstrate below.

national security policy issues are typically among them. Consider the pattern of responses given to opinion pollsters' question, What do you think is the most important problem facing the country today? International issues were typically prominent in Americans' thinking during the height of the Cold War in the 1950s and early 1960s, usually dominating their concerns except for an occasional interruption caused by economic recessions. Not surprisingly, Vietnam emerged during the mid-1960s as the most salient issue in nearly half of the polls taken between 1964 and 1972, with more general foreign policy concerns preeminent three times (Nie, Verba, and Petrocik, 1976: 100–103).

Thereafter, a prolonged period unfolded in which economic needs and issues headed the list of most important problems. The national energy "crisis" (fundamentally a foreign policy problem) was among them, but not until early 1980, in response to events in Iran, did an explicit foreign policy issue emerge as the single most important concern of the American people. Unemployment and, occasionally, other economic problems remained paramount for some time thereafter, but in late 1983, the fear or threat of war and international tensions emerged as salient. They figured prominently in the concerns of the American people as they went to the polls in November 1984 and in the months that followed. Eventually the issue dissipated and drugs emerged as a salient issue.[2] Thus the overall record suggests that foreign policy issues are important to the American people, often rivaling or surpassing their concern for domestic issues. Furthermore, their views and beliefs about who will best handle these issues historically have been important predictors of presidential election outcomes (Gallup, 1985; see also Smith, 1985; Niemi, Mueller, and Smith, 1989; Stanley and Niemi, 1990). Strike a blow in favor of democratic theory!

If the conclusion that the American people are indifferent to foreign policy is questionable, which it is, the relevance of this lack of knowledge is also uncertain. Few people, including corporate executives, legislative aides, and political science majors and their professors, among others, would perform uniformly well on the questions posed by pollsters and journalists that purport to measure the extent to which the public is informed. More important than interest and knowledge is whether the American people are able, in the aggregate, to hold *politically relevant foreign policy beliefs*. These beliefs and the corresponding attitudes that both inform and spring from them may not satisfy political scientists and journalists when they evaluate the theory and practice of American democracy; nonetheless, relatively unsophisticated foreign policy beliefs may be both coherent and politically relevant.[3] One example suffices to make the point:

---

2. A September 1989 *New York Times*/CBS News (*New York Times*, September 28, 1989, p. 26) poll found that only 1 percent of the respondents regarded war as "the most important problem facing this country today," but 54 percent cited drugs as important. By way of contrast, in January 1985, 23 percent had answered that the most important problem was war, nuclear war, and defense, and less than 1 percent mentioned drugs.

3. As one pollster (Hinckley, 1989) put it in commenting on attitudes toward the Soviet Union: "Americans know their opinions about the Soviet Union are generally impressionistic. Nevertheless, whether the knowledge is broad and incomplete or specific and highly detailed, it will be heard in America's political system, which is responsive to public opinion regardless of its knowledge base."

many Americans proved unable during the 1980s to identify where in Central America El Salvador and Nicaragua are or who the United States supported in the long-simmering conflicts there, but they were nonetheless unwavering in their firm conviction that American soldiers should not be sent to fight in the region. From the point of view of policymakers in Washington, the latter was the important, politically relevant datum.

To understand the seeming discrepancy between what Americans know, on the one hand, and how they respond to what they care about, on the other, it is useful to explore the differences between attitudes (opinions) and beliefs.

Foreign Policy Attitudes

In December 1989 a *New York Times*/CBS News poll found that two out of three Americans supported the unification of East and West Germany. Fifty-seven percent of the respondents in the same poll said that the United States should give the same trading privileges to the Soviet Union that it gives other nations, 41 percent thought the Soviet Union would abide by new arms control agreements rather than cheat on them, and a third said President Bush should do more to facilitate the kinds of changes in the Soviet Union sought by Mikhail Gorbachev. *Public opinion* is commonly thought to be captured in responses such as these. Often the *attitudes* they reflect are highly volatile. The character of the issue, the pace of events, new information, or a friend's opinion may provoke change; so may "herd instincts," wherein attitude change is stimulated by the desire to conform to what others (especially opinion leaders) appear to be thinking. Thus, in the short run, Americans' attitudes toward specific issues often appear susceptible to quick and frequent turnabouts.

Public attitudes doubtless change, but they are less erratic in the short run than often presumed. Stability rather than change is demonstrably the characteristic response of the American people to foreign and national security policy issues. For example, one study found that a majority (51 percent) of responses to some 425 identically worded survey items asked between 1935 and 1982 on a broad range of these issues varied less than 6 percentage points from one polling period to the next, and that in nearly half of the remaining instances the percentage change was less than 10 percentage points (Shapiro and Page, 1988: 216–217).[4] Furthermore, even the changes observable over long stretches of time are predictable and understandable—not "formless and plastic," as Almond (1960) once described public opinion toward foreign policy and changes in it.

Consider the issue of defense spending. American opinion was relatively stable—and silent—until the late 1960s, when a "revolt of the masses" (Russett, 1972) erupted and a majority of Americans began advocating, for the first time since World War II, reductions in military spending. The reason, of course,

---

4. See also Graham (1986), Russett and Graham (1988), Wittkopf (1990) and, for a contrasting viewpoint, Holsti (1987).

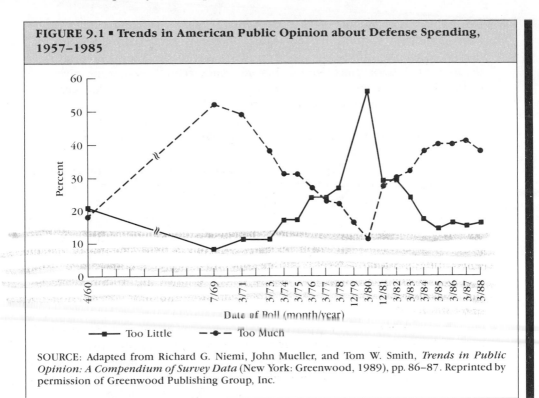

FIGURE 9.1 ▪ Trends in American Public Opinion about Defense Spending, 1957–1985

SOURCE: Adapted from Richard G. Niemi, John Mueller, and Tom W. Smith, *Trends in Public Opinion: A Compendium of Survey Data* (New York: Greenwood, 1989), pp. 86–87. Reprinted by permission of Greenwood Publishing Group, Inc.

was dissatisfaction with the war in Vietnam. The "revolt" turned out to be of relatively short duration, however. By 1977 more Americans supported increased defense spending than reductions, with the level of support for more spending approaching a two-decade peak. The resurgence of support between 1973 and 1978 in the wake of the U.S. withdrawal from Southeast Asia was associated with the rise of conservative thinking in American domestic policies and a resurgence of anti-Soviet and anticommunist sentiments (Kriesberg and Klein, 1980; see also Kriesberg, Murray, and Klein, 1982).

By 1980 both President Jimmy Carter and his presidential challenger, Ronald Reagan, were calling for a greater defense effort. Reagan made this a centerpiece of his commitment to rebuild American defenses that, in his view, had been permitted to deteriorate during a "decade of neglect." Reagan's extreme anti-Soviet rhetoric contributed to public apprehension of Soviet behavior. As a result, support of greater defense spending reached levels unsurpassed since the onset of the Korean War in 1950. As Figure 9.1 illustrates, support subsided thereafter, in part as a result of growing concern for the traditional "guns-versus-butter" tradeoff, which was augmented by mounting federal government deficits. Support for further increases also waned once the Reagan administration's rearmament program gathered speed and public fears that the

U.S. military was lagging receded (see Schmidt, 1983). By the time Reagan left office in 1988, support for additional increases in defense spending had dissipated almost entirely. Over the period of two decades, then, public attitudes demonstrated wide fluctuations—but for understandable reasons given the changed and changing circumstances surrounding America's world role.

Consider as well Americans' internationalist attitudes. The view that the United States ought to take an active role in world affairs has enjoyed persistent public support throughout the post–World War II era (Niemi, Mueller, and Smith, 1989; Shapiro and Page, 1988). Even so, measurable fluctuations in support for a globalist foreign policy posture are also evident. During the 1960s and 1970s, in particular, support for internationalism declined, and reached a low point during the mid-1970s as the Vietnam trauma, the onset of détente with the Soviet Union, and the Watergate episode undermined the international ethos. The wrenching Vietnam experience challenged the assumption that military power by itself could achieve the objectives of American foreign policy; détente called into question the wisdom of the containment foreign policy strategy; and Watergate challenged the belief that American political institutions were uniquely virtuous and that a presidency preeminent in foreign policy continued to be necessary. But support for internationalism rebounded in the decade following Vietnam, with roughly 60 percent of the American people espousing internationalist attitudes at various times in the 1980s, compared with only 44 percent at the time of Carter's election in 1976 (see Figure 9.2). Support, decline, and resurgence are thus once more in evidence. And, as in the case of defense spending, the responses have varied with, and are predictable by reference to, changes in domestic and international circumstances.

War as an instrument of national policy warrants attention as a special case of the cyclical character of public opinion toward foreign policy. Public approval of war appears to occur prior to and just after its inception, followed, predictably perhaps, by a gradual but steady decline in bellicose attitudes and a concomitant rise in pacific attitudes. The wars in Korea and Vietnam illustrate the patterns. During each, enthusiasm was closely related to casualty rates: as the casualty rates went up, support for the wars declined (Mueller, 1971). This suggests that American attitudes toward war are episodic rather than steady; in the context of actual war involvement, public attitudes range from initial acceptance to ultimate disfavor (Campbell and Cain, 1965). As in the case of defense spending and internationalism, however, the reasons underlying their alterations are compelling, which suggests once again that the American people are better able to make prudent political judgments than political pundits would sometimes have us believe.

That conclusion is supported by other information that indicates the public holds firm opinions on issues it cares about, that those opinions are often stable over time, but that if conditions change, public opinion also changes. Again, consider some evidence.

- *Public opinion on salient questions is unwavering: the American people know what matters.* In late 1969, when the United States was

FIGURE 9.2 ▪ Internationalist/Isolationist Trends in American Public Opinion, 1964–1985*

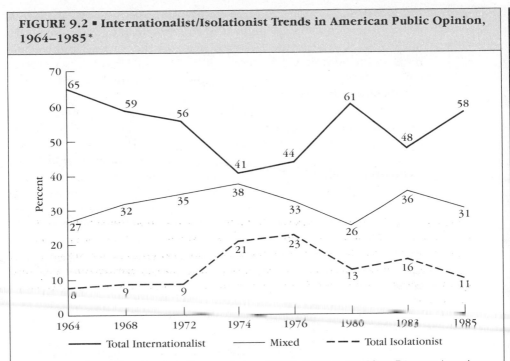

SOURCE: William Watts. Reprinted by permission of William Watts, President, Potomac Associates. The authors gratefully acknowledge the Potomac Associates, the Institute for International Social Research, and the Gallup Organization, who are responsible for collecting the survey data on which these figures rest.

*Trends based on questions asked of national cross-sections of the public in years shown. The figures for 1964 and 1968 are derived from responses to five statements concerning the general posture that the United States should assume in world affairs. The figures for subsequent years reflect responses to the same set of five statements, as well as two new statements regarding possible U.S. military intervention in defense of allies.

†The term *mixed* refers to the proportion of respondents who could not be clearly classified as either internationalists or isolationists.

still mired in Vietnam, two-fifths of the American people felt the war was morally wrong. The proportion grew to 65 percent two years later and remained at that level for more than a decade thereafter (Wittkopf, 1990: 312). Similarly, in 1984 only 30 percent of the American people supported U.S. military aid to the *contras* fighting the Nicaraguan government. The percentage was unchanged four years later, despite concerted presidential efforts to win public approval for the policy (Sobel, 1989: 125). Furthermore, large numbers of Americans attributed the causes of conflict in Central America to indigenous poverty and injustice, not (as the Reagan administration argued) to outside (Soviet and Cuban) interference.

- *Public attitudes change in response to new conditions: the American people learn.* In 1955, 27 percent of the American people agreed that nuclear war between the United States and the Soviet Union would result in the complete destruction of humankind. In 1987, 83 percent believed that the United States and the Soviet Union would both be completely destroyed in an all-out nuclear war (Yankelovich and Harman, 1988: 49). In 1955, two-thirds of the American people thought the Soviet Union would not live up to agreements regarding arms control with the United States, but in 1979, two-thirds supported efforts to conclude an agreement with the Soviet Union to limit nuclear weapons (Wittkopf, 1990: 324, 327). Between 1981 and 1990, the proportion who felt it was likely the United States would get into a nuclear war dropped from 47 to 19 percent, but 54 percent in a 1990 survey indicated they did not believe the Cold War was over (*New York Times*/CBS News Poll, January 1990 release, pp. 12, 13). Still, 59 percent in a 1988 poll responded that economic competitors were a greater threat to U.S. national security than its military adversaries (Americans Talk Security, 1989: 209).

Foreign Policy Beliefs

The stability of public attitudes and the learning they demonstrate are intimately related to changes that have occurred at home and abroad since the 1970s. Although support for active involvement in world affairs rebounded in the 1980s from its nadir in the 1970s, internationalism today wears two faces, a cooperative one and a militant one, which reflects the emergence of new kinds of foreign policy *beliefs* in the wake of the Vietnam tragedy (Wittkopf, 1990). The faces of internationalism grow out of differences among the American people not only on the question of *whether* the United States ought to be involved in the world, which is the central tenet of classical internationalism, but also on *how* it should be involved. The domestic consensus in favor of classical internationalism captured elements of both conflict and cooperation (see Wittkopf and McCormick, 1990a). The United States was willing to cooperate with other nations to solve global as well as national problems, but if need be it would also intervene in the affairs of others, using force if necessary to protect its self-defined national interests. In the years following World War II, a foreign policy consensus emerged in support of these forms of involvement, but in the wake of Vietnam concern about conflict and cooperation came to divide rather than unite Americans. Attitudes toward communism, the use of American troops abroad, and relations with the Soviet Union distinguish proponents and opponents of the alternative forms of internationalism.

Four identifiable *belief systems* flow from these concerns, which inhere among elites as well as the mass of the American people (Holsti and Rosenau, 1990; Wittkopf, 1990). *Internationalists* support active American involvement in international affairs, favoring a combination of conciliatory and conflictual strategies reminiscent of the pre-Vietnam internationalist foreign policy paradigm. *Isolationists*, on the other hand, oppose both types of international involvement, as the term implies. *Hardliners* tend to view communism as a threat to the United States, to oppose détente with the Soviet Union, and generally to espouse an interventionist predisposition. In contrast, *accommodationists* emphasize cooperative ties with other nations, particularly détente with the Soviet Union, and reject the view that the United States can assume a unilateralist, go-it-alone posture in the world. Although accommodationists and hardliners are appropriately described as internationalists, it is clear their prescriptions for the United States' world role often diverge markedly. This has undermined the broad-based domestic support for foreign policy initiatives on which presidents in the Cold War era could count and made the task of coalition building that more recent presidents have faced more difficult.

Beliefs are important in understanding why public attitudes are often less fickle than might be expected. A belief "system" acts as "a set of lenses through which information concerning the physical and social environment is received. It orients the individual to his environment, defining it for him and identifying for him its salient characteristics" (Holsti, 1962).

Belief systems also establish goals and order preferences. They enable people to relate information about one idea to others systematically. This ability is not a function of information or knowledge. In fact, social cognition theory demonstrates that individuals use information shortcuts, based on their beliefs, to cope with ambiguous messages about the external environment. Paradoxically, then, ordinary citizens hold coherent attitude structures not because they possess detailed knowledge about foreign policy but because they lack it: "individuals organize information because such organization helps to simplify the world. Thus, a paucity of information does not *impede* structure and consistency; on the contrary, it *motivates* the development and employment of structure. [Individuals attempt] to cope with an extraordinarily confusing world . . . by structuring views about specific foreign policies according to their more general and abstract beliefs" (Hurwitz and Peffley, 1987).

Because of their nature, beliefs are remarkably stable. Most images concerning foreign affairs are formed during adolescence and remain relatively fixed unless somehow disturbed. Peer group influences and authority figures may exert a modifying impact on images, but only the most dramatic of international events (war, for example) have the capacity to alter completely foreign policy beliefs (Deutsch and Merritt, 1965). Relevant here is the philosopher Charles Sanders Pierce's instructive comment on the dynamics of image change: "Surprise is your only teacher." Thus core beliefs, formed through early learning experiences, serve as perceptual filters through which individuals orient themselves to their environment and structure how they interpret international events encountered later in life. If beliefs do change, they are likely to be replaced by new images that continue to simplify the world, albeit in new terms (the philosopher William James's adage that "most people think they are thinking when they replace one set of prejudices for another" speaks to this principle).

For many Americans—including an entire generation of policymakers—World War II and the events that led to it imprinted their world views indelibly (Neustadt and May, 1986). The message was simple: aggressors cannot be appeased.[5] To others, Vietnam was an equally traumatic event (Holsti and Rosenau, 1984). To them, the lesson was equally simple: there are limits to U.S. power and the utility of military force in international politics.[6] The emergence of the distinctive beliefs associated with cooperative and militant internationalism in the wake of Vietnam conforms to our understanding of how beliefs change.

Do Americans' foreign policy beliefs find expression in the nation's policies? Causation is difficult to trace, but the consistency of public beliefs with the internationalist faces of American foreign policy since Vietnam is undeniable. Many of the policies pursued by the Nixon, Ford, and Carter administrations embraced more accommodationist than hardline positions. President Carter's assertion in 1977 that the inordinate fear of communism had been lifted epitomized the shift to a conciliatory internationalism that tolerated diversity, and a continuation of détente was its manifestation. "That the containment of Communism by the United States was neither possible, nor necessary, nor even desirable . . . was the 'lesson of Vietnam' [drawn by the Carter administration]" (Gershman, 1980). Other elements associated with that fundamental shift included the beliefs that military power was no longer a viable instrument of policy, that the Soviet Union had become a status quo power, that the United States should assist the "forces of change" in the Third World, and that trilateralism, implying a deepening of cooperation, should come to characterize U.S. relations with Europe and Japan (Gershman, 1980).

By the end of Carter's term in office, however, the emphasis shifted from accommodation back to a hardline posture. A critical factor underlying the reversal was the Soviet Union's intervention in Afghanistan in December 1979. With that and with Reagan's election in 1980, any remaining semblance of détente was lost. Reagan pursued a vigorous anti-Soviet and interventionist foreign policy that was the epitome of hardliners' foreign policy prescriptions. Still, he was unable to overcome the accommodationists' opposition to his policies. The best example is found in Central America where, despite concerted presidential efforts to win congressional and public support for a more belligerent approach to the Sandinista regime in Nicaragua, the administration came up short. This illustrates well how public opinion sometimes constrains presidential initiatives in foreign policy, as it does the persistence of accommodationist thinking among political elites and the mass public (see Wittkopf

---

5. The analogy draws on the experience of the late 1930s, when Britain and France agreed to the annexation of a portion of Czechoslovakia by Nazi Germany in the mistaken belief that appeasement would avert war in Europe.

6. A radically different lesson that some drew from Vietnam suggests that war, once entered, should not be prosecuted "with one arm tied behind our back." See May (1973) and Neustadt and May (1986) for examinations of the role that "lessons of the past" play in policy making, and Gershman (1980) for a critical appraisal of the "Vietnam syndrome."

and McCormick, 1990b). Moreover, by the end of his administration, Reagan had once again adopted a conciliatory posture toward the Soviet Union reminiscent of the accommodationist orientation he earlier had so vigorously rejected. The administration also retreated from the unilateralist orientation that had led some to worry about the end of internationalism (Hughes, 1985–1986; Kegley and Raymond, 1989; Keohane and Nye, 1985), finding solace instead in the multilateralism historically central to the internationalist ethos. Cooperative and militant internationalism thus remain as vibrant, competing strains of thinking about the role of the United States in world affairs, and their pull in divergent directions can be expected to become more pronounced as the United States reorients itself toward a post–Cold War world.

The Public ''Temperament'': Nationalistic and Permissive   The responsiveness of the American people—for better or worse—to events and the political information they receive is nowhere more apparent than in the support they accord their political leaders during times of crisis and peril.

Like the citizens of other nations, Americans tend to be *nationalistic*, that is, to value loyalty and devotion to their own nation and promotion of its culture and interests as opposed to those of other nations. Nationalism means that nations are viewed as rivals in a competitive game for power and prestige (Deutsch, 1953). It sometimes includes the ethnocentric belief that the United States is (or should be recognized as) superior to others and should therefore serve as a model for them to emulate.

Although no one would argue that all Americans think nationalistically all the time across all foreign policy issues, there is nevertheless a general predisposition to perceive international problems in terms of in-group loyalty and out-group competition (Rosenberg, 1965). ''Foreign things'' are often viewed with hostility and fear. In the extreme, nationalism results in a world view that accepts the doctrine ''my country, right or wrong.'' Furthermore, because citizens tend to equate loyalty to the nation with loyalty to the prevailing leadership, they sometimes confuse love for the representatives of the government with love for the country and its symbols.

The public's nationalistic temperament also stems from its tendency to view international politics as esoteric, secret, complicated, and unfamiliar—the type of problem better left to ''experts'' who allegedly ''know better'' (and who, in turn, are quite willing to perpetuate the notion)—rendering public attitudes in the realm of foreign policy especially vulnerable to manipulation. People who feel threatened are prone to seek strong leadership to deal with the perceived threatening agent, a tendency long recognized by policymakers.[7] Nationalistic sentiments thus find expression in the way Americans respond to

---

7. It was the Nazi Hermann Goering who expressed the idea by contending, ''Voice or no voice, the people can always be brought to do the bidding of the leaders. That is easy. All you have to do is to tell them they are being attacked and denounce the pacifists for lack of patriotism.'' And a former American secretary of state, John Foster Dulles, expressed the same opinion when he noted: ''The easiest and quickest cure of internal dissension is to portray danger from abroad. Thus group authorities find it convenient always to keep alive among the group members a feeling that their nation is in danger from one or another of the nation-villains with which it is surrounded.''

the foreign policy initiatives of their leaders, especially during real or imagined threats from abroad, when a president tends to realize the widest freedom of action. The reason is that the public's response is typically *permissive* (Almond, 1960; Caspary, 1970); that is, the American people typically acquiesce to and support the decisions of their leaders.

Evidence of the permissiveness of public attitudes is found in the impact that dramatic foreign policy events and initiatives exert on evaluations of presidential performance. Typically they produce rally-'round-the-flag effects that boost a president's popularity with the public. Examples abound. Bush's popularity with the American people climbed nine percentage points following the invasion of Panama in December 1989 and again climbed fourteen percentage points following the dispatch of American troops to the Middle East in response to Iraq's invasion of Kuwait in August 1990. Reagan's notched upward by six points following the bombing of Libya in April 1986; and Carter's jumped by thirteen following the Camp David Middle East accords in September 1978. Such changes are evident across a broad range of foreign policy events, including wars, crises, U.S. peace efforts, summit conferences, and American policy initiatives, all of which demonstrate the nationalistic and acquiescent responses of the American people. In general, the more active a president looks (for example, the frequency of his pronouncements or trips abroad), the greater will be the support he receives at home. Images of decisive, energetic leadership reap domestic rewards, just as crises afford opportunities for presidents to show and benefit from their courage (if not always their wisdom).[8]

But the American people are also discriminating. Reagan's popularity plummeted by sixteen percentage points following the Iran-*contra* revelations in late 1986, the largest drop ever recorded by the Gallup Poll (other polls recorded even steeper declines). Contrast this with Kennedy's experience, who found that his public approval actually rose to its peak (83 percent) in the aftermath of the Bay of Pigs fiasco.[9] Both involved mistakes in judgment, but the way the presidents handled the mistakes appears to have significantly affected public perceptions of the chief executive.[10] More generally, international crises are typically approval-enhancing events, whereas political scandals are approval-diminishing events (Ostrom and Simon, 1989).

---

8. One study (Lee, 1977) of changes in presidential popularity from Franklin D. Roosevelt to Gerald R. Ford shows that, on average, foreign policy events boost presidential ratings a substantial 5.6 percent. Using somewhat different methodology, Lanoue (1989: 497) shows that from 1961 to 1980 international crises increased presidential popularity an average of 4 percent, which is the same boost Reagan received across the various "rally" points he experienced.

9. There are other instances of evident policy failure that actually boosted presidents' popularity. Carter's approval rating shot from 38 to 61 percent following the Iranian hostage incident in late 1979 and, after a prolonged decline, it rose again from 39 to 43 percent following the failed hostage rescue attempt in April 1980. Reagan's popularity increased measurably (but not dramatically) following the Soviet attack on the Korean airline flight 007 in September 1983 and again following the truck-bombing of Marine headquarters in Beirut the following month.

10. In the case of the Iran-*contra* affair, the American people not only disapproved of the sale of arms to Iran, they did not believe the president's version of what happened and thought the administration was engaged in a coverup similar to the Watergate affair (see Ostrom and Simon, 1989).

Presidents care about their popularity because it affects their political latitude. Both the absolute and relative levels of presidents' popularity, evidence suggests (Ostrom and Job, 1986), are important in explaining America's postwar political use of force short of war (recall Chapter 5); the more popular presidents are, the more they are "freed" from domestic constraints to do as they wish abroad. More generally, presidents care about their popularity with the American people because it affects their ability to work their will with others involved in the policy process. (One member of Congress commented on Bush's popularity following the invasion of Panama: "If the President's popularity is at 80 percent, I think [he] can do whatever he wants.") Richard Neustadt (1980) explains: "The Washingtonians who watch a President have more to think about than his professional reputation. They also have to think about his standing with the public outside of Washington. They have to gauge his popular prestige. Because they think about it, public standing is a source of [presidential] influence." In short, the more popular a president is, the more likely he is to accomplish his political agenda. This is the essence of what Dennis M. Simon and Charles W. Ostrom (1988) call "the politics of prestige."

Rally-'round-the-flag events significantly affect presidents' popularity. Indeed, one presidential scholar (Lowi, 1985a) argues that foreign policy comprises the only arena available to presidents that permits them to improve their popularity ratings once in office. The state of the economy is the most potent (environmental) predictor of presidential popularity, but the American people want peace as well as prosperity. Thus foreign policy sometimes figures prominently in the long-term erosion of support as well as short-term boosts that most presidents experience. For Harry S Truman the Korean War was the significant factor explaining the dramatic loss of public confidence in his leadership; for Lyndon B. Johnson, the Vietnam War and riots in the cities were critical; for Richard M. Nixon, it was the continuation of the Vietnam War and Watergate; and for Jimmy Carter, it was his inability to secure the release of Americans held hostage in Iran.

Trends in presidential popularity are described in Figure 9.3. Presidents typically begin with a "honeymoon"—a crucial first few months following an election in which the president is relatively free of harsh public criticism—only to find that in the long-term their popularity declines. As noted, there are often specific reasons for the erosion of presidential support, but it may also be stimulated by growing public dissatisfaction and lost patience with unfulfilled campaign promises, or perhaps by the adage that familiarity breeds contempt.[11] With every presidential decision (or "nondecision"), opposition forms or becomes more vocal, Congress looks increasingly to its own parochial concerns, and the president's support seems to ooze away imperceptibly but methodically. The tendency is symptomatic of the difficulties of running a

---

11. Much of the literature that seeks to explain fluctuations in presidential popularity focuses on the impact of economic variables. The pioneering work incorporating foreign policy was done by Mueller (1973). Ostrom and Simon's (1985, 1989) extension of that work to the impact of political drama generally is especially illuminating.

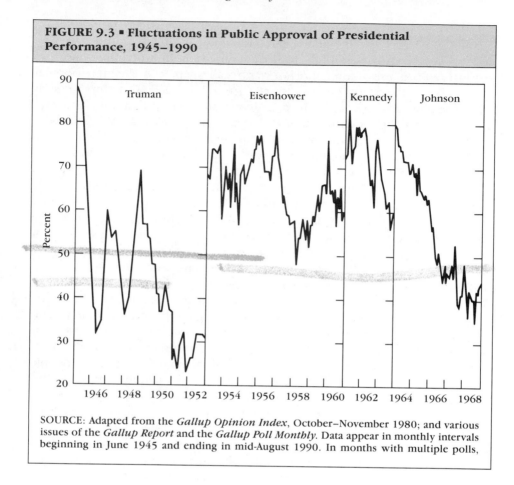

FIGURE 9.3 ▪ **Fluctuations in Public Approval of Presidential Performance, 1945–1990**

SOURCE: Adapted from the *Gallup Opinion Index*, October–November 1980; and various issues of the *Gallup Report* and the *Gallup Poll Monthly*. Data appear in monthly intervals beginning in June 1945 and ending in mid-August 1990. In months with multiple polls,

government and managing the nation's foreign policy in a manner satisfactory to a majority of Americans.

What about Ronald Reagan and George Bush? At first glance both appear to be exceptions to the experience of their predecessors, but on closer examination they fit an established mold. Reagan's popularity followed a predictable decline during his first term, dropping to only 35 percent approval in January 1983 (which prompted political observers at that time to predict Reagan would be a one-term president). But at this point his fortunes were reversed, and little more than a year later Reagan once more enjoyed the approval of a majority of Americans. Things that affected other presidents adversely seemed not to "stick" to Reagan, leading some to describe Reagan's as a "Teflon presidency," implying an immunity from the forces that eroded his predecessors' popular base. The metaphor was reinforced by the paradox that Reagan's personal popularity outstripped public approval of many of his policies and programs, implying his personal charm separated him from the problems people had with his policies (Sussman, 1985).

FIGURE 9.3 ▪ *Continued.*

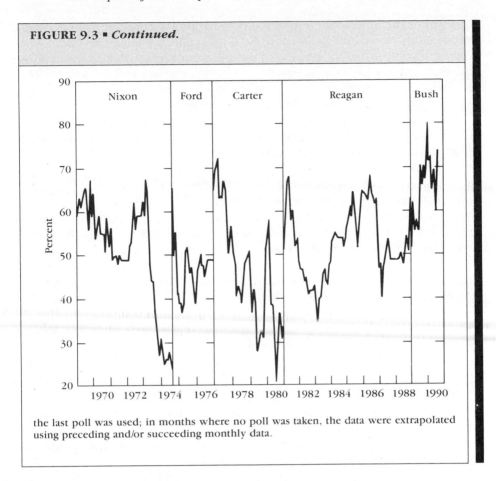

the last poll was used; in months where no poll was taken, the data were extrapolated using preceding and/or succeeding monthly data.

Reagan's popularity continued to climb in his second term. It reached its highest point in April 1986 following the U.S. bombing of Libya, but then fell precipitously when the Iranian arms-for-hostages deal was revealed a few months later. By February 1987 the president's popularity had dropped to nearly the same level as in early 1983. As then, however, approval of "the man in the Teflon suit" (Ostrom and Simon, 1989; see also Lanoue, 1989) once more began a miraculous upward trend as the president's political fortunes were "born again" for the second time. Reagan never regained the lofty popularity ratings he enjoyed before the Iran-*contra* revelations and the Watergate analogy that surrounded it, but, unlike Nixon, he was not destroyed by the scandal's undercurrents.

So how different was Ronald Reagan? To some extent the public did separate its image of the president from his administration (Ferguson with Rogers, 1986). But overall, Reagan's experience was not unique, as the performance of the economy during his two terms in office proved to be the decisive determinant of his popularity (Ostrom and Simon, 1989). "Political drama" in the form of speechmaking, trips abroad, and approval-enhancing international events also mattered, but then so, too, did the disapproval-enhancing Iran-*contra* scandal that corroded the aptness of the teflon metaphor. Perhaps what most distinguished Reagan from his predecessors was the fact that he was the first president since Eisenhower to serve two complete terms in office at a time when positive changes in the domestic political economy redounded to his benefit.[12]

George Bush's experience, too, is less different from his predecessors than is sometimes portrayed. Bush began his presidency with the high level of popular approval (63 percent according to Gallup in February/March 1989) typical of a presidential "honeymoon," but, unlike his predecessors, it remained at that level or higher throughout most of his first year in office and into the second. In one sense that is unusual—presidential "honeymoons" typically last only about a hundred days—but in another it is not inasmuch as Bush enjoyed the fruits of peace and prosperity, much as Reagan and other presidents had. Moreover, a progression of approval-enhancing international events, the most dramatic of which were the invasion of Panama and the militant U.S. response to Iraq's invasion of Kuwait, and the absence of disapproval-enhancing events analogous to Watergate or Iran-*contra*, contributed to a modest upward trend in Bush's popularity. If there was a political payoff to be reaped from developments in Eastern Europe, the Soviet Union, the Middle East, and elsewhere, Bush seemed to be the beneficiary.

Public Opinion and Foreign Policy: An Addendum

The preceding discussion could be expanded in a number of ways. Here we add only a few additional considerations related to Americans' confidence in their political institutions and the political and sociodemographic correlates of their foreign policy attitudes and beliefs.

Confidence in Political Leaders and Institutions

The confidence that Americans repose in the nation's political, economic, and social institutions is

---

12. Reagan is often described as one of the most popular presidents in American history, but that description is inaccurate, as the data below demonstrate (from the *Gallup Report*, January 1989, p. 13). What distinguishes Reagan from his predecessors is that twice during his two-term presidency he was able to stem the decline of support and rebuild it. He also ended his term in office with a higher approval rating than any postwar president, but like all of them he enjoyed less approval upon leaving office than when he entered it.

Presidential Job Approval (percent)

	High	*Low*	*Last*	*Average*
Reagan	68	35	63	52
Carter	75	21	34	47
Ford	71	37	53	46
Nixon	68	24	24	48
Johnson	80	35	49	54
Kennedy	83	57	58	70
Eisenhower	79	49	59	66
Truman	87	23	31	46
Roosevelt	84	54	66	68

closely related to the other developments in public attitudes described above. Jimmy Carter dramatized the trends symptomatic of the changing "public voice" when, in a 1979 nationwide speech, he spoke of "a fundamental threat to American democracy." The threat, he said, was a "crisis of confidence" reflected in "a growing disrespect for government and for churches and for schools, the news media and other institutions." Among the trends was a decline in Americans' sense of political efficacy and a general feeling of despair, alienation, and powerlessness regarding the future. An American public that once appeared to be naive, simplistic, and jingoistic (ultrapatriotic) now seemed more aware of and cynical about foreign policy issues.

Public disclosures of the half-truths regarding U.S. involvement in Vietnam, and the revelations about what was undertaken in the name of national security by presidential staffers, military organizations, and intelligence agencies contributed to Americans' growing cynicism, which was especially evident during and immediately after the Vietnam War. Ronald Reagan helped to rebuild public confidence in political leaders (but not social institutions generally), but it was dealt another blow by the revelations of the Iran-*contra* affair (Lipset and Schneider, 1987; see also Sussman, 1988), which once more raised concerns about the abuse of power in the name of national security. George Bush's prolonged high-level popularity warranted attention in part because of its rarity since the crisis of political confidence brought on by Vietnam and Watergate.

Elites and Masses   One of the sharpest distinctions in public attitudes occurs between elites, on the one hand, and the mass public, on the other. Here the evidence is incontrovertible: elites are markedly more supportive of active involvement in the world than is the mass public. They are also substantially more likely to oppose economic protectionism and to support free-trade principles, basic pillars of postwar internationalism, and to adopt a generally more interventionist orientation toward world affairs than the mass of the American people. But like the mass public, elites also differ among themselves on the question of *how* the United States should be involved in the world. Based on the belief systems derived from the cooperative and militant orientations toward global activism described earlier, elites consistently subscribe to internationalist and accommodationist values in greater proportions than the mass public, which is more likely to hold hardline and isolationist values (Holsti and Rosenau, 1990; Wittkopf, 1990).

Political and Sociodemographic Correlates of Foreign Policy Attitudes
Public attitudes are significantly influenced by, and vary with, many factors, such as age, educational level, gender, political philosophy, party identification, income, occupation, racial background, religious identification, and region of the country. From the point of view of policymakers, knowledge about such factors is often significant politically, in that these factors allow them to court some groups while ignoring others.

Higher-income groups and those with more education generally are more attentive to and better informed about international affairs than lower-income groups and those with less education. Similarly, the better educated and more wealthy, those in professional occupations and those residing in the eastern United States, and self-described liberals are generally more supportive of an internationalist role for the nation than other sectors of society. They are the same societal groups which, when the internationalist consensus split between cooperative and militant internationalism during the 1970s, were most likely to support the policy of détente and to disagree with the proposition that a communist takeover virtually anywhere in the world was necessarily a threat to the vital interests of the United States (Hughes, 1978; Wittkopf, 1990). These differences persisted in various forms into the 1980s. Differences between Republicans and conservatives, on the one hand, and Democrats and liberals, on the other, became especially evident, with the former supporting the kinds of hardline foreign policy positions that the Reagan administration pursued during much of the decade, and the latter more likely to oppose them.

Gender differences on foreign policy issues also became prominent during the Reagan administration. A "gender gap" first became evident in the 1980 election, when Reagan was found to enjoy considerably less support among female voters than among male voters. The differences, which were repeated four years later, appear to have been related to a greater fear among women of Reagan's bellicose foreign policy pronouncements and concerns about his ability to manage the risks of war (Frankovic, 1982; see also Shapiro and Mahajan, 1986; Smith, 1984). Evidence from early in the 1988 presidential campaign indicated that Bush inherited women's distrust of Reagan, but by the time of the election in November 1988 gender differences had largely dissipated (Farah and Klein, 1989; Taylor, 1988).

Generational changes also deserve consideration. Earlier, in commenting on the impact of Vietnam, a contrast was drawn between the Munich generation and the Vietnam generation, which carries with it important implications for the foreign policy thinking that the next generation of policymakers may bring into positions of power (see Holsti and Rosenau, 1980, 1984). The cyclical swings between global activism and withdrawal in American diplomatic history, Frank L. Klingberg (1983, 1990) argues, are largely generational in nature, with oscillations between each mood occurring every twenty-five to thirty years quite independently of public dissatisfaction with particular experiments (such as Vietnam or détente). Although detailed evidence supporting the generational thesis remains problematic (Holsti and Rosenau, 1984; Wittkopf, 1990), the long history of swings between introversion and extroversion Klingberg and others (Holmes, 1985; Schlesinger, 1986) have examined warrants contemplation as the United States looks to the late 1990s and beyond. If the past is a guide, global activism should be the coin of the realm.

A PUBLIC IMPACT ON AMERICAN FOREIGN POLICY?

The foregoing description of the attributes of American public opinion suggests a partial answer to the opinion-policy question: the proposition from democratic theory that foreign policy is merely a reflection of public preferences and beliefs is too crude and simplistic. Public opinion is often described as uninformed, uninterested, acquiescent, apathetic, and manipulable, but we have also seen that it can be resistent to pressure, stable, and capable of learning. Consequently, public opinion provides neither a clear nor a consistent guide to policy making. "To be sure, the results of public opinion polls are usually sufficiently clear that public officials might *claim* that their behavior is consistent with the public will, but such a claim assumes qualities in this opinion not completely borne out empirically" (Weissberg, 1976).[13]

Rather than formulating policy by drawing on public opinion for guidance, policy-making elites are likely to make choices on the basis of other considerations. As a consequence, elites often define their appropriate role as one of leading rather than following. A former Kennedy adviser put it this way: "No president is obliged to abide by the dictates of public opinion. . . . He has a responsibility to lead public opinion as well as respect it—to shape it, to inform it, to woo it, and win it. It can be his sword as well as his compass" (Sorensen, 1963).

The notion that policymakers see public opinion as something to be shaped, not followed, is understandable when we recall the tendency of the public to acquiesce to government decisions. The propensity to accede to leaders' choices and not to mobilize in order to alter them minimizes the impact on foreign policy that the public could exert. The responsiveness of government to public preferences is further reduced by the unwillingness of a passive public to make a meaningful contribution. The conclusion that follows from such a line of reasoning is that the American public participates (through elections, for example) without exercising power. It is involved but does not have influence.

Such a conclusion certainly requires qualification. Rather than asking if there is a direct causal connection between public opinion and the content of foreign policy, it may be more appropriate to inquire into the functions of the public attitudes in the process itself.

Public Opinion as a Constraint on Foreign Policy Innovation

One of the reasons American foreign policy has been so resistant to change since World War II is that public images of international relations have themselves been resistant to change. As noted, fundamental beliefs regarding foreign relations are typically inflexible:

> Almost nothing in the world seems to be able to shift the images of 40 percent of the population in most countries, even within one or two decades. Combinations of events that shift the images and attitudes even of the remaining 50 or 60 percent of the population are extremely rare, and these rare occasions require the

---

13. Among the problems that policymakers face when they seek to interpret opinion polls is that they often measure *nonattitudes* as well as attitudes. The term refers to the fact that individuals often do not have opinions on matters of interest to pollsters, yet, when asked, they will offer an opinion. Clearly such responses are neither strongly held nor meaningful.

combination and mutual reinforcement of cumulative events with spectacular events and substantial governmental efforts as well as the absence of sizable cross-pressures. (Deutsch and Merritt, 1965: 183)

Public opinion thus acts as a brake on policy change, not by stopping innovations, but by restricting "foreign policy modifications because of the perceptions which decision makers have as to the inflexibility of public opinion and its unpredictability" (Peterson, 1971). The constraining impact of the "Vietnam syndrome"—or what has been called a "national first commandment," namely, "there shall be no more Vietnams" (Sussman, 1988)—illustrates the tendency. If decision makers *think* the public voice will not permit certain initiatives and fear that the public may become mobilized against new innovations, that in itself may restrict the kinds of alternatives considered. As one pollster put it, political leaders regard public opinion "as the great gorilla in the political jungle, a beast that must be kept calm" (Sussman, 1988). Their task, then, is to "keep things quiet," which means they seek "to stifle public debate on matters that people care about, or should care about" (Sussman, 1988). It is perhaps for these political and psychological reasons that American foreign policy is perceived by so many analysts and policymakers to be constrained by public attitudes: "Mass opinion may set general limits, themselves subject to change over time, within which government may act" because the "opinion context . . . fixes the limitations within which action may be taken" (Key, 1961). "Fear of electoral punishment," even if unrealistic, serves to limit what decision makers are likely to do, if for no other reason than their (often erroneous) assumption that "the public will never stand for it" (Waltz, 1971).

The inability of the Reagan administration to win support for a firmer posture toward the Sandinistas, noted earlier, is a good example of the constraining influence of public opinion. One observer has gone so far to suggest that public opinion probably prevented Reagan from launching an invasion of Nicaragua (Sussman, 1988). He also argues that public opinion forced Reagan to withdraw the marines from Lebanon in 1984. These assertions are difficult to prove, but it is clear that large numbers of Americans feared that aid to Central America would eventually result in U.S. military involvement in the region and that support for the U.S. role in Lebanon was never great.

Whereas public opinion may serve as a constraint on foreign policy, it would be a mistake to ascribe too much importance to the limits it imposes. The ability of public opinion to constrain foreign policy (by defining a range of permissible policies) is undermined by the acquiescent attitudes of most Americans toward most foreign policy initiatives. If the public sets the outer limits of policy actions, those limits are very broad and elastic.

Indeed, a characteristic closely related to the rally-'round-the-flag phenomenon is the extent to which the public is "blindly obedient" to almost any policy proposed by the government. Consider the following evidence regarding public acceptance of policy changes initiated by the government. Before Johnson announced his Vietnam policy in 1965, only 42 percent of the public favored such an approach. After the announcement, 72 percent favored it. Only 7 percent favored an invasion of Cambodia before it occurred, but after Nixon announced the 1970 "incursion," 50 percent supported it. Fifty-nine percent opposed a U.S. military invasion of Panama to overthrow Panamanian General Manuel Noriega in May 1989, after Noriega had voided Panama's election results. By October the proportion had grown to 67 percent, but following the Bush administration's action in December, 80 percent responded that the United States was justified in sending military forces to invade Panama and overthrow Noriega. Many more examples could be cited.[14]

These data support the proposition that public opinion is inclined to approve of the decisions that leaders make. Moreover, because of the historical tendency of the public to go along with most government actions, decision makers can assume they have public support. The passivity and acquiescence of the mass public would seem to invite presidents to act first and then wait for public approval afterward. Indeed, rather than reflecting on and responding to public opinion, policymakers most of the time seek to create a climate of opinion favorable to contemplated policies and then turn to public opinion to obtain support for policy actions already chosen. Theodore Roosevelt stated it bluntly: "I did not 'divine' what the people were going to think. I simply made up my mind what they ought to think and then did my best to get them to think it." Similarly, George Elsey, former adviser to President Truman, confided, "The president's job is to *lead* public opinion, not to be a blind follower. You can't sit around and wait for public opinion to tell you what to do. . . . You must decide what you're going to do and do it, and attempt to educate the public to the reasons for your action."

Public Opinion as a Stimulus to Foreign Policy Innovation

Exceptions to the general rule of public apathy and powerlessness are rare, but in some instances changes in public opinion precede rather than follow changes in policy. Consider the issue of American policy toward the admission of mainland China to the United Nations. A growing proportion of the public favored admission at the same time that influential segments of the policy-making community remained in rigid opposition to it. In 1950 less than 15 percent of the American public favored admission, but by 1969 over half supported it (Mueller, 1973: 15–17), a level of support which may have made the eventual U.S. decision not to block admission possible. In much the same way, support for the recognition of China by the United States also rose dramatically in the decade before President Carter extended recognition in 1978 (Shapiro and Page, 1988; also Kusnitz, 1984). Thus in the case of China policy, shifts in public preferences preceded foreign policy change.

---

14. See Weissberg (1976) and Brewer (1980) for additional examples, and Sigelman (1979) for a critique of the practice of inferring the impact of governmental action on public attitudes from before and after opinion polls.

Another instance where changes in public attitudes were ahead of policy shifts was the Vietnam imbroglio, where public dissatisfaction with continued intervention was often deeper and more vocal than among government leaders. Similarly, public demonstrations of outrage in 1985 by a small group of activists toward South Africa's racial policy of *apartheid* appeared to rally public opinion and to be critical in bringing congressional pressure to bear on the Reagan administration to abandon its South Africa policy known as "constructive engagement." It may also have contributed to the congressional decision a year later to override a presidential veto to place sanctions on South Africa. Similarly, the rise of popular support of a nuclear freeze and other expressions of fear and dissatisfaction with the military posture of the Reagan administration may have contributed to the administration's willingness to resume nuclear arms control negotiations with the Soviet Union.

Such instances suggest that the public may occasionally serve as a stimulus to policy change, especially when the issue is specific and the public is mobilized. But it would be incautious to suggest that changes in public attitudes *cause* policy innovation. It is probably more accurate to argue that a mobilized public can influence the course of policy only indirectly, by changing "the image of public opinion held by persons capable of affecting policy decisions" or by altering "the image of public opinion held by the public itself" (Rosenberg, 1965). That is, public attitudes may serve as a source of foreign policy by affecting how policymakers think about the international environment, the choices in it, the climate of domestic opinion, and the latitude available for their decisions.

Public Opinion as a Resource in International Bargaining

Countries that make foreign policy through democratic processes enjoy certain advantages. Public attitudes may not only reduce the inclination toward risk and foreign adventure, they may also give policymakers important bargaining advantages when dealing with foreign diplomats. The more unified public opinion, and the more supportive it is of official government policy, the stronger is the leadership's bargaining power with other nations. Here public preferences are seen as a resource to be used by policymakers in the execution of foreign policy. U.S. officials, for instance, may enhance their ability to get their way at the bargaining table by claiming that the American public would never tolerate a proposed concession. Such claims sometimes work because American leaders can describe national opinion to foreigners as they wish and because those leaders may understate their capacity to manipulate public opinion. By describing themselves as victims of popular preferences, policymakers may indeed gain considerable bargaining leverage. "The fact that this decisional process may not in reality originate in the will of the people does not diminish the significance or usefulness of symbolically casting the threshold of national tolerance in terms of public opinion" (Fagen, 1960).

The foregoing observations about the functions of public opinion demonstrate that the links between mass attitudes and foreign policy behavior are complex. "A democratic myth" is what Gabriel A. Almond (1960) called the notion "that the people are inherently wise and just, and that they are the real rulers of the republic." That conclusion is unassailable as far as it goes, but it is also true that the relationship between opinion and policy is affected by a cluster of intervening factors (for example, the nature of the issue, the leadership, policymakers' perceptions, and the international and domestic circumstances prevailing at the time of decision). Rather than viewing decision makers as acting in conformity with the pressures of public opinion, it is often more accurate to say that they formulate their policies independently and then mold public opinion to support them. Moreover, public opinion is characteristically quiescent and influences unobtrusively policymakers' subjective thoughts. But is it also true that, when mobilized, public opinion can exert a comparatively direct and immediate impact.

Finally, we should note that over an extended period a strong correspondence exists between public preferences and the foreign policy goals American leaders choose to make a priority.[15] That may seem paradoxical, since there is considerable evidence supporting the existence of short-run discrepancies between public attitudes and foreign policy behavior. Yet the paradox itself speaks to the indirect nexus that obtains between public opinion and foreign policy, exerting pressure to question how "a policy making system which has mastered all the modes of resistance to outside opinion nevertheless seems, from a long-run perspective, to accommodate to it" (Cohen, 1973). The question is central to efforts to understand the public's impact on foreign policy:

> The troublesome question, which has bedeviled an accurate assessment of the role of public opinion in foreign policy making, may be put as follows: given all the psychological and institutional mechanisms for cushioning, deflecting, and absorbing external opinion so that its day-to-day impact on foreign policy is minimal, and given the apparent immunity of the foreign policy establishment to electoral accountability, how can we account for the occasional but important shifts in the ethos and ideology of foreign policy that seem to follow upon comparable shifts within the larger population? How, in other words, can we reconcile the lack of governmental responsiveness in the short run with an apparent responsiveness in the long run? (Cohen, 1973: 205–206)

We have already suggested some answers to this puzzle, particularly in the ability of decision makers to mold public opinion to fit their preferred policy choices. But that ability also means that in the long run decision makers may become prisoners of their own past efforts to shape public preferences. Public

---

15. Page and Shapiro (1983) conclude from an examination of some "357 instances of significant change in Americans' policy preferences between 1935 and 1979" that opinion and policy are congruent roughly two-fifths of the time. They also argue that in about half of these cases "it is reasonable . . . to infer that opinion change was a *cause* of policy change, or at least a proximate or intervening factor leading to government action, if not the ultimate cause." Monroe (1979) also demonstrates that the congruence between opinion and policy is shown to be higher with respect to foreign than to domestic policy issues.

opinion is thus typically a conservative force, a source of inertia that acts as a restraint on policy innovation. Or, as Alan Monroe (1979) concludes his comparative study of consistency between public preferences and public policy, the policy-making system makes it "more difficult to pass publicly approved changes than to maintain the status quo."

PRESIDENTIAL ELECTIONS AND FOREIGN POLICY CHANGE

Elections are conventionally viewed by the press and public alike as opportunities for policy change, if for no other reason than the prospects they raise for bringing about new leadership. The commonly held assumption is that new leadership will mean new policies and programs. A corollary assumption deserving attention here is that elections enable voters' preferences on foreign policy issues to be translated into policies that reflect those preferences. The question is, Are citizens' votes viable means of expressing policy preferences, thereby rendering electoral processes potent in translating public preferences into policy?

On the one hand, it would seem plausible that decision makers' fear of electoral punishment would lead them to propose policies that would maintain their popularity and thereby enhance their prospects for gaining and retaining office. On the other hand, the "apparent immunity of the foreign policy establishment to electoral accountability" (Cohen, 1973) is notable. Research on the two rival propositions has been extensive. The results have "not, on the whole, been kind to democratic theory," showing "that policy voting is quite rare" and that for a variety of reasons citizens fail to vote for candidates on the basis of policy preferences. "In short, voters are incapable of policy rationality" (Page and Brody, 1972).

Although not altogether consistent, evidence supporting the *issueless politics* hypothesis—that voter choice is determined neither by the nature of the issues nor candidate's positions on them—is abundant (see Asher, 1988). Foreign policy is no exception. Whereas Americans clearly do hold opinions about foreign policy matters, their opinions are not transmitted by elections into the policy-formation process. How do we account for such a failure? One inviting explanation is that although many Americans may regard foreign policy issues as among the most important facing the nation, those issues nevertheless fail to arouse the depth of personal concern raised by issues closer to the populace's daily lives. In addition, foreign policy issues are not the ones that "divide the populace into contending groups. . . . In general foreign issues, involving as they do the United States *versus* others, tend to blur or reduce differences domestically" (Nie, Verba, and Petrocik, 1976).

That does not mean that *party* outcomes are unaffected by foreign policy issues during presidential elections, however. How the public views foreign policy has been shown to be related to the partisan votes cast in each election between 1952 and 1984 (Asher, 1988). Republicans benefited from those perceptions in seven of the nine elections. The 1964 election was the only instance in which voter preferences on foreign policy issues clearly favored the Democrats. In 1984 the Democratic party benefited from public perceptions about nuclear war, the Republicans benefited on the issue of war prevention. The common belief that Republicans produce different policy outcomes (for example, "peace with poverty") than Democrats (for example, "war with wealth") may have something to do with the results.[16]

The 1988 election that pitted George Bush against Michael Dukakis generally reinforced the patterns evident in previous elections. Indeed, one of the "issues" in the campaign was the lack of "issues." This was especially so with respect to foreign policy, where no sharp difference emerged between the candidates (Elshtain, 1989). Lurking in the background, of course, was Ronald Reagan. In many respects the Bush candidacy became a retrospective judgment on the Reagan years (see Abramson, Aldrich, and Rohde, 1990; Farah and Klein, 1989; Pomper, 1989). Peace and prosperity thus redounded to Bush's benefit. Moreover, because Reagan had moved increasingly during his second term toward an accommodationist orientation and away from the hardline foreign policy posture that had characterized his first term—epitomized by his "evil empire" attitude toward the Soviet Union—the ideological differences on foreign policy issues that bore on the electoral outcomes in 1980 and 1984 tended to disappear in 1988. Still, to the extent that voters perceived differences between the candidates on foreign policy issues, particularly their willingness to "stand up for America" (Pomper, 1989), they favored Bush. "Michael Dukakis lost the election," Barbara G. Farah and Ethel Klein (1989) boldly assert, "because the Republicans convinced voters that he would weaken America and Bush would keep the country strong" (see also Abramson, Aldrich, and Rohde, 1990).

Despite this stark conclusion, it is generally difficult to determine the separate effects of particular foreign policy questions on citizens' behavior at the polls. Because most elections involve a variety of different and often overlapping issues, some of those who vote for the winning candidate do so because of his or her stance on particular issues, whereas others do so in spite of it. Foreign policy issues thus become part of a mix of considerations, and often they are a less important ingredient than domestic political issues or retrospective judgments on prior performance (Fiorina, 1981; Abramson, Aldrich, and Rohde, 1986, 1990). As a result, voters' behavior is more likely an aggregate judgment about past performance than a guide to future action.

---

16. These perceptions may be changing. Gallup poll data (Stanley and Niemi, 1990: 153, 154) show that, from the mid-1970s through the mid-1980s, more Americans perceived the Democratic party as better for peace than the Republican party. However, the Republicans did sometimes enjoy an advantage in this respect during the second term of the Reagan administration, a reflection, perhaps, of the abandonment of the hawkish rhetoric of the first term. On the other hand, since 1980 the Republicans have more often than not been perceived as better for prosperity than the Democrats. The ability of the Republicans to command the high ground on issues of peace and prosperity doubtless helps explain why, despite losing at the congressional level, they have been able consistently to win the White House in national elections.

Consider President Carter's electoral fate. The public generally gave Carter high marks on personal attributes (for example, integrity) but low marks on performance. Evaluations of his foreign policy performance were especially critical and generally predicted his electoral fate.[17] Carter's popularity surged in the immediate aftermath of the seizure of American embassy personnel in Teheran in late 1979, but his inability to secure their release fueled public dissatisfaction with his overall performance. His challenger, Ronald Reagan, criticized the policy of détente Carter and his predecessors had promoted, called for substantially increased defense spending, and hammered away at the theme of alleged American impotence in international affairs. In this context "the continuing crisis in Iran came to be seen as a living symbol and constant reminder of all that Reagan had been saying" (Hess and Nelson, 1985).

Four years later, Reagan's reputation for leadership proved a strong force motivating voters to choose the incumbent president over his challenger, Walter Mondale. Certainly there were elements in Reagan's foreign policy record that could be criticized, but four years of relative peace had put to rest fears about Reagan's recklessness. "No longer fearful that the President's policies might lead to war, the public had no compelling reason to abandon him" (Keeter, 1985; see also Abramson, Aldrich, and Rohde, 1990).

Despite the acknowledged importance of retrospective voting, history points to the conclusions that "parties do not offer clear policy alternatives"; "elections are primarily a symbolic exercise that . . . offer the masses an opportunity to participate in the political system, but electoral participation does not enable them to determine public policy"; and a "candidate's election does not imply a policy choice by the electorate" (Dye and Zeigler, 1990). Nevertheless, because policymakers act—evidence to the contrary—*as though* voters make choices on the basis of their policy preferences, they pay attention to the anticipated responses of voters in shaping their policy choices.[18]

The Vietnam episode illustrates many of these conclusions about the mythology of elections as instruments of popular control. In 1964, 1968, and again in 1972, the American electorate had the opportunity to pass judgment on past performance in a way that might have had clear implications

---

17. Compared with his predecessors, Carter ranked poorly in the public's view of his foreign policy performance. A Louis Harris poll taken in January 1981 found that only 5 percent of the public rated Carter best in foreign affairs among the eight presidents holding office between 1933 and 1980. A similar poll taken in 1988 found that only 4 percent ranked him best. At that time Nixon ranked highest (chosen as best by 26 percent of the respondents), followed by Reagan (23 percent) and Kennedy (16 percent). Only Johnson and Gerald R. Ford ranked lower than Carter (Truman and Carter were tied). Interestingly, however, *New York Times*/CBS News polls in 1984 and 1985 showed that 24 percent of the public thought that Carter had done more for world peace than any other recent president, compared with 21 percent for Reagan, and that the 1978 Camp David accords, engineered by Carter, was the most successful foreign policy venture in recent years. Nixon ranked highest as the president who had done most for world peace.

18. Aldrich, Sullivan, and Borgida (1989) have challenged prevailing views of the electorate, which hold that it possesses little information and hold weak attitudes regarding foreign policy. They argue that the public is able to perceive clear differences between candidates on foreign and defense policy issues and that these differences affect their candidate choices (cf. Rattinger, 1989).

for future behavior on the part of their government leadership. Did they vote their preferences on the issue? What was the relationship between those preferences and policy?

Vietnam became a major foreign policy issue in 1964, when President Johnson's overwhelming electoral victory was widely interpreted as a mandate for restraint in the prosecution of the growing U.S. involvement in the Southeast Asian conflict. His Republican opponent, Barry Goldwater, had campaigned on the pledge of pursuing "victory" against communism in all quarters of the globe, but especially in Vietnam by "any means necessary." Johnson's subsequent escalation of the conflict was therefore viewed by some as a violation of his mandate, indeed, as implementation of Goldwater's program. In fact, however, as national surveys indicated:

> There was relatively little relationship between candidate and policy preference, with Johnson winning the support of both "doves" and "hawks." While 63 percent of those favoring withdrawal from Vietnam voted for the President, so did 52 percent of those who favored "a stronger stand even if it means invading North Vietnam" as did 82 percent of those who preferred to "keep our soldiers in Vietnam but try to end the fighting." (Pomper, 1968: 251)

Indeed, the results of that election as it related to Vietnam were so ambiguous as to lead one scholar to conclude: "What could the 1964 vote have told [Johnson] about popular support for various war options? In brief, it could have told him anything he cared to believe" (Boyd, 1972).

By 1968 the war had reached enormous proportions by any measure. The predictable consequence—as we noted above—was growing unpopularity and dissatisfaction with the war as its length increased and its casualty lists grew longer. Campus unrest, mass demonstrations against the war, increasingly vocal minority opposition, including challenges from within the president's own party by Eugene McCarthy and Robert Kennedy—all were indicative of the changing climate of opinion. The widespread popular impression was that Johnson's decision not to run for a second full presidential term was a direct result of this popular opposition. We would expect, therefore, that in 1968 the voters would have made a clear judgment on past performance and would have provided a clear mandate for the future. They didn't.

In terms of Vietnam, the 1968 vote was a clear example of issueless politics. Although "hawks" tended to vote for Nixon in somewhat greater proportion than "doves," overall Vietnam opinions accounted for only between 1 and 2 percent of the variation in voting behavior and "voters did not treat the 1968 election as a referendum on Vietnam policy" (Page and Brody, 1972: 982). This was largely because the electorate (correctly) perceived little difference between the positions of the candidates (Nixon and Hubert H. Humphrey) on Vietnam policy. The voters were in fact deprived of a meaningful foreign policy choice, and the electoral mechanism thus failed to serve as a vehicle for the expression of growing public dissatisfaction with the war.

Hence again in 1968 no clear foreign policy mandate for one course of action over another was provided by the electoral process. Nixon's subsequent shift to what was called "peace with honor" did not emanate from the election. Nor was the promise to end the war promptly fulfilled. An agonizingly slow process ensued. The Vietnamization strategy, announced phased troop withdrawals, and the beginning of peace talks in Paris all came belatedly. It was not until October 1972, shortly (coincidentally?) before the next presidential election, that Secretary of State Henry Kissinger declared to the public that "peace is at hand."

But peace was not *in* hand. So November 7, 1972, became the first election since the Korean War election of 1952 in which foreign policy was the major issue. This time the American electorate cast their votes with Vietnam uppermost in their minds (Miller, et al., 1976). Somewhat less clear-cut, however, was the meaning for Vietnam policy of Nixon's landslide victory. Interpreting the victory as electoral approval for what was perceived, rightly or wrongly, as Nixon's policy of deescalation of the war (Steeper and Teeter, 1976) may be the most compelling way to view the results. But the question of whether the voters voted the way they did because they wanted a negotiated peace or because they desired a military victory remains unanswered.

Given the foregoing discussion of the major characteristics and functions of public opinion, the conclusion that in major electoral contests most Americans tend to support existing government actions should come as no surprise. What is perhaps surprising, however—particularly in light of the nationalistic sentiments of the public and the relative unimportance of foreign policy to most Americans—is that a foreign policy issue became a major item on the electoral agenda at all. The explanation appears to lie in the perceived cost of the war. When foreign policy issues begin to touch significantly the daily lives of Americans, they are likely to be looked upon much more as domestic political issues. Vietnam was precisely such an issue. Mothers and daughters, fathers and sons, taxpayers and draftees—all were intimately touched by Vietnam, a fact which distinguished that war, like others, from most foreign policy questions. Yet the striking fact remains that even in that case, the relationship between public preferences and policy outcomes was essentially an indirect one that does little violence to the general proposition that decision makers lead and the public follows. Little wonder that the characterization holds for the less costly and less disruptive (but infinitely more numerous) issues that comprise the bulk of American foreign policy. Public preferences in general, and during elections in particular, serve as a "source" of American foreign policy, it seems. But they do so more by coloring the vocabulary of decision making than by determining the policy outcomes. Elections are not mechanisms through which the public exercises control over American foreign policy. They are instruments for the selection of personnel, not policy.

THE MASS MEDIA AS A SOCIETAL SOURCE

As suggested earlier, a potentially important component in the public opinion-foreign policy linkage is the role played by the mass media—television, the press, and radio. The mass communications industry plays a central role in the process of policy formulation because (1) public attitudes related to policies are influenced (some would say created) by the information disseminated to the public through the communications network, and (2) the behavior of policy-makers themselves may be affected by the image of the world conveyed by the mass media. From either perspective, the mass media appear to affect the kinds of foreign policies the United States pursues.

In terms of both popular images and policymakers' images, the mass media have been attributed almost dictatorial powers. Many Americans are apparently taken with the notion that the media and the information they disseminate shape public opinion. Indeed, some might even say that the media *are* public opinion.

Policymakers likewise attribute vast powers to the media. They may be right in that the evidence suggests they are able to mold public preferences to support their policies. But policymakers' themselves are less than sanguine about the media. Their own views of the media have ranged from awe and fear to downright hatred. Nixon's claim in 1962 that the press would not have him to "kick around" anymore, followed by his subsequent efforts once in the White House to get revenge on his alleged enemies in journalism, is a case in point. More generally, presidential attitudes perhaps have been captured best in Oscar Wilde's famous remark that "the President reigns for four years, but Journalism reigns forever." Accordingly, presidents actively court the favor of the press, and they ascribe to it the power to make or break government policy. It is no accident, therefore, that many consider the mass media as a fourth branch of the government and often describe it as the "fourth estate."

Although it is hard to deny that the mass media have an effect both on public opinion and on the kinds of policies decision makers choose to pursue, the notion that the media are instrumental in determining foreign policy is not beyond question. The relationships are much more complex. In general, we might ask if the mass media perform more of a mediating than a determining role. We will examine that question by looking, first, at the relationship between the mass media and the public and, second, at the relationship between the mass media and policymakers.

The Mass Media and the Public

The proposition that the mass media exercise overwhelming influence is tempting if for no other reason than that they comprise the primary vehicle for the transmission of knowledge—and "knowledge is power." The industries from which most Americans get their primary information are highly developed. Ninety-eight percent of all American households own at least one television set (which is viewed an average of seven hours a day), and there are nearly 1,650 daily newspapers in the United States, with total daily circulations exceeding sixty-three million. The three major weekly newsmagazines also claim ten million readers. This news establishment has the ability to determine "what the news is": to define behaviors as important actions and thereby to make them into events.

The mass media play an especially important role in setting national agendas. Most people may be inattentive to foreign policy matters most of the time. But when they do show interest in or are exposed to foreign policy issues, the media tell them what to care about. Put succinctly, "the mass media may not be successful in telling people what to think, but the media are stunningly successful in telling their audience what to think about" (Cohen, 1963; see also McCombs and Shaw, 1972). By telling us what to think *about*, however, the media also provide cues as to what to *think* precisely because of their capacity to determine what we think about (Entman, 1989).

The media's influence is greatest in those situations where its audience possesses the least information. Because the mass public often has no prior information on which to rely in forming attitudes about new developments abroad, the media exert a potentially powerful impact on perceptions about events simply because the information they supply is new—and the information is often proffered in a sensational way so as to influence "appropriate" preferences. Americans' understanding of the Soviet Union, for example, is demonstrably limited, with the result that the media's portrayal of Mikhail Gorbachev and his policies of *glasnost* and *perestroika* significantly shaped perceptions of the Soviet Union and its leaders (Hinckley, 1989).

Furthermore, the attention the media give to different issues may contribute to their symbolic significance. During 1987, for example, the United States became increasingly involved in the Persian Gulf war between Iran and Iraq. However, news about the air attack on Iranian bases in the gulf region and the destruction of an Iranian domestic airliner by the *USS Vincennes* in October of that year was dwarfed by news of the dramatic Wall Street stock market crash. In "calmer times," Doris A. Graber (1989) observes, the Persian Gulf incidents "would have been the top stories."

The media not only set the agenda, they also function as "gatekeepers" by filtering the news and shaping the way it is reported.[19] Over the long run "the media tend to reinforce mainstream social values." By serving as gatekeepers, the media transmit "'normal' or legitimate issues and ideas to the public and

---

19. The mass media are widely believed to be dominated by "liberals," and there is evidence to support that view (Lichter and Rothman, 1981; Schneider and Lewis, 1985). Interestingly, however, in 1988 George Bush, the conservative Republican party candidate, was endorsed by 241 daily newspapers (circulation 18,186,225), while Michael Dukakis, the more liberal Democratic party nominee, was endorsed by only 62 newspapers (circulation 11,644,600) (*Editor & Publisher*, November 5, 1988, p. 9). Moreover, a study by the *Los Angeles Times* (Schneider and Lewis, 1985) found that while those who write and edit news stories are overwhelmingly liberal, barely half of those who read these same newspapers could categorize them as either liberal or conservative. It also revealed a "tendency for people to ascribe their own positions to those of their newspaper," suggesting that "readers assume that the newspaper they depend on

[filter] out new, radical, or threatening perspectives" (Bennett, 1980). The gatekeeping role is especially pronounced in foreign affairs, where only seven newspapers (*New York Times, Washington Post, Los Angeles Times, Baltimore Sun, Chicago Tribune, Wall Street Journal*, and *Christian Science Monitor*), the two wire services (Associated Press and United Press International), and the three national television networks (ABC, CBS, and NBC) collect virtually all of the foreign news to which Americans are exposed (Graber, 1989). Furthermore, newspapers such as the *New York Times* provide news to other newspapers, which typically follow their lead in the way news stories about foreign affairs are presented to local audiences. Similarly, "pack journalism"—a troublesome phenomenon that refers to the tendency of most reporters to follow the lead of one or a few others in deciding what is (or is not) news and how to interpret it—often leads to remarkably similar news accounts, particularly among the national print and electronic media (Graber, 1989).

The foregoing ideas demonstrate the powerful role that the media play in American society. Why, then, is the impact of the media on public attitudes toward foreign policy less direct and pervasive than might be expected? Consider the following ideas.

Media Inattention to Foreign Affairs   The ability of the mass media to shape foreign policy attitudes is undermined in part by the media's relative inattention to foreign news and their much greater concern for domestic news. Foreign affairs news coverage in noncrisis periods constitutes less than 10 percent of all stories in American newspapers and less than 20 percent of the stories on national television newscasts (Graber, 1989: 328). The comparatively little treatment that foreign affairs receives is in part because of the absence of a mass market for foreign policy news. For perhaps similar reasons, few reporters are paid to cover international affairs. Television programming, furthermore, is overwhelmingly oriented toward local, not national or international, news.

An exception to the foregoing is the foreign affairs coverage by the so-called prestige press, of which the *New York Times* is the most notable, and the ABC, CBS, and NBC network broadcasts. One study of the news coverage by the *New York Times*, for example, showed that it allotted over 40 percent of its total national and international coverage to foreign news. Network coverage ranged from just under 31 percent for ABC to about 36 percent for NBC (Frank, 1973: 58).[20] How many people consume that coverage and even how much there is to consume remain problematic, however. The circulation of the *New*

---

for information shares their outlook" (Schneider and Lewis, 1985). Finally, an analysis of network and wire service coverage of the 1980 presidential campaign concludes similarly: political reporting, especially of domestic news, "reflects the canons of objectivity more often than the political opinions of the newspeople themselves" (Robinson, 1983).

20. The three national newsmagazines, *Time, Newsweek*, and *U.S. News and World Report*, also give substantial attention to foreign affairs. Frank's data do not extend to the newsmagazines, but Gans (1979) usefully compares these national media to the television networks.

York Times constitutes but a fraction of the nation's newspaper subscribers, and a full transcript of the nightly television network news—foreign and domestic—would not fill half the front page of an average daily newspaper. Yet it is on newcasts that three-quarters of the American people routinely depend for most of their foreign affairs information (Schneider, 1984: 18).[21] The proportion is even higher during times of crisis (Larson, 1990).

Public Inattention to Foreign Affairs   As we noted earlier in this chapter, most Americans are uninterested in and ill informed about foreign affairs because they are inattentive to the world around them. If the American people fail to read or listen to news disseminated by the media, then obviously their opinions cannot be influenced by it. In fact, most Americans are more interested in weekly television entertainment series than in a news commentator's observations on the state of the world.[22] In 1986, for example, less than a third of the American people said they were very interested in following news about other countries, and, as we noted at the beginning of the chapter, less than half were very interested in news of U.S. relations with other countries (Rielly, 1987: 8). Another study found that three-quarters of the public said they paid attention to government and public affairs, but only about a third had above average knowledge on these matters, and over 40 percent were poorly informed (Ornstein, Kohut, and McCarthy, 1988: 53–54). This led the authors to conclude that, "while 75 percent of the people *say* they pay attention to politics, they clearly aren't taking notes."

The Imperviousness of Beliefs   In those instances when people do not begin with the complete absence of preconceptions, behavioral research tells us that people do not change their beliefs very easily, as we noted earlier. What they read in print and see and hear on television does not (popular myths notwithstanding) alter what they think. The reasons are mostly psychological. Beliefs are not a function of information in part because of the pervasive human tendency toward *selective perception*: people search for "comfortable" information that "fits" with preexisting beliefs, whereas information with which one disagrees is screened out or rejected. In short, we see what we want to see, we hear what we want to hear.[23]

---

21. The growing importance of television is suggested by the fact that "most American children begin watching television at the age of three months and, by the time they finish high school, have spent less than 12,000 hours in front of a teacher and more than 22,000 hours in front of a television set" (Ranney, 1983: 4). The correlation of TV-watching with other trends among the nation's emerging generations of foreign policymakers, including, for example, several years of declining Scholastic Aptitude Test scores, may be related to what some (for example, Manheim, 1984) believe to be shallow thinking about politics and a declining interest in public affairs.

22. When given a choice, Doris A. Graber (1989) observes, Americans "do not seek out foreign policy news. For example, when NBC News broadcast a prime-time, hour-long interview with Soviet leader Mikhail Gorbachev in December 1987, just prior to a U.S.-Soviet meeting designed to reduce the danger of war, only 15 percent of the national audience tuned in. Half of the viewers who at that time ordinarily watch NBC's entertainment programs switched to other networks."

Selective perception is partially subconscious, stemming from the nearly universal need to maintain stable images when confronted with inconsistent and confusing information. In the parlance of psychology, everyone seeks to maintain "cognitive balance" (Festinger, 1957), either by screening out information that runs counter to cherished beliefs or by avoiding and suppressing information that challenges preexisting images. An individual subscribing to the simplistic belief that all revolutions and civil disturbances are communist inspired, for instance, is likely to reject or block out information that runs counter to that theory, such as reports that insurgency in Central America stems not from outside intervention, but from indigenous sources.

Selective perception is also pervasive because people are prone to avoid information with which they disagree. Many people choose to read magazines and to listen to news programs that reinforce interpretations consistent with their biases. How many people, for instance, routinely read interpretations *both* from journals reflecting liberal (for example, the *Nation*) as well as conservative (for example, the *National Review*) perspectives? A small proportion, most studies indicate. Thus most people who care about politics and foreign policy are relatively immune to media-induced attitude change. That is *not* to say that most Americans are intellectual bigots. But the propensity for selective perception (reinforced by the related tendency toward "selective recall" of the past) compromises the ability of the mass media to influence attitude change and renders its influence to a subordinate role.[24]

Television's Inadvertent Audience   The pervasiveness of television in the homes and daily lives of millions of Americans requires that we add important caveats to the foregoing conclusions because television has provided the mass of the American people with a huge infusion of foreign policy information that most neither like nor want. Instead, because most who watch television news see what does not interest them as well as what does—they don't "edit" the information television journalists supply by walking away from the set or turning it off—they have become an *inadvertent audience* (Ranney, 1983).

What are the consequences of the intrusive force of television? First, television may explain the decline of confidence in the nation's institutional leadership witnessed during recent decades.[25] As William Schneider (1982), a well-known opinion analyst, has observed, "negative news makes good video.

---

23. See Patterson and McClure's *The Unseeing Eye* (1976) for an examination of the proposition that the broadcasting industry is capable of influencing public opinion. Evidence and critiques of the "minimal-effects" thesis can be found in Iyengar, Peters, and Kinder (1982) and Page, Shapiro and Dempsey (1987). Parenti (1986) provides a wide-ranging critique of the media.

24. This is not meant to imply that the media have no impact on American politics, only that it is more complex and less direct than often presumed. For elaborations on the role of the media in American politics, see Graber (1989, 1990).

25. In the specific case of the presidency, television coverage has been shown to become increasingly negative as a president's term progresses, a finding that may help explain the decline and fall of modern presidents (Smoller, 1986).

Consequently, television presents much of the news as conflict, criticism and controversy. . . . The public responds to this large volume of polarized information by becoming more cynical, more negative, and more critical of leadership and institutions." Less patience with foreign policy initiatives by individuals and institutions about which Americans are cynical and distrustful may be a related consequence of exposure to American involvement in world affairs, which television brings home but which most Americans find confusing and unnecessary.

Second, being uninterested, members of the inadvertent audience are unlikely to have strong convictions about issues, in contrast to those who regularly follow foreign policy issues. "When people with weak opinions are exposed to new information, the impact of that information is very strong. They form new opinions, and if the information they receive is negative or critical, their opinions will develop in that direction" (Schneider, 1982). "There is no evidence that television changes the nature of the public's concerns in the area of foreign policy," observes Schneider (1984). "These concerns remain what they always have been: peace and strength. Television simply intensifies these concerns and creates more negative and unstable public moods."

Third, television has also affected the relationship between the mass public and policymakers in important ways. Members of Congress who wish to make names for themselves (read all), for example, are induced to frame their foreign policy ideas in "one-liners" that will fit into the thirty-, sixty-, or ninety-second slots the evening news allocates to such issues. For the electorate it has meant that "a Presidential candidate without much prior international experience can come to office with a collection of half-minute clichés in his head masquerading as foreign policies" (Destler, Gelb, and Lake, 1984).

Because public opinion is both responsive to events and susceptible to manipulation, it is not surprising to find that policymakers energetically use television to create support for their policies, for "television is the principal means by which elites communicate to masses" (Dye and Zeigler, 1990). A case in point occurred in 1983 when President Reagan was able through a masterful television speech to reverse sentiments about his policies following the death of 241 service personnel in a truck-bombing of marine headquarters in Lebanon and the invasion of Grenada that followed on its heels. Before the speech, 41 percent approved of Reagan's handling of Lebanon; after it, 52 percent approved. Before the speech, 52 percent approved of the invasion of Grenada: after it, 65 percent approved (Sussman, 1988: 70). The American people normally rally 'round the flag—and the president—during times of crisis and peril, as we observed earlier, but the evidence here suggests the president can use the media to help define when those conditions exist.[26]

---

26. Although most crises produce "rally-'round-the-flag" effects, there are exceptions, and the media play a critical role in differentiating them. If recognized opposition leaders fail to criticize a president during a crisis, "press and television accounts of the 'politics' surrounding the event will be unusually full of bipartisan support for the president's actions," and the public will rally

Media Vulnerability to Government Manipulation   To a considerable extent, the media reflect, rather than balance, the government and its interpretation of issues and events. Collusion between the media and the government, conscious and unconscious, is a persistent condition, particularly because policymakers themselves are the principal source of political news reported by the media. The following describes the process.

> Government officials and the press play a game of politics and propaganda which has become as stylized as an 18th century dance. First the officials hand out privileged information to favored journalists ("U.S. intelligence flatly reported that . . ."). Then the journalists pass out the same information, with or without attribution, to their readers. Finally, pro-administration congressmen fill pages of the *Congressional Record* with the same articles to prove that the officials were right. (Draper, 1968: 89)

As these words suggest, the media frequently operate as a conduit for the transmission of information from the governing elite to the American people, rather than as a truly independent source of information about what the government is doing. For a variety of reasons (for example, dependence on government news releases, inability to obtain classified information, use of "privileged" briefings, self-censure, the fact that self-restraint is often in the media's self-interest), the mass media are frequently regarded by the government as vulnerable to manipulation. News, in government parlance, is "manageable,"[27] and what is reported often depends on what is "leaked" by the government for public consumption, rather than on what has occurred behind closed doors. In the extreme, the government effectively censors the news, as the Reagan administration did when it denied reporters permission to observe the Grenada assault force in 1983, an intervention later revealed to be fraught with mistakes. (In a similar vein, reporters covering the 1989 invasion of Panama also complained that the military deliberately kept them away from the action.)

Disclosures about government lies during Watergate and in areas routinely but loosely defined by the government as matters of "national security" appear to have enhanced the ability of the mass media to function as a check

---

behind the president. However, "when opinion leadership does not rally or run for cover, the media must and do report this fact. The public now receives countervailing elite evaluations of presidential performance and, in the aggregate appears to look to the events themselves for information with which to update its judgment of how well the president is handling his job" (Brody and Shapiro, 1989). In cases where dissent occurs, the evidence suggests that the rally phenomenon is either absent or less pervasive (Brody and Shapiro, 1989).

27. The Kennedy administration in particular is often credited with having been extraordinarily successful in having the news its way. However, Kern, Levering, and Levering (1984) suggest that Kennedy's ability to dominate the news varied considerably, depending on the circumstances. Kern (1984) has also compared Carter to Kennedy, finding, not surprisingly, that Carter fared even less well than Kennedy. A number of reasons explain this, including the fact that Carter came to office "on a wave of public and press disillusionment with the strong presidency." An historical overview of the relationship between *The Press and the Presidency* is provided by Tebbel and Watts (1985), who are particularly critical of the Reagan administration's use—and abuse—of the mass media.

on government control. Furthermore, one of the clear lessons of the Iran-*contra* scandal is that covert foreign policy actions cannot long remain secret (Treverton, 1990), regardless of how much the government seeks to hide what it is doing. Still, the fact that abuses of power seem to remain uncovered for extended periods is perplexing in an environment where the media presumably act as a check against governmental excesses. (Noteworthy is that it was the foreign press, not the U.S. media, that first disclosed the Iranian arms-for-hostages deal.) Thus, whereas a more critical and aggressive posture by parts of the "fourth estate" in the wake of Vietnam and Watergate may have helped to rectify compliant tendencies, the media and the government remain intertwined to a considerable extent in a process that invites collusion. Because dependence on news derived from the government itself compromises the ability of the media to oversee government actions in the foreign policy domain, it may be more appropriate to ask not whether the media control public opinion in America, but whether public attitudes are manipulated and structured by the government through the media conduit (see Parenti, 1986).

The Mass Media and Policymakers

The foregoing casts doubt on the thesis that public attitudes are molded by what the mass media report. But the media cannot be dismissed so readily. Important qualifications must be introduced by turning attention from the influence of the media on the attitudes of ordinary citizens to their impact on the attitudes of *policymakers* and *policy influentials* (people who are knowledgeable about foreign affairs and who have access to decision makers, such as the nongovernmental members of the "establishment" described in Chapter 8). The following four observations summarize pertinent evidence on the subject.

Those Who Follow Foreign Policy Events and Who Are Attentive to Foreign Issues Derive Most of Their Information Directly from the Mass Media   American society is structured like a pyramid, with a very small proportion of policy influentials and decision makers at the top (the elite), followed by a larger component comprising the attentive public, with the bulk of the population making up the mass public. The pyramid represents the three strata that make up the aggregate concept *public opinion*. While estimates vary as to the distribution of the public among these three groups, most suggest that the elite (decision makers and policy influentials) comprise less than 2 percent of the population; the attentive public (those knowledgeable about foreign affairs but not necessarily with access to decision makers) between 5 and 10 percent; and the mass public, by definition, the rest.

The distinction among the components of public opinion is important in evaluating the impact of mass media on foreign policy making because such factors as level of education, familiarity with foreign policy issues, and amount of information available are important determinants of one's position within the societal pyramid as well as one's foreign policy attitudes. Television has a leveling effect in that even those who care little about foreign affairs get some information about it. But those making up the elite and attentive public take advantage of a broader array of information, virtually all of it from publicly available sources provided by the mass media in the United States. Accordingly, for those concerned about foreign policy and for those actually involved in the foreign policy-making process, the impact of the mass media is potentially much greater than for the mass public, which pays comparatively less attention to such news, does not seek it, or is only inadvertently an audience for it.

It may appear surprising or even exaggerated to suggest that policymakers rely on the media as a primary source of information—instead of the information provided by the intelligence community, for instance—but they do. The mass media provide policymakers with a basic source of information about what is happening in the world (in part because the press is quicker and more readable than official reports and because it is often perceived as a less biased source of information than government agencies that gather data with a purpose in mind).[28] Especially important in this respect is the prestige press. As Bernard Cohen, a careful student of the subject, put it:

> [The *New York Times*] is read by virtually everyone in the government who has an interest or responsibility in foreign affairs.... One frequently runs across the familiar story: "It is often said that Foreign Service Officers get to their desks early in the morning to read the *New York Times*, so they can brief their bosses on what is going on." This canard is easily buried: The "bosses" are there early, too, reading the *New York Times* for themselves.... The *Times* is uniformly regarded as the authoritative paper in the foreign policy field. In the words of a State Department official in the public affairs field, "You can't work in the State Department without the *New York Times*. You can get along without the overnight telegrams sooner." (Cohen, 1961: 220–221)

Other policymakers and policy influentials corroborate the observation.[29] Thus the media play an important role in disseminating information about foreign affairs to those interested in, and holding positions of power with

---

28. Graber (1989) illustrates the point by noting that President Kennedy "would read the *New York Times* before beginning his official day because stories about foreign affairs often reached him twenty-four hours earlier through the *Times* than through State Department bulletins that had to be coded and then decoded." Interestingly, television has also seemingly come to impact on the process. "Alexander Haig alleges that review of the previous night's newcasts was his first order of business when he served as White House chief of staff, deputy national security adviser, commander of NATO, and secretary of state" (Larson, 1990).

29. Conservative writer William F. Buckley (1970), himself no fond admirer of the news establishment of which he is a part, found himself reporting after hearing a radio bulletin that Egyptian President Gamal Abdel Nasser had died: "I slipped off to telephone *The New York Times* to see if the report was correct (one always telephones *The New York Times* in emergencies). The State Department called *The New York Times*, back in 1956, to ask if it was true that Russian tanks were pouring into Budapest." And John Kenneth Galbraith (1969b), a former American policymaker, has testified to the effectiveness of elite newspapers to gather, as the *New York Times* proclaims, "all the news that's fit to print": "I've said many times that I never learned from a classified document anything I couldn't get earlier or later from *The New York Times*."

respect to, foreign policy making in the United States. To the extent that images of the world depend on the way they are described in the mass media, the media have potentially important input to the policy-making process.

The Mass Media May Stimulate Changes in the Elites' Attitudes, Which Are Then Dispersed throughout Society   That knowledgeable and influential Americans derive most of their information about foreign affairs from the mass media does not mean they are immune to selective perception and foreign policy belief rigidity. Still, attitude change is possible. Indeed, recent American history attests to the fact that the opinions of "the best and the brightest" can shift in response to changing circumstances and new information. When opinion fluctuates within the policy-making and attentive publics, it serves as a stimulus to eventual attitude change among the general populace. The classic explanation of the opinion-making and opinion-circulating process is known as the *two-step flow of communications* theory, according to which, "ideas often flow from radio and print to opinion leaders and from these to the less-active sections of the population" (Katz, 1957). The dynamics of attitude change are best explained, the hypothesis holds, through the crucial channel of face-to-face contact. That is not to suggest that members of the mass public actually sit down and exchange ideas with governing elites or policy influentials. Rather, it suggests that ideas become meaningful only after they have been transmitted farther down the pyramid by such opinion leaders as teachers, the clergy, local political leaders, and others who have an above-average interest in public affairs and occupy positions allowing them to communicate frequently with others. Thus information does not flow directly from the mass media to the general population. Rather, it is transmitted first to opinion leaders (who, incidentally, inevitably distort it) and through them to the less interested or knowledgeable in mass society. Attitude change, according to this view, stems from changes in the thinking of the policy elite and the attentive public, with society at large following sometime later. Face-to-face contacts with opinion leaders and "mobilizables" (Rosenau, 1974) provide a crucial link in the incremental diffusion process. Hence the mass media are not the primary transmitters of ideas; nor are they the primary stimulus of mass attitude change. Rather, the mass media provide information to policy influentials and those attentive to public policy which, when digested in a way that invites attitude change, is then relayed through the political system primarily through interpersonal contact.

Television broadcasting complicates this view. There are few or no apparent intermediaries between evening news anchors and the consumers of their messages. The two-step flow hypothesis is thus clearly overly simple. A *multi-step flow* theory is preferable, for it provides a more accurate description of the opinion-making and opinion-circulating process in an age of mass electronic communication.

> For every field of interest (politics, fashion, economics, moviegoing, etc.) there are apparently certain people who make great use of the media for information

and guidance. The opinion leaders then communicate with each other, crystalliz-ing their views into a consistent stance. Later they transmit this attitude to lesser opinion leaders, who also make use of the mass media but not so much. The recipients compare what they get from the media with what they get from their opinion leaders, then pass the combination on down the line. Eventually the mes-sage reaches that large segment of the population which makes little or no direct use of the media. (Sandman, Rubin, and Sachsman, 1972: 5)

Clearly, though, even in a multistep flow of communications, the media play a crucial role in the transmission of opinions within the political system. Hence they are pivotal in the process of opinion making and opinion diffusion. But because the process of opinion dispersion entails many steps and stages, mass opinion change in American society at large tends to be slow. Neverthe-less, because there is such a process, long-term variations in public opinions are observable.

The Media: Opinion Makers or Reflectors of Policymakers' Opinion?
The role of the media in the opinion-formation process cannot be denied, but their role as an agent of change can be easily exaggerated. We would do well to recall that the mass media are part and parcel of the foreign policy-making "establishment" from which opinion change ultimately springs. That fact undermines the alleged independent role that the press and television might play in fomenting opinion change. During the 1979 Iranian hostage crisis, for example, the media rarely strayed from the government's line about what was happening (Larson, 1990).

Given the relationship between the mass media and the government (the mass media being dependent on the government for information, and govern-ment officials, in turn, comprising the media's major reference group), a con-gruence exists most of the time between the attitudes of the government and the views of the media that seek to scrutinize it. To be sure, conflicts between government officials and media representatives often surface, and they are likely to grow more acute as a president moves beyond the typical "honey-moon" period of popularity into a period of "hard choices." President Carter's comment in 1980 that "I've always been disappointed in two groups—the Ira-nians and the press," is a good example of the feeling every president has that his administration is being victimized by the media. But the ability of govern-ment to manage the news, combined with the media's dependence on the government to get the news, perpetuates a symbiotic (incestuous?) relationship between the two institutions (see Herbers, 1976; Hess, 1984). The mass media are often, then, less a source of opinion change than a mirror image of govern-ment opinion.

Even the familiar news "leak," often used by competing factions within the government to fight their bureaucratic battles publicly through the media, does not alter that conclusion. Indeed, it reinforces it, because reporters typically, in addition to being required by their professional code of ethics to protect the con-fidentiality of "high government sources," must offer such protection in order to be assured of a news story to write or report tomorrow. It is clear from a multitude of sources, moreover, that "high government officials" —meaning White House staffers and members of the cabinet—have often been the source of government "leaks." The "leak" is an American political "institution," a practice rooted in tradition and employed routinely by government officials in every branch and at every level in the government.

The Media Create Foreign Policy Issues That Necessitate Action by Decision Makers   Finally, we might acknowledge again another way in which the mass media affect policy-making behavior and, ultimately, American conduct abroad: through the ability of the mass media to create foreign policy issues, described earlier as the agenda-setting function. By publicizing foreign events or international circumstances, the media draw attention to situations. Frequently that attention forces decision makers to act, rather than to ignore the situation or to choose to keep it hidden. By focusing on or ignoring some circumstance, the media "manufacture" conditions that demand a government response. Thus the media provoke decision making about issues which, had they not attracted attention, would probably have been met with apathy and indifference. As I. M. Destler, Leslie H. Gelb, and Anthony Lake (1984) suggest, the ability of policymakers to determine what is and what is not an important foreign policy issue may be adversely affected by the attention accorded to particular foreign policy problems by the media, especially television.

Moreover, the media intrude into the policy-making process by defining the bounds within which policy debate takes place. The way the media treat an issue, once created, structures how it is perceived and often influences the vocabulary with which it is discussed. The effects of such input cannot, in the long run, be lightly dismissed. Theodore H. White captures the media's influence in setting the agenda by determining what will be discussed and shaping its content:

> The power of the press in America is a primordial one. It sets the agenda of public discussion; and this sweeping political power is unrestrained by any law. It determines what people will talk and think about—an authority that in other nations is reserved for tyrants, priests, parties and mandarins. No major act of the American Congress, no foreign adventure, no act of diplomacy, no great social reform can succeed in the United States unless the press prepares the public mind. (White, 1973: 327)

SOCIETAL SOURCES OF AMERICAN FOREIGN POLICY

By way of conclusion, we are left with the inescapable impression that the mass media play a mediating role in the foreign policy-making process. Although the mass media, through their agenda-setting and gatekeeper functions, condition the way Americans think about foreign affairs only indirectly, they affect more directly the way elite groups perceive the world. Thus they influence the course of U.S. action abroad to the extent that they are able to color the way policymakers, policy influentials, the attentive public, and opinion leaders see the world. When new information enters into the thinking of elite groups and stimulates a change in the attitudes of that stratum of American society that pays attention, then those attitudes gradually tend to affect the way the mass public thinks about foreign affairs. At the same time, the governing elite seeks to use the media to manage the view of the world that various segments of the public hold—an effort that itself attests to the perceived political importance of the media.

As we have seen, however, the impact is neither immediate nor direct. On the one hand, the conduct of American foreign policy is seemingly dependent on the media in the sense that "a large proportion of diplomatic reporting consists of analysis based on the work of journalists. . . . It is only a slight exaggeration to say that the mass media are the eyes and ears of diplomacy" (Davison, 1976). But on the other hand, that dependency does not give the media control over American foreign policy. The media enter into the policy-formation process; but they are less a source from which policy is derived than a cog in the machinery that produces policy decisions and foreign policy actions.

Thus, the question posed at the outset of this (and the preceding) chapter—In what ways do societal factors influence American foreign policy? —has invited a series of additional questions, and, inevitably, provoked a variety of answers. Examination of the potential impact of public opinion, presidential elections, and the mass media suggests that each of those societal factors does indeed intrude upon the policy-making process, and thus each serves as a source of American foreign policy. But the functions they perform explain more about the *process* of formulating American policies toward the external environment than about the objectives of those actions and the particular means chosen to achieve them. The effect of the societal factors we have discussed here in generating foreign actions is rarely if ever exclusively deterministic. Instead, they exert influence primarily as part of the context within which decisions are formulated; in particular, they operate more as forces constraining foreign policy (thereby promoting policy continuity) than as forces stimulating radical departures from the past. Hence, if we assume, for example, that the anticommunist theme in postwar American foreign policy grew out of the Lockean liberal tradition described in the preceding chapter, the way in which the forces we have described in this chapter operate in the policy-making process should help explain why movement away from the traditional anticommunist posture has been so hesitant. More generally, when we add to this the knowledge we have of the effects of the elitist foreign policy-making community and the consequences of pluralized interest group interactions, it should not be surprising that incremental adaptations to evolving international circumstances have been more characteristic of postwar American foreign policy than radical innovations.

Beyond this, however, it is difficult to isolate causal connections between *particular* societal variables and *particular* actions abroad. To pinpoint better the sources of American foreign policy decisions and initiatives, we need to turn from the consideration of factors within American society to an examination of the U.S. government from which most foreign policy initiatives spring.

SUGGESTIONS FOR FURTHER READING

Almond, Gabriel A. (1960) *The American People and Foreign Policy.* New York: Praeger.

Barnet, Richard J. (1990) *The Rockets' Red Glare: When America Goes to War—The President and the People.* New York: Simon & Shuster.

Cohen, Bernard C. (1963) *The Press and Foreign Policy.* Princeton, N.J.: Princeton University Press.

Dye, Thomas R., and Harmon Zeigler. (1989) *American Politics in the Media Age,* 3rd ed. Pacific Grove, Calif.: Brooks/Cole.

Holsti, Ole R., and James N. Rosenau. (1984) *American Leadership in World Affairs: Vietnam and the Breakdown of Consensus.* Boston: Allen & Unwin.

Mueller, John E. (1973) *War, Presidents and Public Opinion.* New York: Wiley.

Parenti, Michael. (1986) *Inventing Reality: The Politics of the Mass Media.* New York: St. Martin's.

Small, Melvin. (1988) *Johnson, Nixon, and the Doves.* New Brunswick, N.J.: Rutgers University Press.

Wittkopf, Eugene R. (1990) *Faces of Internationalism: Public Opinion and American Foreign Policy.* Durham, N.C.: Duke University Press.

Yankelovich, Daniel, and Sidney Harman. (1988) *Starting with the People.* Boston: Houghton Mifflin.

PART V

Governmental Sources of American Foreign Policy

CHAPTER 10

Presidential Preeminence in Foreign Policy Making

As modern bureaucracy has grown, the understanding of change and the formulation of new purposes have become more difficult. Like men, governments find old ways hard to change and new paths difficult to discover.

PRESIDENT RICHARD M. NIXON, 1970

In the areas of defense and foreign affairs, the Nation must speak with one voice, and only the president is capable of providing that voice.

PRESIDENT RONALD REAGAN, 1984

The president of the United States is widely regarded at home and abroad as the most powerful individual in the world. The president commands the ability to unleash destruction beyond anything experienced in history. The president directs political and economic resources without parallel elsewhere in the world. And the president enjoys a level of legitimacy and authority at home that is the envy of political leaders around the world. Moreover, the presidential form of government enjoys advantages over other democratic systems, such as the British parliamentary system; it is able to respond more quickly and pragmatically to emergent challenges (Waltz, 1967). Given that, President Richard M. Nixon's lament about the ability of government to understand change and to formulate new purposes is especially troublesome in a constantly changing world that demands policy adaptation. It is all the more disconcerting when applied to foreign affairs, where the president is largely unencumbered by the many political demands and expectations that typically influence the making of domestic policy.

Could the very size of the government—the incredibly complex organizational structures into which the millions of federal employees fit, and the maze of channels through which innovative ideas must pass before they become new policies—itself be a force working against the understanding of change and the formulation of new purposes? Apart from the cabinet departments, the federal roster includes over 60 different agencies and over 1,250 advisory boards and commissions. Add Congress—which often appears more

325

like 535 separate interests than one unified body—and we can begin to appreciate how the very size of government inhibits prompt policy change in response to new realities.

Consider some simple propositions about the politics of policy making within this maze of multiple and often overlapping institutions. Money and personnel mean political power. Once acquired, institutions seek to protect them. They oppose changes that threaten to erode their sources of influence. Incremental changes at the edge are acceptable, but fundamental reorientations that would require massive budgetary and personnel cuts must be resisted.

The reasons why individuals in organizational settings protect their "fiefdoms" is the subject of Chapter 13. In this chapter and Chapters 11 and 12, we will describe the "fiefdoms" in the "foreign affairs government." The focus throughout these three chapters is how the structure of that part of the U.S. government concerned with foreign policy making—the governmental category—operates as a source of American foreign policy. How the United States organizes itself for the making of foreign policy, in other words, is assumed to shape the nature of American action abroad.

To guide our inquiry, we will draw on a conceptualization of the foreign policy-making process as a series of concentric circles (see Figure 10.1) suggested some years ago by a former policymaker, Roger Hilsman (1967). His view in effect bends the boxes and branches of the standard government organization chart so as to draw attention to the core, or source, of the action. Thus the innermost circle in the policy-making process consists of the president, the president's immediate personal advisers, and such important political appointees as the secretaries of state and defense, the director of the Central Intelligence Agency (CIA), and various under and assistant secretaries who bear responsibility for carrying out policy decisions. The most important decisions involving the fate of the nation are made, in principle, at this level.

The second circle contains the various departments and agencies of the executive branch. If we exclude from that circle the politically appointed agency heads and their immediate subordinates, whom we have already placed in the innermost circle, we can place within the second circle the career bureaucrats who provide continuity in the implementation of policy from one administration to the next, regardless of who occupies the White House. Their primary task—in theory—is to provide top-level policymakers with the information necessary for making decisions and then to carry out those decisions.

The outermost circle is what Hilsman refers to as the "public one," consisting of Congress, domestic interest groups, public opinion, and the mass media. Collectively, the institutions, groups, and individuals at this level are least involved in the day-to-day foreign policy process. Building from this conceptualization, we will take three different approaches to describing the foreign affairs government in the subsequent chapters. First, in this chapter we will examine the way presidential factors, but especially the relationship between

FIGURE 10.1 ▪ The Institutional Setting: The Concentric Circles of Policy Making

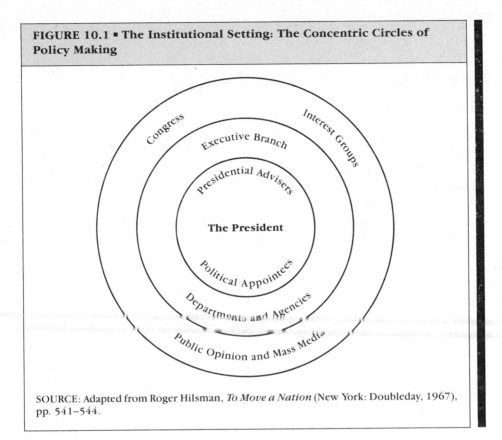

SOURCE: Adapted from Roger Hilsman, *To Move a Nation* (New York: Doubleday, 1967), pp. 541–544.

the president and the president's immediate group of advisers (with special reference to the National Security Council and the president's national security adviser) affect American foreign policy. In a sense, the question addressed is how particular presidential preferences combine with the generalized presidential form of government to promote what may be a distinctively American institutional approach to foreign policy making.

Second, in Chapter 11, the information-gathering and policy-implementation tasks of the most important of the many government organizations involved in the foreign policy-making process will be considered. Although foreign policy making is primarily an executive function, the structural characteristics of the foreign affairs government, which define authority and divide the labor among those responsible for the making and execution of foreign policy, influence presidential decisions and policy performance. The impact of this structure therefore requires examination.

Finally, in Chapter 12, we will examine the governmental sources included in the third concentric circle by examining the policy-making role of Congress.

Here we will explore how the separation of powers—and the sharing of power by separate institutions—is related to foreign policy outcomes.[1]

FOREIGN AFFAIRS AND THE CONSTITUTION

The president's preeminent position in the foreign affairs government derives in part from the authority granted the office by the Constitution. It also flows from the combination of judicial interpretation, legislative acquiescence, personal assertiveness, and custom and tradition that have transformed an otherwise coequal branch of the federal government into the most powerful office in the world.

The Constitution specifically grants the president remarkably few powers with respect to foreign affairs. Article II provides that the president shall have the power, upon the advice and consent of the Senate, to make treaties and to appoint ambassadors and other public ministers and consuls, whereas a later section authorizes the president to receive ambassadors and other ministers. There is little else that deals explicitly with matters of foreign policy.[2]

But the totality of presidential power is much greater than that governing treaties and ambassadors. The Constitution also makes the president the commander in chief of the nation's armed forces,[3] and practice has transformed the president's designation as the nation's chief executive officer into its leading legislative officer. Moreover, the courts have repeatedly conferred on the president a broadly (if ambiguously) defined foreign affairs power by making the president "sole organ" of the nation in its conduct of external affairs.

Those provisions and interpretations have combined with practice to ensure, over time, presidential supremacy in the formulation as well as execution of American foreign policy. Thus the foreign policy of the United States is what the president says it is. And the president says what it is by concluding treaties and other executive agreements with foreign nations; by making public declarations; by recognizing or not recognizing new governments overseas; by

---

1. Because interest groups, the general public, and the mass media were discussed in the two preceding chapters, attention in Chapter 12 to Hilsman's outermost concentric circle will be confined to Congress. This division follows naturally from the organizing framework for the examination of the sources of American foreign policy that structures this book. Whereas some have argued that Congress in particular is the target of intense "lobbying" by the nongovernmental forces elaborated in the two preceding chapters, the governmental-nongovernmental distinction is an important one conceptually. Hence Congress is treated within the governmental source category rather than the societal source category.

2. The absence of additional constitutional provisions led Louis Henkin (1972) to observe, "It seems incredible that these few meager grants support the most powerful office in the world and the multi-varied, wide-flung webwork of foreign activity of the most powerful nation in the world."

3. Arthur Schlesinger (1989a) observes that whereas the president was designated commander in chief of the armed forces, the framers of the Constitution saw this "as conferring a merely ministerial function not as creating an independent and additional source of executive authority." As we will see in Chapter 12, this presidential power has figured prominently in the executive-legislative dispute over war powers, especially since the Vietnam war.

attending international conferences; by deploying military power here or there; by encouraging or denouncing the actions of other nations, and so forth.

If the president's foreign affairs powers have turned out to be enormous, those granted Congress in the Constitution were substantial from the start. Indeed, "the specific grants of authority to the executive in foreign policy were trivial compared with the authority specifically granted to Congress" (Schlesinger, 1989a). The Constitution authorizes Congress to deal with the regulation of international commerce, the punishment of piracies and felonies committed on the high seas and offenses against the law of nations, and declarations of war. Congressional power to appropriate funds from the treasury and to tax and spend for the common defense and the general welfare have also proven tremendously important for the conduct of foreign affairs. And the general legislative powers assigned to Congress grant it nearly limitless authority to affect the flow and form of foreign relations.[4]

The Constitution—often described as an invitation for struggle between the executive and legislative branches of government—is not sufficient in itself to explain the distribution of decision-making authority over foreign affairs shown in Figure 10.1. Authority has derived as well from the ability of the president to act assertively and decisively in the crisis-ridden atmosphere of the post-World War II period. The widely shared consensus that the international environment demanded an active American world role also contributed to the feeling that strong presidential leadership in foreign policy was needed. Together, those factors gave rise to what Arthur M. Schlesinger, Jr. (1973) labeled an "imperial presidency."[5] Moreover, the forces giving rise to the increased power of the presidency went largely unchallenged. The Vandenburg Resolution (1949), in which Congress supported a permanent American alliance with European nations (which later became the North Atlantic Treaty Organization [NATO]), and the Formosa Straits (1955), Middle East (1957), Cuban (1962), Berlin (1962), and Gulf of Tonkin (1964) resolutions, in which Congress gave the president broad power to deal with external conflict situations, fostered presidential supremacy by demonstrating a unity of purpose between the president and Congress. The ascendancy of presidential power in foreign policy making came about not so much because presidents seized power as because Congress itself encouraged executive leadership.

---

4. For details see Henkin (1972: 67–88). See also Henkin (1987–1988) and Schlesinger (1989a) for additional comments on the relative balance of constitutional foreign policy powers in favor of Congress rather than the executive.

5. Theodore Lowi disagrees with the view that the imperial presidency was a radically new departure:

> Schlesinger chose the characterization *imperial* because it connotes a strong state with sovereignty and power over foreigners, as well as rank, status, privilege, and authority, and it also connotes the president's power and responsibility to do whatever he judges necessary to maintain the sovereignty of the state and its ability to keep public order, both international and domestic. The imperial presidency turns out on inspection, therefore, to be nothing more nor less than the discretionary presidency grounded in national security rather than domestic government. (Lowi, 1985b: 189)

But challenges to presidential preeminence grew in the 1960s and early 1970s, fed by discontent with executive policy in Vietnam, the Watergate affair, and revelations of abuses by the intelligence community. In reaction, congressional authority began to be reasserted by those at the other end of Pennsylvania Avenue. Of particular concern was the question of control over American commitments and the president's war powers. The result (discussed in detail in Chapter 12) was a series of assertions of legislative authority that sought to circumscribe the executive's authority: the National Commitments Resolution (1969), the repeal of the Gulf of Tonkin Resolution (1970), the Case Act (1972), and the War Powers Resolution (1973), to name a few. Those congressional assertions have made it more difficult for presidents to initiate war single-handedly and have otherwise circumscribed their foreign policy latitude. But none has removed— and none is likely to remove—the president from the pivotal position in the foreign affairs government. Power remains concentrated in the White House.

It is instructive, in this respect, that the Supreme Court has not sought to resolve the executive-congressional dispute over war powers and related issues because it considers the issues involved to be political rather than legal. Two recent cases reaffirm a long-standing tradition.

In May 1981 several members of Congress brought suit against President Ronald Reagan[6] on grounds that he had violated the Constitution and the War Powers Resolution by sending military advisers to El Salvador. The suit was dismissed with the ruling that a determination of whether U.S. forces in El Salvador were involved in actual or potential hostilities was a political, not a judicial, finding. The ruling was later upheld by the Circuit Court, and the Supreme Court refused to hear the appeal. Six years later, when U.S. forces were involved in a reflagging operation designed to protect Kuwaiti shipping in the Persian Gulf, members of Congress again asked the court to enter the war powers fracas by declaring that the president was required to submit a report to Congress under the War Powers Resolution, but again the court concluded that the issue was a non-justiciable political question.[7]

The doctrine of political questions, which is a judicial construct, ensures that the outcome of the inevitable presidential-congressional tug-of-war therefore will be determined at any one time largely by the resources available to each branch of government. On balance, the resources available to the president are the more formidable, if not overwhelming, as the analysis that follows demonstrates.

THE INNERMOST CIRCLE: THE PRESIDENT AND THE PRESIDENT'S ADVISERS

Executive Organization and Foreign Policy

In principle, the president's greatest resource is the vast executive establishment. Most of the 3.2 million civilian employees of the federal government

---

6. *Crockett v. Reagan*, 558 F. Supp. 893 (D.D.C. 1982).

7. *Lowry v. Reagan*, 676 F. Supp. 333 (D.D.C. 1987).

TABLE 10.1 ▪ U.S. Government Foreign Affairs Personnel, 1984

Department or Agency	Number of Persons in Positions Related to Foreign Affairs
Department of State (U.S. citizens only)	13,500
United States Information Agency (USIA)	8,397
Agency for International Development (AID)	5,016
Arms Control and Disarmament Agency (ACDA)	170
Department of Agriculture	818
Department of Commerce	4,707
Department of Defense (persons with foreign affairs occupational specialties)	827
Department of Energy	127
Department of Labor	166
Department of Treasury	253
Export-Import Bank	327
International Trade Commission	436
National Security Council	56
Overseas Private Investment Corporation	140
Peace Corps (permanent paid staff)	880
United States Trade Representative	131
Total	35,951

SOURCE: Harry F. Young, Bureau of Public Affairs, U.S. Department of State, November 1985.

work in the executive branch, where collectively they bear responsibility for making and executing the full range of American domestic and foreign policies. What proportion of them is concerned primarily with foreign affairs is difficult to determine, however. One compilation, shown in Table 10.1, puts the number of foreign affairs personnel at 36,000. It also names the sixteen federal agencies with clearly identifiable foreign policy interests and activities.[8] But the list is potentially much longer. Another study done in the mid-1970s, for example, identified thirty different federal entities with American nationals employed in international activities (Clark, 1975: 222), and in 1989 the U.S.

---

8. Civilian employment in the Department of Defense stood at 1.1 million in 1989, and the number of military personnel was 2.1 million. A comparison of these numbers with the Department of Defense entry in Table 10.1 suggests how difficult it is to determine what proportion of the "national security establishment" should be considered a part of the foreign affairs government. The difficulty confounds not only the task of defining the foreign affairs government but also of determining who matters within it. The National Aeronautics and Space Administration's (NASA) space shuttle program is illustrative. Although NASA is charged with the peaceful exploration of outer space and has few explicitly overseas activities, the space shuttle has substantial military potential and has been financed in part by the Defense Department.

Office of Personnel Management (1989: 29–32) reported a total of 143,200 civilian employees working abroad for thirty-six executive branch departments and agencies. These compilations include such standards as the Departments of State and Defense (and "standardly" exclude the CIA); but they also identify some unexpected members of the foreign affairs government, including, for example, the Departments of Education and Transportation, the Environmental Protection Agency, the National Labor Relations Board, and the Small Business Administration. Indeed, over three-quarters of the agencies listed in the Office of Personnel Management tabulation are oriented primarily toward domestic policy issues.

For the most part, however, the executive *departments* of government, and the political appointees who head them, are at the core of the policy-making process, particularly the Departments of State and Defense. The former derives its importance from being "first among equals"[9] in the president's cabinet. The secretary of state, in principle at least, is deemed to be the president's foremost foreign policy adviser. In part that is because the State Department is the sole agency of government charged with coordinating the vast range of U.S. activities overseas; in part it is because the department houses the Foreign Service, the professional diplomatic corps of the United States. The tense international political environment of the postwar period, which directed primary emphasis toward military and defense considerations as they relate to foreign policy and national security, has made the Department of Defense especially important as well. The enormous size of the Pentagon, which commands a substantial share of every annual federal budget, gives the Department of Defense clout in a policy-making environment where money and personnel mean political influence.

The importance of the State and Defense Departments warrants more detailed attention; thus in Chapter 11 we explore the way in which they are organized so as to carry out their foreign affairs responsibilities. We will also give attention there to the intelligence community, because that community in general, and the CIA in particular, plays such a central role in the foreign affairs government. Finally, we will consider the responsibilities of some of the primarily domestic departments concerned with aspects of international economic affairs—Treasury, Commerce, Agriculture, and Labor—which have achieved importance in the foreign affairs government as a result of the expansion of American interests in an economically interdependent world. In this chapter we focus on the president and the presidency.

The Executive Office of the President

The president is nominally "boss" of the employees who staff the executive departments and agencies of the foreign affairs government. The president by no means controls them, however, a truism that led Richard Neustadt (1980) to

---

9. The term derives from the fact that the State Department was the first executive agency established under the Constitution in 1789.

describe the president's power as the "power to persuade." The interests of executive branch organizations are not necessarily synonymous with the interests of the president. The people who staff them have often held their positions long before any given president is elected, they are likely to hold them long after any one president leaves, and they frequently equate organizational survival with individual survival. To them the president often appears as a "transient meddler in their business" (quoted in Destler, 1974)—a view attributed to foreign policy professionals by an anonymous National Security Council (NSC) staffer, but one that many others would endorse.

If the president is viewed as a "transient meddler" in the affairs of established organizations, departmental bureaucracies are viewed from 1600 Pennsylvania Avenue as independent, unfamiliar, unresponsive, and inaccessible.

> They are suspected again and again of placing their own, congressional, or special-interest priorities ahead of those communicated to them from the White House. Even the President's own Cabinet members soon become viewed in the same light; one of the strengths of Cabinet members, namely their capacity to make a compelling case for their programs, has proved to be their chief liability with Presidents. (Cronin, 1973: 35)

For these reasons, members of the cabinet have often been described as a president's "natural enemies." Department chiefs become captives of the interests of the departments they administer and of the positions advanced by career bureaucrats within those agencies. And, because they are necessarily advocates for the departments they head, they are often in conflict with one another and sometimes directly with the president. And because cabinet decision making is usually the casualty, the phrase *perennial loser* describes the cabinet (Allison and Szanton, 1976).

Presidents Jimmy Carter and Ronald Reagan both pledged to involve the cabinet more intimately in policy development and implementation. Neither found it particularly useful for those purposes, however—President Reagan was even reported to have catnapped during cabinet meetings—but Reagan did seek better communication between cabinet officials and his White House staff through a series of cabinet councils consisting of selected cabinet heads and members of the White House staff. Initially, five councils were created. The number was reduced to two in Reagan's second term, the Economic Policy Council and the Domestic Policy Council. *Cabinet government* was sometimes used to describe the Reagan's administrative approach, but it is not entirely clear what that meant. "It is true that through the cabinet council system, the administration . . . developed a process for institutionalizing the involvement of the cabinet in routine decisions. However, as a group, the cabinet [did not penetrate] to the heart of presidential decision making" (Benze, 1987). Moreover, cabinet government may have suited Reagan's detached management style, but, as we will examine in detail below, it was also an important contributor to the single most important foreign policy failure of his administration, the Iran-*contra* scandal.[10]

Unlike his two predecessors, George Bush did not talk about cabinet government before assuming the reins of power, but he retained Reagan's economic and domestic policy councils, and six months into his presidency Bush was credited with having formed perhaps "the most influential cabinet since President Eisenhower in terms of the willingness of the president to give cabinet secretaries the latitude within which to operate in their jurisdictions." But "the influence of cabinet secretaries individually . . . did not extend to them as a collectivity," with cabinet meetings used more as briefing sessions than means of policy deliberation (Pfiffner, 1990).

The erosion of cabinet policy making stems in part from the fact that "the cross cutting nature of most presidential policy issues" require "advice from a broader perspective than that of individual department heads" (Pfiffner, 1990). In turn, every American president since World War II has relied increasingly on his own personal staff and the Executive Office of the President for advice and assistance in the development of policies and programs. A kind of presidential subsystem within the executive branch has resulted, which has often led to differences between the presidency, on the one hand, and the established bureaucracies, on the other.

The institutionalization of the presidency began with the Executive Reorganization Act of 1939, which authorized President Franklin D. Roosevelt to create the Executive Office consisting of the White House Office and the Bureau of the Budget. The former unit was to house the president's personal assistants, together with their staffs, while the latter, which was created in 1921 under the jurisdiction of the Treasury Department, ensured presidential control over budgetary matters and later over the president's entire legislative program. Since 1939 the Executive Office has come to include other offices and councils as well. The lists and labels have changed over time; in the Bush administration they included the Office of Management and Budget, the Office of Policy Development, the National Security Council, the Council of Economic Advisers, the Office of Science and Technology Policy, the Council on Environmental Quality, the Office of Administration, the Office of the United States Trade Representative, the Office of National Drug Control Policy, and the National Critical Materials Council.

The growth in the number of official bodies attached to the Executive Office, which has been matched by growth in personnel and funds, is indicative of the extent to which decision-making authority over substantive and operational matters has come to be concentrated in the White House. The institutionalized presidency "has become a powerful inner sanctum of government, isolated from traditional, constitutional checks and balances" (Cronin, 1984).

---

10. See the Tower Board report on the Iran-*contra* scandal, formally the *Report of the President's Special Review Board* (1987). Evaluations of Reagan's cabinet council system can be found in Benze (1987), Campbell (1986), and Pfiffner (1988).

Moreover, an enlarged White House staff designed to increase presidential control of the executive branch becomes "a screen" between the executive and legislative branches that "[cuts] off the President from the government and the government from the President. The staff becomes a shock absorber around the President, shielding him from reality" (Arthur Schlesinger, quoted in the *Wall Street Journal*, January 7, 1981).[11]

This tendency became glaring during the Nixon presidency. Whereas Roosevelt viewed his staff as a channel of communication between himself and his "line" departments and agencies, President Nixon held an entirely different view that led him to utilize his staff less as his "eyes and ears" throughout the government and more as an independent decision-making authority layered between himself and the rest of the executive branch. In contrast to the intent of the Executive Reorganization Act—that presidential assistants should not have power to make decisions in their own right—Nixon's staff became the center of decision making throughout the range of domestic and foreign affairs, and assumed powers that often made them more influential than members of the cabinet. Thus Henry Kissinger, when he was special assistant for national security affairs, was more powerful than the secretaries of state or defense, and H. R. Haldeman and John Ehrlichman, who figured prominently in the Watergate affair, were more powerful than domestic department heads.

Carter pledged that his presidency would never operate as Nixon's had, but he too came eventually to rely heavily on a small group of White House intimates. Similarly, Reagan relied heavily in his first term on a "troika" of key officials (White House counselor Edwin Meese, chief of staff James A. Baker, and deputy chief of staff Michael Deaver) and in his second term on a strong-willed chief of staff (Donald T. Regan). Most recently, the chief of staff in the Bush administration, John H. Sununu, emerged as a commanding, no-nonsense staffer who, in the words of Minnesota Representative Vin Weber, "really does dominate the decision-making process at the White House totally." In this sense each of the Nixon's four successors have followed a well-established trend.

Within the Executive Office the National Security Council is charged with foreign policy matters. It was as head of the NSC staff that Kissinger rose to be more powerful than the secretaries of state or defense. Others had occupied the special assistant post in previous administrations—Robert Cutler and later Gordon Gray under Eisenhower; McGeorge Bundy under John F. Kennedy; and Bundy and Walt W. Rostow under Lyndon B. Johnson. But none achieved the same level of prominence and influence in the foreign affairs government as did Kissinger. Zbigniew Brzezinski's dominance in the Carter administration was less overwhelming than Kissinger's, but he, too, emerged as his boss's key foreign policy adviser. President Reagan initially sought to downgrade the national security adviser's role, but the Iran-*contra* affair demonstrated that the NSC adviser and his staff had embarked upon operational activities that

---

11. See Cronin (1984) and Edwards and Wayne (1985) for additional views on trends in the presidential staffing system.

expanded the role of the NSC system in new and uncharted directions. Brent Scowcroft, President Bush's national security adviser, eschewed operational activities and pursued a role more akin to his pre-Reagan predecessors. Nonetheless, he played an active managerial role in an administration committed to lead with foreign policy as its strong suit.

Presidential preferences explain in part the variations in the way different presidents have drawn on and interacted with their in-house foreign policy advisers.[12] Simultaneously, however, it appears that all recent presidents, regardless of their initial predilections, have found it necessary to exert political control over foreign policy making by institutionalizing it within the White House. "The principal reason for the increasing concentration of foreign policy responsibility in the White House is our increasingly dangerous world," Theodore C. Sorensen (1987–1988), a White House staff member during the Kennedy administration, wrote in the wake of the Iran-*contra* scandal. "Since the days when Dean Acheson could serve as both secretary of state and Truman's personal adviser and coordinator, the overlap between national and international issues, the number and speed of thermonuclear missiles, and the foreign policy pressures from Congress, the press and public, have all mounted to a point where no president can conscientiously delegate to anyone his constitutional responsibilities in foreign affairs."

We can gain an appreciation of the way that presidential style and pressures to exert presidential control over foreign policy have led to its centralization in the White House through a historical examination of the way different presidents have used the National Security Council and its staff. In the process we will gain an understanding of what appears to have become an endemic problem: conflict between the White House and the State Department, and between the national security adviser and the secretary of state, for control over the direction of American foreign policy.

---

12. George (1988) has identified three different presidential management models: competitive, formalistic, and collegial. In the *competitive* model, the president purposely seeks to promote conflict and competition among his advisers, thus forcing problems to be brought to the president's attention for resolution and decision. Roosevelt is the only president to have clearly followed it. In contrast to Roosevelt's approach, a *formalistic* model seeks to establish clear lines of authority and to minimize the need for presidential involvement in the politicking among cabinet officials and key advisers. A chief of staff is often used as a buffer between the president and cabinet heads. Nixon's approach to presidential management took the formalistic model to its extreme, but Harry S. Truman and Eisenhower also followed it. Reagan likewise began with a preference for a formal, chief-of-staff operation with broad delegations of authority, but over time his approach took on some characteristics of the collegial model. Carter also embraced elements of the formalistic and collegial models. Kennedy provides the best illustration of the *collegial* model, which emphasizes teamwork and group problem solving. The president operates like the hub of a wheel with spokes connecting to individual advisers and department heads, who often act as "generalists" rather than "functional specialists" concerned only with parts of particular problems. Bush's style through the first two years of his administration was generally consistent with the collegial model.

THE NATIONAL SECURITY COUNCIL: ORGANIZATION AND EVOLUTION

The National Security Council was created by the National Security Act of 1947[13] to "advise the President with respect to the integration of domestic, foreign, and military policies relating to the national security." Statutory members of the council include the president (as chairman), the vice president, and the secretaries of state and defense. The director of the CIA and the chairman of the Joint Chiefs of Staff (JCS) are statutory advisers. Other participants have included the secretary of the treasury, the attorney general, the U.S. ambassador to the United Nations, the director of the Office of Management and Budget (OMB), heads of such organizations as the United States Information Agency (USIA) and the Agency for International Development (AID), and various presidential advisers and assistants, depending on the issues and presidential predilections.

The president is free to use the NSC as much or as little as he desires, and its deliberations and decisions are purely advisory. As the principal formal mechanism for coordinating the vast federal structure with a view toward producing a single, coherent foreign policy, the council has nevertheless proven useful in tackling problems faced by all presidents: acquiring information; identifying issues; coping with crises; making decisions; coordinating actions; and assuring agency compliance with presidential wishes.

The Early Years, 1947–1961

Although created during his administration, President Harry S Truman did not use the NSC extensively. Truman was fearful that the council might encroach on his constitutional prerogatives by imposing a parliamentary-type cabinet system over foreign policy decision making. He did not even attend NSC meetings prior to the outbreak of the Korean War in 1950, and the professional staff created to service the council remained on the periphery of Truman's relationship with his cabinet officers and departments. As a result, the council was confined to a purely advisory role.

With the outbreak of the Korean War, however, Truman recognized the need for better coordination of policy and action. He therefore directed that major national security policy recommendations come to him via the council. The famous NSC 68 memorandum (discussed in Chapter 5) is perhaps the best example of a major policy proclamation arising from Truman's NSC apparatus. By the end of his term, Truman had also begun using the NSC staff for interagency planning purposes. Both developments presaged the use to which Eisenhower put the NSC.

---

13. The National Security Act, as amended, also created the CIA, the Department of Defense, and the Joint Chiefs of Staff.

Coming from a professional background that emphasized the need for staff work and overall coordination, former General Eisenhower took the rudiments of the NSC structure inherited from Truman and transformed them into a highly formalized system that he viewed as "the central vehicle for formulating and promulgating policy" and "the primary means of imparting Presidential direction and over-all coherence to the activities of the departments and agencies" (Clark and Legere, 1969). A planning board and an operations coordinating board, both eventually chaired by the special assistant for national security affairs (the familiar position created by Eisenhower now called simply the assistant for national security affairs), became part of Eisenhower's NSC system. Those units were charged, respectively, with generating policy recommendations for consideration by the full NSC and with carrying out decisions once made.

For Truman, the National Security Council was primarily a supplementary advisory body. In contrast, Eisenhower sought to place the NSC mechanism at the center of the policy formulation process. Still, formal council meetings were often followed by more intimate "rump" sessions, or the president would convene meetings of a select group of advisers outside the formal NSC structure to deal with urgent matters,[14] a practice used extensively by President Kennedy.

Personalizing the Staff, 1961–1969

By the time Eisenhower left office, the highly institutionalized National Security Council system was being criticized as a "paper mill" that processed policies bearing little relevance to the real issues of the day. Critics also argued that the system tended to reduce, rather than expand, the range of alternatives available for presidential decision.[15] President Kennedy moved rapidly to correct these deficiencies. Shortly after his election in 1960 Kennedy appointed McGeorge Bundy his special assistant for national security affairs and announced that the purpose of Bundy's staff would be "to assist me in obtain-

---

14. These "rump" sessions may explain the apparent incongruity between Eisenhower's emphasis on the NSC system and the widespread belief that Secretary of State John Foster Dulles operated as the chief architect of American foreign policy during most of the Eisenhower years (in contrast, see Greenstein, 1982). Also important is the distinction between long-range planning, which was the primary purpose of the NSC, and day-to-day control of operational matters, which increasingly fell into Dulles's hands (Hoopes, 1973a). Dulles's biographer, Townsend Hoopes, also argues that the close working ties between Eisenhower and Dulles "compromised" Eisenhower's effort to use the NSC system to "orchestrate" the activities of the various foreign policy agencies into a coordinated foreign policy.

15. The hearings of the Jackson Subcommittee on National Security and International Operations of the Senate Committee on Government Operations, published in edited form in Jackson (1965), contain detailed information on both the operations and criticisms of the Eisenhower NSC system. Greenstein's (1982) analysis of the Eisenhower presidency also contains useful information on Eisenhower's NSC apparatus, and Henderson's (1988) recent evaluation of the system is generally more favorable than some earlier analyses.

ing advice from, and coordinating operations of, the government agencies concerned with national security.'' He also announced his intention to strengthen the role of the secretary of state in the area of interagency coordination.

Some observers questioned whether the new president, who had a deep personal interest in foreign affairs, truly wanted the State Department to assume a leadership role in the management of foreign affairs. In any event, insiders' accounts of the Kennedy administration (Hilsman, 1967; Schlesinger, 1965; Sorensen, 1965) indicate clearly that Kennedy was unhappy with the docile role assumed by Dean Rusk, Kennedy's choice as secretary of state, in an otherwise action-oriented administration. The State Department as an organization also proved too sluggish for White House officials. When this happened, the White House staff stepped into the perceived vacuum—not only Bundy's staff but also other members of Kennedy's personal ''team,'' almost all of whom were specifically recruited for his administration rather than drawn from careerists in established bureaucracies.

One of Kennedy's innovations was the use of interagency task forces designed to serve presidential needs rather than the agencies they represented. The 1961 Bay of Pigs fiasco, from which Kennedy learned ''never to rely on the experts'' (Schlesinger, 1965), contributed much to Kennedy's reliance on decision-making groups formulated for reasons other than the institutional affiliations of their members. The most celebrated was the so-called Ex Com (Executive Committee of the NSC), initially comprising some thirteen advisers on whom Kennedy relied heavily in devising a response to the installation of offensive Soviet weapons in Cuba in October 1962. Similar, but less well known, ad hoc groups dealt with the crises in Berlin and Laos, paramilitary experiments being tried in Vietnam, and covert intelligence operations directed against Cuba.

The inclusion of one of Bundy's staff or another presidential assistant was a distinguishing feature of all of those interagency groups. They functioned much more as personal advisers than as staff members belonging to the National Security Council. The importance of the NSC as an institution declined correspondingly. Although formal meetings of the full body were held to discuss long-term policy, the NSC itself was far less important in ensuring presidential control over the making and execution of foreign policy than were these less formal groups.

Kennedy's assassination in November 1963 brought to the White House a man with little interest and less experience in foreign affairs. But as the war in Vietnam escalated, Lyndon B. Johnson and his closest advisers devoted an increasing portion of their attention to Southeast Asia—to the point that by the end of Johnson's term little else seemed to command the energies of top-level decision makers.

The style of Johnson's approach to national security matters more closely resembled Kennedy's informal mode than Eisenhower's institutionalized operation. The NSC as a formal deliberative mechanism languished, a fact which, in the view of one of Johnson's critics, contributed to the Vietnam morass.

The decisions and actions that marked our large-scale military entry into the Vietnam War in early 1965 reflected the piecemeal consideration of interrelated issues, . . . the natural consequence of a fragmented NSC and a general inattention to long-range policy planning. Consultation, even knowledge of the basic facts, was confined to a tight circle of presidential advisers, and there appears to have been little systematic debate outside that group. (Hoopes, 1973b: 7)

The institutional manifestation of the tight inner circle came to be known as the Tuesday Lunch. The participants were the president, Secretaries Dean Rusk and Robert McNamara, the national security adviser (first McGeorge Bundy, then Walt W. Rostow, who replaced Bundy in 1966), and eventually the director of the CIA, the chairman of the JCS, and the president's press secretary. Vietnam was the principal luncheon topic, while the organization itself reflected the president's approach to the war—tight personal control coupled with organizational flexibility.

The cost of Johnson's approach was the exclusion of subordinates on whom the president and his close circle of advisers depended for implementation of top-level decisions. "The top men grew to live in one world, having loyalty primarily to each other, and seeing problems in a context that their subordinates could not understand because they were outside the charmed circle."[16] Contributing to the president's tight handling of the war was his "innate tendency to sniff treason within government walls" (Destler, 1974). The tendency was compounded by the increasingly vocal doubts about government policy that subordinates were suspected of having leaked to the press. Cut off from criticism from within, it took major policy setbacks, such as the enemy's unexpected Tet Offensive at the end of January in 1968 and the poor showing of the incumbent president some six weeks later in the New Hampshire primary, to force a reappraisal of Vietnam policy.

The role of Johnson's national security adviser changed with the appointment of Walt W. Rostow. Rostow continued to manage the flow of information to the president, to communicate presidential wishes to the bureaucracy, and to provide policy analysis and advice. But he did much less in the way of encouraging the free flow of ideas and alternatives to the president than had his predecessor. The result was distrust by governmental agencies of Rostow's ability to present objectively departmental viewpoints to Johnson.[17]

The White House Ascendant, 1969–1981

Noncoherence describes the policy-making legacy Nixon inherited from a divided and demoralized Johnson administration in January 1969. Although the outgoing administration had not been without positive achievements in

---

16. It is useful to note how different this experience was compared with the typical experience presidents have had with their cabinet secretaries, who have come to be viewed as captives of their organization's particular interests.

foreign policy, "its policy-making institutions, formal and informal, had little that would recommend them to its successor" (Destler, 1974).

Nixon moved rapidly to restore coherence by placing the NSC at the hub of the policy-making system. Henry Kissinger, the noted Harvard political scientist named as Nixon's special assistant for national security affairs, was directed to establish an "Eisenhower NSC system" but "without the concurrences" (Destler, 1974). It consisted of numerous top-level interagency committees—all directed by Kissinger—whose jurisdictions covered the entire waterfront of American foreign policy, from arms control negotiations with the Soviet Union (the Verification Panel), to crisis management (the Washington Special Actions Group), to covert operations (the 40 Committee, so named because of the National Security Decision Memorandum that set it up; the group had operated in previous administrations under various names—the Special Group, the 54-12 Group, and the 303 Committee). Their task was to develop alternatives for consideration by the president and the full NSC. Because Kissinger directed all of them, his role in the NSC system was pivotal.

The system fit Nixon's preferred operating style. In contrast to Eisenhower's approach (which encouraged the NSC system to focus on compromises among departments and agencies), and in contrast to the Kennedy and Johnson styles (which used NSC meetings as forums for its members to advocate views), "the Nixon approach was designed to bring all policy options to the table for *subsequent* consideration by the president and, above all, to maintain flexibility for the president" (Esterline and Black, 1975).

Kissinger's influence in the system derived in part from Nixon's preference for solo decision making. It was enhanced by the president's trust in him. Indeed, Kissinger (1979) himself has written that "in the final analysis the influence of a Presidential Assistant derives almost exclusively from the confidence of the President, not from administrative arrangements." He has also described cogently why the influence of presidential advisers seems to grow over time.

> Almost all of [a president's] callers are supplicants or advocates, and most of their cases are extremely plausible—which is what got them into the Oval Office in the first place. As a result, one of the President's most difficult tasks is to choose among endless arguments that sound equally convincing. The easy decisions do not come to him; they are taken care of at lower levels. As his term in office progresses, therefore, except in extreme crisis a President comes to base his choices more and more on the confidence he has in his advisers. He grows increasingly conscious of bureaucratic and political pressures upon him; issues of substance tend to merge in his mind with the personalities embodying the conflicting considerations. (Kissinger, 1979: 40)[18]

17. Hoopes (1973b) provides an especially critical view of Rostow's role in the development of America's Vietnam policy.

18. President Gerald R. Ford (1979) made a similar observation in commenting on why he eventually came to the conclusion he needed a chief of staff: "Because power in Washington is measured by how much access a person has to the President, almost everyone wanted more access that I had access to give."

In the particular case of Kissinger, the confidence Nixon reposed in him was reinforced by the national security adviser's spectacular diplomatic successes in the Middle East and elsewhere, which came at a time when the revelations of Watergate increasingly engulfed and paralyzed the Nixon presidency. The president's efforts to expand Kissinger's authority under such circumstances culminated in Kissinger's appointment as secretary of state, an assignment he held concurrently with his White House role and which placed him unambiguously at the pinnacle of the foreign affairs establishment as the chief architect of American foreign policy.

As Kissinger's personal influence rose, the elaborate NSC system he created was increasingly bypassed. The decisions that led to the 1970 Cambodia incursion, for example, were a product of "catch-as-catch-can" gatherings between Nixon and his advisers outside the formal NSC framework (Destler, 1974). Other major foreign policy initiatives involving China, the Middle East, and Vietnam also evolved outside the NSC system. The "back channel" to the Soviet leadership that Kissinger established is perhaps his most celebrated bureaucratic end-run. It led to a breakthrough in the strategic arms negotiations with the Soviets even while formal negotiations between the two sides' delegations (the "front channel") continued (see Talbott, 1979). Nothing could have made it clearer that Nixon and Kissinger counted much more than the Nixon-Kissinger NSC system. Instructively, Kissinger alone among Nixon's immediate advisers was able to survive the onslaught of Watergate.

One of Gerald R. Ford's first moves on the eve of his inauguration as the first nonelected president was to ask Kissinger to remain as his secretary of state and national security adviser. In that dual capacity Kissinger continued to operate what some felt was a one-person foreign policy show, a role made more apparent because it served a president who was a relative novice in international affairs.

Over time, however, Kissinger's star and the popularity of the policies he engineered began to wane. Much of the criticism came from the right wing of the president's own Republican party—pressure which prompted Ford to drop the word détente from his vocabulary. The president also acquiesced in the inclusion of a plank in the 1976 Republican platform advanced by Ronald Reagan's supporters that was widely interpreted as a repudiation of the incumbent president's foreign policy record. Jimmy Carter, the Democratic presidential nominee, made it clear that Kissinger, his style of operation, as well as some of his policies would be among the first victims of a Democratic victory.

Despite the campaign attacks he had launched against Kissinger's policies and operating style, President Carter's designation of Zbigniew Brzezinski as assistant for national security affairs (which came before he named his secretary of state), reaffirmed the determination of the White House to exercise foreign policy control. Two new NSC committees were created to replace all prior ones. One was the Policy Review Committee. Chaired by a member of the cabinet chosen on the basis of which department had the greatest stake in the issue, the Policy Review Committee was given responsibility for long-term projects.

Short-term projects (including covert intelligence operations and crisis management) were assigned to the Special Coordination Committee, chaired by Brzezinski. The committee eventually emerged as the most influential body within the NSC structure. Over time Brzezinski also emerged as the pivotal foreign policy adviser. Initially he was one of a "collegium" of key advisers that included Secretary of State Cyrus Vance, Secretary of Defense Harold Brown, and U.N. Ambassador Andrew Young. But Young resigned when his contacts with the Palestine Liberation Organization (in violation of established policy) were disclosed, and Vance resigned in the spring of 1980 to protest the president's abortive military rescue of American hostages in Iran.

Vance's resignation was the first time in sixty years that a secretary of state had resigned because of a policy dispute with the president. Although the immediate issue was Iran, the larger issue was conflict between the secretary and the president's national security adviser. Brzezinski stressed a hardline posture toward the Soviet Union and focused on the East-West conflict. Vance stressed détente and appeared more sensitive to North-South relations and global order issues. Carter never seemed able to reconcile the often conflicting thrusts of his principal advisers. Nor did the White House-State Department rift end with Vance's departure. Senator Edmund S. Muskie was chosen as Vance's successor; but he was barely confirmed in office when Carter signed Presidential Directive (PD) 59, which moved U.S. strategic doctrine in the direction of an explicit counterforce posture—and without ever consulting the new secretary of state. The subsidiary role of the State Department compared with the White House staff was affirmed once more.

The rift between Brzezinski and Vance perpetuated what by 1980 had become a recurrent concern. Should the national security adviser be primarily a manager of the decision-making process or primarily a personal adviser to the president and the "resident intellectual"? And what is the proper relationship between the national security adviser and the secretary of state?

Based on the experiences of the five presidents who occupied the Oval Office in the 1960s and 1970s, a degree of consensus emerged among practitioners and scholars as to what the national security adviser should—and should not—be doing (Destler, 1983b).[19] The national security adviser's activities may be viewed as falling along a continuum between, on the one hand, an "inside management" role, where the adviser essentially performs the role of facilitator, and, on the other hand, a "leadership" role, which often places the national security adviser in the potential position as a "second secretary of state." The thrust of the consensus that emerged toward the end of the Carter administration is that the national security adviser should emphasize the "inside" role and eschew the "outside." Exemplary tasks associated with each role are listed in Focus 10.1, which also suggests that some activities midway between the "inside" and "outside" orientations may be acceptable. (It should also be recognized, of course, that everyone may not agree with this list of *do's* and *don'ts*.)

---

19. See also "The National Security Adviser: Role and Accountability" (1980).

FOCUS 10.1 ▪ The National Security Assistant:
The Professionals' Job Description

YES ("Inside Management")	OK In Moderation	NO ("Outside Leadership")
Briefing the president, handling foreign policy in-box	Discreet advice/ advocacy	Conducting particular diplomatic negotia- tions
Analyzing issues and choices:	Encouraging advocacy by NSC staff sub- ordinates	Fixed operational assignments
a. Ordering informa- tion/intelligence	Information and "background" com-	Public spokesperson
b. Managing inter- agency studies	municating with press, Congress, for-	Strong, visible internal advocacy (except of already established
Managing presidential decision processes	eign officials	presidential priori- ties)
Communicating presidential deci- sions and monitor- ing their implemen- tation		Making policy deci- sions
General interagency brokering, circuit- connecting, crisis management		

SOURCE: I. M. Destler, "The Rise of the National Security Assistant," pp. 260–281 in Charles W. Kegley, Jr., and Eugene R. Wittkopf (eds.), *Perspectives on American Foreign Policy: Selected Readings* (New York: St. Martin's, 1983), p. 262.

The argument in favor of the insider rather than outsider orientation is essentially twofold.

First, the assistant's performance of "outside leadership" activities preempts or undercuts other senior presidential advisers and the formally responsible institutions, particularly the State Department and its secretary. Second, it compromises the "honest broker" reputation for balance necessary to performance of the "inside management" functions, most of which (unlike the functions in the right-hand column [of Focus 10.1]) are best handled from within the White House. (Destler, 1983b: 262–263)

The Reagan Administration: From Advocacy to Operations

Ronald Reagan arrived in Washington sensitive to the criticism of prior presidential foreign policy management systems and of the need to redress the balance between the White House and the State Department. Indeed, the new president had promised during his campaign to "restore leadership to U.S. foreign policy by organizing it in a more coherent way."

Reagan's choice of Alexander Haig as secretary of state was spotlighted as an indication of the president's desire to relocate primary control over foreign policy making in the State Department. The former NATO commander had been schooled in the ways of the White House as an assistant to Kissinger and later as chief of staff in the Nixon White House during its Watergate-embattled final days. Moreover, Reagan's implicit campaign pledge to downgrade the importance of the national security adviser's role was affirmed with the selection of Richard V. Allen for the position. Allen not only lacked the intellectual credentials of those who preceded him as national security adviser; he also was denied direct access to the Oval Office, assigned instead to report to the president through the president's White House counselor. Allen's subordinate status reflected his own conception of his assignment, which tracked the "inside management" rather than the "outside leadership" or "second secretary of state" role.

Haig played on Reagan's predilection to place the secretary of state at the forefront of the administration's foreign policy in a lengthy memorandum submitted on inauguration day that would have made him the administration's "foreign policy vicar" by assigning him a role in foreign affairs unprecedented since the days of John Foster Dulles. Haig was rebuffed, however, and no clearly defined organizational structure for the management of foreign policy emerged during the administration's first year, as it gave priority to domestic rather than foreign policy. Robert C. McFarlane, who became Reagan's national security adviser late in 1983, would later testify before Congress that the seeds of the Iran-*contra* scandal were sown in this environment, which was characterized by the absence of an organizational framework within which to engage in a "thorough and concerted governmentwide analysis" of critical foreign policy proposals. "In December 1981, when the CIA presented a proposal for initiating covert action in Nicaragua, there was no framework within which to analyze it," McFarlane testified. "It is immensely important to recognize just how crucial the absence of such a framework proved to be . . . For if we had such a large strategic stake [in Nicaragua], it was clearly unwise to rely on covert activity as the core of our policy." He elaborated by disclosing that people in the Reagan administration "turned to covert action because they thought they could not get Congressional support for overt activities. But they were not forced to think systematically about the fatal risks they were running" (cited in Henderson, 1988). In consequence, the most distinctive characteristic of the NSC system during the Reagan administration became its involvement in operational activities well outside the boundaries established by previous presidents and national security advisers.

An assertive national security adviser might have provoked critical thinking even in the absence of an effective organizational structure designed to promote it, but Allen proved unable to mediate disputes between others in the administration or to broker the competing interests of the bureaucracies comprising the foreign affairs government. Moreover, responsibility for crisis management, previously under the national security adviser's jurisdiction, was placed in the hands of the vice president, George Bush, and neither the NSC staff nor the structure that began to develop during 1981 proved effective. Allen's acceptance of $1,000 from a Japanese journalist set the stage for his replacement in early 1982 by William P. Clark, a former justice on the California Supreme Court then serving as deputy secretary of state. It was the first of what became many personnel changes among Reagan's key foreign policy advisers in an administration plagued by personality conflicts and internecine warfare.

The second casualty was Alexander Haig. Almost from the beginning, Haig became involved in a series of disputes on both organizational and policy matters with members of Reagan's White House staff, with seemingly everyone else in the administration, and with many outside it. Moreover, he seemed not to fit the collegial decision-making style preferred by the president. Haig did experience some initial foreign policy successes, and by and large he was the administration's key foreign policy official. But new disagreements between Haig and others in the administration over the issues of the Israeli invasion of southern Lebanon and the Soviet pipeline to bring Soviet natural gas to Western Europe led Reagan in June 1982 to accept the latest of Haig's threatened resignations.

When Clark first became national security adviser, he hewed to the "inside" description of the job, believing that he could serve as an honest broker for others in the foreign affairs government. It took him almost a year to conclude otherwise and to learn that "Cabinet secretaries are all parochial, so you've got to decide yourself what to do" (cited in Weisman, 1983). Thus he played an increasingly active role across a broad range of issues pertaining to national security policy, even asserting White House control over arms control policy in 1983 when disputes between the State and Defense Departments became overly intense (Lord, 1988).[20] He also enhanced the policy-making role of the NSC generally and increased the number of professional staff serving the council to a level greater than at any time since Kissinger's tenure (Destler, 1983a). Finally, unlike Allen, Clark himself enjoyed direct and frequent access to the president, thus short-circuiting the "troika" of Baker, Deaver, and Meese that had stood between Allen and Reagan.

Clark held strongly conservative ideological convictions that led him to assume a staunchly anti-Soviet foreign policy posture. He believed, with Reagan, that the 1970s represented "a decade of neglect for the security needs of

---

20. See Talbott (1984) for an account of the disagreements and bureaucratic wars over arms control policy during the first Reagan administration.

the United States." Similarly, he advocated stepped-up United States military activity in Central America and was the strongest White House voice favoring increased military spending.

By the summer of 1983, Clark was widely regarded as having become the most influential foreign policy figure in the White House and was credited with having gotten Reagan more deeply involved in foreign affairs. But as the most conservative of the president's inner circle of advisers, he came into conflict with other, more pragmatic White House staffers, particularly Chief of Staff James A. Baker. The squabbling (especially on the issue of defense spending) may have contributed to Clark's sudden and unexpected departure for the Interior Department in October 1983.

Conservative supporters of Reagan saw the national security vacancy as an opportunity to press their policy preferences on the president, and lobbied on behalf of the candidacy of U.N. Ambassador Jeane Kirkpatrick. A committed Reaganite, Kirkpatrick had been a close ally of Clark and had occupied an unusually prominent position in the Reagan foreign policy establishment (she regularly attended of NSC meetings, for example). Baker was another serious candidate, but in the end Reagan chose "Bud" McFarlane. Although McFarlane lacked the academic and intellectual credentials of a Kissinger or Brzezinski, he was an experienced foreign affairs adviser, having served as an NSC staffer under Kissinger and Brent Scowcroft, as a member of the Senate Armed Services Committee staff, and as a troubleshooter for Secretary of State Haig. McFarlane's choice hewed closer to the "middle position" shown in Focus 10.1 than at any other time.

McFarlane inherited from Clark an elaborate NSC organizational structure, which was put into place by a National Security Decision Directive in January 1982. The framework was generally patterned on a plan devised by Johnson but never fully implemented because of the urgency of Vietnam. Three senior interdepartmental groups (SIGs) replaced the cabinet-level Policy Review Committee instituted by the Carter administration. The SIGs were to be chaired by the number-two persons in the State and Defense departments and by the director of central intelligence, with each responsible for conceptually distinct aspects of national security policy, namely, foreign policy, military and defense policy, and intelligence. Policy considerations were to be developed for the SIGs by interdepartmental groups headed by assistant secretaries.

The Reagan NSC system never functioned as it was intended (Lord, 1988). Instead, the real influence appears to have been lodged in the National Security Planning Group, a less formal network consisting of the president's closet personal advisers that emerged as a kind of "executive committee" of the NSC not unlike Johnson's Tuesday Lunch. Moreover, the president himself was largely detached from the foreign policy-making process, preferring instead a hands-off management style.

Few presidents were more passive in policy formulation. Only under great pressure would Reagan reluctantly intervene in his own process, and although in attendance, he apparently almost never chaired NSC meetings. Whereas Presidents Kennedy and Carter sometimes overinvolved themselves in substantive foreign policy matters, President Reagan was often underinvolved. Whereas Nixon overcentralized authority in the White House, Reagan delegated authority excessively, in what he called "cabinet government." . . . The consequent insufficient degree of White House-centralized discipline contributed to a perhaps unprecedented fragmentation of policy. (Clarke, 1989: 7)

The untoward effects of Reagan's lack of involvement and of his failure to utilize the formal policy-making structures that were in place were emphasized by the Tower Board's post mortem on the Iran-*contra* affair: "Established procedures for making national security decisions were ignored. Reviews of the initiative [toward Iran] were not adequately vetted below the cabinet level. . . . The whole matter was handled too informally, without written records of what had been considered, discussed, and decided" (*Report of the President's Special Review Board*, 1987).

The Iran initiative, as the Tower Board called it, included an attempted strategic opening to Iran, the sale of arms to Iran via Israel and by the United States itself in an effort to secure the release of hostages held in Lebanon, and, ultimately, the diversion of profits from the arms sales to the *contras* fighting the Sandinista regime in Nicaragua. The board concluded that the initiative "ran directly counter to the Administration's own policies on terrorism, the Iran/Iraq war, and military support to Iran." Its report went on to suggest how better use of existing structures might have averted the single most damaging foreign policy failure of the Reagan presidency.

At each significant step in the Iran initiative, deliberations among the NSC principals in the presence of the President should have been virtually automatic. . . . The meetings should have been preceded by consideration by the NSC principals of staff papers. . . . These should have reviewed the history of the initiative, analyzed the issues they presented, developed a range of realistic options, presented the odds of success and the costs of failure, and addressed questions of implementation and execution. Had this been done, the objectives of the Iran initiative might have been clarified and alternatives to the sale of arms might have been identified. (*Report of the President's Special Review Board*, 1987: IV-4)

The origins of the clandestine Iran initiative can be traced to 1984 when McFarlane launched an interagency evaluation of U.S. relations with Iran. Eventually, McFarlane secretly visited Teheran armed with a cake shaped like a key and a Bible signed by the president. National security advisers had undertaken secret diplomatic initiatives in the past (technically McFarlane traveled to Iran on behalf of the president and the NSC staff, since by then he had resigned as national security adviser), but as the Iranian affair unfolded it took the NSC staff in a wholly new direction. The record indicates, for example, that Secretary of State George Shultz and Secretary of Defense Caspar Weinberger vigorously opposed the transfer of arms to Iran,[21] that key covert action findings that authorized the arms-for-hostages swap were approved by the president without their knowledge, and that John Poindexter, who succeeded McFarlane as national security adviser in late 1985, authorized the transfer of arms profits to the *contras* without the president's knowledge.[22] Congress was also kept in the dark about what had become a covert operation run out of the White House in apparent contravention of the law, and it was fed false and misleading information by key players in the game, notably McFarlane, Poindexter, and Poindexter's assistant, Lt. Colonel Oliver North (see also Chapter 12).

McFarlane enjoyed some successes as national security adviser, especially in breaking the long deadlock within the administration on arms control policy, but he resigned in late 1985 after becoming "overwhelmed by 'Cabinet government.'"

> He lacked the standing with Reagan to resolve the interminable struggles between Shultz and Weinberger that the president was unable or unwilling to settle himself. His authority dwindled even more after chief of staff Baker switched jobs with Treasury Secretary Donald T. Regan at the beginning of the second term. Regan was jealous of his prerogatives and made it clear to McFarlane and his successor, Rear Adm. John M. Poindexter, that he was first fiddle. An NSC staff member, looking back on what happened, says that Reagan "doubly diminished" the national security adviser's post by subordinating it first to the Cabinet, and then to the White House chief of staff.[23] (Cannon, 1988: 7)

Regan was forced to resign in February 1987 shortly after the Tower Board issued its report on the Iran initiative, in which it charged that Regan, "more than any other Chief of Staff in recent memory, . . . asserted personal control over the White House staff and sought to extend this control to the National Security Advisor."

> He was personally active in national security affairs and attended almost all of the relevant meetings regarding the Iran initiative. He, as much as anyone, should have insisted that an orderly process be observed. In addition, he especially should have ensured that plans were made for handling any public disclosure of the initiative. He must bear primary responsibility for the chaos that descended upon the White House when such disclosure did occur. (*Report of the President's Special Review Board*, 1987: IV-11).[24]

---

21. In testimony before Congress on the Iran-*contra* affair, Shultz described his battle with Poindexter and CIA director William Casey for control over policy making as "guerrilla warfare." He reported that at one point disputes with the White House and intelligence community caused him to submit his resignation as secretary of state.

22. See Henderson (1988) for details on the role of the NSC in the Iran-*contra* affair.

23. The Baker-Regan job switch impacted the national security adviser in another way. An NSC senior interdepartmental group responsible for international economic policy had been created during Clark's tenure, but it was abolished in April 1985 in favor of a new Economic Policy Council chaired by the new treasury secretary.

24. Regan (1988) responded to the charge in his book *For the Record*, by saying "[this paragraph] is mistaken in its assumptions, defective in its evidence, and wrong in its conclusions."

Early assessments of Poindexter's stewardship at the NSC were generally positive, but Poindexter raised another question when he remained on active military duty as a naval admiral. The fear was that placing a military officer in a traditionally civilian policy role might contribute unduly toward a military approach to political problems. The Iran-*contra* affair reinforced the concern, and it was raised again when Lt. General Colin Powell was appointed to succeed Frank C. Carlucci, who had replaced Poindexter following the admiral's forced resignation. Interestingly, Powell's appointment came on the very day that the congressional committees investigating the Iran-*contra* affair voted to recommend that the president's national security adviser "not be an active military officer" (cited in Clarke, 1989). Concern about the status of the national security adviser paralleled concern over whether the NSC staff may not also have become too dependent on professional military personnel.

Midway through the Reagan presidency, an insightful book on the politics of American foreign policy making described the competition between the White House and the State Department as a contest between "courtiers" and "barons," between those "in the White House who gain influence by responding to [presidents'] personal needs and their political priorities," in contrast to senior officials "in formal charge of an important domain within the presidential realm," principally cabinet-level agencies such as the State and Defense Departments. A principal cause of the shift in power from the barons to the courtiers, the authors argue, "has been the triumph of politics and ideology over foreign policy."

> Presidents use foreign policy more frequently for political reasons: Presidents increasingly head political factions committed to distinct, even ideological, policy positions, which they seek to implement once they are in office. This increases their distrust of the bureaucracy and drives them to pull policy control into their own White House. (Destler, Gelb, and Lake, 1984: 237)

Moreover, these experts aver that "greater fluctuation in policy content" has been a consequence of greater dependence on White House courtiers, which "has also made the policy process more personality-dependent, and thus more idiosyncratic, since staff aides are less constrained than Cabinet barons. It has, finally, both encouraged and enabled Presidents to seize personal control of current policy operations" (Destler, Gelb, and Lake, 1984; see also Bock, 1987).

Some elements of the Iran-*contra* affair fit the courtier-baron distinction, but overall it does not lend itself easily to an analysis in these terms, for it was as much a misuse of executive power as it was a competition between the institutionalized presidency and the bureaucratic domains comprising the foreign affairs government. The NSC had become a "government within a government" spurred on by "presidential inattentiveness, ideological fervor, frustration with a Congress that seemed determined to micromanage foreign policy, and the desire of the . . . chief of central intelligence . . . to find an operational channel less vulnerable to congressional scrutiny than the CIA" (Cannon, 1988). Perhaps the "mistakes of the Iran-Contra affair" are best viewed as merely "mistakes in judgment, and nothing more"—as the Republican minority concluded in the congressional report on its investigation of the affair—or merely an "aberration"—as John Tower concluded. Nonetheless, the affair perpetuated what has become an ongoing debate about the role of the White House in the foreign policy-making process and about the characteristics and consequences of the concentration of power in the institutionalized presidency. And it reaffirmed the truism that an effective process is critical to a sound policy. "Issues come and go," observed Colin Powell. "Process is always important."[25]

When Carlucci succeeded Poindexter as national security adviser, he moved quickly to repair the damage the Iran-*contra* affair had inflicted on the NSC system. He replaced about half of the NSC staff, which reportedly had grown to nearly two hundred (Cannon, 1988: 8), abolished the political-military bureau that had been headed by Oliver North, replaced the senior interdepartmental groups with a new Policy Review Group (chaired by the deputy national security adviser, Colin Powell), and received assurances of direct access to the president (Lord, 1988). Reagan in turn signed an order prohibiting further covert operational activities within the NSC.

Powell took over the national security adviser's position in December 1987 when Carlucci replaced Weinberger as secretary of defense. Under his and Carlucci's tutelage, the NSC played an important and positive role in preparing for the Washington and Moscow summits, and the national security adviser once more emerged as an effective facilitator of the foreign affairs policy process (see Kirschten, 1987; Cannon, 1988). "We set out to restore the credibility of the institution, to restore it to its proper role as an interagency body," observed Carlucci. "That is its 'honest broker' role, and we set out to reestablish it. We took the NSC out of operations."

Current History: The Bush Administration

Colin Powell returned to active military duty at the end of the Reagan administration and was later named chairman of the Joint Chiefs of Staff by President Bush. From that vantage point he oversaw the U.S. invasion of Panama in December 1989. There was irony here in that Powell as national security adviser had been involved in the Reagan administration's earlier efforts to force Panamanian strongman Manuel Noriega from power (but had then cautioned against the use of force for that purpose).

Powell was only one of many old faces to reappear in the new administration. Among them was a new "troika" of foreign policy officials: James Baker,

---

25. The problem with the NSC system during the Reagan presidency, it may be argued (Hess, 1988), was not the system itself but the quality of those who were at the head of it: "Reagan was to have six NSC advisers during his two terms and the first four—Allen, Clark, Robert McFarlane, and John Poindexter—were not of the quality of previous occupants of the office, who had tended to be distinguished academics. . . . The cause of the Iran-Contra scandal did not lie in the NSC's institutional shortcomings but in the men who worked there."

Dick Cheney, and Brent Scowcroft. Baker became secretary of state. Earlier he had resigned as Reagan's secretary of the treasury to run Bush's election campaign, just as he had once run Ford's. Cheney became secretary of defense after Bush failed to win Senate approval of former Senator John Tower for the job. Earlier Cheney, too, had served President Ford, as chief of staff. Scowcroft became national security adviser. He had served President Ford in that capacity and was, along with Tower and Edmund Muskie, a member of the Tower Board that investigated the Iran-*contra* affair.

Not only were the three seasoned practitioners of the art of governance; they were also close personal friends, and their experience in the Ford administration (in which Bush served as CIA director), when détente was still in its heyday, gave them a common reference point in coping with the fast-paced changes in Soviet-American relations during the Bush presidency. Baker and Scowcroft also agreed at the outset that "Baker would have the lead on foreign policy, Scowcroft and the NSC would have no operational role and Scowcroft himself would be a low-profile 'honest broker' within the administration." With this they hoped to avoid "niggling disagreements over public speeches, television interviews, ambassadorial visits and the like" (Gergen, 1989), which are precisely the things over which the turf battles between the secretary and state and the national security adviser had been fought in the past.

As a member of the Tower Board, Scowcroft had been an outspoken critic of the NSC operations that led to the Iran-*contra* scandal. He could therefore be expected to seek involvement of the secretaries of state and defense in the policy process and to maintain close contact with the president. The structure of the Bush administration's National Security Council system, illustrated in Figure 10.2, was designed to promote those objectives. The system is somewhat more streamlined at the top than that of previous presidents, but otherwise reveals similar patterns. The Principals Committee consists of the national security assistant (as chair), the secretaries of state and defense, the director of central intelligence, the chairman of the Joint Chiefs of Staff, and the president's chief of staff, with the attorney general and treasury secretary participants when the issues so require. The Principals Committee is charged with reviewing, coordinating, and monitoring the development and implementation of national security policy.

The Deputies Committee, positioned below the Principals Committee in the hierarchy, is the senior sub-cabinet interagency forum for consideration of policy issues. Its members are from the under secretary ranks in the organizations identified above. It, in turn, is served by a series of NSC policy coordinating committees responsible for various geographic regions and functional activities. The committees parallel the interdepartmental groups of previous administrations in both structure and function. Membership on the policy coordinating committees is drawn from the assistant secretary rank, whose tasks include identification and development of policy issues for consideration by the National Security Council.

The key question, of course, is whether the Bush NSC system will be used as intended. The experience of virtually every president since Eisenhower

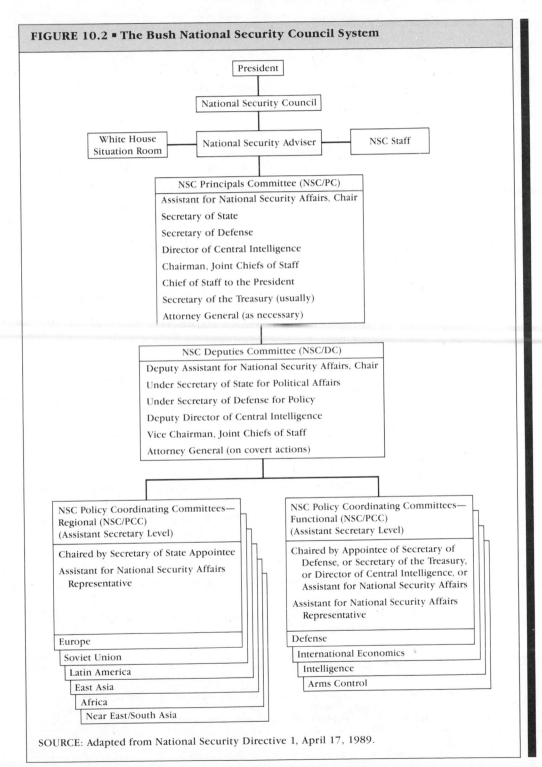

FIGURE 10.2 ▪ The Bush National Security Council System

President

National Security Council

White House Situation Room — National Security Adviser — NSC Staff

NSC Principals Committee (NSC/PC)
Assistant for National Security Affairs, Chair
Secretary of State
Secretary of Defense
Director of Central Intelligence
Chairman, Joint Chiefs of Staff
Chief of Staff to the President
Secretary of the Treasury (usually)
Attorney General (as necessary)

NSC Deputies Committee (NSC/DC)
Deputy Assistant for National Security Affairs, Chair
Under Secretary of State for Political Affairs
Under Secretary of Defense for Policy
Deputy Director of Central Intelligence
Vice Chairman, Joint Chiefs of Staff
Attorney General (on covert actions)

NSC Policy Coordinating Committees—Regional (NSC/PCC)
(Assistant Secretary Level)
Chaired by Secretary of State Appointee
Assistant for National Security Affairs Representative

Europe
Soviet Union
Latin America
East Asia
Africa
Near East/South Asia

NSC Policy Coordinating Committees—Functional (NSC/PCC)
(Assistant Secretary Level)
Chaired by Appointee of Secretary of Defense, or Secretary of the Treasury, or Director of Central Intelligence, or Assistant for National Security Affairs
Assistant for National Security Affairs Representative

Defense
International Economics
Intelligence
Arms Control

SOURCE: Adapted from National Security Directive 1, April 17, 1989.

demonstrates is that the NSC system can easily fall into disuse. The Iran-*contra* affair demonstrates that it can also be misused.

OTHER EXECUTIVE OFFICE FUNCTIONS: MANAGING ECONOMIC AFFAIRS

Before leaving the presidential subsystem, brief mention should be made of other units within the Executive Office that, together with the NSC, are at the immediate disposal of the president, and thereby contribute to presidential preeminence in foreign policy making.[26]

Managing the Budget

The largest of all, with roughly six hundred staff members, is the Office of Management and Budget (OMB). OMB has responsibility for reviewing budgetary and other legislative requests coming from departments and agencies and for examining legislation passed by Congress before it is signed into law by the president. It also assists in devising plans for the organization and management of executive branch functions. Those tasks assign OMB a potentially critical voice in ensuring that agencies' plans and programs are consistent with presidential priorities.

Different presidents have employed different budgetary and management techniques to realize their objectives. In the early 1960s Robert McNamara introduced the Planning, Programming, and Budgeting System (PPBS) into the Defense Department as a procedure for making more informed budgetary choices and evaluating military operations.[27] Lyndon Johnson later ordered that the Bureau of the Budget (as OMB was then called) apply PPBS throughout the government. President Nixon emphasized the concept of "management by objective," which entailed assigning priorities to various objectives over others and choosing some programs over others.

As the 1970s wore on, concern for restraining public spending mounted. In response, Jimmy Carter implemented zero-base budgeting (ZBB), which he had first employed as governor of Georgia. ZBB is a management technique that requires each program to be justified anew each year when money is being requested. It did not prove effective in stemming the flow of public spending, however.

Fueled in part by the priority the Reagan administration gave to rebuilding the nation's defensive posture, budget deficits by the mid-1980s topped

---

26. We will return in Chapter 11 to the CIA, which has roots in, but extends beyond, the Executive Office of the President.

27. See Puritano (1985) for an insider's view of the operation of PPBS at the Defense Department midway through the Reagan administration, and Art (1989) for a discussion of the impact of defense reorganization on Pentagon budgeting processes during the latter part of the Reagan administration.

$200 billion annually and the national debt inched toward $1.5 trillion as the United States became the world's largest debtor nation. President Reagan turned to the Office of Management and Budget to effect budget cuts in domestic programs alongside the administration's supply-side[28] economics in an effort to cope with the deficit problem. It enjoyed some successes, but when it came to trimming the largest and most important foreign affairs item in the budget—national defense—OMB found that other players in the game led with a stronger suit.

As defense spending surged during the 1980s, it was perhaps inevitable that evidence of lax administrative management would surface. Revelations that the Pentagon had paid as much as $1,050 for oil plugs, $640 for toilet seats, and $450 for hammers available at local hardware stores for fractions of those amounts fueled concern about the costs of security (McNaugher, 1989). Understandably, the Reagan administration, which came to Washington committed to curbing government excesses, was embarrassed. Reagan appointed a blue-ribbon panel, known as the Packard Commission,[29] to investigate the charges of procurement mismanagement and abuse. The commission confirmed what had already been revealed through congressional hearings and press coverage and concluded that defects in the application of PPBS within the Defense Department itself contributed to the problem.

In principle, OMB ought to have made the Pentagon tow the line, but for a variety of reasons, as a former associate director of OMB has observed, "OMB imposes far less discipline on the DOD [Department of Defense] budget, and thus on national security decision making, than it does on domestic budgets and decision making" (Szanton, 1985). Among the reasons is the natural tendency of the Pentagon to overestimate threats to the nation's security, which often translates into excessive budgetary requests. OMB is disinclined to challenge such requests because it is likely to lose, for several reasons.

> Directly or indirectly, defense programs employ roughly 1 out of every 10 workers in the United States, and Department of Defense contracts reach suppliers and installations in virtually every congressional district. Inevitably, then, defense programs generate lives and momenta of their own. Bases no longer needed by the army may be politically impossible to close; aircraft not requested by the air force may be procured nonetheless at congressional insistence. To challenge the defense budget, therefore, is to challenge a steamroller. (Szanton, 1985: 107)

Rather than challenge a steamroller, the politically wise strategy is to trim at the margins—a strategy no less astute as the Soviet empire crumbles than

---

28. *Supply-side* economics refers to the assumption that economic growth will be stimulated by reducing government spending and taxation. Supply-side economists argue that by increasing incentives in the private sector, worker productivity and employment will increase and the rate of inflation will decrease. Increased government revenues will result, which will offset any tax reductions.

29. Its report was issued in 1986 under the title *A Quest for Excellence: Final Report to the President by the President's Blue Ribbon Commission on Defense Management*.

before—rather than launch a frontal attack. The result, however, is that OMB is considerably less effective in imposing a presidential imprimatur on the nation's foreign policy spending priorities than might otherwise be expected.

Managing International Economic Policy

Another presidential unit involved in the budgetary process is the Council of Economic Advisers (CEA), which, together with officials from OMB and the Treasury Department, makes economic forecasts on which the income and expenditures of the federal government are based. The CEA has not assumed operational responsibilities, however, serving instead exclusively as a staff arm of its "client," the president (Porter, 1983). The council itself comprises three presidential appointees, usually drawn from the ranks of the most respected academic economists, one of whom is typically assigned international responsibilities. Probably the most important function of the council is the preparation of the influential *Economic Report of the President* presented annually to Congress. More generally, the responsibility to advise the president on economic matters involves the CEA in a variety of policy considerations (such as taxes, commerce, national productivity, and the balance of payments) that can have important foreign policy implications in an economically interdependent world.

As a practical matter, however, the CEA historically has been oriented more toward domestic than international economic questions. That fact has led presidents to devise different means of ensuring top-level coordination of international economic policy making. President Nixon created a Council on International Economic Policy in an unsuccessful effort to achieve dominance in international economic policy making similar to what the National Security Council and its staff has achieved in the foreign policy area. Neither Ford nor Carter emulated Nixon's efforts to create an Executive Office unit with responsibility for international economic affairs, but both found necessary some type of top-level coordinating mechanism to effect policy coherence and control as America's role in the international political economy grew. Ford created an Economic Policy Board chaired by the secretary of the treasury whose purpose was to oversee the entire range of foreign and domestic economic policy. Carter followed with a similarly structured Economic Policy Group. Its form and composition changed over time, but it never achieved the same degree of success as Ford's Economic Policy Board. Carter eventually came to rely on a special presidential representative to facilitate the coordination of international economic policy making. During the Reagan administration the Cabinet Council on Economic Affairs was given responsibility over economic policy, and the administration's NSC apparatus eventually contained a Senior Interagency Group for International Economic Policy. The secretary of the treasury chaired both groups, which contained many of the same participants. The common element among all of the presidents since Nixon is that they have perceived the need for top-level coordination of international economic policy making but have eschewed the use of general purpose, formal entities to exercise economic policy-making control (Porter, 1983). The Bush administration's designation of an NSC policy coordinating committee for international economics (chaired by an assistant secretary of the treasury) conforms to this general pattern.

Managing Trade Policy

Another White House agent involved in managing foreign economic affairs is the Office of the United States Trade Representative (USTR), whose origins date to the Kennedy administration. Headed by a presidential appointee who carries the rank of ambassador as well as membership in the cabinet, the USTR exercises primary responsibility for developing and coordinating the implementation of international trade policy and acting as the principal trade spokesperson in the U.S. government. The office is responsible for directing American participation in trade negotiations with other nations, such as the Uruguay Round of trade negotiations initiated in 1986 under the aegis of the General Agreement on Tariffs and Trade (GATT), and in other international forums such as the United Nations Conference on Trade and Development (UNCTAD) and the Organization for Economic Cooperation and Development (OECD).

The trade representative's role in setting and managing trade policy was enhanced during the Carter administration, when Robert Strauss played a key role in bringing the Tokyo Round of multilateral trade negotiations to successful conclusion. Strauss was particularly successful not only in promoting American interests internationally but also in negotiating with important affected industries in the United States and in placating congressional concerns. The result was a reorganization of the trade office in 1980 that gave it a greater voice among the many government agencies involved in determining overall U.S. trade policy.

President Reagan pledged that his trade representative would continue to play a dominant role in orchestrating the nation's trade policies, but as the nation's once preeminent position in the global trade network began to deteriorate in the early 1980s, he proposed creation of a new cabinet-level trade department, which would combine the roles of policy development (exercised by the U.S. Trade Representative) and policy implementation (exercised by the Commerce Department). The proposal was never pushed vigorously by the White House, and when it failed to win congressional support the matter languished (see Cohen, 1988). Thereafter the administration chose a generally benign approach to trade policy.

Congress, however, became increasingly agitated about the nation's accelerating trade imbalances and about the administration's unwillingness to undertake corrective action. In 1986 it began consideration of a new trade bill designed to deal with a wide range of issues underlying the nation's deteriorating position in the global trade regime. The measure finally came to fruition two years later in the form of a massive trade bill known as the Omnibus Trade and Competitiveness Act of 1988. The bill that finally passed both houses of Congress and won presidential approval contained no radical new departures from existing U.S. trade policy, despite the fact that during its long gestation period many highly protectionist measures figured prominently in the deliberations. The bill did, however, remove any ambiguity about where authority and responsibility over trade policy rest by statutorily lodging both in the USTR.

The new trade law also enhanced the role of the USTR in dealing with other nations. It grants the trade representative authority to decide whether foreign trade practices are "unfair"; requires it to take retaliatory actions against other nations in certain instances; and also requires it to identify foreign trade practices, and the countries who engage in them, that inhibit the growth of U.S. exports. All of these are controversial responsibilities from the point of view of other nations, but they effectively solidify the role of the USTR as the principal trade policy actor within the U.S. government in a way not previously done.

The record of White House efforts to coordinate foreign economic policy making is clearly a mixed one, and in no way matches its efforts to master foreign and national security policy making. As I. M. Destler (1980) argues, one explanation is the ambivalence various administrations have shown toward the *foreign* and *economic* aspects of the policy area. Such ambivalence necessarily brings one bureaucratic agency (such as the State Department) to the forefront of policy making at one time, another agency (such as the Department of Agriculture) at another. Without clear and consistent direction from the White House, interagency politics are likely to dominate the process and ultimately the outcome.

Why does the White House fail to give clear and consistent direction? Why, in other words, does it not dominate the outcome as overwhelmingly as it has sought to do in national security affairs? Two intersecting lines of reasoning seem plausible.

First, although the line between foreign and economic policy is often ambiguous, "the substance of most foreign economic policy issues relates more closely to domestic economic policy concerns than to foreign policy ones" (Porter, 1983). One consequence is that foreign economic policy making necessarily involves many organizations, whereas on national security matters the principal actors are often confined to the State and Defense Departments and the White House. International economic matters typically involve a much wider network: the Department of Agriculture on food policy, the Department of Commerce on trade issues, and the Department of the Treasury on monetary issues. Each of those agencies, in turn, has important domestic roots and networks and often powerful congressional allies. The number of actors the White House would have to control is therefore substantial, encompassing domestic as well as foreign interests. Moreover, those interests and the goals they reflect are usually in conflict. Withholding grain from the Soviet Union can deprive American farmers of an important overseas market; lowering trade barriers on imported autos can cost Detroit assembly-line workers their jobs; manipulating the value of the dollar abroad can affect the competitiveness of American goods in overseas markets and interest rates at home. For presidents to decide among the conflicting objectives and to achieve sustained control over such diverse foreign and interests requires a greater expenditure of political capital than most are willing to make. As the complex challenges of the interdependent global political economy become more potent, their management becomes more difficult and less rewarding politically.

Second, postwar presidents historically have emphasized the "high politics" of national security policy, not the "low politics" of foreign economic affairs. That emphasis reflects the perceived realities of the postwar political environment, where political and military challenges, particularly Soviet communism, were deemed foremost. For four decades economic issues were understandably treated as secondary to that overriding reality. Many of the policy problems of the 1970s seemed to challenge that pecking order, only to see it reassert itself during the 1980s. As the Soviet empire disintegrates, however, economic issues are likely to vie for top billing on the policy making agenda. This augurs well for a determined effort to assert White House control of foreign economic policy making in the 1990s, but the force of domestic politics will create inertia for leaving things as they are.

Because presidents are inherently political animals always with an eye toward either the next election or their place in history, no organizational framework for managing foreign economic policy is likely to emerge if the president determines its activities are detrimental to the president's own political fortunes. And since foreigners neither vote in American elections nor write American history books (at least ones widely read by Americans), it is likely that organizational adaptations will continue to be made but that in the area of foreign economic policy—where foreign and domestic politics overlap in important and fundamental ways—domestic political interests will typically dominate the politics of policy making.

PRESIDENTIAL PREEMINENCE AND PRESIDENTIAL POWER

Continued and direct White House involvement in matters of foreign policy beyond that which any president might manage personally has doubtless become a permanent feature of the institutional setting within which American foreign policy is made and executed. The reason is especially clear in matters of "high politics": with so much at stake in the nuclear age, the president cannot afford to let someone else decide. To the extent that the United States seeks to exercise control over external problems that have grown increasingly complex, and to the extent that established departments and agencies seek to protect their own interests in coping with those problems, no one institution is fully equipped to protect the interests of the person who bears final responsibility— the president. "When things don't go well they like to blame presidents—and that's what presidents are paid for," observed John F. Kennedy. In such an environment, a personalized staff, infused with the authority and prestige that only the president can claim, becomes an indispensable tool. For as Richard Nixon noted, presidents are chosen to make things happen.

In a larger sense, a personalized staff also assists the president in the roles of ultimate decider, ultimate coordinator, and ultimate persuader. The danger, of course, is that the presidential subsystem may so cut off the president from other elements of the institutionalized foreign affairs government (or even from American society) that the ability of the president to exercise responsibility may be impaired seriously. That appears to be precisely what happened to the Nixon presidency, to which the entire Watergate affair now stands in giant testimony, and it was repeated during the Iran-*contra* scandal as a "junta" of the president's staff acted in his name but apparently without the involvement or knowledge of the members of his cabinet or even the president himself (Draper, 1990). Secrecy may be desirable from the viewpoint of managing the nation's security, but because what stimulates as well as what constrains foreign policy are much greater forces than any one or a few are able to manage alone, secrecy and solo performances may be ultimately counterproductive. As Henry Kissinger concluded, "No foreign policy—no matter how ingenious—has any chance of success if it is born in the minds of a few and carried in the hearts of none."

SUGGESTIONS FOR FURTHER READING

Bock, Joseph G. (1987) *The White House Staff and the National Security Assistant: Friendship and Friction at the Water's Edge*. New York: Greenwood.

Brzezinski, Zbigniew. (1983) *Power and Principle: Memoirs of the National Security Adviser 1977–1981*. New York: Farrar, Straus, & Giroux.

Destler, I. M., Leslie H. Gelb, and Anthony Lake. (1984) *Our Own Worst Enemy: The Unmaking of American Foreign Policy*. New York: Simon & Schuster.

George, Alexander L. (1980) *Presidential Decisionmaking in Foreign Policy: The Effective Use of Information and Advice*. Boulder, Colo.: Westview Press.

Henkin, Louis. (1987–1988) "Foreign Affairs and the Constitution," *Foreign Affairs* 66 (Winter): 284–310.

Kissinger, Henry. (1979) *White House Years*. Boston: Little, Brown.

Lowi, Theodore J. (1985) *The Personal President: Power Invested, Promise Unfulfilled*. Ithaca, N.Y.: Cornell University Press.

Sorensen, Theodore C. (1987–1988) "The President and the Secretary of State," *Foreign Affairs* 66 (Winter): 231–248.

Watson, Richard A., and Norman Thomas. (1988) *The Politics of the Presidency*. Washington, D.C.: CQ Press.

CHAPTER 11

The Role of Executive Departments and Agencies in Foreign Policy Making

It's inevitable that control over foreign policy should gravitate to the White House. It's simply impossible to shape foreign policy from the vantage point of the State Department for the very reason foreign policy is . . . an amalgam of defense, intelligence, mass persuasion, and all of these things can be coordinated from close proximity to the president.
FORMER ASSISTANT FOR NATIONAL SECURITY AFFAIRS ZBIGNIEW BRZEZINSKI, 1983

At last count some 46 agencies were running international programs, and . . . every one of them seems to have its own foreign policy agenda. This can—and often does—create an impression of chaos.
FORMER FOREIGN SERVICE INFORMATION OFFICER FITZHUGH GREEN, 1984

Globalism is a pattern of American foreign policy. Recall from Chapters 4 and 5 its manifestations: billions of dollars in military and economic assistance and in military sales; military weapons and personnel spread worldwide, with a corresponding capacity to strike militarily virtually anywhere; diplomatic relations with nearly every foreign government; participation in scores of international organizations; and trade and investment connections with the rest of the world far out of proportion to the nation's percentage of the world's population.

Whose activities are reflected in such involvements? Whose responsibility is it to protect the interests they represent? The president and the presidency are the easy answers; the executive departments and agencies of the federal government, and especially the State and Defense departments, are the more accurate ones.

The distinction made in the preceding chapter between executive branch agencies (the second concentric circle of policy making) and the presidential subsystem (the innermost concentric circle) is not entirely clear-cut. The heads of executive departments and agencies appointed by the president together with their immediate subordinates make up the innermost circle of advisers. Thus the various secretaries of state, defense, and treasury who have served the nation since World War II were simultaneously members of the inner circle as

361

well as heads of the large, complex organizations found in the second concentric circle. Such organizations are important to those in the innermost circle because the president and the closest presidential advisers depend heavily on them and on the literally thousands of career professionals who manage America's day-to-day foreign affairs activities. Hence the scope and magnitude of the responsibilities of major organizations in the second concentric circle must be examined.

THE DEPARTMENT OF STATE

As the "first among equals" in the foreign affairs government, the Department of State is the executive agency bearing primary responsibility for the conduct of American foreign relations. Its activities range from negotiation of treaties and other agreements with other nations, to representing the nation in more than four dozen international organizations, to making policy recommendations and taking steps to implement them on all aspects of America's foreign relations and interests. In the late 1980s the State Department was operating a network of 300 posts throughout the world—141 embassies, 11 missions, 73 consulates general, 29 consulates, 45 consular agencies, and 1 branch office.

The State Department is organized in the typical bureaucratic pyramid, with the secretary of state perched on top of a series of lesser offices and bureaus that divide the labor within the department. As shown in Figure 11.1, that division reflects the department's orientation to the major geographic regions of the world, on the one hand, and the necessity to cope with functional problems that transcend geographic boundaries (for example, economic and agricultural affairs, intelligence and research, and politico-military affairs) together with those associated with the internal administration of any large government organization, on the other.

As Figure 11.1 shows, three organizations attached to the State Department are the Arms Control and Disarmament Agency (ACDA), the United States Information Agency (USIA), and the Agency for International Development (AID).[1] ACDA conducts research on arms control and disarmament policy and participates in negotiations with other nations on those subjects. USIA is responsible for the nation's public diplomacy; that is, the cultural and informational activities directed at overseas audiences (see Chapter 5). AID is responsible for administering U.S. economic assistance programs in more than sixty different countries. Overseas personnel of all three agencies are typically

---

1. Technically, AID is a subsidiary unit of the International Development Cooperation Agency (IDCA), which is the government's coordinating unit for U.S. economic relations with developing nations. Other component agencies of IDCA include the Trade and Development Program and the Overseas Private Investment Corporation (OPIC). The former is responsible for promoting simultaneously the economic development of Third World countries and the sale of U.S. goods and services to them, and the latter assists American investors' ability to make profitable investments in Third World countries.

FIGURE 11.1 ▪ The Department of State Organization Chart

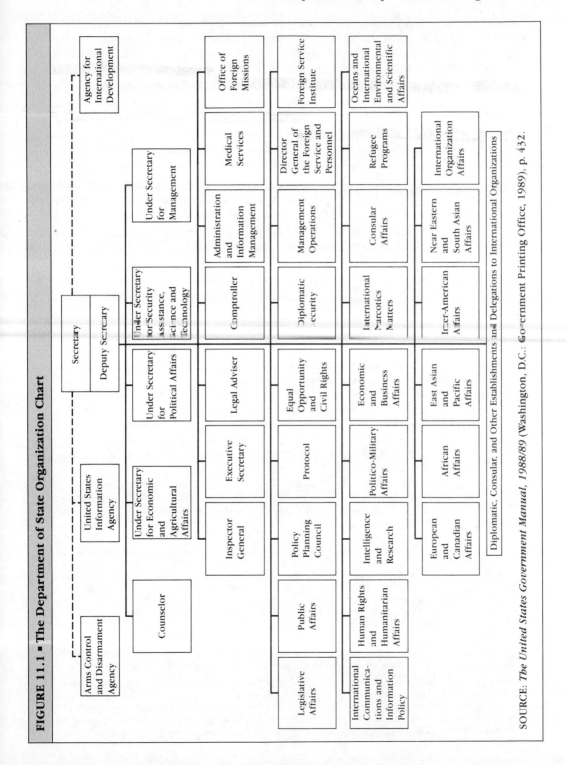

SOURCE: *The United States Government Manual, 1988/89* (Washington, D.C.: Government Printing Office, 1989), p. 432.

attached to the field mission abroad, over which the State Department, usually through the person of the ambassador, bears primary responsibility.[2]

Decision-making responsibility within the State Department itself follows the hierarchical pattern of its organization chart. The most important decisions are made by the secretary, the deputy secretary, and the under secretaries who occupy the seventh floor of the State Department offices in the area of Washington, D.C., known as Foggy Bottom, and who frequently interact with the White House and other government agencies. Routine decisions, important more in the implementation than in the development of policy, are made at the levels below the seventh floor, with responsibilities assigned to various regional and functional bureaus at different levels in the State Department's hierarchy (see Rubin, 1985).

Decision making begins with the regional assistant secretary and works down from there to the country directors and desk officers within each regional bureau who bear responsibility for coordinating U.S. policy toward particular countries abroad. In practice the responsibilities of the regional bureaus have been greatly diluted by the involvement of several dozen other federal agencies in the management of foreign affairs (Warwick, 1975).[3] But within the State Department itself,

> if one reviews decision-making in the Department of State in terms of a continuum of five decision categories—minor, routine, significant, fundamental and critical—it is clear, first, that country directors are engaged principally in *minor* decision-making, although they make resource inputs [e.g., give information on and interpretations of current political developments] to routine and significant decision-making concerning "their" countries. Second, assistant secretaries are limited principally to *routine* decisions affecting their geographical areas, although they make resource inputs to significant decisions involving their areas and, occasionally, other geographical areas through inputs which propose alternative policy positions. . . . Third, few *significant* decisions are made below the level of the seventh floor, and many significant decisions—probably the bulk—are made in consequence of interactions with the White House . . . and the bureaucracies of other foreign policy agencies. Fourth, all *fundamental* and *critical* foreign policy decisions involve the White House. (Esterline and Black, 1975: 63)[4]

---

2. The legal mandate that the ambassador supervise the activities of other U.S. agencies attached to the field mission abroad has been described as a "polite fiction" (Pringle, 1977–1978). Even within the State Department, the power of ambassadors has declined as modern telecommunications and travel have increased Washington's capacity to handle a broad range of foreign affairs details. As one Foreign Service officer commented wryly upon resigning his post in the Moscow embassy in 1980, "We don't need an ambassador in Moscow . . . because he has nothing to do" (cited in Rubin, 1985).

3. Less than 30 percent of the fifteen thousand Americans stationed at U.S. missions abroad work for the State Department (Spiers, 1985a: 3; 1988: 3). The practical consequence is that a substantial proportion of its personnel are involved in serving agencies other than their own.

4. One must be careful not to assume from that description, which pertains more to the development than to the implementation of policy, that the State Department and other bureaucratic agencies are unimportant foreign policy actors. On the contrary, the dependence of decision makers on bureaucratic organizations for policy implementation gives such organizations considerable opportunity to shape policy to fit their preferred positions, as we shall explain in more detail in Chapter 13.

Within this structure the individuals who matter most are the Foreign Service officers (FSOs). Accounting (in 1989) for about forty-two hundred of the more than twenty-six thousand employees of the State Department, this elite corps of professional diplomats has traditionally held the most important positions within State (outside the political appointments made by the president) both at home and abroad.

The Foreign Service Subculture

The popular image of the Foreign Service, based partly on legend and partly on historical fact (see Garnham, 1975; Harr, 1969), is that of a remarkably homogeneous diplomatic corps comprising upper-class men from the Northeast with degrees from Ivy League colleges. In recent years the Foreign Service officers corps has sought to open itself to a broader geographical, educational, ethnic, and socioeconomic spectrum, and has encouraged women and minorities to join its ranks in order to rectify what Ronald Spiers, under secretary of state for management during the Reagan administration, termed a "serious" problem. "Still, if the Foreign Service is no longer a smug men's club, it is more like one than any other part of the U.S. government" (Rubin, 1985). Epithets that describe foreign service officers as "effete, snobbish, striped-pants cookie pushers" (Rubin, 1989) reflect evaluations of the composition as well as performance of the Foreign Service.

The corps' distinctiveness is reinforced by a personnel system that is separate from the Civil Service, of which most federal employees are a part. And because it is an elite corps, other groups, such as State's Civil Service employees, are, by definition, nonelite. This has been the source of continuing personnel problems within the State Department for decades (Warwick, 1975). Non-FSOs have voiced complaints about their inferior status and their feeling of neglect within the department. In 1989 female Foreign Service officers won a class-action suit against the State Department that charged it discriminated against women by hiring more men for the Foreign Service and giving them better career assignments, performance ratings, and honors awards.

The Foreign Service has developed a distinctive subculture and mode of operation that have important ramifications for the State Department's policy-making role. This elitist subculture promotes respect for tradition, precedent, and conformity above all else.

One characteristic of the subculture is resistance to ideas from the outside. As one officer put it, "'The Foreign Service officer believes that his is an arcane craft which people on the outside cannot hope to understand.' We listen carefully and politely but seldom change our views" (*Diplomacy for the 70's*, 1970). Another is timidity in delineating State's jurisdiction within the foreign affairs government, which would be acceptable if other organizations were unaggressive—but they are not. As a result, leadership has tended to gravitate elsewhere. Yet the norms of the Foreign Service subculture militate against a more vigorous role. Especially important are three beliefs prevalent in the subculture.

- The only experience that is relevant to the activities of the Department of State is experience gained in the Foreign Service.
- The really important aspects of the foreign affairs of the United States are the political and traditional ones—negotiation, representation, and reporting.[5]
- Overseas operations of the kind conducted by DOD, AID, USIA, and CIA are peripheral to the main foreign policy task (Destler, 1974: 163, quoting Scott, 1969; see also Clarke, 1989).[6]

These beliefs and the norms of the subculture may satisfy the short-term needs of the career service and the individuals within it, but they do not necessarily satisfy the long-term needs of the Department of State or the requirements of U.S. foreign policy (Scott, 1970).

Within the Foreign Service itself, the subculture creates pressures to avoid rocking the boat—to avoid expressing controversial views that may be viewed as challenges to the wisdom of one's superiors, and to avoid dress and behavior that deviate from the norms of the group. Those pressures derive partly from the assignments of the typical Foreign Service officer. Viewed as a generalist rather than a specialist, an FSO's career pattern usually involves two- or three-year tours of duty both in Washington and abroad in a variety of operating and functional positions. Whether one's star is allowed to shine in an assignment to political affairs in Paris rather than budgetary affairs in Ouagadougou is thus heavily dependent on the outcome of one's evaluation by superiors.

The fiercely competitive nature of the Foreign Service has been reinforced historically by the "up-or-out" promotion system, under which an FSO has to advance beyond his or her present rank within a specified time or be "selected-out." That principle, together with the exceptional importance of the efficiency rating, tends, as one influential departmental self-study put it, "to stifle creativity, discourage risk-taking, and reward conformity" (*Diplomacy for the 70's*, 1970).

Over the years a number of developments within the Foreign Service and outside of it have had disruptive effects on the professional diplomatic corps. Preeminent among them were the effects of McCarthyism. "I have in my hand a list of 205 that were known to the Secretary of State as being members of the Communist party and who, nevertheless, are still working and shaping the policy in the State Department." With those words, spoken in the winter of 1950, Senator Joseph McCarthy launched an all-out attack against suspected—

---

5. As one FSO observed, "substantive knowledge" is the competency most highly valued in the Foreign Service. "It doesn't matter if it was a junior officer hoping for tenure, an FS-1 seeking to get into the Senior Foreign Service, or an ambassador or assistant secretary, the qualities judged begin with reporting, analysis, and policy. In the second and third competencies are leadership and managerial skills" (Bushnell, 1989).

6. One FSO reports that Foreign Service promotion panels tend to penalize those who seek experience outside "the admittedly stagnant mainstream" of State Department or embassy assignments (Pringle, 1977–1978).

but never proved—"disloyalty" in the Foreign Service. The immediate thrust was against those charged with responsibility for the "loss" of China. Eventually the entire corps of Foreign Service officers suffered the grueling humiliation of the security investigations engendered by an atmosphere of hysterical anticommunism. Harry S Truman's loyalty program reflected deference to McCarthyism. And unhappily for those involved, the career-shattering and head-rolling trauma continued to plague the State Department for nearly two years following the election of Dwight D. Eisenhower (see Hoopes, 1973a).

McCarthyism's impact on the Foreign Service was long-term and devastating:

> Talented officers resigned or were drummed out of the service. Field reports began to be couched in bland and roundabout language. Few dared to list Communist countries as career preferences, while East Asian specialization became a wasteland. Rumors and gossip were rampant in the corridors, reinforced by the spot visits of McCarthy's assistants. The virtues inculcated were caution, conformity, discretion, and prudence. (Warwick, 1975: 20)[7]

Extraordinary security consciousness and an elaborate system of horizontal clearances resulted. The latter in particular has made State's operating procedures among the most complex of all federal agencies. "Clearing" and "coordinating" with other comparably placed offices within the department and other agencies are necessary before an item can go up the chain of command. The result is "a most cautious way of doing business. It reflects an institutionalized desire to diffuse responsibility among many different offices and colleagues rather than to accept responsibility oneself" (Campbell, 1971).

Even as the effects of McCarthyism recede into the past, structural problems have emerged to plague the professional diplomatic corps. One is a bulge at the top of the Senior Foreign Service (from which are chosen the most prized positions career service personnel can hold, including ambassadorships) as more career officers are promoted to senior ranks than can be placed in meaningful positions.[8]

---

7. McCarthyism tragically robbed a later generation of decision makers of much-needed expertise on Asia at the very time that the emergent Vietnam War and the China tangle demanded knowledge of that area. The State Department's Bureau of Far Eastern Affairs (now East Asian and Pacific Affairs) in 1961 "was notorious for its rigidity and its resistance to policy change. For the Bureau had been one of McCarthyism's central targets; and the endless Congressional and Executive Branch investigations of the early '50s had largely destroyed, through harassment and dispersal, the China career professionals of the wartime and pre-war years . . . . By 1961 'FE' was a Bureau dominated by Cold Warriors and staffed largely by the cowed" (Thomson, 1972).

8. The expectation underlying the Senior Foreign Service when created by the Foreign Service Act of 1980 was that most FSOs would retire from the corps after twenty years, leaving only a small cadre from which the highest career appointments would be made. Instead, more have been promoted than have been absorbed into productive new assignments. In 1985, for example, the Senior Foreign Service comprised 17 percent of the Foreign Service officers corps, compared to a Senior Executive Service consisting of 1 percent of the Civil Service officers of comparable grades and an even smaller fraction among the comparable military ranks (Spiers, 1985b: 35). The current surplus may in the long run turn to shortage (Steigman, 1985), but there is little question

The second problem, directly related to the first, is the growth in the number of political appointments to top jobs from outside the Foreign Service. The 1980 Foreign Service Act specified that ambassadorial appointments will "normally" go to career officers, for example, but since the law was passed the proportion of political appointments has actually increased.[9] This trend exacerbates the "senior surplus" by reducing the opportunities available to career officers at the prime of their careers when their potential to make a meaningful contribution is greatest. The propensity to make political appointments reflects the profound distrust of "careerists" by "politicians," who often believe the former are not only disloyal to the latter's policies but also actively seek to undermine them. Such suspicions derive in part from State's bureaucratic subculture and from the requirement that careerists support policy, whatever it may be, objectively and without partisanship. "Since they are representing the views of the U.S. government rather than their own," Barry Rubin (1985) observes, "FSOs are supposed to become vessels of communication, without personal views. Many of them learn to radiate blandness and to censor their own opinions. An ideal pose is to give the impression of great knowledge while revealing little of substance." Such apparent lack of conviction does not sit well with those placed in office by voters or presidents, for whom partisan loyalty and, sometimes, ideological purity are important yardsticks. Often, however, the demands political appointees make on those expected to serve them are contradictory.

> They want the career staff to be detached, but accuse it of being bland; they demand discipline, but can brand this as lack of imagination; they require experienced judgment, but may call this negativism. One FSO complains, "Presidents and their aides need scapegoats. They can't blame the administration so they blame the secretary of state and if they can't blame the secretary of state they criticize the department's staff." (Rubin, 1985: 242)

---

that the bloated Senior Foreign Service resulted in "a demoralizing phenomenon for those consigned to 'makework' or overcomplement status after reaching the prime of their careers" (Spiers, 1985a).

The other side of the coin is that many talented FSOs are forced into early retirement when they fail to be promoted to the Senior Foreign Service. To the extent that ambassadorships and other top-level positions are filled by political appointees rather than Senior Foreign Service officers, which, as we note below, occurred frequently during the Reagan administration, the positions available at the top shrink even further, thus causing larger numbers of officers to be "selected out" of the service.

Mention should also be made of concern within the Foreign Service for preserving its traditional structure and career patterns in a sociocultural environment where two-career families are increasingly the norm, and where the incidence of terrorism abroad has reduced the willingness of officers and their families to accept demanding and dangerous assignments overseas. Noteworthy in this respect is that, since the Korean War, more ambassadors have been killed while on duty than generals and admirals (Spiers, 1989).

9. During the first Reagan administration, more than 40 percent of the ambassadorships went to noncareer officials (read political appointees), compared with 27 percent for Jimmy Carter and 32 percent for Richard M. Nixon and Eisenhower (Perry, 1984: 21; also Spiers, 1985a). During the early months of the Bush presidency the proportion increased even farther, as George Bush made more political appointments than had his predecessors at comparable periods in their administrations (*New York Times*, July 20, 1989, p. 20).

The State Department in the Foreign Affairs Government

The subculture of the State Department and its interaction with related extraor-
ganizational factors are critical in explaining why an organization that theoretically sits center stage in the foreign affairs government is in fact ill equipped to
play a leadership role. "As long as the norms of the subculture prescribe
organizational accommodation rather than combat, and caution rather than
venturesomeness, and as long as the ideology assures members of the subculture that they are doing a good job, it is vain to expect bold and innovative
policy" (Scott, 1969). As an instructive example, Lt. Colonel Oliver North, the
key National Security Council (NSC) operative in the Iran-*contra* scandal, gave
the State Department the code name "Wimp" (Sorensen, 1987–1988).

　　Two additional factors help explain State's compromised capacity to exert
leadership. Both are linked to the subculture but extend beyond it. One is that
secretaries of state in the postwar era often chose to remove themselves from
the department rather than giving it the kind of vigorous attention that might
have enabled it to be more intimately involved in the policy process. Secretary
of State John Foster Dulles, for example, reportedly told Eisenhower he would
become secretary only if he did not have to be responsible for the management
of the department and the Foreign Service; in the case of Dean Rusk, time pressures, his own personality, and his preoccupation with Vietnam prevented a
more effective use of State's expertise (*Diplomacy for the 70's*, 1970). The
record for subsequent secretaries—Henry Kissinger, Cyrus Vance, Edmund
Muskie, Alexander Haig, George Shultz and James A. Baker—contains little to
suggest they were able to bridge effectively the chasm between top officials and
the careerists in such a way as to involve the latter actively in the policy-making
process. Kissinger took many of his NSC staffers with him to Foggy Bottom
when he left the White House, but one of the hallmarks of his stewardship was
the amount of time he spent out of town. Vance was apparently more popular
at State, "partly due to memories of his predecessor—tales of Kissinger mis-
treating FSOs and ashtray-throwing tantrums [were] legion" (Rubin, 1985)—
but eventually Vance became enmeshed in a bureaucratic duel with the White
House, which he ultimately lost. Haig, Ronald Reagan's first secretary of state,
likewise resigned when he found himself outside the charmed circle of White
House advisers in an administration otherwise known for its friction with the
career staff. If there was an exception, it was Shultz, Haig's successor, whose
very survival suggested he was better able to satisfy the competing demands of
organization man and presidential adviser. But even he found himself under
attack by right-wing Reaganites who sought his ouster on grounds he had
become captive of the State Department's "liberal" foreign service establishment, and hence insufficiently responsive to the president's policy preferences.
Noteworthy in this respect is that Shultz was a vigorous critic of the Reagan
administration's initiative toward Iran, as discussed in Chapter 10.

　　By way of contrast, Baker, Shultz's successor, reopened the chasm separating the secretary of state from the department's career professionals. Whereas
Shultz "used the brightest stars of the career Foreign Service as the core of his

policy-making team,'' Baker's style was to keep them at arm's length. ''Many Foreign Service officers [complained] that Baker and his coterie of insiders . . . turned the department's seventh-floor executive suite into an inaccessible redoubt where even the most senior professional diplomats [felt] unwelcome and ignored'' (Goshko, 1989). ''He's running a mini-NSC, not State,'' complained one senior diplomat. ''We learn what our policy is when we read it in the newspapers.''

A second important reason for the State Department's inability to lead in foreign policy making is its relative lack of political resources and bureaucratic muscle in Washington's intensely politico-bureaucratic environment. As one Foreign Service officer (Pringle, 1977–1978) put it, although the secretary of state ''is [the] most senior of cabinet members, and is charged (in theory) with responsibility for the coordination of all foreign policy activities, he presides over a bureaucratic midget.'' The State Department's expenditures in 1989 were $3.8 billion, compared with $311.5 billion for the Defense Department, $244.6 billion for Health and Human Services, and what is widely thought to be in excess of $10 billion for the intelligence community. No other cabinet-level department spends less. The State Department's twenty-six thousand employees (many of whom are foreign nationals working in field missions abroad) likewise make it one of the smallest cabinet agencies. Even so, the resources devoted to foreign affairs came under close scrutiny during the Reagan administration, which led to turmoil and demoralization in the State Department as hundreds of foreign affairs professionals faced an uncertain future.

Increasing centralization of foreign policy making in the White House— described by three close observers as ''the triumph of politics and ideology over foreign policy'' (Destler, Gelb, and Lake, 1984)—has been one of the consequences of State's lack of leadership. Ironically, such centralization has further undermined State's capacity for leadership, for it ''has meant exclusion of the bureaucracy from most of the serious, Presidential foreign-policy business'' (Destler, Gelb, and Lake, 1984). And both circumstances reflect the State Department's lack of attunement to presidential needs, especially the need to be sensitive to domestic political considerations. ''Once a president comes to believe that Foggy Bottom is not attuned to politics, they are doomed to being ignored'' (Gelb, 1983).

Part of the reason for the belief that the State Department is insensitive to a president's political needs is that the department necessarily represents the interests of other countries, who are its ''clients,'' in the councils of government. ''From a White House perspective, efforts to accommodate the legitimate concerns of other countries are often viewed as coming at the expense of American interests, and the accommodationists are viewed as not being tough enough. Presidents usually do not have much patience with this kind of advice, find they cannot change State's penchant for it, and soon stop listening'' (Gelb, 1983).

White House dominance over foreign policy also stems from the State Department's lack of responsiveness. There is a ''widespread feeling'' within the State Department, John Kenneth Galbraith (1969a) complained to President

John F. Kennedy, "that God ordained some individuals to make foreign policy without undue interference from presidents and politicians." More specific presidential complaints are that the State Department produces bad staff work and is slow to respond, resistant to change, reluctant to follow orders, and incapable of putting its own house in order. Although in some respects those problems are a product of internal State Department politics, they also demonstrate that the department is not unlike other large government organizations whose parochial viewpoints often lead them to put their own functions and programs ahead of broad policy considerations. If there is a charge that is unique to State, it is that the department is insensitive to domestic politics. It is not surprising, therefore, that other government entities (the Defense Department, the Central Intelligence Agency [CIA], the White House staff) have exercised greater leadership and made more important and innovative contributions to recent American foreign policy than has the Department of State.

THE DEPARTMENT OF DEFENSE

During the 1960s, when White House dominance over foreign policy first began to emerge partly in response to the State Department's inability to lead (see also Chapter 10), the Office of International Security Affairs (ISA) emerged as an influential Defense Department voice in the foreign affairs government.[10] Once described as the "little State Department," the influence of ISA in the development and coordination of Department of Defense (DOD) policies and positions on decisions lying at the intersection between foreign and national security policy, and in the foreign affairs government generally, reached its apogee during Robert McNamara's tenure as defense secretary (1961–1967). In part this was because of McNamara's ability to effect civilian control over the mammoth military complex, which others had been unable to do; in part it is also because the principal foreign policy problem of the era—Vietnam—was also a formidable military problem. Thereafter ISA's influence waned as the constellation of forces that had sustained its influence shifted (see Piller, 1983). A 1979 reorganization created a new under secretary of defense for policy as the assistant to the defense secretary in matters relating to international security policy and political-military affairs. Later, the Reagan administration created two units at the assistant secretary level to deal with political-military affairs, one

---

10. Just as McGeorge Bundy's NSC staff became influential because of the State Department's lack of responsiveness, ISA's influence was in part a response to the sluggishness of the professional military, particularly the Joint Chiefs of Staff (described later in this chapter). Paul Nitze, whose involvement in the national security establishment spans four decades, compared ISA and the Joint Chiefs during the Kennedy years: "It sometimes would take them [the joint chiefs] three days to blow their nose. We [ISA] would sometimes be able to get a position together within an hour. When you get into a rapidly moving situation, when the house is burning down, every president likes to see something reasonable put forward for his consideration promptly" (cited in Piller, 1983).

(International Security Policy) with responsibility for the North Atlantic Treaty Organization (NATO) and arms control, the other (International Security Affairs) with responsibility for other geographical regions. Both performed useful roles, but no Defense Department unit has emerged to wield the kind of influence that ISA once did. The importance of the department as a whole, however, remains unambiguous, all the more so in a foreign policy-making environment where national security issues historically figured prominently in creating what has been dubbed a "security culture" (Hughes, 1981).

The secretary of defense together with the secretary of state and the chairman of the Joint Chiefs of Staff (JCS) bear the heaviest responsibility for advising the president on matters relating to the national security of the United States. In contrast to the secretary of state, however, the defense secretary commands (nominally, at least) an organization so thoroughly interwoven into the fabric of American social, political, and economic life that the secretary's recommendations regarding national security influence greatly not only the foreign environment but the domestic one as well. Moreover, each of the branches of the armed forces has developed important and influential allies in private industry and in Congress, particularly in the armed services committees. The "iron triangles" linking defense contractors, defense bureaucrats, and Congress often enable the uniformed services to fight for policies and programs (weapons systems, for example) that are at variance with the wishes of the civilian leadership. Those comprising the "iron triangles," who thrive on information, access, influence, and money (Adams, 1988), sometimes exacerbate long-standing rivalries among the branches of the armed services and contribute to the defense establishment's image as a fragmented rather than unified actor. Still, in the larger context of policy making, the ability of the military establishment to draw on support from influential sectors of business and government contributes to its importance in the making of foreign policy.

The National Security Establishment and Defense Reform

The Department of Defense is a product of the National Security Act of 1947, which created a "national security establishment" that sought to balance civilian and military elements. Efforts at defense reform since then have typically sought to increase civilian control, as embodied in the office of the secretary of defense. The Defense Reorganization Act of 1958 augmented the secretary's authority over the sprawling defense department. In practice the secretary's ability to exercise that prerogative has been less than complete, but the determination to put the secretary in charge was reaffirmed by the Defense Reorganization Act of 1986, the first major reorganization of the Defense Department in thirty years and the most sweeping change since it was created. The law, popularly known as the Goldwater-Nichols Act after its congressional architects, also clarified the functions of the civilian secretaries who, operating under the authority of the secretary of defense, head each branch of the separately organized military services (see Figure 11.2). But greater attention

FIGURE 11.2 ■ The Department of Defense Organization Chart

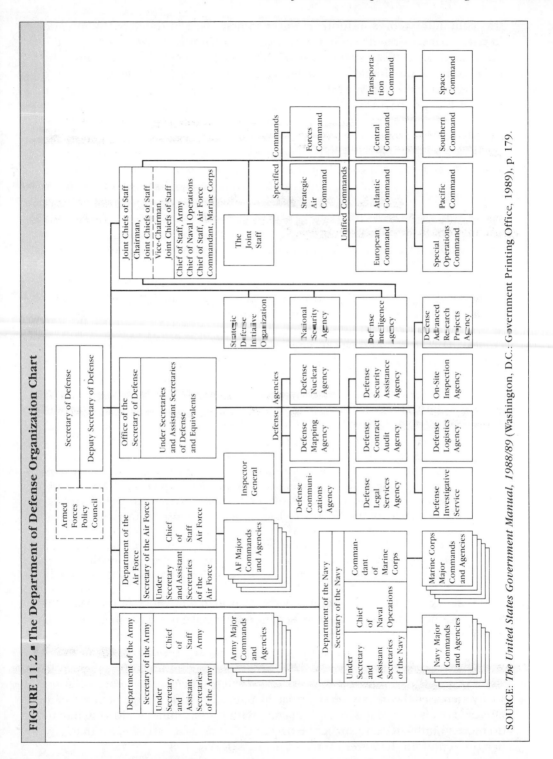

SOURCE: *The United States Government Manual, 1988/89* (Washington, D.C.: Government Printing Office, 1989), p. 179.

was paid in the reorganization act to the military side of the department, and in particular to strengthening the role of the institutions associated with the Joint Chiefs of Staff at the expense of the separate service organizations. The intent was to ameliorate the interservice rivalry that has long plagued the defense establishment by shifting power from the separate services to those responsible for coordinating them.

The Joint Chiefs of Staff consists of the senior military officer within each uniformed service and a chairman appointed by the president, who serves as the nation's chief military officer. Each service chief—the chief of staff of the army, the chief of staff of the air force, the chief of naval operations, and the commandant of the Marine Corps (who heads a separate service in the Navy Department)—is responsible for advising the civilian secretary on military matters and for maintaining the efficiency and operational readiness of the military forces under the chief's command. Until the 1986 reorganization, the joint chiefs were assisted in that task by a joint staff comprising some four hundred officers selected from each branch of the armed forces. Now, however, the joint staff explicitly serves as the chairman's staff, operating solely under the chairman's direction, authority, and control. A newly created "joint specialty" designed to make service on the joint staff more rewarding professionally was also mandated by the Goldwater-Nichols Act, as was creation of a new vice chairman of the JCS who is to serve as the nation's number-two military officer. Civilians also now serve on the joint staff, which numbers roughly sixteen hundred.

In another change, the chairman of the Joint Chiefs of Staff is now the principal military adviser to the president, the National Security Council, and the secretary of defense. Prior to passage of the Goldwater-Nichols Act, that task fell to the joint chiefs as a collective body, but no longer.

> The chairman had previously been merely a committee chairman—albeit with substantial prestige and opportunities for persuasion. The overall JCS was the committee, and the chairman's old role was faithfully to report and reflect the collective judgment of that body, which often amounted to an arithmetic lesson on lowest common denominators. The new law did stipulate that the chairman's advice should take into account the perspectives of the other JCS members. . . . But the law stripped away from the service chiefs the privilege of initiating access to the president, the NSC, and the secretary of defense. (Davis, 1987: 188–189)

The law did not, however, make the chairman a member of the National Security Council, as some had proposed; nor did it make him a commander with direct control over U.S. combat forces, a move many believed would have undermined the primacy of civilian control over the military. Instead, the chairman's position was solidified as the chief military "thinker" in the government, with others assigned the primary roles as "doers." Nonetheless, the reorganization vastly increased the role of the chairman by putting him "in charge of broad new ranges of decision making in the Pentagon, with responsibilities allowing him to do more to influence and shape the overall U.S. defense establishment than any person in uniform had ever exercised before" (Davis, 1987).

The Policy-Making Role of the Joint Chiefs of Staff   The importance of these changes can be appreciated through a brief sketch of the policy-making role the JCS has played historically and the factors giving rise to the perceived need to tackle once more the difficult problem of defense reform.

In the immediate postwar period, President Truman used the JCS to defend major political as well as military decisions, including the NATO alliance, his firing of General Douglas MacArthur, and the carrying out of "limited" war in Korea. Under Eisenhower the joint chiefs provided political support for the administration's military strategy of massive retaliation, but their overall prominence was somewhat reduced, presumably because President Eisenhower was his own best military adviser.

During the early part of Robert McNamara's term as defense secretary, a combination of President Kennedy's disenchantment with the advice of the joint chiefs at the time of the Bay of Pigs fiasco and McNamara's mastery of modern management techniques led influence within the Pentagon to gravitate toward the civilian leadership and away from the professional military, as was the intention of the 1958 reorganization act. The trend was reversed during the Vietnam War, when the joint chiefs reemerged as a voice for the military independent of the secretary of defense, as manifested by the eventual inclusion of the chairman of the JCS in President Lyndon D. Johnson's Tuesday Lunch group (a move rumored to have been made to counterbalance McNamara's increasingly dovelike stand on the war).

Richard M. Nixon and Gerald R. Ford likewise gave the JCS a relatively prominent role, but once again it was challenged during the Carter administration. Under the tutelage of Harold Brown, the secretary's Office of Program Analysis and Evaluation, which McNamara's management analysts known as "whiz kids" had used to assert civilian control over the military, grew to be bigger and more powerful than at any time since the 1960s. (Brown himself was one of the original "whiz kids.") As a consequence, the secretary of defense often appeared not to advocate the military's views or to defend them at the White House. The Joint Chiefs of Staff opposed the Carter administration's decision to cancel the B-1 bomber, for example, and also its decision (later reversed) to withdraw American troops gradually from South Korea. Subsequently, the Reagan administration sought to give the joint chiefs a greater role in policy development and management, but Defense Secretary Caspar Weinberger likewise either ignored or went against the joint chiefs on such major issues as the basing mode for the MX missile and the Rapid Deployment Force.

The Defense Reform Movement   At issue is the quality of advice that the joint chiefs provided civilian leaders (which Harold Brown once described as "worse than nothing") and, more broadly, their capacity to command the separate and powerful military services. General David C. Jones, chairman of the Joint Chiefs of Staff from 1978 to 1982, became a catalyst to a 1980s defense reform movement when, in his final testimony before Congress, he charged that "the fundamental balance of influence within the defense establishment is oriented too much toward the individual services," and concluded that "fundamental defense deficiencies cannot be solved with dollars alone." A year later, General Edward C. Meyer, chief of staff of the army, sounded a similar theme: "If we were trying to convince an enemy that we were able to go to war with a system that works like this, he would laugh." Robert W. Komer, under secretary of defense for policy in the Carter administration, predicted that "a system which is so inadequate in peacetime will perform even worse in crisis or war." A 1985 study by the staff of the Senate Armed Services Committee confirmed that prognosis when it blamed poor interservice coordination for the failure of the 1980 Iranian hostage rescue mission and for shortcomings in the 1983 invasion of Grenada. These events, plus the truck-bombing of marine headquarters in Beirut in 1983, were the principal forces behind Congress's determination to take the lead in defense reform.

Interservice rivalry and parochial interests were the primary factors underlying the seeming paralysis of the JCS system. "Dual hatting" sums up much of the problem. This refers to the fact that each service chief wears two hats, one as the leader of a branch of service, the other as a member of the joint chiefs. This required that the chiefs be able, in the words of General John W. Vessey, a former chairman of the joint chiefs, "to hang their service loyalties and prejudices on the hat rack outside the Joint Chiefs' meeting room" so as to give military advice from a "national perspective." Under the new system, that responsibility now rests squarely with the chairman, thus relieving the cross pressures under which the individual chiefs previously operated.

A related problem permeated the joint staff. Called "purple-suiters" because they were expected to represent all of the services with impartiality (as opposed to the "green-suiters" [the army], "white-suiters" [navy], and "blue-suiters" [air force], who typically reflect the views of their respective services), members of the joint staff ran the risk of being "too purple," of forgetting what the colors of their uniforms really meant, to the detriment of their own careers. Because the individual services, not the joint chiefs, controlled promotions, money, and personnel, there were "few incentives . . . for an officer assigned to joint duty to do more than punch his or her ticket and then get back into a service assignment" (Jones, 1984). Moreover, the best officers often sought assignments elsewhere. Now, however, with the creation of a "joint specialty" for those serving the chairman as a member of the joint staff, purple-suiters have their own incentives and rewards, and the evidence suggests that talented officers are seeking "joint specialty" assignments (Locher, 1988).

A related problem that has plagued the JCS system is that the senior military officers who make up the joint chiefs do not command combat forces in the field. They are essentially an administrative unit outside the operational chain of command. The actual command of combat forces in the field rests with ten commanders in chief (CINCs),[11] who receive their orders from the

---

11. The unified commands are the Atlantic, Pacific, European, Southern, and Central commands, the Forces, Transportation, Special Operations, and Space commands, and the Strategic Air Command.

president as commander in chief through the secretary of defense. The Joint Chiefs of Staff have no independent role in this chain of command, despite its often bizarre twists and turns. The Marine Corps commandant on the scene when marine headquarters in Beirut was blown up in 1983, for example, was not responsible for security there. Instead, the marines reported to officers off-shore, who reported to unified commanders in London, Naples, Stuttgart, and Brussels, who in turn were responsible to Defense Secretary Weinberger and President Reagan (Hiatt, 1984).

The Goldwater-Nichols Act moved very tentatively on this issue. As noted, the chairman of the Joint Chiefs of Staff was not assigned command responsibilities, but was given authority to transmit orders from the president or the secretary of defense to the CINCs. The CINCs of unified commands, in turn, were not given complete command over forces assigned to them, but were given "operational command." The issue is a touchy one, as it bears directly on "an emotionally charged philosophical debate over how to define the relationship between the CINCs of unified commands and their subordinate forces" (*Congressional Quarterly Almanac, 1986,* 1987). That debate bears heavily on the bureaucratic politics of defense reform.

Opponents of the more unified military system sought by the 1986 Defense Reorganization Act, which included the secretaries of defense and the navy, among others, argued that such a system would cut civilian policymakers off from competing viewpoints. The Navy Department—which "in more than two hundred years had never met a centralization proposal that [it] liked" (Davis, 1987)—was an especially vigorous opponent of any change that might undercut the "services-dominated architecture" of the defense establishment. As the most strategically independent of the three service branches, with its own air force (naval aviation) and army (the Marine Corps), the navy had potentially more to lose by strengthening the "jointness" of the Defense Department than either the army or air force.

On paper the Defense Reorganization Act of 1986 moves boldly forward in enhancing the roles of the Joint Chiefs of Staff and its chairman and, with that, in reducing the interservice rivalries that have historically contributed to shortcomings in the nation's military performance. But there are important reasons to doubt whether significant change will occur. More than three decades ago President Eisenhower "sought to create truly unified war-fighting commands through a combination of legislation and presidential directions," but "the Pentagon never complied" (Locher, 1988). In fact, reinforced by the organizational debacle during the Grenada invasion, the issue figured prominently in the Goldwater-Nichols Act, which suggests how difficult change is. What is the more remarkable is that the reorganization was a distinctly congressional initiative and product. Congress, a key element in the "iron triangle," is typically an obstacle to defense innovation (see also Chapter 12), but in this case the cause triumphed despite determined opposition throughout the executive branch. Perhaps the victory over seemingly insurmountable odds is what led the no-nonsense Senator Barry Goldwater to exclaim of the bill at the twilight of his long and distinguished career, "It's the only goddamn thing I've done in the Senate that's worth a damn."

The Defense Establishment in the Policy Process

Whatever strengths or weaknesses the present system of military advice, command, and coordination may have, a more fundamental question is how much influence the defense establishment exerts in the policy-making process. Concern that military officers may dominate key policy-making institutions, as was true of the National Security Council staff during much of the Reagan administration (see Chapter 10), is sometimes warranted, but since the Vietnam War military professionals have typically been cautious about military interventions because of their heightened sensitivity to the costs and risks involved.[12] (But they also believe if the military instrument is chosen, the United States should "go all out to win.")

Civilian leaders, on the other hand, often approach international problems "in a specially tough, macho, or militaristic spirit" that stresses the use of raw military power and lets questions of strategy dominate diplomacy (Kattenburg, 1980). The roots of military machismo are lodged in the psychological reactions of individuals to the circumstances they experience in their environments and to the beliefs they maintain about those experiences (see also Chapter 14). Among the beliefs and experiences shared by civilian policymakers since World War II have been a "deep respect for military effectiveness and efficiency"; a "belief in the capacity of U.S. military forces to accomplish virtually any mission"; "fear of being perceived as weak"; "fear of losing policy control to military leaders"; and a "belief that the fame of states was a game of men" (Kattenburg, 1980).

Historically, the anticommunist consensus and the widespread belief that the Soviet Union posed a military threat to United States reinforced the preference of civilian policymakers for military solutions to political problems. As Adam Yarmolinsky, a former Defense Department official, observed, "It is hard to conceive, under the circumstances, how reasonable men in the executive branch could have developed or espoused any policies other than those emphasizing military security, enemy capabilities, and readiness for worst contingencies." In such a context, deference to the military establishment "was merely one by-product of the forces that produced the policies themselves" (Yarmolinsky, 1971).

Yarmolinsky also observes that the involvement of the Pentagon and the military in foreign policy making had the effect of intertwining rationales for certain foreign policies with rationales for increased defense spending. As defense spending increased, "the abundant availability and pervasiveness of

---

12. Secretary of State Shultz, for example, was a strong Reagan administration advocate of using military force as an instrument of diplomacy, and it was the State Department that pushed for American intervention in Grenada, which the Joint Chiefs of Staff resisted. Similarly, national security adviser Robert McFarlane (a retired Marine Corps lieutenant colonel) was a strong advocate of American intervention in Lebanon, and both he and Shultz favored retaliation for the October 1983 suicide truck-bombing of U.S. Marines in Beirut; Defense Secretary Weinberger and the joint chiefs opposed retaliation.

all forms of military power" (Kattenburg, 1980) also increased. So, too, did domestic political support for the maintenance of a large military establishment, even in peacetime, as hundreds of thousands of Americans became dependent directly or indirectly on the Pentagon for their livelihoods.

The disintegration of the Soviet external empire and the denouement of the ideological contest between East and West do not guarantee a more peaceful world, but policymakers have determined that they call for a contraction of the defense effort put forth heretofore. That will not be easy politically, however, as local communities and their senators and representatives in Congress seek to cushion themselves against the "price of victory." Closing a military base or canceling a weapons system has always been difficult and will remain so even as the nation moves beyond the Cold War.[13] Meanwhile, the influence that the military establishment exerts on foreign policy will continue to depend on "the extent to which civilians in the executive branch, in Congress, and among the public bear in mind or forget General George C. Marshall's maxim that political problems, if thought about in military terms, become military problems" (Yarmolinsky, 1971).

THE INTELLIGENCE COMMUNITY

Like the military, the intelligence community has played a prominent role in postwar American foreign policy because of the preferences of elected officials and their advisers. As Bobby Inman, a former deputy director of central intelligence, observed on his retirement from government service in 1982, "Every administration ultimately turns to the use of covert operations when they become frustrated about the lack of success with diplomatic initiatives and are unwilling to use military force."

The intelligence community itself is a vast complex of operating agencies and interagency and oversight committees. The agencies involved are depicted in Figure 11.3,[14] which also suggests that primary responsibility for managing

---

13. Under a 1988 plan, eighty-six military bases were slated for closure, and Secretary of Defense Dick Cheney announced in early 1990 that "extensive" new closures were in the offing. In addition, the Bush administration's fiscal 1991 budget request called for a reduction of 38,000 active duty military personnel and 5,000 civilian employees of the Defense Department, and it projected an eventual overall reduction of 300,000, two-thirds military personnel and one-third civilian. It also slated a number of weapons systems for termination whose combined costs would reduce military expenditures by more than $42 billion in the fiscal 1991–1994 period. ("Cheney's Spending Blueprint Faces Welter of Changes," *Congressional Quarterly Weekly Report*, February 3, 1990, pp. 336–337). However, as noted in previous chapters, the Iraq-Kuwait crisis stalled executive and congressional efforts to downsize the military establishment.

14. The term *intelligence community* "connotes a good deal more harmony and commonality of goals and views than actually exists. Indeed, tribal and feudal metaphors often seem more appropriate in describing how the various collection, processing, and analytic organizations interact with one another and with policymakers" (Flanagan, 1985). Similarly, the visual impression conveyed by Figure 11.3 belies the complexity of the community. See Richelson (1989) for a detailed description of the complex network of institutions that are involved in the U.S. intelligence effort.

FIGURE 11.3 ■ **The Intelligence Community**

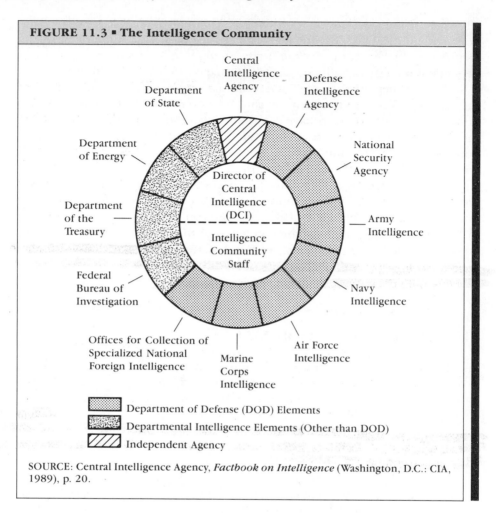

SOURCE: Central Intelligence Agency, *Factbook on Intelligence* (Washington, D.C.: CIA, 1989), p. 20.

---

the community rests with the director of central intelligence (DCI), who is also director of the Central Intelligence Agency (although, as will be seen, the director's managerial role is less overwhelming than the figure perhaps suggests). The director's authority is exercised through the role of chair of the National Foreign Intelligence Board (NFIB), the body made up of the principals of operating agencies comprising the intelligence community, and the director, in turn, is responsible to the National Security Council, and through it, to the president. Oversight is provided by two citizen advisory bodies, the Intelligence Oversight Board (IOB) and the President's Foreign Intelligence Advisory Board (PFIAB). The former, established by President Ford in 1976 in response to congressional investigations of the intelligence community, has from time to time been given responsibility for determining the legality of intelligence operations of questionable propriety;[15] and the latter, established by President Eisenhower in 1956 (but disbanded for a time during the Carter administration), gives general counsel on the conduct of the intelligence community. Under Reagan the board reportedly focused attention on technology-transfer and counter-intelligence issues (Flanagan, 1985), but neither it nor the IOB plays a central role in the intelligence community (Johnson, 1989).

Finally, oversight is exercised by the House and Senate select committees on intelligence. They authorize appropriations for the intelligence community, receive reports on intelligence analysis and production, and oversee the conduct of covert activities once the executive has presented a *presidential finding* on the need for such activities. More broadly, the president is required by law to keep Congress "fully and currently informed" of all intelligence activities, and Congress as a whole appropriates all money for the intelligence community, including money for intelligence activities secretly tucked away in the Pentagon's budget.

Secrecy in a democracy necessarily poses a paradox, but the concern for control, legality, and oversight of the intelligence community stems more immediately from revelations of abuses committed over the past quarter-century by intelligence agencies, including illegal activities against American citizens as well as questionable operations abroad.[16] During the 1970s in particular, a number of institutional reforms were put in place in an effort to prevent a recurrence of the abuses. For the Central Intelligence Agency, the key intelligence institution, the result was an "identity crisis" that made the agency unsure of itself and its mission and that may have affected adversely the willingness of intelligence officers to take risks in pursuit of their convictions (Turner and Thibault, 1982).[17] Resources also dwindled, which may have impaired the nation's overall intelligence capabilities, especially in the area of human intelligence (HUMINT, otherwise better known as espionage). Inman testified before Congress in 1982, for example, that "the intelligence establishment was cut back sharply in the 1960s and 1970s after a major buildup in the 1950s, losing 40 percent of its personnel from 1964 to the mid-1970s."[18]

---

15. The IOB was charged during the Carter administration with determining both the legality and propriety of covert actions, but under Reagan it was restricted to the former issue, despite the fact that the 1975–1976 congressional hearings on the CIA questioned the propriety of its actions as much as their legality. See Clarke and Neveleff (1984) and Turner and Thibault (1982) for evaluations of this and other changes made during the Reagan administration in regulations governing the intelligence community.

16. Many trace the roots of intelligence abuses to the top-secret report that Lt. General James Doolittle submitted to President Eisenhower in 1954, which urged the Central Intelligence Agency to become "more ruthless" than the Soviet KGB, and which asserted that "if the United States is to survive, long-standing American concepts of 'fair-play' must be reconsidered."

17. The issue surfaced again in 1989, when U.S. officials failed to assist an attempted coup against Panamanian dictator Manuel Noriega apparently because they believed it might lead to Noriega's assassination. U.S. participation in political assassinations has been banned since President Ford issued an executive order to that effect in 1976. The ban on assassinations has been reaffirmed by subsequent presidents.

18. The contraction of intelligence support became a matter of public controversy when President Reagan in 1984 asserted that "the near destruction of our intelligence capability" was partly responsible for the car bombing of the U.S. embassy in Beirut in September of that year. He later explained to Jimmy Carter, who demanded an apology for the comment, that he had not meant to suggest that "you or your Administration was responsible for the decline in intelligence-

Following the election of Ronald Reagan, a number of restrictions were lifted, and the intelligence community, with the CIA at the vanguard, enjoyed a resurgence not only as a servant of American foreign policy, but also sometimes as a substitute for it, notably in Central America, Southwest Africa, and Southwest Asia. According to one estimate (*New York Times*, June 11, 1984, p. 1), covert operations under Reagan experienced "a fivefold increase since the last year of the Carter administration to over 50 continuing operations." Moreover, by the mid-1980s, previous cutbacks in budgets and personnel had been restored and probably surpassed (Taubman, 1984); the intelligence community's budget grew 17 percent annually during the first three years of the Reagan administration (*Newsweek*, October 10, 1983, p. 38). Thereafter, however, Congress reportedly began to trim back administration requests.

Indicative of the new mood was the intelligence oversight legislation passed in 1980. What began in 1978 as a comprehensive bill designed to provide a statutory basis for the national intelligence activities of the United States ended up as "no more than a few fence posts around which the intelligence agencies may pass with little effort" (Johnson, 1980). The principal change was the repeal of the 1974 Hughes-Ryan Amendment, which required that covert CIA operations be reported to as many as eight congressional committees "in a timely fashion." The new Intelligence Oversight Act stipulated that only the Senate and House intelligence committees need be informed of covert actions (but did require that *all* covert actions be reported, not just CIA operations). And while it reaffirmed the principle of congressional oversight, it also permitted the president discretion to limit prior congressional notification and specifically denied Congress the right to disapprove covert operations.

The matter of timely notification figured in the Iran-*contra* scandal, when it became evident that the president failed to reveal to Congress a retroactive presidential finding that authorized the secret sale of arms to Iran. Ten months passed before Reagan formally notified Congress of the operation, and then only after a Beirut newspaper had revealed the secret.

The Iranian initiative and the revelation that it resulted in the diversion of funds to the *contras* was the culmination of a series of events involving Nicaragua that led Congress to conclude that, despite legal restraints and verbal assurances, it had repeatedly been deluded by key intelligence personnel.

For some time following the Sandinistas' rise to power in 1979, the CIA had been engaged in a "secret" effort to subvert the new government by means little short of supporting widespread warfare against the Nicaraguan regime. The insurgent army fighting the Sandinistas, the *contras*, were the creation of the

---

gathering capability" or for the Beirut bombing. A White House spokesperson later suggested that Reagan had been talking about "a decade-long trend and climate in Congress." Senator Daniel P. Moynihan responded that the comment "undermines—I am prepared to say betrays—almost a decade of sustained bipartisan efforts in Congress to reconstruct an intelligence community whose budgets had run down steadily through the first half of the 1970s and began to rise sharply in the second." For a discussion of Congress's part during the latter part of Carter's administration in reversing the downward trend in the intelligence community's funding, see Pickett (1985).

CIA, and in 1984 the agency supported their mining of Nicaragua's harbors—but it did so without properly informing Congress as required by law, which, as noted above, obliges the intelligence community to keep Congress "fully and currently informed" of all intelligence activities, including "any significant anticipated activity." In addition, the 1982 Boland amendment (to the 1983 appropriations act) specifically prohibited the use of CIA or Defense Department funds "for the purpose of overthrowing the Government of Nicaragua."

The congressional response to the CIA's defiance of the relevant legal requirements was reminiscent of the Vietnam years. Barry Goldwater, chair of the Senate's Intelligence Committee, castigated the CIA's director, William Casey, for the Nicaraguan operation, and Norman Mineta, a member of the House Intelligence Committee, expressed the perennial congressional dilemma with the observation, "We are like mushrooms. They keep us in the dark and feed us a lot of manure."[19] Shortly thereafter the administration sold arms to Iran in violation of its own policies about dealing with terrorists and without seeking prior congressional approval of the sale (see also Chapter 12). Moreover, not only was Congress not given prior notification of the Iranian initiative, but, as noted, the White House also decided to keep details of the operation from Congress for nearly a year. Finally, the diversion of funds to the *contras* was a violation of the spirit if not the letter of congressional intent regarding *contra* aid. These and other revelations from the Iran-*contra* affair fueled Congress's ire and broke the trust that the Reagan administration had sought to build with Congress on the sensitive issue of covert operations and intelligence activities generally. As a result, questions about propriety, legality, secrecy, and control once more emerged as central issues surrounding the role of intelligence activities in American foreign policy.

Intelligence Operations and the Department of Defense

Apart from the administrative units that make up the intelligence community, its size in terms of money and personnel remains uncertain because of the secrecy in which the community and its activities are shrouded. Most estimates for the period from the 1970s through the late-1980s converge around $10–13 billion as the size of the budget and 150,000–160,000 as the number

---

19. Congressional pique was fueled by revelations in October 1984 that the CIA had produced a psychological warfare manual that recommended to the *contras* the use of violence, perhaps assassination, to achieve their political goals in Nicaragua. Such methods were perceived to be in violation of the CIA's policies and of presidential orders as stated in President Reagan's Executive Order 12333.

    Despite that order (which states that "no person employed by or acting on behalf of the United States government shall engage in, or conspire to engage in, assassination"), Bob Woodward (1987) reports that CIA director Casey played an active role in an attempted assassination of Muslim leader Sheikh Fadlallah, the leader of the Party of God, Hizbollah, in Beirut in March 1985. Eighty people were killed and some two hundred wounded, but Fadlallah escaped unharmed. Woodward also reports that deliberations in 1982 involving the CIA, the State Department, and the National Security Council staff about coping with terrorism were at one point "nearly an invitation to assist in an assassination of [Libyan leader Muammar] Qaddafi."

of personnel.[20] These are likely to be conservative estimates, however, since they do not include intelligence funds hidden in the budget of the Defense Department, whose magnitudes are unknown, and various contract employees and foreign agents, whose numbers are also unknown (perhaps even to the CIA; Marchetti and Marks, 1974).[21]

What is clear is that the Department of Defense is the largest component of the intelligence community, consuming anywhere from two-thirds to three-quarters of the federal intelligence budget (see also *Final Report*, 1, 1976: 328–340). The DOD's intelligence responsibilities are discharged by intelligence units within the various branches of the armed services and by the Defense Intelligence Agency (DIA) and the supersecret National Security Agency (NSA). The latter, which operates under the authority of the secretary of defense, is the biggest spender.

Created by a classified presidential directive in 1952, the NSA was not even generally acknowledged as a government organization until 1957. Even today, references to it in government documents are hard to find and deficient in detail (its initials are sometimes said to stand for "No Such Agency"). Some sense of the magnitude of its operation is suggested by the fact that the Capitol in Washington, which houses the legislative body of the world's largest democracy, contains 718,740 square feet. In contrast, NSA's headquarters in Fort George Meade, Maryland, encompasses 1,912,000 square feet (Pett, 1984: B8). Moreover, its budget may be far greater than the $4–6 billion that would be assumed from its estimated share of the intelligence community budget. Signals intelligence (SIGINT), communications security, and cryptology—code breaking and code making—are NSA's main responsibilities, particularly as they relate to Soviet military capabilities. One report puts the amount Congress appropriated for these functions in 1989 at "between $10 and $15 billion," with "[NSA] and its military surrogates, the Army Intelligence and Security Command, the Naval Security Group Command and the Air Force Electronic Security Command" the recipients (Lardner, 1990b: 6; see also Bamford, 1983: 109).

NSA's operations are extraordinarily technology-intensive, requiring massive supercomputers to discharge its responsibilities in the areas of "intercepting, 'traffic analyzing,' and cryptanalyzing the messages of all other nations,

---

20. For more precise estimates, see Bamford (1983), Carver (1990), Esterline and Black (1975), Johnson (1989), Marchetti and Marks (1974), *Newsweek* (February 6, 1978, October 10, 1983), Richelson (1989), Taubman (1983, 1984), *U.S. News & World Report* (June 25, 1984), and the annual issues of *Congressional Quarterly Almanac*.

21. According to one of the supplementary staff reports of the Senate Select Committee to Study U.S. Intelligence Activities (the Church Committee), "Such statistics provide some indication of the size of the immediate intelligence community within the Federal government but, of course, ignore the commitment of resources to intelligence efforts, on one hand, by front groups, proprietary organizations [e.g., Radio Free Europe and Radio Liberty], and informers, and, on the other hand, by sub-national government agencies, and other Federal entities (such as Department of Agriculture overseas attachés, National Aeronautics and Space Administration satellite launching systems, and the products of the National Weather Service). With these additional components identified, the pervasive nature of the intelligence organization begins to become more apparent" (*Final Report*, 4, 1986: 290–291).

presumably friend as well as foe," and ensuring the security of U.S. messages (Ransom, 1970). The ability of the United States to deal confidently with the Soviet Union in arms control negotiations, which requires detailed knowledge of Soviet military capabilities, rests in large measure on NSA's sophisticated signals intelligence capabilities. "No Such Agency" is hypersecretive about what precisely those capabilities are. It supported the Iran-*contra* initiative by intercepting scores of messages over a sixteen-month period ending in December 1986, many of which involved eavesdropping on Iranian officials' phone conversations. But this evidence was never admitted into the criminal trials of the Iran-*contra* principals because of NSA's objection that the admission of classified material relating to the agency's functions in intercepting communications would compromise national security (Lardner, 1990a).[22]

NSA's SIGINT capabilities are supported by the National Reconnaissance Office (NRO), whose existence was first revealed in 1973 when its name was inadvertently included in a declassified congressional document (Richelson, 1989). Even so, the office remains a secret or "black" agency in that its existence is not officially recognized.

NRO manages the nation's satellite reconnaissance programs. It operates under the "cover" of the air force, which reportedly pays the bills for the extremely costly photographic and electronic reconnaissance satellites and the rockets necessary to put them into orbit. Replacing the spy planes (for example, the SR-71) and spy ships (for example, the *Pueblo*) of previous decades, reconnaissance satellites have become the single most important source of technical intelligence data gathered by the United States. Employing high-resolution and wide-angle cameras, the photographic satellites have for years provided enormous amounts of detailed information on military and related strategic developments within the Soviet Union and elsewhere, while the electronic sensing tasks of the reconnaissance satellites have been oriented toward gathering data on missile testing, on radars and the emissions of other electronic equipment, and on communications traffic.

Like NSA, the Defense Intelligence Agency also operates under the authority of the secretary of defense. Created by Robert McNamara in 1961, the DIA was intended to consolidate the various intelligence units of the armed services. The latter are involved in the collection of "departmental" intelligence as opposed to "national" intelligence; that is, in collecting information germane to their tactical missions. In so doing, however, their intelligence product has often been skewed in the direction preferred by their parent organizations for "budgeteering" purposes.

Thus the air force saw the development of a "bomber gap" and then a "missile gap" which never materialized. The navy was inclined to exaggerate Soviet naval power, and the army was often found estimating a number of Russian army divisions that

---

22. Although NSA operates under the authority and control of the secretary of defense, it reportedly refused to advise the secretary of the role it had played in intercepting Iranian communications on grounds he did not need to know (Johnson, 1989).

existed only on paper. All of these activities tended to inflate budgetary requests and fundamentally to challenge the decision-making authority of the Secretary of Defense, particularly vis-à-vis Congress. (Ransom, 1970: 103–104)

The DIA was designed to provide direct intelligence assistance to the secretary of defense and the Joint Chiefs of Staff, an assignment that required improved coordination and management of Defense Department intelligence resources. Moreover, it was assumed that the DIA would take over many of the functions of the armed forces intelligence units. This has never happened. Although the functions assigned the DIA appear to place it in a superior position compared with the army, navy, and air force, the DIA collects little information on its own, relying instead on the service intelligence agencies for its raw intelligence data. Thus the service intelligence units continue to flourish, with the result that they and DIA often duplicate efforts. These and other problems have led critics to question the need for DIA's continued existence, but at least one observer concludes that, because the DIA continues to enjoy the backing of the secretary of defense, "who enjoys higher official status in the government than the director of the CIA," the agency "remains a formidable bureaucratic rival of other intelligence agencies—and sometimes an incorrigible underling to its titular civilian overseer, the DCI" (Johnson, 1989). Moreover, improved analytical skills and experience have contributed to DIA's capabilities and growing political clout in the bureaucratic politics of intelligence (Johnson, 1989).

Intelligence Operations and the Department of State

The Bureau of Intelligence and Research (INR) is the State Department's representative in the intelligence community. The department's intelligence functions arise naturally out of its general foreign affairs responsibilities, and much of what the department routinely does in the way of analyzing and interpreting information might be regarded as intelligence work. INR is the focus of such activity as it relates to the larger intelligence community, for it is through that bureau that State makes its input into the various interagency committees that seek to guide intelligence operations.[23] The director of the Bureau of Intelligence and Research is also the senior in-house intelligence adviser to the secretary of state.

In addition to representing the State Department within the intelligence community, INR's primary objective is to introduce a "diplomatic sensitivity to intelligence reports," and its own reports "are among the most highly regarded in the government—some say the best" (Johnson, 1989). But INR does not engage in the collection of intelligence other than through normal

---

23. Paralleling the earlier discussion of the State Department's bureaucratic subculture, Rubin (1985) observes that "because INR is seen as a specialized and research-oriented bureau outside the policy-making chain of command, many FSOs consider an INR assignment detrimental to their careers."

cable traffic and reporting from overseas posts. Instead, it depends on input from other agencies, which its small staff then turns into finished intelligence reports. Within the intelligence community, therefore, the State Department has been more a consumer than a producer of intelligence. That fact combined with its comparatively small size lead to the suspicion that the State Department is in a relatively disadvantageous position in the highly competitive intelligence community.

Intelligence Responsibilities of Other Departments and Agencies

The Treasury Department, the Energy Department, and the Federal Bureau of Investigation (FBI) are the remaining officially designated members of the intelligence community. All play an important role in intelligence operations, although none is concerned primarily with the collection of foreign intelligence.

Treasury's intelligence activities derive in part from the collection of foreign economic intelligence by its overseas attachés. More specific intelligence activities derive from the department's responsibilities for protecting (by the U.S. Secret Service) the president, presidential candidates, and certain foreign dignitaries, for controlling (through the Bureau of Alcohol, Tobacco, and Firearms and the U.S. Customs Service) illegal trafficking in alcohol, tobacco, firearms, and other articles entering international trade and for protecting against terrorism in international transportation facilities; and for ensuring compliance (through the Internal Revenue Service) with the internal revenue laws. Executing those functions has often resulted in the use of undercover personnel, paid informants, and electronic surveillance operations (*Final Report*, 4, 1976).[24]

The Department of Energy, operating through an assistant secretary for defense programs, is responsible for conducting nuclear weapons research, development, production, and surveillance programs. In the latter capacity, it is responsible for verifying compliance with treaties limiting nuclear tests and with foreign nuclear weapons technology analysis. Historically, that function has involved it in monitoring nuclear explosions abroad through overseas listening posts and measuring radioactivity in the atmosphere. The department

---

24. Since the targets of such activities have often been American citizens, it would be inappropriate to label all of the activities as relating to the making and execution of foreign policy. As a practical matter, the line between foreign and domestic intelligence gathering is an amorphous one, which opens the intelligence community to charges of abuse. It was revealed in congressional testimony, for example, that for a time during the Nixon presidency the Internal Revenue Service operated a Special Service Staff (SSS) initially designed to ensure that dissident groups were complying with the tax laws. By the time it was disbanded in 1973, a total of 11,458 SSS files had been generated on 8,585 individuals and 2,873 organizations. Those files were reportedly used as "a reference source for White House intelligence actors" as well as a means of identifying subjects for IRS scrutiny (*Final Report*, 4, 1976: 288–289). Alleged abuse of various intelligence agencies are detailed in *Final Report*, 2 (1976); see also U.S. Commission on CIA Activities within the United States, published in 1975.

is also responsible for the overt collection of intelligence on energy policies and developments abroad that may affect the United States, and for monitoring compliance with nuclear nonproliferation policies.

The Federal Bureau of Investigation, like the Treasury Department, historically has not engaged directly in overseas intelligence operations, although it does assign agents to posts abroad and cooperates with the CIA on counterintelligence matters outside the United States. Domestic counterintelligence is the FBI's major intelligence function, and the bureau has jurisdiction in the investigation of espionage, sabotage, treason, and other internal security matters. Its activities in these areas are not always benign or free of controversy, however. In 1981, for example, the FBI began investigating a coalition of organizations called the Committee in Solidarity with the People of El Salvador (CISPES), which became the leading citizens' organization protesting U.S. policies in El Salvador. The FBI defended its surveillance, which continued for several years, saying it was investigating alleged criminal activity, but its actions were widely interpreted as an effort to intimidate the administration's political opponents and may have violated their civil rights.

Although not formally designated members of the intelligence community, mention should be made of the Justice Department's Drug Enforcement Administration (DEA) and of the Department of Commerce. Intelligence relating to illicit drug trafficking is a primary concern of the former. Both foreign and domestic aspects of narcotics production and trafficking fall within its jurisdiction. The Commerce Department is concerned with technology-transfer issues. The Office of Intelligence Liaison links the department to the intelligence community in matters involving technology-transfer intelligence (Richelson, 1989). Heightened national concern with drug trafficking and the protection of high-tech secrets also led the CIA under William Casey to become involved in these issues. The Bush administration's declaration of war on drugs contributed even further to the salience of the drug issue. On the other hand, the rapid changes that have taken place in Eastern Europe and the Soviet Union have reduced the breadth of technology-transfer controls insofar as they relate to potential military applications.

The Central Intelligence Agency

Placing the Central Intelligence Agency last in our discussion of executive intelligence agencies underscores the fact that the most widely known and controversial intelligence organization is far from the only one. Indeed, based on estimates of the size of the intelligence community, the CIA constitutes less than a quarter of its expenditure and an even smaller percentage of its employees. Its attention thus derives more from its reputation for "dirty tricks" and its assumption of the primary responsibility for covert political operations than from its size.

The CIA's Intelligence Responsibilities   As the *central* in its name implies, the CIA was originally designed for something other than covert operations as its primary function. Successor to the World War II Office of Strategic Services

(OSS), the CIA was conceived as the center of the various intelligence community activities and the coordinator of an integrated and coherent national intelligence operation. The Japanese attack on Pearl Harbor on December 7, 1941, revealed the necessity for such a centralized operation. Evidence of the impending Japanese aggression was available, but its form was so fragmented and its location so diffuse as to be useless for purposes of decision making.

The CIA was created by the National Security Act of 1947 as a subsidiary of the National Security Council with responsibilities for (1) advising the NSC on intelligence matters relating to national security; (2) making recommendations to the NSC for coordinating the intelligence activities of the various federal executive departments and agencies; (3) correlating and evaluating intelligence and providing for its dissemination; and (4) carrying out such additional services, functions, and duties relating to national security intelligence as the NSC might direct. Those responsibilities reflect the fact that the concept of a central intelligence organization evolved out of concern for the quality of intelligence analysis available to policymakers. Yet within a year of its creation, the CIA was charged with the conduct of covert psychological, political, paramilitary, and economic activities. The acquisition of a covert mission had a profound impact on the subsequent activities of the agency and ultimately on its relative political stature within the government.

The initial impetus for covert activity was provided by the increasingly hostile international political environment of the late 1940s and early 1950s. Subsequent policy directives and organizational adaptations contributed to the extensiveness of such activity. (The consequences in terms of external actions are discussed in Chapter 5.) Internally, the relative importance of clandestine activities within the CIA itself is documented by the fact that between 1962 and 1970, the budget of the Clandestine Services of the CIA averaged 52 percent of the agency's total budget, while roughly 55 percent of its personnel were assigned to such activities (*Final Report*, 1, 1976: 121).

The years 1971 to 1975 were a transition period. Vietnam, public disclosures of CIA abuses of power (spurred in part by a more assertive Congress), and the shifting distribution of international power and officials' perceptions of the nation's role within the emergent power structure all contributed to an erosion of the foreign policy assumptions on which CIA clout within the policy-making community had come to be based. "The consensus that had existed among the press, the informed public, the Congress, and the Executive branch and that had both supported and protected the CIA broke down" (*Final Report*, 1, 1976).

An outward manifestation of the crisis was a rapid succession of directors of central intelligence—Richard Helms, James Schlesinger, William Colby, George Bush, Stansfield Turner, and William Casey. Schlesinger and Colby, in particular, were concerned with carrying out management reforms that would enhance the CIA's communitywide role and provide improved intelligence to policymakers (for details, see *Final Report*, 4, 1976: 84–88; see also Flanagan, 1985). Colby's appointment was inopportune, however, since it coincided with public disclosures of CIA domestic spying (in violation of its foreign intelligence charter), including, for example, operation CHAOS (which was directed against domestic political dissidents from 1967 to 1974) and a massive mail-rifling program conducted in partial cooperation with the FBI.

Clandestine activities also continued to be the bread and butter of the CIA. Despite reductions and reorientations, by 1975 clandestine activities still constituted 37 percent of the agency's total budget,[25] and its covert capabilities were still intact—as illustrated by CIA activities against the Marxist Allende government in Chile (*Final Report*, 1, 1976: 123). Those facts led the Senate committee examining foreign and military intelligence to conclude:

> The activities of the Clandestine Service have reflected not what the Agency can do well but what the demands of American foreign policy have required at particular times. The nature of covert operations, the priority accorded them by senior policymakers, and the orientation and background of some DCIs have made the clandestine mission the preeminent activity within the organization. (*Final Report*, 1, 1976: 124)

The CIA and the Management of Intelligence   Allen Dulles, Richard Helms, and William Casey are known to have been intimately involved in the CIA's clandestine activities. Such involvement may cause conflicts of interest within the intelligence community and erode its credibility elsewhere in the government (Flanagan, 1985). At the same time, the coordination function implied by the *central* in CIA's name has taken a back seat. "The CIA's primary task is not to coordinate the efforts of U.S. intelligence or even to produce finished national intelligence for policy-makers," observe Victor Marchetti and John D. Marks (1974). "Its job is, for better or worse, to conduct the government's covert foreign policy." Correspondingly, the other activities of the agency have tended to overlap with those of other intelligence organizations. Although created in part to rectify the problem of duplication among the departmental intelligence services, the CIA has contributed to the problem rather than minimizing it by becoming yet another source of intelligence production. Moreover, the bureaucratic subculture operative in the CIA and elsewhere in the intelligence community militates against change.

---

25. Loch K. Johnson (1980: 145) cites a report by former CIA Director Colby that covert actions—called "special activities" by both the Carter and Reagan administrations—consumed only 5 percent of the CIA's budget, presumably during the Carter administration (see also Johnson, 1989: 103, for an assessment of this figure in a larger historical context). The *Wall Street Journal* (January 11, 1985, p. 9) used the same figure in a 1985 article in obvious reference to the Reagan administration. Robert M. Gates (1987–1988: 216), deputy director of central intelligence in the Reagan administration, also reported that "only about three percent of the CIA's people are involved in covert action." Because accurate and reliable data are simply unavailable, it is difficult to know how to evaluate these numbers. However, because the budget figures cited here represent such a sharp decline from the proportions reported for earlier time periods, there is reason to wonder whether they are comparable. Since covert actions constitute only one type of clandestine operation—the secret gathering of intelligence also falls into this category—the 5 percent cited by Colby and others may cover only a restricted portion of the budgetary expenditure on clandestine activities.

> Intelligence officers often compartmentalize data collected by the sensitive methods of one agency and restrict dissemination to the rest of the community. This practice is rationalized by narrowly interpreting the "need-to-know" security guidelines. But the bottom line is that the bureaucratic culture underlying the American intelligence system does not . . . guarantee that all of what is collected is subject to community-wide, objective, and rigorous analysis. (Goodman, 1984–85: 173)

Although the CIA has been ineffective in communitywide coordination of the national intelligence function,[26] it has played an integral role in the various interagency groups responsible for coordinating and overseeing the making and executive of foreign policy. Principal among those groups, of course, is the National Security Council and its network of interagency committees, in which the director of central intelligence has historically played a key role.

As a practical matter, neither the president nor the NSC exercises control over the day-to-day management of the intelligence community. As noted earlier, the DCI is formally charged with this responsibility, which has been exercised in different ways and through different institutional mechanisms historically. Under Turner and Casey, the National Foreign Intelligence Board assisted the DCI in the production of "national" intelligence (as distinct from "departmental" intelligence), and in establishing intelligence policy, requirements, plans, and priorities. Among the DCI's management tools in the production of national intelligence is the National Intelligence Council (NIC), consisting of a group of analysts and writers who bear special responsibility for National Intelligence Estimates (NIEs), routinely prepared on various parts of the world, and Special National Intelligence Estimates (SNIEs), prepared in response to specific requests by top-level policymakers. These reports are the "best judgments" of the intelligence community on their respective subjects.

The national foreign intelligence budget in principle gives the DCI a second important lever on management responsibilities, but in practice the DCI has been unable to control the budget effectively. The DCI exercises independent authority only over the CIA's budget, which, according to available data, is a comparatively small portion of the whole pie. This has placed the DCI at a competitive disadvantage in dealing with the other intelligence agencies whose activities the DCI in principle is to coordinate. Indeed, a congressional committee, noting that the DCI controlled "less than 10 percent of the combined national and tactical intelligence efforts," described his influence over the allocation of the other 90 percent as limited to that of "an interested critic" (cited in Bamford, 1983).

Ultimately, the issue is control of the intelligence community by the president, for whom the DCI is principal foreign intelligence adviser. Different presidents have approached the issue differently. President Nixon first charged the DCI with making recommendations for a consolidated national foreign

---

26. For a discussion of the coordination process in action, see the testimony in "The Role of Intelligence in the Foreign Policy Process" (1980).

intelligence budget; President Ford sought to enhance further the DCI's role in the allocation of national intelligence resources; and President Carter went furthest in giving the DCI "full and exclusive authority over approval of the National Intelligence Program budget submitted to the President." To accomplish this task, the size of the intelligence community staff that assists the DCI (as suggested in Figure 11.3) was considerably enlarged.

Not surprisingly, the other intelligence agencies were less than enthusiastic with the efforts of Carter's DCI to expand this communitywide role. They won the day when those who joined Reagan's administration with a strong preference for the military were able to curb the DCI so as to preserve DOD's historic independence. Reagan issued an executive order upon his election that "cast the DCI more in the role of a coordinator, rather than a manager, of Community affairs," and William Casey, his director of central intelligence, "adopted a more collegial, 'board of directors' approach" to the National Foreign Intelligence Board whose members are responsible for intelligence collection and production (Flanagan, 1985).

Intelligence Gathering and Analysis   Critics often argue that bringing the tasks of intelligence gathering, analysis, and coordination under the authority of the head of the CIA may have a detrimental impact on the ultimate intelligence product.

> This consolidation exposes the entire intelligence community to the same political and cultural pressures, and reinforces the tendency of all elements to sway together with the mood of the moment. It has fostered a type of "group-think" where the pressures for unanimity override individual mental faculties—somewhat analogous to what occurs in a jury room. (Ellsworth and Adelman, 1979: 158)

The inability of the CIA to foresee the fall of the Shah of Iran in 1979 may have been related to the centralization of intelligence functions. As noted in a study by the House Intelligence Committee, the CIA was essentially caught in a conflict of interests: "On the one hand, the CIA had historically considered itself the Shah's booster. On the other hand, it was supposed to provide sound intelligence analysis of the Iranian political situation." The merging of intelligence gathering and analysis in the DCI did little to enable the agency to separate its estimates of the Shah's survivability from its confidence in him, since the director of the CIA was simultaneously head of the agency that collected the information and the president's chief adviser in determining what the information meant. The Iranian intelligence failure thus bore similarities to the 1961 Bay of Pigs fiasco, in which the CIA was responsible for both gathering intelligence and planning a program of action based on that information. Ultimately, its commitment to the program led it to discount information that might have caused it to abandon the military option.

Iran and Cuba are only two instances of thirty or more intelligence failures investigated by Congress or the media since 1960 (Goodman, 1984–1985:

162). Perhaps such failures are inevitable (Betts, 1978), but explaining why they occur is still important.

Iran and Cuba suggest that the inability of the intelligence establishment to provide policymakers with objective, timely, and accurate intelligence contributes to policy failures. Furthermore, bureaucratic culture, as we suggested earlier, doubtless contributes to intelligence shortcomings by favoring (and rewarding) some kinds of analyses more than others (Goodman, 1984–1985). It is also true, however, that policymakers may disregard objective intelligence or otherwise seek to skew it to their purposes (Johnson, 1983). During the Vietnam War, for example, CIA Director Richard Helms received an estimate only thirteen days before the American military incursion into Cambodia that suggested an invasion would not deter continued North Vietnamese involvement in the war, but he did not bring it to the attention of the White House. Similarly, the CIA provided information during the summer of 1990 suggesting an imminent Iraqi invasion of Kuwait, but the information was discounted because it ran counter to the view of Saddam Hussein's intentions regarding Kuwait then dominant in the National Security Council and the upper echelon of the State Department. Contrariwise, the resignation of two senior CIA analysts during the first Reagan term because, they claimed, William Casey pressured them to rewrite their Central American assessments to make them more consonant with existing U.S. policy points to what then Senate Minority Leader Robert Byrd described as "a shocking use of the CIA for political purposes."

Casey's role in the Reagan administration became especially controversial not only because he was a vigorous champion of the covert option, which he was, but also because he was the first DCI to enjoy cabinet rank (he also enjoyed close personal ties with the president). This meant, in effect, that he was assigned to roles that simultaneously placed him in the position of advocating policy and providing assessments on which policy was to be based. As in the case of the Bay of Pigs fiasco, the dual responsibilities contributed to the failure of the initiative toward Iran.

As we noted in Chapter 10, John Tower, chair of the commission that investigated the Iran-*contra* affair, concluded it was little more than an "aberration." Others disagreed, finding in it evidence of long-standing weaknesses in the nature and control of U.S. intelligence operations. "Throughout the postwar period the structures, attitudes, and loopholes that led to the Iran-*contra* affair have contributed to many other failures and abuses," according to Allan E. Goodman (1987), who has held several senior staff positions in the CIA. "In this latest fiasco . . . the CIA made mistakes that are not unique to the politics and personalities involved . . . but that represent major defects in the country's system of intelligence support to foreign policy." Included among them, Goodman continues, are "long-standing problems stemming from the intrusion of politics into intelligence collection and analysis."

Robert M. Gates (1987–1988), deputy director of central intelligence during the Reagan administration (and an NSC adviser in the Bush administration), wrote shortly after the Iran-*contra* affair became public that "policymakers have always liked intelligence that supported what they want to do, and they often try to influence the analysis to buttress the conclusions they want to reach. They ask carefully phrased questions; they sometimes withhold information; they broaden or narrow the issue; on rare occasions they even try to intimidate. The pressures can be enormous."[27] But, he added, "There is no charge to which those in the CIA are more sensitive than that of cooking intelligence—of slanting its reports to support policy," which would "transgress the single deepest ethical and cultural principle of the CIA." It is clear nonetheless that the line between intelligence and advocacy is often slender. The Tower Board found, for example, that members of the National Security Council staff were so actively involved with CIA officials in the preparation of a May 1985 SNIE on Iran that their "strong views" may have been "allowed to influence the intelligence judgments" contained in it. "It is critical that the line between intelligence and advocacy of a particular policy be preserved if intelligence is to retain its integrity and perform its proper function," the Board continued. "In this instance, the CIA came close enough to the line to warrant concern."

Other examples specifically related to the fact that the director of central intelligence and the director of the CIA are one and the same can be cited (Goodman, 1987). The problem will persist until the roles are split, with the job as director of the CIA divorced from the job as the president's chief intelligence adviser (Goodman, 1987).

Management and Oversight of Covert Actions   A common and related thread running through many inquiries into intelligence operations has to do with the control of covert operations. Responsibility for approval and supervision of "special activities" during the Reagan administration initially rested with the National Security Planning Group. Later, a secret interagency committee was established at the deputy under secretary level to oversee the growing number of covert operations initiated by the administration (Tyler and Ottaway, 1986). Sometimes called the 208 Committee because it met in Room 208 of the Old Executive Office Building across from the White House, the committee reportedly assumed responsibilities akin to those of the 40 Committee, which had managed U.S. covert operations during the 1970s. Decisions of the group were ratified by the National Security Planning Group. The fact that the presi-

---

27. The example of the exercise of political pressure to change *objective intelligence* cited above implicates the director of the CIA. In another case, it appears the White House was responsible for applying political pressure to the CIA. A 1983 CIA estimate

> concluded that the controversial Soviet oil pipeline to Western Europe would fail to make our allies vulnerable in any significant way to Soviet pressures, as argued by the Reagan administration. A senior staffer on the National Security Council (NSC) telephoned the CIA, complaining that "it is not helpful to have an NIE (National Intelligence Estimate) suggesting disagreement with White House policy." The thinly-veiled implication was: deep-six the estimate. When told of the call, CIA deputy director John McMahon reportedly responded with searing scatological advice for the NSC staffer. On this occasion the NIE stood. (Johnson, 1983: 183)

dent actually participated in the latter's meetings made it the highest-level group ever employed for the approval of covert operations. During the Carter administration, the NSC Special Coordination Committee was responsible for this task. The committee was a successor to President Ford's Operations Advisory Group, which in turn was a refurbished and restyled 40 Committee bearing policy-making responsibility for overseeing clandestine political operations during the Nixon administration and the early months of Ford's. The Bush administration's NSC Principals Committee is the current analogue to each of these.

Part of the impetus for sensitivity to the need to pinpoint responsibility for covert operations came from Congress. The Hughes-Ryan Amendment to the 1974 Foreign Assistance Act (repealed by the 1980 Intelligence Oversight Act) required the president to certify to Congress that an executive-approved covert action is "important to the national interests of the United States." The DCI was to inform Congress of the presidential finding in a "timely manner."[28] The process of informing Congress did not have to be completed prior to the implementation of the covert action, however (within twenty-four hours became the understanding). The requirement was a response to the prior concept of *plausible denial*, which meant that covert operations were formulated and approved in such a manner that the president could be saved the embarrassment of a "blown" covert operation. Secretary of State Kissinger testified before Congress that from 1972 to 1974 President Nixon personally and directly approved all covert operations, and that he believed with "almost certain knowledge" that the same had been true previously (House Select Committee on Intelligence, cited in *Final Report*, 1, 1976). Other testimony before Congress, however, indicated that "one means of protecting the President from embarrassment was not to tell him about certain covert operations, at least formally. . . . The concept of 'plausible denial' was taken in an almost literal sense: 'The government was authorized to do certain things that the President was not advised of'" (*Final Report*, 1, 1976). It surfaced once more during the Iran-*contra* affair, as hearings before Congress demonstrated that some of those involved, notably National Security Adviser John Poindexter, undertook actions in the president's name without his explicit knowledge. "Although convinced the president would approve the use of proceeds from the Iranian arms sales for the contras as an 'implementation' of his policy, Poindexter 'made a very deliberate decision not to ask the President' so that he could

---

28. In practice, the requirement meant informing the House and Senate committees on intelligence, armed services, appropriations, and foreign affairs and relations. Theoretically, this meant that anywhere from roughly forty-five to perhaps as many as two hundred members of Congress and their staffs could be knowledgeable about impending covert actions, which is one reason why the number of committees needing to be informed was cut to only two in the 1980 Intelligence Oversight Act. Underlying the perceived need to trim the number of committees was the belief that Congress cannot keep a secret. Although widespread, it does not hold up well under scrutiny, either before the Intelligence Oversight Act was passed (Johnson, 1980), or since. In fact, the evidence indicates that the executive branch is more often responsible for leaks of sensitive information than is Congress (see Goodman, 1987).

'insulate [him] from the decision and provide some future deniability'" (Treverton, 1990, citing testimony before Congress).

Available evidence suggests other ways top-level management of covert operations has been lax. The Senate's extensive inquiry in the mid-1970s into the intelligence community found that verbal checks by telephone rather than extensive face-to-face discussions were used to approve proposals, for example. When formal meetings and extended discussions did occur, they were directed primarily at new departures rather than thorough examinations of ongoing projects. During 1975, for example, the 40 Committee met nine times to discuss Angola (compared with one National Security Council meeting on the subject), and an Interagency Working Group on Angola met twenty-four times between August 1975 and January 1976 (*Final Report*, 1, 1976: 55).

The Senate hearings, which took place during the Ford administration, pointed out that Ford's reorganization of the intelligence community did little to define the criteria by which covert operations were brought forth for top-level executive approval. There is no evidence that Carter's reorganization accomplished anything more, and what little is available for the Reagan administration suggests less stringency, not more.[29] Previously, it had been the director of central intelligence who decided whether an operational program should be submitted to the 40 Committee for approval. "Political sensitivity" of the project was one criterion guiding the decision. Cost was another. Projects involving "large" sums of money—defined as $25,000 or more—were apparently more likely to be brought before the 40 Committee.

Given those rules, many clandestine political operations were outside the purview of most top-level officials. The Senate's report (*Final Report*, 1, 1976: 56) indicates that 409 covert projects were approved by the 40 Committee and its predecessors between March 1955 and February 1967 (104 under Eisenhower, 163 under Kennedy, and 142 under Johnson). Contrast those numbers with a CIA study that showed that of the 550 Clandestine Services projects existing in 1962, only 86 were separately approved or reapproved by Kennedy's 40 Committee predecessor, the Special Group, during that year (*Final Report*, 1, 1976: 57). Projects not receiving explicit consideration were viewed as low-risk, low-cost operations. There apparently was also a tendency by the CIA to view specific projects not reviewed by the 40 Committee as having received prior approval under broader program guidelines. As one observer commented in reference to the Carter administration, "A tendency reportedly has grown within the CIA to forward only a few broad covert action categories

---

29. Drawing on the historical record from the inception of the CIA in 1947 through 1982, Harry Howe Ransom (1983) argues that "the state of relations with the Soviet Union determines the degree of accountability imposed upon intelligence operations. The greater the hostility between the U.S. and the U.S.S.R., and the stronger the consensus about threats to national security, the fewer the restrictions, audits, and controls that will be imposed upon the CIA." Thus the increase in Soviet-American tensions evident in the early 1980s "produced a domestic political climate within the United States more tolerant of the intelligence agencies" than had been true in the immediate wake of Vietnam and Watergate.

to the president and make in-house decisions on all the supposedly routine ones. Although these routine operations are allegedly offsprings of earlier presidential findings, this permits the agency to by-pass the White House and Congress" (Johnson, 1980). In all, the number of specific covert operations subjected to top-level interagency scrutiny appears to have been small.[30]

The scope of the presidential finding that certifies covert actions to Congress, as required by the Intelligence Oversight Act, can have an important impact on their control. In particular, whether findings are conceived in broad or narrow terms is a matter of concern to both Congress and the executive branch. Stansfield Turner, DCI during the Carter administration, explains:

> Under a broad finding, an operation can be expanded considerably; with a narrow one, the CIA has to go back to the President to obtain a revised finding if there is any change of scope. The Congress is wary of broad findings; they can easily be abused. The CIA is afraid of narrow findings; they can be a nuisance. What has evolved is a working understanding that whenever the activity being carried out under a finding is widened past the original description to the Congress, the CIA will advise the committee. (Turner, 1985: 169)[31]

Even in this respect, however, there is room for interpretation and possible abuse. Take the issue of the CIA's mining of Nicaragua's harbors in 1984.

> On January 31, 1984, DCI William Casey met with the House Intelligence committee and mentioned the mining, though the meeting was primarily about releasing funds for the overall contra project. The House committee apparently did not share its information with its Senate colleagues. . . .
>
> Casey first met with the full Senate Intelligence committee on March 8, for over an hour, but this meeting too dealt primarily with authorizing the release of funds, over which the Intelligence committee was fighting a jurisdictional battle with Appropriations. Only one sentence dealt with the mining, and it, like the rest of the briefing, was delivered in Casey's inimitable mumble. Many on the committee did not learn of the mining until a month later, and then almost by accident. (Treverton, 1990: 83)

Technically, Casey nodded to the letter of the law with his reference to what became a politically explosive covert operation. The episode angered even Republican members of Congress, such as Senator Barry Goldwater (see

---

30. See Johnson (1989) and Treverton (1987) for discussions of the process whereby covert actions are approved. Both authors point out that the attitudes of those involved in the process can significantly affect the way it operates.

31. The distinction between what the CIA regards as "important" and "routine" covert actions is related to the nature of presidential findings. The former require a presidential finding, while the latter flow from existing findings (Johnson, 1980). In an environment where covert actions are a preferred mechanism of policy, as they were during the Reagan administration, we would expect presidential findings to be very broad indeed. The joint congressional committee investigating the Iran-*contra* affair concluded this was the case when it noted that under DCI Casey "CIA personnel attempted to craft Findings in terms so broad that they could not limit the CIA's freedom to act" (cited in Johnson, 1989).

also Chapter 12), who had supported the adminstration's desire to bring covert actions back into service of the nation's foreign policy, for it seemed to flaunt the idea that even those actions are subject to democratic governance, difficult though that may be. The Iran-*contra* revelations reinforced Congress's concern and led it to insist that all presidential findings approving covert actions and all significant changes in them be made in writing. Congress also pushed toward being notified of such operations within specified time periods, but this effort was set aside (at least temporarily) by mutual agreement between the legislative and executive branches early in the Bush administration. In the meantime, it fell to William H. Webster, in his first year as DCI in the Bush administration, to concentrate on the primary task — "clean up Casey's mess" (Clarke, 1989).

In a high-risk world of push and shove, threat and counterthreat, there is no question that policymakers demand the best available information about the present and future status, capabilities, and intentions of foreign powers. Nor is there question that national security often requires policy making behind closed doors. But what are the consequences for democratic control of foreign policy making? Can a democratic society long absolve itself from responsibility for the conduct of its government officials without also running the risk of losing sight of who is serving whom, for what purpose, and in pursuit of what ideals? These questions go to the heart of a fundamental democratic dilemma: effective intelligence requires secrecy, yet democracy depends on public scrutiny of the government's exercise of power. Those responsible for the management of the intelligence community and its operations must wrestle with that continuing dilemma.

ECONOMIC AGENCIES: AGENTS OF POLITICAL ECONOMY

The State and Defense Departments are the preeminent executive departments concerned with foreign policy and national security. In a complex and economically interdependent world, however, their jurisdiction, particularly the former's, impinges on, and is infringed on by, other executive departments whose policy responsibilities spill over into international affairs. A brief look at four essentially domestically oriented departments that are also concerned with foreign economic affairs provides additional evidence about the complexities of the foreign affairs government.

The Department of the Treasury

Concern for the position of the U.S. dollar in the international monetary system gives Treasury a keen interest in international affairs. Its responsibilities include tax policy, tariffs, the balance of trade and payments, exchange rate adjustments, and the public debt. Those responsibilities make Treasury the principal department through which domestic and international financial and fiscal policy recommendations are formulated. Stephen D. Cohen (1988) describes the ascendancy of the Treasury Department to a position of power in the area of international economic policy making as "the outstanding organizational feature of U.S. international economic policy since the end of World War II." He attributes Treasury's rise to the position of "an organizational superpower" to three overarching factors: "the relative international decline of U.S. economic strength, as measured in the deterioration of the U.S. balance of payments and two subsequent dollar devaluations; the increased impact of the external sector on domestic economic policy management; and the increased interest in Washington in achieving a broad range of economic policy goals."

The importance of the Treasury Department has often brought the secretary of the treasury, who serves as the chief financial officer of the United States, into the most intimate circle of presidential advisers, where the secretary has been able to influence foreign as well as domestic policy making. The roster of influentials would take us all the way back to Alexander Hamilton. In the postwar period, it includes George M. Humphrey, Douglas Dillon, John Connally, William Simon, Michael Blumenthal, G. William Miller, James A. Baker, and Nicholas F. Brady, among others.

The secretary's role as chair of major White House economic policy coordinating bodies, such as President Bush's Cabinet Council on Economic Policy and President Nixon's Council on International Economic Policy, is an institutional manifestation of the secretary's position in government-wide economic policy issues. Other key roles derive from the secretary's duties as the U.S. governor of the International Monetary Fund, the World Bank, and the Inter-American, Asian, and African development banks. Those assignments give the Treasury secretary and department a major voice in decisions regarding U.S. participation in, and the level of contributions to, multilateral lending institutions, which have been the focus of considerable debate in recent years,[32] as well as in the larger issues involved in the maintenance and operation of the complex international monetary system. Included is a mandate in the Omnibus Trade and Competitiveness Act of 1988 requiring the secretary of the treasury to pursue a more stable exchange rate for the dollar as a means of both national economic policy and trade policy.

The office of the assistant secretary for international affairs is the main unit within Treasury through which the department's international functions are carried out. It is organized into subunits responsible for monetary affairs, developing nations, trade and investment policy, and Arabian Peninsula affairs. Through these groups the office assists the secretary of the treasury and the under secretary for monetary affairs in the formulation and execution of international financial, monetary, commercial, energy, and trade policies and programs. The office is also responsible for providing assistance to the secretary in the roles of cochair of the U.S.-Saudi Arabian Joint Commission on Economic Cooperation, the U.S.-Israel Joint Committee for Investment and Trade, the U.S.-China Joint Economic

---

32. See Schoultz (1982) for a discussion of the decision-making structure governing U.S. participation in multilateral banks and an examination of its voting record in them.

Committee, and chair of the National Advisory Council on International Monetary and Financial Policies. In the past this office has also played a key role in institutional arrangements and policies governing commercial ties between the United States and the Soviet Union and Eastern Europe.

Other subdivisions in the Treasury Department include the Bureau of Alcohol, Tobacco, and Firearms, the U.S. Customs Service, and the U.S. Secret Service. In carrying out their functions, each of those units performs limited intelligence activities relevant to foreign affairs, as noted earlier.

The Department of Commerce

Foreign economic policy is also the bailiwick of the Commerce Department insofar as it is concerned with international affairs, particularly that portion relating to the expansion and protection of American commerce abroad. Unlike the secretary of the treasury, however, the secretary of commerce and the Commerce Department as a whole historically have not been principal actors in foreign policy making. Instead, as indicated in Chapter 10, the U.S. Trade Representative plays the lead role in trade policy. Since 1980, however, when the government's trade-related responsibilities were reorganized, the Commerce Department has been the principal agency with operating responsibilities in the trade area except in matters involving agricultural trade.

Specific trade responsibilities of the Commerce Department include administration of countervailing duty and antidumping statutes,[33] foreign commercial representation and export promotion, implementation of the GATT multilateral trade negotiations agreements, trade policy analysis, and foreign compliance with trade agreements. Those duties are discharged by the International Trade Administration, headed by the under secretary for international trade, whose general charge is to promote world trade and to strengthen the position of the United States in the global network of trade and investment. Another unit, the Bureau of Export Administration, is responsible for directing the nation's export control policy, which includes enforcement of export licensing and U.S. export laws.

Illustrative of the way in which foreign economic affairs, which encompass issues both foreign and domestic in nature, have eroded the primacy of the traditional foreign policy agencies is the fact that the Commerce Department rather than the State Department is now responsible for U.S. commercial representation. The U.S. and Foreign Commercial Service is responsible for commercial representation and trade promotion overseas, a position affirmed by Congress in the 1988 omnibus trade bill. It combines some four dozen

---

33. *Countervailing duties* are import taxes that offset the special advantages that imports have because of subsidies provided by the exporting nation; they are designed to place subsidized imports on the same price footing as other imports and domestic products. *Dumping* means selling exports for prices below those in the exporter's own domestic market. Antidumping regulations are designed to make up the difference between the exporter's price and the foreign market value when the selling price is less than the fair value.

district offices in the United States with posts located in more than sixty countries throughout the world, thus bringing together in one organization those seeking to encourage American firms to sell abroad and those who deal with the potential buyers of American products. The service also supports the Caribbean Basin Initiative, the program of tariff reductions and tax incentive designed to promote economic growth and trade in the region.

Despite the enhanced role of the Commerce Department in trade policy implementation since 1980, it remains a comparatively weak actor in the councils of government. In part this reflects a historical aversion to close ties between the manufacturing sector and government bureaucrats, with the result that the department plays "more of an operational than a policymaking role" (Cohen, 1988). The distinction is in part an institutional reflection. As Malcolm Baldrige (1983) observes, "Trade is the only major Cabinet function where policy is made in one department (the United States trade representative) and carried out in another (Department of Commerce)." As a result, "trade policy has to be 'brokered' among the other Cabinet departments, instead of being advocated."

Baldrige was secretary of commerce when President Reagan in 1983 proposed creation of a Department of International Trade and Industry. Designed to eliminate the split between who makes and who implements policy, it is perhaps no accident that the acronym for the proposed department—DITI—bore striking resemblance to Japan's Ministry of International Trade and Industry—MITI—after which the new agency was presumably modeled. The proposed department failed to receive congressional support during Reagan's first term, and although the administration gave lip service to the proposal in its second term, Congress moved instead to enhance the role of the U.S. Trade Representative in overall trade policy. The result is that the Commerce Department remains more of an implementor than advocate of United States trade policy.

The Department of Agriculture

In 1987 the value of U.S. agricultural exports stood at $28.6 billion. Although substantial, the amount is less than two-thirds of what it was at its peak in 1981, as worldwide recession, an overvalued dollar, and increased trade competitiveness caused American export sales to decline and the U.S. share of world agricultural trade to fall. At the same time, American exports of particular products (such as grain and soybeans) continue to account for a substantial share of total world exports, and U.S. dependence on export markets for these products is in turn substantial. Agricultural exports thus continue to figure prominently in the world marketplace and to contribute measurably to domestic farm income and to the nation's overall trade balance with the rest of the world. Those facts attest to the importance of the United States in the world marketplace and to the importance of agriculture in the domestic economy. Necessarily, therefore, the Department of Agriculture has a major stake in the administration of foreign economic policy. Particular departmental interests include promotion of the sale of agricultural commodities abroad, including the sale or distribution of government-owned surplus commodities under Public Law (PL) 480, which includes the Food for Peace Program; allocation of import quotas for certain agricultural commodities; collection of information about agricultural developments overseas; and participation in international negotiations relating to world trade in agricultural products.

The Foreign Agricultural Service (FAS), operating under the authority of the under secretary for international affairs and commodity programs, is the principal subdivision of the department concerned with international affairs. Its primary purpose is promoting sales of American agricultural commodities overseas. Toward that end, it maintains agricultural counselors and attachés in some sixty American embassies overseas covering 110 different foreign countries. The FAS is responsible for formulating, administering, and coordinating Agriculture Department policies and programs as they relate to multilateral conventions and organizations, such as the General Agreement on Tariffs and Trade (GATT) and the Food and Agriculture Organization (FAO) of the United Nations, and for providing support for U.S. agricultural representatives during international negotiations.

FAS is also responsible for managing agricultural functions under the Food for Peace Program, which is aimed at the long-run improvement of developing nations' economies. Included under PL 480 are long-term credit sales for American dollars, whereby the government dispenses commodity surpluses purchased by the government to support the American farmer. Donations for humanitarian purposes to foreign governments, voluntary relief agencies, and international institutions, such as the World Food Program of the United Nations, are included. The Agriculture Department carries out provisions of PL 480 in cooperation with the Agency for International Development (AID).

Finally, the department's Office of International Cooperation and Development is responsible for the Agriculture Department's contribution to the Caribbean Basin Initiative, and it directs the department's international development and technical cooperation efforts. That task involves the department simultaneously with American universities and other domestic organizations, foreign governments, and international organizations.

The Department of Labor

Gathering information, proffering advice, administering selected programs, and participating in international negotiations (especially in the International Labor Organization [ILO], the General Agreement on Tariffs and Trade, and the Organization for Economic Cooperation and Development)—those are the international affairs functions of the Labor Department, but with a view toward their importance for the American wage earner rather than the agricultural, business, or financial communities. They are carried out by the Bureau of International Labor Affairs headed by the deputy under secretary for international affairs. Among other things, the department's authority traditionally has carried with it a special concern for immigrant labor. It also has involved the department with the State Department in the provision of labor attachés for assignment abroad and with the Agency for International Development in the execution of technical assistance activities overseas. The department also bears responsibility for the administration of the trade adjustment assistance programs for workers under the Trade Act of 1974. The act provides that workers adversely affected by foreign trade competition are entitled to restitution.

THE POLITICS OF POLICY MAKING: RETROSPECTIVE AND PROSPECTIVE OBSERVATIONS

The executive agencies that are part of the foreign affairs government are so numerous and multifaceted that no brief description could adequately capture either the breadth of their interests or the depth of their involvement in matters of foreign policy. As a way of explicating governmental sources of American policy, however, the description provided here should demonstrate what clearly has become a distinguishing characteristic of American foreign policy making—decision making by and within a disparate set of exceedingly large and complex organizational structures. Affecting control over them and dealing with the consequences of their decision-making behavior have become important parts of the way in which the president and the presidential advisers within the innermost concentric circle of policy making seek to make American foreign policy. Hence we will return later (in Chapter 13) to a further examination of the characteristics and consequences of decision making by and in organizations.

The jurisdictions of the executive agencies necessarily catapult them into the forefront of the political processes through which the nation's external conduct ultimately becomes visible. Determining which are preeminent among those agencies is therefore important. On the basis of the diplomatic and historical record examined in Chapters 3, 4, and 5, the Defense Department and the CIA appear to have been in a commanding political position throughout the postwar period. Certainly the stimuli coming from what was widely perceived to be a hostile external environment, which buttressed widely shared fears of Soviet communism, were important in promoting Defense and CIA influence within the policy-making community—to the point, in fact, that preferences for military might and interventionist means have become distinctive patterns of American foreign policy. The fact that the CIA often controlled the information on which policy decisions had to be based, and that both the CIA and the military often had ready alternatives available from which decision makers could choose, also contributed to their commanding political positions.

Beyond those factors, the ties between government agencies and the larger societal system within which they reside also become important in understanding who matters within the policy-making community. In fact, if we think of the institutions of government as filters through which the other

source variables must ultimately pass if they are to affect foreign policy outcomes, the way in which the government agencies described in this chapter
both reflect and respond to the other source categories illuminates the role they
play in that process. In that context, the nongovernmental groups that government agencies serve, and with which they often are therefore identified,
become important sources of agencies' political power. That fact helps explain
why the State Department—which is the only agency of government that bears
responsibility for the totality of American relations with other nations—has
not assumed a more commanding position within the foreign affairs government. There is virtually no substantive area of foreign policy in which the State
Department does not become involved. But it often lacks the political
resources and domestic support to go along with its formal authority that
would make it a more dominant force.

As a practical matter, the State Department is involved in the range of substantive items that are the stuff of foreign policy through its extensive consultation and coordination with other agencies. The State Department's relative
lack of political resources means that in those interagency contacts that do
occur, it is frequently likely to be bargaining from a position of weakness rather
than strength. Our earlier discussion of the relative advantages of the Defense
Department compared to the State Department is relevant here. It is also germane to State's position with regard to the economic agencies, whose importance in the policy-making process derives from the changing position of the
United States in the transitional political economy discussed in Chapter 7. John
Franklin Campbell cogently summarizes the point:

> State speaks to a broad but weak national constituency, whereas the domestic eco-
> nomic departments represent narrower but more vocal special interest groups.
> These inherent conflicts of point of view are expressed in a complex series of
> interagency committees in which State is one voice among many, and generally a
> minor voice in the debate. The reasons for this are twofold. Business, farm, and
> labor lobbies bring considerable pressure to bear on the other departments of
> government, which by custom respond to those interests more passionately than
> does the Foreign Affairs Department. Second, economic policy is but one of many
> foreign policy concerns of State, whereas it is the central issue with the other
> departments concerned in the process. Treasury, not State, is the "expert" on
> monetary matters; Agriculture is the "expert" on U.S. farm surpluses; Commerce
> is the "expert" on American industry; while State speaks for a foreign policy that
> may seem quite remote if not abstract in comparison to these immediate home
> issues. State's logical domestic ally in these debates would often be the American
> consumer, who is unfortunately the least organized of the actors in our interest
> group domestic politics. (Campbell, 1971: 220).

Congress frequently is an intimate part of the complex interagency politicking in which government agencies often become engaged. Indeed, Congress, or, more correctly, congressional committees and subcommittees, often
behave much like domestic clientele groups in protecting government agencies
from attack by "outsiders," which in this context may include those making

up the presidential subsystem. The convenient alliance between certain bureaucracies and their congressional allies helps explain, for example, the political functions of bureaucratic "leaks" to the press. They become mechanisms for cueing others within the political system, such as Congress, of impending changes in policies or programs, which they can then attack or defend. In the political struggle between Congress and the president, however, the president is generally in the more commanding position when it comes to foreign policy. Exploring why that is so is the subject of the next chapter.

SUGGESTIONS FOR FURTHER READING

Bamford, James. (1983) *The Puzzle Palace: A Report on America's Most Secret Agency*. New York: Penguin.

Clarke, Duncan L. (1989) *American Defense and Foreign Policy Institutions: Toward a Solid Foundation*. New York: Harper & Row.

Cohen, Stephen D. (1988) *The Making of United States International Economic Policy: Principles, Problems, and Proposals for Reform*, 3rd ed. New York: Praeger.

Gates, Robert M. (1987–1988) "The CIA and American Foreign Policy," *Foreign Affairs* 66 (Winter): 215–230.

Ikenberry, G. John, David A. Lake, and Michael Mastanduno (eds.). (1988) *The State and American Foreign Economic Policy*. Ithaca, N.Y.: Cornell University Press.

Johnson, Loch K. (1989) *America's Secret Power: The CIA in a Democratic Society*. New York: Oxford University Press.

Newsom, David D. (1987) "The U.S. Foreign Affairs Structure in a Changing World," *Washington Quarterly* 10 (Summer): 203–214.

Richelson, Jeffrey T. (1989) *The U.S. Intelligence Community*, 2nd ed. Cambridge, Mass.: Ballinger.

Rubin, Barry. (1985) *Secrets of State: The State Department and the Struggle over U.S. Foreign Policy*. New York: Oxford University Press.

Yarmolinsky, Adam. (1971) *The Military Establishment: Its Impact on American Society*. New York: Harper & Row.

CHAPTER 12

The Role of Congress in Foreign Policy Making

In the last twenty years we've witnessed a departure from the way in which this nation has conducted its foreign policy for nearly two centuries. Congress has asserted an increasingly influential role in the day-to-day micromanagement of foreign policy and even of foreign operations.

VICE PRESIDENT GEORGE BUSH, 1987

Congress . . . is a conservative organization—cautious and reluctant to initiate change. It responds to old stimuli better than new. When it opposes the Executive, it is usually to protect some interest group or some aspect of the status quo rather than to initiate action . . . . Sometimes a member of Congress will take the initiative, or a group of members will, but Congress as an institution will not.

REPRESENTATIVE LES ASPIN, 1976

Member of Congress Les Aspin's description of Congress's role in foreign policy making lends support to the old adage that "the president proposes, Congress disposes." To many, Congress primarily plays a negative role—functioning as a public critic of the executive and otherwise placing limits on its behavior. But especially since Vietnam, Congress has also sought actively to shape various policies and policy-making procedures, as demonstrated by the following:

- In 1970 Congress "repealed" the Gulf of Tonkin Resolution, which had given President Lyndon B. Johnson, as interpreted by him, a "blank check" for prosecuting an undeclared war in Southeast Asia.
- In 1973 Congress overrode President Richard M. Nixon's veto to write the War Powers Resolution into law, thus requiring the president to consult Congress prior to dispatching troops abroad.
- In 1974, Congress embargoed, over the Ford administration's objection, arms sales to Turkey in retaliation for its invasion of Cyprus.
- In 1974 Congress refused to permit the president to extend most-favored-nation (MFN) trade treatment to the Soviet Union by linking MFN to the free emigration of Soviet Jews.

- In 1975 Congress ensured American withdrawal from the Vietnam war by denying the president authority to provide the South Vietnamese government emergency military aid to forestall its imminent collapse to communist forces.
- In 1976 Congress prohibited continued Central Intelligence Agency (CIA) expenditures to bolster anti-Marxist forces fighting in Angola.
- In 1978 the Senate adopted a reservation to the Panama Canal neutrality treaty allowing the United States to use military force in Panama to reopen the canal if it were closed for any reason.
- In 1979 more than two dozen senators challenged President Jimmy Carter's right to abrogate without congressional approval the U.S. defense treaty with Taiwan.
- In 1980 Congress passed legislation asserting its right to prior notice by the executive branch of covert intelligence activities abroad.
- In 1982 Congress denied the Defense Department and the CIA funds for the purpose of overthrowing Nicaragua's government.
- In 1983 Congress invoked provisions of the War Powers Resolution to limit the time military forces could remain in Lebanon.
- In 1985 Congress cut from two hundred to fifty the number of land-based MX missiles to be deployed in fixed silos.
- In 1986 Congress overrode a presidential veto to place economic sanctions on South Africa.

These examples of congressional assertiveness in response to the so-called imperial presidency of the Vietnam era reflect the effort of Congress to ensure itself a greater voice in policy making. By writing certain conditions into legislation bearing on the nation's foreign relations, Congress, historically submissive, sought to expand its control over foreign policy making, often at the expense of the president. As Under Secretary of State William D. Rogers lamented in 1979, "Foreign policy has become almost synonymous with law-making. The result is to place a straitjacket of legislation around the manifold complexity of our relations with other nations."

Policy-making procedures affect policy substance, but the impact of legislative involvement is not clear-cut. Nonetheless, it is feared and decried in the White House. "We have got to get to the point where we can run a foreign policy without a committee of 535 telling us what we can do," Ronald Reagan exclaimed in 1985. The attitude perhaps explains why the Reagan administration challenged a broad array of laws and procedural reforms that Congress earlier had put into place to assert its foreign policy prerogatives. For its part, Congress did little to address the underlying issues of shared power by separate institutions that the administration's actions provoked, preferring instead to rely on "parliamentary gimmickry and legislative 'ad hocery'" to deal with the various crises that had to be faced (Warburg, 1989). In many respects, therefore, the 1980s might be regarded as a "counterreformation" that "curbed many legislative prerogatives that were central to the congressional revolution of the previous decade'' (Warburg, 1989).[1] Congress continues to assert its foreign policy authority in various ways, but it has been wary of restricting presidential flexibility in foreign policy making. Thus the overall thrust of executive-legislative relations during the 1980s reinforced rather than undermined the long-standing propensity for the president to propose and Congress to dispose.

This chapter will explore the initiator-respondent relationship between the executive and Congress by examining those institutional characteristics of Congress that favor its more passive role vis-à-vis the executive. We then probe Congress's conduct with respect to treaties, war, and money—three areas wherein the Constitution gives Congress especially formidable powers—and inquire into the appropriateness of the initiator-respondent label in these special policy areas. As a preface, we first trace the postwar record of executive-legislative interactions in foreign policy making.

PAST EXECUTIVE-LEGISLATIVE INTERACTIONS

Although *initiator-respondent* generally describes the relationship between the executive and Congress, its precise nature is more complex than the label conveys. Not infrequently, ideas are born on Capitol Hill for which the president subsequently receives political credit when they are brought to fruition. Moreover, whereas presidential dominance was especially evident prior to the Vietnam buildup in 1965, since then congressional assertiveness in foreign policy has been more characteristic. In fact, extending the chronology suggested by Frans R. Bax (1977), six relatively distinct phases of postwar executive-legislative relations can be delineated.

Accommodation describes the pattern of relations from roughly 1943 to 1951. The nation's goals of globalism, anticommunism, and containment of perceived Soviet expansionism were forged during that time through a variety of specific foreign policy initiatives and programs in which Congress willingly participated.[2] Bipartisanship (discussed more fully later in this chapter) captures the essence of the accommodative atmosphere of the period.

Accommodation was followed by *antagonism*, a phase that lasted from 1951 to 1955. McCarthyism fell within that period. So, too, did congressional recriminations over who ''lost'' China, disenchantment with ''limited'' war in Korea and the firing of General Douglas MacArthur, who independently sought

---

1. During the post-Vietnam revolutionary ferment of the 1970s, ''a system of *policy codetermination*'' or ''a sharing of the decision-making process'' came to characterize executive-legislative relations (Franck and Weisband, 1979).

2. That is not to say Congress unanimously supported the premises on which American postwar strategy was predicated. Despite the prevailing consensus, some (such as Senator Robert Taft from Ohio) opposed continuation of America's international involvement and advocated a return to America's isolationist tradition (recall Chapter 3). This neo-isolationist sentiment represented a minority view, however.

to expand that war, and growing concern over the cost of foreign aid and Harry S Truman's commitment of troops to Europe. Efforts by the Senate to curb presidential treaty-making powers symbolized the antagonisms of the period.

For nearly a decade thereafter, from 1955 to 1965, congressional *acquiescence* in foreign policy making prevailed. During this period Congress passed the "area resolutions" granting the president broad authority to deal with external conflict situations, such as those in the Middle East, Berlin, Cuba, the China straits, and Vietnam. A bipartisan spirit was again dominant as Congress agreed with most of the specific foreign policy decisions made by the three presidents who held office during these years. Any lingering doubts Congress may have had about some of them were "simply swallowed," as Congress preferred "not to share the responsibility of decision with the president" (Bax, 1977). But by backing presidential decisions in a manner that legitimated them to the public, Congress helped to build a broad-based, anticommunist foreign policy consensus.

Presidents, for their part, encouraged the acquiescent congressional mood, for a passive role made consultation with or deference to "mere congressmen" unnecessary. Following the massive Vietnam buildup in 1965, however, congressional docility began to dissipate. Highly publicized hearings by the Senate Foreign Relations, chaired by J. William Fulbright, raised questions that fed the growing perception that the war in Vietnam was a major mistake. Still, Congress refused to exercise the constitutional prerogatives at its disposal to constrain presidential behavior. Congress was in a state of *ambiguity*.

President Nixon's decision to expand the Vietnam war into Cambodia in the spring of 1970 transformed ambiguity into *acrimony*. During the next three years the Senate passed a variety of measures that would have curtailed the president's ability to keep or use American troops in Indochina. The House generally failed to go along with these, but in 1971 both chambers did adopt language that proscribed the use of funds authorized or appropriated by Congress "to finance the introduction of United States ground combat troops into Cambodia, or to provide United States advisors to or for Cambodian military forces in Cambodia." Significantly, the bill was passed only *after* the 1970 spring offensive had been completed. Other efforts to restrict expenditures were also largely symbolic. Nevertheless, Congress had begun to participate in the termination of America's role in the tragic Indochina conflict.

The high point of congressional acrimony was reached in 1973, when the War Powers Resolution (discussed later in this chapter) was passed over President Nixon's veto. Ever since, congressional *assertiveness* has prevailed as Congress has sought to be treated as a coequal branch of government and to be heard as a coequal voice in the making of foreign policy. Disenchantment with the Vietnam quagmire and later the Watergate abuses was the critical catalyst giving rise to changed and changing congressional mood.

In a larger sense, however, the emerging mood was rooted in a collapse of the conditions on which congressional acquiescence of the 1950s and 1960s had been based. Acquiescence is possible only when a substantial national consensus on the general purposes of policy exists, and when the specific means chosen by the president to pursue those purposes are generally successful (Bax, 1977). That those conditions should crumble in the wake of Vietnam is significant, for a notable cyclical pattern is evident here: an assertive congressional mood has typically coincided with and followed each major American war, much as congressional dissatisfaction in the 1950s coincided with the Korean War. Congressional activity in the post-Civil War Reconstruction era and in the post-World War I "return to normalcy" period are striking parallels. More generally, the post-World War II record shows that "when Congress has agreed with the general thrust of presidential policy, it has acquiesced in the use or even the enlargement of presidential power. When it has disagreed, it has asserted it own prerogatives" (Crabb and Holt, 1989).

Still, important changes have occurred in executive-legislative relations that cannot be dismissed. Recognizing that the presidential-congressional struggle to shape the nation's foreign policy displays a distinctively cyclical variation, one long-time Capitol Hill staff member nonetheless concludes that "since the end of the Nixon administration, this enduring battle has developed new characteristics. In no previous era of congressional ascendancy has the United States borne the burdens of world leadership. And in no previous era of presidential counterreformation has the White House confronted such a formidable array of procedural weapons at the legislature's disposal" (Warburg, 1989).

Bipartisanship

The proposition that "politics stops at the water's edge"—long a part of the nation's cherished political mythology—has been a sure victim of the changed and changing nature of executive-legislative relations since Nixon.

Bipartisanship is the practical application of the "water's edge" consensual ideal. As noted above, it has often been used to describe the cordial and cooperative relationship between Congress and the executive during the Roosevelt, Truman, and Eisenhower presidencies. It was then that the United States rejected isolationism, embraced internationalism, and developed the postwar strategy for containment of the Soviet Union. Congress and the president often acted as partners in these efforts, especially on matters involving Europe. The famous conversion of Arthur Vandenberg, Republican senator from Michigan who coined the "water's edge" aphorism, symbolized the emergent bipartisan spirit. Once a staunch isolationist, as chair of the Senate Foreign Relations Committee after World War II, Vandenberg engineered congressional support for the North Atlantic Treaty Organization (NATO) and the Marshall Plan. Partisan and ideological differences were never absent during the heyday of bipartisanship, but the anticommunist consensus muted them. It was not until the Vietnam War challenged the premises of the anticommunist consensus that the premises of bipartisanship itself were challenged. Thereafter foreign policy increasingly became a topic over which factional and partisan interests fought. No longer did politics stop at the water's edge.

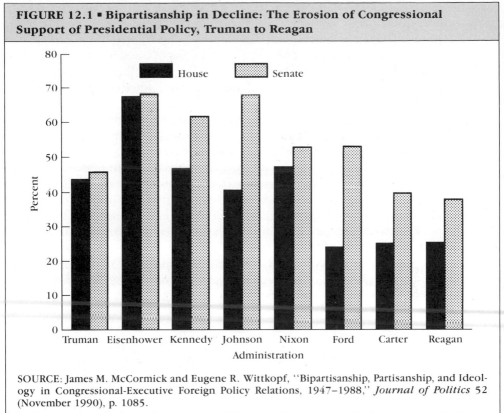

FIGURE 12.1 ▪ Bipartisanship in Decline: The Erosion of Congressional Support of Presidential Policy, Truman to Reagan

SOURCE: James M. McCormick and Eugene R. Wittkopf, "Bipartisanship, Partisanship, and Ideology in Congressional-Executive Foreign Policy Relations, 1947–1988," *Journal of Politics* 52 (November 1990), p. 1085.

NOTE: Each bar represents the percentage of foreign policy votes on which a majority of both parties supported the president's position.

Although the precise meaning of bipartisanship is not altogether clear,[3] one outward measure is how often a majority of the two parties have agreed with the president's position on foreign policy issues on which they have voted in Congress. Figure 12.1 traces this measure through time. It exhibits a gradual decline following the Eisenhower presidency, which then changes abruptly with the Ford presidency, especially in the House.

Underlying these changes are shifts in the partisan and ideological support accorded different presidents. Democratic presidents have consistently won their greatest support on foreign policy issues not only from their own partisans

---

3. One definition associates bipartisanship with "unity in foreign affairs" as reflected in "policy supported by majorities within each political party;" another depicts it as a set of "practices and procedures designed to bring about the desired unity" (Crabb, 1957). For a review of the idea and practice of bipartisanship, see Collier (1989).

but also from liberals, regardless of party. Dwight D. Eisenhower also enjoyed support from liberal Democrats as well as from members of his own party. Since Eisenhower, however, Republican presidents have tended to receive their greatest support from conservatives. The changing patterns of foreign policy voting suggest that a realignment of partisan áttachments and ideological predispositions has transpired since the 1970s such that they now reinforce one another. Republicans have become the party of conservative internationalism and Democrats the party of liberal internationalism, thus bringing both of them into alignment with their postures on domestic policy (McCormick and Wittkopf, 1990a). In this climate bipartisanship has become a more elusive goal.

Presidents invariably appeal for bipartisanship to win political support for their programs, and they often use bipartisan commissions as a vehicle to that end. Prominent examples include those Reagan appointed to seek alternative policies for Central America, strategic defense, and military base closings. George Bush underscored the importance he attached to bipartisanship when he called in his inaugural address for "a new engagement . . . between the executive and the Congress." "There's grown a certain divisiveness," he lamented. "And our great parties have too often been far apart and untrusting of each other. It's been this way since Vietnam. That war cleaves us still . . . . A new breeze is blowing—and the old bipartisanship must be made new again."

The urge to restore bipartisanship to foreign policy making stems from a desire to restore the halcyon mood of the early postwar era. But beyond this, advocates of bipartisanship see it as a vehicle promoting the policy coherence and consistency necessary to an effective foreign policy (Kissinger and Vance, 1988; Winik, 1989). This view presupposes broad-based agreement within American society about the appropriate American role in world affairs of the sort that deeply held anticommunist values once provided. Critics, on the other hand, argue that bipartisanship is a tool used to stifle the expression of divergent viewpoints that is the heart of democratic governance (Falk, 1983; see also Nathan and Oliver, 1987). Too often, they say, its appeal is motivated by the goal of blurring the separation of powers that assigns different foreign policy making responsibilities to Congress and the president. Yet, as Justice Louis Brandeis wrote (in *Myers v. United States*, 1926), the purpose of the separation-of-powers doctrine is "not to avoid friction but . . . to save the people from autocracy."

Numerous policy issues illustrate the increasingly antagonistic congressional attitude that emerged in the wake of Vietnam and Watergate. Prominent among them are Congress's embargo of arms sales to Turkey and its denial of funds to affect political outcomes in Angola during the Ford administration; the numerous reservations Congress expressed when the two Panama Canal treaties came up for ratification during the Carter administration; and the prohibition against sending foreign aid to states that refused to abide by international nuclear nonproliferation safeguards mandated during the Reagan administration.

To illuminate executive-legislative relations in the post-Nixon era, let us consider congressional efforts to shape American arms sales policy during the

Carter and Reagan presidencies and to influence U.S. policy toward Nicaragua during the Reagan administration (with particular attention to the question of providing aid to the *contras*).[4] Both stories demonstrate how Congress has used procedure to assert its prerogatives, how the perceived need to protect presidential flexibility to promote America's world position constrained congressional assertiveness, and how partisan and ideological concerns colored both.

Congress and Arms Sales Policy

The Nixon Doctrine provided the background to congressional involvement in arms sales policy. As the value of foreign military sales skyrocketed during the Nixon presidency, Congress became concerned about the Nixon Doctrine's consequences, which rationalized providing sophisticated equipment to Third World countries (and particularly Israel and the Arab countries opposed to it). In 1975 Congress passed a law, later incorporated into the Arms Export and Control Act, requiring that the executive inform Congress of prospective major arms sales and enabling Congress to veto them within a specified time period.[5] Significantly, that law stipulated that congressional disapproval need only be expressed in a concurrent resolution of the two houses of Congress, thus avoiding the threat of a presidential veto. The procedure, whose origins date to the early 1930s, is known as a *legislative veto* (see Fisher, 1987).

In 1983 the Supreme Court ruled in the *Chadha* case that the legislative veto based on concurrent resolutions was unconstitutional.[6] Congress responded in 1985, when it decided that the enactment of a joint resolution, rather than a concurrent resolution, would be required to block an arms sale. Since a joint resolution is subject to presidential veto, this would effectively

---

4. See the Congressional Quarterly (1986) and Destler (1984) for accounts that focus on El Salvador, which, until the election of José Napoleón Duarte in May 1984, preoccupied the administration and Congress. Our subsequent discussion of U.S. policies toward Nicaragua draws on the Congressional Quarterly (1986).

5. Eventually the law set the period for congressional consideration at thirty days. By mutual agreement, since 1976 presidents have been expected to give Congress twenty days advance notice before submitting a formal proposal for approval to allow the two branches to reach compromises on politically sensitive issues. In the mid-1980s the notice and veto provisions applied to arms sales packages of $50 million or more, to sales of individual weapons worth $14 million or more, and to sales of military construction services worth $200 million or more (Congressional Quarterly, 1990: 81).

6. *Immigration and Naturalization Service v. Chadha*, 103 S. Ct. 2764 (1983). The Court's ruling applied to cases in which Congress had expressly granted administrative power to the executive. Since not all legislation fit the conditions addressed by the Court, the import of the *Chadha* case is more restricted than once thought; applicability to the legislative veto provisions of the War Powers Resolution remains unresolved.

Although the legislative veto had come to be viewed as a necessary instrument to protect Congress from the executive's usurpation of legislative prerogatives, the record shows that the president willingly accepted legislative veto provisions in exchange for the flexibility Congress granted the president in exchange (Fisher, 1987). Noteworthy in this regard is that since 1983 Congress has written a legislative veto into more than one hundred laws that have been signed by the president. Most of these are committee and subcommittee vetoes. Thus the evidence indicates that the device continues to be useful to both the legislative and executive branches.

mean that Congress is now able to stop a major arms sale only if a two-thirds majority in both houses votes to block it. This substantially alters the procedural balance of power in favor of the president, who now needs only to find a third-plus-one minority in either the House or the Senate to move an arms sale forward—or the president can simply veto Congress's action. Instructively, however, Congress never exercised its powers to veto major arms sales prior to the *Chadha* ruling—nor has it done so successfully since. Nevertheless, the possibility of a veto has encouraged presidents to make significant alterations in controversial arms sales proposals to avoid congressional disapproval.

Jimmy Carter pledged during the 1976 presidential campaign to restrain the excessive trade in arms in which the United States had become involved, but he quickly learned once in the White House that the nation's interests and commitments required continued reliance on foreign military sales. Early in his administration he exempted from his own arms restraint policies an Iranian request to purchase advanced-technology airborne warning and control system aircraft (AWACS). Congressional approval of the deal was secured only after the administration agreed to strict conditions that would govern the sophisticated technology's delivery and use. A year later, in 1978, in what was considered a major political achievement, the administration again won congressional support for a massive arms package involving Israel, Egypt, and Saudi Arabia, but this time only after agreeing to increase the number of warplanes destined for Israel.

The electoral tide that swept Ronald Reagan into office included a mandate for sharply increased military spending (which, in fact, Carter had already put in motion) and for a more assertive foreign policy posture generally. The restraining influences of a Congress protective of its own prerogatives were not to be dismissed, however, and it was on an arms sale issue that Reagan first encountered congressional resistance.

The Carter administration's 1978 Middle East arms package included the sale to Saudi Arabia of F-15 aircraft, the most sophisticated jet fighters in the American arsenal, but to secure congressional approval of the deal in the face of strong opposition by the pro-Israeli lobby, the planes were not equipped with bomb racks or air-to-air missiles. The Saudis chafed under the restrictions and repeatedly sought the additional equipment. Upon assuming office, the Reagan administration determined the Saudis should have them, and, in addition, sought to sell them AWACS. The administration thereby pitted itself against the Israeli lobby headed by the powerful American Israel Public Affairs Committee (AIPAC) and its congressional supporters, who generally concur with the view of the Israeli lobby that "arms sales to the Arabs endanger Israel, threaten the stability of the Middle East, and perpetuate the arms race" (Bard, 1988; see also Crabb and Holt, 1989; Tivnan, 1987).

As expected, the Democratically controlled House voted against the sale proposed by the administration shortly after it was brought before Congress. To win approval of the sale, the White House then launched an intensive campaign in the Senate that targeted a handful of senators considered maneuverable.

Seven Republican senators who had earlier opposed the AWACS deal decided to switch, and in a dramatic 48–52 vote the Senate rejected a resolution to disapprove the arms deal. Thus Reagan won his first major foreign policy test with Congress—but it was a victory that required the expenditure of an extraordinary amount of political capital and that was secured only after Reagan elevated the issue by describing it as a test of the credibility of a presidential commitment. Members of Congress also learned the costs of taking on the powerful Israeli lobby, as many of the senators who supported the arms sale lost their reelection bids.

Three years later, in 1984, Reagan again faced formidable opposition—to a proposed sale of a portable antiaircraft missile called the Stinger to Jordan and Saudi Arabia. This time, to the surprise of many, Reagan chose not to fight. Reagan's retreat "was the first time in the 16-year history of direct congressional involvement in arms sales that a president had withdrawn an arms sales proposal without stating that he would resubmit it to Congress at a future date" (*Congressional Quarterly Almanac, 1984*, 1985). Interestingly, however, the administration shortly thereafter sent Stingers to Saudi Arabia under the president's emergency power, thereby bypassing Congress. This was only the second time Congress's role in a major arms sale had been circumvented by this unusual procedure.[7]

Reagan did fight on a third important Mideast arms package, however. Saudi Arabia was again the intended arms recipient, and once more intensive White House lobbying was necessary to save the weapons deal. In this case the effort was directed at sustaining a presidential veto of a measure that would have blocked a $258 million sale from going forward. The president prevailed by a single vote when, in June 1986, thirty-four members of the Senate gave the president the minimum number he needed to reverse an earlier decision blocking the Saudi sale. Some who switched their votes indicated they had done so because of the president's argument that his ability to manage foreign policy was at stake. Others suggested that, by deleting certain weapons from the arms package (notably Stinger missiles), their earlier objections no longer mattered. Significantly, however, the case represented the first time that both houses of Congress had moved to block a major arms sale, thus requiring a sustained presidential veto to proceed with the sale.

Late in 1986 it was revealed that at the same time the administration was seeking congressional approval for the sale of arms to Saudi Arabia, it was engaged in a secret arms deal with Iran that circumvented Congress altogether. Eventually the arms-for-hostages deal came to be known as the Iran-*contra* affair because of the administration's clandestine diversion of funds from the sale of weapons to Iran to the counterrevolutionaries fighting the Sandinistas in Nicaragua. As details spilled into the public limelight, congressional attention

---

7. The first occurred in 1979, when the Carter administration sent military equipment to North Yemen, which at that time was involved in an escalating war with South Yemen's Marxist-oriented government.

riveted on possible violations of congressional prohibitions against covert actions against the Sandinista regime and whether the president had violated the constitutional provision granting Congress power to appropriate funds. In the first instance, however, the question was whether the president had violated the Arms Control and Export Act, which required congressional assent to major arms sales. Congress eventually concluded he had.

The Iran-*contra* affair clouded consideration of the administration's proposals in 1987 to sell Saudi Arabia sixteen hundred Maverick air-to-ground missiles and other weapons, including advanced F-15 fighters. Time-worn arguments about threats to Israeli security again figured in these cases, as did an Iraqi missile attack on the *USS Stark* in the Persian Gulf that killed thirty-seven U.S. sailors. Congressional opposition to the sale was so widespread that in both cases the administration withdrew the proposals before they were ever acted on. Eventually, the administration did score a victory, when a compromise proposal to sell the fighter aircraft but not the missiles was approved. Evidence that the Saudis had become more cooperative with Washington on its Persian Gulf policies and that they were turning to Britain as a source of arms softened resistance from Capitol Hill. So, too, did the political tactics adopted by the new national security team headed by national security adviser Frank Carlucci, who sought a compromise with congressional leaders before the battle lines were drawn. Ironically, the Iran-*contra* affair may actually have helped as the compromise worked out ''was a spirit born of shared burnout'' over the ''seemingly unending'' scandal and ''reflected a recognition by pro-Israeli legislators and AIPAC strategists that it was not a good time to pile on a staggering Reagan administration'' (Warburg, 1989).

Despite this victory and others in 1988 involving the sale of fighter-bombers and missiles to Kuwait, by the end of the Reagan administration neither the president nor Congress was satisfied with the state of arms sales procedures. The executive branch had come to expect opposition to its proposals, which led it to keep pending sales secret as long as possible and otherwise to approach Congress in a confrontational manner. Major arms sales proposals were made without giving Congress the additional twenty-day grace period before a formal notification was filed, as had become customary, and members of Congress chose routinely to introduce resolutions of disapproval as soon as the administration announced the proposals. Prior consultation between the president and Congress rarely occurred. For its part, Congress felt hamstrung in the post-*Chadha* environment in its ability to play an effective overseer role at the same time that members of Congress felt increasingly beleaguered by lobbyists armed with promises of campaign funds or political threats (Warburg, 1989).

By the time Ronald Reagan departed the White House, ''there was consensus throughout Washington that the process was 'broke.' But conflict proved insurmountable when efforts were made to fix it'' (Warburg, 1989). Meanwhile, the president continues to propose arms sales to other countries, and Congress continues to dispose of them—but in a way that typically gives the president much of what he wants.

Congress and the Reagan Administration's Nicaraguan Policy

Unlike the Reagan administration's experience with arms sales, in the case of Nicaraguan *contra* aid the president often got little of what he wanted, and by the end of his second term he had largely abandoned efforts to win congressional approval of his preferred policies. Nicaragua also differed in that resistance centered in the House of Representatives rather than the Senate. In the case of arms sales to Arab countries, the Reagan administration generally abandoned efforts to win support in the Democratically controlled House, preferring instead to concentrate on the Senate, where it had a greater chance of avoiding outright defeat. In the case of *contra* aid, on the other hand, every major battle from mid-1983 onward was determined in the House, where typically nearly all of the Republicans supported the president and a (narrow) majority of Democrats opposed him. The president's only significant victory in the House came in 1986, as we note below.

The *contra* aid story began in 1979 when the dictatorial regime of Anastasio Somoza, long supported by the United States, collapsed. It was succeeded by an anti-Somoza coalition known as the Sandinista National Liberation Front (FSLN). Alarmed by what it believed to be growing Cuban and Soviet influence in Nicaragua (and in Central America generally), the Reagan administration in 1981 authorized CIA support and training for Nicaraguan exiles in Honduras, known as *contras*, who earlier that year had begun fighting the allegedly marxist Sandinistas. With U.S. support the *contras* grew in numbers, and their actions became bolder. In 1984, with the help of the CIA, they mined Nicaraguan ports, leading the Sandinistas to bring suit against the United States in the World Court on a charge of violating international law.

Meanwhile, Congress grew apprehensive about America's efforts to overthrow an internationally recognized and established government. The CIA's covert actions were rationalized as a method for protecting Nicaragua's neighbors from the leftist regime, but it became increasingly clear that the *contras* themselves sought nothing less than the overthrow of the Sandinista regime.

Congress moved against that objective. Reagan administration officials denied U.S. policy sought the overthrow of the Nicaraguan government, arguing instead its purpose was the interdiction of Soviet and Cuban supplied arms to leftist insurgents in El Salvador. House Democrats nonetheless succeeded in December 1982 in passing the so-called Boland amendment, which prohibited the use of CIA and Defense Department funds for operations specifically aimed at overthrowing the Nicaraguan government.[8]

---

8. The Boland amendment, named after its sponsor, Edward P. Boland, Democratic representative from Massachusetts and chair of the House Intelligence Committee until 1984, figured prominently in the Iran-*contra* affair, in which a central question was whether the restrictions contained in the amendment applied to the president and the National Security Council. Although Reagan signed the Boland amendment into law, he maintained "it so happens that it does not apply to me."

Actually, there were several Boland amendments that reflected the changes in congressional concern about providing military aid to the *contras*. Congress first approved covert funding for

The executive-legislative tug-of-war over Central American policy continued throughout Reagan's first term in office and into his second. Congress repeatedly fought expanded U.S. involvement through covert actions and direct military aid. As noted, the Democratically controlled House, where the specter of "another Vietnam" was repeatedly raised, typically led the fight against administration proposals, only to be checked by the Republican-controlled Senate. Then, in 1984, following the mining episode that led to Nicaragua's World Court suit, the Senate joined the House in refusing to approve additional funds to undermine the Sandinista regime. The turnabout was animated less by a change of heart than by the belief that the CIA had shirked its legal responsibility to keep Congress "fully and currently informed" about covert operations.[9] A year later, in April 1985, Congress refused to resume U.S. aid to the *contras*, agreeing only later to provide $27 million in nonmilitary assistance. The funds were made available through March 1986 and specifically excluded the CIA and Defense Department from participation in their distribution. In April 1986 the House once again voted against a presidential request for renewal of aid to the *contras*. The decision reflected public sentiments on the issue of *contra* aid, as poll after poll indicated that a majority of the American people sided with Congress, not the president (Sobel, 1989; Wittkopf and McCormick, 1990b).

The Reagan administration mounted an intensive lobbying campaign to reverse the House decision. Eventually it succeeded. In June 1986 the House narrowly approved a $100 million aid package for the *contras*, including $70 million in military aid. The president thus prevailed over the Democratic leadership in the House, which, drawing an analogy with Vietnam, opposed military aid out of fear that it would be the first step toward direct U.S. military involvement. As House Speaker Thomas P. "Tip" O'Neill argued, "I see us becoming engaged step-by-step in a military situation that brings our boys directly into fighting."

---

contra military activities in 1981, and this was continued in some form until the first Boland amendment, cited here, was passed. Congress passed a second Boland amendment covering the period from December 1983 to September 1984, which limited not only CIA and Defense Department military aid to the *contras*, but also aid from "any other agency or entity" involved in intelligence activities. It passed a third amendment covering the period from October 1984 to September 1985, which prohibited the use of funds available to the CIA, the Defense Department, or "any other agency or entity of the United States involved in intelligence activities" for "supporting, directly or indirectly, military or paramilitary operations in Nicaragua." Subsequent versions of the amendment limited *contra* aid to humanitarian assistance until, in 1986, Congress approved $100 million with no strings attached. However, in the wake of the Iran-*contra* affair, Congress placed a six-month moratorium on $40 million in aid, during which time the administration was to account for funds previously provided to the *contras*. A later effort to prohibit expenditure of the money failed.

9. Senator Barry Goldwater, chair of the Senate Intelligence Committee, expressed the resentful congressional mood in a pithy "Dear Bill" letter to CIA Director William Casey, in which he remarked, "I've been trying to figure out how I can most easily tell you my feelings about the discovery of the President having approved mining some of the harbors in Central America."

"It gets down to one, little, simple phrase: I am pissed off."

He continued: "Bill, this is no way to run a railroad and I find myself in a hell of a quandary. . . . The President has asked us to back his foreign policy. Bill, how can we back his foreign policy when we don't know what the hell he is doing?" (*Congressional Quarterly Weekly Report*, April 14, 1984, p. 833).

The administration's victory in the House required the investment of considerable presidential capital. Reagan appealed his case directly to the American people by going over the heads of Congress in nationally televised appeals. The "Great Communicator" referred to the *contras* as "freedom fighters" and "our brothers," while those opposing aid to the insurgents were labeled "new isolationists" who "hide their heads in the sand and pretend the strategic threat in Nicaragua will go away." "They are courting disaster and history will hold them accountable," Reagan warned. The president and other top administration officials described the "strategic threat" in dire terms: "another Cuba"; "a privileged sanctuary for terrorists and subversives just two days driving time from Harlingen, Texas"; "a permanent staging ground for terrorism, a home away from home for Khadafy, and the Ayatollah, just three hours by air from the U.S. border." Ultimately, the president asked rhetorically in March 1986, "Will we give the Nicaraguan democratic resistance the means to recapture their betrayed revolution, or will we turn our backs and ignore the malignancy in Managua until it spreads and becomes a mortal threat to the entire New World?" "Those who would compromise must not compromise the freedom fighters' lives nor their immediate defensive needs," he continued. "They must not compromise freedom."

No new military aid was approved in 1987, but additional humanitarian aid was provided through February 1988. The Reagan administration remained adamant in its determination not to abandon the *contras*, but Congress increasingly emphasized the need for a political settlement. Jim Wright, Democratic Speaker of the House, helped formulate a bipartisan peace plan that involved him in negotiations with Nicaraguan officials.[10] Shortly thereafter Costa Rican President Oscar Arias Sanches formulated a peace proposal, endorsed by the other Central American governments, whose objective was a negotiated political settlement (and which eventually won Arias the Nobel Peace Prize). Congress generally supported that process, while the Reagan administration remained skeptical, but Congress's support of the *contras* waned once the Arias proposals became the focus of diplomatic efforts. Reagan urged without success renewal of military aid for the *contras* in his 1988 State of the Union message. The administration did not try again.

In March 1988 the Sandinistas and the *contras* agreed to a cease-fire and the eventual inclusion of the *contras* in Nicaraguan political life. As in most political accords designed to end violent conflict, much controversy and many setbacks lay ahead of the agreement. Efforts to negotiate a bipartisan accord on *contra* aid failed in the summer of 1988, and as the fall congressional and presidential elections approached, placing blame for the possible future "loss" of Nicaragua to communism colored the debate over Nicaraguan policy. But neither party capitalized on the theme, and both wearied from the long *contra* aid battle from which neither benefited politically.

---

10. Wright's efforts led to charges that he violated the Logan Act, a controversial but seldom invoked law passed in 1799 that makes it illegal for any private citizen to negotiate with a foreign government.

George Bush seemed to recognize as much. Early in 1989 he struck a bipartisan accord with Congress to provide $66.6 million in nonmilitary aid to the *contras* until February 1990, by which time the Sandinista government was to hold free elections. With that agreement, Congress and the executive joined hands in seeking to move U.S. policy toward Nicaragua from the battlefield to the negotiating table. Surprisingly, Nicaraguan President Daniel Ortega, the Sandinista candidate, lost in the February elections. With that, a new chapter in American foreign policy toward Central America opened. But the one it closed warrants attention, for it demonstrated the continuing reluctance of American leaders to become involved in conflict situations that might require the commitment of U.S. troops. Both Congress and the executive resorted to procedural gimmickry to keep a politically unpopular program alive, but in the end Congress abandoned a program whose objectives were vague and chances of success remote. "Congress will support success and abandon failure: Skepticism about the efficacy of the Contra effort repeatedly hamstrung the President's aid requests. . . . Anticommunism remains a potent rallying cry. But an effective program is still a sine qua non for maintaining a long-term national commitment of troops or money" (Warburg, 1989).

OBSTACLES TO CONGRESSIONAL FOREIGN POLICY MAKING

Although historically Congress at times has played an assertive role (notably following war), and at others an acquiescent role, neither description overrides the fact that as an institution Congress is poorly equipped to compete effectively with the executive when it comes to directing America's conduct abroad. Three interrelated factors explain this: parochialism, organizational weaknesses, and lack of expertise.

Parochialism

Congress is more oriented toward domestic than foreign affairs. All 435 members of the House are up for reelection every two years, as is a third of the Senate. Continual preoccupation with reelection (especially on the House side) creates pressure to attend more to domestic than international concerns. Whereas the president has a national constituency, all 535 members of Congress have much more narrowly construed electoral bases and correspondingly restricted constituency interests.

Because senators and representatives depend for their survival on satisfying their constituents' rather limited interests, "being national-minded can be a positive hazard to a legislative career" (Sundquist, 1976). "With their excessively parochial orientation," Senator J. William Fulbright explains, "congressmen are acutely sensitive to the influence of private pressure and to the excesses and inadequacies of a public opinion that is all too often ignorant of the needs, the dangers, and the opportunities in our foreign relations."[11] Thus a foreign policy problem may be viewed from a representative's Polish, Israeli, or Irish constituent viewpoint. Similarly, military needs may be weighed by the benefits of industries located within a House member's state or district. "Asked one day whether it was true that the navy yard in his district was too small to accommodate the latest battleships," Henry Stimson (chair of the House Naval Affairs Committee early in the century) replied, 'That is true, and that is the reason I have always been in favor of small ships'" (cited in Sundquist, 1976).

The president's vantage point is much different. Because the president has a nationwide constituency, the outlook from the White House on foreign policy problems is broader. A president can usually afford to alienate some local or narrow interests (by closing a military base, for example) without fear of electoral retribution, and is rewarded for thinking in terms of the long run, rather of the problems of the moment. A senator or representative is not. In the words of former Under Secretary of State William D. Rogers (1979), "With the fate of the entire House and a third of the Senate in the hands of the voters every 730 days, Congress is beholden to every short-term swing of popular opinion. The temptation to pander to prejudice and emotion is overwhelming."

Interest in and attention to foreign policy issues by senators and representatives is typically short-lived, influenced by their newsworthiness (Crabb and Holt, 1989). According to Senator Daniel J. Evans of Washington, the legislative process has degenerated into "reading yesterday's headlines so that we can write today's amendments so that we can garner tomorrow's headlines." Often amendments are passed with little expectation they will become law. As one Senate aide observed, "It has come to be an accepted part of the game that amendments are passed and press releases claiming credit are issued, with the understanding that most of these items will be tossed in the wastebasket when the bill goes to conference with the House." The "100 barons phenomenon" —all senators want to be seen as directing the nation's foreign policy—explains the seemingly pointless behavior (Oberdorfer and Dewar, 1987).

Parochialism is reinforced by the congressional committee system, in which the institution's real work is done. Members of Congress serve on committees to enhance their prospects for reelection, expand their influence within chambers, devise good public policy, and position themselves for new careers (Fenno, 1973; see also Smith and Deering, 1984). Although distinguished performance in congressional committees may further each of those goals, reelection depends primarily on constituent service. To perform such service, gaining a committee assignment relevant to constituencies' interests is critical. For this reason,

---

11. Noteworthy is that Fulbright and two of his successors as chair of the Senate Foreign Relations Committee, Frank Church of Idaho and Charles Percy of Illinois, were defeated in reelection bids at least in part because they had assumed leadership roles in foreign rather than domestic affairs.

farm state members want to deal with agriculture while city people do not, so the agriculture committees are rural and proagriculture in their composition. The military affairs committees are dominated by partisans of the military, urban affairs committees by members from the cities, interior committees by prorecla-mation westerners, and so on. By custom, the judiciary committees are made up exclusively of lawyers. Within each committee, there is further specialization of subcommittees and of individual members. The decisions of the specialists have to be accepted by their colleagues most of the time without more than a cursory examination; a fresh and exhaustive review of every question by every member is obviously impossible. And through logrolling, the advocates of various local interests form coalitions of mutual support. (Sundquist, 1976: 600)

Given these incentives and the behaviors they encourage, congressional attention to foreign affairs is often fleeting and shallow.

Organizational Weaknesses

Power and responsibility within Congress are fragmented. President Truman's famous quip, "The buck stops here!" has no counterpart in Congress, where authority is dispersed. Over half of the standing committees in both the House and Senate have broadly defined jurisdictions that give them some kind of foreign affairs responsibility (see Table 12.1). Unlike the executive branch, where policy debates take place in private with a single individual, the president, often making the final choice, congressional debates are perforce public, with final choices made by counting yeas and nays, and with decision making diffuse. Under these conditions, policy consistency and coordination are most unlikely. Structurally, Congress rarely speaks with a single voice.

During the 1970s Congress undertook a number of procedural reforms that decentralized power from the committee to the subcommittee level, encouraged challenges to the seniority system, and reduced the importance of leadership positions.[12] As a consequence it became more difficult than ever to locate power and authority in Congress. "There are 165 different people in the House and Senate who can answer to the proud title 'Mr. Chairman,' having been given committees or subcommittees of their own" (Broder, 1986: 9). Accordingly, the congressional leadership cannot speak for the institution as a whole, and individual members of Congress can take foreign policy initiatives and set agendas. For example, the legislative veto on military sales and the Turkish arms embargo were the product of initiatives taken by individuals outside the congressional foreign policy "establishment" (Franck and Weisband, 1979).

The rise of single-issue politics—which subjects members of Congress to evaluation not on the basis of their entire record but only their performance on particular issues—has exacerbated the problems associated with the diffusion

---

12. See Cavanagh (1982–1983) and Smith and Deering (1984) for examinations of changes in Congress since the 1960s, and Drischler (1985) and Lindsay (1988, 1987) for insight into the importance of these changes for the enactment of foreign affairs legislation.

TABLE 12.1 ▪ Foreign Affairs Responsibilities of Committees in the House and Senate

Senate Committee	Foreign Affairs Responsibility	House Committee
Agriculture, Nutrition and Forestry	Foreign agricultural policy and assistance	Agriculture
Appropriations	Appropriation of revenues, rescission of appropriations	Appropriations
Armed Services	Defense, national security, national security aspects of nuclear energy	Armed Services
Banking, Housing and Urban Affairs	Foreign commerce, international economic policy, export and foreign trade promotion	Banking, Finance and Urban Affairs; Energy and Commerce
Budget	Budgetary matters	Budget
Commerce, Science and Transportation	Merchant marine, marine fisheries, oceans, coastal zone management, nonmilitary space sciences and aeronautics	Merchant Marine and Fisheries; Science, and Technology
Energy and Natural Resources	International energy affairs, global climate changes, nonmilitary aspects of nuclear energy	Energy and Commerce; Science, Space and Technology
Environment and Public Works	Environmental policy, ocean dumping, environmental aspects of outer continental shelf lands	Science, Space and Technology
Finance	Revenue measures, customs, foreign trade agreements, tariffs, import quotas	Ways and Means
Foreign Relations	Relations with foreign nations, treaties, executive agreements, international organizations, foreign assistance, intervention abroad, declarations of war, terrorism	Foreign Affairs
Governmental Affairs	Organization and reorganization of the executive branch, organization and management of nuclear export policy	Government Operations
Intelligence	Intelligence activities, covert operations	Intelligence
Judiciary	Immigration and refugees	Judiciary
Labor and Human Resources	Regulation of foreign laborers	Education and Labor

NOTE: Descriptions of the foreign affairs responsibilities are derived from the jurisdictions of the Senate committees in the 101st Congress, with the corresponding jurisdictions of House committees matched to those as closely as possible. All of the committees are standing committees of the respective houses of Congress except the Intelligence committees, both of which are select committees.

of power. Noting that the 385 committees and subcommittees of Congress are scouted by more than thirteen hundred registered lobbyists, one former official lamented that instead of a two-party system Capitol Hill resembles "a 385-party system" (cited in Crabb and Holt, 1989).

The dispersion of power and sharing of responsibility within Congress frustrate executive-legislative consultation and coordination and make Congress appear irresponsible. When facing a skeptical electorate, for example, these conditions enable individual senators and representatives to deflect criticism with the defense, "I didn't do it; it was everyone else." Individual accountability is reduced further by the congressional penchant for dealing with issues in procedural terms rather than confronting them directly. A striking illustration was provided during the Senate's consideration of the two controversial Panama Canal treaties designed to cede American control of the waterway to Panama. Senators took record votes on over fifty amendments, nearly twenty reservations, a dozen understandings, and several conditions— nearly ninety proposals for change of one kind or another (Congressional Research Service, 1979: viii–xi).

The temptation to deal with matters procedurally is often irresistible. In the Panama Canal case, for example, a common procedural practice was to bill many of the proposed changes "improvements," which made it easier to vote for a politically unpopular document. In other words, procedure becomes a useful tool for coping with single-issue politics because through it members of Congress can conceal their positions and votes and thereby deflect potential electoral criticism. (In the case of the Panama Canal, however, it is noteworthy that over half of the thirty-eight senators who supported the treaties lost in their next campaigns for reelection). They can also avoid direct confrontation with the executive by couching their opposition in procedural arguments to which the executive branch has no retort.

> If done directly, a Congressional decision—for example, to disapprove money for a new aircraft carrier—would require that more than half of all Congressmen conclude that the Navy can do with fewer carriers . . . . This would involve a stark confrontation with expertise that would be very uncomfortable for a Congressman. If a showdown is reached on the carrier issue, the vote is almost certain to be cloaked in procedures (motions to table, etc.) that would allow the Congressman to justify his vote, if he needed to, on a procedural question rather than on the merits of the case. The end-the-war vote in the House in 1972, for example, was in fact a motion to table, a motion to instruct the conferees to insist on the House version of the Defense Authorization bill in the light of the Legislative Reorganization Act of 1970. Nobody's constituents would ever be able to figure that one out. (Aspin, 1976: 165)

Procedure, then, is purposely used to avoid direct responsibility. This does not mean that members of Congress are incapable of performing their jobs. On the contrary, by masking their votes' real effects in procedural gobbledygook, they more readily can take the road of conscience rather than the road of convenience.

Another form of irresponsibility is found in the frequent tendency of members of Congress to "leak" information. A glaring example of the recurrent problem took place in 1987, when the Senate Intelligence Committee voted not to make public a report on the closed-door hearings it conducted on the Iran-*contra* affair, only to have NBC News acquire the first half of it three days later. Within two weeks the other half appeared in the *New York Times*. Senator Patrick J. Leahy later resigned as vice chair of the committee when it was learned he had leaked the unclassified committee report—and at precisely the time the committee was trying to demonstrate that Reagan administration officials were more often responsible for news stories based on classified government information than were members of congress.

Congressional leaks arise from the independence that senators and representatives prize and the benefits they can realize by placing issues in the mass media's spotlight. One of the consequences is that the president often has used "executive privilege" to conceal information—particularly classified information—thereby preventing congressional involvement in policy making. In the extreme, the president may also choose to ignore Congress altogether, as Reagan did in his clandestine arms-for-hostages operation orchestrated by Robert McFarlane, his national security adviser. Lt. Colonel Oliver North, the National Security Council (NSC) staffer primarily responsible for managing the Iran-*contra* deal, argued in defense of the initiative that secrecy was necessary because of Congress's penchant to leak information, even though the initiative itself may have been illegal because it violated the Arms Control and Export Act.

Finally, congressional irresponsibility of a different sort arises out of the very sluggishness of the legislative process. Slow, deliberative procedures may be inherent in a body charged with reconciling disparate views, but delays are prolonged by the dispersion of power and responsibility between two houses, their further fragmentation within a complex structure of committees and subcommittees, and the erosion, even absence, of party discipline.[13] "The result is that any piece of legislation must surmount an obstacle course of unparalleled difficulty . . . . Few things happen quickly. Policies eventually adopted are often approved too late . . . . And in the process of overcoming the countless legislative hurdles, policies may be compromised to the point of ineffectiveness" (Sundquist, 1976). Contrast that picture with the president's proven ability to act quickly and decisively, as rapidly moving international developments frequently seem to require. "Presidents can procrastinate too," James L. Sundquist (1976) observes, "but unlike Congress they are not compelled to by any institutional structure."

---

13. The Senate's cloture rule requiring an extraordinary majority for terminating debate presents another restraint on initiative. As former Senate Majority Leader Robert Byrd put it in the context of the Senate's debate of President Carter's energy proposals: "It would be impossible for Jesus Christ to do anything without unanimous consent."

Lack of Expertise

A third organizational weakness contributing to Congress's "respondent" relationship with the executive derives from the White House's relatively greater command of technical expertise and from its ability to control the flow of information. This fact should be apparent from the discussion in Chapter 11 of the departments and agencies comprising the policy-making system's second concentric circle, all of which are *executive* branch organizations. Although such organizations sometimes resist presidential orders in foreign affairs (see Chapter 13), the agencies contribute enormously to presidential supremacy over Congress, which must depend on the executive branch for vital information on which to make policy recommendations (see West and Cooper, 1990).

Congress has sought to overcome its lack of expertise in several ways. It periodically has expanded the overseer role of the General Accounting Office, and it created the Office of Technology Assessment to evaluate scientific and technical proposals and the Congressional Budget Office to assist in analyzing budget options and preparing the annual budget resolution. More important, perhaps, the size of the professional staff serving congressional committees and individual members of Congress has grown enormously in recent years. The most explosive growth occurred in the 1970s, but some occurred in the 1980s, bringing the total number of personal and committee staff employees to nearly fifteen thousand (Ornstein, Mann, and Malbin, 1990: 125). Staff resources have given Congress a greater capacity to assert an independent congressional position and the means to become involved in policy questions where previously congressional interest and expertise may have been lacking (Crabb and Holt, 1989). To that could be added the ability of congressional staffs, in an atmosphere where knowledge is power, to exercise greater influence over the direction of policy.

Committee staffs are most important because of their influence over legislation. The technical experts filling staff roles, and the networks of communications and coalitions that have developed among them, operate as an "invisible force in American lawmaking" in steering policy (Fox and Hammond, 1977). But whether congressional staff growth has enhanced Congress's ability to cope with the complex issues of foreign policy is uncertain. Clearly the increase in staff size has led to a corresponding increase in the information available to members of Congress, but that is no guarantee that the information will be used wisely to improve policy making. In any large, politicized organization, information will be somewhat biased. Just as Congress must be wary of information provided by the executive, now it also must determine whether the information it receives from its own staffs may not be designed to serve some special interest (Malbin, 1977).

Individual members of Congress do themselves develop considerable policy expertise. The committee system and the corresponding congressional preference for allocating positions of authority according to the rules of seniority (despite challenges to it) mean that some senators and representatives often spend their entire legislative careers specializing in their committees' areas. Some congressional careers have spanned more than a quarter-century —much longer than any postwar president is allowed by the Constitution to remain in office. Historically, specialization by entrenched members of Congress has been especially prominent in the House and Senate Armed Services committees, where southern Democrats, in particular, have claimed considerable expertise on national security issues. Members of these committees also now receive substantial amounts of intelligence from the CIA, which contributes to their ability to arrive at policy judgments independent of the president.[14]

At the same time, the committee and seniority systems facilitate the patron-client relationships between Congress and the foreign policy bureaucracy described in Chapter 11. Such relationships often subvert presidential interests, but they do provide Congress power vis-à-vis the executive.

> Every Congressman of seniority has cultivated numbers of career civil servants, military, foreign service, or intelligence officers throughout those agencies dealing in his areas of committee or constituent interest. The pattern of such symbiotic relationships typically stretches over three or more administrations. For the bureaucrat, the relationship yields benefits (or protection) to his agency or bureau office, or perhaps to his job. It can assist in promotion and even such things as service academy appointments to favored sons. The Congressman of course gains access to information and an influence on the day-to-day application to policy. (Lehman, 1976: 33)

But all members of Congress cannot be experts on all matters of policy. The executive, however, can be and is. When expertise is lacking, people look to the experts—that is, the executive. That tendency is especially pronounced in matters of foreign policy and national security. Moreover, members of Congress are especially ill equipped to acquire the kinds of information that would enable them to better monitor, and hence influence, decision making in times of crisis. Following the Ford administration's use of marines to rescue the ship *Mayaguez* from its Cambodian captors in May 1975, for example, a survey of members of Congress revealed that for many the press was their principal source of information; this applied to even a majority of those serving on congressional committees directly concerned with foreign military and political affairs. Little wonder that one anonymous member of congress cynically observed that "the actions of the United States are not secret to other nations, only to Congress and the American people" (*Congressional Quarterly Weekly Report*, November 13,

---

14. CIA Deputy Director Robert M. Gates (1987–1988) argues that, in addition to Vietnam and Watergate, a primary change that has affected the balance of power between Congress and the president on national security issues has been "the obtaining, by Congress in the mid-1970s, of access to intelligence information essentially equal to that of the executive branch." He notes that "virtually all CIA assessments go to the two congressional intelligence committees. Most go also to the appropriations, foreign relations and armed services committees. Eight congressional committees get the CIA's daily national intelligence report. In 1986 the CIA sent some 5,000 intelligence reports to Congress and gave many hundreds of briefings" (Gates, 1987–1988: 224).

1976). Little wonder also that Congress's role is largely negative, with Congress functioning primarily as a public critic of what the executive has already done. The same relationship characterizes the exercise of congressional powers with respect to treaties, war, and money.

THE POWERS OF CONGRESS AND FOREIGN POLICY MAKING

On the surface, the Constitution appears to give to Congress more far-reaching foreign policy powers than it gives the president. In particular, congressional authority over treaties, war, and money would appear to give it a commanding position, enabling it to set overall policy much like a board of directors does in private enterprise. But the reality is quite different.

Treaties

Treaty-making powers rest in the Senate, whose advice and consent by a two-thirds vote (which effectively gives control to only 34 of the 535 members of Congress) is necessary before the president can enter into a treaty with another country. The Senate Foreign Relations Committee bears primary responsibility for conducting the hearings and investigations on which senatorial advice and consent are based. These and the other foreign policy responsibilities at one time made the Foreign Relations Committee the most prestigious of all Senate committees, but in recent years it has been racked by ideological divisions that have prevented it from speaking with a single voice. Its prestige and influence have declined as a result. (Simultaneously, the House Foreign Affairs Committee, whose constitutionally based powers are more limited, has gained in stature.) Still, the Senate Foreign Relations Committee remains a primary forum for the discharge of Congress's foreign policy responsibilities.

Despite the importance of the Constitution's treaty clause, the precise mechanism whereby senatorial advice and consent is to be proffered the president is ambiguous. The result is that from the very beginning of the Republic the provision has been controversial. In barest form the process works when the president, through representatives, negotiates a treaty with another nation as the nation's chief diplomat, which the Senate then merely votes up or down. More frequently, advice is given in written communications between the executive and the legislature or through the inclusion of members of Congress on the treaty-negotiation team. The latter practice has been widespread ever since the Senate's rejection of the Versailles treaty, which would have brought the United States into the League of Nations, and which had been negotiated without senatorial representation on the Peace Commission.

Consent to treaties is still established by a two-thirds vote, but the Senate has also adopted the practice of attaching reservations to treaties. These may take the form of amendments that require the executive to renegotiate the terms of the treaty with other signatories—a potentially inhibiting obstacle, particularly with the increase in the number of multilateral treaties. Alternatively, reservations or "conditions" may simply incorporate the Senate's interpretation of the treaty without any binding effect on the parties to it. Other variants are reservations that apply only to the United States. Perhaps the most celebrated example is the so-called Connally Amendment to the Statute of the International Court of Justice, whereby the United States reserves for itself determination of whether matters falling under the compulsory jurisdiction clause of the court are essentially within the domestic jurisdiction of the United States.

The Senate's role in the treaty-making process became the subject of a sharp dispute in 1987 between the Reagan administration and Congress over the administration's announced reinterpretation of the 1972 Anti-Ballistic Missile (ABM) treaty. The reinterpretation would have permitted the administration to test technology as part of its Strategic Defense Initiative (SDI) previously thought to be prohibited by the ABM treaty. SDI was the immediate issue, of course, but broad constitutional questions were also at stake. Although treaty interpretation is understood to be an executive function, conformity to senatorial understanding is expected. A reinterpretation that would significantly revise a prior understanding could constitute an amendment of sufficient gravity as to again require the Senate's advice and consent. Without the Senate's ability to rely on the executive branch for reliable information about treaty negotiations, the Senate's constitutional prerogatives in the treaty-making process would be severely impaired.

The State Department's legal adviser contended that nothing in the original ratification record precluded a broad interpretation of what was permitted under the ABM treaty. However, nearly all of those who had participated in the actual negotiation of the treaty disputed this, and, after studying the negotiating record, Senator Sam Nunn (chair of the Armed Services Committee) concluded that the document submitted by the Nixon administration fifteen years earlier permitted only a narrow interpretation (see Nunn, 1987; Sofaer, 1987). Nunn spearheaded an effort to block the broad interpretation, and the Senate placed restrictions on SDI tests and funds that had the effect of enforcing a narrow interpretation. In addition, it attached a reservation to the ratification resolution for the Intermediate-Range Nuclear Forces (INF) treaty stating that (1) the treaty should be interpreted in accordance with the understanding common between the president and the Congress at the time the Senate gave its advice and consent, and (2) any subsequent reinterpretation would again require the Senate's advice and consent. Reagan questioned the reservation's constitutionality but proceeded with the ratification process nonetheless. Thus the Senate protected its treaty-making powers and warned future presidents against unilateral treaty reinterpretations.

Despite the ABM confrontation, the Senate's treaty ratification record has on the whole been quite positive. Since 1900 only six treaties have failed to receive the two-thirds vote necessary for Senate advice and consent (Congressional Research Service, 1984: 117). Only two rejections occurred in the postwar period. This record attests simultaneously to congressional deference to presidential initiatives and to general agreement between the president and Congress on most foreign policy issues. What the historical record fails to show is also noteworthy, namely, those occasions when treaties were not presented for a vote because of known legislative opposition. The Carter administration's decisions not to proceed with a comprehensive test ban treaty and to shelve the Threshold Test Ban Treaty and the Peaceful Nuclear Explosives Treaty are examples (Warburg, 1989).

The president's ability to sidestep congressional restraints on international agreements is considerable. A novel example occurred in 1977. When it became apparent that the Strategic Arms Limitations Talks (SALT) II treaty would not be concluded before the five-year interim SALT I accord expired, the Carter administration declared that the United States would continue to abide by the terms of SALT I until a new agreement was completed. (The Soviets did likewise.) Later, an analogous tactic was used to ensure compliance with the signed but unratified SALT II treaty (which the Senate opposed after the Soviet invasion of Afghanistan). The Reagan administration even voluntarily dismantled older nuclear submarines as the new Trident came on line, rather than violate the accord's limits on strategic weapons, despite the fact that Reagan had campaigned against the treaty in 1980. Eventually, Reagan decided to exceed the SALT II limits. Interestingly, by that time the Senate had gone on record urging the president to maintain the "do not undercut" policy toward the treaty that both Carter and Reagan had hitherto followed.

Executive agreements are the usual method used by presidents to make international agreements that avoid the necessity of securing the advice and consent of the Senate altogether.[15] Although these government-to-government agreements have essentially the same legal force as treaties, and thus become part of the "supreme law of the land," they may be concluded without legislative scrutiny. Early examples include the agreements governing the Lend-Lease Act of 1941, under which the U.S. provided war materials to its World War II allies, and Truman's aid to Greece and Turkey in the late 1940s. More recent ones include the Paris peace agreement on Ending the War and Restoring Peace in Vietnam (1973); the SALT I accords (1972); and various bilateral agreements covering American military base rights in Spain, the Azores, Diego Garcia, Bahrain, and Iceland.

These illustrations show that executive agreements often cover important aspects of America's foreign relations. Their quantity indicates that they have been a preferred mechanism for reaching international accords. Roughly 95 percent of the more than ten thousand international agreements concluded in

---

15. The term *executive agreement* has come to be used to refer to any international agreement that is not submitted to the Senate. In fact, however, even that definition is ambiguous; see Johnson (1984), Johnson and McCormick (1977), and Stevens (1977) for useful discussions of executive agreements and of congressional efforts to curtail their use or otherwise assert greater congressional controls over them.

the four decades following World War II have been executive agreements and hence not subject to the formal approval procedures of the Senate.[16] Although many of these are based on statutory directives, while others are entered into pursuant to treaty provisions, both of which require legislative input, the vast number of agreements made without the expressed advice and consent of the Senate indicate the president's wide latitude to negotiate international agreements unrestrained by constitutional checks and balances.

That executive agreements represent a potential challenge to congressional oversight is attested to by Congress's periodic attempts to block such maneuvers. One of the most sustained of those endeavors occurred in 1953–1954, when Senator John Bricker of Ohio proposed a constitutional amendment that would have greatly restricted the president's treaty-making powers and ability to manage the day-to-day conduct of foreign affairs. The proposal fell one vote short of the two-thirds majority necessary for Senate approval (a necessary condition in the long process of constitutional revision).

Two decades later, while the nation was still deeply mired in the Vietnam War, the congressional assault on executive prerogatives resulted in a statute (known as the Case Act after its sponsor, Senator Clifford Case of New Jersey) requiring the president to submit to Congress all international agreements within sixty days of their execution. The enactment represented the culmination of a process begun in the late 1960s, when the Senate passed the National Commitments Resolution prohibiting commitments without the approval of Congress. Thereafter a Senate investigation unearthed the breadth and depth of overseas commitments entered into by the executive without the knowledge of Congress. Not only were secret agreements and de facto understandings discovered, but knowledge was also gained about covert activities and paramilitary operations authorized by the executive with neither the knowledge nor approval of Congress. The essence of the findings was that the executive had repeatedly made commitments to foreign governments in secret talks while downplaying their importance at home.

The Case Act provided Congress a mechanism through which to be informed of international agreements entered into by the executive; it helped establish a baseline for determining when international agreements should be in the form of treaties rather than executive agreements; and it ensured authori-

---

16. Enumerations of executive agreements often differ because of the difficulty of defining exactly what constitutes an executive agreement. The following quip by a former secretary of state illustrates the problem:

> Secretary of State John Foster Dulles . . . said at the Bricker Amendment hearings that "every time we open a new privy, we have to have an executive agreement." Pointing out that with every treaty or agreement listed in the Executive Agreement Series there were numerous concomitant unlisted agreements, he estimated that about 10,000 such informal agreements accompanied the North Atlantic Treaty alone. Probably the number was picked out of the air, but Dulles was doubtless including informal understandings in letters, notes, and even oral conversations and routine transactions reflecting some element of consensus. (Henkin, 1972: 420, n. 1)

zation by the State Department of agreements made by other U.S. government agencies (Collier, 1988). But it did little to redress the imbalance between presidential and congressional authority over treaty making in general or executive agreements in particular. The president remains the initiator of agreements with other nations, determines which are to be treaties and which executive agreements, and is still not required to obtain congressional advice or consent before doing either. Moreover, the law protects the secrecy of executive agreements by providing that they need be forwarded only to the relevant Senate and House committees, under an injunction of secrecy, if the president determines that public disclosure would endanger national security.[17] Thus the statute may have complicated the president's role, but it has not substantially restricted presidential freedom.

Beyond the Case Act, little has been done to strengthen the position of Congress in the treaty-making enterprise. The president continues to exercise treaty-making leadership, and the historical record—which now covers more than seventy years of attempts to alter the treaty-making provisions of the Constitution—indicates that the president will remain the initiator and Congress the respondent.

War

With respect to war-making powers, the Constitution would appear to be clear; it states in Article I, Section 8, that "the Congress shall have power . . . to declare war." Elsewhere, however (Article II, Section 2), the Constitution specifies that "the President shall be Commander-in-Chief of the Army and Navy of the United States." Of the two provisions, the latter has proved the more important, for the president has used that provision to defend the stationing of troops all over the world. The provision was also used to justify American military intervention in Korea (1950–1953), Lebanon (1958), the Dominican Republic (1965–1966), Vietnam (1965–1973), Grenada (1983), and Panama (1989). Yet in none of those cases was military action accompanied by a formal declaration of war.

Protracted American involvement in Vietnam prompted congressional efforts to redress the war-making balance. At issue was whether President Johnson had exceeded his constitutional powers by repeatedly escalating the nation's involvement without a corresponding congressional mandate. Johnson argued that his authority rested on the Gulf of Tonkin Resolution, passed by Congress in August 1964. The joint resolution gave the president congressional approval "to take all necessary measures to repel any armed attack against the forces of the United States and to prevent further aggression."

---

17. As of January 1, 1990, 5,843 executive agreements had been transmitted to Congress pursuant to the Case Act. Of those, 328 were transmitted under the injunction of secrecy provision of the statute (Treaty Affairs, Office of the Legal Advisor, U.S. Department of State, personal communication, January 1990).

As the quagmire of Vietnam deepened, the meaning of the Gulf of Tonkin Resolution became the source of intense debate. With hindsight, it is now recognized that Congress was duped by a president who controlled the information, and hence the policy.[18] On four previous occasions Congress had authorized the president to use armed forces to defend certain geographical areas (in the 1955 Formosa Straits Resolution, the 1957 Eisenhower Middle East Doctrine Resolution, the 1962 Cuban Resolution, and the 1962 Berlin Resolution), but the magnitude and duration of U.S. military involvement in Vietnam and the Johnson administration's insistence that the resolution was the "functional equivalent" of a declaration of war made this situation different.

Johnson's interpretation was repudiated by Congress when it passed the National Commitments Resolution in 1969 and formally repealed the Gulf of Tonkin Resolution in 1970. Further concrete steps to limit presidential war-making prerogatives were embodied in the War Powers Resolution passed by Congress over President Nixon's veto in 1973. Several of its provisions were designed to ensure congressional consent in decisions to deploy American troops abroad. First, the resolution stipulates that the president should inform Congress of the introduction of forces "into hostilities or into situations where imminent involvement in hostilities is clearly indicated by the circumstances." This provision triggers a second that prohibits troop commitments by the president to extend beyond sixty days without specific congressional authorization (although this period can be extended up to ninety days if the safety of American troops is at stake). Third, any time American forces become engaged in hostilities without a declaration of war or a specific congressional authorization, the law enables Congress to direct the president to disengage such troops by a concurrent resolution of the two houses of Congress. Because such a measure would not require the president's signature to take effect, it constitutes a legislative veto and may no longer be constitutional because of the Supreme Court's *Chadha* ruling in 1983. Presumably that provision of the War Powers Resolution is now null and void. The sixty-day limit and various consulting and reporting requirements remain intact.

In his veto message President Nixon questioned the constitutionality of the War Powers Resolution and criticized its practical consequences. He contended that the sixty-day limit and the concurrent resolution provisions "purport to take away, by a mere legislative act, authorities which the President has properly exercised under the Constitution for almost 200 years." They are unconstitutional, he contended, because "the only way in which the constitutional powers of a branch of government can be altered is by amending the Constitution—and any attempt to make such alterations by legislation alone is clearly without force." He also claimed the resolution would "seriously under-

---

18. To sell the Tonkin Resolution to Congress, events were well staged and the timing of the resolution carefully calculated; a draft of the resolution "had been reposing in Assistant Secretary of State William P. Bundy's drawer for several months" (Kattenburg, 1980). For accounts of the affair, see Goulden (1969) and Austin (1971).

mine the nation's ability to act decisively and convincingly in times of international crisis'' and that it would ''give every future Congress the ability to handcuff every future President.''

If the constitutionality of the War Powers Resolution is tested directly in the courts, the judiciary probably will retreat to its traditional position that the issues raised are fundamentally political, not juridical, in nature. In the meantime, even though the resolution remains a monument to Congress's assertive reaction to the so-called imperial presidency, it has not effectively restrained the president's use of force abroad without congressional involvement. The United States has used its armed forces abroad more than two dozen times since the resolution was passed. In twenty-one of these instances (as of January 1, 1990) the president submitted reports to Congress under the resolution, but rarely has Section 4(a)(1) that would set the sixty-day clock in motion been cited or reference been made to actual or imminent hostilities. For its part, Congress has invoked the provisions of the resolution only once, in 1983 when in connection with the deployment of U.S. Marines to Lebanon it declared that Section 4(a)(1) had become operative—but it went on to authorize the marines to stay in Lebanon for eighteen months (Collier, 1990: 1).

Nearly every president since Nixon has claimed the War Powers Resolution is unconstitutional. Thus, when President Bush ordered military forces into Panama in December 1989, his report to Congress claimed the intervention was ''consistent with the War Powers Resolution'' but neither cited the provision of the act that would limit the duration of force deployments nor recognized the legitimacy of the resolution itself.[19] His seemingly defiant attitude and unwillingness to be burdened by congressional interference was signaled by his assertion that ''I have an obligation as President to conduct the foreign policy of this country as I see fit.''

Beyond the constitutionality question, two other interrelated issues have plagued the applicability of the resolution since its inception: what constitutes ''consultation,'' and what constitutes ''imminent hostilities''?

The War Powers Resolution seeks to ensure greater congressional participation in decisions authorizing the use of force by requiring consultation between the executive and legislative branches ''in every possible instance'' prior to committing U.S. forces to hostilities or to situations likely to result in hostilities. Presidents generally claim to have met this requirement, but rarely if ever has serious and meaningful debate between the two branches occurred prior to a presidential decision on the use of force, and seldom has Congress sought to limit the use of force once set in motion. The rescue of the *Mayaguez* authorized by President Gerald R. Ford in 1975 and the abortive attempt to

---

19. However, Bush did announce in his 1990 State of the Union address his determination to withdraw combat forces from Panama before the end of February. This would mean U.S. troops would be removed within the sixty-day time period specified in the War Powers Resolution, which was in fact accomplished. Bush followed the same reporting strategy when he advised Congress on the dispatch of U.S. troops to the Persian Gulf several months later.

rescue American hostages in Iran authorized by President Carter in 1980 both proceeded without prior consultation. However, congressional criticism of Ford's unwillingness to consult Congress was generally muted, despite the loss of forty-one marines in a mission designed to "rescue" thirty-nine crew members who had already been released by their Cambodian captors. In the case of the Iranian operation, Congress generally accepted Carter's contention that the need for secrecy plus the fact that the troops were engaged in a rescue operation rather than a military exercise precluded consultation with Congress.[20]

The invasion of Grenada in October 1983 again raised questions about the applicability of the War Powers Resolution and the president's compliance with both its letter and spirit. Some congressional leaders were informed about the invasion, but the administration did not consult Congress before deploying the troops (Rubner, 1985–1986). Furthermore, because the report the president sent to Congress about the invasion claimed only to be "consistent with the War Powers Resolution," it did not recognize the right of Congress to prior consultation. Nor did it explicitly state that U.S. troops were being introduced into actual or potential hostilities, which would have set in motion the sixty-day clock requiring withdrawal of U.S. troops without explicit congressional authorization. In any event, the administration described the Grenada mission as a "rescue" operation, and the actual conflict was of short duration and popular at home. All of these factors militated against a concerted congressional effort to assert its war-making prerogatives (see also Rubner, 1985–1986).

The prior consultation issue surfaced again in April 1986 when U.S. warplanes made a surprise nighttime attack on Tripoli and Benghazi to punish Libyan leader Muammar Qaddafi for his alleged support of international terrorism. Republican House leader Robert H. Michel, one of the dozen or so lawmakers briefed by the White House just before the Libyan raid, expressed the sentiment that "we really ought to have some sort of vehicle for getting Congress into the mix, so we're not left out in the cold." "We are in a war," he continued. "It's a new kind of war. It's a terrorist war. We're going over a threshold, we're ploughing new ground, and we have to think what comes next." The result was a proposal to establish a special consultative group within Congress to which the president could turn in future situations. The measure was not acted on at the time, but the idea has been advanced periodically since. Meanwhile, there still exists no agreed-on mechanism to ensure that congressional views will be weighed by the president before a decision to use force is made, and once such decisions are implemented Congress's power remains severely

---

20. Although the Ford administration, like Nixon's, held the view that the War Powers Resolution was unconstitutional, it nevertheless complied with the reporting procedures embodied in the law not only in the case of the *Mayaguez*, but also earlier, when it conducted a series of rescue missions from Danang, Saigon, and Phnom Penh as American forces withdrew from Indochina. The Carter administration likewise submitted a report to Congress after the Iranian rescue mission was aborted and did not contest the constitutionality of the War Powers Resolution (Crabb and Holt, 1989).

circumscribed.[21] Congress cannot effectively make war against a president's war-making powers.

The Reagan administration's decision to send military advisers to El Salvador in 1981 illustrates these constraints on congressional involvement. Several senators and representatives perceived a parallel between Reagan's action and the incremental process through which the United States was drawn into the Vietnam quagmire. Accordingly, a number of resolutions were introduced in the House and Senate asserting the administration's move required a report under the provisions of the War Powers Resolution on grounds that the advisers were being sent into a situation of imminent hostilities. Although the administration never conceded the applicability of the resolution,[22] it did agree that the number of advisers would not exceed fifty-five and that they would not be assigned combat roles.

The Reagan administration's Central American policies provoked some members of Congress to assert that the War Powers Resolution applied in a number of other situations,[23] but the most serious challenges it faced over the resolution came in 1983 during the crisis in Lebanon and in 1987 following an Iraqi missile attack on the *USS Stark*.

American marines were first sent to Lebanon in 1982 (under the president's authority as commander in chief) with the expectation that their presence would be required for only a short time. A year later they were still in Lebanon, and as conditions worsened the question arose as to whether the U.S. troops were subject to imminent hostilities that should trigger the sixty-day War Powers Resolution clock. In August 1983 the marines suffered two fatalities and several casualties. Reagan submitted to Congress a report on the hostilities consistent with the War Powers Resolution and shortly thereafter entered negotiations with Congress to secure authorization for the marine presence in Beirut. In the weeks that followed, U.S. forces were drawn more actively into the Lebanese civil conflict. Meanwhile, negotiations between Congress and the president resulted in a compromise, passed by both houses and signed by Reagan in mid-October, that authorized the marines to stay in Lebanon for eighteen months. In signing the Lebanon resolution, however, Reagan did not concede the applicability of the War Powers Resolution: ''I do not and cannot cede any

---

21. Noteworthy in this respect is that President Bush informed members of Congress at 6:00 P.M. on December 19, 1989, after the decision had been made but before its implementation, of his intention to invade Panama (Collier, 1990). The actual invasion began seven hours later, at 1:00 A.M., December 20.

22. Reagan did submit reports under the War Powers Resolution pertaining to other conflict situations: one relating to U.S. observers in the Sinai desert, three relating to marines in Lebanon, one on assistance to Chad, one on Grenada, one on Libya, and six on actions in the Persian Gulf (Collier, 1990: 1).

23. Among them was the revelation in 1984 that the CIA had assisted in the mining of Nicaraguan harbors; the administration's decision in 1985 to use U.S. helicopters to ferry Honduran combat troops to the Nicaraguan border; and its deployment of U.S. airborne troops to Honduras following an alleged invasion of Honduras by Sandinista forces seeking to destroy anti-Sandinista guerrillas. In these and other instances Congress sought to place various restrictions on the executive but never invoked the provisions of the War Powers Resolution as such (Collier, 1990, 1987b).

of the authority vested in me under the Constitution as President and as Commander in Chief of the United States Armed Forces. Nor should my signing be viewed as any acknowledgment that the President's constitutional authority can be impermissibly infringed by statute.''

The controversy heightened a few weeks after the resolution passed when terrorists truck-bombed marine headquarters in Beirut, killing 241 marines and navy personnel. In the months following the tragedy, Reagan defended his policies against his congressional critics by accusing them of wanting to ''cut and run.'' Then, in a dramatic about-face, he announced in February 1984 that the marines would be stationed on ships offshore. Not long thereafter a complete evacuation from Lebanon was ordered.

Both Reagan and Secretary of State George Shultz alleged that the debate over the applicability of the War Powers Resolution and other congressional misgivings about the American presence in Lebanon contributed to the terrorism there. Reagan chastised Congress for abandoning the bipartisan accord on Lebanon and second-guessing his decision to keep U.S. forces there. Shultz was more broadly critical of the War Powers Resolution, arguing, much as President Nixon had when he vetoed the measure, that the provisions that U.S. troops must be withdrawn from conflict situations unless Congress authorizes their continued presence ''practically invite an adversary to wait us out.''

The controversy over Lebanon had barely subsided when the administration's Persian Gulf policies came under attack. In May 1987 an Iraqi warplane fired two Exocet missiles at the *USS Stark*, killing thirty-seven U.S. sailors. The *Stark* was part of a large and growing naval presence in the Persian Gulf whose mission included protection of Kuwaiti oil tankers (reregistered to carry American flags) from attacks in the protracted Iran-Iraq war. The decision to reflag and protect the Kuwaiti tankers was motivated by the desire to prevent Iranian expansionism from threatening other states in the region who were friendly to the United States, and to keep the Soviet Union from expanding its influence in the region. Member of Congress, however, were concerned that they had not been consulted on the reflagging operation, and they continued to press in the months following the *Stark* incident for a greater voice in Persian Gulf policies.

The *Stark* incident prompted a vigorous debate in Congress about the applicability of the War Powers Resolution. Secretary Shultz argued in a report to Congress on the *Stark* incident that the United States had maintained a naval presence in the Persian Gulf under the president's authority as commander in chief for nearly forty years. Unconvinced, both houses of Congress introduced legislation that sought to invoke the War Powers Resolution. When these failed, over one hundred members of the House and Senate sought (unsuccessfully) to have a U.S. district court compel the president to file a report under its provisions. Meanwhile, as the tanker war in the Persian Gulf escalated and the United States increasingly became involved in military operations, Senators Lowell Weicker and Mark Hatfield introduced legislation declaring that the provisions of the resolution had been triggered, but it failed, too, to enjoy majority support. Clearly Congress itself was badly divided.

> The harder Congress tried to achieve a policy consensus, the more deeply it became entangled in procedural questions. By the end of 1987, the very mention of another war powers debate brought groans from Republican and Democratic cloakrooms alike. The law itself had become an embarrassment to a majority in Congress. Thus, legislators chose to do nothing rather than choose between challenging the White House on Gulf policy or forcing a legal showdown over the War Powers Act's provisions. (Warburg, 1989: 139)

The Reagan administration never conceded the applicability of the War Powers Resolution, but it did begin in the fall of 1987 to submit reports to Congress on developments in the Persian Gulf consistent with the resolution. Eventually six reports on Persian Gulf activities were submitted, including one in July 1988 on the downing by the *USS Vincennes* of an Iranian civilian airliner mistakenly believed to have been a hostile Iranian military plane. Then, in August 1988, a cease-fire in the Iran-Iraq war removed the circumstances causing the executive-legislative disagreement, as U.S. military forces were gradually withdrawn from the Gulf region.

The prolonged clash over Persian Gulf policy set the stage for efforts in 1988 to amend the War Powers Resolution itself. Of particular concern was how to define criteria for determining when hostilities were imminent enough to require invoking the resolution's procedures. In the end these, too, failed to produce any changes. In part this is because members of Congress themselves continued to be divided about the wisdom of the War Powers Resolution itself, as they had been in the past. Some felt the resolution was an ill-advised, unnecessary intrusion on the president's authority; others believed that the law had worked in the sense that it gave Congress some leverage over policy that it otherwise lacked; and still others believed it had failed because it was not invoked in a situation where U.S. forces were in danger of imminent hostilities. Underlying these differing viewpoints were partisan and ideological differences over the wisdom of particular policies that, in turn, affected perceptions of the procedural issues over which Congress and the president differed. As one expert concluded, "Decisions to invoke the War Powers Resolution are likely to be based on broad political judgments about the role of Congress in U.S. foreign and security policy or about the particular situation under consideration, rather than measurable facts on whether forces are in hostilities or imminent hostilities" (Collier, 1987a). This was nowhere more evident than in the fall of 1990 when Bush dispatched troops to the Persian Gulf with barely a whisper from Congress, only to find that as the objectives of the mission became clouded Congress increasingly expressed concern about its constitutional prerogatives.

Jacob K. Javits, architect of the War Powers Resolution, wrote shortly before his death that the resolution "did not, and does not, guarantee the end of presidential war, but it does present Congress with the means by which it can stop presidential war if it has the will to act" (Javits, 1985). In most instances it appears that Congress lacks the will, in part because short, decisive military actions by the president tend to be politically popular at home—as in the case of the interventions in Grenada in 1983 and Panama in 1989 and the attack on Libya in 1986. Even a prolonged engagement, as in the Persian Gulf conflict with Iraq over Kuwait, may not provoke a congressional backlash as long as the involvement remains popular with the American people.

And so the debate continues. But while it continues, the historical record demonstrates that the War Powers Resolution has failed in its intention to redress the balance between Congress and the president because, quite simply, no president has conceded he is bound by its provisions and because Congress cannot ensure enforcement. "What *should* Congress do when the president fails to consult them before committing the nation to battle?" asked one observer rhetorically. "How *should* Congress respond when the president fails to comply with the provisions of the law of the land?" (Warburg, 1989).[24] In the end, the president remains preeminent in the initiation and execution of war.

Money

What about the power of the purse? Since Congress has the exclusive power to appropriate funds for foreign as well as domestic programs, we should expect that here, more than in any other area, Congress would assert its authority over foreign affairs. And, in some respects at least, that has been the case.[25]

Managing Foreign Aid Expenditures   The perennially unpopular foreign aid program is a case in point. It has been a favored target of Congress's exercise of the power of the purse, and Congress has often substantially cut the president's foreign aid request. Part of the reason is that, unlike many other areas of the budget, foreign aid cuts are unlikely to affect adversely local constituents' interests. Moreover, as we noted in Chapter 4, Congress characteristically "earmarks" foreign aid funds for particular countries. Special-interest groups and ethnic lobbies are important in determining who gets how much, with the result that the executive's flexibility in its use of this long-standing policy instrument is severely impaired.

The aid program enables Congress to scrutinize periodically the executive's conduct of foreign policy, and through such scrutiny to place a legislative stamp on certain aspects of U.S. behavior overseas.

> Since there is no guarantee that a major arms sale, a treaty question, or a war powers dispute will arise in a given year, the foreign aid measure is the one vehicle upon which legislators know they can make manifest their international concerns . . . . Even the most junior legislator can easily reshape U.S. interna-

---

24. Theodore Lowi (1985b) has argued that the War Powers Resolution does not give Congress power to participate in war-making decisions it did not already have, but that it does in effect give the president "blanket power to use military force for sixty days, without legislative authorization," which "legitimizes a war-making power that heretofore had been based on customary practice and precedent."

25. See Turner (1988) for a critical view of Congress's use of the power of the purse to affect foreign and national security policy.

tional relations through irresponsible but irresistible floor amendments. Here is where a host of foreign spending projects on a State Department or Pentagon wish list can be pared. Here is where legislators can attempt to steer foreign procurement contracts toward local firms. Here is where the specter of "535 secretaries of state" is inevitably raised by critics of an aggressive congressional role. (Warburg, 1989: 234–235)

In addition to "earmarking," in recent years "conditionality"—the various directives, provisos, and restrictions that Congress writes into the annual foreign aid bill—has become the centerpiece of congressional-presidential struggles over foreign aid funding (Warburg, 1989). These conditions may take many different forms. Bans on aid to countries taking certain actions—such as human rights violations, seizure of U.S. fishing vessels, the granting of sanctuary to terrorists, and the like—are commonplace. Aid has also been made conditional on recipients meeting certain standards, such as cooperating with the United States in the interdiction of drug trafficking, as required by the Anti-Drug Abuse Act of 1986, holding free elections, or voting in agreement with the United States on United Nations resolutions. The list goes on. In fact, Congress reportedly directs where half of all development loan funds and over 90 percent of all U.S. security assistance is to go (Kondracke, 1990: 20). Often in recent years the aid bill has become so encumbered with conditions that it has simply failed to be approved. The regular annual foreign aid authorization bill passed only twice during the eight-year Reagan presidency, with various stop-gap measures required to keep the aid program alive.

Congress has increasingly resorted to various reporting requirements to ensure executive compliance with legislative restrictions built into the foreign assistance act and other foreign policy legislation, as witnessed by the fact that the number of reporting requirements mushroomed from two hundred in 1973 to more than eight hundred in 1988 (Collier, 1989: 37). From Congress's point of view, reporting requirements serve a number of purposes. They provide Congress with information (as has come to be the practice with the reporting requirements in the War Powers Resolution); promote consultation (the Refugee Assistance Act of 1980, for example, defines particular means of executive-legislative consultation); focus attention on a problem (as occurs with the annual required publication of human rights practices in other countries); provide a means of control (the Fishery Conservation Management Act of 1976 requires that fisheries agreements be submitted to Congress within a specified time period); and oversee implementation (as with provisions in the Anti-Apartheid Act of 1986 passed over Reagan's veto) (Collier, 1988). The number of reporting requirements is now so great, however, that "Congress has difficulty keeping track of them, the executive branch agencies fulfilling them, and members and staff reading the submitted reports" (Collier, 1988). Moreover, from the executive's point of view, the required reports and certifications create inappropriate congressional "micromanagement"—that is, excessive legislative interference in the conduct of America's foreign relations. Congress has imposed nearly three hundred individual reporting requirements on the

Agency for International Development (AID), for example, which has led AID employees in Third World countries to "complain that they spend so much time filling out reports for Congress . . . that they have only an afternoon a week to help the poor" (Kondracke, 1990).

Conditions imposed by Congress often mean that the president must balance priorities in such a way that American policy sometimes seems contorted if not outright contradictory.[26] The Anti-Drug Abuse Act, for example, made it necessary for the Reagan administration to certify that Panama under the leadership of Manuel Noriega was cooperating in drug traffic control when in fact it was known to be the center of massive drug trafficking and money laundering operations (Kempe, 1990). "Yet the President was reluctant to let fly the guillotine on aid to Panama—in part because of concern about the security of the Panama Canal, and in part because of fears that Noriega would embarrass the United States with revelations about his former long-standing relationship with the CIA and the Contras" (Warburg, 1989).

Often the president is able to avoid such situations by taking advantage of loopholes Congress typically provides, the most general of which permits the president to ignore most restrictions if the president finds that the security interests of the United States are compromised. The provision of such a large loophole fits Congress's tendency to permit the president a degree of flexibility at the same time that it seeks to exercise some influence over the overall direction of policy (while escaping responsibility—and criticism—for its management). Concern for possible adverse effects on the nation's security and interests underlies such seemingly contradictory impulses.

Managing Military Expenditures   Military spending is another budgetary area in which Congress can and does play a major role. During the 1950s and 1960s, Congress often voiced its views on the defense budget by appropriating *more* for defense than was asked for by the president. But as executive-congressional relations moved from acquiescence to ambiguity and then to acrimony, Congress began cutting administration requests substantially, much as it has done in the foreign aid area. Moreover, its "micromanagement" of the Pentagon has steadily increased. A Bush administration White Paper complained that "some 30 committees and 77 subcommittees claim some degree of oversight . . . and more than 1,500 congressional staffers devote nearly all of their time to defense issues." The result (in 1988) was some eighteen thousand letters sent by Congress to the Defense Department, which, in turn, spent

---

26. Effectiveness is another issue. For example, despite congressional restraints on providing aid "to the government of any country which engages in a consistent pattern of gross violations of internationally recognized human rights," the actual relationship between aid allocations and the pattern of humans rights fails to show that congressional intentions were met (see Carleton and Stohl, 1985; McCormick and Mitchell, 1989; Mitchell and McCormick, 1988; and Schoultz, 1981). Similarly, the 1986 effort to link U.S. foreign assistance to the voting behavior of aid recipients in the United Nations fell far short of the goals envisioned by its supports (see Kegley and Hook, 1990).

245,000 hours answering the mail (*Wall Street Journal*, December 18, 1989, p. A10).

The congressional penchant to "micromanage" was especially evident during the Reagan administration. What became the most ambitious peacetime military buildup in American history led Congress eventually to ask, how much is enough? The buildup of Soviet military forces during the 1970s stimulated support for substantial U.S. spending increases, as did specific events, such as the December 1979 Soviet invasion of Afghanistan. Congress nonetheless often trimmed Reagan's extraordinary appropriation requests, particularly as the administration sought to reduce domestic spending and concern for mounting federal government budget deficits began to grow. Rarely, however, did Congress target specific programs or weapons for major reductions; more often the cuts were spread so widely as to have inconsequential programmatic consequences (see Congressional Quarterly, 1983). The MX missile was, with some qualifications, an exception.

The Carter administration became convinced that the MX was necessary to replace the increasingly vulnerable intercontinental ballistic missile (ICBM) force made up principally of aging Minuteman III missiles. The basing modes for the projected mobile missile proved to be extraordinarily costly, however, not only financially but also environmentally and politically. The Reagan administration scrapped the mobile design but never found an alternative basing mode among the dozens that were examined that was acceptable to Congress and the defense community. In December 1982 Congress refused to appropriate the funds necessary for production of the first five MX missiles. It was the first time since the Vietnam War that Congress had denied funds for a major weapons system requested by the president (Congressional Quarterly, 1983).

In January 1983 Reagan appointed the bipartisan Scowcroft Commission to review the administration's strategic modernization program with special emphasis on the land-based missile system and its basing mode. The commission recommended building a new single-warhead mobile missile, which it called Midgetman, but it could not find an alternative to a fixed-basing mode for the MX, which it proposed to assign to existing Minuteman silos. This seemed to belie the very purpose for which the MX was first proposed, namely, to reduce the vulnerability of the land-based leg of the strategic triad. Congress then handed Reagan a stunning political defeat when in 1985 it reduced from two hundred to fifty the number of MX missiles authorized for production until a survivable basing mode was devised. "Never before had a major strategic weapons program been cut back so drastically by binding legislation" (Warburg, 1989).

Congressional skepticism about the MX basing mode and about Reagan's claim that the missile would enhance the administration's bargaining leverage in arms control talks with the Soviet Union were major reasons for Congress's action. But as dramatic as it was, the decision was a deferral, not an outright cancellation of the MX. Indeed, the MX has proved to be remarkably durable and is a graphic illustration of the fact that Congress rarely defeats presidents' proposals for weapons systems. In this case the link that Ford, Carter, and Reagan drew between the missile and the Soviet Union's arms buildup enhanced its survivability. Uncertainty over nuclear security issues strengthened the presidents' hands. "There is a kind of reverence to strategic issues," Senator Gary Hart observed. "Strategic issues are of a different order, a higher order. It's survival; it's the whole ball game if things go wrong." By the time George Bush moved into the White House, the MX was being proposed as a rail-garrisoned weapon, Midgetman was still alive, the Reagan administration's Strategic Defense Initiative (proposed at precisely the time MX seemed to be dead) was still being funded, and a new, exceedingly expensive weapon system was moving from the research and development to the production stage—the B-2 Stealth radar-evading bomber designed to penetrate Soviet air defenses in the 1990s and beyond at a cost of $70 billion, or nearly $600 million for each copy of the advanced technology aircraft.

Congress's inability to grapple effectively with the overarching issues of national security policy that the MX and related strategic weapons raise applies broadly to its treatment of the defense budget. As already noted, rather than focusing on the big picture, Congress has increasingly "micromanaged" the defense budget. Between fiscal 1970 and fiscal 1987, for example, the number of congressional directives and line-item adjustments in the Pentagon budget skyrocketed from just over a hundred to nearly fifteen hundred (Lindsay, 1988: 61). "Congress now changes more than 60 percent of the line items in the Pentagon's annual budget request" (*Wall Street Journal*, December 18, 1989, p. A10).

The motivation to micromanage is tied directly to the factors that differentiate the perspective of members of Congress on foreign and national security policy issues from that of the president. Political grandstanding for electoral purposes is a powerful incentive. Congress debated (and voted on) virtually all of the important strategic and many conventional weapons systems requiring production decisions during the 1980s, including not only MX, SDI, and the Stealth bomber program, but also antisatellite systems, chemical weapons, the Trident II submarine, the B-1 bomber, cruise missiles, nuclear powered aircraft carriers, and antiaircraft guns and tactical aircraft. But whereas earlier decisions on these systems would typically have been made in congressional committees, during the 1980s they became the object of much activity on the floor of the respective chambers of Congress, where members debated them to enhance their visibility. As Senator Gaylord Nelson noted wryly, "The floor is being used as an instrument of political campaigning far more than it ever was before." Electoral incentives in the form of financial contributions and constituency support also multiplied as the guns-instead-of-butter spending priorities of the Reagan administration contributed to politicizing defense policy (Lindsay, 1987).[27]

---

27. As noted in Chapter 8, defense procurement is typically regarded as a pork barrel issue that members of Congress can use to cultivate constituency support. During the debate on the B-1 bomber, for example, the air force and its industrial allies lobbied members of Congress with the

Parochialism that stimulates the desire for committee service by members of Congress is also a closely related reason for micromanagement of the defense budget, as members of Congress have incentives to be sensitive to the impact of defense spending on their constituencies. Neglect of long-term policy is a natural consequence. As a former staff member of the House Armed Services Committee has observed, "There is a natural constituency for concentration on weapons systems in the here and now. It is difficult for members to focus on the big issues because of the lack of time, because of the need to get reelected, and because of the fact that constituency service, not policy oversight, is what is necessary today to stay in office" (cited in Art, 1985).

The question is how to get Congress to focus on policy, not programs. In Pentagon jargon, "policy oversight" is captured in issues of "force structure" or "force design." The consensus is that on these issues, Congress does not do well (Art, 1985). As a former House Armed Services Committee staff member observed, "Members of Armed Services get into policy but only obliquely. For example, on the Lehman power projection or sea control issue . . . we made a decision in favor of the former by authorizing a 600-ship navy, but we did it this way: We justified a carrier by stating the policy behind it rather than the reverse. We did not debate which policy we needed and then determine the best weapons systems to achieve it. The members of the committee thus back into policy" (cited in Art, 1985).

Neglecting policy oversight may undermine Congress's capacity to exercise the power of the purse effectively, but for individual members such avoidance is politically astute.

> The only thing worse than taking on an issue that will not make a legislator look good is taking on one that will make him look bad. Most issues of general policy oversight . . . involve longstanding and fairly intractable problems, ones in which the risk of looking bad is high . . . . The political incentives as they are structured on Capitol Hill today put the bias on the short term, the specific, the details, the programs that can be grabbed, manipulated, changed, and sold. (Art, 1985: 240)

Constraints on the Power of the Purse   Congressional actions on the foreign aid and defense budgets demonstrate that Congress is not unwilling to exercise its power of the purse, even if its instruments for doing so are not finely honed and its motives sometimes circumspect. Elsewhere, however, the frequency with which Congress has sought to deal with a dominant executive

---

argument that they would profit from the project with increased jobs and dollars in their states and congressional districts (Kotz, 1988; Ornstein and Elder, 1978). Interestingly, however, congressional votes on strategic weapons issues are best explained not by constituency interests (as the military-industrial complex thesis would argue) but instead on the basis of the political ideology of members of Congress (Lindsay, 1990). Evidence shows that foreign and domestic policy issues may be more similar than dissimilar in terms of how members of Congress treat them. Partisanship and ideology often reign supreme in the domestic domain, whereas foreign and national security policy is thought to be above politics. For evidence to the contrary, see Bernstein (1989), Bernstein and Anthony (1974), Fleisher (1985), McCormick and Black (1983), McCormick (1985), McCormick and Wittkopf (1990a, 1990b), Moyer (1973), and Wayman (1985).

through its fiscal powers has been remarkably irregular. There have been examples, of course, as in the winter of 1975–1976 when the Clark amendment to the 1976 appropriations bill barred the use of funds in the bill "for any activities involving Angola directly or indirectly" (the amendment was repealed in 1985) and in the early 1980s when the Boland amendment sought to prevent covert activities in Central America. But historically, such actions are the exception rather than the rule. Indeed, the Angolan and Nicaraguan stories demand attention as much for their uniqueness as for their illustration of congressional assertiveness.

More characteristic of executive-legislative relations is the fate of the much publicized Cooper-Church amendment, which sought to cut off funds for U.S. war efforts in Cambodia following Nixon's "incursion" into the country in 1970. The amendment failed. In fact, Congress cut off Cambodian war funds only after (then known) U.S. military activity had ceased, and Congress never failed to appropriate the funds for the war that the Johnson and Nixon administrations sought.

The largely symbolic Cooper-Church amendment illustrates the difficulty inherent in getting even a majority of 535 independent-minded lawmakers to agree on a specific proposal—a prospect made all the more difficult when the proposal is at variance with the president. More generally, however, the extent to which money can be used to affect the nation's foreign policy is limited. Simply put, it is difficult to legislate foreign policy, or to equate lawmaking with foreign policy making. Programs, but not necessarily policies, require appropriations. Hence some of the most important aspects of America's foreign relations do not require specific and direct appropriations of money. The Nixon and Carter Doctrines are excellent cases in point. Both were essentially statements of intent that created important expectations both at home and abroad quite independently of fiscal activities Congress was asked to undertake at the time. Moreover, the division of congressional responsibility among many different committees, alongside the breakdown of party unity and the erosion of leadership in Congress, militates against a more effective use of congressional powers. This fact is nowhere more evident than in the funding process, where, within each house of Congress, authorizations for expenditures are specified by the substantive committees having jurisdiction over particular programs but the actual appropriations are made by another committee.

In 1974 Congress passed the Budget and Impoundment Control Act in an attempt to consolidate some control over the purse, as it requires Congress to specify overall spending guidelines and otherwise broadens the ability of Congress to scrutinize the president's budgetary requests. In principle, Congress is now required to face squarely the unwelcome political task of weighing federal spending against federal income. In practice, Congress continues to postpone the tough choices. The budget resolution process itself extends several months into each session of Congress, with the result that disagreements over budget priorities protract the authorization and appropriations process. The problem has been compounded by the Gramm-Rudman-Hollings deficit reduction amendment signed into law in 1985. The amendment provides mandatory and declining targets for the federal deficit with a view toward their eventual elimination. Achieving the required deficit reduction targets has inspired imaginative means of postponing tough choices, especially those that involve a tradeoff between national security and domestic welfare, both of which involve values highly prized at both ends of Pennsylvania Avenue.

Even if there are no built-in impediments to the use of congressional spending powers to affect foreign affairs, the devices that the executive has developed to spend as it pleases, irrespective of congressional wishes and oversight, give the president substantial fiscal independence. Impoundment, which is a presidential refusal to spend money appropriated by Congress, is one mechanism. Others include discretionary funds and reprogramming decisions. Each enables the executive to undertake activities that may well be at variance with congressional wishes and intent. *Discretionary funds*, for example, are monies provided the president to deal with situations unforeseen at the time of the annual budgetary process, but they have often been used for purposes other than emergencies. Johnson used $1.5 billion in contingency funds embedded in the Defense Department budget to finance military operations in Southeast Asia during 1965 and 1966 (Nathan and Oliver, 1976: 495–496), for example, and the Reagan administration used $10 million in CIA discretionary funds to finance the *contras* during its first term (Copson, 1988: 4).

Reprogramming provides executive flexibility by allowing funds within an appropriation to be moved from one purpose to another (for example, from shipbuilding to submarine construction). The device is widely used by the Defense Department. "Major" reprogramming actions require some congressional committee oversight (but *not* approval by the whole Congress), whereas "minor" reprogramming decisions are at the internal discretion of the Defense Department. Reprogramming is one of several nonstatutory control mechanisms Congress and the executive have devised to deal with contingencies that neither branch is able to anticipate in the annual budgetary cycle (Fisher, 1987). The sums involved are often substantial, which opens the mechanism to charges that it is but one more device used by the executive to undermine Congress's constitutional power of the purse.

Constraining the executive's flexibility in using funds appropriated by Congress was a principal purpose of the Budget Control and Impoundment Act. It specifies that the president has two avenues by which to impound funds, both subject to congressional review. Temporary spending delays, which can extend up to twelve months, are known as *deferrals*; permanent efforts to cancel budget authority are known as *rescissions*. The role of Congress in each of these executive decisions is now clear (see Ellwood and Thurber, 1981; Ellwood, 1985), but how well Congress has used them to constrain executive latitude is not easily determined. The overall record suggests, however, that even as Congress has sought to tighten politically its control in an area where it appears dominant constitutionally, it has done so in a way that has not substantially reduced presidential flexibility.

One area in which Congress has been especially reluctant to fix leaks from the fiscal faucet is in the financing of the intelligence community. Indeed, intelligence funding remains the best-known example of dollars provided the executive by Congress that remain outside the direct control of Congress as a whole.[28] The House and Senate Intelligence Committees have been empowered to authorize expenditures by the intelligence community—which presumably means that committee members know what the funding figures are—but the periodic efforts by some members of Congress to have the actual costs of intelligence operations released publicly have routinely failed. The reasons derive from the familiar—and often legitimate—concern for security.

What could not be anticipated from the practice of intelligence appropriations is that the executive might engage in covert intelligence activities by bypassing the congressional funding process altogether. Yet this is exactly what happened during the Iran-*contra* affair. Between $3 and $4 million in profits from the sale of arms to Iran in early 1986 was diverted to the *contras* at precisely the time the Boland amendment banned U.S. government support for the guerrillas. According to the Tower Board inquiry into the affair, the act raised important questions about law as well as propriety. It also became clear as the entire Iran-*contra* affair unfolded that staff members of the president's National Security Council had solicited millions of dollars in funds from private contributors in the United States and from foreign governments to keep the *contras* afloat at the same time that Congress had in effect determined that the United States should distance itself from the anti-Sandinista cause.

Lt. Colonel Oliver North testified before Congress that, in his opinion, the withholding of appropriations by Congress did not prevent the president from pursuing his foreign policy objectives using private or foreign-donated funds. Admiral John Poindexter, North's boss at the NSC, concurred, arguing that the executive branch could circumvent Congress by using nonappropriated funds. Furthermore, he defended the withholding of information from Congress on grounds that the NSC was using private and third-country funds, not money appropriated by Congress.

Poindexter also testified that President Reagan had not been informed of the diversion of funds to the *contras*, but he quickly added that he believed Reagan would have approved of the scheme. Finally, it was revealed during the congressional inquiry into the Iran-*contra* affair that William Casey, director of central intelligence during the Reagan administration until his death in 1987, had expressed interest in creating an off-the-shelf, stand-alone, self-financed

---

28. The Senate Select Committee on Intelligence (*Final Report*, 1, 1976: 470) noted that the CIA's budget is contained within the Defense Department budget and reported that "the CIA spends approximately 70 percent more than it is appropriated, with the additional funds coming from advances and transfers from other agencies." It went on to note that "the use of advances and transfers between agencies is a common governmental practice." Although intelligence expenditures continue to be buried in the Defense Department budget, the practice of spending more than is appropriated may no longer be widespread because the charters for the House and Senate Intelligence Committees contain provisions prohibiting appropriations that have not been authorized.

intelligence organization capable of conducting covert activities without ever being held accountable to Congress or anyone else.

The Constitution of the United States places the power of the purse directly in the hands of Congress. The logic used by North and Poindexter would have undermined the system of checks and balances between the executive and legislative branches of government that is the essence of the American political system. By "placing in the same branch the ability to make war and fund it," Louis Fisher (1988), an expert on the powers of Congress and the president, writes, "executive use of funds obtained outside the appropriations process would create a government the framers feared the most: union of sword and purse." As James Madison wrote, "Those who are to *conduct a war* cannot in the nature of things, be proper or safe judges, whether a war ought to be *commenced, continued*, or *concluded*. They are barred from the latter functions by a great principle in free government, analogous to that which separates the sword from the purse, or the power of executing from the power of enacting laws" (cited in Fisher, 1988).

"To preserve the system of checks and balances," concludes Fisher (1988), "foreign policy must be carried out with funds appropriated by Congress. Allowing foreign policy to be conducted with funds supplied by private parties and foreign governments would open the door to widespread corruption, compromise, and loss of public accountability. This type of outside financing would fundamentally subvert the Constitution and undermine the powers of Congress as a coequal branch." Secretary of State Shultz, a vigorous critic of the Iran-*contra* connection, agreed: "You cannot spend funds that the Congress doesn't either authorize you to obtain or appropriate. That is what the Constitution says, and we have to stick to it. . . . We have this very difficult task of having a separation of powers that means we have to share power. Sharing power is harder, . . . but that's the only way" (cited in Henderson, 1988).

IS CONGRESS EITHER ABLE OR WILLING?

Congress is a central component of the exceedingly complex institutional labyrinth in which American foreign policy is made, but in the process whereby policy emanates from this maze, the resources available to the White House are clearly more formidable than those available to Congress. In the areas of treaties, war, and money, the Constitution would appear to make Congress, not the president, preeminent, but the reverse has in fact been true. Congress has made some strides toward coping with its structural inadequacies, but power remains diffused, the ability to assume and discharge responsibility remains fragmented, and the incentives continue to favor attention to parochial needs rather than the broader picture. Moreover, the powers of the institutionalized presidency are so vastly superior to those of the legislature that Congress is far more likely to be co-opted by the wishes of the president than vice versa. That conclusion was reinforced countless times during the 1980s, as Congress by choice or necessity retreated from the more acrimonious posture it had assumed during the 1970s. Hence there is little that warrants a revision of the initiator-respondent view of executive-legislative relations. Congress remains relatively far removed from the center of power; it has authority, but it follows more than it leads.

Many would argue that Congress functions most appropriately when it is removed from day-to-day activities. Even J. William Fulbright (1979), once an outspoken critic of presidential dominance in foreign policy making, has argued that the role of Congress is "in the authorization of military and major political commitments, and in advising broad policy directions, while leaving to the executive the necessary flexibility to conduct policy within the broad parameters approved by the legislature." But such a view should not obscure the fact that Congress can make a difference and a positive contribution. As member of Congress Les Aspin (1976) observes, Congress functions reasonably well as an avenue for the expression of constituent and other views and interests; as an overseer of government policies and resource allocations; and as a "guardian" of the processes of government. In the latter capacity, in particular, Congress is often able to shape significantly the processes through which policies evolve and hence to influence the composition of the contestants who engage in the debate. The creation by Congress of the National Security Council and the Defense Department and, more recently, its augmentation of the roles of the chairman of the Joint Chiefs of Staff and the U.S. Trade Representative in the policy process are cases in point.

Similarly, the actions that Congress takes in executing its negative, limit-setting functions often can shape significantly the content of debate about the goals and means of foreign policy. The provisions in the 1988 omnibus trade bill requiring that the president play a more assertive role in promoting U.S. interests vis-à-vis its trade partners are illustrative. In the process of asserting its prerogatives, Congress often inhibits the prospects for a hasty revision of the direction of American foreign policy. In the final analysis, then, Congress affects most the way in which policy is debated within the executive branch; it becomes part of the ultimate decision-making process, even if only by affecting the various political forces involved there. Hence the existence of a coequal legislative branch may require even a preeminent president to defer to what often becomes a relatively public policy-making process. It is a process that is perhaps unique even among democratic societies.

SUGGESTIONS FOR FURTHER READING

Bax, Frans R. (1977) "The Legislative-Executive Relationship in Foreign Policy: New Partnership or New Competition?" *Orbis* 20 (Winter): 881–904.

Bleachman, Barry M. (1990) *The Politics of National Security: Congress and U.S. Defense Policy.* New York: Oxford University Press.

Collier, Ellen C. (1989) "Bipartisan Foreign Policy and Policymaking Since World War II," *CRS Report for Congress*, November 9. Washington, D.C.: Congressional Research Service.

Crabb, Cecil V., Jr., and Pat M. Holt. (1989) *Invitation to Struggle: Congress, the President and Foreign Policy*, 3rd ed. Washington D.C.: CQ Press.

Fisher, Louis. (1987) *Constitutional Conflicts Between Congress and the President*, 2nd ed. Princeton, N.J.: Princeton University Press.

Franck, Thomas M., and Edward Weisband. (1979) *Foreign Policy by Congress*. New York: Oxford University Press.

Johnson, Loch K. (1989) "Covert Action and Accountability: Decision-Making for America's Secret Foreign Policy," *International Studies Quarterly* 33 (March): 81–109.

Turner, Robert F. (1988) "The Power of the Purse: Controlling National Security by Conditional Appropriations," *Atlantic Community Quarterly* 26 (Spring): 79–96.

Warburg, Gerald Felix. (1989) *Conflict and Consensus: The Struggle between Congress and the President over Foreign Policymaking*. New York: Harper & Row.

West, William F., and Joseph Cooper. (1990) "Legislative Influence v. Presidential Dominance: Competing Models of Bureaucratic Control," *Political Science Quarterly* 104 (Winter): 581–606.

PART VI

Roles and Foreign Policy Making

The Process of Decision Making: Rationality and the Impact of Bureaucratic Organization

In so many of the ex post facto *investigations, [outsiders] take individual documents and assume that people sat around the table in a seminar-type discussion, having all the facts. . . . But that is rarely the case. Usually decisions are made in a very brief time with enormous pressure and uncertain knowledge.*

FORMER SECRETARY OF STATE HENRY KISSINGER, 1977

The process was the author of the policy.

UNDER SECRETARY OF STATE GEORGE W. BALL, 1962

Many different people, widely dispersed throughout the government, make American foreign policy. We have examined the offices and their overall organization—the governmental superstructures. We now consider the decision making *process*— how the roles or formal positions within the superstructure influence the policymakers occupying those roles, and, ultimately, their foreign policy decisions.

ROLES AS A SOURCE OF FOREIGN POLICY

According to role theory, policymakers' actions and attitudes are largely determined by the positions they occupy; individuals are not unimportant, but institutional roles constrain and mold their behavior.

Role theory recognizes that any individual's actual behavior can be distinguished from the role he or she occupies. Nonetheless, each role (or position) carries with it certain expectations and demands of how it should be performed. Such pressures, including each position's functions and the rules governing how the job is to be handled, affect attitudes and actions. These images and requirements are assumed to influence *anyone* filling a particular role; every individual acts somewhat similarly to others who have previously occupied the same role.

To suggest that roles influence thoughts and behavior should not be disturbing. Everyone plays many roles in life; unless we are hermits, we sometimes find ourselves in social situations with which we have had no prior experience. We typically respond to such new circumstances by behaving according to our image of appropriate conduct. Witness the changes observable when people shift from the role of student to employee, or to new parent or even politician; they subconsciously act in the manner they think is expected. Their vocabulary and ideas undergo subtle change, as does their outlook. The various roles each of us play in life, evidence suggests, explain and predict our attitudes and behavior.[1]

Policymakers are not immune from this phenomenon. Each decision-making role carries with it certain expectations, obligations, and images of appropriate behavior—pressures that tend to make the new occupant of an office think and act like his or her predecessor. Whereas an individual's style and mannerisms may be markedly different from that of the person who held the job previously, orientations on crucial issues tend to be consistent.[2] "It's an old story in Washington that where you stand depends on where you sit. That's a practical acknowledgment of the fact that people's views change as they change responsibilities," political journalist David Broder observed. An example: while campaigning, Jimmy Carter criticized Henry Kissinger's "personal diplomacy" and advocated less emphasis on private talks with foreign leaders. Yet in the first seven months in office, Carter played host to no fewer than eighteen foreign heads of state. The discrepancy between advocated and actual behavior changed once the role was actually assumed.

Of course, there are clear limits to role theory's ability to explain policy-making behavior. A forceful personality may actually redefine the role so as to extend the boundaries of permissible behavior, as Franklin D. Roosevelt is pictured having done by his expansion of the office of the presidency. Ronald Reagan's habit of taking many naps and frequent vacations—a propensity that reflected his relaxed style in an office that heretofore demanded sleepless attention to the duties of governance—similarly transcended customary role restraints. Moreover, particular roles permit more than one interpretation, and

---

1. Examples of this propensity come readily to mind. Consider the professor who receives a large Defense Department research grant and then ceases to write articles critical of defense spending; or take the labor organizer promoted to a major corporate position who overnight begins to see the "necessity" for "right to work" laws and for wage controls. Likewise, the military officer may return home from work, take off the uniform, become spouse and parent, and change his or her behavior accordingly.

2. Research has conclusively demonstrated a causal relationship between policymakers' attitudes and roles (Lieberman, 1965; Singer, 1965). For example, it has been shown that people promoted in the armed services develop more favorable attitudes toward the army than those who are not promoted, and that commissioned officers are more pro-army than draftees (Stouffer et al., 1949); the length of service in the U.S. House of Representatives affects members' attitudes toward foreign aid (Rieselbach, 1964); in addition, the role requirements (that is, committee experience) of U.S. senators shapes their attitudes toward the secretary of state (Rosenau, 1980).

some roles have boundaries so wide and elastic that individual behavior within them is almost unpredictable. Although high positions allow several interpretations—as evidenced, for example, by the contrast between Dwight D. Eisenhower's and John F. Kennedy's concept of the presidency (or between Carter's and Reagan's or Reagan's and George Bush's)—each interpretation is, in effect, a specific role.[3] Variations in behavior will still depend on which role interpretation a new occupant of a policy-making position adopts. And certain types of people become their roles easily—they are prone to adopt whatever role they inherit (Snyder, 1980).

Yet the capacity for alternative role definitions to be framed attests to one of the ways in which the individual source category (elaborated in Chapter 14) affects foreign policy making. For example, consider how various role conceptions led each postwar president to organize and use his White House foreign policy staff somewhat differently (described in Chapter 10). The consequences, as shown in particular by Lyndon B. Johnson's approach to the Vietnam War and Richard M. Nixon's insulation from the larger foreign affairs government, can be significant. Even leaders who may at times be given considerable leeway to act as they wish usually acquiesce to the prevailing norms associated with their position. Behavioral conformity is especially evident in the formal roles in government positions, where norms governing performance are backed by legal obligations and sanctions and not merely social pressures. Watergate is a case in point: Richard Nixon discovered the system's intolerance for illegal conduct even by the president.

The implications of this line of reasoning for American foreign policy are substantial. Role theory's premise—that people's conduct conforms with their roles—means that to understand the sources of American foreign policy we must examine the behavior most often associated with foreign policy-making roles in addition to examining individuals.

A focus on decision-making roles also enables us to understand foreign policy change, because policy discontinuities may derive from changes in the major policy-making roles. Because roles shape goals, policy modification may be produced by role transformations. That is, changes in the system by which decisions are made and the roles that induce those decisions may lead to policy revisions and redirection.

This chapter will investigate two interpretations of roles often assumed to be descriptive of American decision-making procedures: the proposition that American foreign policy is made through a *rational* decision process, and the rival image of a decision-making process governed by *bureaucratic politics*.

---

3. These pressures were illustrated by George Bush's confession in November 1989 at a White House reception honoring Ronald Reagan that he had difficulty adjusting to his new role as president after serving as Reagan's vice president: "When the announcer said 'Mr. President,' well, I fell back to where I comfortably was for eight years. It seemed most appropriate."

FOREIGN POLICY MAKING AS A RATIONAL PROCESS

President Carter's campaign strategists attempted to portray a particular image of their candidate when he was running for reelection in 1980. In an often-televised commercial, Carter was photographed in the Oval Office, working industriously late into the night, pouring over documents. He was pictured a deep thinker, intellectually absorbed in the tasks of the office—making the decisions that only he could make, formidable choices on which the nation's destiny would ultimately depend. Viewers were asked to compare his qualifications—his intelligence, experience, dedication, energy, and diligence—with those of his opponent.

The footage did more than attempt to sell the candidate, though. It also reinforced a popular view of the policy-making process at the nation's nerve center on Pennsylvania Avenue: that fateful decisions are made by *rational* actors engaged in orderly, contemplative processes. In this view American foreign policy results from a deliberate intellectual process, in which the central figures carefully seek to choose what is best for the country and to select tactics that promote its national interests.

Thus, the question, Is foreign policy making rational?, actually may seem a curious one to ask. We tend, almost instinctively, to think, How could it be otherwise? Indeed, it is disconcerting to picture something as important as foreign policy choice, where the stakes are the survival of the nation and perhaps civilization itself, governed by incoherence, emotions, or irrational impulses. The notion of rational policy making is much more comforting. Moreover, leaders try to cultivate public images of themselves as capable of decisiveness, unfettered by subconscious psychological drives, able to manage the stress and burden of their position, endowed with limitless energy, and prepared to guide the country safely through crises while pursuing the country's best interests. Their efforts are frequently successful because we prefer to think of our leaders' decisions as the product of rational deliberation.

What comprises rationality as it applies to foreign policy decision making? Although *rationality* is loosely used in a variety of ways, it generally refers to "actions chosen by the nation . . . that will maximize strategic goals and objectives" (Allison, 1971). This implies purposeful, goal-directed behavior that occurs when "the individual responding to an international event . . . uses the best information available and chooses from the universe of possible responses that alternative most likely to maximize his goals" (Verba, 1969).

Rationality is often relied on as a standard for evaluating the processes by which policies are formulated, because a counter model, premised on *nonrational* behavior (in which actions are derived exclusively from emotional predispositions, subconscious impulses, and nonintellectual forces) is not very useful.

The Rational Actor Model

The rational actor model treats the nation-state as a *unitary-actor*, a single homogeneous entity, and presumes that all policymakers go through the same rational thought processes to make value-maximizing choices defining national interests and options. This assumption

> allows one to consider all decision-makers to be alike. If they follow the [decision] rules, we need know nothing more about them. In essence, if the decision-maker behaves rationally, the observer, knowing the rules of rationality, can rehearse the decisional process in his own mind and, if he knows the decision-maker's goals, can both predict the decision and understand why that particular decision was made. (Verba, 1969: 225)

Scholars who study decision making and advise policymakers on ways to improve their policy-formulation skills have described the perfect rationality role model as a sequence of decision-making activities involving the following intellectual steps:

1. *Problem recognition and definition*. The necessity for decisions begins when policymakers perceive the existence of a problem with which they must deal and attempt to define objectively its distinguishing characteristics. They must see the situation as it actually exists and not as they merely assume it to be. Accuracy requires full information about international conditions and about other actors' actions, motivations, and capabilities. The search for such information must be exhaustive; *all* the facts relevant to the problem must be gathered.
2. *Goal selection*. Next, rational actors must define how they want the perceived problem resolved. This disarmingly simple requirement is often difficult. It requires ranking values in terms of the degree to which they are preferred. This is often challenging because many national interests are incompatible and their relative value can vary across situations. Yet to set priorities rationally requires that *all* goals be identified and ranked in a hierarchy from most to least preferred. For example, rationality would require policy makers to decide which of many attractive goals—promoting democracy, world order, human rights, self-defense, economic growth, and so forth—should receive priority.
3. *Identification of alternatives*. Rationality requires that an exhaustive list of *all* policy alternatives be compiled and the costs associated with each alternative estimated.
4. *Choice*. Finally, rational decision making necessitates selecting from among these competing options the single alternative with the best prospect of achieving the desired goal(s). For this purpose a rigorous means-ends, cost-benefit analysis must be conducted, guided by an accurate prediction of the probable success of each possible option.

Clearly, the requirements of perfect rationality are stringent. Nonetheless, policymakers often describe their own decision-making procedures as rational. A former Kennedy adviser, for example, described an eight-step process for policy making that the Kennedy administration sought to follow that is consistent with the rational model we have described: (1) agreement on the facts; (2) agreement on the overall policy objective; (3) precise definition of the problem; (4) canvassing of all possible solutions; (5) listing of the possible consequences flowing from each solution; (6) recommendation of one option; (7) communication of the option selected; and (8) provisions for its execution (Sorensen, 1963).

Elements of this idealized version of decision making have in fact been exhibited, or at least approximated, in past situations. For example, American policy making during the 1962 Cuban missile crisis reveals several ways in which the deliberations of the key advisers concerned with the issue of Soviet missiles in Cuba adhered to the principles of a rational process. On recognizing the emergent problem, President Kennedy charged the crisis decision-making group he formed to "set aside all other tasks to make a prompt and intensive survey of the dangers and all possible courses of action" (Allison, 1971). Six options were ultimately identified: (1) do nothing; (2) exert diplomatic pressure; (3) make a secret approach to Castro; (4) invade Cuba; (5) launch a surgical air strike against the missiles; (6) blockade Cuba. Choosing among these six required that goals be defined clearly. Was removal of the Soviet missiles, retaliation against Castro, or maintenance of the balance of power the goal? Or did the missiles pose no serious threat to America's vital interests? "Do nothing" could not be eliminated as an option until it was determined that the missiles did indeed represent a real security threat. Once it was agreed that the goal was to eliminate the missiles, discussion turned to evaluating the options of a surgical air strike or naval blockade. The latter was eventually chosen, presumably because of its perceived advantages, among which were the demonstration of U.S. firmness it permitted and the flexibility with respect to further choices it allowed both parties.

Often, however, it would appear that rational decision making is more an idealized standard by which to evaluate behavior than it is an actual description of real-world decision making. One participant in the Cuban missile crisis decision process, Theodore Sorensen, suggested why rational procedures are difficult to follow:

> Each step cannot be taken in order. The facts may be in doubt or dispute. Several policies, all good, may conflict. Several means, all bad, may be all that are open. Value judgments may differ. Stated goals may be imprecise. There may be many interpretations of what is right, what is possible, and what is in the national interest. (Sorensen, 1963: 19–20)

In addition, rational decision-making processes are often compromised by other constraints. During the Cuban missile crisis, for example, choices were determined by politicking among the crisis decision-making team (the ExCom) and were affected by the willingness and ability of bureaucratic organizations to implement the options considered.[4] Thus the surgical air strike ceased to be seen as a feasible option when three of the president's most trusted advisers (Robert McNamara, Robert Kennedy, and Theodore Sorensen) opposed it and the air force admitted it could not guarantee 100 percent success in taking out the missiles.

Let us examine the impediments to rational decision making in more detail, in order to clarify why it does not describe accurately the ways in which most foreign policy decisions are reached.

Rationality and Reality: The Limits to Rational Choice

The realities of actual decision making often depart from the idealized rational model. Rational procedures and principles are rarely strictly followed in practice. Here we note the conspicuous discrepancies.

Tardy Problem Recognition   Decision makers often neglect evidence of an impending problem until it confronts them directly or reaches crisis proportions, as people seldom foresee improbable events (Boffey, 1983). The reason is that people are prone psychologically to deny the existence of troublesome problems (even when they might be partially responsible for them), and often avoid facing information suggesting the necessity for difficult decisions.

Inadequate Information   Henry Kissinger observed that "when the scope for action is greatest, the knowledge on which to base such action . . . is at a minimum." The information required to define a problem is often incomplete, outdated, or unavailable, and critical variables such as others' intentions are not open to scrutiny. In addition, "information overload"—the availability of too much information—may also undermine rationality. Discrepant and contradictory information makes distinguishing the significant from the irrelevant difficult.

Inaccurate Information   The information on which decision makers base policy is screened, sorted, and rearranged by their advisers. Distortion is compounded by the tendency of advisers to tell their superiors what they want to hear rather than supplying them with the cold, hard facts, and by policymakers' all-too-human tendency to reject unfamiliar or disturbing information.

---

4. Dean Rusk called the Cuban missile crisis "the most dangerous crisis the world has ever seen." Assessments of the episode suggest that policymakers can absorb new information quickly under great pressure and take calculated risks through deliberate, rational planning, but that personality factors color outcomes, rationality does not assure caution, and "rational models . . . are not enough" (Blight, Nye, and Welch, 1987).

Deficient Information Gathering   Policymakers rarely search for *all* pertinent information; instead, they base decisions on partial information.[5] Rationality is compromised because, had an exhaustive search generated additional information, conceivably a different set of policy choices would be given consideration. Moreover, rather than admit error, leaders are prone to cling to bad decisions and to search energetically for new information that justifies their previous, mistaken choices (Wilensky, 1967).

Ambiguous National Interests   In facing a policy problem, it is not sufficient to insist that the national interest be served. That merely begs the question. The more difficult intellectual task requires "prioritizing" *all* possible goals in terms of their ability to promote the nation's welfare.

Rational identification of what is best is obscured by the fact that every goal has costs associated with it as well as possible unanticipated long-run consequences. Therefore rational goal selection frequently means choosing the lesser of two evils. For instance, if a leader's goals include (1) the economic development of impoverished countries, and (2) the enhancement of America's standard of living, one national interest may be achieved only at the expense of the other. Or consider the goals of (1) fostering human rights worldwide, and (2) protecting American allies; the latter may undermine the former by rationalizing support of repressive regimes.

Time Pressures   Because policymakers work constantly with overloaded agendas and short deadlines, time is rarely available for careful identification of possible courses of action and for a cool-headed assessment of their consequences. "There is little time for leaders to reflect. They are locked in an endless battle in which the urgent constantly gains on the important. The public life of every political figure is a continual struggle to rescue an element of choice from the pressure of circumstance" (Kissinger, 1979).

If some options are not identified, they cannot be considered, for as Thomas Schelling asks, "How do you make a list of things you would never have thought of?" (cited in Bloomfield, 1974). In fact, instead of identifying options themselves, presidents usually are presented with an abbreviated list of "feasible" options by their advisers and by bureaucratic agencies. During a crisis in particular, the pressure is intense to shorten the search for options, which limits the range of alternatives considered to the first ones that come to mind (usually those derived from prior analogous situations).

"Satisficing"   Rational decision making is compromised most by the way foreign policy *choices* tend to be reached in practice. Evidence demonstrates

---

5. This may not be entirely illogical; Anthony Downs (1957) suggests that the rational voter cannot afford to gather all the information available about all candidates prior to deciding for whom to vote: the costs involved are too high for the resultant payoff. Instead, voters base decisions on partial information, such as the candidate's party label.

that policymakers do not choose the option or set of options that has the maximum chance of realizing desired goals (Lindblom, 1959; March and Simon, 1958). Instead, they settle for the first course of action that satisfies minimal requirements or expectations—they engage in what Herbert Simon (1957a) has labeled "satisficing." Rather than seeking to "optimize," decision makers select any choice that meets minimally acceptable or satisfactory standards; that is, the typical decision maker engages in "optional stopping": he or she evaluates one option at a time but terminates the evaluation as soon as an option is discovered that appears to be superior to those previously considered (Slovic, Fischhoff, and Lichtenstein, 1977). Had they acted rationally by engaging in maximizing behavior, they would choose the one "best" choice capable of producing the results preferred.[6]

The great difficulties of ascertaining correctly the payoff probabilities of each available option reduce the prospects for rational choice (and promote "satisficing" instead). Even in the best of circumstances—even if policymakers could obtain full information and were able to identify all the options available to realize the preferred goal—"guesstimates" about the relative utility and efficacy of each alternative still often guides the choice.

Because rationally determining the best choice is difficult, optimal solutions are seldom sought in practice; what is perceived feasible and pragmatic is chosen through a "muddling-through" decision-making approach. And this may in fact be reasonable. "A wise policy-maker," Charles E. Lindblom (1959) summarizes, "expects that his policies will achieve only part of what he hopes and at the same time will produce unanticipated consequences he would have preferred to avoid. If he proceeds through a succession of incremental changes, he avoids serious lasting mistakes." Some past leaders have themselves been known to advocate this less-than-comprehensive, trial-and-error method for making difficult decisions. "It is common sense," noted Franklin D. Roosevelt "to take a method and try it; if it fails, admit it frankly and try another."

Psychological Restraints   Foreign policy is made not by states but by human beings acting on behalf of states. Hence decision-making processes cannot be separated from psychodynamics (Simon, 1985), and decisions, therefore, may be rooted less in logic than in the subconscious needs and drives of

---

6. It is tempting to speculate that the more important the decision, the less likely it is that the decision will be based on pure rationality (and, conversely, the more likely "satisficing" behavior will be exhibited). Notice how little effort is put into acquiring information, considering alternatives, and making choices for the really big life decisions one makes, like choosing a career or a marriage partner. Here people seem to slide into the path of least resistance and to settle for the first available alternative, rather than conducting a thorough search and selecting that alternative which best fulfills one's basic values. More intellectual effort and rational behavior may typically be put into buying a car or a six-pack of beer, where at least people shop comparatively and gather some information. It is worth asking if the same pattern exists in the realm of foreign policy decisions, where it appears more time and energy are sometimes given to choosing seating arrangements for a diplomatic reception than to evaluating the effectiveness of the latest weapons system proposed by the Department of Defense.

the decision maker (see Chapter 14). The need to be liked, the desire to be popular, and the temptation to look decisive, even heroic, may interfere with rational judgment and ultimately sacrifice the nation's welfare. Decision makers also tend to be overconfident about their judgments and analytical skills and to overestimate their abilities and wisdom so as to maintain their "illusion of control" (Langer, 1975).

Personal emotional needs and passions may also lead decision makers to confuse their own goals with those of the nation. If they come to see themselves as indispensable to the nation's welfare, they may equate what is good for them with what is good for the country. When this happens, foreign initiatives may be undertaken to maintain or to strengthen the leader's power and popularity, possibly at the expense of America's self-interest.[7]

The foregoing review of some of the ways policymakers make decisions in real life warrants the conclusion that the ideal requirements of rational problem solving cannot be met in practice (see Focus 13.1). Preconceived notions pass for facts. Decisions are made to satisfy immediate, not long-term, needs. The task of formulating a coherent strategy is avoided. There is a natural reluctance to reach decisions, and a strong temptation to pass the buck. Only a small number of alternatives are usually considered, and only a restricted number of consequences pondered. Full knowledge is rarely achieved, even though the volume of information may be staggering. Decisions are generally reached under conditions of "bounded rationality," with only the information regarded as most relevant to the decision scanned. Fear of public criticism discourages making unpopular but necessary choices. And often before a final decision is reached or announced, information is gathered to justify the preferred option (that is, a decision is reached first and reasons found to support it only later). The result is not rationality, with each step leading logically to a value-maximizing decision, but something that appears quite different—a haphazard, trial-and-error, seat-of-the-pants decision-making process conducted in a rush, based on "gut-it-out," best-guess calculations, and influenced strongly by social pressures (Anderson, 1987). Serious "information pathologies" are generated (Holsti, 1989). The process thus looks decidedly indecisive and improvisational; the degree of rationality in foreign policy decision making "bears little relationship to the world in which officials conduct their deliberations" (Rosenau, 1980).

What are the implications of such a conclusion? If comprehensive rationality and even the notion of planning in foreign policy can be questioned (Bloomfield, 1978), then we are forced to reject descriptions of American foreign policy making as based purely on rational calculations. For it is simply inaccurate to think of the nation's actions as the response of public officials

---

7. Examples are numerous, and it is probably safe to regard leaders' confusion of personal and national interests as a recurrent problem. Richard Nixon, for instance, at times went on foreign trips (for example, to Beijing in 1972) not to bring about some long-cherished diplomatic goal, but instead to augment his public popularity (Ball, 1976). Similarly, President Johnson is said to have consciously sought to schedule international negotiations during the Vietnam War to diffuse criticism of his policies at home and to divert attention from protest demonstrations.

FOCUS 13.1 ▪ Foreign Policy Decision Making in Theory and Practice

The Ideal Process	Actual Performance
Accurate, comprehensive information	Distorted, incomplete information
Clear definition of national goals	Personal motivations and organizational interests bias national goals
Exhaustive analysis of all options	Limited number of options considered, none thoroughly analyzed
Selection of optimal course of action most capable of producing desired results	Selection of course of action by political bargaining and compromise
Effective statement of decision and its rationale to mobilize domestic support	Confusing and contradictory statements of decision often framed for media consumption
Instantaneous evaluation of consequences followed by correction of errors	Superficial policy evaluation, uncertain responsibility, poor follow-through, and delayed correction

---

laden with exceptional skills and cognitive powers, untiring in the collection of accurate information on which to base decisions, and logical in the derivation of conclusions designed to maximize the country's national interests. The facts do not support the image.

But knowing that rational foreign policy is more an ideal than a description of reality, we can nevertheless assume that policymakers aspire to rational decision-making behavior, which they may even occasionally approximate. Indeed, as a working proposition, it is useful to assume rationality in analyzing how the decision-making process *should* work as well as in describing the elusive principles which policymakers seek.

> Officials have some notion, conscious or unconscious, of a priority of values; . . . they possess some conceptions, elegant or crude, of the means available and their potential effectiveness; . . . they engage in some effort, extensive or brief, to relate means to ends; and . . . therefore, at some point they select some alternative, clear-cut or confused, as the course of action that seems most likely to cope with the immediate situation. (Rosenau, 1980: 304–305)

Administrative Theory and Foreign Policy Rationality

Before we accept the idea that less-than-rational decision making is responsible for America's problems in world affairs, we should probe a competing thesis: that the U.S. foreign policy-making machinery enhances rational decision making (even if the ideal is not always realized). It is not possible for one, two, or a few officials to make a superpower's foreign policy. Given America's incredibly varied global interests, large-scale *bureaucracy* is necessary. Neither sufficient time nor resources are available to manage foreign relations without the support of large organizations, which facilitate rational decision making in ways that would otherwise be impossible (Goodsell, 1985). Let us briefly examine these contributions.

The idea that modern bureaucracy—by virtue of the roles it creates—enhances the prospects for rational decision making stems from the German scholar Max Weber's influential theories. Large-scale bureaucracies contribute to efficient administration and rationality, Weber reasoned, through the ways in which they are organized and operate:

- Structured on the principle of division of labor, bureaucracies make each individual in the machinery a specialist, even an expert, at his or her job; functional division between agencies as well as within them (as, for example, in the separation of diplomatic and defense responsibilities between the State and Defense Departments) assigns different tasks to different qualified people.
- Authority is distributed hierarchically, and jurisdictions stipulate a clear chain of command. It is easier to get things done when everyone has a clear notion of who is subordinate to whom, of who has authority over whom, and what role is to be performed by each cog in the machinery. Precious time does not have to be devoted to deciding who has the power to decide.
- Rules specify how each major function or task is to be performed and prescribe standard operating procedures for each role. Hence, rather than deliberating about the best method for handling a problem, the career professional can concentrate on mastering those methods.
- Bureaucracies rely on a system of records managed by reference to written documents systemically gathered and stored, in order to facilitate intelligence retrieval, provide a data bank of past decisions, and increase the amount of information available for making future decisions.
- In principle, bureaucracies recruit "the best and brightest" personnel on the basis of achievement and aptitude, rather than on the basis of ascriptive criteria such as wealth, gender, ethnicity, or family background.
- Similarly, bureaucracies place decision-making responsibility in the hands of the most competent by compensating and promoting personnel on the basis of achievement criteria; "merit" governs who is "selected up" and who is "selected out" (rather than criteria such as longevity, personal characteristics, ingratiation, or repayment for favors to superiors).
- Large bureaucracies divide authority among competing agencies, which enhances the probability that all policy options will be consid-

ered before decisions are reached. "Multiple advocacy" (George, 1972) results from interagency bargaining because the process requires defending positions and negotiation prevents any one actor from making a major policy decision unilaterally.

- Administrative norms allow some specialists the luxury of engaging in *forward planning*. Unlike the president, whose role requires that attention be focused on the crisis of the moment, bureaucracies can consider long-term future needs.

This theoretical portrayal of the bureaucratic policy process suggests that bureaucracies contribute to the rational decisional procedures described above. However, before jumping to the conclusion that bureaucratic decision making is a modern panacea, we should emphasize that these propositions tell us how, according to organization theory, decision making *should* occur. They do not tell us how bureaucratic agencies actually make decisions. Bureaucratic practice and the foreign policy outcomes it produces suggest that bureaucracies cause problems as well as solve them.

THE CASE AGAINST BUREAUCRATIC FOREIGN POLICY MAKING

In principle, bureaucracies exist to help the president carry out executive responsibilities and presidential policies. In practice, the president is dependent on those comprising the foreign affairs government to get things done. Thus, as Henry Kissinger advised, "To understand what the government is likely to do, one has to understand the bureaucratics of the problems."

What are some of the consequences of presidential dependency on bureaucracies? Is presidential power over American foreign policy limited? Are bureaucracies "ruling servants," in control of policy by virtue of their power to impede? Indeed, does the bureaucracy rule while the president merely reigns?

Those troublesome questions have been raised by past presidents' recurrent complaints that they were unable to persuade and coerce their own bureaucracy to go along with policy decisions (see Focus 13.2). Subordinates have often appeared insubordinate; rather than helping to get things done, they have opposed presidential directives.

Although it is perhaps an exaggeration to speak of the "bureaucratic captivity" of the president, the occupant of the Oval Office is heavily reliant on the bureaucracy for information, for the identification of problems, for the advocacy of solutions, and most important, for the implementation of presidential orders. Correspondingly, the president's leeway is considerably constrained by the government the president is elected to run.

The very size of the enormous federal bureaucracy is a constraint. The federal civilian and military work force totaled 5.3 million in 1990. The employees were ensconced in roughly two thousand separate but overlapping

---

FOCUS 13.2 ▪ Bureaucratic Agencies: Policy Servants or Policy Saboteurs?

You know, one of the hardest things in a government this size is to know that down there, underneath, is that permanent structure that's resisting everything you're doing.

President Ronald Reagan, 1985

I thought I was used to all sorts of back-knifing from my years in private industry, but I wasn't prepared for this [level as head of the State Department]. Why, down here they literally search your back for soft spots.

Secretary of State George Shultz, 1985

There is nothing more frustrating for a President than to issue an order to a Cabinet officer, and then find that, when the order gets out in the field, it is totally mutilated. I have had that happen to me, and I am sure every other President has had it happen.

President Gerald R. Ford, 1980

I underestimated the inertia and the momentum of the Federal bureaucracy. . . . It is difficult to change.

President Jimmy Carter, 1977

To a degree, the needs of bureaucrats and President are incompatible. The better one is served, the worse will be the other.

Former presidential adviser Richard E. Neustadt, 1963

---

government agencies. Whereas presidents come and go, these bureaucrats remain. Only about thirty-three hundred officials are policymakers, that is, individuals appointed by and capable of being fired by the president (although many of those are "in-and-outers" "whose career stakes are tied neither to party politics nor to government administration" [Heclo, 1988]). Consequently, foreign policy decisions necessarily are made by many individuals within a massive but fragmented governmental structure, most of whom are beyond the immediate reach of elected public officials. As Woodrow Wilson put it in a timeless description, "Nobody stands responsible for the policy of government . . . a dozen men originate it; a dozen compromises twist and alter it; a dozen offices put it into execution."

Major Attributes of Bureaucratic Behavior

How do people behave in complex organizational settings? Does administrative theory hold in practice? Or it is like the model of rational choice more an ideal than an accurate description of reality?

FOCUS 13.3 ▪ Agency Interests versus National Interests

In 1945, with George Ball, Paul Nitze, other notables, and a staff of several hundred, I was assigned to the study of the effect of strategic air attacks on the German war economy—the United States Strategic Bombing Survey. The results were impressive. Great and extremely costly attacks . . . raised no enduring difficulty for the Germans. . . . After major attacks on all the German aircraft plants in 1944, aircraft production was promptly reorganized and in ensuing months greatly increased.

These findings were seen by the Air Force as deeply inimical to its mission. As a consequence, though published after acrimonious discussion, they were ignored. The further and historically important consequence was that strategic air attacks went forward on North Korea and North (and South) Vietnam with similar but perhaps even greater military inconsequence.

SOURCE: John Kenneth Galbraith, *American Heritage* 40 (December 1989), p. 58.

At least eight characteristics and policy consequences of administrative decision making, identified here, are important to an understanding of bureaucratic behavior.[8]

Parochialism   Each federal agency shares three distinct characteristics with every other administrative unit: it seeks to pursue its own purposes, promote its own power, and enhance its own position in the governmental hierarchy.

Bureaucracies are driven to protect their jurisdiction. They define issues and take stands on them in order to promote their agency's self-interests. Indeed, "since a public bureaucracy is concerned with special and limited aspects of public policy, to a degree it resembles the ordinary private pressure group" (Freeman, 1965). As James M. Fallows, President Carter's major speech writer, observed, "The chief force motivating most top bureaucrats, Cabinet secretaries, and even some White House aides is job security—you can predict a bureaucrat's reaction to almost any issue by the way it will affect their job or fiefdom. That's what comes first."

"Since each [bureaucratic organization] has, by definition, less than government-wide responsibilities and hence less than a society-wide constituency . . . to a degree such parochialism is useful, for the department head must retain credibility with his constituency (and the congressional committees responsible to it) if he is to be effective" (Destler, 1980). Yet bureaucratic parochialism can be detrimental to the nation's larger interests (see Focus 13.3).

---

8. The inventory of characteristics that follows summarizes the so-called bureaucratic politics model of foreign policy decision making. For discussions, see Allison (1971), Allison and Halperin (1989), C. Hermann (1988, 1983) and Hilsman (1990); for a critique, see Krasner (1988).

In part the efforts by the White House to centralize control over foreign policy making is a response to that problem.

Competitiveness   Far from being neutral or impartial administrators that obediently carry out presidential orders, the agencies that comprise the foreign affairs government frequently compete with one another for influence. As a former deputy assistant defense secretary noted, organizations take stands on issues that advance their interests and maneuver to protect them against other organizations and senior officials, including the president (Halperin, 1971). Not intentionally malicious, many agency heads nonetheless confuse their organization's welfare with the country's. In the words of Richard J. Barnet, another former adviser:

> National security managers have a personal investment in the health and aggrandizement of their own bureaucratic organizations. They equate the national interest and their organization's interest as a matter of course. They will fight to maintain an obsolete air base, build redundant weapons systems, proliferate arms around the world by certifying that the nation's "vital interests" are at stake when it is merely their own budgets. (Barnet, 1972: 122)

Heads of bureaucratic organizations are not incapable of putting the nation's interests ahead of their organization's; more accurately, although struggle among bureaucracies often characterizes policy debates, what is best for the country dominates the bargaining dialogue. Still, the incidence with which agency officials propose policies that blatantly benefit their own agency attests to the parochial outlook and selfish concerns that dominate bureaucratic thinking.[9]

The reasons for such competitive intragovernmental politics are numerous. Henry Kissinger (1969) suggests one: "The decision-maker will always be aware of the morale of his staff. . . . [He] cannot overrule it too frequently without impairing its efficiency. . . . Placating the staff then becomes a major pre-occupation of the executive." Another reason is that most agency heads are not only tied *to* their own organization but also *by* it: "A Secretary of a Federal Department almost invariably becomes more the agent of the permanent bureaucracy under his command than a free agent, mainly because he must rely upon the permanent officials for expert information and analysis" (MacMahon, 1951). Thus caught in the middle between higher-level executives and the

---

9. In 1962, for example, on the issue of rescinding a promise to give Great Britain the Skybolt missile, the position of the Defense Department was defined by the budgetary strains involved; the air force interpreted the idea as a threat to one of its missions—the piloted bomber; the secretary of state viewed the proposal as potentially disruptive of close American-British relations; the State Department's Bureau of European Affairs saw in the proposal a chance to seduce Great Britain out of the strategic weapons business; and the president wanted to reconcile such conflicts and avoid congressional resistance to Skybolt's cancellation. Thus, in each case, the major agencies involved sought to deal with the issue in a manner beneficial to its own interest. The consequence was competition among those involved for acceptance of their preferred definition of the national interest (Halperin, 1971; Neustadt, 1970).

career professionals in an organization, the typical agency head must try to satisfy both. The pressures encourage competition with other agencies for scarce resources and power. Policy success in such an atmosphere tends very quickly to be defined less in terms of national interests than in terms of organizational interests.

Imperialistic Task Expansion   Driven to protect and promote their own influence, bureaucratic agencies invariably seek to enlarge their budgets and staffs, both absolutely and in relation to other agencies. Size is a sign of security, expansion an indicator of importance, and, to some extent, prestige and influence can be conferred only by growth. Other things being equal, larger bureaucracies have greater access, greater credibility, greater resources, greater durability—and greater influence. (Such organizations usually have more enemies as well.) Thus most organizations strive to maintain and enhance their budget and personnel. Historically, bureaucratic agencies have also sought to increase their prerogatives and functional powers along with their employees and budgets. That is, bureaucratic organizations have a marked tendency whenever possible to expand the conception of their tasks (but always to preserve their original mission). Correspondingly, a candid list of the criteria by which career professionals judge their success would have to include such things as salary, number of people under their command, opportunities for advancement, and the size of their office and its distance from the parking lot. Somewhere in that list the nation's interest would presumably be included.

The *raison d'être* of administrative organization is efficiency through the performance of various tasks by independent units. A division of labor that clearly differentiates functions permits experts to specialize in performing particular roles. This rationale led in 1947 to creation of a separate Central Intelligence Agency (CIA), whose ostensible purpose was to coordinate the gathering of foreign intelligence, and in 1961 to creation of the Agency for International Development (AID), to specialize in the administration of foreign aid and technical assistance.

Practice, however, frequently has not conformed to theory. Imperialistic bureaucracies seek to perform the tasks for which other agencies have been assigned responsibility. That inclination provides one reason why the Council on International Economic Policy created by President Nixon did not become an effective coordinator of economic policy making: it became merely another competitor jockeying for a piece of the policy action among those preexisting units needing coordination. Bureaucratic imperialism also explains why so many different agencies are independently involved in gathering roughly the same intelligence information (for example, the State Department, the Defense Department, and the CIA, among others), and why the three military services have found it "absolutely essential" that each develop its own capabilities in areas where the other services specialize (as evidenced by the army's accumulation of more support aircraft than the air force). The result: instead of a bureaucratic division of labor, functions are often duplicated.

Endurance   Bureaucracies are survival-oriented. Both the number and size of administrative units responsible for America's globalist postwar foreign policy have increased enormously. More new units have been created or added to than phased out or cut back. Once created, they usually persist, even in the face of great adversity.[10]

Historically, organizational "reforms" have often created *new* agencies to coordinate and regulate the activities of existing organizations. The result is not streamlining, but the addition of new layers to a burgeoning bureaucracy. As Secretary of the Navy John Lehman complained in 1985: "It would be impossible for me or anyone to accurately describe to you the system with which, and within which, we must operate. There are thousands upon thousands of offices and entities and bureaus that have been created over the years to deal episodically with aspects of defense."

Secrecy and Exclusiveness   Bureaucratic agencies seek to minimize interference in and regulation of their operations. To the extent possible, they keep their proceedings secret from potential enemies, including the president, who might use such knowledge to attack publicly their operations (Franck and Weisband, 1974), and to conceal activities that can injure their public image. "There are no secrets in Washington," President Kennedy observed, "except the things I need to know." Conversely, bureaucratic secrets are "leaked" selectively for propaganda purposes when their release is politically advantageous.

Attitudinal Conformity   Every bureaucracy tends to develop, over time, a shared mind-set, or dominant way of looking at reality, which few challenge. The process of recruitment and self-selection brings together individuals who already share many basic attributes and attitudes. The Foreign Service, for instance, has sought for employees "young people they consider most like the successful officers already in the system" (Harr, 1969). Free thinkers or people who might rock the boat or make waves are not welcomed; instead, those

---

10. Herbert Kaufman (1976) found that of 175 organizations extant in 1923, fully 148 (nearly 85 percent) were still active in 1973. Federal agencies endure, Kaufman argues, because (1) most agencies are established by law or are accorded statutory recognition; (2) congressional allies and "committee staffs tend to develop possessive and protective attitudes toward them"; (3) agencies' budgets are usually increased each year, rather than calculated anew from a base of zero, and budgetary momentum protects appropriations from one year to the next; (4) presidents and cabinet officers typically pass from the scene far more rapidly than do most agencies or their congressional allies, thus federal agencies are relatively insulated from White House control; (5) inasmuch as the reputations of agency leaders are linked to their organizations' fate, "the mysterious forces of organizational loyalty and commitment to program" promote organizational preservation; (6) when trouble arises, clientele groups and outside supporters marshall political support on behalf of the threatened agency; and (7) when threats to an agency surface, support also can be expected from the professional and trade associations outside a particular agency with whom the dominant occupational group within that agency is identified—whether lawyer, doctor, or professional soldier.

subscribing to the agency's dominant values are preferred.[11] The process is reinforced in small-group decision-making situations, where social pressures toward conformity to group norms often produce "groupthink," a cohesiveness and solidarity of outlook that may lead to dysfunctional policy choices, as in the case of the 1961 Bay of Pigs decision (Janis, 1982).

Once an individual enters a bureaucracy, socialization reinforces belief conformity. Recruits are quickly educated into their role and the acceptable attitudes that go with it. Nonconformity can result in loss of influence or, in the extreme, the loss of employment. On the other hand, those who conform to peer-group attitudes, who are perceived as team players, are rewarded; "promotions are awards given to bureaucrats for accepting organizational myths" cynically describes this phenomenon.

Institutional mind-sets discourage creativity, dissent, and independent thinking, and thereby undermine rational policy making. The Department of State, for instance, has found in numerous self-studies that pressures producing uniformity of thought and stifling creativity have been persistent problems.

Deference to Tradition Because decision making in complex organizations is conducted according to *rules*, rather than by invention of a new way to deal with a new problem, bureaucrats are prone to defer to standard procedures and tradition. "A man comes to an assignment," Charles Frankel (1969) observed, "and he is told what policy is. He must find a way to navigate through the storms, to resist the pressures of people and events, and to turn over the policy to his successor in the same condition in which it was when he received it from his predecessor." A former staff member of the National Security Council (NSC) dubbed this respect for ritual and precedent the "curator mentality" (Thomson, 1988).

Reliance on Historical Analogies When a decision point is reached, policymakers are prone to search history impressionistically for parallels that suggest options for dealing with the emergent problem. That tendency—which often results in a misreading of historical lessons (Neustadt and May, 1986)—helps account for the postwar continuity of American foreign policy. The Munich analogy, for example, was drawn on by a generation of policymakers—including George Bush at the time of the 1990 Iraq-Kuwait crisis—as evidence that it is impossible to appease aggressors. The analogy refers to the 1938 British and French agreement that permitted Nazi Germany to annex a large part of Czechoslovakia in return for what British Prime Minister Neville Chamberlain

---

11. Some organization theorists note that *new* units within administrative agencies recruit ideologues and risk takers, whereas old ones recruit cautious, security-conscious personnel who are more likely to be motivated to protect their stakes in the present scheme of things, rather than to express their policy preferences and push reforms. An example of the former was the State Department's Bureau of Human Rights under Carter.

called "peace in our time." In fact, war broke out in Europe a year later, with the apparent lesson that an aggressor cannot be stopped short of war.[12]

Other attributes also describe the bureaucratic behavior and other aspects of decision making by group methods that become relevant under particular conditions and in response to certain kinds of issues (see Hermann, 1988; Simon, 1957a). The preceding brief survey suggests, however, a general proposition: the decision-making system influences the behavior of those who occupy institutionally defined decision-making roles. Given this, let us shift attention to some of the major policy consequences of those attributes.

POLICY CONSEQUENCES OF ORGANIZATIONAL DECISION MAKING

Because American foreign policy is a product of bureaucratic behavior, it is useful to consider how the organizational decision-making process shapes policy making. Some conspicuous repercussions of bureaucratic policy-making processes are discussed in this section.

Bureaucratic Competition and Foreign Policy Inertia

As described in earlier chapters, a major feature of postwar American foreign policy has been the resistance of its grand vision to change. Core assumptions and policy reactions to external events have conformed to long-established precedents and have changed only slowly and incrementally.

Innovation in American policy has been constrained by many factors. Among them, bureaucratic restraints are powerful and explain well why American foreign policy has seemed so "gradualist." The overwhelming complexity of the foreign affairs machinery, with its entrenched and competing bureaucracies, has limited what leaders could do and cast doubt on Washington's capacity to act expeditiously. Because policy is formulated and implemented by a large number of individuals situated in a complex institutional arrangement, obtaining consensus and taking decisive action has been inhibited. Career professionals in charge of the different agencies usually disagree: they want different policies and define situations differently because of their differing vantage points. The result is that policy formulation often boils down to a tug-of-war among competing agencies, a political game with high stakes, in which differences are settled at the minimum common denominator. As Henry Kissinger described the process:

---

12. The lessons of the 1930s also led policymakers to conclusions about the appropriateness of interventionist and noninterventionist trade policy regarding manufactured and agricultural goods (Goldstein, 1989). The result, as we noted in Chapter 7, is that international trade in the industrial and agricultural sectors developed quite differently.

Each of the contending factions within the bureaucracy has a maximum incentive to state its case in its most extreme form because the ultimate outcome depends, to a considerable extent, on a *bargaining process*. The premium placed on advocacy turns decision-making into a *series of adjustments among special interests*—a process more suited to domestic than to foreign policy. This procedure neglects the long-range because the future has no administrative constituency and is, therefore, without representation in the adversary proceedings. Problems tend to be slighted until some agency or department is made responsible for them. . . . The outcome usually depends more on the pressures or the persuasiveness of the contending advocates than on a concept of over-all purpose. (Kissinger, 1969: 268; emphasis added)

In addition, fundamental or far-reaching choices are discouraged by a relentlessly politicized process involving many constituencies in decisions. The inclination among career officials to "go along in order to get along" encourages acceptance of prevailing policies and the status quo. Moreover, the sheer size of the foreign affairs government inhibits policy change, because, in general, the larger and more complex the institutional machinery, the greater will be the force of policy inertia.

Bureaucracies typically administer programs created by prior decisions. Most career professionals, therefore, see their role as being loyal, even unquestioning, implementors of past policies, rather than the creators of their own. The greater the loyalty to specific administrative tasks, the greater the commitment to the policy being implemented. "To try and believe in what one is doing, . . . to see broader problems in narrow terms derived from one's own specific activities," is a natural part of a bureaucrat's role, but the result is that "the information and judgments bureaucrats provide for use in the making of policies tend to be strongly biased in favor of the continuation, rather than the modification, much less the reversal, of existing policies. . . . Thus a bureaucracy inevitably comes down heavily on the side of established policies and strongly resists change" (Reischauer, 1968). Some bureaucrats, of course, fight inertia, and in some areas of domestic policy bureaucracies have engineered policy innovation (see Britan, 1981). But such efforts are the exception.

Bureaucratic Sabotage of Presidential Foreign Policy Initiatives

The popular impression that American foreign policy is little more than what the president says it is in fact is very misleading. The president alone does not make foreign policy; policy must not only be pronounced but carried out, and for that task the chief executive must rely on the executive bureaucracy. Hence what the government's various executive agencies choose to implement becomes American foreign policy; policy is what is done, not just what is said.

Because bureaucracies are by nature exclusive, parochial, and interested primarily in protecting their own power and authority, we should not be

surprised to discover that few agencies cheerfully carry out presidential directives that they perceive to be harmful to their organizations. When threatened,
bureaucrats are inclined to put themselves first and to defend their own welfare. The result: the often intractable foreign affairs machinery is capable of disloyalty to the president it ostensibly serves. And because change, or the
prospect of change, is often threatening (because policy change almost invariably entails some redistribution of influence in the government hierarchy),
bureaucratic agencies typically resist top-level executive policy proposals.

Nearly every postwar president has complained on occasion that the federal bureaucracy ostensibly designed to serve him undercut his policy by refusing to carry out orders expeditiously. Witness President Truman's prediction
prior to General Eisenhower's succession to the White House: "He'll sit here
and he'll say, 'Do this! Do that!' *And nothing will happen.* Poor Ike—it won't
be a bit like the Army. He'll find it very frustrating." Or reflect on President
Kennedy's observation that giving the State Department an instruction was like
dropping it in the dead-letter box. As Dick Cheney, Bush's secretary of defense,
put it when he was President Ford's chief of staff, "There is a tendency before
you get to the White House or when you're just observing it from the outside
to say, 'Gee, that's a powerful position that person has.' The fact of the matter
is that while you're here trying to do things, you are far more aware of the constraints than you are of the power. You spend most of your time trying to overcome obstacles to getting what the President wants done."

Most often, lack of bureaucratic responsiveness and action manifest themselves as lethargy. The government machinery grinds slowly, and sometimes
appears motionless.[13] Procrastination appears endemic, and can easily be interpreted as intentional, when in fact it is often inadvertent. It simply takes time to
get things moving, and delay is routine in getting even the simplest requests
completed (see Focus 13.4). An impatient president can easily mistake the crawl-
ing pace for insubordination, even sedition (because the effect—braking or
abrogating policy decisions—is the same). But everyday bureaucratic inaction
should not be confused with planned foot dragging; the differences between
slothful protraction and disobedient noncompliance are meaningful.

But then again, willful bureaucratic sabotage is not a mere figment of
leaders' imaginations, and it can take several forms. Bureaucracies can withhold or slant vital information. They can provide advice showing reasons why
recommended policy changes will not work, and they can circulate that advice
to those in a position to challenge the policy change (such as Congress). They
can discreetly contact interest groups capable of mobilizing opposition against
a directive the bureaucrats find intolerable. Or they can delay policy implementation by demanding time to study the problem thoroughly (that is, to death)
—a tactic known as "paralysis by analysis"—or by complexifying it into incom-

---

13. To quote the tongue-in-cheek characterization of James H. Boren, founder of the International Association of Professional Bureaucrats: "One must always remember that freedom from
action and freedom from purpose constitute the philosophical basis of creative bureaucracy."

FOCUS 13.4 ▪ **Bureaucratic Inaction "in Action"**

Once upon a time in Camelot, Robert F. Kennedy was commuting daily through the Virginia countryside and was irritated to see a road sign directing any passing motorist to CIA headquarters at Langley. He complained to his brother the President. "Get somebody to take that sign down," JFK ordered an aide. A call went out to the Interior Department. Days passed. Nothing happened. Bobby repeated the complaint. JFK repeated his order. Again, nothing happened. Finally, exasperated, the President short-circuited the bureaucratic chain of command and put in a direct call to the man in charge of signs in the Virginia suburbs. "This is Jack Kennedy," he said, looking at his watch. "It's 11 o'clock in the morning. I want that sign down by the time the Attorney General goes home tonight, and I'm holding you personally responsible." He returned the receiver, still smoking, to its cradle. "I now understand," he said, "that for a President to get something done in this country, he's got to say it three times."

SOURCE: *Newsweek*, January 26, 1981, p. 41.

---

prehensibility. And bureaucracies can buck a presidential directive by interpreting it in such a way that it can be administered differently than proposed or with a change in emphasis. The result, of course, is no result. It has been said in this context that bureaucracies never change the course of the ship of state; they just adjust the compass.

Sometimes bureaucratic sabotage can be direct and immediate, as President Kennedy discovered in the midst of the 1962 Cuban missile crisis. While the president sought to orchestrate American action and bargaining, his bureaucracy in general, and the Navy Department in particular, was in fact controlling events by doing as it wished. The bureaucracy was

> choosing to obey the orders it liked and ignore or stretch others. Thus, after a tense argument with the Navy, Kennedy ordered the blockade line moved closer to Cuba so that the Russians might have more time to draw back. Having lost the argument with the President, the Navy simply ignored his order. Unbeknownst to Kennedy, the Navy was also at work forcing Soviet submarines to surface long before Kennedy authorized any contact with Soviet ships. And despite the President's order to halt all provocative intelligence, an American U-2 plane entered Soviet airspace at the height of the crisis. When Kennedy began to realize that he was not in full control, he asked his Secretary of Defense [Robert McNamara] to see if he could find out just what the Navy was doing. McNamara then made his first visit to the Navy command post in the Pentagon. In a heated exchange, the Chief of Naval Operations suggested that McNamara return to his office and let the Navy run the blockade. (Gelb and Halperin, 1973: 256)

Another example of bureaucratic disobedience occurred during the tense period *preceding* the Cuban missile crisis in 1962. President Kennedy had concluded in March 1961 that Jupiter missiles in Turkey should be removed. He felt they were obsolete and exacerbated Soviet fears of encirclement and possible American attack from just beyond the Soviet border. The president therefore instructed the State Department to negotiate withdrawal of the American missiles. But Turkish officials disapproved of the proposal, so the State Department reasoned that the diplomatic thing to do was to comply with the Turkish request that the missiles stay. The president, however, convinced that the benefits of removing the missiles far outweighed the costs, reiterated his command. Kennedy then "dismissed the matter from his mind," Robert Kennedy (1971) reported, because "the President believed he was President and that, his wishes having been made clear, they would be followed and the missiles removed." But to his amazement, President Kennedy discovered months later during the Cuban missile crisis that the State Department had ignored his instructions—the missiles were still in Turkey. Because the crisis centered on the issue of weapons on the adversary's periphery, the president was, needless to say, angry about the risks this blatant disregard of his orders caused.[14]

These incidents illustrate the extent to which bureaucracies can perceive themselves as autonomous agents. Untethered, they contribute to the appearance of the United States as a rudderless ship of state.

In the realm of broad foreign policy conceptions and goals, the president and the executive bureaucracies may be natural enemies. Because many upper-echelon career officials have retained their positions for years, sometimes even decades, their long-held assumptions about American foreign policy may be as deeply entrenched as the bureaucracies for which they work. Those fundamental assumptions—about Soviet motives, the need for globalism, the utility of force, and other themes that have defined American foreign policy for five decades—have become bureaucratic conventional wisdom, often viewed as unworthy of further reexamination. But presidents intermittently come to power with fresh ideas about foreign policy essentials and are intent to implement new departures. The inevitable result is a clash between politicians and bureaucrats, between new and old, between policy innovation and policy continuity—with the former more frequently the loser. President Carter's experience with the State Department (see Focus 13.5) suggests that failures to change foreign policy can be attributed in part to a bureaucracy's refusal to support a new administration's new ideas. It was perhaps recognition of this that prompted George Bush to pledge at the 1989 Malta summit with Mikhail Gorbachev that to achieve arms control agreements he would "kick our bureaucracy and push it as fast as I possibly can."

---

14. The Turkish missiles have long figured prominently in the Cuban missile story. Kennedy was believed to have been intransigent on the issue of trading U.S. missiles in Turkey for Soviet missiles in Cuba, but a transcript of a crucial meeting of the ExCom declassified twenty-five years after the event reveals that Kennedy was more willing to compromise on withdrawal of the U.S. missiles than previously thought. He apparently worried about how he could justify going to nuclear war over missiles his own advisers considered obsolete (Bundy and Blight, 1987–1988).

FOCUS 13.5 ▪ President versus Bureaucracy: An Insider's Look at the State Department's Reaction to Jimmy Carter

Since the Georgia team had little built-in expertise in foreign affairs, it acquiesced in the appointment of some State Department officials who had more loyalty to their résumés than to Carter.

Moreover, the permanent bureaucracy at State has watched Presidents come and go and is not much moved by each new Administration's inevitable exercises in rediscovery of the obvious. . . . Some of the older generation of diplomats openly didn't and don't believe in the efficacy or wisdom of such notions as campaigns for human rights or restraint in arms sales abroad. They have used arms as the sweetener with recalcitrant client states for so long that they see them as irreplaceable tools of the diplomatic trade. As for human rights concerns, there are those at State who believe that torture is not something that gentlemen discuss, publicly or privately. They fully expected that most of the new initiatives would soon be dropped, and they did everything they could to see that the day of abandonment came sooner rather than later. . . . The career Foreign Service obstructors of the new policies often made more converts among the appointees than the newcomers were able to convert to the President's policies.

SOURCE: Hodding Carter III, "Life inside the Carter State Department," *Playboy* 28 (February 1981), pp. 96ff.

Managing Bureaucratic Intransigence

The "bureaucratic captivity" of American foreign policy can easily be exaggerated. While presidents' policies are in bureaucracies' grip, presidents are not powerless. They may employ a variety of methods to handle recalcitrant agencies and obstructionist officials.

First, consider the strategy employed by the "master" at managing federal bureaucracies, Franklin D. Roosevelt. His approach may be termed "planned disorganization and confusion." An astute politician, Roosevelt overcame policy-implementation obstacles through a divide-and-rule strategy:

> He deliberately organized—or disorganized—his system of command to insure that important decisions were passed on to the top. His favorite technique was to keep grants of authority incomplete, jurisdictions uncertain, charters overlapping. The result of this competitive theory of administration was often confusion and exasperation on the operating level; but no other method could so reliably insure that in a large bureaucracy, filled with ambitious men eager for power, the decisions, and the power to make them, would remain with the President. . . . Franklin allowed no one to discover the governing principle. (Schlesinger, 1958: 527)

In short, Roosevelt sought to control policy by denying control to those around him.

The "Kissinger solution" represents a second rather blunt but highly effective strategy: punish the disobedient agency by excluding it from future decision making or circumvent it by creating a smaller, substitute unit. Removing a bureaucracy from influence by bypassing or omitting it during important policy deliberations, especially on issues that vitally concern it, can therapeutically induce a hostile agency's reform and make it submissive and less intent on opposing presidential policy every time its own parochial interests are at stake.[15]

Kennedy employed a third tactic: causing disturbance *within* a recalcitrant agency by skipping the normal chain of command and dealing directly with lower-echelon officials. By upsetting standard operating procedures and going through unusual channels of communication, Kennedy was able to obtain needed information and avoid bureaucratic bottlenecks.[16]

Nixon practiced yet a fourth strategy, described best by his words to George Shultz when the latter was director of the Office of Management and Budget:

> You've got to get us some discipline, George. You've got to get it, and the only way you get it, is when a bureaucrat thumbs his nose, we're going to get him. . . . They've got to know, that if they do it, something's going to happen to them, where anything can happen. I know the Civil Service pressure. But you can do a lot there. There are many unpleasant places where Civil Service people can be sent.

This punitive approach requires a stomach for vindictiveness, because dismissals, forced resignations, or an insubordinate's demotion risk adverse publicity and are time consuming. Not only are grievance proceedings protracted and embarrassing, but even identifying the individual responsible for the insubordination among the faceless bureaucracy can be a challenge. (John Roche, a Johnson policy adviser, once recommended the chief executive "fire the s.o.b." who had sabotaged one of the president's pet programs. "Fire him!" screamed Johnson. "I can't even find him!") These obstacles may explain why politeness is often preferred to punishment; the common approach is to remove an obstructionist employee by giving him or her a promotion or special assignment to a prestigious-sounding but meaningless position. To "squeeze" an intransigent bureaucrat from a position, the victim is "layered over" by assigning others to perform his or her duties.

---

15. Isolation from policy influence by denying access to the "magic circle" of power may also have been employed by President Reagan to contain the open feud that erupted between Secretary of State Alexander Haig and Secretary of Defense Caspar Weinberger. Exasperated by the lack of attention and authority he felt were due him, Haig resigned, protesting that "at times it seems that the secretary of state is nothing but an errand boy" (Haig, 1984).

16. Another Kennedy tactic was to encourage a recalcitrant official's voluntary resignation by hinting that he or she was no longer in favor, a strategy described thus: Kennedy "would plant newspaper reports that the official was planning to resign. After reading a sufficient number of these reports, the official would grasp what was happening and turn in his resignation" (Berkley, 1978).

Behind the impulse to punish obdurate staff is the belief that changing people can solve disloyalty problems and get the bureaucracy moving. "Let me control personnel," George F. Kennan once said, "and I will ultimately control policy. For the part of the machine that recruits and hires and fires and promotes people can soon control the entire shape of the institution." In practice, however, those presidents who have carefully picked their "own" people and instructed them to get their agencies to obey executive orders often have discovered that instead "their" people have, in Nixon aide John Ehrlichman's words, "married the natives." Typically, cabinet officers come to see their role as spokespersons for the departments they run instead of servants of the presidents who appointed them. The problem is not simply that obstructionist individuals are at fault. The roles within the policy-making process create incentives for disobedience.

President Carter practiced a fifth method by attacking causes instead of symptoms. In his 1976 campaign for office he proposed regaining control of government by reorganizing it: "We must give top priority to a drastic and thorough revision and reorganizing of the federal bureaucracy."

Reorganization attempts have been frequent in the postwar era and were stressed not only by Carter but also by Truman, Johnson, Nixon, and Reagan. Symptomatic of the magnitude of the problem—and indicative of why such solutions are improbable—is the fact that reorganization seldom demolishes existing bureaucracies. As noted earlier, entrenched bureaucracies have usually perfected survival tactics. (As former Secretary of State James F. Byrnes noted, "The nearest thing to immortality on Earth is a government bureau.") Evidently, reorganization (or even what Secretary of the Navy John Lehman termed "de-organization"—not greater centralization and unification of authority, but decentralization and greater accountability) is not a final solution, as Carter and others have learned.

Carter also sought revision of the regulations governing civil servants' employment in 1978 with the Civil Service Reform Act, which put some seven thousand top bureaucrats into a Senior Executive Service, entitled them to earn bonuses for outstanding job performance, but separated them from job tenure. This reform permitted the chief executive and cabinet officers to reassign upper-middle management personnel and, where deemed necessary, to replace those not moving quickly enough or in the right direction. Similar reforms followed in the Foreign Service with the creation of the Senior Foreign Service. These innovations considerably augmented the president's managerial capabilities, but they did not guarantee agency responsiveness to presidential orders.

Like his predecessors, President Reagan sought to exercise greater control over the federal bureaucracy. His campaign for office openly opposed the government he sought to run by berating its size and by promising to reduce, reorganize, and streamline it. "Government is not the solution, it is the problem," Reagan said in his first inaugural speech.

Reagan largely failed to live up to his own promises. During his presidency big government got bigger: federal spending went up, not down, as budget outlays as a percent of the gross national product rose to peacetime records. Moreover, while reductions in some agencies' forces were implemented, over-all the number of federal civilian and military employees grew by 7 percent between 1980 and 1987, from to 4.9 million to 5.3 million.

In addition to seeking to *redistribute* various agencies' budget, person-nel, and policy authority, Reagan sought to control the bureaucracy by infiltrat-ing it with political operatives. To gain a top government post candidates were required to pass an "ideological censorship" test (Barber, 1985). The number of political appointees increased by a third, from roughly twenty-two hundred to more than thirty-three hundred (Struck, 1985: 31). The program was predi-cated on the belief that patronage would purchase loyalty from those whose jobs depended on the president—for these are the only personnel who can eas-ily be relieved of their duties. The goal was driven by the perceived need, in the words of Navy Secretary Lehman, "to roll back the accretion of layers of cen-tralized bureaucracy and restore a crisper accountability."

That goal appears to remain as elusive as ever. Indeed, whether the federal bureaucracy can be made measurably more tractable is questionable, and whether the foreign affairs government's capacity for responsiveness and for taking direction can be increased remains uncertain. "Those who think we're powerless to do anything about the greenhouse effect," George Bush warned in 1988, "are forgetting about the White House effect. As President, I intend to do something about it." But well into his presidency, Bush learned the power of the "bureaucratic effect" as his "Commerce and Interior departments waged constant guerrilla warfare against any effort to make good on the President's prior commitments" (Talbott, 1989b).

Compartmentalized Policy Making and Foreign Policy Inconsistency

Because each agency in the foreign affairs government has its *own* definition of proper goals, incompatible foreign policies are sometimes pursued by the United States.

Foreign policy tends to lack cohesion in part because the "facts" govern-ing the interpretation of any situation are colored by the role positions indi-viduals occupy. Where one sits shapes one's vision and version of reality. And because facts are less important than what is perceived, individuals often differ about the nature of the circumstances confronted and about what should be done to meet the challenges posed. The compartmentalized division of labor in the foreign affairs government, therefore, often produces competition among the bureaucratic units involved and, on occasion, culminates in one unit's challenge of another's policies. When such contests become public, American foreign policy looks as if it were working at cross-purposes and lacks a clear sense of mission.

An example was provided during the final days of the Shah's rule in Iran that set the stage for the takeover of the American embassy and the illegal incarceration of American diplomatic personnel. The U.S. response to the unfolding drama was clouded by a quarrel that developed between the National Security Council staff in Washington and the State Department representatives in Teheran, a dispute rooted in how different the relevant "facts" looked to those in the White House compared with those in the field. According to William Sullivan, the American ambassador to Tehran at the time, the divergent views, and the interagency bickering and struggle they produced, led to a tragic outcome: "[This] division of perceptions within the Washington bureaucracy . . . extended to the . . . instructions that were sent to the embassy or, more often, to the absence of any instructions whatsoever. . . . By November 1978 [national security adviser] Brzezinski began to make his own policy and established his own embassy in Iran . . . . It soon became apparent that [my] views were no longer welcome at the White House" (Sullivan, 1980). The White House ignored Ambassador Sullivan's recommendation that, upon the Shah's fall from power, the U.S. should not cast its fate with the Bakhtiar government because, in his view, it "was a chimera the shah had created to permit a dignified departure, that Bakhtiar himself was quixotic and would be swept aside by the arrival of Khomeini and his supporters in Teheran" (Sullivan, 1980). As history records, Sullivan's dire predictions proved correct even while Brzezinski's policy prevailed. Iran fell into revolution and American personnel became its target. But the ambassador sought to negotiate with the revolutionaries to prevent the Americans' capture. His words describe the sequence of events that, in his view, sealed the U.S. fate and insured that disaster would result:

> Well into the night, I worked with our contacts among the revolutionaries to arrange for the extraction of these Americans from the bunker in which they were trapped. Just as I was at the point of achieving their rescue, I received a telephone call in the clear over the international circuit from Washington relaying a message from Brzezinski who asked whether I thought I could arrange a military coup against the revolution. I regret that the reply I made is unprintable. (Sullivan, 1980: 186)

Another example of the untoward effects of bureaucratic struggle occurred in response to the Laotian situation in 1960, when the State Department and the CIA gave aid to opposing armies. How bureaucratic competition can lead to policy inconsistency has been described in the disturbing recollections of a former American official.

> The Agency [CIA] supported Indonesian rebels against Sukarno while State was trying to work with Sukarno. It supplied and emboldened the anticommunist Chinese guerrillas in Burma over the protests of the Burmese Government and the repeated protestations of the State Department in Washington and our ambassador in Burma that we were doing no such thing. In Vietnam, too, CIA and State . . . worked at cross-purposes.
>
> But the [CIA] has not confined its activities to unstable countries. It has meddled elsewhere, to the consternation of the State Department and friendly governments. In the mid-1950s, its agents intruded awkwardly in Costa Rica, the

most stable and democratic country in Latin America. While the Agency was trying to oust José Figueres, the moderate socialist who became the Costa Rican President in a fair election in 1953, the State Department was working with him and our ambassador was urging President Eisenhower to invite him to the United States to enhance his prestige. So it went the world around. (Simpson, 1967: 103)

Turf battles and the pursuit of incompatible objectives may be endemic to the policy-making process. The differences early in the Bush administration about what to do with, for, and about Mikhail Gorbachev illustrated the entrenched nature of this consequence. While President Bush and Secretary of State James A. Baker spent their time attempting to convince the Soviets (and the American public) that they truly wished Gorbachev's domestic reforms and foreign policy redirection to succeed, Secretary of Defense Cheney and Vice President Dan Quayle publicly proclaimed their reservations about Gorbachev's prospects and peaceful intentions, and a secret team was established in the White House to discredit Gorbachev's credibility. Because the professed goal of "ending the Cold War" was not endorsed by all of the administration's factions, during the Bush administration's first year in office initiatives to end that conflict appeared timid, tardy, and inconsistent.

Bureaucratic Pluralism and Foreign Policy Making by Compromised Solution

Bureaucratic pressures diminish presidents' ability to assert control and lead. Rather than selecting policies from alternative recommendations and turning to the bureaucracy to implement them, presidents often choose among agreed-on bureaucratic solutions and then seek to mobilize their movement on the decisions reached.

That image does not conform to the popular view of policy goals determined by presidents through rational processes. But few, if any, presidential decisions are unaffected by the options bureaucracies present to the president. Hence policy determination is more realistically pictured as produced by bargaining through an accommodative political process that reconciles conflicting recommendations, with presidents necessarily playing the role of "power broker" to resolve their competing agencies' conflicting demands. Policy results from compromise, not from the president's values.

Seen in this way, the chief executive is an arbitrator of interagency disputes, and policy making entails settling jurisdictional struggles. Addressing the State Department's senior officials at the beginning of the Kennedy administration, Secretary of State Dean Rusk noted that "the process of government has sometimes been described as a struggle for power among those holding public office." The observation follows the spirit of Dean Acheson's memorable remark that a secretary of state's most essential quality was "the killer instinct."

The decision the president makes must reconcile divergent claims in order to maintain a modicum of harmony within the government. In many ways the president's role is primarily to govern by managing the executive bureaucracy. "The president is beset with too many often conflicting opinions," James A. Baker observed in 1987 when he was Reagan's chief of staff, "and he spends an inordinate time resolving differences among his advisers who are there because their existence has been legislated."

It is that aspect of policy making that led Grant McConnell (1962) to say of President Kennedy that "perhaps his greatest achievement lay in holding the diverse elements of his administration together and creating a façade of unity in government." How to get bureaus to do what is needed and prevent their rebellion dominates presidents' attention. "Somehow a President must try to make a ministry out of what is at best a coalition" (Lowi, 1967).

If we view foreign policy formulation from the perspective of the role any president must play, the reasons for compromise, incrementalism, and caution become apparent. On a daily basis the president is surrounded by advisers, including members of the cabinet, who so interpret their jobs as to make maximum claims on their agencies' behalf. Having heard from one agency the extreme of one side of the policy dispute, and then the other extreme from another agency, the president must forge the terms of settlement.

But look at the setting in which the president must make a choice. "The President . . . has to operate in a world populated with countervailing organizations which believe his every move is of concern to them, and must therefore be cleared with them" (Cleveland, 1959). Those embracing competing viewpoints must be allowed to struggle regularly, and all contestants must attempt to remain friends. The politicized situation encourages the participants to make maximum claims as bargaining points, but all expect a compromise settlement, in part because the president must give everyone something in the hopes of eliciting their cooperation. Thus the president is driven to satisfy most groups somewhat, rather than a few agencies fully; to keep future options open by appearing neutral and hedging, rather than by allowing the opposition to become adamant or allied; and to deal in increments and adjustments, inching toward fundamental goals step by step, gaining a little but also losing a little. Permitting foes to save face is also an important part of this game. Because policy making involves constant struggle, with much give and take, "the profusion of so many centers of power makes building the kind of consensus necessary for positive action a formidable task" (Hilsman, 1990). The resistance of postwar American foreign policy to adaptive change may flow not from the concentration of power but from its diffusion. The welter of policy-making centers and the increases in their number decreases presidents' capacity to take visionary initiatives. Because policy directions were set through long-established bargains, reflecting the established distribution of influence, policy disruptions are unlikely unless the distribution of influence itself is changed.

Some Other Effects of Decision Making
in Large-Scale Organizations

The preceding discussion has identified some basic consequences of policy making by organizational procedures. Certainly that list is incomplete. Decision making by and within organizations produce still other effects.

Among them is *ad hoc decision making*. Preoccupied with each day's immediate crisis, leaders rarely think long-term. Often, they confront issues only after they have reached crisis proportions. Piecemeal adjustments as a substitute for long-term planning often have been evident. As one State Department official described the Carter administration's decision making: "Adhocracy gone mad seemed too often to be the order of the day, with policy careening from crisis to crisis with no more certain guide than the decisions of the moment" (Carter, 1981). The same criticism was leveled by some critics of the Bush administration's response to Iraq's invasion of Kuwait in 1990, which seemed to evolve piecemeal as the crisis unfolded. The unattractive pictures suggest policy by improvisation instead of planning. Rather than choices being made in light of carefully considered national goals, trial-and-error policy responses to problems as they surface have at times been characteristic.

A related consequence of bureaucratic behavior is *decision avoidance*. Most of us think of presidents as decisive, and presidents cultivate this image. Recall Harry S Truman (1966): "The greatest part of the President's job is to make decisions—big ones and small ones. . . . The President—whoever he is—has to decide. He can't pass the buck to anybody. No one else can do the deciding for him. That's his job."

Unfortunately, relatively few presidents adhere to Truman's advice. Many, quite proficient at passing the buck, manage not to decide. "Presidents are, in the eyes of bureaucrats, notorious for putting off decisions or changing their minds. They have enough decisions to make without looking for additional ones. In many cases, all the options look bad and they prefer to wait" (Gelb and Halperin, 1973).

The psychological incentives for ignoring problems or postponing confronting them are enormous. Not taking direct action or letting the force of momentum determine policy outcomes avoids criticism and opposition. Particularly in the realm of foreign policy, where the wrong decision can mean the difference between life and death for millions,[17] it is tempting to seek refuge from decision-making burdens by simply denying a problem's existence.

Another possible effect of group decision making is the *risky-shift* phenomenon. In contrast to what was argued above, under some circumstances the decisions made by groups may actually entail greater risks than those cautious ones that individual members would have made had they been acting alone. Groups, in other words, may be more inclined to take dangerous, bold, and

---

17. For an incisive analysis showing how policy may evolve from the inertia of previous decisions and a *fait accompli* from the depths of the bureaucracy, see Schilling (1973).

aggressive actions than individuals. People deciding in groups (recall "group-think") are prone to reinforce and support each other's extreme positions, especially when an *esprit de corps* exists among them. They are reluctant to appear overly cautious or, worse, fearful.[18] People act differently together than when they act alone; for psychological reasons they reach shift-to-risk decisions under peer-group pressure, and groups, it has been argued, are usually dominated by their most neurotic (and reckless) member. "Madness," Friedrich Nietzsche argued, "is the exception in individuals but the rule in groups." People will sacrifice themselves for and take chances on behalf of others that they would not normally take when acting merely for themselves. When decision responsibilities are shared, risky alternatives are more likely because no member of the group making the risky decision can be held personally responsible for proposing a policy that produces failure. Hence, although the general effect of bureaucracy is to encourage caution and restraint, when policy making becomes centralized in the hands of a small group, as it is prone to do when the nation faces an external threat, that penchant for caution may be overcome and even reversed (decision making in crisis situations is explored in Chapter 15).

Yet another product of decision making in large, complex organizations is the increased likelihood of *unmanaged policy initiatives*. Organizational size reduces the ability of the foreign affairs machinery to maintain strict control over the behavior of subordinates through a clear chain of command. Many individuals occasionally have the opportunity to take unilateral initiatives. "In the intricate sticky webs of paperwork, the principle of accountability flutters and expires. Responsibility gets diffused; finally it disappears. Everyone is responsible; therefore no one is responsible. It is 'the system'" (Kilpatrick, 1985). If policy making is really determined at the implementation stage, and not at the declaratory stage (when the president or presidential staff proclaims the policy), then what bureaucrats actually do defines the real policy. In a sense, then, every bureaucrat has the opportunity to be a policymaker. The debate over who has authority to control the nuclear missiles on U.S. submarines, navy personnel or only the president (see Meyer, 1984), illustrates that the issue of command and control is not a trivial one.

A revealing illustration occurred during the Vietnam War. After President Nixon finally declared a cessation of the bombing over North Vietnam in 1972 in the hope of encouraging bargaining concessions from the North Vietnamese, General John D. Lavelle of the air force took it upon himself to order hundreds of pilots to attack North Vietnamese territory, and over a three-month period

---

18. "One of the first lessons a national security manager learns . . . is that toughness is the most highly prized virtue. Some of the national security managers of the Kennedy-Johnson era, looking back on their experience, talk about the 'hairy chest syndrome.' The man who is ready to recommend using violence against foreigners, even where he is overruled, does not damage his reputation for prudence, soundness, or imagination, but the man who recommends putting an issue to the U.N., seeking negotiations, or, horror of horrors, 'doing nothing,' quickly becomes known as 'soft'" (Barnet, 1972). Case in point: President Johnson had the habit of addressing his resident-dove adviser Bill Moyers: "Well, here comes Mr. Stop-the-Bombing."

he continued to order the drops in clear violation of the president's official policy. To the North Vietnamese, not surprisingly, the president's policy proclamation mattered little: American policy had not changed.

The most dramatic recent example of policy making by a low-level subordinate is provided by the covert actions of Lt. Colonel Oliver North in the Iran-*contra* affair. A gung-ho underling intoxicated with the desire to pursue Cold War confrontation by any means necessary, North "seized upon the 'neat idea' of using profits made in [clandestine arms sales to what Secretary of State George Schultz had termed a terrorist regime—the anti-American government of Iran] to support the contras" fighting the leftist Sandinista government in Nicaragua. Moving "under cover," North set up an illegal plan to divert secret funds from the arms sales in order to provide the *contras* clandestine military support. His operation established a "secret government" or "government within a government" to conduct a "secret war." This "junta" felt it "had been forced to manipulate the real [U.S.] government in order to get what they wanted" because it could not secure public approval or congressional authorization for its action (Draper, 1990). In the end the carefully crafted plan backfired at the same time that it jeopardized basic democratic principles. "There was a concern," Johnson's former adviser Clark Clifford put it, "that our nation not resort to the tactics of our enemies in order to resist them." Convicted of lying to Congress (even though he claimed to have received the tacit approval of President Reagan), North was given a light sentence by presiding Judge Gesell, who, in pronouncing the sentence, "reiterated the jurors' view that North was not a leader but a 'low-ranking subordinate' who presumably was not entirely responsible for what he did" (Fitzgerald, 1989).

Some allege that the cruelest and most inhumane features of American conduct abroad have been caused not by evil people, but by the institutions in which evil behavior is sometimes bred. Bureaucratic decision making, in other words, not deficiencies of those who work in those settings, accounts for past immoral decisions or *the dehumanization of foreign policy.*

Here observers note that specialization discourages the humanitarian's role in the policy making process. An army of technocrats—individuals who only know how to perform certain specific tasks but who feel no responsibility for anything beyond the narrow confines of their job—carry out decisions. More often than not they give unquestioning loyalty to their agency without doubting its motives. Bureaucratic policy-making conceals the overall content of the policy; and bureaucrats who evaluate the ethics of their assigned mission find that their judgment and loyalty is questioned. Even the managers, the agency heads, are isolated from the policy product; a manager's true product is management.

Additionally, the foreign affairs machinery's size spreads decision responsibility, so that assigning credit—or blame—for what the United States does abroad becomes a hopeless task. Without clear-cut responsibility for policy initiatives, bureaucrats are shielded from the fact that they had a hand in producing foreign actions which, on a personal level, they might otherwise regard as morally repugnant or socially harmful. The anonymity of the policy-making process, critics note, produced Vietnam: a reading of *The Pentagon Papers* (1971) gives the impression that no one was to blame for the way the war was ruthlessly prosecuted. It was the faceless bureaucratic system, and not people, that produced the product.

When foreign policies emanate through a division of labor from "the activities of thousands of human beings organized into bureaucratic structures," the chilling consequence—what is termed "bureaucratic homicide" waged abroad—may occur.

> In general, those who plan do not kill and those who kill do not plan. The scene is familiar. Men in blue, green, and khaki tunics and others in three-button business suits sit in pastel offices and plan complex operations in which thousands of distant human beings will die. The men who planned the saturation bombings, free fire zones, defoliation, crop destruction, and assassination programs in the Vietnam War never personally killed anyone.
>
> The bureaucratization of homicide is responsible for the routine character of modern war, the absence of passion, and the efficiency of mass-produced death. Those who do the killing are following standing orders. . . . An infantryman, aware that even old men, women, and children will shoot or lay booby traps for foreigners who burn their village, sprays machine-gun fire randomly into a crowd of cowering "Vietcong sympathizers." . . . The man who does the killing or terrorizing on behalf of the United States has been sent by others—usually men he has never seen and over whom he has no control.
>
> The complexity and vastness of modern bureaucratic government complicates the issue of personal responsibility. At every level of government the classic defense of the bureaucratic killer is available: "I was just doing my job!" The essence of bureaucratic government is emotional coolness, orderliness, implacable momentum, and a dedication to abstract principle. Each cog in the bureaucratic machine does what it is supposed to do. The Green Machine, . . . the military establishment, kills cleanly, and usually at a distance. America's highly developed technology makes it possible to increase the distance between killer and victim and hence to preserve the crucial psychological fiction that the objects of America's lethal attention are less than human. For the bureaucratic killer destruction is almost hygienic provided one does not have to lay hands on his victim. (Barnet, 1972: 13–14)

THE PROCESS OF DECISION MAKING: A BALANCE SHEET OF CREDITS AND DEBITS

The preceding discussion raises serious doubts about the proposition that American foreign policy is the end product of a logical chain of reasoning. Although the official histories we are likely to read in a high-school civics text make everything that happened sound rational, the memoirs of past participants in the decision-making process—including presidents—and an objective treatment of the diplomatic record create quite a different impression. To people there at the

time, as well as to many who subsequently have probed the record of events, those happenings often did not look orderly or rational. At times they seemed more like scenes stolen from the theater of the absurd. To some, the American process of foreign policy decision making has contributed to its recurrent failures (Etheredge, 1985); to others, the decisional process has made the
• United States its "own worst enemy" (Destler, Gelb, and Lake, 1984).

How valid is the villain image of foreign policy-making procedures and the corollary hypothesis that the decision-making process within large-scale organizations is characterized by malaise? The symptoms are numerous. Recall some of them: bureaucracies constantly driven to expand the boundaries of their own power; parochial bureaucracies that define objectives in light of their own needs and traditions; agencies that reward blind loyalty and pursue fierce interagency competition; institutions that promote the obedient, unimaginative, and cautious but ostracize the questioner, the doubter, and the reformer; deference to ritual and precedent; machinery that avoids risk and honors the status quo; groups composed of "yes-men" intolerant of divergent viewpoints; a government of technocrats; bureaucracies dedicated to doing whatever they were assigned initially regardless of its present usefulness; institutions resisting control from above while perfecting it from within; and decision making by mechanical procedure rather than by reflection. The words commonly associated with bureaucracies are not flattering: *backlogs, waste, foulups, overstaffed, overpaid* and *underworked, duplication, special interests. Bureaucrat* has seldom been a word commanding respect; to many it is a term of derision.

Recall as well some of the processes' policy consequences: inaction; decision sabotage; policy by compromise; inertia and incrementalism, where continual nibbling becomes a substitute for a good bite; decisions based on biased, self-serving information and oversimplifications, which make policymakers captives of their advisers; policy by delay; policy without a vision of the future and that deals only with the present and thus "muddles through" problems instead of anticipating and averting them; a process that strips leaders of real authority and encourages them to try to be everything to everyone instead of leading; a process in which major policy may occasionally percolate upward from the decisions of people at the machinery's bottom; policies insensitive to human needs or inattentive to the protection of life itself; a process that deals with methods of handling problems instead of programs for preventing them; and, of course, methods of implementation so notoriously sluggish that *bureaucracy* and *red tape* are practically synonymous.

These symptoms are readily recognizable in contemporary American foreign policy. Many of the things that are wrong, and that go wrong, are clearly attributable to the way the government organizes itself for the making of foreign policy decisions and the kinds of role-induced behavior that organizations promote. "We overorganize, overman, overspend, and underaccomplish," was the way former Deputy Secretary of Defense David Packard described his department's performance—and his words seem to describe well the way most people think of bureaucratic performance in general. Inefficiency stems, so it seems, from the institutional arrangements and sheer size of the government itself and their consequent impact on the behavior of those individuals working in the foreign affairs government.

But such a conclusion may grossly overstate or misrepresent the impact of large-scale organizations on the making of American foreign policy and the motives and contributions of the career professionals who comprise them. This picture must be balanced by the clear advantages of modern bureaucracy. The foreign affairs bureaucracy provides more than liabilities. *Bureaucrat* need not be a dirty word. In fact, the conduct of diplomacy would not be possible without a modern bureaucracy and the kind of organizational support that it alone can provide. For no president could successfully manage a globalist foreign policy without the assistance of a large bureaucracy.

Often the assistance of America's foreign affairs government has proved invaluable. One example perhaps makes the point. India and China, a critical neutral and a (then) proclaimed adversary, went to war during the Cuban missile crisis. Because President Kennedy was necessarily preoccupied with events in Cuba, the bureaucracy had to act—almost unilaterally—to protect American interests in South Asia. The actions taken proved successful (in contrast with the 1971 India-Pakistan war when President Nixon and Secretary of State Kissinger were in charge). Incidents such as that suggest that the image of the bureaucracy-as-enemy can easily be overdrawn and may often be simply inaccurate. Some kind of bureaucracy is necessary; it can often be beneficial to effective policy making. The question, therefore, is not whether to have foreign policy made in a group context, but rather how to make that context more responsive.

Indeed, it is *not* the huge size of the bureaucracy that alone makes it appear that officials are continually tripping over each other (although that is part of the problem). Nor is the propensity for the policy-making system to stumble and blunder due merely to self-serving people (although they contribute to the problem as well). It is at least partly the formidable challenges posed by today's complex and threatening world environment that make bureaucratic government so necessary even while it often looks so inept. "Inveighing against big government," observes syndicated columnist George Will, "ignores the fact that government, though big, is often too weak." What may be needed is more government, not less (Alperovitz and Faux, 1984). Though deficient in many respects, bureaucratic government is nonetheless indispensable to a great power's practices. The solution, therefore, is not to do away with bureaucratic government. It is to run it efficiently and shape its power to national purposes. For that, leadership is required. In the final analysis, then, bringing out the best that the foreign affairs governments has to offer seemingly rests with the president and the president's principal advisers. But can presidents make a difference? Or was the great sociologist Max Weber correct when he argued, "In a modern state the actual ruler is necessarily and unavoidably the bureaucracy"? To address that question, we must consider yet another potential source of American foreign policy: individual leaders.

SUGGESTIONS FOR FURTHER READING

Allison, Graham T. (1971) *Essence of Decision: Explaining the Cuban Missile Crisis.* Boston: Little, Brown.

Anderson, Paul A. (1987) "What Do Decision Makers Do When They Make a Foreign Policy Decision?" pp. 285–308 in Charles F. Hermann, Charles W. Kegley, Jr., and James N. Rosenau (eds.), *New Directions in the Study of Foreign Policy.* Boston: Allen & Unwin.

Hermann, Charles F. (1988) "New Foreign Policy Problems and Old Bureaucratic Organizations," pp. 248–265 in Charles W. Kegley, Jr., and Eugene R. Wittkopf (eds.), *The Domestic Sources of American Foreign Policy: Insights and Evidence.* New York: St. Martin's.

Hilsman, Roger. (1990) *The Politics of Policy Making in Defense and Foreign Affairs: Conceptual Models and Bureaucratic Politics,* 2nd ed. Englewood Cliffs, N.J.: Prentice-Hall.

Janis, Irving L. (1982) *Groupthink: Psychological Studies of Policy Decisions and Fiascoes,* 2nd ed. Boston: Houghton Mifflin.

Krasner, Stephen D. (1988) "Are Bureaucracies Important? A Re-examination of Accounts of the Cuban Missile Crisis," pp. 215–226 in Charles W. Kegley, Jr., and Eugene R. Wittkopf (eds.), *The Domestic Sources of American Foreign Policy: Insights and Evidence.* New York: St. Martin's.

Simon, Herbert A. (1957) *Administrative Behavior: A Study of Decision-Making Processes in Administrative Organizations,* 2nd ed. New York: Macmillan.

Walker, Stephen G. (1987) "Role Theory and the Origins of Foreign Policy," pp. 269–284 in Charles F. Hermann, Charles W. Kegley, Jr., and James N. Rosenau (eds.), *New Directions in the Study of Foreign Policy.* Boston: Allen & Unwin.

Wheeler, Nicholas, and Phil Williams. (1988) "United States Foreign Policy-Making: Chaos or Design?," pp. 464–481 in Steven L. Spiegel (ed.), *At Issue: Politics in the World Arena,* 5th ed. New York: St. Martin's.

Wilson, James Q. (1989) *Bureaucracy: What Government Agencies Do and Why They Do It.* New York: Basic Books.

CHAPTER 14

Leader Characteristics and Foreign Policy Performance

If I have learned anything in a lifetime in politics and government,
it is the truth of the famous phrase, "History is biography"—that
decisions are made by people, and they make them based on what
they know of the world and how they understand it.

VICE PRESIDENT GEORGE BUSH, 1987

One of the most unsettling things for foreigners is the impression that
our foreign policy can be changed by any new president on the basis
of the president's personal preference.

FORMER SECRETARY OF STATE HENRY KISSINGER, 1979

Picture a president sitting alone in the White House, wrestling with a crisis threatening the nation's very survival, possessing the power by virtue of the president's position to unleash massive destruction. Assume that this individual is impulsively competitive, prone to act brashly to attract attention, inclined to take risks to exploit opportunities, motivated by the view that the world is a jungle and that it demands that one perpetually claw and scratch in a struggle for power, distrustful of others, contemptuous of adversaries, and a person of quick temper. Assume also that this same person is driven by a fear of failure stemming from low self-esteem, a fear overcome in the past by dramatic and successful actions that restored self-confidence. How is such a person likely to respond to the immediate crisis? It is hard to imagine that the response will not be significantly affected by the person's uniquely individual characteristics—background, beliefs, and personality traits—and that the nation's destiny will therefore also not be so affected. Indeed, to understand why the United States acts the way it does in world affairs, clearly we must take into account the characteristics of those responsible for the conduct of the nation's foreign policy.

This chapter examines individuals as a source of foreign policy. It looks at the leaders themselves, the people who occupy the decision-making roles at the highest echelons of government, and explores the extent to which leaders' idiosyncracies—their personal aspirations, convictions, anxieties, and experiences and memories—influence America's foreign policy.

493

INDIVIDUALS AS A SOURCE OF FOREIGN POLICY

Properly speaking, nation-states are incapable of acting or thinking; they are inanimate symbols for collectivities—the people within a state's borders. Leaders, on behalf of states, make foreign policy decisions that influence national destinies. For that reason, the personal characteristics of those empowered to make national decisions are crucial.

Foreign policy choices are often made by a remarkably small number of individuals, most conspicuous of whom is the president. "The management of foreign affairs," Thomas Jefferson maintained, is "executive altogether." Harry S Truman concurred by exclaiming "I make American foreign policy."

Given the president's prominence and power, it is tempting to think of foreign policy as determined exclusively by presidential preferences and to personalize government by identifying a policy with a leader (even though foreign policy is implemented by many people). Ralph Waldo Emerson's aphorism "There is properly no history, only biography" dramatizes the popular impression of individual leaders as movers of history. With regard to American foreign policy, this "hero in history" claim equates American action with the wishes and choices of its highest elected officials. Names of presidents are commonly attached to policies as if the men were synonymous with the nation itself, and foreign affairs successes and failures are routinely attributed to the administration in which they occurred. New leaders are assumed to make a difference. The view that changes in leadership matter is reinforced by the efforts of each new administration to distinguish itself from its predecessor and to highlight policy departures in order to convey the impression that it has engineered a new era. The media's tendency to label presidential actions "new" abets those efforts. Hence leadership is seen as policy and policy making, and changes are perceived as the result of the predispositions of the leadership. From this viewpoint, Truman's doctrine, Dwight D. Eisenhower's massive retaliation, John F. Kennedy's frontiersmanship, Richard M. Nixon's détente, and Jimmy Carter's human rights initiative were simply products of the leaders whose names they bear.

Consideration of the idiosyncratic characteristics of individuals draws attention to the important psychological foundations of human conduct. Perceptions, personal needs, and drives are all important determinants of the way people act. Correspondingly, decision makers' inner traits influence how they respond to various situations—the cognitions and responses of decision makers are determined not by "the 'objective' facts of the situation . . . but [by] their 'image' of the situation," that is, they "act according to the way the world appears . . . not necessarily according to the way it 'is'" (Boulding, 1959). That principle correctly suggests that images shape foreign conduct. Perceptions are not simple reflections of what is passively observed; instead, they are influenced by the memories, values, needs, and beliefs the observer brings to the situation (see Falkowski, 1979; Jönsson, 1982a). All individuals' perceptions are to some extent biased by personality predispositions and inner drives, as well as by prior experiences and future expectations. What occurs in decision makers' heads is therefore important.

As we shift attention from the way issues are debated to the debaters themselves, we must ask if contrasts among decision makers make a difference in policy—in content as well as in style. Does the type of person elected to or selected for policy-making positions affect the country's international conduct? Do the particular personal qualities of the people holding policy positions determine the course the nation charts for itself in foreign affairs? Or would others holding those positions during the same period have acted similarly? Do changes in leadership promote changes in foreign policy? If so, in what ways, and under what conditions? We now turn to this set of important questions.

ASSESSING THE "CHARACTER" OF LEADERS

No two individuals are identical; every person differs in some way from every other. This personal diversity is exhibited by the major figures in postwar American foreign policy. Compare "give 'em hell" Harry Truman, soft-spoken Ike Eisenhower, charismatic Jack Kennedy, "tricky Dick" Nixon, "down home" Jimmy Carter, Hollywood "Dutch" Reagan, and, most recently, "prep pie" George Bush. Nevertheless, apparent differences in policy elites' personalities may mask important similarities. The relevant question, therefore, is not how different are the individuals who make American foreign policy, but, instead, what impact leaders' peculiar traits have on their decisions.

Linking Personal Characteristics to Foreign Policy Behavior

Although it is difficult to generalize, it is easily demonstrated that policymakers' personal characteristics often influence their behavior, because in-depth case studies of particular decision makers abound, especially in the era of the "personal president" (Lowi, 1985a).[1] Most such studies probe the life histories of public officials to describe their psychological makeup and world views. Almost invariably, such psychobiographies assume that leaders' personalities are determined by such factors as their early childhood experiences, their relationships with parents and peers, and their self-conceptions. Such background factors are presumed to mold the leaders' personalities, beliefs, and decision styles and their subsequent adult and policy-making behavior.

Consider the psychological consequences of President Woodrow Wilson's stern and often punitive childhood. Wilson's inability to please his rigid father during childhood is hypothesized to have created an all-consuming need in later

---

1. The studies by Barber (1985), Donovan (1985), and Stoessinger (1985) provide insights on the personalities and beliefs of the postwar presidents that are particularly relevant to foreign policy formulation.

life to attain self-esteem; that need accounts for most of Wilson's idealistic policy programs. As president, Wilson may have compulsively striven for great deeds to compensate for his fear of rejection. Most notable was his intense battle to create the League of Nations, a passion best explained by Wilson's overwhelming need to attain a puritanic "state of grace" (George and George, 1964).

The first American secretary of defense, James Forrestal, is the object of another illustrative psychobiography (Rogow, 1963). Driven and worrisome, Forrestal became obsessed by paranoid fantasies. He not only feared foreigners, but distrusted his own friends and coworkers. His career came to a tragic end with suicide.

The possible relationship between a leader's psychological profile and his policy behavior has been suggested by investigations of the ways President Kennedy's personality may have been instrumental in the decisions he made during the Cuban missile crisis. According to one (admittedly controversial) interpretation (Mongar, 1974), Kennedy suffered most of his life from a neurotic conflict between an overpowering fear of failure, on the one hand, and an overwhelming need for assistance, on the other. The first stemmed from his inability to compete successfully with his older brother (Joe, Jr.), a sibling given unfair advantage in a contrived competitive family environment. Joe, Jr., was introduced by his father to friends as a future president of the United States, and his mother held him up as a model for the other children, especially Jack, and gave him a free hand in disciplining them. In that atmosphere it became impossible for Jack to attain an equal portion of attention, recognition, and affection from his parents: "No matter how hard he tried, Jack could neither conquer his older brother nor equal his competitive triumphs outside the family arena." Consequently, the younger Kennedy lacked self-assurance. To overcome these psychological fears of failure, he "hit upon the strategy of feigning helplessness as a way of avoiding the costs of competitive failure." A succession of childhood illnesses permitted him to avoid fruitless competition, and he resorted to "the manipulation of fantasy to protect his [preferred self-] image of greatness." Thus self-deception is hypothesized by Mongar to have served as a defense mechanism to protect him from his fears of weakness.

Maturity, Mongar argues, helped young Jack Kennedy strengthen his self-image. As his personality took shape, Kennedy nonetheless retained a need to prove his personal worth; his search for adventure, and his restlessness, intellectualism, and acceptance of difficult tasks reflected this abiding need. To protect his preferred self-image, he habitually disarmed criticism "by modestly calling attention to minor shortcomings. This witty self-derision, which reflected a merciless introspection, undermined criticism early and at the same time elicited reassurance and support from other people."

Kennedy's words and actions as president during the Cuban missile crisis, Thomas Mongar avers, can be traced to his unresolved inner conflicts. That crisis became a "game," an opportunity to recover self-esteem; Kennedy's actions were made for psychotherapeutic rather than for strategic reasons (such as preventing a change in the nuclear balance of power). The risks were not trivial. When asked about the probability of nuclear war and the destruction of civilization resulting from risky U.S. actions, Kennedy coolly replied, "about one in three." Kennedy's major decisions, Mongar argues, were greatly shaped by his personal motives.

Is Kennedy's situation unique, or is the response of other policymakers to foreign policy situations influenced strongly by their emotional and personality needs? Consider the case of Henry Kissinger, a decision maker whose story "refutes the myth that individuals are of little importance in the world politics of the nuclear age. . . . Indeed, history may show that Henry Kissinger was the most powerful individual in the world in the 1970s" (Isaak, 1975).

That could hardly have been predicted twenty years earlier. Kissinger's remarkable childhood deviated far from the usual route to power: escape from Nazi persecution in his native Germany; study in high school at night while working all day; service as a draftee in the army; college at Harvard; and then, college professor and presidential foreign policy adviser, culminating in his appointment as the first Jewish secretary of state.

Arguably, Kissinger relied to a considerable extent on ideas developed during his early experiences to deal with analogous personal and national problems later in life. In particular, Kissinger's formative experiences inculcated pessimism and mistrust that affected his image of world affairs. Words unfamiliar to other foreign policy analysts, such as *ambiguity, irony, paradox, nuance,* and *tragedy,* punctuated his writings; "instinctively he knew that truth in the modern nuclear age was more a question of constant change, indeterminacy, and relativity, than of fixed boundaries, roles, and unambiguous situations and positions. Yet, even so, he longed to know the limits of knowledge and his own limits" (Isaak, 1975).

Personally insecure, yet egocentric, Kissinger felt that uncertainty was the very essence of international politics. As a decision maker he consistently acted on his belief that people are limited in what they can do and that because of the complexity of life many imponderables make history move. Ironically, however, the principle of uncertainty that supported his pessimistic world view may have been the source of his successes, for Kissinger's achievements may be attributed in part to his ability to use ambiguity, negotiated compromise, and secrecy—as well as public relations strategies ingeniously devised to enhance his own image—in his conduct of diplomacy.[2]

Then, too, much of Kissinger's posture toward international affairs can be traced to his assumptions about interpersonal relations as those were shaped by

---

2. Woodward and Bernstein (1979) provide a less than flattering glimpse of this man who otherwise was successful as a diplomat. They note the alienation of Kissinger from his own staff, which became over time increasingly "disillusioned with both the Kissinger policies and his personality. . . . He seemed to thrive on trouble, hysteria, fright, uncertainty. He raged at his secretaries. He appeared to take pleasure in humiliating his aides." And he was judged unable "to manage either personal relationships or staff organization." For another highly critical appraisal, see Hersh (1983). For overviews of Kissinger's world view and "operational code" and an assessment of their impact on Kissinger's policy performance, see Caldwell (1983) and Walker (1977).

the distinctive nature of his past. His philosophy of *realpolitik*—stressing the expectation of conflict, not collaboration, between states, the need to increase power relative to one's adversaries, the inadequacy of moral precepts as a guide to foreign affairs, and distrust of others' motives—finds a counterpart in the "lessons" he derived from his personal experiences during the crucial formative period of his political awakening. Could it be that Kissinger's disdain for moralism and his corresponding preference to ask not What is right and what is wrong? but Who is strong and who is weak? was rooted in the views he formed in his uncertain, insecure youth?

The preceding case studies illuminate the varied personalities of those who have risen to positions of power, the impact of their needs, background, and prior experience on their subsequent outlook, and the ways in which these characteristics may have molded their subsequent policy-making conduct. We can explore this notion further by looking specifically at the relationship between presidential character and presidential performance.

Presidential Character: Types and Consequences

When we move from observation of individuals to observation of *types* of leaders, it is easier to generalize about the relationship between leaders' characters and their expected policy-making performance. Here James David Barber's (1985) analysis of presidents' personal traits and leadership styles is most informative.

Barber suggests that presidents can be understood best by observing the energy they put into the job (active or passive) and their personal satisfaction with their presidential duties (negative or positive). The first dimension captures a president's image of the duties of the job. Active presidents are movers and shakers, energetically engaged in the challenge of leading, eagerly attentive to the responsibilities of office, and willing to accept the tasks of policy formulation and management. Conversely, passive presidents prefer to steer an even course, maintaining existing arrangements and avoiding the conflict that invariably accompanies changes in policy. The second dimension reflects a president's level of contentment with the job. This varies because some presidents have not enjoyed the position they achieved and have looked with disfavor on the burden of awesome responsibility. Such negative types, Barber notes, tend to have had childhood experiences that make them dutifully accept but not enjoy the demands that go with holding power.

Thus the character of each president may be classified in one of four categories: passive-negative (Calvin Coolidge, Dwight D. Eisenhower); passive-positive (Warren G. Harding, William Taft, Ronald Reagan); active-negative (Woodrow Wilson, Herbert Hoover, Lyndon B. Johnson, Richard M. Nixon); and active-positive (Franklin D. Roosevelt, Harry S Truman, John F. Kennedy, Gerald R. Ford, Jimmy Carter, George Bush). Barber distinguishes among the tendencies represented by these categories thus:

Active-positive Presidents want most to achieve results. Active-negatives aim to get and keep power. Passive-positives are after love. Passive-negatives emphasize their civic virtue. The relation of activity to enjoyment in a President thus tends to outline a cluster of characteristics, to set apart the adapted from the compulsive, compliant, and withdrawn types. (Barber, 1985: 10)

For understandable reasons, Barber contends that presidents with active-positive characters are best equipped to direct foreign policy and meet challenges and crises. Active-positives are self-respecting and happy, open to new ideas, and able to learn from their mistakes; their energies are no longer consumed with conquering the developmental traumas associated with youth but instead are directed outward toward achievement. As policymakers, therefore, active-positives have the greatest capacity for growth and flexibility.

Barber's analysis demonstrates that the behavior of leaders with similar skills and values can be quite different, depending on the type of character possessed. A leader's inner self, and especially the degree of self-confidence and self-esteem, critically affect performance. Barber shows that psychic attributes developed during childhood influence all decision makers' careers and conduct. Let us consider some examples.

Harry S Truman   An active-positive president, Truman took "massive initiatives at a time when such initiatives seemed unlikely, given the circumstances of his accession to office, his own qualifications, and the condition of the country" (Barker, 1985). Why? Many of Truman's bold foreign policy initiatives (the Truman Doctrine, the Marshall Plan, the North Atlantic Treaty Organization, and the Korean intervention) arguably stemmed from Truman's decisive character.

Dwight D. Eisenhower   Although he submits that Eisenhower is difficult to categorize, Barber concludes Eisenhower was a passive-negative. The passive side was reflected in the fact that Eisenhower "did not feel a duty to save the world or become a great hero, but simply to contribute what he could the best he was able." The negative side of Eisenhower's character, Barber observes, was reflected in his feelings that he was imposed on by an unnecessarily heavy schedule; Eisenhower claimed his heart attack in September 1955 was triggered "when he was repeatedly interrupted on the golf links by unnecessary phone calls from the State Department" (Barker, 1985).

John F. Kennedy   Similarly, Barber maintains that Kennedy's active-positive character may (Mongar's analysis notwithstanding) have contributed to his crisis-management capabilities. He was able to learn from his prior mistakes and disastrous experience in the Bay of Pigs fiasco of April 1961. By the time of the Cuban Missile Crisis in October 1962, "In command, in the assessment of information, in the technique of consultation, and in the empathy with his opponent, clearly John Kennedy had grown. He was, at that point, a professional president" (Barber, 1985).

Lyndon B. Johnson   Barber concludes Johnson was an active-negative president. The activism in Johnson's character was exhibited in the "fantastic pace of action in his presidency," motivated by humanitarian concerns and a commitment to the pursuit of happiness and creation of a better world. But the negativism of Johnson's character was evidenced in the "tough, hard, militaristic" posture he assumed toward his enemies, as shown in his 1952 statement while a member of the U.S. Senate that "he was prepared to reduce Moscow to rubble to stop Communist aggression anywhere."

Richard M. Nixon   An active-negative president, Nixon provides a revealing contrast to Truman and Kennedy. "The danger in his Presidency," Barber (1977) wrote while Nixon was still in the White House, "is the same as the danger Wilson, Hoover, and Johnson succumbed to: rigid adherence to a failing line of policy." Nixon's decision to widen the Vietnam War by invading Cambodia in the spring of 1970 was symptomatic: "To see in President Nixon the character of Richard Nixon—the character formed and set early in his life—one need only read over his speech on the Cambodian invasion, with its themes of power and control, its declaration of independence, its self-concern, its damning of doubters, and its coupling of humiliation with defeat" (Barber, 1977). Nixon reached this momentous decision without urging from his advisers, and the manner in which the president announced his decision "flabbergasted" his defense secretary, Melvin Laird. Indeed, to many in Washington

> the process by which the President had decided and acted was . . . as scary as the invasion itself. As the story of the crisis decision-making came out—the fact that senior State Department officials had been suddenly cut off from key cablegrams, that military orders were issuing directly from the White House, and especially the nearly complete isolation of the President from Congressional opinions as he stepped out beyond his most sanguine military advisors—the President's judgment as a professional came into question. (Barber, 1977: 439)

Extreme personal isolation ultimately destroyed the Nixon presidency.

Gerald R. Ford   Entering office in the wake of Watergate and Richard Nixon's resignation, Barber notes that Ford exceeded the generally low expectations many held for his presidency, and showed a capacity to grow and learn. Although "a step-by-step thinker," Ford approached the task of policy making with the positive attitude and activism characteristic of active-positives: "Just as all the props were collapsing in Vietnam, he unrealistically called for hundreds of millions more in military aid. He turned foreign policy over to a wizard of dramatic negotiation [Henry Kissinger] whose *ad hoc* successes obscured deepening world chaos."

Jimmy Carter   Noting that Carter came to Washington full of high expectations at a time of low hopes, Barber predicted that the energetic, "up and at 'em" active-positive Carter would enjoy life in the Oval Office and would find that it could be fun. But Barber also warned that Carter's troubles would spring "from an excess of an active-positive virtue: the thirst for results." His prophecy proved accurate.

With hindsight, it appears that Carter's character eventually led him impatiently to pursue too many goals simultaneously—a penchant that lent credibility to the frequent charges that he was inconsistent and indecisive, that he lacked a clear sense of priorities, and that he abandoned policy objectives almost as soon as they were announced in favor of still newer objectives, which then also were shelved. Carter's eagerness for results led to hyperactivity without follow-through, which produced dreaded failure. Critics and friends alike laid much of the blame for Carter's policy failures and unsuccessful reelection bid to his self-defeating tendencies; few linked them to the president's lack of effort or vision (his energy, drive, and natural intelligence were extraordinary) or to improper intentions or motives.

Ronald Reagan   Reagan's personality and ideology reveal inconsistent traits. "What makes it difficult to sort out Reagan's operative world view," observed Barber (1981) on the day of Reagan's first inauguration, "is his peculiar way with rhetoric. Obviously, it dominates his political style." But although Reagan's way with words concealed his true feelings, Barber concluded Reagan is basically "a passive person," a take-it-easy type. And, as everyone has noticed, he is an optimist, a booster, a smiler, a genial fellow. In my jargon, that combination makes Reagan a "passive-positive," that is, "the receptive, compliant, other-directed character whose life is a search for affection as a reward for being agreeable and cooperative rather than personally assertive." (Barber, 1981: 8)

Other ascribed passive-positive aspects of Reagan's character include his pronounced sentimentality and nostalgic infatuation with the past and his lack of a coherent ideology. "His conservatism is an attitude, not a theory," Barber concludes; it "has been circumstantial, not visceral." Indeed, Reagan adhered to a simple "black-and-white" outlook and was uninterested in facts and unaffected by them (see Dallek, 1984; Glad, 1983). Reagan also displayed an apparent need to avoid close personal contact and to distance himself from others. As demonstrated in the Iran-*contra* affair, he preferred to delegate responsibility to his staff and he depended on his advisers' decisions for guidance. Moreover, Reagan's life had been spent playing roles, an experience that may have colored his conception of the presidency. As he once revealingly commented: "Politics is just like show business. You have a hell of an opening, coast for a while and then have a hell of a close."

George Bush   Bush presents a challenging case for character assessment. Like his quiet, unobtrusive career in public service (as U.S. representative to China, Central Intelligence Agency director, vice president), Bush's performance

performance in the White House does not lend itself to easy interpretation as his words and actions fail to disclose a consistent pattern. From one perspective, Bush clearly is a man of ambition, drive, and dedication who has eagerly accepted the responsibilities of power. Before becoming president he assumed many government posts happily and carried out their responsibilities without complaint. But in none of these did Bush personally push for innovative policy changes. However, in temperament, "George Bush is not a political neurotic; he is well-adjusted," Barber mused, "and will not use the presidency for personal therapy."[3] "Mr. Bush wants a mission. It is important that he likes normal, ordinary politics, that he invests much energy in that work. His character is active-positive, a pattern that means he is ready to learn, to change, to develop in office, as distinct from fixated types such as Richard Nixon or Lyndon Johnson" (Barber, 1989). "Well-meaning," "well-organized," "self-confident" describe his general orientation to his duties.

From a second perspective, Bush was often criticized for his lack of creativity, curiosity, and ingenuity—in a word, for a lack of vision. "A philosophy of do your best and don't look back is characteristic of Bush's decision-making style" (Woodward, 1989). Instinctively cautious, once in the White House he showed respect for prudence and pragmatism and a disdain for ideology and impulsive innovation. "Never . . . known for imaginative ideas, probing insights or creative brilliance" (Beckworth, 1988), Bush was, prior to becoming president, largely a follower of someone else, not a leader. As one expert summarized, "Combined with President Bush's need for affiliation is a tendency to see the world in zero-sum terms which . . . makes him prone to perceiving criticism where it does not exist. . . . Once President Bush decides a situation is threatening, he will be difficult to persuade otherwise. Because he believes he has little control over events, President Bush allows situations to dictate to him rather than the reverse. This type of behavior leads to more reactive and slow policymaking" (Hermann, 1989). As one observer put it, "Bush is hostage to the status quo. . . . What all this professionalism adds up to is not exactly leadership. It is more like management. Bush's policies have been reactive. The United States responds, cautiously and reluctantly, to other's proposals. It is an in-box approach to governing. You respond to problems as they reach your desk (Schneider, 1990).

A third facet of Bush's character is his "great personal need for support and affiliation" (Hermann, 1989). This congeniality influences his managerial style. Able to give allegiance himself, Bush is perceived intolerant of disagreement and disloyalty from subordinates, a person who craves consensus. "My philosophy," Bush explained in 1988, "is that when you're part of an Administration you don't jump out and try to take credit. You are part of a team." To curtail conflict, Bush is prone to practice private, personal diplomacy, by-passing lower-level advisers and "micro-managing" information and events

---

3. James David Barber, personal interview, December 1, 1989.

rather than delegating authority (Seib, 1989). "With Reagan decisions were made from the bottom up. . . . With Bush they are made from the top down. He dominates everything" (Dowd, 1989a). A "Lone Ranger" president, cut in the Kissinger and Nixon mold, Bush has been seen as "probably our last President of the World War II generation, after the United States called the world's shots" (Grady, 1990). Bush's "I'm in charge" style were conveyed by his pronouncements that "some things will be conducted in secrecy" and that "I have an obligation to conduct the foreign policy of this country in the way I see fit." And his ability to take charge decisively was illustrated by the way he personally orchestrated worldwide support for economic sanctions and the possible use of force in response to Saddam Hussein's invasion of Kuwait.

Bush's personal traits converged to shape his presidential performance somewhat differently in different decision-making situations. This may explain why the mass media characterized his performance in such contradictory ways—why they ascribed to him distinct "personalities": wimp, healer, meanie, Mr. Affability, Mr. Timid, and a "trigger-happy" decision maker (Keene, 1990). These diverse styles do not provide a firm basis for anticipating their subsequent policy consequences, beyond the prediction that Bush would move cautiously to avoid making major mistakes.

Differentiating "Crusaders" and "Pragmatists"

Barber's typology of leader types has proven able to predict foreign policy performance. But his popular categorical approach is not the only way of assessing the impact of individual differences on decisions and policies. John Stoessinger has provided another, which looks exclusively at the nexus between leaders' personalities and their foreign policy behavior. Stoessinger maintains that two kinds of decision makers may be distinguished—*crusaders* and *pragmatists*. He characterizes the first type in this way:

> The crusader tends to make decisions based on a preconceived idea rather than on the basis of experience. Even though there are alternatives, he usually does not see them. If the facts do not square with his philosophy, it is too bad for the facts. Thus, the crusader tends toward rigidity and finds it difficult, if not impossible, to extricate himself from a losing posture. He does not welcome dissent and advisers will tend to tell him what he wants to hear. He sets out to improve the world but all too often manages to leave it in worse shape than it was before. (Stoessinger, 1985: xiii)

Pragmatists, on the other hand, come closer to fitting the "perfectly rational" decision maker described in Chapter 13. A pragmatist seeks facts, welcomes advice, accepts criticism, considers alternatives, and cherishes the flexibility that permits adjusting policy to new realities and changing its course where necessary (but without inflicting damage on his or her self-esteem in the process). Not surprisingly, Stoessinger feels that the country has been best served when pragmatists have held the reins of power. But this conclusion should not lead one to conclude that pragmatists never make mistakes.

> They often do. But as a general rule, such mistakes are more easily reversible than those of the crusaders. It is also true that a pragmatist may lack an overall blueprint or design for American foreign policy. But this does not mean that the pragmatic mind is unable to conceive a general philosophy. The crucial difference is this: the pragmatist always tests his design against the facts of his experience. If the design does not hold up against the facts, the design will have to change. The crusader, on the other hand, tends to sacrifice unwelcome facts on the altar of a fixed idea. (Stoessinger, 1985: 317–318)

Stoessinger maintains that America's foreign policy leaders in the twentieth century have included both crusaders and pragmatists. Crusaders, by his account, are those whose policies generally ended in failure, namely, Woodrow Wilson, John Foster Dulles, General Douglas MacArthur, Lyndon B. Johnson, and Richard M. Nixon. Among the pragmatists were Harry S Truman, John F. Kennedy, and, to some extent, Henry Kissinger—leaders whose policies largely engineered successful accommodations to the exigencies of the times in which they held power. Jimmy Carter is depicted as falling somewhere between the crusader and the pragmatist, and Franklin D. Roosevelt is held up as the ideal—unique in combining the qualities of the two basic personality types by tempering idealistic concern with an overriding concern for doing what worked. Ronald Reagan, on the other hand, stands as "the classic crusader."

> President Reagan's foreign policy was based on deeply held ideological convictions: of these, the most important was anti-communism. . . . During his first term, the President did not seek to correct this devil image with new facts. He surrounded himself with like minded men. Not only did he choose not to visit Soviet Russia, but he was content to receive a series of one-page "mini-memos" summarizing foreign and defense problems and a foreign policy paper of ten pages or more once a month. Facts would only confuse these powerful convictions, rooted deeply in Ronald Reagan's past. . . . Ronald Reagan's shallow knowledge of history and foreign policy thus snared him into several serious mistakes, but he was never trapped as Lyndon Johnson was. The crusader and the actor inhabited his soul in equal measure. (Stoessinger, 1985: 312, 314)

Stoessinger concludes that the best foreign policymakers are those whose pragmatic realism predominates over the compulsion to play the role of crusading evangelist. The conclusion is not beyond dispute, of course. But as Barber's and Stoessinger's interpretations indicate, past leaders have undoubtedly left their imprint on history, as Stoessinger observes, "for better or for worse."

PERSONALITY TRAITS AND FOREIGN POLICY ORIENTATIONS: AN ALTERNATIVE APPROACH

An analogous approach to assessing the impact of individual idiosyncracies is to investigate personality traits and the foreign policy beliefs associated with them.

The number of available personality-trait classifications is large. Unfortunately, most are based almost exclusively on samples of the entire U.S. population instead of elites. Nevertheless, ten types of personalities, representing clusters of traits, are especially important in foreign policy-making:[4]

- *The Nationalist.* Nationalism is a state of mind that gives primary loyalty to one nation-state to the exclusion of other possible objects of affection (such as family, other countries, or extranational entities like the European Community or a religion). Nationalists glorify their own nation and exaggerate its virtues, while denigrating others. Because nationalists develop an ego involvement with their state, they tend to defend its right to superiority (Stagner, 1971).
- *The Militarist.* Militarism defines the individual's attitude toward aggression. The militarist views hostility as unexceptional and accepts the use of force as a legitimate means to achieve national goals. Research offers little support for the often popular impression that aggressiveness is rooted in human nature (Maslow, 1966). On the contrary, an individual's predisposition toward aggressiveness is a learned trait.
- *The Conservative.* Conservatism is a psychological concept denoting a cluster of interrelated personality characteristics rather than a political philosophy. It refers to hostility and suspicion, rigidity and compulsiveness, intolerance, and perceptual and judgmental inflexibility. Included is the inclination to condemn others' weakness and imperfection and to blame the disadvantaged for their misfortunes. Lacking compassion, the conservative has a need to discern hierarchy and rank and to resolve self-doubts by exaggerating others' inferiorities (''I'm OK—you're so-so''). The conservative is said to greet new ideas not with curiosity but with fear. Conservative dispositions are found most often among the uninformed, the poorly educated, the less intelligent, and among those who are socially isolated yet conforming, submissive, and wanting in self-confidence (McClosky, 1958).
- *The Pragmatist.* Expediency, intellectualism, impatience, eagerness, ambition, detachment, experimentalism, and tough-minded bravado are characteristic of a pragmatic temperament. ''Pragmatists are interested in what works; their prime criterion of value is success. It is the very definition of pragmatism to turn away from a belief in fixed principles toward the truth of concrete results'' (Miroff, 1976). Pragmatists' need for control overwhelms their fear of power; indeed, they are drawn to it, tempted by it, and eager to exercise it to get things done without regard for ideals and morality. As Kennedy may illustrate (Miroff, 1976), pragmatists' dispassionate pursuit of rational solutions

---

4. Useful elaborations of the personality types discussed below can be found in Hermann with Milburn (1977), Hopple (1982), Kreml (1977), Levinson (1957), McClosky (1958), Rokeach (1960), and Stagner (1971). Note that the categories are based on individuals' attitudes, motives, decision styles, personalities, role perceptions, beliefs, and values; the approach assumes that all of those factors are interrelated in the delineation of types of dispositions.

and promising results may violate moral principles and rationalize the violation with the classic excuse that "the ends justify the means."

- *The Paranoid.* Paranoia is a psychoneurotic disorder characterized by excessive suspicion, fear, and distrust of others. Paranoids believe that people are out to "get" them, and their expectation becomes the driving force behind their behavior. Normally, we do not expect politicians to manifest such symptoms. But under stressful conditions they may be prone to display some characteristics of the disorder, the effects of which can impair the performance of their roles. As mentioned earlier, the first secretary of defense, James Forrestal, is an example (Rogow, 1963). A dogmatic sense of certainty, superiority, and self-confidence are aspects of the paranoid temperament that coexist alongside mistrust and fear of deception (as psychobiographies of classic paranoids, Adolf Hitler and Joseph Stalin, reveal). The tendency of some Americans holding positions of power to think conspiratorially has provoked inquiry into *The Paranoid Style in American Politics* (Hofstadter, 1965), as one classic work on the subject is titled. Paranoids fear both foreigners and citizens of their own country.

- *The Machiavellian.* Deriving its name from the philosopher to the prince of Florence in Renaissance Italy, Machiavellianism is a personality syndrome emphasizing strategy and manipulation over principle and sentiment. The need to acquire power, and to exercise it effectively, dominates the Machiavellian's attention above all other values; indeed, conventional morality, love for and empathy toward others, and ideological goals may all be sacrificed if they interfere with the ability to control others. For it is the cold exploitation of others that gives greatest satisfaction to the Machiavellian. Politicians who display that syndrome are motivated most by the desire to win and by the fear of losing; they seek to exercise influence for the satisfaction, prestige, and arousal of emotions it provokes in others, and not for the sake of demeaning opponents or to carry out a policy program. Because taking advantage of others is their primary motive, Machiavellians provoke competition and take risks in order to create opportunities for gaining concessions (Christie and Geis, 1970). This trait is strongly associated with the psychological need for power (McClelland, 1975).

- *The True Believer. Fanatic, ideologue, terrorist,* and *crusader* are words often associated with true believers. They are the joiners of mass religious, political, or ideological movements. Whether militant Christians, nationalists, ideological terrorists, communists, or fascists, true believers share with others of like mind the need to join a cause and to sacrifice themselves for its advancement. Their willingness is not necessarily animated by the power of ideas, for true believers will join any movement that fulfills their need for something to worship and perhaps for which to die. The need to join a cause—any cause—is rooted in personal frustration, low self-esteem, a sense of humiliation, a craving for status, and a search for control of one's life. Adherents seek to lose themselves in a glorified mass movement and to regain a sense of personal worth by identifying totally with the doctrine or group, the status and power of which will confer status and power on them. Because true believers need to believe in the absolute truth and virtue of their chosen movement, they are motivated to coerce people to their way of life and to compete with all other movements outside it. For instance, fanatical patriots (that is, extreme nationalists or chauvinists) who place their country above everything else (including themselves) are intolerant of foreigners and seek to spread their nation's way of life worldwide. Eric Hoffer's (1951) *The True Believer* remains the definitive exposition of this mentality.

- *The Authoritarian*. Authoritarianism is a constellation of predispositions including the propensity to conform and to adhere to conventional values while condemning those who reject such values. Authoritarians crave authority; they submissively and uncritically obey leaders while abusing the rights of subordinates. Authoritarians think in terms of stereotypes; they see themselves as victims, are cynical about other people's motives, and value force and order (Adorno et al., 1950).

- *The Antiauthoritarian*. In contrast to the preceding category, antiauthoritarianism refers to a partially integrated attitude syndrome exhibited by introspective people uncomfortable with order and power. Antiauthoritarians impulsively embrace left-wing political views emphasizing idealism, optimism, and a preference for change (Kreml, 1977).

- *The Dogmatist*. The dogmatic personality has a closed mind. Dogmatists, who typically are prisoners of past attitudes, form opinions and refuse to modify them despite contrary evidence. Unreceptive to forming new images, they are intolerant of ambiguity and inconsistent information. Perceptual inflexibility is particularly endemic, as is passionate attachment to authority figures. Established doctrines are important to the dogmatist; hence, dogmatism is equated with rigidity (Rokeach, 1960).

These ten personality syndromes are examples of categories of personality traits that may have relevance to foreign policy. The types are neither exhaustive nor mutually exclusive, as some are often associated with others. Additional constructs relevant to policy making have also been identified. For example, Harold D. Lasswell (1930) examined politicians' attitudes and dispositions and deduced the existence of three basic types of figures: the agitator, the administrator, and the theorist. Similarly, Jeane Kirkpatrick (1974), Reagan's first ambassador to the United Nations, has differentiated four types of (female) politicians: the leader, the personalizer, the moralizer, and the problem solver.

Distinguishing among personality traits is important because the categories provide tools for explaining leaders' behavior and for making predictions. Predictions are possible (though not always accurate) because the traits possessed by a leader influence his or her response to international events (Pruitt, 1965). Personality traits also operate as a prime determinant of foreign policy attitudes. Some illustrations of the more firmly substantiated findings may suffice to indicate how a leader's traits may affect views taken toward international affairs.

Nationalism and Foreign Aggressiveness

Generally speaking, the more nationalistic the policymaker, the more warlike and aggressive will be the person's foreign policy attitudes. Leaders maintaining strong attachments to their nation are prone to emit hostility, loathing, and toughness toward foreigners. They frequently perceive international conflict and competition as inevitable and therefore appropriate. Nationalists oppose transcendent policies that compromise national sovereignty and privilege. They also oppose foreign aid when given for others' benefit. On the other hand, nationalists tend to advocate policies that promote their nation's immediate self-interests over others' welfare, and they promote policies that accentuate differences between their country and others. In general, nationalists advocate national self-interest as the supreme foreign policy principle.

Authoritarianism and Policy Consistency

Authoritarians form and maintain attitudes in conformity with the groups of which they are a part. They reject new information running counter to prior images and search for information that reinforces existing beliefs. Such individuals base actions on opinion and affections rather than facts and inquiry. Once committed to a position, they are reluctant to change it. With respect to foreign policy, the goals of a state controlled by an authoritarian individual (for example, Germany under Hitler) are unlikely to show significant change. The reason is that the behavior of authoritarians is governed by the psychological need for consistent images. Their emphasis on protocol and rule-based procedures reinforces policy consistency. States run by authoritarian personalities are thus not inclined toward foreign policy innovation. Authoritarianism also correlates with isolationist foreign policy attitudes, Cold War thinking, and resistance to international conciliation (Levinson, 1957; Rosenberg, 1967).

Conservatism and Isolationism

The conservative personality holds a pessimistic view of both human nature and the human prospect and accordingly sees inequality between nations as an inevitable, if not preferable, feature of international affairs. Foreigners are seen as threatening outsiders. The best way to deal with other nations, the conservative personality would believe, is to avoid them. Both isolationists and conservatives are reluctant to become involved with others or to assume responsibility for them. They oppose the rearranging of institutions for the purpose of correcting imbalances or promoting social and economic equality. They resist legislation that might interfere with a man's (or a nations's) autonomy and the disposition of his property, and they are, for the most part, inhospitable to social change. There is in both conservatism and most forms of isolationism the . . . same implicit belief that one's own good fortune—and, by extension, the nation's good fortune—is part of the natural order of things. (McClosky, 1967: 84)

Isolationism is also closely correlated with aversive (tending to avoid, shut out, deny) dispositions rather than appetitive (tending to embrace, reach out, accept) temperaments. Generally, members of the mass public endorse isolationist policies more enthusiastically than do American leaders, and isolationist attitudes are most prevalent among the less educated segments of society (McClosky, 1967; Wittkopf, 1990).

These illustrations barely scratch the surface in describing the potential correlation between personality traits and foreign policy beliefs. The danger with such suggestive correlations is that they tempt one to assume that they can be used safely to predict the behavior of each individual. The correlations describe relationships based on collectivities and do not necessarily hold for each individual within them. But if we want to anticipate the foreign policy orientation of a particular leader, we can classify him or her by observation of personality traits and then predict the expected foreign policy orientation, providing we recognize the limitations of this approach. To illustrate how a leader's personality traits may influence policy preferences, let us consider an example.

John Foster Dulles and the Soviet Union   According to an authoritative interpretation (Holsti, 1962), former Secretary of State John Foster Dulles's behavior toward the Soviet Union was driven by his prior beliefs rather than Soviet conduct. "Built on the trinity of atheism, totalitarianism, and communism, capped by a deep belief that no enduring social order could be erected upon such foundations," his belief system was predicated on three strong convictions: (1) whereas the Russian people were basically good, the Soviet leaders were irredeemably bad; (2) Soviet national interest, which sought to preserve the state, was good, in contrast to implacably bad atheistic international communism; and (3) the Soviet state was good whereas the Communist party was bad (Holsti, 1962).

What were the sources of Dulles's beliefs? His perceptions were shaped in part by his childhood experiences, his relationship with his parents and his peer groups, and his psychological needs and personal predispositions—his basic personality. Dulles came from a celebrated, well-connected elite background that boasted two previous secretaries of state. He presumably inherited his moralistic, evangelic attitude toward most issues from his father, a stern Presbyterian minister. Indeed, Dulles was perhaps the most unabashed moralist ever to sit in the office of the secretary of state (Barnet, 1972), for whom the purpose of policy was the pursuit of morality. He believed that the Cold War was basically a moral, rather than a political, conflict. To his frame of mind, the "insincere," "immoral," and "brutal" Soviet leadership was hateful because its creed was "godless." Two universal faiths competed, one good and the other evil; symbolically, Dulles routinely carried a copy of the New Testament in one coat pocket and a copy of Marx's *Communist Manifesto* in the other (Hoopes, 1973a). No compromise could be made with a philosophy opposed to religion.

Other aspects of Dulles's background may also have affected his later outlook. For instance, Dulles's early training and practice in business law may have inculcated an aggressive "can do" attitude, "an inspired ability to calculate risks and gamble on them," and a habit of mind that "carried over into his diplomacy, where countries 'were all instinctively rivals and opponents of his own client, America' " (Barnet, 1972). Moreover, his personal views may have been a product of his "establishment" and elitist background. As Dulles's biographer Richard S.M. Goold-Adams observes:

> [Dulles] was never in touch with people who knew hunger, poverty, or personal failure. Believing in addition that everyone must make the most of themselves in life and that those who do not have something wrong with them, he never seriously tried to understand the people whose misfortune it is to get left on the bottom rungs of the ladder. (cited in Barnet, 1972: 59)

A self-described conservative with a strong authoritarian bent, Dulles's conduct exhibited the traits associated with those personality types. His attitude toward the weak and poor was indicative of his conservative mind: adversity and poverty are the fault and character weaknesses of the victim and serve as a measure of their worth. His authoritarianism as secretary of state was legendary: back your superior, buck your subordinates. Dulles "demanded what he called 'positive loyalty' from all employees of the State Department, but he felt none himself toward subordinates who were unjustly attacked by McCarthy" (Barnet, 1972) for their alleged but unverified communist sympathies.

As secretary of state, Dulles's rigid, doctrinaire beliefs and personality traits predetermined his reactions to the Soviets, and led him to distort information so as to reduce any discrepancies between his knowledge and his perceptions (Holsti, 1962). Dulles's psychological need for image maintenance led him to reject all information that conflicted with his preexisting belief that the Soviet Union could not be trusted. Friendly Soviet initiatives were seen as deception rather than as true efforts to reduce tension. For example, Soviet military demobilizations were attributed to necessity (particularly economic weakness) and bad faith (the released men would be put to work on more lethal weapons); similarly, the Austrian State Treaty[5] was explained as Soviet frustration (the failure of its European policy) and weakness (their system was "on the point of collapse") (Holsti, 1962). Thus in Dulles's image the Soviets could do

---

5. The Austrian State Treaty, initiated by the Soviet Union, called for the peaceful withdrawal of Soviet and American occupation forces from Austria in return for the promise that the Austrians would maintain a policy of neutrality in the East-West dispute.

only harm and no good. If they acted cooperatively, it was either because they were dealing from a position of weakness or because they were trying to deceive the United States into a position of unpreparedness. When they did anything bad, it supported Dulles's prior image that the Soviets were incapable of virtuous behavior. The Cold War policies of John Foster Dulles, it is safe to say, were derived largely from his entrenched negative beliefs—what Henry Kissinger (1962) termed an "inherent bad faith" model of the Soviet leadership.

Dulles's inflexible image and his unwillingness to accept any uncomfortable information was reinforced by his extreme faith in his own judgment and lack of respect for that of others, whom he regarded as his inferiors. Dulles felt "he was uniquely qualified to assess the meaning of Soviet policy. This sense of indispensability carried over into the day-to-day operations of policy formulation, and during his tenure as Secretary of State he showed a marked lack of receptivity to advice" (Holsti, 1962).

Dulles's policy conduct thus was greatly rooted in his belief system and personality traits. The Dulles example makes a convincing case for the influence of individual variables on policy behavior.

Other Examples The diplomatic record is replete with other examples demonstrating that personality influences foreign policy making. There was, for instance, Johnson's intense need to be loved and feel in control of his fate, and his subsequent penchant during the Vietnam War to surround himself with advisers who provided him information he wanted to hear—that his popularity with the American people was enduring, and that the war was going well (Kearns, 1976).[6] Or take Henry Kissinger's need for personal acceptance, his reputed distrust of democratic foreign policy, and his intolerance of dissent, and note in turn his insistence on secrecy, his "taste for solo performances," and his substitution of private for public diplomacy (Starr, 1984).

Consider as well Truman, a president who "was prone to back up his subordinates to an extent that was indiscriminate" (DeRivera, 1968). A decisive person, Truman expected loyalty and was intolerant of disrespect. Hence when he was confronted with blatant insubordination from General Douglas MacArthur (an authoritarian who wanted to call the shots and expand the war with the communists in Asia), the president dealt with this insubordination decisively: "You're fired!" Able to give loyalty himself, Truman expected and demanded it from others.

---

6. Equally evident was Johnson's immense ego involvement with affairs of state, which led him, like other presidents, to "personify" the policies he devised for the nation and to think of himself as the embodiment of the nation itself. The "personalization" of foreign policy was illustrated by Johnson's statements regarding his Vietnam policies: "By 1965, Johnson was speaking of 'my Security Council,' 'my State Department,' 'my troops.' It was *his* war, *his* struggle; when the Vietcong attacked, they attacked *him*. On one occasion, a young soldier, escorting him to an army helicopter, said: 'This is your helicopter, sir.' 'They are *all* my helicopters, son,' Johnson replied" (Stoessinger, 1985). "The White House machinery became the President's psyche writ large" (Kearns, 1976).

President Eisenhower illustrates the difficulties of evaluating the psychological bases of diplomatic conduct. His style is not easily interpreted because his low-profile approach produced results that were not at the time recognized as a part of his design. Historians have reevaluated his presidency and now see strength and command where previously they perceived inattention and indifference to the duties of office (see Ambrose, 1983). Eisenhower's personality contributed to his "hidden hand" (low-key, publicity-avoiding) managerial approach and its quiet effectiveness (see Greenstein, 1982).

And the perplexing case of Richard Nixon lingers. Some of Nixon's conduct, both in and out of office, appears explicable only in terms of his private conflicts and emotional problems. Consider David Abrahamsen's (1977) psychoanalytic probing, which diagnosed Nixon as a disturbed personality, at war with himself since the traumatic events and parental disputes of his unhappy childhood. Those conflicts were never resolved, making Nixon unstable, indecisive, and, above all, self-consciously unsure of himself; they account for Nixon's obvious discomfort in the White House, his inability to maintain warm personal relationships, his paranoid distrust of those around him, his self-absorption, and his competitive, adversarial approach toward his political opponents. By conquering and destroying in order to become the "victor," Nixon could temporarily remove his self-doubts and submerge his private conflicts. But those personal problems may have subconsciously attracted Nixon to failure, because inwardly he felt inadequate and suspected that he did not deserve better. Decisions motivated by such personal factors may have led to the tragedies of Vietnam and Watergate (Abrahamsen, 1977).

These examples certainly suggest that the content and conduct of American foreign policy may in some instances be profoundly influenced by the personal characteristics of U.S. policymakers. But the occasions when that influence might be felt and the extent to which it might be felt will be limited by a variety of factors.

LIMITS ON THE EXPLANATORY POWER OF INDIVIDUAL FACTORS

Can continuities and change in postwar American foreign policy be traced to leaders' personal attributes? As intuitively inviting as that interpretation might be, it ignores the fact that individuals are only one of several sources of American foreign policy, any one of which can limit severely the impact that leaders exert on the direction of foreign policy. The question, then, is under what conditions are leaders' individual characteristics likely to be influential?

When Are Individual Factors Influential?

In general, the influence of personal characteristics on policy-making conduct *increases* in particular circumstances:

- *The higher the individual is in the decision-making structure.* The higher one climbs in the hierarchy of the foreign affairs government, the more the occupant's personality will affect policy.
- *The more ambiguous and complex the decision-making situation.* Because people respond to bewildering and uncertain situations emotionally rather than rationally and calmly, perceptions of circumstances are important. At least four types of foreign policy situations bring psychological (nonlogical) drives into play because they are especially ambiguous: new situations, in which the individual has had little previous experience and few familiar cues to assist in the definition of the situation; complex situations, which involve a large number of different factors; contradictory situations, which encompass many inconsistencies and incompatibilities; and situations devoid of social sanctions, which permit freedom of choice because societal definitions of appropriate options are unclear (DiRenzo, 1974).
- *The greater the self-confidence and ego of the individual.* Decision makers' subjective faith in their own ability to control events—their self-esteem, self-confidence, and belief in themselves—strongly determines the extent to which they will dare to allow their own preferences to set policy directions (DeRivera, 1968). Conversely, when such assurance (or narcissistic ego inflation) are absent, self-doubt will inhibit risk-taking and leadership.
- *The greater the personal involvement of the individual in the situation.* When people believe their own interests and welfare to be at stake, their response is governed primarily by their private psychological needs. They cease to appear cool and rational and begin to act emotionally. Compare student behavior when mechanically taking class notes during a lecture with behavior when called on to recite or when negotiating with a professor over an exam grade. Likewise, when policymakers assume personal responsibility for policy management (and become ego involved in outcomes), their reactions frequently display heightened emotion and their personality is revealed. Contrast President Johnson's behavior with respect to Vietnam in 1963 (cautious) with his behavior in 1968 (excited, compulsive), by which time the war had become "his war."
- *The less information available.* When facing a decision in which pertinent information is unavailable, gut likes or dislikes tend to dictate policy choices. Conversely, "the more information an individual has about international affairs, the less likely is it that his behavior will be based upon non-logical influences" (Verba, 1969). Other things being equal, ample information may reduce the probability that decisions will be based on psychological drives and personal needs.
- *The more recent or dramatic the assumption of power.* When an individual first enters office, the formal requirements of the role are least likely to circumscribe what he or she can do. That holds true espe-

cially for newly elected presidents, who routinely are allowed a "honeymoon" period during which they are relatively free of criticism and extraordinary pressure. So, too, cabinet officials and other top-level officials usually experience a brief period during which their personal freedom is great and their decisions encounter little resistance. Moreover, when a leader comes to office following a dramatic event (a landslide election or the assassination of a predecessor), "the new high-level political leader can institute his policies almost with a free hand. Constituency criticism is held in abeyance during this time" (Hermann, 1976).

Thus, while interpretations of American conduct in light of individual idiosyncrasies are useful in some circumstances, they can be misleading in others. Innate drives and personal predispositions are not all-powerful determinants of foreign policy behavior in all contexts. Rather, they vary in terms of the nature of the concrete decision, the decision maker's psychological disposition toward the situation, and his or her subjective definition of its importance.

We can carry such reasoning one step further by suggesting a corollary hypothesis: the potency of leaders' personal characteristics as policy determinants will increase when those decisions center on broad, abstract conceptions of the nation's basic policy goals. That is, unlike occasions when a policymaker is asked to find a pragmatic solution to a specific problem, when attention focuses on doctrinal and ideological issues, leaders' values, fundamental beliefs and inner needs will be especially influential.

Consider the divergent postures assumed by past presidents on the issue of containing communism. In the specific context of Indochina, where five different presidents were confronted with the necessity of deciding if and how a "war" with communism should be waged, personality became a visible influence on how each reacted. As a former policy planner illustrates:

> Truman was obdurate, tough, and determined to demonstrate these traits in his policies. . . . [He] felt challenged by the rise of communism in Southeast Asia and became determined to arrest it. Eisenhower, far more at ease in the office, accustomed to high command, and not in need of establishing his credentials as a tough leader with the Congress, was relatively relaxed and more aloof. He alone among the five presidents involved was able to absorb a defeat to communism in Indochina [that of the French] and to provide such a defeat with a domestic appearance of success by way of gradually increasing U.S. responsibility in Southeast Asia. . . . Kennedy was sophisticated, eager, and daring to the point of adventurousness. He accordingly did not shy away from undertaking new commitments. . . . Johnson suffered from the combination of an enormous inferiority complex in regard to handling affairs of state, and an enormous feeling of superiority, experience, and self-confidence in handling and manipulating the movers, shakers, and sleepers in American politics. His inferiority complex . . . put him in wholly unwarranted awe of the national security and foreign affairs expert advisers he inherited from Kennedy [and] the intellectuals who surrounded him. . . . Accordingly, Johnson accepted the ill-conceived scenarios of the graduated escalation school of thought in regard to Vietnam. . . . Finally,

> Nixon's negative manipulative traits of a highly insecure (proto-paranoid) but extremely ambitious power-seeker . . . led him to deceive the public into believing he was withdrawing from Vietnam when in fact he was not only continuing but intensifying the war. . . . He managed also to convince the public that he was turning defeat in Vietnam into standoff . . . by changing the most fundamental premise of American foreign policy, namely, the coequation in the U.S. public's mind of American security with the defeat of communism everywhere. (Kattenburg, 1980: 227)

Personality factors thus influenced significantly the approach five different presidents took toward the same basic challenge, namely, how best to react to the perception of a communist threat in Southeast Asia. Although the problem was roughly the same, their reactions were quite different.

In addition to the argument that personal predispositions influence policy when the focus is on abstract principles, the proposition that individual factors become especially powerful policy determinants under conditions of national crisis is compelling. It is not an accident that the great leaders of history have customarily arisen during periods of extreme challenge. The moment may make the person, rather than the person the moment, in the sense that crisis can liberate a gifted leader from the constraints that normally would inhibit his or her capacity to engineer change. During crises, decision making tends to be centralized and handled exclusively by the top leadership. The situation is ambiguous and threatening. Elites become personally involved in policy management and perceive themselves responsible for its outcome. And crucial information is usually unavailable. At such times the individual leader's personality has often been determinative especially because the usual institutional barriers to decisive action are suspended. In a situation that simultaneously challenges the will of a nation and the self-esteem of the president, governmental decision processes can easily become fused with the chief executive's psychodynamic processes; and the resolution of a policy crisis under such circumstances could depend ultimately on the outcome of a personal, emotional crisis (DiRenzo, 1974).[7]

It is instructive to note in this context that the influence of personality on the decisions of American foreign policymakers have been especially strong when the use of force has been involved (Etheredge, 1978). Conversely, under more routine circumstances, the policymakers' personalities have been much less influential. The interesting question is, therefore, how different are the personalities of those in the decision-making elite?

Do Policy-Making Elites and Politicians Have Similar Personality Profiles?

In terms of background and experience, a remarkably homogeneous collection of people have made up America's postwar foreign policy establishment. Recall

---

7. We will return in Chapter 15 to a more thorough discussion of decision making in crisis situations.

from Chapter 8 the similarities of those who have managed American foreign policy since 1945. To be sure, America's postwar presidents and advisers have displayed different personality predispositions and espoused different beliefs (Holsti and Rosenau, 1984; Wittkopf, 1990). But these elite differences nonetheless mask important similarities. Several considerations support that observation.

It is commonly assumed that positions of power and prestige command respect and honor and therefore are naturally desired by nearly everyone. ("In America, anyone can grow up to be President.") But are they? It may be more realistic to recognize that only a small proportion of the American public even desires the power of public office. Moreover, those who do become involved or active politically constitute a very small portion of the citizenry.

When we carefully examine America's postwar foreign policymakers, we discover that they share a distinctive set of personal characteristics that set them apart from the average person. Participation in politics and political aspiration may be functions of personality, with the consequence that those who seek top positions share psychological traits that make them more like one another and less like "average" Americans.

Those attracted to political careers conventionally are thought to possess an instinct for power; political leaders are power seekers. They choose to struggle in the corridors of power. What motivates their choice? The classic psychological interpretation sees "political man" attempting to overcome poor self-images: "The power seeker . . . pursues power as a means of compensation against deprivation. *Power is expected to overcome low estimates of the self*, by either changing the traits of the self or of the environment in which it functions" (Lasswell, 1974). Accordingly, politicians seek positions of power that confer attention and that command deference, respect, and status, in order to overcome their personal sense of inadequacy. Erich Fromm has argued in a similar vein that "the lust for power is rooted in weakness and not in strength, and that fundamentally this motive is a desperate attempt to gain secondary strength where genuine strength is lacking" (cited in DiRenzo, 1974).

The disturbing suggestion here is that policymakers are power-hungry. Though they may claim they enter politics to do good and serve the public, in fact they subconsciously seek leadership to compensate for their personal insecurities and to bolster their own self-esteem by holding power over others. Bruce Buchanan describes this conventional view of presidential aspirants' motives.

> Recent national experience—and common sense—tell us that those who make the final presidential sweepstakes are men of near fanatical personal ambition who show themselves willing to sacrifice health, family, peace of mind, and principle in order to win the prize. To the question, "What price success?" presidential candidates are near-unanimous in responding: "Any price." (Buchanan, 1978: 154)[8]

---

8. "This kind of preoccupation with personal success," adds Buchanan (1978), "is neither characteristic of, nor does it favor the prospects of, moderate or temperate people. Rather it suggests that aggressive types—some positive, some negative—will prevail."

This image of leaders' psychological motives can easily be exaggerated. Although politicians may be similar in their need and desire for power,[9] clear differences in motivation and belief are also evident, as a comparison of Jimmy Carter's preference for accommodation, Cyrus Vance's emphasis on principled conduct, and Zbigniew Brzezinski's concern for power politics illustrates.

Generalizations about the *response* of people to the acquisition of power are less risky, perhaps. For if the motives that drive individuals to seek positions of authority are mixed, their reactions to the privileges and ascribed importance of the office are relatively patterned. Those with power, whether conferred by election or appointment to high positions, tend to become personally absorbed in the roles they play, to let their egos and identity become involved with these roles, and to become intoxicated with the sense of power, purpose, and importance they derive from the experience. After all, they find themselves making history, attended by press and public. Even the most self-assured individuals can easily confuse personal identity with the role played and to mistake the power conferred by the position for personal power. The next step is to inflate their own importance in the overall scheme of things: to think that they have made things happen when in fact things have happened only because of the power they control, or to assume that, being powerful, they are indispensable. Individuals playing roles often become in their own mind the masks they wear. As John Kenneth Galbraith observes, bureaucrats and officials

> enjoy power not by personal right but from association. An official of the Pentagon or the State Department is dispensing authority that derives not from his personal qualities but from the majesty and power of the United States. There is interesting proof of the point in the life style of . . . an American ambassador to a country of more than marginal consequence [who] is accorded considerable deference by most people, including himself, until the day he retires. Then he disappears. . . . It was the United States . . . that made the man important and not, unhappily, any quality of the man himself. This fact, not surprisingly, quite a few organization men fail to grasp. In consequence, they parade the power under the impression it is their own. The contrast between the biggest authority and the smallest man is an unpleasant thing to see. (Galbraith, 1973: 315)

Galbraith's point is important in understanding the alleged influence of individuals on the nation's destiny: the office can make the person as much as the person can make the office. People become elites only because they occupy elite positions and not because, as they sometimes assume, they are inherently special. In that respect the impact of the office on the office-holder makes those in the foreign policy elite more alike than different.

---

9. Even that generalization must be qualified by cognizance of the existence of "power seekers" in other occupations as well.

Do Individuals Make a Difference?
Psychological Limits on Policy Change

> In a sense, I had known that "power" might feel like this, just as I had known, before I ever had a drink, that whiskey goes to the head. The taste of power, or whatever it was that I tasted that first day, went to my head too, but not quite as I had been warned it would. I had come into the office with projects and plans. And I was caught in an irresistible movement of paper, meetings, ceremonies, crises, trivialities. There were uncleared paragraphs and cleared ones, and people waiting for me to tell them what my plans were, and people doing things that had nothing to do with my plans. I had moved into the middle of a flow of business that I hadn't started and wouldn't be able to stop. There were people in place to handle this flow, and established machinery in operation to help me deal with it. The entire system was at my disposal. In a word, I had power. And power had me. (Frankel, 1969: 5–6)

This recollection by a new policymaker of his first day in office illuminates the connection between policymaker and policy position. The policy-making system influences the behavior of those who work within it.[10] Although we cannot speak precisely about what makes a politician a politician, our discussion in the previous chapter documented the similarity of outlook among those who occupy roles within the foreign affairs government—regardless, by implication, of the idiosyncratic variations among the individuals themselves and their projects and plans. As individuals enter new groups, they experience enormous pressure to conform to the prevailing and preexisting views of that group. They find that they must "go along to get along." Rewarded for accepting the views of their superiors and predecessors, and punished or ostracized for questioning them, few resist.[11] Authority and tradition are seldom challenged.

---

10. Zbigniew Brzezinski, President Carter's national security adviser, describes these influences thus:

> To succeed at the top in government you need strong nerves and a thick skin. Public officials today are so exposed that they're subjected to continuous criticism from within the government and outside it—and a lot of it tends to be ad hominem—so a thick skin is an absolute prerequisite.
>
> You are also continuously under pressure. If you are at the very top in the White House, you are working 15 to 16 hours a day in 5-to-7 minute fragments, occasionally interspersed with sessions of up to an hour that shift from topic to topic, from event to event. That imposes enormous strains.
>
> When the pressure is high, it's essential to be very low-key and to cool everybody's moods rather than contribute to a heightened sense of anxiety and tension. . . .
>
> It's important not only to have control over your emotions but also over your schedule and work habits. That means discriminating about what you want to do and, once you have made that decision, acting expeditiously. Never let your desk be cluttered or your briefcase overflow.
>
> Beyond that, it's crucial to come into government with a larger perspective of what you wish to accomplish, with clear priorities because, once in office, you tend to be so overwhelmed by events that it is very easy to lose perspective and get absorbed in specifics. You can become increasingly responsive to situations rather than using your power to shape situations and to define outcomes. (*U.S. News & World Report*, May 20, 1985, p. 65)

This psychological tendency to accept the views of those with whom individuals interact frequently is sobering. It suggests that certain types of situations elicit certain uniform behaviors regardless of the different kinds of personalities involved. Because people behave differently when in different groups and when engaged in different activities, it is uncommon for all but those with unusually strong personalities to resist group pressures and role demands. All people are inclined to adapt themselves and sometimes their personalities to their roles or positions (see Lieberman, 1965), each of which has certain expected ways of behaving and attitudes associated with it and each of which is governed to a large extent by a preexisting set of decision norms embedded in and reinforced by the force of a social process within an institutional structure. All occupants of those roles tend to conform to the rituals, vocabulary, and beliefs defined by them.[12] That applies to the office of the presidency as well. In fact, the formal and informal norms of that office in particular—the demands of the job, its constitutional obligations, and its public pressures—may permit less freedom of individual expression than almost any other. "Both its prominence and its symbolic functions make the presidential office a more important molder of its incumbents than any other in the nation" (Truman, 1951). Indeed, "the historical consistency of the president's responsibilities produces a like consistency in the kinds of exposures he will encounter as he goes about the business of performing his functions" (Buchanan, 1978). "The higher a man stands in the social scale," Leo Tolstoy observed, "the more manifest is the predetermination and inevitability of his every act."

These pressures suggest a powerful explanation for the persistence and continuity characteristic of postwar American foreign policy: for nearly five decades the individuals who have been part of the policy-making establishment accepted the prevailing image of the world and bent their behavior, and

---

11. The classic research on the tendency of most individuals to conform to the perceived will of the majority was conducted by Asch (1951), who demonstrated that people often yield to group images even when they are perceived to be contrary to fact. This disturbing tendency indicates that independent judgment is often nonexistent in many decision-making situations, but especially in those, like situations involving foreign policy, in which decisions are routinely made in groups. See Janis (1982) for a discussion of this phenomenon in the context of foreign policy making.

12. A review of the research on this phenomenon concludes:

> If there has been one important lesson coming from all the research in social and personality psychology in the past few years, it is that situations control behavior to an unprecedented degree. It is no longer meaningful, as it once was, to talk in terms of personality "types," of persons "low in ego strength," or of "authoritarians"—at least it is not meaningful if we wish to account for any substantial portion of an individual's behavior. . . . Rather, we must look to the situation in which the behavior was elicited and is maintained if we hope ever to find satisfactory explanations for it. The causes of behavior we have learned are more likely to reside in the nature of the environment than inside the person. And although the operation of situational forces can be subtle and complex in the control of behavior, it can also be extremely powerful. . . . Research . . . seems to indicate that . . . [in] "real life" we are often faced with a situation or role which demands behavior of a certain kind and, over a period of time, our beliefs are likely to change in a way consistent with this situation or role behavior. (Haney and Zimbardo, 1973: 40–42)

ultimately their beliefs, to that of their predecessors. As James N. Rosenau (1980) concluded, "Even the President must function within narrowly prescribed limits, so much so that it would be easier to predict the behavior of any President from prior knowledge of the prevailing state of that role than from data pertaining to his past accomplishments, orientations, and experiences." There are definite limits to the amount of change individual leaders can engineer. The external environment, societal factors, governmental characteristics, and role-induced constraints restrict the range of permissible policy choices. Durable policy prescriptions have been advanced for decades, despite changing international circumstances. The names of the actors may have changed in the postwar era, but the script has remained the same.

Additional Restraints on Individual Initiative and Policy Innovation

If the constraints discussed above are not enough, other considerations properly falling within the individual source category also narrow the range of alternatives available to leaders. Among them are the following:

- The tendency of policymakers, like the general public, to maintain preexisting images and to view and interpret new information so as to preserve, rather than change, their perceptual models of reality.
- The propensity of policymakers to avoid decision-making responsibilities altogether by relying on reassuring illusions and rationalizations (Janis, 1989).
- The impact of "organizational norms, routines, and standard operating procedures [which] may . . . constrain the manner in which issues are defined, the range of options that may be considered, and the manner in which executive decisions are implemented by subordinates" (Holsti, 1976).
- The legacy of past policies—in the form of treaties signed with other countries, previous budgetary decisions, prior commitments, and the like—which may reduce considerably the range of available choice and limit changes in existing policy to only incremental revisions.
- The tendency of decision makers to feel subjective, if subconscious, loyalties toward pet programs (and the people associated with them), with the result that they are often reluctant to withdraw support from them despite their diminishing utility.
- The tendency for acquiescent personalities (people who are "team players") to make it to positions of power and for "rugged individualists" and reformers to be systematically selected out.
- The preference of individuals for incremental change, which is encouraged by the tendency of most to focus attention on familiar experiences and to shy away from the unfamiliar.

- The desire of policymakers to be loved and respected together with their concern for earning a "place in history," which instills the preference to do what is popular even if it is unwise.
- The reliance of policymakers on established rules and procedures for decision making.
- The stagnating effect promoted by length in public service—as President Nixon said in 1972, "It is inevitable [that] when an individual has been in a Cabinet position or, for that matter, holds any position in government, after a certain length of time he becomes an advocate of the status quo; rather than running the bureaucracy, the bureaucracy runs him."

When these psychological and circumstantial restraints on policy initiatives are added to the many domestic and external factors discussed in the preceding chapters, we can appreciate why policy "change, as it occurs, does so in acts of renewing, repairing, or improving existing relationships or commencing new ones that correspond to familiar patterns [and why] diplomacy . . . normally resembles more the act of gardening than of bulldozing" (Seabury, 1973).

THE QUESTIONABLE UTILITY OF THE "HERO IN HISTORY" THESIS

The interpretation at the beginning of this chapter articulated a potentially powerful source of change in American foreign policy: since so much authority is concentrated in the hands of so few, it is logical to assume that the decision-making elite in charge of foreign policy can, with relative ease, choose to revise, indeed, revolutionize, America's foreign policy. Change the people in charge, it is assumed, and the policy itself will often change in turn. In other words, when leadership changes, a change in American behavior toward other countries may be expected.

The theory and evidence summarized in this chapter force one to question the utility of this so-called hero in history theory of American foreign policy.[13] At the very least, that theory appears much too simple. By attributing policy variation to a single source, the theory seeks to explain everything and succeeds in explaining little.

Why? To recapitulate, we find that the people who make American foreign policy are not that different from one another after all. Only certain types of people seek positions of power, and top leaders are recruited from similar backgrounds and rise to the top in similar ways. Consequently, they share many

---

13. The terminology is borrowed from the timeless "great man" versus "Zeitgeist" debate. At the core of the controversy is the perhaps unanswerable question of whether the times must be conducive to the emergence of great leaders, or whether, instead, great people would have become famous leaders regardless of when and where they lived. For a discussion, see Greenstein (1969).

attitudes and personality characteristics. Moreover, once in office, their behaviors are shaped by the positions they occupy; they often see their options differently from within the system than they did outside it. They typically conform to the beliefs of their peers and their predecessors, as the pressures imposed by the office and decision-making setting elicit similar policy responses from diverse personalities. The result: different individuals often pursue their predecessors' policies and respond to international events consistently. Postwar American policymakers thus have displayed a propensity for incremental change, perpetuation of established routines of thought and action, and preservation of established policies.

This reasoning invites the conclusion that, even though the president and the immediate circle of presidential advisers constitute one of the most powerful institutions in the world, and even though, in principle, they have the resources to bring about prompt and immediate change by the decisions they make, the fact is that those powers are seldom exercised. In today's complex world, it is difficult for great leaders to ''emerge.'' The consequence: momentous decisions are rare. Personal characteristics influence the style with which decisions are reached, but the overall thrust of American foreign policy has remained patterned. As Ole R. Holsti (1973) puts it, ''Names and faces may change, interests and policies do not.'' Thus Henry Kissinger's comment in 1976 about the forthcoming election remains a timely and telling observation: ''The essential outlines of U.S. policy will remain the same no matter who wins the [next] U.S. Presidential election.''

SUGGESTIONS FOR FURTHER READING

Barber, James David. (1985) *The Presidential Character: Predicting Performance in the White House*, 3rd ed. Englewood Cliffs, N.J.: Prentice-Hall.

Buchanan, Bruce. (1978) *The Presidential Experience: What the Office Does to the Man*. Englewood Cliffs, N.J.: Prentice-Hall.

DeRivera, Joseph H. (1968) *The Psychological Dimension of Foreign Policy.* Columbus, Ohio: Charles E. Merrill.

Etheredge, Lloyd S. (1978) *A World of Men: The Private Sources of American Foreign Policy.* Cambridge, Mass.: MIT Press.

Greenstein, Fred I. (ed.). (1989) *Leadership in the Modern Presidency.* Cambridge, Mass.: Harvard University Press.

Hermann, Margaret G. (1988) ''The Role of Leaders and Leadership in the Making of American Foreign Policy'' pp. 266–284 in Charles W. Kegley, Jr., and Eugene R. Wittkopf, eds., *The Domestic Sources of American Foreign Policy: Insights and Evidence.* New York: St. Martin's.

Janis, Irving L. (1989) *Crucial Decisions: Leadership in Policymaking and Crisis Management.* New York: Free Press.

Kellerman, Barbara, and Ryan J. Barilleaux. (1991) *The President as World Leader.* New York: St. Martin's.

Kelman, Herbert C. (ed.). (1965) *International Behavior: A Social-Psychological Analysis*. New York: Holt, Rinehart and Winston.

Stoessinger, John G. (1985) *Crusaders and Pragmatists: Movers of Modern American Foreign Policy*, 2nd ed. New York: Norton.

PART VIII

Pattern and Process in American Foreign Policy

The Sources of Continuity and Change in American Foreign Policy: A Synthesis and Interpretation

If one looks at this postwar period as a whole, one sees that [American] foreign policy . . . includes a good deal of continuity.
FORMER SECRETARY OF STATE DEAN RUSK, 1989

As if stupefied by the pace of events, many members of the American foreign policy establishment behave like the orphans of containment—clinging to the remains of an obsolete strategy.
HARVARD UNIVERSITY POLITICAL SCIENTIST STANLEY HOFFMANN, 1989

This book's opening chapters documented the narrow range in which America's post–World War II foreign policy has varied. Although nine different presidents have occupied the Oval Office during this period, their core foreign policy assumptions about the need for globalism, anticommunism, containment, military might, and interventionist means have not greatly differed. Those assumptions and the goals they rationalized have remained remarkably continuous, even though profound changes have substantially altered the challenges confronting America's national interests from beyond its borders. Their shadow colors the turbulent diplomatic climate of the 1990s and continues to frame debate about the available options.

In this chapter we explore why policy innovation since the late 1940s has been so unusual by linking the postwar pattern of American foreign policy to the process by which it is formulated and implemented. In so doing we may also gain insight into those forces that may stimulate new patterns—not mere incremental adjustments—as the United States moves toward the new millenium.

EXPLAINING POSTWAR AMERICAN FOREIGN POLICY PATTERNS

As Secretary of State, Henry Kissinger (1977) reflected that American foreign policy emerges "from an amalgam of factors: objective circumstances, domestic pressures, the values of [American] society and the decisions of individual

527

leaders. The relative weight to be given to each," he concluded, shapes "our nation's foreign policy."

Kissinger's timely and timeless rumination reveals a policymaker's acute awareness that the course of American foreign policy is determined by multiple factors. Moreover, it serves to stimulate thinking about the central question to which this book is addressed: What accounts for continuity and change in America's policy response to global developments?

Previous chapters provide some potential answers. In reviewing the independent impact of various causal forces, let us explore whether each explanatory factor is of equal importance and whether their rank in order of importance varies with time and circumstance.

In Chapter 2, we identified five policy sources in a "funnel of causality" (see Figure 2.1) that pictured external, societal, governmental, role, and individual sources combining as inputs into the foreign policy-making process to account collectively for the outputs of that process, namely, U.S. foreign policy conduct. After describing the substance of postwar American foreign policy, that is, its historic pattern, the subsequent chapters then treated each of those major sources in turn, demonstrating how each independently serves to influence the prospects for policy continuity (or change). The presentation began with the most complex set of interrelated variables, the external environment, and worked from there through societal, governmental, role, and individual determinants of policy outcomes. These "inputs" and "outputs" are illustrated in Figure 15.1, which recasts the "funnel of causality" shown in Figure 2.1.

Beginning at the bottom, Figure 15.1 pictures each of the interrelated sources of American foreign policy as "nested" within an ever larger set of variables. The framework views individual decision makers as constrained by their policy-making roles, roles defined by their positions within America's foreign policy-making institutions. Those governmental variables are cast within a more encompassing societal setting, which, in turn, is part of an even larger international environment comprising other nations, nonstate actors, and global trends and issues to which the United States as a global actor responds.

Let us review briefly the influence of each of those source categories so that some observations about their relative potency in explaining patterns in postwar American international behavior may be advanced.

Do Individuals Make a Difference?

Change the people who make the policy, and the policy itself will probably change, so one view has it. However, perusal of this intuitively appealing theory is not altogether persuasive. Henry Kissinger asserted during the 1976 presidential campaign that it really doesn't make a difference who is elected president—the essential outlines of foreign policy will remain the same regardless—and that viewpoint appears to be the more cogent one. Why? As we have seen, similar types of individuals have usually been recruited into

FIGURE 15.1 ▪ The Hierarchy and Interrelationship of the Sources of Foreign Policy

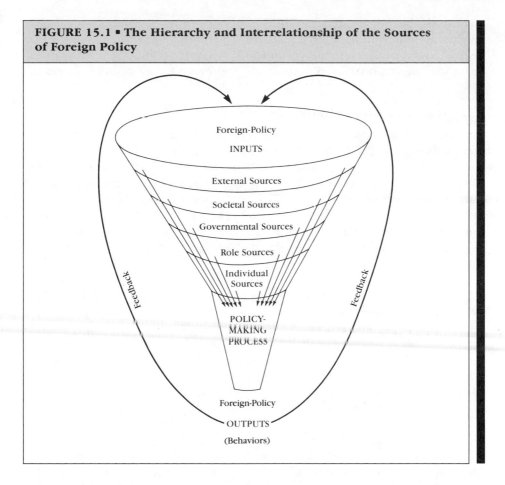

decision-making positions. And many of the same people have held various top-level posts, having entered in one administration and returned through a metaphorical revolving-door to serve in another (carrying their previous policy thinking with them). Moreover, once in office, individuals tend to be shaped by, more than they are able to shape, the roles they occupy. As a result, a policymaker's individuality is reduced: new decision makers often act like and advocate the same kinds of policies as their predecessors. Although changes in personnel often produce changes in style, rhetoric and tactics, such surface changes should not be mistaken for fundamental changes in values and images that give rise to new foreign policy objectives. In short, radical departures from ongoing policy trends are unlikely to result from changes in personnel.

Whereas policy change may be stimulated by action initiated by single individuals, their attempts to engineer policy change seldom succeed without reinforcement from supporting influences emanating from other sources. The type of leader *can* matter greatly (as the exceptional case of Soviet President

Mikhail Gorbachev illustrates). But the exercise of true, visionary leadership may require extraordinary circumstances. The times make leaders; stable times restrain their capacity to move policy in new directions, whereas rapidly changing international conditions create opportunities for policy innovation.

The Organizational Network

Because American foreign policy is decreed and implemented by many government officials, role and governmental variables are influential in shaping the decisions policymakers reach and how they are carried out. Different people have the capacity to act differently, but leaders' roles mold their outlook and restrain their latitude for choice. Thus the policy-making process is greatly influenced by the kinds of behavior bred by the government's roles and institutional structures (behavior encapsulated by President John F. Kennedy's description of Washington—''Southern efficiency, Northern charm'').

Bureaucratization encourages presidential delay, punishes taking a stand, rewards marking time, and spreads responsibility so that no one is blamed for failures. The institutional setting breeds parochialism (agencies pursuing their own narrowly defined purposes) and attitudinal conformity (creativity, dissent, critical thinking, and long-range planning are discouraged, whereas conservatism, timidity, and procrastination are rewarded). In addition, bureaucratic roles are conditioned by intragovernmental politics. Because contending bureaucracies want different things, policy formulation emerges from competitive bargaining, a tug-of-war in which interagency differences are resolved through compromises rather than a careful weighing of the merits of the options.

Other properties also reduce efficiency and constrain presidential initiative. Bureaucratic unresponsiveness to presidential direction is exacerbated by the huge size of the institutional apparatus coupled with its penchant for growth. The fragmentation of power within the multiple channels of this institutional maze is another inertial force. Ironically, the power of the ''sole organ'' of American foreign policy, the president, is circumscribed by the executive branch's own departments and agencies, which limit the president's ability to act. Authority among individual departments is blurred, with the result that policy coordination is difficult. The sometimes clumsy, contradictory, and counterproductive record of postwar American foreign policy actions may be attributed at least in part to these institutional features (Destler, Gelb, and Lake, 1984).

Belief in the efficacy of military and clandestine solutions to political problems gave rise to an immense peacetime military establishment and sprawling intelligence community, both of which achieved great political clout in a policy-making environment where money and personnel mean influence. Once acquired, political influence tends to be self-perpetuating, because players with relatively greater influence win intragovernment contests. Since winning means choosing the option most consonant with one's organizational goals and expertise, a cycle is set into motion that helps to explain why today's policies are considerably shaped by the legacy of past decisions.

The American People

American foreign policy is also conditioned by such important if relatively stable societal characteristics as America's geographical size and political culture. America's internal characteristics are influential because decision makers can tap the nation's vast resources to cope with international problems (capabilities which, in economic and military terms, have been extraordinarily abundant during much of the postwar era). In addition, the more volatile societal policy sources, such as public opinion, elections, the mass media, and interest groups, also impact policymakers' beliefs and behavior. Moreover, American political culture shapes their attitudes before, during, and after their assumption of power, affecting how they perceive, judge, and act. The general values embraced by American society delimit the options from which decision makers choose, thereby defining the range of permissible action. These public preferences have traditionally been rationalized in liberal values stressing a concern for liberty, prosperity, moral virtue, self-determination, and peace for the world's peoples.

We also know, however, that leaders do not passively internalize beliefs endorsed widely in American society—they also shape them. This applies especially to public opinion. The American people are generally uninformed about and uninterested in international affairs, but they are still capable of forming stable, politically relevant foreign policy beliefs. At they same time, they are acquiescent toward presidential policy initiatives and reward the president with their approval (when deserved). Thus leaders have the opportunity to "manage" public opinion rather than merely follow it—with the result that over time public attitudes converge with leaders' preferences. The electoral process contributes to the process. The net result is that officials influence opinion as much as they respond to it. There are exceptions, of course. Moreover, public opinion can constrain policy innovation—not because a mobilized public interferes with presidential leadership, but because leaders are prone to overestimate the public's agreement and power, and this perception instills caution and restraint. In the final analysis, then, public preferences and public policy tend to be the same.

Situated midway between decision makers and the public, the mass media simultaneously shape public preferences and judge leaders' choices. However, evidence suggests that the mass media do not determine the public's foreign policy opinions because most people are habitually inattentive to foreign affairs and relatively impervious to new information. The media do, however, help to set agendas by influencing the issues people think *about*.

The media's impact is mediated by a multiple-step communications flow. Media information defines agendas for the attentive public and policymakers. If information results in changes in those select groups' attitudes, they then are likely to be transmitted through these opinion leaders to the general American public. Hence the mass media *do* contribute to popular attitudes, but that impact is not direct. Television is a partial exception to this generalization because it disseminates information to American homes, and, even though most Americans prefer to ignore it, they cannot avoid it and their impressions about international realities are accordingly affected.

The mass media themselves are part of the foreign policy-making establishment from which opinion change must ultimately derive because the media are dependent on the government for information. It is not surprising, therefore, to often find considerable congruence between the opinion of policymakers and media opinion.

Likewise, interest groups and political action committees seldom exercise effective influence over the policy-making process. Because many contending interest groups coexist, they tend to offset each others' influence. Moreoever, groups committed to preserve the status quo are generally more successful than those that seek to change policy.

The pluralist model of interest group interaction describes the countervailing forces of competing groups whose efforts constrain policymakers' ability to engineer policy change. By way of contrast, the elitist policy-making model sees policy consistency emanating from stable "establishment" preferences—foreign policy is of the elite, by the elite, and for the elite. "The national interests pursued by a nation or stated by its official leaders are simply the interests of the dominant groups or classes. It is this transmutation of private interests into national interests that is the essence of the elitist tradition" (Berkowitz, Bock, and Fuccillo, 1977). The military-industrial complex allegedly fits this model, promoting policies beneficial to its own parochial, profit-motivated interests. Precisely because so many people have a stake in high military spending, reductions have been resisted by those benefiting from its perpetuation, even when military threats have waned.

On balance, then, societal factors operate as a status quo force, encouraging halting, incremental, and remedial policy adjustments to evolving circumstances.

The International Environment

The very existence of an external environment over which nation-states have no absolute control gives rise to the need for foreign policy. But how important is the external environment in the process whereby everyday decisions are made? "Not very" has appeared applicable for many years. "The traditional mind-set in [the United States], derived from nearly a century of global dominance and a virtually self-sufficient continental economy, has been to adopt whatever public policies and corporate strategies fit the domestic environment," observes international economist C. Fred Bergsten (1990). "The rest of the world was largely ignored in the formation of policy." Moreover, the United States depended throughout most of the postwar era much less on the state of the world than the state of the world depended on it. It was this largely hospitable global setting that made the U.S. global policeman role possible. In turn, extraordinary U.S. capabilities coupled with America's globalist foreign policy did much to create the kind of international environment that currently exists.

That situation is changing; in fact, American preeminence has been eroding since 1945. In the immediate postwar years the United States was the only superpower; that unipolar period gave way to tight bipolarity and eventually to a bipolycentric international distribution of power. A truly multipolar world may now be on the horizon. This transformation has accompanied the decline of American power relative to other nations. The United States continues to stand center stage, but other actors now join it.

Closely related to this geostrategic shift has been the growing importance of nonmilitary issues, nonsuperpower relations, and the Newly Industrialized Countries and intensely nationalistic Third World nations—actors whose interests and objectives often diverge from those of the United States and the other major powers. Additionally, the presence and assertiveness of nonstate actors—some pacific (international organizations), others violent (terrorists)— comprise features of the contemporary global environment with which the United States must deal. The world has become more complex and interdependent, thereby inhibiting the ability of the United States to follow its own preferences unrestrained by the demands of others, including those of powerful domestic actors. The rise of transnational problems (migration, trade, debt, environment, drugs, and energy) that cannot be addressed by any one nation is indicative of a changing world, in which unilateral approaches fail and multilateral cooperation is imperative. The international environment of the twenty-first century will doubtless include other changes that will stimulate the need for policy adaptations.

Rapidly changing international conditions appear destined to force reassessments of the fundamental assumptions on which postwar American foreign policy has been based. As the dramatic changes that occurred in 1989 and 1990 in the Soviet Union, Germany, and elsewhere in Europe illustrate, new directions in the American response to the world may follow, and be pushed by, revolutionary changes in the international system in the wake of the Cold War. At a minimum, changes in America's external environment will determine the issues on policymakers' future agendas. Shifting global conditions and "issue cycles" (Vasquez and Mansbach, 1983) create incentives for policy adjustments to new realities. As Edmund Burke warned in the eighteenth century, "A state without the means of some change is a state without the means of its preservation."

THE SOURCES OF AMERICAN EXTERNAL BEHAVIOR: A COMPARATIVE ASSESSMENT

The forces that determine the course of American Foreign policy are myriad. Five interacting source categories have been posited to affect the rate of change in that policy. Under most conditions they work to sustain foreign policy continuity and to ensure that policy change, when it has occurred, has come slowly and incrementally. Policy innovation has been rare; more often, remedial adjustments devoid of fundamental reevaluations of the untested assumptions on which present policies rest have been evident.

But how influential are the source categories in comparison with one another? What is their relative impact? The policy-making process combines many causal factors whose interaction defies precise definition. Still, the mental exercise of exploring the source categories' relative influence can provoke thought about the determinants of postwar American foreign policy.

To organize inquiry, the following rank order of the causal impact of the sources of American foreign policy is hypothesized: (1) role, (2) governmental, (3) societal, (4) external, and (5) individual.

In essence this ranking of the relative explanatory power of the policy sources advances a skeleton *theory* of the influences that have shaped postwar American foreign policy. It avers that policy continuity has been sustained more by role variables than by any other factor and that individual sources have been the least powerful, with governmental, societal, and external factors—in that order—exerting an intermediate impact. More important, perhaps, the ranking raises questions about alternate ways of weighing the impact of the source categories' relative causal influence and prompts recognition that *all* the factors affect policy outcomes in very complex ways. There exists a multitude of ways in which different factors may combine with one another, and the precise balance among them may fluctuate in conjunction with an almost infinite set of conditions. For example, the relative weight assigned to the five sources may be different with respect to American policy toward a particular actor (the Soviet Union) than it is for others (Japan, Germany, Israel, the North Atlantic Treaty Organization, the Organization of Petroleum Exporting Countries, the United Nations). A plethora of circumstantial factors might modify these weights (for instance, are they different in election years?). Nonetheless, by asking which source categories predominate over the others, the relative potency of each source under different circumstances can be estimated. Ranking the source categories to construct alternate theories of American behavior forces consideration of the conditions under which any hypothesized ranking might or might not hold and the ways in which they might promote policy continuity or change in the 1990s and beyond.

CRISIS: AN INTERVENING VARIABLE?

Crisis conditions measurably modify peoples' behavior and often induce them to engage in actions they would not otherwise perform. Crises also change the way governments make decisions and influence the kinds of decisions they reach. Because crises upset "business as usual," they often upset the influences that otherwise affect how foreign policy is made.

A foreign policy crisis is "a situation that (1) threatens high-priority goals of the decision-making unit [for example, foreign policymakers], (2) restricts the amount of time available for response before the decision is transformed,

and (3) surprises the members of the decision-making unit by its occurrence''
(Hermann, 1972b).

When such a situation arises, how do decision makers proceed? And what
happens to the way in which decisions are reached? Charles Hermann (1969b:
416–417) hypothesizes the following:

- The highest level of government officials will make the decision(s)
  (because of the perceived threat to national goals or interests).
- Bureaucratic procedures usually involved in foreign policy making will
  be side-stepped (because high-ranking officials can commit the government to action without the normal deference to bureaucracies).
- Information about the situation is at a premium (because time limits
  decision makers' ability to acquire new information).
- The basis for selecting among options is often something other than
  information about the immediate situation (for example, because of the
  short time, analogies with prior situations).
- Personal antagonisms and disagreements among policymakers will
  remain subdued (because of the urgent need for consensus).
- Extreme responses are encouraged (because of limited information and
  the enhanced importance of the policymakers' personalities).
- Substantial energy following the decision is devoted to gaining support
  for it from allies and others (because of uncertainty about the decision's
  outcome).

Case studies of particular crises and experimental research support these
hypotheses. For our purposes, the most important finding is that in crisis situations ad hoc decision-making groups form and are given broad authority (Hermann and Hermann, 1989). In crises, decision-making elites truly govern.
Bureaucratic procedures are short-circuited and decision responsibility is redis-
tributed from the usual centers of government power. Hence one of the greatest
role-induced constraints on decision makers is circumvented.

Moreover, a ''crisis alters organizational plans and objectives by disrupting
the regular schedule of activities''; as a result, ''personnel assignments are real-
located and top-level decision-makers focus their attention exclusively on the
crisis, postponing action on other matters that may originally have had a higher
priority on their scale of values'' (Robinson, 1972). During the Cuban missile
crisis, for example, some of the members of the ad hoc crisis-management team
were ''relieved'' of their organizational affiliations. Assigned the role of ''skeptical generalists,'' ''they were charged with examining the policy problem as a
whole, rather than approaching the issues in the traditional bureaucratic way
whereby each man confines his remarks to the special aspects in which he considers himself to be an expert and avoids arguing about issues on which others
present are supposedly more expert than he'' (Janis, 1982).

Finally, the Korean and Cuban situations suggest that during international
crises the domestic political implications of policy options are not given their
usual intense consideration (Paige, 1972). That is not to say that domestic

politics cease to affect leaders' policies, for decisions may be greatly influenced by calculations of their internal consequences (see Hampson, 1988).[1] But the influence of societal factors in policy making recedes in crisis situations compared to general (for example, the Nixon Doctrine) or administrative (for example, whether to recognize a new government) decision situations.

Crisis conditions create unusual decision-making procedures and open the door to new initiatives. In short, *crises are opportunities for foreign policy innovation*. Hence crises, which erupt from external disturbances, have the capacity to transform the nation's policies.[2] Under such circumstances—and ignoring the external source category for a moment—the relative potency of the (four) explanatory source categories might be altered as follows: (1) individual, (2) role, (3) governmental, and (4) societal.

Again this ranking is merely suggestive. It illuminates how policy determinants vary across circumstances, and reasons that in crises, individual factors are most potent because crises lead to ad hoc decision making by small groups and because the existence of a crisis situation is determined typically by the president, whose personal perceptions shape definitions of situations. Role factors are next in importance because, despite circumvention of the usual bureaucratic constraints, policy-making roles still shape leaders' images and conduct. The presidential form of government ensures that the executive branch of government will bear primary, probably exclusive, responsibility for dealing with crises, and that makes governmental variables a factor. Last in importance are societal factors. The conditions of short time and surprise (to which we might add secrecy) preclude active involvement by interest groups, the mass media, and the attentive public. Hence societal influences will become important only to the extent that presidents take them into account.

Most difficult to place is the external source category. Its ranking varies, depending on how one conceptualizes a crisis. Crises may be viewed as "situational variables," where the decisions themselves are the responses to those external stimuli crises generate (Hermann, 1969a). In that conceptualization, the external source category is the most important because it is external developments that set in motion crisis decision-making procedures.

In the decision-making process itself, however, the external environment may be somewhat less important. As argued in Chapters 6 and 7, global circumstances help to shape foreign policy options by defining what is possible and

---

1. The perception of the 1962 Cuban situation as a crisis was reportedly influenced by President Kennedy's feeling that Nikita Khrushchev had reneged on his promise not to complicate the president's delicate domestic political situation at the time of the forthcoming congressional elections (the president's Republican opponents were calling for sterner measures against Castro's Cuba).

2. Some historians, for example, have interpreted the Cuban missile crisis as the point at which U.S. foreign policy turned away from the instinct toward nuclear brinkmanship; others see it as the impetus for détente, because it sparked realization of the mutuality of Soviet and American interests (see Blight and Welch, 1989). An analogous policy-transforming event occurred with President Jimmy Carter's definition of the 1979 Soviet invasion of Afghanistan as a crisis and with his subsequent policy reorientation in response to what he labeled "the most serious threat to peace since the Second World War."

probable. But the constraints and opportunities posed by the external environment become relevant only insofar as decision makers perceive them. In other words, because policy ultimately derives from what policymakers choose, policymakers themselves must perceive the external environment as affecting their choices for the external factor to influence their decisions.

Even in a system punctuated by periodic crises since 1945, it would appear that American leaders seldom perceived external circumstances in a way that constrained their definition of policy options. The Cuban missile crisis and Vietnam stand as giant testimonies to the danger of this view—and may continue to restrain the options future American leaders consider.[3] But generally, even in crisis situations the external environment would appear not to be a more powerful policy determinant than individual factors because of the inherent importance of leaders' perceptions in defining national interests.

So it does matter who is elected or who is appointed to top-level foreign policy positions—at least in crisis situations. The characteristics of the president and the men and women who surround the president thus critically affect the potential for future policy change. Such characteristics cannot, as previously suggested, be disregarded.

Although crisis situations are occasions that invite policy change, it is questionable whether crises in fact produce such results. Suspicions that they may cause disturbances but not real changes in policy are aroused when we note how endemic crises are to international politics. One compilation (Brecher and Wilkenfeld, 1991) identified 251 international crises between 1945 and 1985; nearly all of these system-disrupting threats to postwar stability affected America's global interests, and 12 Soviet-American crises in the period directly threatened U.S. security. Hence international crises have been recurrent, erupting an average of more than six times annually; yet during this forty-year period American foreign policy exhibited great continuity. Thus crises did not lead to policy revision as theorized. On the contrary, this evidence suggests that *whereas crises do indeed present opportunities for policy innovation, the opportunities are seldom seized*. Rather than stimulating new departures, more often crises are "managed" in a way that preserves existing policy. The propensity for American foreign policy to bounce from one crisis to another—without a fundamental change in orientation—appears to continue. Recurrent crises— the Angolan War, the Soviet invasion of Afghanistan, the seizure of American diplomats by Iran, the terrorist bombing of U.S. Marines in Lebanon, the Panama invasion—did not precipitate major policy changes. Even the response to the Iraq-Kuwait crisis, while stimulating for the first time deployment of American ground forces to the volatile Middle East, was little more than an extension of the Carter Doctrine which had been enunciated more than a decade earlier.

---

3. Congressional fear about U.S. military involvement in Angola in the mid-1970s leading to "another Vietnam" is perhaps a case in point, as were the situations in El Salvador and Nicaragua in the 1980s (both the Reagan and Bush administrations were reluctant to expand American involvement).

The reasons crises seldom produce policy changes are varied. Ironically, although crisis situations remove many of the impediments to policy innovation, the limited time frame within which decisions must be reached precludes a full search for options. Under pressure, policymakers rely on historical analogies for guidelines and alternatives (May, 1973; Neustadt and May, 1986). For example, when faced with the Soviet pressures on Iran, Turkey, and Greece, which ultimately led to the Truman Doctrine, the Truman administration viewed those events as analogous to developments prior to World War II (especially the Manchurian, Italo-Ethiopian, and Czechoslovakian crises). In the case of the Vietnam embroilment, several inferred historical parallels contributed to American involvement—the "loss" of China, the French defeat at Dien Bien Phu in Vietnam, concern for the success of communist-inspired wars of national liberation, Korea, and communist behavior in the Quemoy-Matsu, Berlin, and Cuban crises.[4] More recently, the Munich analogy once again informed the decision process as the Bush administration framed a response to Iraq's invasion of Kuwait. Thus crisis decisions are bound by memories of the past.

Nor can policymakers completely escape role constraints in crises. Whereas role expectations are perhaps less potent in crises than in other situations, decision makers nevertheless remain confined by them. Among the primary role constraints under which they operate are their predecessors' prior commitments, goals, and orientations. In fact, faced with the perceived need to do something in crises, decision makers will be especially sensitive to established commitments and policy orientations if for no reason other than that the high-priority goals threatened by crisis situations are embedded within existing policy goals. The tendency to equate successful crisis management with the restoration of pre-crisis conditions may also be operative.

Nor can we dismiss the role constraints bureaucracies impose. For example, middle-level watch officers in the State Department's Operations Center play a critical role in selecting and filtering information about potential or actual crisis situations before it is passed on to higher-level decision makers (Lentner, 1972). That enables them to "subtly but surely affect the outcome" (Hermann, 1972a). And again, as the Cuban missile crisis suggests, in crises bureaucracies carry out their tasks according to standard operating procedures.

---

4. The important question, then, is how well decision makers are able to use the past. Ernest May (1973) is skeptical: "Policy-makers ordinarily use history badly. When resorting to an analogy, they tend to seize upon the first that comes to mind. They do not search more widely. Nor do they pause to analyze the case, test its fitness, or even ask in what ways it might be misleading. Seeing a trend running toward the present, they tend to assume that it will continue into the future, not stopping to consider what produced it or why a linear projection might prove to be mistaken."

May speaks kindly of Kennedy's imaginative thinking about historical analogies at the time of the Cuban missile crisis, and especially Kennedy's awareness of the dangers of fallacious historical inference. Even in that instance, however, one might be skeptical, for Kennedy, too, relied on historical analogies to guide his response. In his announcement to the nation of the presence of Soviet missiles in Cuba, for example, Kennedy branded the Soviet move a provocative and unjustified change in the "status quo, which cannot be accepted by this country if our courage and our commitment are ever to be trusted again by either friend or foe. The 1930s taught us a clear lesson: aggressive conduct, if allowed to go unchecked and unchallenged, ultimately leads to war."

Because the limited time available during crises precludes development of new procedures to deal with new problems, the bureaucracies' existing repertoires define policymakers' range of available choices.

It would also be inappropriate to discount the potential impact of external and societal constraints. Even if we regard crises as situations that make decisions necessary, in the actual decision phase of a specific crisis situation, policymakers' calculations of the costs and benefits of alternative options are influenced by their images of international circumstances. Again, in the Cuban missile crisis, decision makers' estimates of the likely reaction of allies and adversaries to each alternative brought the external environment into the decision-making calculus.

Such implicit calculations are likely to be more pronounced than are considerations of domestic political consequences, particularly because decision makers can usually count on broad-based support for the actions they initiate. But that does not mean that all societal forces will be inoperative. The public, the mass media, and interest groups (at least according to the pluralist model) may not be directly involved (but certainly interested—to the extent the crisis is public knowledge) in the decision process. But to the extent that decision makers are drawn from the same political culture (usually from a relatively limited pool of elite members of the "establishment") and go through similar learning processes, societal factors, too, will constrain decision makers' vision of the viable courses of action.

In the final analysis, then, whereas the individual source category is perhaps the most potent policy determinant in crisis situations, the range of choice is constricted by other constraints. More often than not, whereas the advent of an international crisis enhances dramatically the prospects for policy innovation, crises typically have been managed in such ways as to preserve the parameters of existing policy rather than to alter them.

AN ADDITIONAL CAVEAT: ISSUES AND ISSUE-AREAS

The preceding discussion of policy making in crisis situations suggests how difficult it is to trace the relative influence of multiple sources of foreign policy. Valid generalizations are not easily discovered because of the large number of factors that intervene in the policy-formation process.

Although many confounding factors exist that can alter the hypothesized ranking of the source categories, the effects of issues stand out in particular. Let us briefly consider their potential impact on our hypothesized ranking of the source categories.

We have used the term *foreign policy* to refer to the goals a nation's officials seek to attain abroad, the values that give rise to those objectives, and the means (instruments) whereby America pursues them. Although we examined particular features of America's postwar external objectives (particularly in Part II), generally speaking we have not given attention to specific substantive issues and policymakers' day-to-day responses to them. A macrotheoretic explanation of broad policy goals and methods, and of the forces that contribute to their continuity, has been provided to the exclusion of discrete foreign policy issues and America's evolving postures toward them.

This macro approach conceals the daily work of government, which is largely issue-focused. At that level (and certainly from the viewpoint of America's foreign policy managers), *persistence* and *continuity* do not describe the short-range process through which foreign policy is made and implemented. Indeed, any particular policy issue or subset (such as immigration policy) may be in a state of flux, whereas in another area (such as deterrence strategy) persistence is an apt description. Hence it is appropriate to think of policy responses to different issues, or issue-areas, as undergoing differential rates of change over the same period.

And over longer periods of time, definitions of "critical" foreign policy issues may be subject to cyclical variation, with moods determining the degree and length of time in which any particular issue receives attention (Vasquez, 1985). If the salience of an issue peaks and declines in a cyclical fashion, then the sources of American foreign policy would also be expected to vary in their relative influence depending on the phase of the cycle at any particular point in time. For instance, how the sources interact to shape policy would be different during those periods when America is threatened militarily than during a stage in which energy scarcities or trade deficits become the preoccupations of the moment.

Presumably, the five policy sources also contribute to cyclical swings in the attention given to discrete foreign policy issues. Whereas in the long run the five source categories collectively promote stability in policy assumptions, in the shorter run they may stimulate cyclical changes in the attention paid to particular policy issues. Thus continuity in the premises underlying American foreign policy may coexist with cyclical variation in the salience of particular foreign policy issues.

Several examples illustrate these short- and long-term processes. For instance, American strategic doctrine has fundamentally shifted from compellence to deterrence, while the nation's commitment to a strong defense posture has remained constant. Similarly, American support for human rights was momentarily awakened in the late 1970s, only to have waned in the 1980s, while the globalist impulse never reverted to isolationist withdrawal. With respect to international institutional development, American policy again shows ambivalence: it strongly supported international organizations (the United Nations, the World Court, the United Nations Educational, Scientific, and Cultural Organization) from 1947 through the 1970s, but subsequently eschewed multilateral problem solving during the period of the Reagan administration's attack on international institutions. The picture that emerges is one of uneven change, with historical continuity in some areas and discontinuity in others. Issues are given only episodic attention.

Turning from issue-cycles to issue-areas poses analytic difficulties. A set of theoretical propositions satisfactorily delineating relationships between issue-areas and the sources of foreign policy has evaded scholarship.[5] Yet at least two ideas derived from analysis of issue-areas are useful in exploring change and changelessness in foreign policy. One addresses the source categories' relative influence, the other relationships between different issue-areas.

The core idea of the issue-area concept is simple: policies determine politics. That means that the specific issue or policy at stake will determine who will become involved in policy making.[6] If different individuals, groups, or institutions actively influence one set of specific policies (while neglecting others), the effect could be to alter our hypothesized ranking of the source categories' relative policy impact. Consider, for example, the differences between the processing of a "routine" foreign policy decision, such as whether to recognize a new military government in a small African state, as compared to a "nonroutine" situation, such as the prosecution of war as in Korea and Vietnam. In the first case, decision makers would normally be allowed to make their own final choices relatively unaffected by societal forces. But in the latter, where the issues more intimately touch Americans' daily lives, we would expect the matter to be processed much like a domestic issue. In the former case the issue engages a relatively small proportion of the total political system, primarily the specialized foreign affairs government. In the latter a number of individuals, groups, and institutions both within and outside government actively attempt to influence the outcome. Because many Americans' resources and welfare are affected by a protracted war, we would expect large segments of the general public, the attentive public, the mass media, and so forth to attempt to influence the government's choice of means and ends.

If we extend this reasoning to a more general range of substantive questions, we can hypothesize that matters falling into a category called "noncrisis military-security issues" will generally be processed by the foreign affairs apparatus (that is, both role and governmental forces will predominate), with little consideration given to other factors (except perhaps external pressures). Included here would be questions of whether to deploy troops to country A, withdraw them from country B, and replace outmoded weapons system X with system Y.

An alternative generalized set of substantive issues might be labeled simply economic. In those the foreign affairs government would still be critically important, but the societal category would probably supersede the external in

---

5. A persuasive case for the empirical utility of the issue-area concept is provided in Ripley and Franklin (1987). Theoretical arguments relevant to the concept can be found in Evangelista (1989), Lowi (1972, 1967, and 1976), Mansbach and Vasquez (1981), Rosenau (1967, 1980), and Zimmerman (1973).

6. Note that for a particular actor, an issue will become a factor only when a problem is defined as an issue that needs resolution. Thus issues are relevant only when they are recognized as such by decision makers.

importance. Most aspects of foreign economic policy would fit here. Military-security issues insofar as they relate to domestic resources and relationships would also fit. Included, for example, would be questions relating to the procurement of new weapons systems and the allocation of initial prime contract awards. Those stand in contrast to routine decisions to continue funding an ongoing weapons system, which are typically made in an incremental fashion. In short, some combination of considerations relating to "routine-nonroutine," "military-security," and "economic policy" issues would help to account for variations in the relative weight of the policy sources when we move beyond (or below) the macrotheoretic view of policy construed in its broadest sense.

The second implication derived from the issue-area concept is the need to consider the effects that change in one issue-area might have on other issue-areas. In the long run, variation in any one component of American foreign policy—however gradual—has implications for other components. Discontinuity in any one area of policy (for example, budget deficits) may accelerate the rate of change in other areas (for example, the issue of American troops in Europe). Conversely, significant continuity in a particular area may decrease the prospects for change in other areas.

The history of American efforts to contain Soviet influence illustrates some of these interconnections. Détente was more than the simple relaxation of tensions: accommodations in the military-security sphere were linked inextricably to shifts in the diplomatic and the economic spheres. The 1972 wheat deal was tied to the Strategic Arms Limitations Talks (SALT), and both were tied to the level of diplomatic consultation evolving at least since creation of the "hot line" in 1963. Conversely, but still to the point, some critics (for example, Pisar, 1977) argue that President Carter's push for human rights in the Soviet Union, which was vigorously opposed by Soviet leaders, impeded progress in achieving long-term Soviet-American agreements on limiting strategic arms. During the Reagan presidency, developments in the military, diplomatic, and economic spheres of Soviet-American relationships were often explicitly linked as the administration first pursued a confrontational posture to the Soviet Union and later a more accommodative mode of interaction. And during the Bush administration, changes in Soviet domestic and foreign policies paved the way for cooperative efforts to deal with the Iraq-Kuwait crisis.

Change in any one part of American foreign policy may not immediately stimulate change in others; however, over time, significant change in one issue-area may substantially affect others. Thus a dramatic change toward a particular issue may generate substantial pressure to modify policy toward other issue-areas as adjustments to the new circumstances engendered by the original policy change are made. The dramatic rate of increase in the price of oil during the OPEC decade, for example, which was tied to the rapid growth of domestic energy consumption since World War II, arguably stimulated major changes in the American posture toward the dangerous political situation in the Middle East. Likewise, the growing awareness of ecological threats to the global environment in the 1990s pushed for revisions of the way national security was defined.

And perhaps most profoundly, the dizzying pace of change in the Soviet Union and Eastern Europe may have prompted the Bush administration to proclaim in 1989 the end of the Cold War and the need to move beyond containment.

The point is that the different issue-areas that American foreign policy addresses may contain within them the seeds of policy change. The overall pattern may be one of persistence and continuity, but altered conditions in any one issue-area may ultimately stimulate change in another. The result may be fundamental adaptation in America's overall approach to its external environment. Or, conversely, a cycle of attention and neglect of particular policy issues may follow.

In addition to shifts within issue-areas, policy change might be generated by fundamental changes within one or some combination of the five source categories that influence foreign policy. Despite the fact that the source categories examined in this book in general have promoted persistence throughout the postwar era, if policy change is to occur, significant and fundamental change in one or more of the five sources is a necessary condition.

What are the prospects for change in postwar American foreign policy generated by changes in the sources of it? Have domestic and international circumstances changed so substantially in the early 1990s that revision of orthodox assumptions is now probable? If so, will American policymakers respond to the new opportunities by framing adaptive new orientations? Or will they, instead, resist change and reaffirm the assumptions on which the postwar pattern of American foreign policy behavior has rested? Our concluding chapter will probe these questions about the probable future of American foreign policy.

SUGGESTIONS FOR FURTHER READING

Evangelista, Matthew. (1989) "Issue-Area and Foreign Policy Revisited," *International Organization* 43 (Winter): 147–171.

Hermann, Charles F. (ed.). (1972) *International Crises: Insights from Behavioral Research*. New York: Free Press.

Rosenau, James N. (1990) *Turbulence in World Politics: A Theory of Change and Continuity*. Princeton, N.J.: Princeton University Press.

Roberts, Jonathan M. (1988) *Decision-Making during International Crises*. New York: St. Martin's.

Smith, Steven M. (1981) *Foreign Policy Adaptation*. New York: Nichols.

Vasquez, John A. (1985) "Domestic Contention on Critical Foreign Policy Issues: The Case of the United States," *International Organization* 39 (Autumn): 606–643.

Wiarda, Howard J. (1990) *Foreign Policy without Illusion*. Glenview, Ill.: Scott, Foresman/Little Brown.

Wilkenfeld, Jonathan, Gerald W. Hopple, Paul J. Rossa, and Stephen J. Andriole. (1980) *Foreign Policy Behavior*. Beverly Hills, Calif.: Sage.

Zimmerman, William. (1973) "Issue Area and Foreign Policy Process: A Research Note in Search of a General Theory," *American Political Science Review* 67 (December): 1204–1212.

CHAPTER 16

Toward the Year 2000: The Bush Administration and the Future of American Foreign Policy

As the most powerful democracy, . . . we can be a force for freedom and peaceful change unlike any other in this world. But if we fail to do so, we will not be able to run or to hide from the consequences.
SECRETARY OF STATE JAMES A. BAKER, 1989

While freedom has made great gains, we have not entered an era of perpetual peace.
PRESIDENT GEORGE BUSH, 1990

The second half of the twentieth century has witnessed accelerating change. Yet during this turbulent period American foreign policy has displayed a remarkable degree of continuity. The world has changed dramatically, but the American approach to it has resisted change. Today, more so than at any time since the Truman Doctrine set the course for postwar American foreign policy, the assumptions underlying that world view are being challenged.

To many, the revolutionary changes that swept the world in 1989 have set the stage for the United States to rethink the foreign policy axioms of the past half-century and frame a fresh approach. Furthermore, President George Bush's repeated statements about the need to look over the horizon and prepare for the year 2000 raised expectations that reorientations would be forthcoming. As Bush put it in March 1989, "The essential question today is, what are we doing to prepare for the new world that begins eleven short years from now? That is what my agenda is all about." That pronouncement, and others like it, implied a recognition that a once-reasoned policy may have become "a conditioned reflex" (Ball, 1976) and that a new vision was now an imperative.

Still, as the Bush administration positioned itself for the 1992 presidential election campaign, it remained unclear whether a new policy adequate for the new century would indeed be forged. George Bush is not the first postwar president to call for a new foreign policy, and, like his predecessors, he discovered that inherited policy precepts often have a life of their own. Even a determined president finds he cannot change the course of American foreign policy quickly or by command. Thus to some extent, and despite the convulsive changes that have recently transformed the world, the conditioning force of the sources of foreign policy analyzed in this book limit the extent to which *any* administration can hope to orchestrate policy change. Moreover, the actual behavior of the Bush administration as it approached the mid-point of its term in office often belied the president's seeming commitment to engineer policy changes.

THE BUSH ADMINISTRATION'S FOREIGN POLICY

In his campaign for office, and as president, George Bush frequently portrayed himself as a pragmatic, adaptive leader, but he seemed unable to frame a comprehensive plan for adjusting American foreign policy to the radically transformed international environment that abruptly emerged as he took command in the Oval Office. Despite his promise to pursue "prudent approaches," his initial moves evoked "the ghost of indecisiveness . . . carried out . . . without vision" (Hyland, 1989).

The emphasis on pragmatism departed from the ideologically inspired style of the Reagan administration. Bush—a man who claims to value loyalty above all else (Dowd, 1989b)—did assert in his campaign for office in 1988 that "the most important mission in my life is to complete the mission [Ronald Reagan and I] started in 1980." But revolutionary changes in circumstances forced a reevaluation of that policy mission. "The task before us," the president exclaimed in December 1989, "is to provide the architecture for continued peaceful change." Still, he remained silent about the kind of world he wanted and his plans to create it.

The president himself seemed to be aware of the potential problem of missed opportunities for lasting superpower harmony and mindful of the danger of protracted delay when in January 1989 he observed, in the context of criticism of his cautious reaction to Mikhail Gorbachev's overtures, "What I don't want is to have it look like foot-dragging, or sulky refusal to go forward, . . . [But] I would be imprudent if I didn't have our team take a hard look at everything." Subsequently, in May 1989 Bush explained why he felt a slow response was necessary: "In an era of extraordinary change, we have an obligation to temper optimism . . . with prudence. I know," he added, "that some are restless with the pace I have set . . . but I think it is the proper pace."

"There are no maps," Bush confessed in 1990, "to lead us where we are going in this new world of our own making." In fact, the review that follows illustrates that the administration often returned to conceptualizations that had been formulated decades earlier, with the result that established goals were pursued in ways that entailed only marginal policy modifications.

Globalism

From the beginning the Bush administration repeatedly reaffirmed its commitment to America's global role. Priority was given to projecting American power abroad and to demonstrating the nation's resolve to protect its global interests. Unlike Jimmy Carter and many others who had warned that the nation's ability to manage an interdependent world had eroded, Bush maintained that global disengagement was not acceptable. Preeminence was to be preserved.

The administration's advocacy of global diplomacy was captured by Bush's attack in August 1988 on the positions of his presidential campaign opponent, Michael Dukakis, that he called "a rejection of America's role as a world leader and a repudiation of the Truman Doctrine and the vision of John Kennedy." Thus, the Bush administration's activism represented a frontal attack on the view that American splendor was mortal (Mead, 1987). Bush, like Reagan before him, rejected the claim that U.S. commitments were "over-stretched" (Kennedy, 1987). He responded to the so-called declinists by asserting that "America is not in decline. America is a rising nation." By implication, the country's missionary role abroad, which the Reagan administration had revived after the disrepute it had suffered in the wake of Vietnam, was heralded as a centerpiece of American foreign policy as the Bush administration assumed responsibility for the triumph of freedom and the preservation of peace around the world. "It's a question as to whether the United States will continue to lead," Bush observed, explaining "You see, I don't believe any other country can pick up the mantle."

George Bush, like his predecessors, had been schooled in the logic of *realpolitik*; and for those steeped in this philosophy, assertive American leadership is a given. Secretary of State James Baker's 1989 pledge that the United States *would* steer the future reflected the conviction that was to guide American policy making. Disengagement was not an option. The Nixon Doctrine, which had acknowledged America's diminished capacity either to control global developments everywhere or to assume responsibility for them, was repudiated. Believing that the United States was "bound to lead" (Nye, 1990), the Bush administration also returned to an embrace of multilateral approaches to global problems and once again treated international institutions as useful instruments for the promotion of American national interests. Thus the Bush administration endorsed former national security adviser Zbigniew Brzezinski's (1970) belief that the American "commitment to international affairs on a global scale [has] been decided by history. It cannot be undone, and the only remaining relevant question is what its form and goals will be." Accordingly, the symbols of stature and power were highlighted to communicate the nation's continuing intention to direct the course of history.

This reaffirmation of globalism was not foreordained, however. Recall that during the 1970s and 1980s a neoisolationist mood had arisen, punctuated by talk of suspending the U.S. commitments to its allies and of "decoupling" the United States from Europe. That neoisolationist mood was sometimes accompanied by a strain of unilateralism and an attack on multilateral institutions, as the values embodied in the "internationalist ethos" and in political idealism became "the objects of derision and contempt" (Hughes, 1985–1986). The mood was fed by American frustration with its loss of influence;

the go-it-alone posture represented in part a reaction to the strain that an unrestrained globalist foreign policy had placed on the nation's resources and to the resistance the country's efforts to exercise leverage abroad had encountered. A contraction in the scope of America's global involvements appeared to some to be inevitable; accordingly, the challenge was perceived to be one of discovering how to accommodate the nation to the reality of deteriorating influence without jeopardizing U.S. security. The Reagan administration did not accept this, however, and sought boldly to reassert American influence abroad.

By lowering the ideological stridency with which the American model and U.S. preeminence were extolled, Bush departed from Reagan's evangelical style. He made the idealist face of the American diplomatic tradition a more prominent feature of American foreign policy, especially in his advocacy of democratic ideals as the principle that would guide post-Cold War American policy. As communism collapsed and the number of erstwhile authoritarian states embracing democratic and market principles increased, the spread of American political institutions was aggressively promoted worldwide as much by example as by forceful assertion.

Anticommunism

Throughout the postwar period, discussions of American national interests persistently had been couched in the language of ideology—of opposition to communism's supposedly expansionist global impulses. Indeed, the diplomatic pronouncements of American leaders indicate that in the wake of World War II, communism had become, as President Carter once described it, "an inordinate fear" and an "obsession." Policymakers riveted their attention on the communist threat to the exclusion of other important issues that had no direct bearing on the competition between democracy and communism, capitalism and socialism.

The grip of anticommunism was rarely stronger than during the Reagan presidency. Reagan chose to view nearly every international development through the prism of anticommunist ideology; all events disrupting the global status quo were traced to the revolutionary activities of a coordinated communist front. Whether an uprising by leftists against their oppressors or terrorism by nationalists pursuing the cause of self-determination, the interpretation was the same: communism was responsible. Behind the U.S. fear and ideological opposition to communist beliefs was a Manichean world view that perceived the battle for people's hearts and minds as a zero-sum fight between the forces of good and evil.

But in 1989 communism—proclaimed by Reagan as the "focus of evil in the modern world"—was repudiated by the Soviet Union itself and by its East European allies. The West's so-called "victory" over communism was widely interpreted as a historical watershed that brought the ideological contest between communism and democratic capitalism to an end. "History" had "ended," a prominent State Department official declared (Fukuyama, 1989).

Because "the communist experiment [had] failed both in communist countries and in developing countries [and] the model it represented for development [had] lost its influence everywhere" (Kreisberg, 1989), the need for the United States to remain energetically opposed to it seemed irrelevant, anachronistic even. Conditions had indeed changed, although their ultimate consequences were difficult to envision.

> For decades [the anticommunist] principle justified every aspect of American foreign policy from the composition of its alliances to the size of its foreign aid program. Almost as important, it served as a tool to discipline critics, whether in Congress or alliance councils. Deprived of this principle, American foreign policy will lack direction. It is inevitable, therefore, that the country will face a major debate over the future course of American foreign policy. (Maynes, 1990: 8)

Still, it would be premature to assert that the anticommunist impulse has been exorcised from the American polity or from American foreign policy. Anticommunism may have receded in importance, but it is not forgotten. Even in decline, communism is seen as a profound threat to the American way of life. To recognize that "communism has proven to be a false god," as Assistant Secretary of State Richard Schifter put it, does not mean that anticommunism no longer influences thinking about the ends and means of American foreign policy. Whereas an "inordinate fear" is no longer overpowering, fear of a communist revival (especially if Mikhail Gorbachev's reforms fail) remains.

It is also axiomatic that American leaders continue to remain fearful of left-wing governments, whether communist or socialist, and continue to define combatting the spread of these philosophies and institutions as a policy goal. A Cold War orientation continues to shape American leaders' interpretations of unrest in the Third World. In the view of many, communism as a force on the world's stage may have died, but the ghost of Stalin continues to haunt American policymakers' images of the primary threats facing the United States in the post-cold War system (see Iklé, 1990).

Containment

Since the conclusion of World War II, America's primary diplomatic mission had been the containment of the Soviet Union's power. The abiding relevance of that focus has been challenged by the Soviet economy's careening bankruptcy, the potential political fragmentation of the Soviet Union's internal empire, the withdrawal of the its presence from beyond its borders, and by the de facto dissolution of the Warsaw Pact. "Even some of the most . . . hard-line experts . . . doubt that Gorbachev's Kremlin or any imaginable successors will undertake foreign adventures while the home front is in a state of such crisis, as it will be for a long, long time to come. A new consensus is emerging, that the Soviet threat is not what it used to be" (Talbott, 1990b). Simultaneously, resource constraints in the United States combined with other urgent foreign policy problems (such as nuclear proliferation, international drug-trafficking, the international debt crisis, and pollution and other forms of environmental degradation) have reduced the salience of America's Soviet-centric foreign policy focus and concomitantly increased the need to follow through with President Bush's promise to move "beyond containment."

Although the Bush administration paid lip service to these hitherto neglected problems (such as the environment), it continued to concentrate its attention on the problematic future role of the Soviet Union in world affairs. Whereas Bush readily recognized that collaboration with the Soviet Union was possible and could pay dividends at home and abroad, he made clear his view that on many issues the U.S. relationship with the Soviet Union was certain to be conflictual, declaring that whereas the United States "must be bold enough to seize the opportunity of change," it must at the same time be prepared for "protracted conflict" (Broder, 1988). Uppermost in the Bush administration's thinking was the fear, as Bush phrased it in May 1989, that "Soviet 'new thinking' [had] not yet totally overcome the 'old.'" Containment of the global influence of America's primary military rival remained a cornerstone of his policy.

This mistrustful posture crystallized early and remained a potent force in the administration's thinking. Bush at first dismissed as premature what appeared to most observers to be unprecedented opportunities to collaborate in areas where American and Soviet interests intersected, and he responded negatively to many of Mikhail Gorbachev's dramatic concessions (for which the Soviet leader scored great public relations victories). Secretary of State Baker captured the administration's apprehension in April 1989 when he counseled: "I think it is too soon to conclude that the Soviet policies most troubling to the West are in fact gone forever." An administrative directive issued in 1990, an update of the Defense Planning Guidance report, warned of intense superpower tensions in the 1990s, asserting that "fundamental Soviet objectives in the Third World do not appear to have changed" (cited in Tyler, 1990). The same theme was expressed in the Defense Department's 1991 annual assessment of Soviet objectives and capabilities, *Soviet Military Power*. Thus, the Bush administration feared that the Soviet Union under Gorbachev was not necessarily less threatening than it had been at the height of the Cold War—a precept publicly expressed by Secretary of Defense Richard Cheney, who in 1989 predicted that Gorbachev's reforms would not succeed. The comment raised doubts as to whether the administration at that time truly wanted Gorbachev to succeed.

Instructively, and as a precursor of the policy rhetoric that followed, Bush's practice of containment during his first year in office "came to be known by the oxymoronic slogan 'status quo plus,' and the administration was widely accused of harboring nostalgia for the Cold War" (Omestad, 1990). The administration's time-consuming review of Soviet policy during the first four months in office proved indicative: "We have the initial results from the study," Brent Scowcroft, President Bush's national security adviser, concluded, "and it's probably not surprising that the future looks a lot like the present in a straight line projection." Critics and even some supporters were moved to ask at the time whether this assessment represented, as Edward N. Luttwak (cited in Friedman, 1989) maintained it did, "a classic case of cultural lag: a President applying 1970s thinking to a 1990 situation"?

Bush later sought to dispel the image of unresponsiveness to changes in the Soviet Union and in the Soviet-American relationship when he announced that "our goal [is] integrating the Soviet Union into the community of nations." Thus the goal of containing Soviet power continued, but through a less confrontational and more political approach. The vow harkened back to the 1970s era of détente, when the United States had sought to create in the Soviet Union a "vested interest in restraint." The means chosen by Bush paralleled the earlier strategy known as *linkage* (Hyland, 1989), which geared the superpower dialogue toward the search for reciprocal concessions across different issues, including arms control, trade expansion, technology transfer, and management of regional conflicts bilaterally and through the United Nations. The administration early on asserted that it distrusted words and respected only Soviet deeds and laid down "'tests' to be passed before the Kremlin could 'earn' a better relationship" (Schlesinger, 1989b), but it later relaxed these requirements as superpower cooperation became more evident.

Bush's pledge at the annual meeting of the North Atlantic Treaty Organization in May 1989 to "move beyond the era of containment" signalled the beginning of the linkage strategy; he promised that the United States would "match [the Soviet Union's] steps with steps of our own." This initiative was motivated in part by the need to assuage the fears of America's allies that the United States alone clung to the perception that the military threat from the East was as dangerous as ever, and in part to counter Gorbachev's popularity. It was also inspired by the need to comply with what public opinion worldwide strongly endorsed. Negotiations did proceed eventually on reducing strategic nuclear forces and conventional weapons and troop levels in Europe (culminating in a major conventional force treaty signed in November 1990).

Lurking behind the linkage strategy was a long-standing belief embraced by successive generations of American decision makers about what Soviet leaders understand best—military might. Bush believed that Gorbachev sought to end the Cold War because he had no choice as a result of America's awesome weapons (Seib and Walcott, 1988). From this stemmed a corollary approach toward containing Soviet influence: preserving the strategic advantage in military power the United States had acquired through the Reagan administration's military rearmament program. Bush insisted that the United States must be prepared for the danger that "a retrograde Soviet leadership [might] *once again* threaten the rest of the world with military intimidation if not conquest" (Talbott, 1990b). To this end, the administration sought to rehabilitate "the mutually assured destruction doctrine that had been stigmatized as evil and unworkable by Reagan" (Hoagland, 1989). This return to orthodox deterrence stemmed from many of the same kinds of "worst case" analyses on which previous Cold War confrontational policies had been based.

Thus, the salience of the goal of containment has receded in prominence as the Soviet challenge has diminished, but the goal has not disappeared. The important question for the future is how American foreign policy will evolve if, as appears likely, the Cold War has truly ended. The future is uncertain. But we can predict with confidence that should Gorbachev's reforms fail and Soviet communism and power again pose a challenge, the logic of containment in its classical sense can be expected to reassert itself. And we can expect the United States to remain concerned about the Soviet Union's influence in world affairs, even if it totally abandons communist principles; as a great power, it remains, as de Tocqueville predicted, a natural rival.

Military Might and Interventionist Means

Like nearly all postwar presidents, Bush favored reliance on a strong military in order to deter potential challenges to American hegemony. The relaxation of tensions with the Soviet Union did not change that priority.

Bush echoed the orthodox faith in military prowess in October 1990 when he restated, as he had on many occasions, his belief that strength and clarity lead to peace—weakness and ambivalence lead to war. He pledged in his campaign for office to "continue our policy of strength" and insisted "it is not sound" "to cut the Defense Department . . . and put the money into domestic spending." Further suggestive of Bush's thinking was his depiction in 1990 of a strong U.S. military as the "secure bridge" that "can lead [America] to the promise of a lasting peace."

The priority Bush attached to military preparedness was signalled by the continuing budgetary commitments made to support a strong defense. In an era of staggering deficits and debt and Soviet military retrenchments, the Pentagon remained a favored agency in the distribution of America's limited resources.

The criteria governing how defense allocations should be made evolved piecemeal. The Bush administration first placed primary emphasis on its desire to upgrade the land-based missile leg of the nation's strategic triad. Development of both the rail-mobile MX and the Midgetman intercontinental missiles was supported and was followed with a push for funding the expensive Trident II submarine-launched missile. Furthermore, Bush announced in June 1989 that he planned to go ahead with the Stealth bomber program—potentially the most expensive in Pentagon history, with a price tag for 132 bombers at $70 billion—even though Secretary of Defense Cheney had expressed reservations about the program's cost and quality, and despite the resumption of negotiations with the Soviet Union to reduce the number of nuclear warheads, bombers, and missiles in each nation's arsenal. The costly and technologically unproven Strategic Defense Initiation (SDI)—popularly known as Star Wars—was also fervently supported. Moreover, Bush opposed a ban on nuclear weapons testing at the same time that he confessed that "the fact of the matter is we have a massive survivable nuclear deterrent right now." These commitments led observers at the time to question whether Bush was capable of meeting a weapons system he didn't like (Seib and Carrington, 1988). Dedicated to "modernization"—"a euphemism for breeding a whole aviary of brand-new weapon systems" (Talbott, 1990a)—Bush also pledged to strengthen conventional capabilities: "What we don't have is the kind of strong conventional defense capability we must have, and that is going to be my top priority as president." Without question, military preparedness was to remain a paramount goal.

The administration also continued America's postwar propensity to prepare for and engage in military intervention. One careful student of presidential character (Barber, 1989) predicted on the day of Bush's inauguration that "Turning to a military cause, even beyond the dimension of the Grenada invasion that Mr. Bush helped to orchestrate, [would] be a temptation for this President." The prognosis proved well founded. Shortly thereafter Bush pledged to continue supporting anti-communist rebels (Seib and Walcott, 1988), thereby reaffirming his faith in the Reagan Doctrine. And in December 1989 he ordered a military invasion of Panama to overthrow Manuel Noriega. That intervention paled in comparison with the magnitude of Operation Desert Shield, when the President committed himself to dispatch more than 400,000 troops to the Persian Gulf to reverse Iraq's conquest of Kuwait. This bold step affirmed the U.S. role as a superpower. In mid-October 1990 Secretary of Defense Richard Cheney pledged that American troops would stay "as long as the Saudis want us . . . as long as it takes to get the job done."

Both the president's pronouncements and his actions thus emphasized a martial conception of the means to exert American influence throughout the globe. In addition to concern for conventional weapons, Bush voiced renewed support for enhanced counterinsurgency and counterterrorist capabilities and rapidly deployable forces; the Carter Doctrine, which pledged the use of military force if necessary to maintain a free flow of oil from the Persian Gulf region, was reaffirmed and acted on; and efforts were made to expand intelligence gathering capabilities. In addition, Bush sought to increase the economic aid package for Third World countries, especially in security-supporting assistance.

In all of these ways the Bush team sought to dispel doubt that the United States was averse to the exercise of military or other forms of influence. The administration's posture unambiguously reaffirmed a cluster of firmly entrenched beliefs: strength produces peace, the capacity to destroy is the capacity to control, weapons superiority can both deter and compel, the price of military preparedness is never too high, arms control negotiations should proceed from a position of relative strength, and political problems are susceptible to military solutions. A centrist, Bush showed little inclination to depart from the center of a beaten path.

That conclusion must be tentative, however, as the potential for surprising policy reversals is also in Bush's character (Barber, 1989). During the 1980 presidential campaign, for example, Bush "said he believed there could in fact be a winner in a nuclear exchange between the United States and the Soviet Union'' (Warnke, 1988). But a decade later, his administration suggested, in a letter submitted before the 1990 NATO summit, that whereas Bush believed that nuclear weapons should only be used as a last resort (which seemed to reaffirm NATO's long-standing support of a ''first use'' nuclear weapons principle), he also stressed the importance of ''modifying flexible response to reflect a reduced reliance on nuclear weapons.'' Bush also was the primary catalyst to a NATO initiative designed to have the Cold War alliances establish some type of diplomatic liaison. The Bush administration thus has shown a capacity to advocate adaptive changes in military strategy. Hence with respect to defense policy, substantial continuities but also policy changes are probable as America's needs and circumstances undergo change in the post-Cold War world.

THE SOURCES OF CONTINUITY IN AMERICAN FOREIGN POLICY

What forces reinforced Bush's embrace of the same policy tenets on which his postwar predecessors relied? Are those forces so potent as to preclude the possibility of reorienting American foreign policy in a world undergoing profound transformation? Or from those same forces can there emanate conditions sufficiently ripe for fundamental reorientations in American foreign policy?

The balance sheet on forces now at work at home and abroad yields no sure conclusions. Nonetheless, a reading of prevailing trends and constraining factors suggests that the core assumptions on which the postwar policy pattern has been based are unlikely to be jettisoned.

What is the basis for this prediction? As has been argued throughout this book, the constraints on fundamental foreign policy change contained in the confluence of individual, role, societal, governmental, and external variables that condition foreign policy decisions are formidable—and they will remain so.

Any administration's foreign policy will reflect the character of the person sitting in the innermost sanctuary of power, the Oval Office. A president's *individual* or idiosyncratic qualities influence policy style. But this impact is also reduced by numerous constraints. All recent presidents have found it necessary to bend to the force of competing political pressures and to apply their energies to rallying support for their policies. Successful presidential performance requires not only strong convictions but also a willingness to satisfy political constituents. That is the art of politics. But sometimes the art of politics leads historians to portray presidents as chameleons whose capacity to lead is compromised by the exigencies of the moment.

The Bush experience illustrates the power of these pressures and the policy inertia they create. In George Bush we have a president whose personality has disposed him strongly to seek public approval, to back away from domestic confrontation, and to reconcile contending factions' differences. We also have an individual with a history of adherence to precedents and an inclination to make decisions piecemeal. More reactive than proactive throughout his long career as a public servant, Bush's instinctive urge has been to take the middle road, to wait for events to hit his desk, to let their course set his agenda (Schneider, 1990), and "to postpone hard choices on issues that may cry out for action" (Broder, 1989).

In short, George Bush has not shown himself to be a force for change; under him marginal policy adjustments and ad hoc reactions to problems have been more characteristic. The status quo has had an ally in his White House. As Reagan speech writer Larry Speakes put it, "The bottom line is [Bush is] the perfect team player, the perfect yes man. . . . With Bush, the popular image may be accurate: That he does not have a strong philosophical base, that he is not decisive, that he is not willing to take stands on the big issues" (*U.S. News and World Report*, May 23, 1988, p. 22).

A president is not the personification of the state, and Bush's capacity to move in new directions is also restricted by his predecessors' prior commitments and policies, the actions and preferences of the individuals already in position to implement policy, and his own conception of how he is expected to perform the role of president.

The backgrounds of those appointed to fill foreign policy-making *roles* invariably govern the decisions that are made. In this respect, it is important to note that Bush's advisers (and many of their immediate subordinates) are almost all veterans of previous Republican administrations. James A. Baker, Larry Eagleberger, Brent Scowcroft, Dick Cheney, Nicholas Brady, and even the president himself are products of the habits of mind developed in the formative stage of their careers and strengthened by the coaching they received as understudies from their mentors (among whom Richard M. Nixon and Henry Kissinger were prominent). They carry with them well-worn conceptual baggage. Members of the Eastern "establishment" who have guided American foreign and defense policy for nearly a half century, these foreign policy managers who have been insiders before agree on the principles that should guide policy making—a consensus that helps to explain why their response to many decisions has often sprung from a common perspective shaped by Cold War precepts. They are unlikely to throw away their scripts in the future.

Bush selected key personnel on the basis of their ability to be loyal team players. Instructively, however, loyalty to the president's formulations of the national agenda did not prevent the inevitable struggle for power among ambitious men and women from surfacing. True to role theory, the president's players at times disagreed about positions on key issues. The differences between Secretary of Defense Cheney and Assistant for National Security Affairs Scowcroft in 1989 on choices regarding the MX and Minuteman missiles and between Vice President Quayle and Secretary of State Baker on the nature of the Soviet menace were illustrative (although the friction paled in comparison with that which ignited between Cyrus Vance and Zbigniew Brzezinski in the Carter administration and between George Shultz and Caspar Weinberger in the Reagan administration). Policy innovation is usually not a product of such conflict-ridden processes. Compromise and delay are.

As before, bureaucratic struggles also are likely to restrain future efforts to bring about policy innovation and redirection. This was illustrated in 1989 budget hearings when top level Pentagon officials in testimony before Congress deliberately withheld information about Soviet cuts in defense spending so as to ensure funding of their requests (McCartney, 1989).

Implementation of new policy initiatives also will be circumscribed by the *governmental* structure Bush was elected to run. But the elaborate, overlapping organizational machinery of the foreign affairs government is resistant to streamlined management and coordination. Often this is for good reason. As one observer put it in commenting on Ronald Reagan's vow to "get government off the backs of people":

> Bureaucrats do not climb onto the backs without a boost from interest groups and members of Congress. They do not write regulations because they are malevolent but because someone wants those rules on the books. . . . Congress, in the interest of appearing responsive to public revulsion with large and complicated government, may tinker a little here and streamline a little there, but the basic structure of alliances will remain intact. (Baker, 1981: 160)

Nevertheless, to a considerable extent, the governmental machinery is beyond presidential control.

> Presidents operate on the brink of failure and in ignorance of when, where, and how failure will come. They do not and cannot possibly know about even a small proportion of government activity that bears on their failure. They can only put out fires and smile above the ashes. They don't know what's going on—yet they are responsible for it. And they feed that responsibility every time they take credit for good news not of their own making. (Lowi, 1985b: 190)

Add to this an independent-minded Congress with a propensity to act as a brake on proposed policy change, and the prospects for legislative support of presidential policy initiatives appear at best remote. Bush's stress on bipartisanship was initially medicinal, but polarizing forces within Congress reduced the president's capacity to win and preserve goodwill on Capitol Hill. The fact that Bush was the first newly elected president to have a cabinet choice (John Tower, nominated as secretary of defense) rejected by the Senate attested to the power of a determined Congress, as did the often-critical hearings held by Congress regarding the administration's Persian Gulf policies.

Whereas Congress is unlikely to facilitate policy changes sought by the president, it could itself become a source for changes in policy priorities in the post–Cold War political climate: "the balance of power between the executive and the legislature is . . . likely to shift with the Cold War's end. For as security policy receives less attention, economic policy, environmental concerns and human rights should achieve greater salience. In all three areas Congress is likely to play a greater role than it has in security policy" (Maynes, 1990).

Ultimately, the ability of the president to work his will in Congress is influenced by the support his policies enjoy among the American people. Indeed, the potential influence of *societal* forces in a globally interdependent world is especially potent, for under such circumstances foreign policy is often little more than an extension of domestic policy. Many groups within American society have great incentives to influence foreign policy, and presidents are tempted to take foreign policy positions primarily for their public impact—in a highly politicized domestic environment presidents are inclined to resist everything but temptation. Politics does not stop at the water's edge.

The American public's definition of national priorities is also likely to be driven by concerns about the economic foundations of national prosperity. The potential impact of these concerns was nowhere more apparent than in the domestic debate that arose over the basic question that Bush was forced to confront: whether guns and butter (military spending and economic prosperity) are incompatible in the long run (and whether one could be obtained without sacrifice of the other).

The failure of the Reagan administration to increase military spending without incurring deficits speaks to the inherent tension between the goals. Reagan's borrowing at home and abroad to fund the government's massive arms buildup succeeded in making America stand tall—by standing on a mountain of debt. Bush's ability to continue that approach is doubtful, especially as the economy slides toward another recession. The national interest may require corrective action. As Senator Daniel Patrick Moynihan in 1989 warned, "It is an iron law of history that power passes from debtor to creditor." American power will wane if its status as the world's greatest debtor is not corrected. That will require painful adjustments of prevailing policy priorities.

Whether or not those adjustments can be made in the American political setting is problematic. Moreover, it is not clear that the American public knows where Bush stands on these issues. The president's 1988 election was a personal victory without a mandate. Opinion polls revealed that many Americans who voted for Bush did not understand the specifics of his philosophy, particularly in a vicious campaign that neglected to spell out positions. "The vote itself . . . cannot be read as an endorsement of Bush's program" (Pomper, 1989). Moreover, single-issue, special-interest groups and political action committees continue to press their causes. And public opinion, always potentially fickle, may be expected to turn sharply against the president if the economy sours, disapproval-enhancing events crop up, or the costs of adjusting to the nation's deficits, debt, and stationing of troops in the explosive Middle East come to be perceived as too burdensome or risky. The status quo, accordingly, is preserved by the cross pressures exerted by contending groups in a pluralistic society and the preference of political leaders to hew a middle course.

The paradox exists that whereas the American public clearly desires and rewards presidential leadership, the fragmented American political system thwarts its exercise. The public "mood," moreover, is prone to cyclical oscillations between internationalism and isolationism and between idealism and realism. Together these discordant rhythms, both evident in the 1980s and 1990s, point toward potentially divergent future paths as the relative costs and benefits of options are weighed. Some will find the interventionist thrust that Reagan and Bush advocated in the 1980s palatable; others will recoil from it. Regardless of the direction in which public opinion swings in the 1990s, however, it is unlikely that opinion will mobilize permanently around a conception of U.S. national interests sufficiently radical to push American foreign policy outside the boundaries within which it has fluctuated since the end of the World War II.

How peace and prosperity are best protected and promoted is, of course, a matter of opinion. Some nations in America's *external* environment do not share its world view, and their growing economic and political power arguably could serve as a powerful catalyst to its revision. At a time when interdependence among nations is growing rapidly and Japan and a uniting Europe (and united Germany) have become viable economic competitors to the United States, some of America's closest allies strongly differ with recent American administrations' picture of global priorities and professed definitions of the global agenda. Instead of conceding these concerns and downplaying some vulnerabilities, Bush followed the path blazed by the author of the Reagan Doctrine. It spent "more on the 'Operation Just Cause' Panama invasion than the entire yearly budget of Bush's so called 'drug war'" (Wicker, 1990). Dire consequences, some predicted, could flow from this sense of priorities: "Like the Soviet Union, but unlike Japan and Germany, the United States has systematically sacrificed economic strength to the accumulation and projection of military power. In the process the sinews of nationhood have become frayed" (Barnet, 1990).

The United States does maintain unmatched military strength and doubtless continues to exercise disproportionate political influence over international affairs. In this sense one can easily agree with former editor of the *London Times* Henry Brandon's contention in 1983 that "the presumed retreat of American never happened." But that conclusion ignores the decline of the resource base of the United States relative to that of other nations, however measured. The erosion of America's economic output, productivity, and competitiveness has made it increasingly difficult for the United States to exercise political leverage. "The idea that the United States, acting alone in an interdependent world, can somehow renew the mythical golden era of the immediate postwar years when [the United States] seemed invulnerable to international political or economic developments," Secretary of State Alexander Haig observed in 1985, "is a dangerous illusion." "Today," former U.N. ambassador Jeane Kirkpatrick warned in June 1990, the superpowers "are no longer undisputed captains of their teams. . . . We have already experienced decentralization of decision-making powers. I wonder," she added, "if the superpower leaders fully understand the limits on their ability to speak for the alliances they head."

Clearly, many of the challenges of the 1990s do not fit well with a foreign policy designed for the circumstances of the late 1940s. A post-World War II vision is not very suitable to a post-Cold War system. "We must recognize," former Secretary of Defense and CIA director James R. Schlesinger urged in testimony before Congress in 1990, "that the international environment has now been transformed. We must not go on doing what we have done in the past on the premise, why change a successful strategy? Were we to do so, it would prove self-defeating."

Will the Bush administration live up to the lofty standard it has set for itself, and pragmatically adjust its policy approach to the world taking shape in 2000?

THE PROBLEMATIC FUTURE

Former Secretary of State Dean Acheson once noted that "there are fashions in everything, even in horrors . . . and just as there are fashions in fears, there are fashions in remedies." To the extent that that telling aphorism is true, global trends can be expected eventually to distance American foreign policy from the approach it has relentlessly pursued for nearly five decades and move it toward a broadened conception of national security. But resistance to acceptance of new fashions is evident.

It is nonetheless clear that as Soviet power recedes in the aftermath of the Cold War, an auspicious opportunity for superpower accommodation has emerged. In the early-1950s, the creator of the Office of Strategic Services, William Donovan, predicted, "one day the Iron Curtain will lift and the captive nations of the East will become part of a United Europe. Even Russia, purged by future events of its desire to bully and subdue its neighbors, will be a member and, given the innate genius of the Russian people, a highly respected and involved member." This vision appeared far-fetched then, but not so much so today. Still, the United States has yet to construct a long-term strategy for a post-Cold War era, or to develop a blueprint for working *with* the Soviets and others on problems it cannot solve alone.

As before, at issue today is whether the conventional assumptions that have guided American foreign policy making since World War II are warranted. Although reaffirmed as sacred truths during the Reagan years, their appropriateness, given the transformed international system and the large number of unconventional economic and environmental threats that urgently need to be addressed, is certain to be questioned. Today's world necessitates many hard choices. "There are periods of history," Stanley Hoffmann (1989) observes, "when profound changes occur all of a sudden. . . . We are now in one of those periods, which obliges the United States to rethink its role in the world, just as it was forced to do by the cataclysmic changes that followed the end of the Second World War." "What is in order," Irving Kristol (1990) urges, "is some new, imaginative thinking about America's role in the world, and not a mere projection of yesterday's role and policy." Whether changes will occur depends, in part, on the capacity of democracy to recruit into office farsighted, courageous leaders able to offer a positive vision of the future and a program for reaching it. Trend is *not* destiny. The world that will be inherited will be influenced by the assumptions policymakers make about global realities and on their capacity to act decisively and wisely in responding to emerging challenges. That capacity is again being tested.

The person empowered to make the fundamental choices, the president, is, of course, only one determining element in the outcome. The factors that collectively drive the policy process will give direction to the eventual policy that emerges. Indeed, the process—more so than the individuals involved in it—will parent the policy. For the policy-making process and the conditions that influence it will not only stimulate efforts to cope with external challenges, but also constrain a president's ability to implement the design chosen. "All of [the nation's past presidents], from the most venturesome to the most reticent, have shared one disconcerting experience: the discovery of the limits and restraints—decreed by law, by history, and by circumstances—that sometimes can blur their clearest designs or dull their sharpest purposes," noted Emmet John Hughes (1972). "I have not controlled events, events have controlled me" was a telling lament that President Lincoln expressed.

"The really surprising thing about [the United States]," noted Henry Brandon in 1983, "has been the basic stability of [postwar] American foreign policy. There has been a continuity that, in fact, nobody could have predicted." The assumptions made by American policymakers in the immediate aftermath of World War II have proven to be remarkably resilient for almost five decades. But now, however, the structure of the postwar system has collapsed. Turbulent global changes call for a new American foreign policy. Although past policy has the force of momentum behind it, and that force is awesome, the question for the 1990s is whether the United States has the will to chart new foreign policy directions. Will the parameters of American foreign policy be redrawn, and can accommodative adjustments to the new realities be expected? On the answers may depend the security and prosperity of the United States in the new millennium.

SUGGESTIONS FOR FURTHER READING

Bundy, McGeorge. (1990) "From Cold War Toward Trusting Peace," *Foreign Affairs* 69 (No. 1): 197–212.

Hoffmann, Stanley. (1989) "What Shall We Do in the World?" *Atlantic Monthly* 264 (October): 84–96.

Hyland, William G. (1990) *The Cold War is Over.* New York: Times Books.

Maynes, Charles William. (1990) "America Without the Cold War," *Foreign Policy* 78 (Spring): 3–25.

Mead, Walter Russell. (1990) "On the Road to Ruin: Winning the Cold War, Losing the Economic Peace," *Harper's* 280 (March): 59–64.

Mearsheimer, John G. (1990) "Why We Will Soon Miss the Cold War," *Atlantic Monthly* 266 (August): 35–51.

Nye, Joseph S., Jr. (1990) *Bound to Lead: The Changing Nature of American Power.* New York: Basic Books.

Ravenal, Earl C. (1990–1991) "The Case for Adjustment," *Foreign Policy* 81 (Winter): 3–19.

Rizopoulos, Nicholas X., ed. (1990) *Sea-Changes: American Foreign Policy in a World Transformed.* New York: Council on Foreign Relations Press.

von Vorys, Karl. (1990) *American National Interest: Virtue and Power in Foreign Policy.* New York: Praeger.

Wattenberg, Ben J. (1991) *The First Universal Nation: Leading Indicators and Ideas of the Surge of America in the 1990s.* New York: The Free Press.

References

Abrahamsen, David. (1977) *Nixon vs. Nixon: An Emotional Tragedy.* New York: Farrar, Straus & Giroux.

Abramson, Jill, and Brooks Jackson. (1990) "Debate over PAC Money Hits Close to Home as Lawmakers Tackle Campaign-Finance Bill," *Wall Street Journal,* March 7, p. A20.

Abramson, Paul R., John H. Aldrich, and David W. Rohde. (1990) *Change and Continuity in the 1988 Elections.* Washington, D.C.: CQ Press.

_____. (1986) *Change and Continuity in the 1984 Elections.* Washington, D.C.: CQ Press.

Acheson, Dean. (1969) *Present at the Creation.* New York: Norton.

Adams, Gordon. (1988) "The Iron Triangle: Inside the Defense Policy Process," pp. 70–78 in Charles W. Kegley, Jr., and Eugene R. Wittkopf (eds.), *The Domestic Sources of American Foreign Policy: Insights and Evidence.* New York: St. Martin's.

Adelman, Kenneth L. (1981) "Speaking of America: Public Diplomacy in Our Time," *Foreign Affairs* 59 (Spring): 913–936.

Adorno, Theodore W., Else Frenkel-Brunswik, Daniel J. Levinson, and R. Nevitt Sanford. (1950) *The Authoritarian Personality.* New York: Harper.

Aho, C. Michael, and March Levinson. (1988) *After Reagan: Confronting the Changed World Economy.* New York: Council on Foreign Relations.

Aldrich, John H., John L. Sullivan, and Eugene Borgida. (1989) "Foreign Affairs and Issue Voting: Do Presidential Candidates 'Waltz before a Blind Audience'?" *American Political Science Review* 83 (March): 123–141.

Allison, Graham T. (1971) *Essence of Decision: Explaining the Cuban Missile Crisis.* Boston: Little, Brown.

Allison, Graham T., and Morton H. Halperin. (1989) "Bureaucratic Politics: A Paradigm and Some Policy Implications," pp. 378–409 in G. John Ikenberry (ed.), *American Foreign Policy: Theoretical Essays.* Glenview, Ill.: Scott, Foresman.

Allison, Graham T., and Peter Szanton. (1976) "Organizing for the Decade Ahead," pp. 227–270 in Henry Owen and Charles L. Schultze (eds.), *Setting National Priorities: The Next Ten Years.* Washington, D.C.: Brookings Institution.

Almond, Gabriel A. (1960) *The American People and Foreign Policy.* New York: Praeger.

_____. (1954) *The Appeals of Communism.* Princeton, N.J.: Princeton University Press.

Alperovitz, Gar. (1989) "Do Nuclear Weapons Matter?" *New York Review of Books* 36 (April): 57–58.

_____. (1985) *Atomic Diplomacy: Hiroshima and Potsdam—The Use of the Atomic Bomb and the American Confrontation with Soviet Power,* rev. ed. New York: Penguin.

Alperovitz, Gar, and Jeff Faux. (1984) "Think Again: What We Need Is More Government, Not Less," *Washington Post National Weekly Edition,* October 22, p. 23.

Alsop, Joseph, and David Joravsky. (1980) "Was the Hiroshima Bomb Necessary? An Exchange," *New York Review of Books* 27 (October 23): 37–42.

Ambrose, Stephen E. (1988) *Rise to Globalism: American Foreign Policy since 1938,* 5th ed. New York: Penguin.

_____. (1983) *Eisenhower.* New York: Simon & Schuster.

Americans Talk Security. (1989) *Compendium.* Boston: Americans Talk Security.

Amuzegar, Jahangir. (1987) "Dealing with Debt," *Foreign Policy* 68 (Fall): 140–158.

Anderson, Paul A. (1987) "What Do Decision Makers Do When They Make a Foreign Policy Decision?" pp. 285–308 in Charles F. Hermann, Charles W. Kegley, Jr., and James N. Rosenau (eds.), *New Directions in the Study of Foreign Policy.* Boston: Allen & Unwin.

Anjaria, S. J. (1986) "A New Round of Global Trade Negotiations," *Finance & Development* 23 (June): 2–6.

Arnold, Fred. (1990) "International Migration: Who Goes Where?" *Finance & Development* 27 (June): 46–47.

Arnson, Cynthia J., and Philip Brenner. (1990) "The Limits of Lobbying: Interest Groups, Congress and Aid to the Contras." Paper presented at the conference on "Public Opinion and U.S. Foreign Policy: The Case of Contra Funding," the Woodrow Wilson School of Public and International Affairs, Princeton University, Princeton, N.J., May 4–5.

Art, Robert J. (1989) "The Pentagon: The Case for Biennial Budgeting," *Political Science Quarterly* 104 (Summer): 193–214.

———. (1985) "Congress and the Defense Budget: Enhancing Policy Oversight," *Political Science Quarterly* 100 (Summer): 227–248.

Asch, Seymour E. (1951) "Effects of Group Pressure upon the Modification and Distortion of Judgment," pp. 177–190 in Harold Guetzkow (ed.), *Groups, Leadership and Men*. Pittsburgh: Carnegie.

Asher, Herbert B. (1988) *Presidential Elections and American Politics*. Homewood, Ill.: Dorsey.

Aspin, Lee. (1976) "The Defense Budget and Foreign Policy: The Role of Congress," pp. 115–174 in Franklin A. Long and George W. Rathjens (eds.), *Arms, Defense Policy, and Arms Control*. New York: Norton.

Atkinson, Rick, and Fred Hiatt. (1985) "Oh, That Golden Safety Net: The Pentagon Never Met a Defense Contractor It Wouldn't Bail Out," *Washington Post National Weekly Edition*, April 22, pp. 6–8.

Austin, Anthony. (1971) *The President's War*. Philadelphia: Lippincott.

Baker, Ross K. (1981) "Outlook for the Reagan Administration," pp. 142–169 in Gerald Pomper, Ross K. Baker, Kathleen A. Frankovic, Charles E. Jacob, Wilson Carey McWilliams, and Henry A. Plotkin, *The Election of 1980: Reports and Interpretations*. Chatham, N.J.: Chatham House.

Balassa, Bela, and Marcus Noland. (1988) *Japan in the World Economy*. Washington, D.C.: Institute for International Economics.

Baldrige, Malcolm. (1983) "At Last, Hope for Coherent Policy," *New York Times*, June 19, p. F2.

Ball, Desmond. (1989) "Can Nuclear War Be Controlled?" pp. 284–290 in Charles W. Kegley, Jr., and Eugene R. Wittkopf (eds.), *The Nuclear Reader: Strategy, Weapons, War*, 2nd ed. New York: St. Martin's.

Ball, Desmond, and Robert C. Toth. (1990) "Revising the SIOP: Taking War-Fighting to Dangerous Extremes," *International Security* 14 (Spring): 65–92.

Ball, George. (1984) "White House Roulette," *New York Review of Books* 31 (November 8): 5–11.

———. (1982) *The Past Has Another Pattern: Memoirs*. New York: Norton.

———. (1976) *Diplomacy for a Crowded World: An American Foreign Policy*. Boston: Atlantic–Little, Brown.

Bamford, James. (1983) *The Puzzle Palace*. New York: Penguin.

Barber, James David. (1989) "George Bush: In Search of a Mission," *New York Times*, January 19, p. A31.

———. (1985) *The Presidential Character: Predicting Performance in the White House*, 3rd ed. Englewood Cliffs, N.J.: Prentice-Hall.

———. (1981) "Reagan's Sheer Personal Likability Faces Its Sternest Test," *Washington Post*, January 20, p. 8.

———. (1977) *The Presidential Character*, 2nd ed. Englewood Cliffs, N.J.: Prentice-Hall.

Bard, Mitchell. (1988) "The Influence of Ethnic Interest Groups on American Middle East Policy," pp. 57–69 in Charles W. Kegley, Jr., and Eugene R. Wittkopf (eds.), *The Domestic Sources of American Foreign Policy: Insights and Evidence*. New York: St. Martin's.

Baritz, Loren. (1985) *Backfire: A History of How American Culture Led Us into Vietnam and Made Us Fight the Way We Did*. New York: Morrow.

Barnet, Richard J. (1990) *The Rockets' Red Glare: When America Goes to War—The Presidents and the People*. New York: Simon & Schuster.

———. (1981) "The Search for National Security," *New Yorker* 57 (April 27): 50–52ff.

———. (1972) *Roots of War: The Men and Institutions behind U.S. Foreign Policy*. Baltimore: Penguin.

———. (1969) *The Economy of Death*. New York: Atheneum.

Barnet, Richard J., Lester R. Brown, Robert S. Browne, Hodding Carter III, Stephen F. Cohen, Jeff Faux, Randall Forsberg, Archibald L. Gillies, Stanley B. Greenberg, Ann F. Lewis, Robert B. Reich, Carl Sagan, and Ronald Steel. (1989) "American Priorities in a New World Era," *World Policy Journal* 6 (Spring): 203–237.

Barnet, Richard J., and Ronald E. Müller. (1974) *Global Reach: The Power of the Multinational Corporations*. New York: Simon & Schuster.

Bauer, Raymond A., Ithiel de Sola Pool, and Lewis Anthony Dexter. (1972) *American Business and Public Policy*, 2nd ed. Chicago: Aldine-Atherton.

Bax, Frans R. (1977) "The Legislative-Executive Relationship in Foreign Policy: New Partnership or New Competition?" *Orbis* 20 (Winter): 881–904.

Beckworth, David. (1988) "What to Expect," *Time*, November 21, pp. 28–30.

Beirne, Kenneth J. (1988) "Hope for the Homeless—Local and State Response," pp. 67–75 in *Assisting the Homeless: State and Local Responses in an Era of Limited Resources*. Washington, D.C.: Advisory Commission on Intergovernmental Relations.

Bell, J. Bowyer. (1990) "Explaining International Terrorism: The Elusive Quest," pp. 178–184 in Charles W. Kegley, Jr. (ed.), *International Terrorism: Characteristics, Causes, Controls*. New York: St. Martin's.

Bennett, Scott. (1989) "George's Tears Are for American People," *State* (Columbia, S.C.), October 30, p. A10.

Bennett, W. Lance. (1980) *Public Opinion in American Politics*. New York: Harcourt Brace Jovanovich.

Benze, James G., Jr. (1987) *Presidential Power and Management Techniques: The Carter and Reagan Administrations in Historical Perspective*. New York: Greenwood.

Bergsten, C. Fred. (1990) "The World Economy After the Cold War," *Foreign Affairs* 69 (Summer): 96–112.

_____. (1988) *America in the World Economy: A Strategy for the 1990s*. Washington, D.C.: Institute for International Economics.

_____. (1987) "Economic Imbalances and World Politics," *Foreign Affairs* 65 (Spring): 770–794.

Berkley, George E. (1978) *The Craft of Public Administration*. Boston: Allyn & Bacon.

Berkowitz, Morton, P. G. Bock, and Vincent J. Fuccillo. (1977) *The Politics of American Foreign Policy*. Englewood Cliffs, N.J.: Prentice-Hall.

Bernstein, Robert A. (1989) *Elections, Representation, and Congressional Voting Behavior: The Myth of Constituency Control*. Englewood Cliffs, N.J.: Prentice Hall.

Bernstein, Robert A., and William Anthony. (1974) "The ABM Issue in the Senate, 1968–1970: The Importance of Ideology," *American Political Science Review* 68 (September): 1198–1206.

Berry, Jeffrey M. (1984) *The Interest Group Society*. Boston: Little, Brown.

Berry, John M. (1989a) "Dampening Dollar Demand or Money Down the Drain?" *Washington Post National Weekly Edition*, October 16–22, p. 22.

_____. (1989b) "Next Time, World Bankers May Not Rush to Our Rescue?" *Washington Post National Weekly Edition*, December 26, 1988–January 1, 1989, pp. 20–21.

Betts, Richard K. (1978) "Analysis, War and Decision: Why Intelligence Failures Are Inevitable," *World Politics* 31 (October): 61–89.

Bissell, Richard E. (1990) "Who Killed the Third World?" *Washington Quarterly* 13 (Autumn): 23–32.

Blachman, Morris J., and Donald J. Puchala. (1991) "When Empires Meet: The "Long Peace" in Long-Term Perspective," pp. 177–201 in Charles W. Kegley, Jr. (ed.), *The Long Postwar Peace*. New York: HarperCollins.

Blake, David H., and Robert S. Walters. (1987) *The Politics of Global Economic Relations*, 3rd ed. Englewood Cliffs, N.J.: Prentice-Hall.

Blechman, Barry M., and Stephen S. Kaplan, with David K. Hall, William B. Quandt, Jerome N. Slater, Robert M. Slusser, and Philip Windsor. (1978) *Force without War*. Washington, D.C.: Brookings Institution.

Blight, James F., Joseph S. Nye, Jr., and David A. Welch. (1987) "The Cuban Missile Crisis Revisited," *Foreign Affairs* 66 (Fall): 170–188.

Blight, James G., and David A. Welch. (1989) *On the Brink: Americans and Soviets Re-examine the Cuban Missile Crisis*. New York: Hill & Wang.

Bloomfield, Lincoln P. (1978) "Planning Foreign Policy: Can It Be Done?" *Political Science Quarterly* 93 (Fall): 369–391.

_____. (1974) *The Foreign Policy Process: Making Theory Relevant*. Beverly Hills, Calif.: Sage.

Blumenthal, Sidney. (1988) *The Rise of the Counter Establishment*. New York: Harper & Row.

Bock, Joseph G. (1987) *The White House Staff and the National Security Assistant: Friendship and Friction at the Water's Edge*. New York: Greenwood.

Bodenheimer, Thomas, and Robert Gould. (1989) *Rollback! Right-wing Power in U.S. Foreign Policy*. Boston: South End Press.

Boffey, Philip M. (1983) "'Rational' Decisions Prove Not to Be," *New York Times*, December 6, pp. C1,C7.

Boulding, Kenneth E. (1959) "National Images and International Systems," *Journal of Conflict Resolution* 3 (June): 120–131.

Boyd, Richard W. (1972) "Popular Control of Public Policy: A Normal Vote Analysis of the 1968 Election," *American Political Science Review* 66 (June): 429–449.

Brady, Linda P. (1978) "The Situation and Foreign Policy," pp. 173–190 in Maurice A. East, Stephen A. Salmore, and Charles F. Hermann (eds.), *Why Nations Act*. Beverly Hills, Calif.: Sage.

Brecher, Michael, and Jonathan Wilkenfeld. (1991) "International Crises and Global Instability: The Myth of the 'Long Peace,'" pp. 85–104 in Charles W. Kegley, Jr. (ed.), *The Long Postwar Peace*. New York: HarperCollins.

Breslauer, George W. (1983) "Why Détente Failed: An Interpretation," pp. 319–340 in Alexander L. George (ed.), *Managing U.S.-Soviet Rivalry*. Boulder, Colo.: Westview.

Brewer, Garry D., and Paul Bracken. (1984) "Who's Thinking about National Security?" *Worldview* 27 (February): 21–23.

Brewer, Thomas L. (1980) *American Foreign Policy*. Englewood Cliffs, N.J.: Prentice-Hall.

Britan, Gerald M. (1981) *Bureaucracy and Innovation: An Ethnography of Policy Change.*" Beverly Hills, Calif.: Sage.

Broad, Robin, and John Cavanagh. (1988) "No More NICs," *Foreign Policy* 72 (Fall): 81–103.

Broder, David S. (1989) "Bush Hasn't Met Leadership Challenge," *State* (Columbia, S.C.), December 6, p. A10.

_____. (1988) "Bush Skeptical about Détente," *State* (Columbia, S.C.), July 17, p. A6.

_____. (1986) "Who Took the Fun Out of Congress?" *Washington Post National Weekly Edition*, February 17, pp. 9–10.

Brody, Richard A., and Catherine R. Shapiro. (1989) "A Reconsideration of the Rally Phenomenon in Public Opinion," pp. 77–102 in Samuel Long (ed.), *Political Behavior Annual*, vol. 2. Boulder, Colo.: Westview.

Bronfenbrenner, Urie. (1961) "The Mirror Image in Soviet-American Relations," *Journal of Social Issues* 17 (No. 3): 45–56.

Brown, Lester R. (1990) "The Illusion of Progress," pp. 3–16 in Lester R. Brown, Christopher Flavin, Sandra Postel, Linda Starke, Alan Durning, Jodi Jacobson, Michael Renner, Hilary F. French, Marcia D. Lowe, and John E. Young, *State of the World 1990*. New York: Norton.

_____. (1972) *World without Borders*. New York: Vintage.

Brown, Lester R., Christopher Flavin, Sandra Postel, Linda Starke, Alan Durning, Jodi Jacobson, Michael Renner, Hilary F. French, Marcia D. Lowe, and John E. Young. (1990) *State of the World 1990*. New York: Norton.

Brown, Lester R., and John E. Young. (1990) "Feeding the World in the Nineties," pp. 59–78 in Lester R. Brown, Christopher Flavin, Sandra Postel, Linda Starke, Alan Durning, Jodi Jacobson, Michael Renner, Hilary F. French, Marcia D. Lowe, and John E. Young, *State of the World 1990*. New York: Norton.

Brownstein, Ronald, and Nina Easton. (1983) *Reagan's Ruling Class*. New York: Pantheon.

Brzezinski, Zbigniew. (1990) *The Grand Failure: The Birth and Death of Communism in the Twentieth Century*. New York: Collier Books.

_____. (1970) *Between Two Ages: America's Role in the Technetronic Era*. New York: Viking.

Buchanan, Bruce. (1978) *The Presidential Experience: What the Office Does to the Man*. Englewood Cliffs, N.J.: Prentice-Hall.

Buckley, William F. (1970) "On The Right," *National Review*, October 24, pp. 1124–1125.

Bunce, Valerie. (1985) "The Empire Strikes Back: The Transformation of the Eastern Bloc from a Soviet Asset to a Soviet Liability," *International Organization* 39 (Summer): 1–46.

Bundy, McGeorge. (1990) "From Cold War to Trusting Peace," *Foreign Affairs* 69 (No. 1): 197–212.

_____. (1988) *Danger and Survival*. New York: Random House.

Bundy, McGeorge, and James G. Blight. (1987–1988) "October 27, 1962: Transcripts of the Meetings of the ExComm," *International Security* 12 (Winter): 30–92.

Bundy, McGeorge, George F. Kennan, Robert S. McNamara, and Gerald Smith. (1982) "Nuclear Weapons and the Atlantic Alliance," *Foreign Affairs* 60 (Spring): 753–768.

Burch, Philip H., Jr. (1980) *Elites in American History: The New Deal to the Carter Administration*. New York: Holmes and Meier.

Burgess, John. (1988) "America on the Block," *Washington Post National Weekly Edition*, March 7–13, pp. 6–7.

Burki, Shahid Javed. (1983) "UNCTAD VI: For Better or for Worse?" *Finance & Development* 20 (December): 16–19.

Bushnell, Prudence. (1989) "Leadership at State: The Neglected Dimension," *Foreign Service Journal* 66 (September): 30–31.

Caldwell, Dan. (ed.). (1983) *Henry Kissinger: His Personality and Policies*. Durham: Duke University Press.

Califano, Joseph A., Jr. (1975) *A Presidential Nation*. New York: Norton.

Callison, C. Stuart. (1990) "Development and the National Interest," *Foreign Service Journal* 67 (January): 28–33.

Campbell, Angus, Philip E. Converse, Warren E. Miller, and Donald E. Stokes. (1960) *The American Voter*. New York: Wiley.

Campbell, Colin. (1986) *Managing the Presidency: Carter, Reagan, and the Search for Executive Harmony*. Pittsburgh: University of Pittsburgh Press.

Campbell, Joel, and Leila Cain. (1965) "Public Opinion and the Outbreak of War," *Journal of Conflict Resolution* 9 (September): 318–329.

Campbell, John Franklin. (1971) *The Foreign Affairs Fudge Factory*. New York: Basic Books.

Cannon, Lou. (1988) "An 'Honest Broker' at the NSC," *Washington Post National Weekly Edition*, August 22–28, pp. 6–8.

Carleton, David, and Michael Stohl. (1985) "The Foreign Policy of Human Rights: Rhetoric and Reality from Jimmy Carter to Ronald Reagan," *Human Rights Quarterly* 7 (May): 205–229.

Carnesale, Albert. (1985) "Special Supplement: The Strategic Defense Initiative," pp. 187–205 in George E. Hudson and Joseph Kruzel (eds.), *American Defense Annual 1985–1986*. Lexington, Mass.: Heath.

Carr, E. H. (1939) *The Twenty-Years' Crisis 1919–1939: An Introduction to the Study of International Relations*. London: Macmillan.

Carter, Hodding, III. (1981) "Life inside the Carter State Department," *Playboy* 28 (February): 96ff.

Caspary, William R. (1970) "The 'Mood Theory': A Study of Public Opinion," *American Political Science Review* 64 (June): 536–547.

Carver, George A., Jr. (1990) "Intelligence in the Age of Glasnost," *Foreign Affairs* 69 (Summer): 147–166.

Cavanagh, Thomas E. (1982–1983) "The Dispersion of Authority in the House of Representatives," *Political Science Quarterly* 97 (Winter): 623–637.

Centre on Transnational Corporations. (1987) *Direct Foreign Investment, the Service Sector, and International Banking*. New York: United Nations.

Chace, James, and Caleb Carr. (1988) *America Invulnerable: The Quest for Absolute Security from 1812 to Star Wars*. New York: Summit Books.

Cheney, Dick. (1990) *Annual Report to the President and the Congress*. Washington, D.C.: Government Printing Office.

Childs, Harold L. (1965) *Public Opinion: Nature, Formation, and Role*. Princeton, N.J.: Van Nostrand.

Christie, Richard, and Florence L. Geis. (1970) *Studies in Machiavellianism*. New York: Academic Press.

Clairmonte, Frederick, and John Cavanagh. (1982) "Transnational Corporations and Global Markets: Changing Power Relations," *Trade and Development: An UNCTAD Review* 4 (Winter): 149–182.

Clark, James W. (1975) "Foreign Affairs Personnel Management," pp. 181–222 in *Commission on the Organization of the Government for the Conduct of Foreign Policy*, Vol. 6, Appendix P. Washington, D.C.: Government Printing Office.

Clark, Keith C., and Laurence J. Legere. (eds.). (1969) *The President and the Management of National Security: A Report by the Institute for Defense Analyses*. New York: Praeger.

Clarke, Duncan L. (1989) *American Defense and Foreign Policy Institutions: Toward a Sound Foundation*. New York: Harper & Row.

Clarke, Duncan L., and Edward L. Neveleff. (1984) "Security, Foreign Intelligence, and Civil Liberties: Has the Pendulum Swung Too Far?" *Political Science Quarterly* 99 (Fall): 493–513.

Cleveland, Harlan. (1959) "Dinosaurs and Personal Freedom," *Saturday Review* 42 (February 28): 12–14ff.

Clymer, Adam. (1985a) "Perception of America's World Role Ten Years after Vietnam: Assertiveness Caused by Reagan, Trust and Sex." Paper presented at the Annual Meeting of the American Political Science Association, New Orleans, August 29–September 1.

_____. (1985b) "Polling Americans," *New York Times Magazine*, November 10, pp. 37ff.

Coate, Roger A. (1988) *Unilateralism, Ideology and U.S. Foreign Policy: The United States in and out of UNESCO.* Boulder, Colo.: Lynne Rienner.

Cohen, Benjamin J. (1989) "A Global Chapter 11," *Foreign Policy* 75 (Summer): 109–127.

Cohen, Bernard C. (1983) "The Influence of Special-Interest Groups and the Mass Media on Security Policy in the United States," pp. 222–241 in Charles W. Kegley, Jr., and Eugene R. Wittkopf (eds.), *Perspectives on American Foreign Policy.* New York: St. Martin's.

_____. (1973) *The Public's Impact on Foreign Policy.* Boston: Little, Brown.

_____. (1963) *The Press and Foreign Policy.* Princeton, N.J.: Princeton University Press.

_____. (1961) "Foreign Policy Makers and the Press," pp. 220–228 in James N. Rosenau (ed.), *International Politics and Foreign Policy.* New York: Free Press.

_____. (1959) *The Influence of Non-Governmental Groups on Foreign Policy.* Boston: World Peace Foundation.

Cohen, Stephen D. (1988) *The Making of United States International Economic Policy: Principles, Problems, and Proposals for Reform*, 3rd ed. New York: Praeger.

Collier, Ellen C. (1990) "War Powers Resolution: Presidential Compliance," CRS Issue Brief 81050, January 2. Washington, D.C.: Congressional Research Service.

_____. (1989) "Bipartisan Foreign Policy and Policymaking since World War II," *CRS Report for Congress*, November 9. Washington, D.C.: Congressional Research Service.

_____. (1988) "Foreign Policy by Reporting Requirement," *Washington Quarterly* 11 (Winter): 75–84.

_____. (1987a) "War Powers and the Persian Gulf," *Congressional Research Service Review*, November/December, pp. 23–24.

_____. (1987b) "The War Powers Resolution: Fifteen Years of Experience," *CRS Report for Congress*, August 3. Washington, D.C.: Congressional Research Service.

Commager, Henry Steele. (1983) "Misconceptions Governing American Foreign Policy," pp. 510–517 in Charles W. Kegley, Jr., and Eugene R. Wittkopf (eds.), *Perspectives on American Foreign Policy.* New York: St. Martin's.

_____. (1965) "A Historian Looks at Our Political Morality," *Saturday Review* 48 (July 10): 16–18.

Commission on the Organization of the Government for the Conduct of Foreign Policy. (1975) Washington, D.C.: Government Printing Office.

Commission on Transnational Corporations. (1986) "Recent Developments Related to Transnational Corporations and International Economic Relations," U.N. Doc. E/C.10/1986/2, United Nations Economic and Social Council.

Congressional Quarterly. (1990) *The Middle East*, 7th ed. Washington, D.C.: Congressional Quarterly, Inc.

_____. (1986) *U.S. Foreign Policy: The Reagan Imprint.* Washington, D.C.: Congressional Quarterly, Inc.

_____. (1984) *Trade: U.S. Policy since 1945.* Washington, D.C.: Congressional Quarterly, Inc.

_____. (1983) *U.S. Defense Policy.* Washington, D.C.: Congressional Quarterly, Inc.

Congressional Quarterly Almanac, 1986. (1987) Vol. 42. Washington, D.C.: Congressional Quarterly, Inc.

Congressional Quarterly Almanac, 1984. (1985) Vol. 40. Washington, D.C.: Congressional Quarterly, Inc.

Congressional Research Service. (1989) "Soviet-U.S. Relations: A Briefing Book." *CRS Report for Congress*, October. Washington, D.C.: Congressional Research Service.

_____. (1984) *Treaties and Other International Agreements: The Role of the United States Senate.* Prepared for the Committee on Foreign Relations, United States Senate. 96th Congress, 2nd Session. Washington, D.C.: Government Printing Office.

_____. (1979) *Senate Debate on the Panama Canal Treaties: A Compendium of Major Statements, Documents, Record Votes and Relevant Events.* Prepared for the Committee on Foreign Relations, United States Senate. 96th Congress, 1st Session. Washington, D.C.: Government Printing Office.

Conway, M. Margaret. (1985) *Political Participation in the United States.* Washington, D.C.: CQ Press.

Cooper, Richard N. (1988) "International Economic Cooperation: Is It Desirable? Is It Likely?" *Washington Quarterly* 11 (Spring): 89–101.

Copson, Raymond W. (1988) "The Reagan Doctrine: U.S. Assistance to Anti-Marxist Guerrillas," *CRS Issue Brief*, March 11.

Cox, Arthur Macy. (1976) *The Dynamics of Détente*. New York: Norton.

Crabb, Cecil V., Jr. (1986) *Policy Makers and Critics: Conflicting Theories of American Foreign Policy*, 2nd ed. New York: Praeger.

Crabb, Cecil V. (1957) *Bipartisan Foreign Policy: Myth or Reality*. Evanston, Ill.: Row, Peterson.

Crabb, Cecil V., Jr., and Pat M. Holt. (1989) *Invitation to Struggle: Congress, the President and Foreign Policy*, 3rd ed. Washington, D.C.: CQ Press.

Craig, Paul P., and John A. Jungerman. (1986) *Nuclear Arms Race*. New York: McGraw-Hill.

Crenshaw, Martha. (1990) "Is International Terrorism Primarily State-Sponsored?," pp. 163–169 in Charles W. Kegley, Jr. (ed.), *International Terrorism: Characteristics, Causes, Controls*. New York: St. Martin's.

Cronin, Thomas E. (1984) "The Swelling of the Presidency: Can Anyone Reverse the Tide?" pp. 345–359 in Peter Woll (ed.), *American Government: Readings and Cases*. Boston: Little, Brown.

———. (1973) "The Swelling of the Presidency," *Saturday Review of the Society* 1 (February): 30–36.

Dallek, Robert. (1984) *Ronald Reagan: The Politics of Symbolism*. Cambridge, Mass.: Harvard University Press.

———. (1983) *The American Style of Foreign Policy: Cultural Politics and Foreign Affairs*. New York: Knopf.

Davis, Vincent. (1987) "Organization and Management," pp. 171–199 in Joseph Kruzel (ed.), *American Defense Annual, 1987–1988*. Lexington, Mass.: Lexington Books.

Davison, W. Phillips. (1976) "Mass Communication and Diplomacy," pp. 388–403 in Gavin Boyd, James N. Rosenau, and Kenneth W. Thompson (eds.), *World Politics*. New York: Free Press.

DeRivera, Joseph H. (1968) *The Psychological Dimension of Foreign Policy*. Columbus, Ohio: Merrill

Destler, I. M. (1986) *American Trade Politics: System under Stress*. Washington, D.C.: Institute for International Economics.

———. (1984) "The Elusive Consensus: Congress and Central America," pp. 319–335 in Robert S. Leiken (ed.), *Central America*. New York: Pergamon.

———. (1983a) "The Evolution of Reagan Foreign Policy," pp. 117–158 in Fred I. Greenstein (ed.), *The Reagan Presidency*. Baltimore: Johns Hopkins University Press.

———. (1983b) "The Rise of the National Security Assistant," pp. 260–281 in Charles W. Kegley, Jr., and Eugene R. Wittkopf (eds.), *Perspectives on American Foreign Policy*. New York: St. Martin's.

———. (1980) *Making Foreign Economic Policy*. Washington, D.C.: Brookings Institution.

———. (1974) *Presidents, Bureaucrats, and Foreign Policy: The Politics of Organizational Reform*. Princeton, N.J.: Princeton University Press.

Destler, I. M., Leslie H. Gelb, and Anthony Lake. (1984) *Our Own Worst Enemy: The Unmaking of American Foreign Policy*. New York: Simon & Schuster.

Destler, I. M., and C. Randall Henning. (1989) *Dollar Politics: Exchange Rate Policymaking in the United States*. Washington, D.C.: Institute for International Economics.

Destler, I. M., and John S. Odell. (1987) *Anti-Protection: Changing Forces in United States Trade Politics*. Washington, D.C.: Institute for International Economics.

De Tocqueville, Alexis. (1969) (Originally published in 1835) *Democracy in America*. New York: Doubleday.

Deutsch, Karl W. (1974) *Politics and Government*. Boston: Houghton Mifflin.

———. (1953) "The Growth of Nations: Some Recurrent Patterns of Political and Social Integration," *World Politics* 5 (January): 168–195.

Deutsch, Karl W., and Richard L. Merritt. (1965) "Effects of Events on National and International Images," pp. 132–187 in Herbert C. Kelman (ed.), *International Behavior*. New York: Holt, Rinehart and Winston.

Diplomacy for the 70's: A Program of Management Reform for the Department of State. (1970) Washington, D.C.: Department of State.

DiRenzo, Gordon J. (ed.). (1974) *Personality and Politics*. Garden City, N.Y.: Doubleday-Anchor.

Dobbs, Michael. (1990) "How to Make a Comeback after Your Empire Folds," *Washington Post National Weekly Edition*, September 17–23, pp. 16, 18.

Dolbeare, Kenneth M., and Patricia Dolbeare. (1971) *American Ideologies*. Chicago: Markham.

Dolbeare, Kenneth M., and Murray J. Edelman. (1985) *American Politics*, 5th ed. Lexington, Mass.: Heath.

Domhoff, G. William. (1984) *Who Rules America Now?* Englewood Cliffs, N.J.: Prentice-Hall.

———. (ed.) (1980) *Power Structure Research*. Beverly Hills, Calif.: Sage.

———. (1971) "Who Made American Foreign Policy, 1945–1963?" pp. 95–114 in Douglas M. Fox (ed.), *The Politics of U.S. Foreign Policy Making*. Pacific Palisades, Calif.: Goodyear.

Donovan, Hedley. (1985) *Roosevelt to Reagan*. New York: Harper & Row.

Donovan, John C. (1974) *The Cold Warriors: A Policy-Making Elite*. Lexington, Mass.: Heath.

Dowd, Maureen. (1989a) "Basking in Power's Glow: Bush's Year as President," *New York Times*, December 31, pp. 1, 15.

———. (1989b) "Bush's Fierce Loyalty Raises Debate on Whether It Hinders His Judgment," *New York Times*, March 10, p. B6.

Downs, Anthony. (1957) *An Economic Theory of Democracy*. New York: Harper & Row.

Draper, Theodore. (1990) *A Present of Things Past*. New York: Hill & Wang.

———. (1968) *The Dominican Revolt*. New York: Commentary.

Drischler, Alvin Paul. (1985) "Foreign Policy Making on the Hill," *Washington Quarterly* 8 (Summer): 165–175.

Drucker, Peter F. (1986) "The Changed World Economy," *Foreign Affairs* 64 (Spring): 768–791.

Duffy, Michael. (1989) "Mr. Consensus," *Time*, August 21, pp. 16–21.

Dulles, John Foster. (1952) "A Policy of Liberation," *Life*, May 19, pp. 19ff.

———. (1939) *War, Peace and Change*. New York: Harper & Row.

Durning, Alan B. (1990) "Ending Poverty," pp. 135–153 in Lester R. Brown, Christopher Flavin, Sandra Postel, Linda Starke, Alan Durning, Jodi Jacobson, Michael Renner, Hilary F. French, Marcia D. Lowe, and John E. Young, *State of the World 1990*. New York: Norton.

Dye, Thomas R. (1990) *Who's Running America?: The Bush Era*, 5th ed. Englewood Cliffs, N.J.: Prentice-Hall.

———. (1978) "Oligarchic Tendencies in National Policy-Making: The Role of the Private Policy-Planning Organizations," *Journal of Politics* 40 (May): 309–331.

Dye, Thomas R., and John W. Pickering. (1974) "Government and Corporate Elites," *Journal of Politics* 36 (November): 900–925.

Dye, Thomas R., and Harmon Zeigler. (1990) *The Irony of Democracy*, 8th ed. Pacific Grove, Calif.: Brooks/Cole.

Easterbrook, Gregg. (1986) "Ideas Move Nations," *Atlantic Monthly* 257 (January): 66–80.

Edwards, George C., III, and Stephen J. Wayne. (1985) *Presidential Leadership*. New York: St. Martin's.

Ehrlich, Paul R., and Anne H. Ehrlich. (1990) *The Population Explosion*. New York: Simon & Schuster.

Ehrlich, Paul R., John Harte, Mark A. Harwell, Peter H. Raven, Carl Sagan, George M. Woodwell, Joseph Berry, Edward S. Ayensu, Anne H. Ehrlich, Thomas Eisner, Stephen J. Gould, Herbert D. Grover, Rafael Herrera, Robert M. May, Ernst Mayr, Christopher P. McKay, Harold A. Mooney, Norman Myers, David Pimentel, and John M. Teal. (1983) "Long-Term Biological Consequences of Nuclear War," *Science* 222 (December 23): 1293–1300.

Ehrlich, Paul R., Carl Sagan, Donald Kennedy, and Walter Orr Roberts. (1985) *The Cold and the Dark: The World after Nuclear War*. New York: Norton.

Eisenhower, Dwight D. (1963) *The White House Years: Mandate for Change 1953–1956*. Garden City, N.Y.: Doubleday.

Elazar, Daniel J. (1972) *American Federalism: A View from the States*. New York: Crowell.

———. (1970) *Cities of the Prairie*. New York: Basic Books.

Elliott, Kim Andrew. (1989–1990) "Too Many Voices of America," *Foreign Policy* 77 (Winter): 113–131.

Ellsworth, Robert F., and Kenneth L. Adelman. (1979) "Foolish Intelligence," *Foreign Policy* 36 (Fall): 147–159.

Ellwood, John W. (1985) "The Great Exception: The Congressional Budget Process in an Age of Decentralization," pp. 315–342 in Lawrence C. Dodd and Bruce I. Oppenheimer (eds.), *Congress Reconsidered*, 3rd ed. Washington, D.C.: CQ Press.

Ellwood, John W., and James A. Thurber. (1981) "The Politics of the Congressional Budget Process Re-examined," pp. 246–271 in Lawrence C. Dodd and Bruce I. Oppenheimer (eds.), *Congress Reconsidered*, 2nd ed. Washington, D.C.: CQ Press.

Elshtain, Jean Bethke. (1989) "Issues and Themes in the 1988 Campaign," pp. 111–126 in Michael Nelson (ed.), *The Elections of 1988*. Washington, D.C.: CQ Press.

Emerson, Steven. (1988) *Secret Warriors: Inside the Covert Military Operations of the Reagan Era*. New York: Putnam.

Entman, Robert M. (1989) "How the Media Affect What People Think: An Information Processing Approach," *Journal of Politics* 51 (May): 347–370.

Epstein, Joshua M. (1983) "Horizontal Escalation: Sour Notes of a Recurrent Theme," pp. 649–660 in Robert J. Art and Kenneth N. Waltz (eds.), *The Use of Force*. Lanham, Md.: University Press of America.

Erikson, Robert S., Norman R. Luttbeg, and Kent L. Tedin. (1988) *American Public Opinion*, 3rd ed. New York: Macmillan.

Esterline, John H., and Robert B. Black. (1975) *Inside Foreign Policy: The Department of State Political System and Its Subsystems*. Palo Alto, Calif.: Mayfield.

Etheredge, Lloyd S. (1985) *Can Governments Learn? American Foreign Policy and Central American Revolutions*. New York: Pergamon.

———. (1978) *A World of Men: The Private Sources of American Foreign Policy*. Cambridge, Mass.: MIT Press.

Etzioni, Amitai. (1984) "Military Industry's Threat to National Security," *New York Times*, April 6, p. A35.

Evangelista, Matthew. (1989) "Issue-Area and Foreign Policy Revisited," *International Organization* 43 (Winter): 147–171.

Fagen, Richard R. (1975) "The United States and Chile: Roots and Branches," *Foreign Affairs* 53 (January): 297–313.

———. (1960) "Some Assessments and Uses of Public Opinion in Diplomacy," *Public Opinion Quarterly* 24 (Fall): 448–457.

Falk, Richard. (1983) "Lifting the Curse of Bipartisanship," *World Policy Journal* 1 (Fall): 127–157.

Falkowski, Lawrence S. (ed.). (1979) *Psychological Models in International Politics*. Boulder, Colo.: Westview.

Farah, Barbara G., and Ethel Klein. (1989) "Public Opinion Trends," pp. 103-128 in Gerald M. Pomper, Ross K. Baker, Walter Dean Burnham, Barbara G. Farah, Marjorie Randon Hershey, Ethel Klein, and Wilson Carey McWilliams, *The Election of 1988: Reports and Interpretations*. Chatham, N.J.: Chatham House.

Farnsworth, Elizabeth. (1974) "Chile: What Was the U.S. Role? More Than Admitted," *Foreign Policy* 16 (Fall): 127–141.

Feis, Herbert. (1966) *The Atomic Bomb and the End of World War II*. Princeton, N.J.: Princeton University Press.

Feldstein, Martin. (1985) "American Economic Policy and the World Economy," *Foreign Affairs* 63 (Summer): 995–1008.

Fenno, Richard F., Jr. (1973) *Congressmen in Committees*. Boston: Little, Brown.

Ferguson, Thomas, with Joel Rogers. (1986) "The Myth of America's Turn to the Right," *Atlantic Monthly* 257 (May): 43–53.

Festinger, Leon. (1957) *A Theory of Cognitive Dissonance*. Evanston, Ill.: Row, Peterson.

Final Report of the Select Committee to Study Governmental Operations with Respect to Intelligence Activities. (1976) U.S. Senate, 94th Congress, 2nd Session, Books 1–4. Washington, D.C.: Government Printing Office.

Finlayson, Jock A., and Mark W. Zacher. (1988) *Managing International Markets: Developing Countries and the Commodity Trade Regime*. New York: Columbia University Press.

Fiorina, Morris P. (1981) *Restrospective Voting in American National Elections*. New Haven, Conn.: Yale University Press.

Fisher, Louis. (1988) "Foreign Policy Powers of the President and Congress, *The Annals* 449 (September): 148–159.

———. (1987) *The Politics of Shared Power: Congress and the Executive*, 2nd ed. Washington, D.C.: CQ Press.

Fitzgerald, Francis. (1989) "Annals of Justice: Iran-Contra," *New Yorker* 65 (October 16): 51–84.

Flanagan, Stephen J. (1985) "Managing the Intelligence Community," *International Security* 10 (Summer): 58–95.

Fleisher, Richard. (1985) "Economic Benefit, Ideology, and Senate Voting on the B-1 Bomber," *American Politics Quarterly* 13 (April): 200–211.

Ford, Gerald R. (1979) *A Time to Heal*. New York: Harper & Row.

Foreign Military Sales, Foreign Military Construction Sales and Military Assistance Facts. (1989) Washington, D.C.: Defense Security Assistance Agency.

Fossedal, Gregory A. (1989) *The Democratic Imperative: Exporting the American Revolution*. New York: Basic Books.

———. (1985) "The Military-Congressional Complex," *Wall Street Journal*, August 8, p. 22.

Foster, Gregory D. (1989) "Global Demographic Trends to the Year 2010: Implications for U.S. Security," *Washington Quarterly* 12 (Spring): 5–24.

Fox, Harrison W., Jr., and Susan Webb Hammond. (1977) *Congressional Staffs: The Invisible Force in American Lawmaking.* New York: Free Press.

Frank, Charles R., Jr., and Mary Baird. (1975) "Foreign Aid: Its Speckled Past and Future Prospects," *International Organization* 29 (Winter): 133–167.

Frank, Robert S. (1973) *Message Dimensions of Television News.* Lexington, Mass.: Lexington Books.

Franck, Thomas M., and Edward Weisband. (1979) *Foreign Policy by Congress.* New York: Oxford University Press.

———. (eds.) (1974) *Secrecy and Foreign Policy.* New York: Oxford University Press.

Frankel, Charles. (1969) *High on Foggy Bottom.* New York: Harper & Row.

Frankovic, Kathleen A. (1982) "Sex and Politics—New Alignments, Old Issues," *PS* 15 (Summer): 439–448.

Free, Lloyd A., and Hedley Cantril. (1968) *The Political Beliefs of Americans.* New York: Simon & Schuster.

Freeman, J. Leiper. (1965) "The Bureaucracy in Pressure Politics," pp. 23–35 in Francis E. Rourke (ed.), *Bureaucratic Power in National Politics.* Boston: Little, Brown.

Frieden, Jeff. (1981) "Third World Indebted Industrialization: International Finance and State Capitalism in Mexico, Brazil, Algeria, and South Korea," *International Organization* 35 (Summer): 407–431.

Friedman, Thomas L. (1989) "As Ideology Recedes, the U.S. Rearranges Its Global Struggles," *New York Times*, December 31, p. E2.

Froman, Creel. (1984) *The Two American Political Systems: Society, Economics, and Politics.* Englewood Cliffs, N.J.: Prentice-Hall.

Fukuyama, Francis. (1989) "The End of History?" *National Interest* 16 (Summer): 3–18.

Fulbright, J. William. (1979) "The Legislator as Educator," *Foreign Affairs* 57 (Spring): 719–732.

Fulbright, J. William, with Seth P. Tillman. (1989) *The Price of Empire.* New York: Pantheon.

Funabashi, Yoichi. (1988) *Managing the Dollar: From the Plaza to the Louvre.* Washington, D.C.: Institute for International Economics.

Gaddis, John Lewis. (1991) "Great Illusions, the Long Peace, and the Future of the International System," pp. 25–55 in Charles W. Kegley, Jr. (ed.), *The Long Postwar Peace.* New York: HarperCollins.

———. (1990) "Coping with Victory," *Atlantic Monthly* 265 (May): 49–60.

———. (1987–1988) "Containment and the Logic of Strategy," *National Interest* 10 (Winter): 27–38.

———. (1982) *Strategies of Containment: A Critical Appraisal of Postwar American National Security Policy.* New York: Oxford University Press.

———. (1972) *The United States and the Origins of the Cold War, 1941–1947.* New York: Columbia University Press.

Galbraith, John Kenneth. (1973) "The Decline of American Power," pp. 311–350 in Lloyd C. Gardner (ed.), *The Great Nixon Turnaround.* New York: New Viewpoints.

———. (1970–1971) "The Plain Lessons of a Bad Decade," *Foreign Policy* 1 (Winter): 31–45.

———. (1969a) *Ambassador's Journal.* Boston: Houghton Mifflin.

———. (1969b) "The Power of the Pentagon," *Progressive* 33 (June): 29.

Gallup, George, Jr. (1985) *The Gallup Poll: Public Opinion 1984.* Wilmington, Del.: Scholarly Resources.

Gans, Herbert J. (1979) *Deciding What's News.* New York: Vintage.

Gardner, Lloyd C. (1984) *A Covenant with Power: America and World Order from Wilson to Reagan.* New York: Oxford University Press.

Garnham, David. (1975) "Foreign Service Elitism and U.S. Foreign Affairs," *Public Administration Review* 35 (January/February): 44–51.

Garten, Jeffrey E. (1985) "Gunboat Economics," *Foreign Affairs.* Special issue *America and the World 1984* 63 (No. 3): 538–559.

Gasiorowski, Mark J. (1987) "The 1953 Coup d'État in Iran," *International Journal of Middle East Studies* 19 (August): 261–286.

Gates, Robert M. (1987–1988) "The CIA and American Foreign Policy," *Foreign Affairs* 66 (Winter): 215–230.

Gati, Charles. (1990) *The Bloc That Failed: Soviet-East European Relations in Transition.* Bloomington: Indiana University Press.

Gelb, Leslie H. (1983) "Why Not the State Department?" pp. 282–298 in Charles W. Kegley, Jr., and Eugene R. Wittkopf (eds.), *Perspectives on American Foreign Policy.* New York: St. Martin's.

_____. (1976) "What Exactly Is Kissinger's Legacy?" *New York Times Magazine* (October 31): 13ff.

Gelb, Leslie H., and Morton H. Halperin. (1973) "The Ten Commandments of the Foreign Affairs Bureaucracy," pp. 250–259 in Steven L. Spiegel (ed.), *At Issue: Politics in the World Arena.* New York: St. Martin's.

George, Alexander L. (1988) "Presidential Management Styles and Models," pp. 107–126 in Charles W. Kegley, Jr., and Eugene R. Wittkopf (eds.), *The Domestic Sources of American Foreign Policy: Insights and Evidence.* New York: St. Martin's.

_____. (ed.) (1983) *Managing U.S.-Soviet Rivalry: Problems of Crisis Prevention.* Boulder, Colo.: Westview.

_____. (1972) "The Case for Multiple Advocacy in Making Foreign Policy," *American Political Science Review* 66 (September): 751–785.

George, Alexander L., and Juliette L. George. (1964) *Woodrow Wilson and Colonel House: A Personality Study.* New York: Dover.

Gergen, David. (1989) "The Bush Administration's Three Musketeers," *Washington Post National Weekly Edition*, April 17–23, pp. 23–24.

Gershman, Carl. (1980) "The Rise and Fall of the New Foreign-Policy Establishment," *Commentary* 70 (July): 13–24.

Gilpin, Robert. (1987) "American Policy in the Post-Reagan Era," *Daedalus* 116 (Summer): 33–67.

_____. (1981) *War and Change in World Politics.* New York: Cambridge University Press.

Glad, Betty. (1989) "The United States's Ronald Reagan," pp. 200–229 in Barbara Kellerman and Jeffrey Rubin (eds.), *Leadership and Negotiation in the Middle East.* New York: Praeger.

_____. (1983) "Black-and-White Thinking: Ronald Reagan's Approach to Foreign Policy," *Political Psychology* 4 (March): 33–76.

Glaser, Charles L. (1989) "Managing the Transition from Offense to Defense," pp. 223–232 in Charles W. Kegley, Jr., and Eugene R. Wittkopf (eds.), *The Nuclear Reader: Strategy, Weapons, War*, 2nd. ed. New York: St. Martin's.

Goldberg, Andrew C. (1989) "Offense and Defense in the Postnuclear System," pp. 121–128 in Charles W. Kegley, Jr., and Eugene R. Wittkopf (eds.), *The Nuclear Reader: Strategy, Weapons, War*, 2nd ed. New York: St. Martin's.

Goldstein, Judith. (1989) "The Impact of Ideas on Trade Policy: The Origins of U.S. Agricultural and Manufacturing Policies," *International Organization* 43 (Winter): 31–71.

Goldstein, Joshua. (1988) *Long Cycles: Prosperity and War in the Modern Age.* New Haven: Yale University Press.

Goldstein, Joshua S., and John R. Freeman. (1990) *Three-Way Street: Strategic Reciprocity in World Politics.* Chicago: University of Chicago Press.

Goodman, Allan E. (1987) "Reforming U.S. Intelligence," *Foreign Policy* 67 (Summer): 121–136.

_____. (1984–1985) "Dateline Langley: Fixing the Intelligence Mess," *Foreign Policy* 57 (Winter): 160–179.

_____. (1975) "The Causes and Consequences of Détente, 1949–1973." Paper presented at the National Security Education Seminar, Colorado College, Colorado Springs, Colorado, July.

Goodsell, Charles T. (1985) *The Case for Bureaucracy*, 2nd ed. Chatham, N.J.: Chatham House.

Goodwin, Jacob. (1985) *Brotherhood of Arms: General Dynamics and the Business of Defending America.* New York: Times Books.

Goshko, John M. (1989) "Foreign Policy in Turmoil—or Transition?" *Washington Post National Weekly Edition*, March 13–19, p. 7.

_____. (1988) "On U.S. Aid, It's a Battle of the Haves and the Have-Nots," *Washington Post National Weekly Edition*, January 18–24, p. 32.

Goulden, Joseph C. (1969) *Truth Is the First Casualty: The Gulf of Tonkin Affair.* Chicago: Rand McNally.

Graber, Doris A. (1989) *Mass Media and American Politics*, 3rd ed. Washington, D.C.: CQ Press.

_____. (ed.) (1990) *Media Power in Politics*, 2nd ed. Washington, D.C.: CQ Press.

Grady, Sandy. (1990) "A Lone Ranger President," *State* (Columbia, S.C.), January 11, p. A15.

Graham, Thomas W. (1986) "Public Attitudes towards Active Defense: ABM and Star Wars, 1945–1985." Cambridge, Mass.: Center for International Studies, Massachusetts Institute of Technology.

Gray, Colin S. (1984) *Nuclear Strategy and Nuclear Planning.* Philadelphia: Foreign Policy Research Institute.

Gray, Colin S., and Keith Payne. (1980) "Victory Is Possible," *Foreign Policy* 39 (Summer): 14–27.

Greenberg, Edward S. (1985) *Capitalism and the American Political Ideal*. Armonk, N.Y.: Sharpe.

Greenberger, Robert S. (1989) "Baker Is Pressing 'Linkage' with Soviets, Even Though Policy Has Limitations," *Wall Street Journal*, March 6, p. A8.

Greenstein, Fred I. (1982) *The Hidden Hand Presidency: Eisenhower as Leader*. New York: Basic Books.

———. (1969) *Personality and Politics*. Chicago: Markham.

Haig, Alexander M., Jr. (1984) *Caveat: Realism, Reagan, and Foreign Policy*. New York: Macmillan.

Halberstam, David. (1972) *The Best and the Brightest*. New York: Random House.

Halperin, Morton H. (1971) "Why Bureaucrats Play Games," *Foreign Policy* 2 (Spring): 70–90.

Hampson, Fen Osler. (1988) "The Divided Decision-Maker," pp. 227–247 in Charles W. Kegley, Jr., and Eugene R. Wittkopf (eds.), *The Domestic Sources of American Foreign Policy*. New York: St. Martin's.

Handbook of Economic Statistics, 1989. (1989) Washington, D.C.: Central Intelligence Agency.

Haney, Craig, and Philip Zimbardo. (1973) "Social Roles, Role-Playing, and Education," *Behavioral and Social Science Teacher* 1 (No. 1): 24–45.

Hansen, Roger D. (1980) "North-South Policy—What's the Problem?" *Foreign Affairs* 58 (Summer): 1104–1128.

Harr, John Ensor. (1969) *The Professional Diplomat*. Princeton, N.J.: Princeton University Press.

Harris, John B., and Eric Markusen. (1986) "Nuclear Weapons and Their Effects," pp. 24–26 in John B. Harris and Eric Markusen (eds.), *Nuclear Weapons and the Threat of Nuclear War*. San Diego: Harcourt Brace Jovanovich.

Hartz, Louis. (1955) *The Liberal Tradition in America*. New York: Harcourt Brace and World.

Head, Ivan L. (1989) "South-North Dangers," *Foreign Affairs* 68 (Summer): 71–86.

Helco, Hugh. (1988) "The In-and-Outer System: A Critical Assessment," *Political Science Quarterly* 103 (Spring): 37–56.

Henderson, Phillip G. (1988) *Managing the Presidency: The Eisenhower Legacy—From Kennedy to Reagan*. Boulder, Colo.: Westview.

Henkin, Louis. (1987–1988) "Foreign Affairs and the Constitution," *Foreign Affairs* 66 (Winter): 284–310.

———. (1972) *Foreign Affairs and the Constitution*. Mineola, N.Y.: Foundation Press.

Henry, James S. (1988) "Poor Man's Debt, Rich Man's Loot," *Washington Post National Weekly Edition*, December 19–25, pp. 24–25.

———. (1987) "Brazil Says: Nuts," *New Republic*, October 12, pp. 28–29.

———. (1986) "Where the Money Went," *New Republic*, April 14, pp. 20–23.

Herbers, John. (1976) *No Thank You, Mr. President*. New York: Norton.

Herken, Gregg. (1982) *The Winning Weapon: The Atomic Bomb in the Cold War, 1945–1950*. New York: Vintage.

Hermann, Charles F. (1988) "New Foreign Policy Problems and Old Bureaucratic Organizations," pp. 248–265 in Charles W. Kegley, Jr., and Eugene R. Wittkopf (eds.), *The Domestic Sources of American Foreign Policy*. New York: St. Martin's.

———. (1983) "Bureaucratic Constraints on Innovation in American Foreign Policy," pp. 390–409 in Charles W. Kegley, Jr., and Eugene R. Wittkopf (eds.), *Perspectives on American Foreign Policy*. New York: St. Martin's.

———. (ed.). (1972a) *International Crises: Insights from Behavioral Research*. New York: Free Press.

———. (1972b) "Some Issues in the Study of International Crisis," pp. 3–17 in Charles F. Hermann (ed.), *International Crises: Insights from Behavioral Research*. New York: Free Press.

———. (1969a) *Crises in Foreign Policy*. Indianapolis: Bobbs-Merrill.

———. (1969b) "International Crisis as a Situational Variable," pp. 409–421 in James N. Rosenau (ed.), *International Politics and Foreign Policy*. New York: Free Press.

Hermann, Margaret G. (1989) "Defining the Bush Presidential Style," *Mershon Memo* (Spring): 1.

———. (1976) "When Leader Personality Will Affect Foreign Policy: Some Propositions," pp. 326–333 in James N. Rosenau (ed.), *In Search of Global Patterns*. New York: Free Press.

———. (1974) "Leader Personality and Foreign Policy Behavior," pp. 201–234 in James N. Rosenau (ed.), *Comparing Foreign Policies*. New York: Sage/Halsted Press.

Hermann, Margaret G., and Charles F. Hermann. (1989) "Who Makes Foreign Policy Decisions and How," *International Studies Quarterly* 33 (December): 361–389.

Hermann, Margaret G., with Thomas W. Milburn. (eds.) (1977) *A Psychological Examination of Political Leaders*. New York: Free Press.

Hersh, Seymour. (1983) *The Price of Power: Kissinger in the Nixon White House*. New York: Summit Books.

Hess, Stephen. (1988) *Organizing the Presidency*, rev ed. Washington, D.C.: Brookings Institution.

_____. (1984) *The Government/Press Connection*. Washington, D.C.: Brookings Institution.

Hess, Stephen, and Michael Nelson. (1985) "Foreign Policy: Dominance and Decisiveness in Presidential Elections," pp. 129–154 in Michael Nelson (ed.), *The Elections of 1984*. Washington, D.C.: CQ Press.

Hiatt, Fred. (1984) "The War within the Pentagon," *Washington Post National Weekly Edition*, August 6, pp. 6–7.

Hiatt, Fred, and Rick Atkinson. (1985) "The Defense Boom: Uncle Sam Is a Cream of a Customer," *Washington Post National Weekly Edition*, April 29, pp. 19–22.

Hilsman, Roger. (1990) *The Politics of Policy Making in Defense and Foreign Affairs: Conceptual Models and Bureaucratic Politics*, 2nd ed. Englewood Cliffs, N.J.: Prentice-Hall.

_____. (1967) *To Move a Nation*. New York: Doubleday.

Hinckley, Ronald H. (1989) "American Opinion Toward the Soviet Union," *International Journal of Public Opinion Research* 1 (No. 3): 242–257.

Hoagland, Jim. (1989) "The Return of Nuclear Deterrence," *Washington Post*, June 27, p. A23.

Hoffer, Eric. (1951) *The True Believer*. New York: Harper & Brothers.

Hoffmann, Stanley. (1989) "What Should We Do in the World?," *Atlantic Monthly* 264 (October): 84–96.

_____. (1984) "Détente," pp. 231–262 in Joseph S. Nye, Jr. (ed.), *The Making of America's Soviet Policy*. New Haven, Conn.: Yale University Press.

_____. (1978) *Primacy or World Order: American Foreign Policy since the Cold War*. New York: McGraw-Hill.

Hofstadter, Richard. (1965) *The Paranoid Style in American Politics and Other Essays*. New York: Knopf.

Holmes, Jack E. (1985) *The Mood/Interest Theory of American Foreign Policy*. Lexington: University Press of Kentucky.

Holsti, Ole R. (1989) "Models of International Relations and Foreign Policy," *Diplomatic History* 13 (Winter): 15–43.

_____. (1987) Public Opinion and Containment," pp. 20–58 in Terry L. Deibel and John Lewis Gaddis (eds.), *Containing the Soviet Union*. Washington, D.C.: Pergamon-Brassey's.

_____. (1976) "Foreign Policy Formation Viewed Cognitively," pp. 18–54 in Robert Axelrod (ed.), *Structure of Decision: The Cognitive Maps of Political Elites*. Princeton, N.J.: Princeton University Press.

_____. (1973) "Foreign Policy Decision-Makers Viewed Psychologically." Paper presented at the Conference on the Successes and Failures of Scientific International Relations Research, Ojai, California, June 25–28.

_____. (1962) "The Belief System and National Images: A Case Study," *Journal of Conflict Resolution* 6 (September): 244–252.

Holsti, Ole R., and James N. Rosenau. (1990) "The Structure of Foreign Policy Attitudes: American Leaders, 1976–1984," *Journal of Politics* 52 (February): 94–125.

_____. (1984) *American Leadership in World Affairs: Vietnam and the Breakdown of Consensus*. Boston: Allen & Unwin.

_____. (1980) "Does Where You Stand Depend on When You Were Born? The Impact of Generation on Post-Vietnam Foreign Policy Beliefs," *Public Opinion Quarterly* 44 (Spring): 1–22.

Hoopes, Townsend. (1973a) *The Devil and John Foster Dulles: The Diplomacy of the Eisenhower Era*. Boston: Little, Brown.

_____. (1973b) *The Limits of Intervention*. New York: McKay.

Hopple, Gerald. (ed.). (1982) *Biopolitics, Political Psychology and International Politics*. New York: St. Martin's.

Horelick, Arnold L. (1990) "U.S.-Soviet Relations: The Threshold of a New Era," *Foreign Affairs* 69 (No. 1): 51–69.

Horowitz, David. (1965) *The Free World Colossus*. New York: Hill & Wang.

Houghton, Neal D. (ed.). (1968) *Struggle against History: U.S. Foreign Policy in an Age of Revolution*. New York: Washington Square Press.

House, Karen Eliot. (1989) "As Power Is Dispersed among Nations, Need for Leadership Grows," *Wall Street Journal*, February 21, pp. A1, A10.

Hufbauer, Gary. (1989–1990) "Beyond GATT," *Foreign Policy* 77 (Winter): 64–76.

Hughes, Barry B. (1978) *The Domestic Context of American Foreign Policy*. San Francisco: Freeman.

Hughes, Emmet John. (1972) *The Living Presidency*. New York: Coward, McCann and Geoghegan.

Hughes, Thomas L. (1985–1986) "The Twilight of Internationalism," *Foreign Policy* 61 (Winter): 25–48.

———. (1981) "Up from Reaganism," *Foreign Policy* 44 (Fall): 3–23.

Huntington, Samuel P. (1988–1989) "The U.S.—Decline or Reviewal" *Foreign Affairs* 67 (Winter): 76–96.

Hurwitz, Jon, and Mark Peffley. (1987) "How Are Foreign Policy Attitudes Structured? A Hierarchical Model," *American Political Science Review* 81 (December): 1099–1120.

Hyland, William G. (1989) "Bush's Foreign Policy: Pragmatism or Indecision?" *New York Times*, April 26, p. A27.

Ignatius, David. (1988) "Is This Any Way for a Country to Buy Weapons?" *Washington Post National Weekly Edition*, July 4–10, p. 23.

Iklé, Fred Charles. (1990) "The Ghost in the Pentagon," *National Interest* 19 (Spring): 13–20.

Immerman, Richard H. (1982) *The CIA in Guatemala: The Foreign Policy of Intervention*. Austin: University of Texas Press.

Insel, Barbara. (1985) "A World Awash in Grain," *Foreign Affairs* 63 (Spring): 892–911.

International Monetary Fund. (1987) *World Economic Outlook*. Washington, D.C.: International Monetary Fund.

Isaak, Alan C. (1985) *Scope and Methods of Political Science*, 4th ed. Chicago: Dorsey.

Isaak, Robert A. (1977) *American Democracy and World Power*. New York: St. Martin's.

———. (1975) *Individuals and World Politics*. North Scituate, Mass.: Duxbury Press.

Iyengar, Shanto, Mark D. Peters, and Donald R. Kinder. (1982) "Experimental Demonstrations of the 'Not-So-Minimal' Consequences of Television News Programs," *American Political Science Review* 76 (December): 848–858.

Jackson, Henry M. (1965) *The National Security Council: Jackson Subcommittee Papers on Policy-Making at the Presidential Level*. New York: Praeger.

Jacobson, Harold K. (1984) *Networks of Interdependence: International Organizations and the Global Political System*. New York: Knopf.

Jacobson, Jodi L. (1989) "Abandoning Homelands," pp. 59–76 in Lester R. Brown, Christopher Flavin, Sandra Postel, Linda Starke, Alan Durning, Lori Heise, Jodi Jacobson, Michael Renner, and Cynthia Pollock Shea, *State of the World 1989*. New York: Norton.

Janis, Irving L. (1989) *Crucial Decisions: Leadership in Policymaking and Crisis Management*. New York: Free Press.

———. (1982) *Groupthink: Psychological Studies of Policy Decisions and Fiascoes*, 2nd ed. Boston: Houghton Mifflin.

Javits, Jacob K. (1985) "War Powers Reconsidered," *Foreign Affairs* 64 (Fall): 130–140.

Jervis, Robert. (1984) *The Illogic of American National Strategy*. Ithaca, N.Y.: Cornell University Press.

Jervis, Robert, Richard Ned Lebow, and Janice Stein. (1988) *Psychology and Deterrence*. Baltimore: Johns Hopkins University Press.

Johnson, Loch K. (1989) *America's Secret Power: The CIA in a Democratic Society*. New York: Cambridge University Press.

———. (1984) *The Making of International Agreements*. New York: New York University Press.

———. (1983) "Seven Sins of Strategic Intelligence," *World Affairs* 146 (Fall): 176–204.

———. (1980) "Controlling the Quiet Option," *Foreign Policy* 39 (Summer): 143–153.

Johnson, Loch K., and James M. McCormick. (1977) "Foreign Policy by Executive Fiat," *Foreign Policy* 28 (Fall): 117–138.

Jones, David C. (1984) "What's Wrong with the Defense Establishment," pp. 272–286 in Asa A. Clark, IV, Peter W. Chiarelli, Jeffrey S. McKitrick, and James W. Reed (eds.), *The Defense Reform Debate*. Baltimore: Johns Hopkins University Press.

Jönsson, Christer. (1982a) *Cognitive Dynamics and International Politics*. New York: St. Martin's.

———. (1982b) "The Ideology of Foreign Policy," pp. 91–110 in Charles W. Kegley, Jr., and Pat McGowan (eds.), *Foreign Policy: USA/USSR*. Beverly Hills, Calif.: Sage.

Kahler, Miles. (1990) "The International Political Economy," *Foreign Affairs* 69 (Fall): 139–151.

Kaplan, Morton A. (1957) *System and Process in International Politics*. New York: Wiley.

Kattenburg, Paul. (1980) *The Vietnam Trauma in America Foreign Policy, 1945–75*. New Brunswick, N.J.: Transaction Books.

Katz, Elihu. (1957) "The Two-Step Flow of Communications," *Public Opinion Quarterly* 21 (Spring): 61–78.

Kaufman, Herbert. (1976) *Are Government Organizations Immortal?* Washington, D.C.: Brookings Institution.

Kearns, Doris. (1976) *Lyndon Johnson and the American Dream*. New York: Harper & Row.

Keene, Karlyn. (1990) "Bush: Man of the Common Sense People," *Wall Street Journal*, January 15, p. A22.

Keeny, Spurgeon M., Jr., and Wolfgang K. H. Panofsky. (1981) "MAD vs. NUTS: Can Doctrine or Weaponry Remedy the Mutual Hostage Relationship of the Superpowers?" *Foreign Affairs* 60 (Winter): 287–304.

Keeter, Scott. (1985) "Public Opinion in 1984," pp. 91–111 in Gerald M. Pomper, Ross K. Baker, Charles E. Jacob, Scott Keeter, Wilson Carey McWilliams, and Henry A. Plotkin, *The Election of 1984: Reports and Interpretations*. Chatham, N.J.: Chatham House.

Kegley, Charles W., Jr. (ed.). (1990) *International Terrorism: Characteristics, Causes, Controls*. New York: St. Martin's.

Kegley, Charles W., Jr., and Steven W. Hook. (1990) "American Foreign Aid and UN Voting: Did Reagan's Leakage Strategy Buy Deference or Defiance?" *International Studies Quarterly* (forthcoming).

Kegley, Charles W., Jr., and Gregory A. Raymond. (1990a) "The End of Alliances?" *USA Today* 118 (May): 32–34.

_____. (1990b) *When Trust Breaks Down: Alliance Norms and World Politics*. Columbia: University of South Carolina Press.

_____. (1989) "Going It Alone: The Decay of Alliance Norms," *Harvard International Review* 12 (Fall): 39–43.

Kegley, Charles W., Jr., and Eugene R. Wittkopf. (1989) *World Politics: Trend and Transformation*, 3rd ed. New York: St. Martin's.

Kempe, Frederick. (1990) *Divorcing the Dictator: America's Bungled Affair with Noriega*. New York: Putnam.

_____. (1983) "Terrorist Attacks Grow but Groups Are Smaller and Narrower Focus," *Wall Street Journal*, April 19, pp. 1, 19.

Kennan, George F. (1977) *The Cloud of Danger*. Boston: Little, Brown.

_____. (1976) "The United States and the Soviet Union, 1917–1976," *Foreign Affairs* 54 (July): 670–690.

_____. (1967) *Memoirs*. Boston: Little, Brown.

_____. (1954) *Realities of American Foreign Policy*. Princeton, N.J.: Princeton University Press.

_____. (1951) *American Diplomacy, 1900–1950*. New York: New American Library.

_____. ["X"]. (1947) "The Sources of Soviet Conduct," *Foreign Affairs* 25 (July): 566–582.

Kennedy, Paul. (1987) *The Rise and Fall of the Great Powers*. New York: Random House.

Kennedy, Robert F. (1971) *Thirteen Days*. New York: Norton.

Keohane, Robert O. (ed.). (1986) *Neorealism and Its Critics*. New York: Columbia University Press.

Keohane, Robert O., and Joseph S. Nye, Jr. (1989) *Power and Interdependence: World Politics in Transition*, 2nd ed. Glenview, Ill.: Scott, Foresman/Little, Brown.

_____. (1985) "Two Cheers for Multilateralism," *Foreign Policy* 60 (Fall): 148–167.

_____. (1975) "International Interdependence and Integration," pp. 363–414 in Fred I. Greenstein and Nelson W. Polsby (eds.), *International Politics: Handbook of Political Science*, Vol. 8. Reading, Mass.: Addison-Wesley.

Kern, Montague. (1984) "The Press, the Presidency, and International Conflicts: Lessons from Two Administrations," *Political Psychology* 5 (March): 53–68.

Kern, Montague, Patricia W. Levering, and Ralph B. Levering. (1984) *The Kennedy Crises*. Chapel Hill: University of North Carolina Press.

Key, V. O. (1961) *Public Opinion and American Democracy*. New York: Knopf.

Kidder, Rushworth M. (1990) "Why Modern Terrorism?" pp. 135–138 in Charles W. Kegley, Jr. (ed.), *International Terrorism: Characteristics, Causes, Controls*. New York: St. Martin's.

Kilpatrick, James J. (1985) "An Overstuffed Bureaucracy," *State* (Columbia, S.C.), April 23, p. A8.

Kirkpatrick, Jeane. (1974) *Political Women*. New York: Basic Books.

Kirschten, Dick. (1987) "Competent Manager," *National Journal* 19 (February 28): 468–469 passim.

Kissinger, Henry. (1979) *White House Years.* Boston: Little, Brown.

———. (1977) "Remarks by the Honorable Henry A. Kissinger, Secretary of State, before the National Press Club, Washington, D.C., January 10, 1977." State Department Press Release. January 11, No. 3.

———. (1974a) *American Foreign Policy*, expanded ed. New York: Norton.

———. (1974b) "Statement on U.S.-Soviet Relations," News Release of the Bureau of Public Affairs, Department of State, Office of Media Service. Special Report, September 19.

———. (1969) "Domestic Structure and Foreign Policy," pp. 261–275 in James N. Rosenau (ed.), *International Politics and Foreign Policy.* New York: Free Press.

———. (1962) *The Necessity of Choice.* Garden City, N.Y.: Doubleday.

Kissinger, Henry, and Cyrus Vance. (1988) "Bipartisan Objectives for American Foreign Policy," *Foreign Affairs* 66 (Summer): 899–921.

Klare, Michael. (1990a) "An Arms Control Agenda for the Third World," *Arms Control Today* 20 (April): 8–12.

———. (1990b) "Who's Arming Who? The Arms Trade in the 1990s," *Technology Review* 93 (May/June): 45–50.

———. (1989) "Subterranean Alliances: America's Global Proxy Network," *Journal of International Affairs* 43 (Summer/Fall): 97–118.

———. (1988–1989) "Deadly Convergence: The Perils of the Arms Trade," *World Policy Journal* 6 (Winter): 141–168.

———. (1984) *American Arms Supermarket.* Austin: University of Texas Press.

Kline, John. (1983) *State Government Influence in U.S. International Economic Policy.* Lexington, Mass.: Lexington Books.

Klingberg, Frank L. (1990) "Cyclical Trends in Foreign Policy Revisited in 1990," *International Studies Notes* 15 (Spring): 54–58.

———. (1983) *Cyclical Trends in American Foreign Policy Moods: The Unfolding of America's World Role.* Lanham, Md.: University Press of America.

Knudsen, Baard B. (1987) "The Paramount Importance of Cultural Sources: American Foreign Policy and Comparative Foreign Policy Research Reconsidered," *Cooperation and Conflict* 22 (No. 2): 81–113.

Kober, Stanley. (1990) "Idealpolitik," *Foreign Policy* 79 (Summer): 3–24.

Koch, Noel. (1986) "U.S. Security Assistance to the Third World: Time for a Reappraisal," *Journal of International Affairs* 40 (Summer): 43–57.

Kolko, Gabriel. (1968) *The Politics of War.* New York: Random House.

Kondracke, Morton. (1990) "How to Aid A.I.D.," *New Republic*, February 26, pp. 20–23.

Kotz, Nick. (1988) *Wild Blue Yonder.* Princeton, N.J.: Princeton University Press.

Kovic, Ron. (1977) *Born on the Fourth of July.* New York: Pocket Books.

Krasner, Stephen D. (1989) "Realist Praxis," *Journal of International Affairs* 43 (Summer/Fall): 143–160.

———. (1988) "Are Bureaucracies Important? A Re-examination of Accounts of the Cuban Missile Crisis," pp. 215–226 in Charles W. Kegley, Jr., and Eugene R. Wittkopf (eds.), *The Domestic Sources of American Foreign Policy.* New York: St. Martin's.

———. (1985) *Structural Conflict: The Third World against Global Liberalism.* Berkeley: University of California Press.

———. (1982) "Structural Causes and Regime Consequences," *International Organization* 36 (Spring): 185–206.

Krauthammer, Charles. (1985) "The Reagan Doctrine," *Time*, April 1, pp. 54–55.

———. (1983) "From OPEC to ODEC," *New Republic*, November 28, pp. 19–21.

Kreisberg, Paul H. (1989) "Containment's Last Gasp," *Foreign Policy* 75 (Summer): 146–163.

Kreml, William P. (1977) *The Anti-Authoritarian Personality.* Oxford: Pergamon Press.

Kriesberg, Louis, and Ross Klein. (1980) "Changes in Public Support for U.S. Military Spending," *Journal of Conflict Resolution* 24 (March): 79–110.

Kriesberg, Louis, Harry Murray, and Ross A. Klein. (1982) "Elites and Increased Public Support for U.S. Military Spending," *Journal of Political and Military Sociology* 10 (Fall): 275–297.

Kristol, Irving. (1990) "The Map of the World Has Changed," *Wall Street Journal*, January 3, p. A6.

Kuczynski, Pedro-Pablo. (1987) "The Outlook for Latin American Debt," *Foreign Affairs* 66 (Fall): 129–149.

Kurth, James R. (1989) "The Military-Industrial Complex Revisited," pp. 196–215 in Joseph Kruzel (ed.), *American Defense Annual, 1989–1990*. Lexington, Mass.: Lexington Books.

Kusnitz, Leonard A. (1984) *Public Opinion and Foreign Policy: America's China Policy, 1949–1979*. Westport, Conn.: Greenwood.

Kwitny, Jonathan. (1985) *Endless Enemies: The Making of an Unfriendly World*. New York: Congdon & Weed.

LaFeber, Walter. (1976) *America, Russia, and the Cold War 1945–1975*. New York: Wiley.

Langer, E. J. (1975) "The Illusion of Control," *Journal of Personality and Social Psychology* 32 (No. 6): 311–328.

Lanoue, David J. (1989) "The 'Teflon Factor': Ronald Reagan & Comparative Presidential Popularity," *Polity* 21 (Spring): 481–501.

Lardner, George, Jr. (1990a) "Dragging the NSA into the Glare of the Court," *Washington Post National Weekly Edition*, March 26-April 1, pp. 7–8.

———. (1990b) "No Such Agency," *Washington Post National Weekly Edition*, March 26-April 1, pp. 6–7.

Larson, Deborah Welch. (1985) *Origins of Containment: A Psychological Explanation*. Princeton, N.J.: Princeton University Press.

Larson, James F. (1990) "Television and U.S. Foreign Policy: The Case of the Iran Hostage Crisis," pp. 301–312 in Doris A. Graber (ed.), *Media Power in Politics*, 2nd ed. Washington, D.C.: CQ Press.

Laski, Harold J. (1947) "America—1947," *The Nation* 165 (December): 641–644.

Lasswell, Harold D. (1974) "The Political Personality," pp. 38–54 in Gordon J. DiRenzo (ed.), *Personality and Politics*. Garden City, N.Y.: Doubleday-Anchor.

———. (1962) "The Garrison State Hypothesis Today," pp. 51–70 in Samuel P. Huntington (ed.), *Changing Patterns of Military Politics*. New York: Free Press.

———. (1930) *Psychopathology and Politics*. Chicago: University of Chicago Press.

Lasswell, Harold D., and Daniel Lerner. (1952) *The Comparative Study of Elites*. Stanford: Stanford University Press.

Ledeen, Michael. (1985) *Grave New World: The Superpower Crisis of the 1980s*. New York: Oxford University Press.

Lee, Jong R. (1977) "Rallying around the Flag: Foreign Policy Events and Presidential Popularity," *Presidential Studies Quarterly* 7 (Fall): 252–256.

Lehman, John. (1976) *The Executive, Congress, and Foreign Policy: Studies of the Nixon Administration*. New York: Praeger.

Leng, Russell, J. (1984) "Reagan and the Russians," *American Political Science Review* 78 (June): 338–355.

Lentner, Howard H. (1972) "The Concept of Crisis as Viewed by the United States Department of State," pp. 112–135 in Charles F. Hermann (ed.), *International Crises: Insights from Behavioral Research*. New York: Free Press.

Levinson, Daniel J. (1957) "Authoritarian Personality and Foreign Policy," *Journal of Conflict Resolution* 1 (March): 37–47.

Levy, Jack S. (1991) "Long Cycles, Hegemonic Transitions, and the Long Peace," pp. 147–176 in Charles W. Kegley, Jr. (ed.), *The Long Postwar Peace*. New York: HarperCollins.

Lewis, Flora. (1989) "Nonaligned Nations in Crisis," *State* (Columbia, S.C.), September 6, p. A10.

Lewy, Guenter. (1978) *America in Vietnam*. New York: Oxford University Press.

Lichter, S. Robert, and Stanley Rothman. (1981) "Media and Business Elites," *Public Opinion* 4 (October/November): 42–46, 59–60.

Lieberman, Seymour. (1965) "The Effects of Changes in Roles on the Attitudes of Role Occupants," pp. 155–168 in J. David Singer (ed.), *Human Behavior and International Politics*. Chicago: Rand McNally.

Lindblom, Charles E. (1959) "The Science of Muddling Through," *Public Administration Review* 19 (Spring): 79–88.

Lindsay, James M. (1990) "Parochialism, Policy, and Constituency Constraints: Congressional Voting on Strategic Weapons Systems," *American Journal of Political Science*, 34 (November): 936–960.

———. (1988) "Congress and the Defense Budget," *Washington Quarterly* 11 (Winter): 57–74.

———. (1987) "Congress and Defense Policy: 1961 to 1986," *Armed Forces and Society* 13 (Spring): 371–401.

Lipset, Seymour Martin, and William Schneider. (1987) "The Confidence Gap during the Reagan Years, 1981–1987," *Political Science Quarterly* 102 (Spring): 1–23.

Lipsitz, Lewis, and David M. Speak. (1989) *American Democracy*, 2nd ed. New York: St. Martin's.

Liska, George. (1978) *Career of Empire: America and Imperial Expansion over Land and Sea.* Baltimore: Johns Hopkins University Press.

Locher, James. (1988) "Organization and Management," pp. 171–190 in Joseph Kruzel (ed.), *American Defense Annual, 1988–1989.* Lexington, Mass.: Lexington Books.

Lord, Carnes. (1988) *The Presidency and the Management of National Security.* New York: Free Press.

Louscher, David J. (1977) "The Rise of Military Sales as a U.S. Foreign Assistance Instrument," *Orbis* 20 (Winter): 933–964.

Lovell, John P. (1970) *Foreign Policy in Perspective.* New York: Holt, Rinehart and Winston.

Lowi, Theodore J. (1985a) *The Personal President: Power Invested, Promise Unfulfilled.* Ithaca, N.Y.: Cornell University Press.

————. (1985b) "Presidential Power: Restoring the Balance," *Political Science Quarterly* 100 (Summer): 185–213.

————. (1979) *The End of Liberalism.* New York: Norton.

————. (1972) "Four Systems of Policy, Politics, and Choice," *Public Administration Review* 32 (July/August): 298–310.

————. (1967) "Making Democracy Safe for the World," pp. 295–331 in James N. Rosenau (ed.), *Domestic Sources of Foreign Policy.* New York: Free Press.

————. (1964) "American Business, Public Policy, Case Studies and Political Theory," *World Politics* 16 (July): 677–715.

Lowi, Theodore J., and Benjamin Ginsberg. (1990) *American Government.* New York: Norton.

Luckham, Robin. (1984) "Militarisation and the New International Anarchy," *Third World Quarterly* 6 (April): 351–373.

Lundestad, Geir. (1988) "Uniqueness and Pendulum Swings in U.S. Foreign Policy," pp. 444–464 in Steven L. Spiegel, ed., *At Issue: Politics in the World Arena*, 5th ed. New York: St. Martin's.

Lyon, Peter. (1989) "Marginalization of the Third World?" *Jerusalem Journal of International Relations* 11 (September): 64–73.

MacMahon, Arthur W. (1951) "The Administration of Foreign Affairs," *American Political Science Review* 45 (September): 836–866.

Maechling, Charles, Jr. (1990) "Washington's Illegal Invasion," *Foreign Policy* 79 (Summer): 113–131.

Magdoff, Harry. (1969) *The Age of Imperialism.* New York: Monthly Review Press.

Magnuson, Ed. (1988) "The Pentagon Up for Sale," *Time*, June 27, pp. 16–18.

Malbin, Michael J. (1977) "Congressional Committee Staffs: Who's in Charge Here?" *Public Interest* 47 (Spring): 16–19.

Malcolm, Andrew H. (1989) "More Americans Are Killing Each Other," *New York Times*, December 31, p. 14.

Malone, Gifford D. (1985) "Managing Public Diplomacy," *Washington Quarterly* 8 (Summer): 199–213.

Manheim, Jarol B. (1984) "Can Democracy Survive Television?" pp. 131–137 in Doris A. Graber (ed.), *Media Power in Politics.* Washington, D.C.: CQ Press.

Mansbach, Richard W., and John A. Vasquez. (1981) *In Search of Theory: A New Paradigm for Global Politics.* New York: Columbia University Press.

March, James G., and Herbert M. Simon. (1958) *Organizations.* New York: Wiley.

Marchetti, Victor, and John D. Marks. (1974) *The CIA and the Cult of Intelligence.* New York: Knopf.

Maslow, Abraham H. (1966) "A Comparative Approach to the Problem of Destructiveness," pp. 156–159 in Janusz K. Zawodny (ed.), *Man and International Relations: Contributions of the Social Sciences to the Study of Conflict and Integration*, Vol. 1. San Francisco: Chandler.

Mathews, Jessica Tuchman. (1989) "Redefining Security," *Foreign Affairs* 68 (Spring): 162–177.

Mathias, Charles McC., Jr. (1981) "Ethnic Groups and Foreign Policy," *Foreign Affairs* 59 (Summer): 975–998.

May, Ernest R. (1984) "The Cold War," pp. 209–230 in Joseph S. Nye, Jr. (ed.), *The Making of America's Soviet Policy.* New Haven, Conn.: Yale University Press.

————. (1973) *"Lessons" of the Past.* London: Oxford University Press.

Maynes, Charles William. (1990) "America without the Cold War," *Foreign Policy* 78 (Spring): 3–25.

McCartney, James. (1990a) "Soviet Expert Warns of Peril for Gorbachev," *State* (Columbia, S.C.), January 18, pp. A1, A11.

_____. (1990b) "Washington May Let European Reform Fizzle," *State* (Columbia, S.C.), (March 11), pp. D1, D5.

_____. (1989) "Pentagon Resists Cuts in Spending," *State* (Columbia, S.C.), December 18, p. A14.

McClelland, David C. (1975) *Power: The Inner Experience*. New York: Irvington.

McClosky, Herbert. (1967) "Personality and Attitude Correlates of Foreign Policy Orientation," pp. 51–109 in James N. Rosenau (ed.), *Domestic Sources of Foreign Policy*. New York: Free Press.

_____. (1958) "Conservatism and Personality," *American Political Science Review* 52 (March): 27–45.

McClosky, Herbert, and John Zaller. (1984) *The American Ethos: Public Attitudes toward Capitalism and Democracy*. Cambridge, Mass.: Harvard University Press.

McCombs, Maxwell E., and Donald L. Shaw. (1972) "The Agenda-Setting Function of Mass Media," *Public Opinion Quarterly* 36 (Summer): 176–185.

McConnell, Grant. (1962) *Steel and the Presidency*. New York: Norton.

McCormick, James M. (1985) "Congressional Voting on the Nuclear Freeze Resolutions," *American Politics Quarterly* 13 (January): 122–136.

McCormick, James M., and Michael Black. (1983) "Ideology and Voting on the Panama Canal Treaties," *Legislative Studies Quarterly* 8 (February): 45–63.

McCormick, James M., and Neil J. Mitchell. (1989) "Human Rights and Foreign Assistance: An Update," *Social Science Quarterly* 70 (December): 969–979.

McCormick, James M., and Eugene R. Wittkopf. (1990a) "Bipartisanship, Partisanship, and Ideology in Congressional-Executive Foreign Policy Relations, 1947–1990," *Journal of Politics* 52 (November): 1077–1100.

_____. (1990b) "Bush and Bipartisanship: The Past as Prologue?" *Washington Quarterly* 13 (Winter): 5–16.

McGowan, Patrick J. (1975) "Meaningful Comparisons in the Study of Foreign Policy," pp. 52–87 in Charles W. Kegley, Jr., Gregory A. Raymond, Robert M. Road, and Richard A. Skinner (eds.), *International Events and the Comparative Analysis of Foreign Policy*. Columbia: University of South Carolina Press.

McManus, Doyle. (1989) "President Comes Away from Eastern Europe with 'Bush Doctrine' Taking Form," *Los Angeles Times*, July 14, p. 14.

McNamara, Robert S. (1984) "Time Bomb or Myth: The Population Explosion, *Foreign Affairs* 62 (Summer): 1107–1131.

McNaugher, Thomas L. (1989) *New Weapons, Old Politics: America's Military Procurement Muddle*. Washington, D.C.: Brookings Institution.

Mead, Walter Russell. (1990) "On the Road to Ruin: Winning the Cold War, Losing Economic Peace," *Harper's* 280 (March): 59–64.

_____. (1989) "American Economic Policy in the Antemillennial Era," *World Policy Journal* 6 (Summer): 385–468.

_____. (1988–1989) "The United States and the World Economy," *World Policy Journal* 6 (Winter): 1–45.

_____. (1987) *Mortal Splendor: The American Empire in Transition*. Boston: Houghton Mifflin.

Mearsheimer, John J. (1990a) "Back to the Future: Instability in Europe after the Cold War," *International Security* 15 (Summer): 5–56.

Mearsheimer, John J. (1990b) "Why We Will Soon Miss the Cold War," *Atlantic Monthly* 266 (August): 35–50.

Meier, Kenneth J. (1987) *Politics and the Bureaucracy*, 2nd ed. Monterey, Calif.: Brooks/Cole.

Melanson, Richard A. (1983) *Writing History and Making Policy: The Cold War, Vietnam and Revisionism*. Lanham, Md.: University Press of America.

Melman, Seymour. (1974) *The Permanent War Economy*. New York: Simon & Schuster.

Merelman, Richard M. (1984) *Making Something of Ourselves: On Culture and Politics in the United States*. Berkeley: University of California Press.

Meyer, John W., and W. Richard Scott. (1983) *Organizational Environments: Ritual and Rationality*. Beverly Hills, Calif.: Sage.

Meyer, Lawrence. (1984) "The Navy's Very Own Nuclear Button," *Washington Post National Weekly Edition,* October 15, pp. 6–7.

Milbrath, Lester W. (1967) "Interest Groups and Foreign Policy," pp. 231–252 in James N. Rosenau (ed.), *Domestic Sources of Foreign Policy*. New York: Free Press.

Miles, Rufus E., Jr. (1985) "Hiroshima: The Strange Myth of Half a Million American Lives Saved," *International Security* 19 (Fall): 121–140.

Miller, Arthur H., Warren E. Miller, Alden S. Raine, and Thad A. Brown. (1976) "A Majority Party in Disarray: Policy Polarization in the 1972 Election," *American Political Science Review* 70 (September): 753–778.

Millett, Allan R., and Peter Maslowski. (1984) *For the Common Defense.* New York: Free Press.

Mills, C. Wright. (1956) *The Power Elite.* New York: Oxford University Press.

Miroff, Bruce. (1976) *Pragmatic Illusions: The Presidential Politics of John F. Kennedy.* New York: McKay.

Mitchell, Neil J., and James M. McCormick. (1988) "Economic and Political Explanations of Human Right Violations," *World Politics* 40 (July): 476–498.

Modelski, George. (ed.). (1987) *Exploring Long Cycles.* Boulder, Colo.: Lynne Rienner.

Mongar, Thomas M. (1974) "Personality and Decision-Making: John F. Kennedy in Four Crisis Decisions," pp. 334–372 in Gordon J. DiRenzo (ed.), *Personality and Politics.* Garden City, N.Y.: Doubleday-Anchor.

Monroe, Alan D. (1979) "Consistency between Public Preferences and National Policy Decisions," *American Politics Quarterly* 7 (January): 3–19.

Moon, Bruce. (1985) "Consensus or Compliance? Foreign Policy Change and External Dependence," *International Organization* 39 (Spring): 297–329.

Morgan, Dan. (1979) *Merchants of Grain.* New York: Viking.

Morgan, Edmund S. (1988) *Inventing the People: The Rise of Popular Sovereignty in England and America.* New York: Norton.

Morgenthau, Hans J. (1985) *Politics among Nations,* revised by Kenneth W. Thompson. New York: Knopf.

———. (1969) "Historical Justice and the Cold War," *New York Review of Books* 13 (July 10): 10–17.

Morin, Richard. (1989a) "PACing in the Bucks for Incumbents," *Washington Post National Weekly Edition,* April 10–16, p. 37.

———. (1989b) "The Public May Not Know Much, But It Knows What It Doesn't Like," *Washington Post National Weekly Edition,* January 23–29, p. 37.

Morse, Edward L. (1986) "After the Fall: The Politics of Oil," *Foreign Affairs* 64 (Spring): 792–811.

Mossberg, Walter S. (1983) "Some Congressmen Treat Military Budget As Source of Patronage," *Wall Street Journal,* April 15, pp. 1, 22.

Moyer, Wayne. (1973) "House Voting on Defense: An Ideological Explanation," pp. 106–142 in Bruce Russett and Alfred Stepan (eds.), *Military Force and American Society.* New York: Harper & Row.

Moynihan, Daniel Patrick. (1990) *On the Law of Nations.* Cambridge, Mass.: Harvard University Press.

Mueller, John F. (1991) "Deterrence, Nuclear Weapons, Morality, and War," pp. 69–97 in Charles W. Kegley, Jr., and Kenneth L. Schwab (eds.), *After the Cold War: Questioning the Morality of Nuclear Deterrence.* Boulder, Colo.: Westview Press.

———. (1990) "A New Concert of Europe," *Foreign Policy* 77 (Winter): 3–16.

———. (1973) *War, Presidents and Public Opinion.* New York: Wiley.

———. (1971) "Trends in Popular Support for the Wars in Korea and Vietnam," *American Political Science Review* 65 (June): 358–375.

Nathan, James A., and James K. Oliver. (1987) *Foreign Policy Making and the American Political System,* 2nd ed. Boston: Little, Brown.

———. (1976) *United States Foreign Policy and World Order.* Boston: Little, Brown.

"The National Security Adviser: Role and Accountability." (1980) *Hearings Before the Committee on Foreign Relations, United States Senate.* 96th Congress, 2nd Session, April 17. Washington, D.C.: Government Printing Office.

Nau, Henry R. (1990) *The Myth of America's Decline: Leading the World Economy in the 1990s.* New York: Oxford University Press.

Neustadt, Richard E. (1980) *Presidential Power.* New York: Wiley.

———. (1970) *Alliance Politics.* New York: Columbia University Press.

Neustadt, Richard E., and Ernest R. May. (1986) *Thinking in Time: The Uses of History for Decision Makers.* New York: Free Press.

Nichols, Bruce, and Gilburt Loescher. (eds.) (1989) *The "Moral Nation": Humanitarianism and U.S. Foreign Policy Today.* Notre Dame, Ind.: University of Notre Dame Press.

Nichols, John Spicer. (1984) "Wasting the Propaganda Dollar," *Foreign Policy* 56 (Fall): 129–140.

Nie, Norman H., Sidney Verba, and John R. Petrocik. (1976) *The Changing American Voter.* Cambridge, Mass.: Harvard University Press.

Niebuhr, Reinhold. (1947) *Moral Man and Immoral Society.* New York: Scribner's.

Niemi, Richard G., John Mueller, and Tom W. Smith. (1989) *Trends in Public Opinion: A Compendium of Survey Data.* New York: Greenwood.

Nincic, Miroslav. (1989) *Anatomy of Hostility: The U.S.-Soviet Rivalry in Perspective.* Chicago: Harcourt Brace Jovanovich.

Nivola, Pietro S. (1990) "Trade Policy: Refereeing the Playing Field, pp. 201–253 in Thomas E. Mann (ed.), *A Question of Balance: The President, the Congress, and Foreign Policy.* Washington, D.C.: Brookings Institution.

Nowzad, Bahram. (1990) "Lessons of the Debt Decade," *Finance & Development* 27 (March): 9–13.

Nunn, Sam. (1987) "The ABM Reinterpretation Issue," *Washington Quarterly* 10 (Autumn): 45–57.

Nye, Joseph S., Jr. (1990) *Bound to Lead: The Changing Nature of American Power.* New York: Basic Books.

Nye, Joseph S., Jr., and Robert O. Keohane. (1971) "Transnational Relations and World Politics: An Introduction," *International Organization* 25 (Summer): 329–349.

Oberdorfer, Don, and Helen Dewar. (1987) "The Capitol Hill Broth Is Being Seasoned by a Lot of Cooks," *Washington Post National Weekly Edition*, October 26, p. 12.

O'Brien, Conor Cruise. (1990) "Impediments and Prerequisites to Counter-Terrorism," pp. 201–206 in Charles W. Kegley, Jr. (ed.), *International Terrorism: Characteristics, Causes, Controls.* New York: St. Martin's.

O'Brien, Patrick M. (1988) "Agricultural Productivity and the Global Food Market," pp. 394–408 in Charles W. Kegley, Jr., and Eugene R. Wittkopf (eds.), *The Global Agenda: Issues and Perspectives*, 2nd ed. New York: Random House.

Omestad, Thomas. (1990) "Bush Still Plays Follow the Leader," *State* (Columbia, S.C.), February 14, p. A15.

———. (1989) "Selling Off America," *Foreign Policy* 76 (Winter): 119–140.

Ornstein, Norman J., and Shirley Elder. (1978) *Interest Groups, Lobbying and Policymaking.* Washington, D.C.: CQ Press.

Ornstein, Norman J., Andrew Kohut, and Larry McCarthy. (1988) *The People, the Press, and Politics.* Reading, Mass.: Addison-Wesley.

Ornstein, Norman J., Thomas E. Mann, and Michael J. Malbin. (1990) *Vital Statistics on Congress, 1989–1990.* Washington, D.C.: Congressional Quarterly, Inc.

Ornstein, Norman J., and Mark Schmitt. (1990) "Dateline Campaign '92: Post-Cold War Politics," *Foreign Policy* 79 (Summer): 169–186.

Osgood, Robert E. (1953) *Ideals and Self-Interest in America's Foreign Relations.* Chicago: University of Chicago Press.

Ostrom, Charles W., Jr., and Brian L. Job. (1986) "The President and the Political Use of Force," *American Political Science Review* 80 (June): 541–566.

Ostrom, Charles W., Jr., and Dennis M. Simon. (1989) "The Man in the Teflon Suit: The Environmental Connection, Political Drama, and Popular Support in the Reagan Presidency," 53 (Fall): 353–387.

———. (1985) "Promise and Performance: A Dynamic Model of Presidential Popularity," *American Political Science Review* 79 (June): 334–358.

Owen, Oliver S. (1989) "The Heat Is On: The Greenhouse Effect and the Earth's Future," *Futurist* 23 (September-October): 34–40.

Oye, Kenneth A., Robert J. Lieber, and Donald Rothchild. (eds.). (1983) *Eagle Defiant: United States Foreign Policy in the 1980s.* Boston: Little, Brown.

Oye, Kenneth A., Donald Rothchild, and Robert Lieber. (eds.). (1979) *Eagle Entangled: U.S. Foreign Policy in a Complex World.* New York: Longman.

Paarlberg, Robert L. (1988) "U.S. Agriculture and the Developing World: Opportunities for Joint Gains," pp. 119–138 in John W. Sewell and Stuart K. Tucker, *Growth, Exports, and Jobs in a Changing World Economy: Agenda 1988.* New Brunswick, N.J.: Transaction Books.

Packenham, Robert A. (1973) *Liberal America and the Third World.* Princeton, N.J.: Princeton University Press.

Page, Benjamin I., and Richard A. Brody. (1972) "Policy Voting and the Electoral Process: The Vietnam War Issue," *American Political Science Review* 66 (September): 979–995.

Page, Benjamin I., and Robert Y. Shapiro. (1983) "Effects of Public Opinion on Policy," *American Political Science Review* 77 (March): 175–190.

Page, Benjamin I., Robert Shapiro, and Glenn R. Dempsey. (1987) "What Moves Public Opinion?" *American Political Science Review* 81 (March): 23–43.

Paige, Glenn D. (1972) "Comparative Case Analysis of Crises Decisions: Korea and Cuba," pp. 41–55 in Charles F. Hermann (ed.), *International Crises: Insights from Behavioral Research.* New York: Free Press.

Parenti, Michael. (1989) *The Sword and the Dollar: Imperialism, Revolution and the Arms Race.* New York: St. Martin's Press.

———. (1988) *Democracy for the Few*, 5th ed. New York: St. Martin's.

———. (1986) *Inventing Reality: The Politics of the Mass Media.* New York: St. Martin's.

———. (1981) "We Hold These Myths to be Self-Evident," *Nation* 232 (April): 425–429.

———. (1969) *The Anti-Communist Impulse.* New York: Random House.

Parkinson, C. Northcote. (1972–1973) "The Five Other Rules," *Foreign Policy* 9 (Winter): 108–116.

Parry, Robert, and Peter Kornbluh. (1988) "Iran-Contra's Untold Story," *Foreign Policy* 72 (Fall): 3–30.

Paterson, Thomas G. (1979) *On Every Front: The Making of the Cold War.* New York: Norton.

Patterson, Bradley H., Jr. (1988) *The Ring of Power.* New York: Basic Books.

Patterson, Thomas E. (1990) *The American Democracy.* New York: McGraw-Hill.

Patterson, Thomas E., and Robert D. McClure. (1976) *The Unseeing Eye.* New York: Putnam.

The Pentagon Papers as Published by the New York Times. (1971) Toronto: Bantam Books.

Perle, Richard. (1991) "Military Power and the Passing Cold War," pp. 33–38 in Charles W. Kegley, Jr. and Kenneth L. Schwab (eds.), *After the Cold War: Questioning the Morality of Nuclear Deterrence.* Boulder, Colo.: Westview.

Perry, Jack. (1984) "The Foreign Service Is in Real Trouble, But It Can Be Saved," *Washington Post National Weekly Edition,* January 16, pp. 21–22.

Perry, James M. (1989) "Reagan's Last Scene Blaming the 'Iron Triangle' for U.S. Budget Deficit Draws Mixed Reviews," *Wall Street Journal*, January 5, p. A12.

Peterson, Sophia. (1971) "International Events, Foreign Policy-Makers, Elite Attitudes, and Mass Opinion." Paper presented at the annual meeting of the International Studies Association, San Juan, March 17–20.

Petras, James F., and Robert LaPorte, Jr. (1972) "Can We Do Business with Radical Nationalists? Chile: No," *Foreign Policy* 7 (Summer): 132–158.

Pett, Saul. (1984) "Spy vs. Spy," *State* (Columbia, S.C.), April 22, pp. B1, B8.

Pfiffner, James P. (1990) "Establishing the Bush Presidency, *Public Administration Review* 50 (January/February): 64–73.

———. (1988) *The Strategic Presidency: Hitting the Ground Running.* Chicago: Dorsey.

Pickett, George. (1985) "Congress, the Budget, and Intelligence," pp. 157–179 in Alfred C. Maurer, Marion D. Tunstall, and James M. Keagle (eds.), *Intelligence: Policy and Process.* Boulder, Colo.: Westview.

Pilisuk, Marc, and Thomas Hayden. (1965) "Is There a Military-Industrial Complex Which Prevents Peace? Consensus and Countervailing Power in Pluralistic Society," *Journal of Social Issues* 21 (July): 67–117.

Piller, Geoffrey. (1983) "DOD's Office of International Security Affairs: The Brief Ascendancy of an Advisory System," *Political Science Quarterly* 98 (Spring): 59–78.

Pincus, Walter. (1985a) "The Military's New, Improved 'Revolving Door,'" *Washington Post National Weekly Edition*, March 18, p. 33.

Pine, Art. (1990) "Sensitive Technology War Shifting to Third World," *Sunday Advocate* (Baton Rouge, La.), June 24: 15A.

Pisar, Samuel. (1977) "Let's Put Détente Back on the Rails," *New York Times Magazine*, September 25, pp. 31ff.

Pomper, Gerald M. (1989) "The Presidential Election," pp. 129–152 in Gerald M. Pomper, Ross K. Baker, Walter Dean Burnham, Barbara G. Farah, Marjorie Randon Hershey, Ethel Klein, and Wilson Carey McWilliams, *The Election of 1988: Reports and Interpretations.* Chatham, N.J.: Chatham House.

———. (1968) *Elections in America: Control and Influence in Democratic Politics.* New York: Dodd, Mead.

Porter, Roger B. (1983) "Economic Advice to the President: From Eisenhower to Reagan," *Political Science Quarterly* 98 (Fall): 403–426.

Preeg, Ernest H. (1989a) "The GATT Trading System in Transition: An Analytic Survey of Recent Literature," *Washington Quarterly* 12 (Autumn): 201–213.

———. (1989b) "Trade, Aid, and Capital Projects," *Washington Quarterly* 12 (Winter): 173–185.

Pringle, Robert. (1977–1978) "Creeping Irrelevance at Foggy Bottom," *Foreign Policy* 29 (Winter): 128–139.

Proxmire, William. (1970) *Report from Wasteland*. New York: Praeger.

Pruitt, Dean G. (1965) "Definition of the Situation as a Determinant of International Action," pp. 393–432 in Herbert C. Kelman (ed.), *International Behavior*. New York: Holt, Rinehart and Winston.

Puritano, Vincent. (1985) "Resource Allocation in the Pentagon," pp. 359–374 in Robert J. Art, Vincent Davis, and Samuel P. Huntington (eds.), *Reorganizing America's Defense: Leadership in War and Peace*. Washington, D.C.: Pergamon Brassey's.

Quijano, Alicia M. (1990) "A Guide to BEA Statistics on Foreign Direct Investment in the United States," *Survey of Current Business* 70 (February): 29–37.

Rai, Kul B. (1980) "Foreign Aid and Voting in the UN General Assembly, 1967–1976," *Journal of Peace Research* 17 (No. 3): 269–277.

Rankin, Robert A. (1989) "New Era's Wars to Be Economic," *State* (Columbia, S.C.), July 23, pp. G1, G5.

Ranney, Austin. (1983) *Channels of Power*. New York: Basic Books.

Ransom, Harry Howe. (1983) "Strategic Intelligence and Intermestic Politics," pp. 299–319 in Charles W. Kegley, Jr., and Eugene R. Wittkopf (eds.), *Perspectives on American Foreign Policy*. New York: St. Martin's.

———. (1970) *The Intelligence Establishment*. Cambridge, Mass.: Harvard University Press.

Rattinger, Hans. 1989 "Domestic and Foreign Policy Issues in the 1988 Presidential Election: Some Parts of the Audience Watch the Waltz, Others the Rock'n Roll," mimeo.

Raymond, Gregory A. (1975) "Comparative Analysis and Nomological Explanation," pp. 41–51 in Charles W. Kegley, Jr., Gregory A. Raymond, Robert M. Rood, and Richard A. Skinner (eds.), *International Events and the Comparative Analysis of Foreign Policy*. Columbia: University of South Carolina Press.

Reed, Julia. (1988) "The New American Establishment," *U.S. News & World Report*, February 8, pp. 37–40 ff.

Regan, Donald T. (1988) *For the Record: From Wall Street to Washington*. San Diego: Harcourt Brace Jovanovich.

Reich, Robert B. (1985) "How Much Is Enough?" *New Republic*, August 12 and 19, pp. 33–37.

Reifenberg, Jan. (1990) "Economies Built on Arms," *World Press Review* 37 (January): 22–23.

Reischauer, Edwin O. (1968) "Redefining the National Interest: The Vietnam Case." Paper delivered at the annual meeting of the American Political Science Association, Washington, D.C., September 2–7.

Report of the President's Special Review Board. (1987) Washington, D.C.: Government Printing Office.

Reutlinger, Shlomo. (1985) "Food Security and Poverty in LDCs," *Finance & Development* 22 (December): 7–11.

Richelson, Jeffrey T. (1989) *The U.S. Intelligence Community*, 2nd ed. Cambridge, Mass.: Ballinger.

Rielly, John E. (ed.) (1987) *American Public Opinion and U.S. Foreign Policy 1983*. Chicago: Chicago Council on Foreign Relations.

———. (ed.) (1979) *American Public Opinion and U.S. Foreign Policy 1979*. Chicago: Chicago Council on Foreign Relations.

Rieselbach, Leroy N. (1964) "The Demography of the Congressional Vote on Foreign Aid, 1939–1958," *American Political Science Review* 58 (September): 577–588.

Ripley, Randall B., and Grace A. Franklin. (1987) *Congress, the Bureaucracy, and Public Policy*, 4th ed. Homewood, Ill.: Dorsey.

Rizopoulos, Nicholas X., (ed.). (1990) *Sea-Changes: American Foreign Policy in a World Transformed*. New York: Council on Foreign Relations Press.

Robinson, James A. (1972) "Crisis: An Appraisal of Concepts and Theories," pp. 20–35 in Charles F. Hermann (ed.), *International Crises: Insights from Behavioral Research*. New York: Free Press.

Robinson, Michael Jay. (1983) "Just How Liberal Is the News? 1980 Revisited," *Public Opinion* 6 (February/March): 55–60.

Robock, Alan. (1990) "Nuclear Winter Confirmed," *National Forum* 70 (Winter): 17–19.

Rogers, William D. (1979) "Who's in Charge of Foreign Policy?" *New York Times Magazine*, September 9, pp. 44–50.

Rogow, Arnold A. (1963) *James Forrestal: A Study in Personality, Politics, and Policy*. New York: Macmillan.

Rokeach, Milton. (1960) *The Open and Closed Mind: Investigations into the Nature of Belief Systems and Personality Systems*. New York: Basic Books.

"The Role of Intelligence in the Foreign Policy Process." (1980) *Hearings before the Subcommittee on International Security and Scientific Affairs of the Committee on Foreign Affairs, House of Representatives*. 96th Congress, 2nd Session, January 28, February 8, 11, 20. Washington, D.C.: Government Printing Office.

Rose, Richard. (1989) "How Exceptional Is the American Political Economy?" *Political Science Quarterly* 104 (Spring): 91–115.

Rosecrance, Richard. (1990) *America's Economic Resurgence: A Bold New Strategy*. New York: Harper & Row.

Rosen, Steven. (ed.) (1973) *Testing the Theory of the Military-Industrial Complex*. Lexington, Mass.: Heath.

Rosenau, James N. (1980) *The Scientific Study of Foreign Policy*. New York: Nichols.

———. (1974) *Citizenship between Elections*. New York: Free Press.

———. (1973) "Paradigm Lost: Five Actors in Search of the Interactive Effects of Domestic and Foreign Affairs," *Policy Sciences* 4 (December): 415–436.

———. (1967) "Foreign Policy as an Issue-Area," pp. 11–50 in James N. Rosenau (ed.), *Domestic Sources of Foreign Policy*. New York: Free Press.

———. (1966) "Pre-Theories and Theories of Foreign Policy," pp. 27–92 in R. Barry Farrell (ed.), *Approaches to Comparative and International Politics*. Evanston, Ill.: Northwestern University Press.

Rosenberg, Milton J. (1967) "Attitude Change and Foreign Policy in the Cold-War Era," pp. 278–334 in James N. Rosenau (ed.), *Domestic Sources of Foreign Policy*. New York: Free Press.

———. (1965) "Images in Relation to the Policy Process: American Public Opinion on Cold War Issues," pp. 277–336 in Herbert C. Kelman (ed.), *International Behavior*. New York: Holt, Rinehart and Winston.

Rothstein, Robert L. (1988) "Epitaph for a Monument to a Failed Protest? A North-South Retrospective," *International Organization* 42 (Autumn): 725–748.

Rowe, Edward T. (1974) "Aid and Coups d'État: Aspects of the Impact of American Military Assistance Programs in the Less Developed Countries," *International Studies Quarterly* 18 (June): 239–255.

Rowen, Hobart, and Jodie T. Allen. (1989) "When Corporations, Not Countries Will Matter," *Washington Post National Weekly Edition*, March 27–April 2, pp. 23–24.

Rubenstein, Richard L. (ed.) (1987) *The Dissolving Alliance: The United States and the Future of Europe*. New York: Paragon House.

Rubin, Barry. (1989) "Legacy of State," *Foreign Service Journal* 66 (September): 32–34.

———. (1985) *Secrets of State: The State Department and the Struggle over U.S. Foreign Policy*. New York: Oxford University Press.

Rubner, Michael. (1985–1986) "The Reagan Administration, the 1973 War Powers Resolution, and the Invasion of Grenada," *Political Science Quarterly* 100 (Winter): 627–647.

Russett, Bruce Martin. (1991) "An Acceptable Role for Nuclear Weapons?" pp. 121–145 in Charles W. Kegley, Jr., and Kenneth L. Schwab (eds.), *After the Cold War: Questioning the Morality of Nuclear Deterrence*. Boulder, Colo.: Westview.

———. (1989) "The Real Decline in Nuclear Hegemony," pp. 177–193 in Ernst-Otto Czempiel and James N. Rosenau (eds.), *Global Changes and Theoretical Challenges*. Lexington, Mass.: Lexington Books.

———. (1972) "The Revolt of the Masses: Public Opinion on Military Expenditures," pp. 299–319 in Bruce M. Russett (ed.), *Peace, War, and Numbers*. Beverly Hills, Calif.: Sage.

Russett, Bruce, and Thomas W. Graham. (1988) "Public Opinion and National Security Policy Relationships and Impacts," pp. 239–257 in Manus Midlarsky (ed.), *Handbook of War Studies*. London: Allen & Unwin.

Sachs, Jeffrey. (1989) "Making the Brady Plan Work," *Foreign Affairs* 68 (Summer): 87–104.

Safire, William. (1989) "Europe's Nascent 'Superpower'," *State* (Columbia, S.C.), November 14, p. A12.

Sagan, Carl. (1983–1984) "Nuclear War and Climatic Catastrophe: Some Policy Implications," *Foreign Affairs* 62 (Winter): 257–292.

Sampson, Anthony. (1977) *The Arms Bazaar.* New York: Bantam Books.
_____. (1975) *The Seven Sisters*, New York: Viking.
Sanders, Jerry W. (1983) *Peddlers of Crisis: The Committee on the Present Danger and the Politics of Containment.* Boston: South End Press.
Sandman, Peter M., David M. Rubin, and David B. Sachsman. (1972) *Media.* Englewood Cliffs, N.J.: Prentice-Hall.
Schattschneider, F. E. (1960) *The Semisovereign People.* New York: Holt, Rinehart and Winston.
Schell, Jonathan. (1984) *The Abolition.* New York: Knopf.
_____. (1982) *The Fate of the Earth.* New York: Avon Books.
Schelling, Thomas C. (1966) *Arms and Influence.* New Haven, Conn.: Yale University Press.
Schilling, Warner R. (1973) "The H-Bomb Decision: How to Decide without Actually Choosing," pp. 240–260 in Morton H. Halperin and Arnold Kanter (eds.), *Readings in American Foreign Policy.* Boston: Little, Brown.
Schlagheck, Donna M. (1990) "The Superpowers, Foreign Policy, and Terrorism," pp. 170–177 in Charles W. Kegley, Jr. (ed.), *International Terrorism: Characteristics, Causes, Controls.* New York: St. Martin's.
Schlesinger, Arthur M., Jr. (1989a) "The Legislative-Executive Balance in International Affairs: The Intentions of the Framers," *Washington Quarterly* 12 (Winter): 99–107.
_____. (1989b) "Somebody Tell Bush We've Won the Cold War," *Wall Street Journal*, May 17, p. A18.
_____. (1986) *The Cycles of American History.* Boston: Houghton Mifflin.
_____. (1984) "In the National Interest," *Worldview* 27 (December): 5–8.
_____. (1983) "Foreign Policy and the American Character," *Foreign Affairs* 62 (Fall): 1–16.
_____. (1977) "America: Experiment or Destiny?" *American Historical Review* 82 (June): 505–522.
_____. (1973) *The Imperial Presidency.* Boston: Houghton Mifflin
_____. (1965) *A Thousand Days: John F. Kennedy in the White House.* Boston: Houghton Mifflin.
_____. (1958) *The Coming of the New Deal.* Boston: Houghton Mifflin.
Schlesinger, James. (1990) "Oil and Power in the Nineties," *National Interest* 19 (Spring): 111–115.
_____. (1989) *America at Century's End.* New York: Columbia University Press.
Schlozman, Kay Lehman, and John T. Tierney. (1986) *Organized Interests and American Democracy.* New York: Harper & Row.
Schmidt, William E. (1983) "Poll Shows Lessening of Fear That U.S. Military Is Lagging," *New York Times*, February 6, p. 1.
Scholl, Russell B. (1989) "The International Investment Position of the United States in 1988," *Survey of Current Business* 69 (June): 41–49.
Schneider, Barry R. (1989) "Invitation to a Nuclear Beheading," pp. 291–301 in Charles W. Kegley, Jr., and Eugene R. Wittkopf (eds.), *The Nuclear Reader: Strategies, Weapons, War*, 2nd ed. New York: St. Martin's.
Schneider, William. (1990) "The In-Box President," *Atlantic Monthly* 265 (January): 34–43.
_____. (1984) "Public Opinion," pp. 11–35 in Joseph S. Nye, Jr. (ed.), *The Making of America's Soviet Policy.* New Haven, Conn.: Yale University Press.
_____. (1982) "Bang-Bang Television: The New Superpower," *Public Opinion* 5 (April/May): 13–15.
Schneider, William, and L. A. Lewis. (1985) "Views on the News," *Public Opinion* 8 (August/September): 6–11, 58–59.
Schoultz, Lars. (1982) "Politics, Economics, and U.S. Participation in Multilateral Development Banks," *International Organization* 36 (Summer): 537–574.
_____. (1981) "U.S. Foreign Policy and Human Rights Violations in Latin America: A Comparative Analysis of Foreign Aid Distributions," *Comparative Politics* 13 (January): 149–170.
Schulzinger, Robert D. (1985) *The Wise Men of Foreign Affairs: The History of the Council on Foreign Relations.* New York: Columbia University Press.
Schwartz, Richard. (1989) "U.S. Interest in Europe's 1992 Process: An Analytic Survey," *Washington Quarterly* 12 (Summer): 205–213.
Scott, Andrew M. (1970) "Environmental Change and Organizational Adaptation: The Problem of the State Department," *International Studies Quarterly* 14 (March): 85–94.
_____. (1969) "The Department of State: Formal Organization and Informal Culture," *International Studies Quarterly* 13 (March): 1–18.
Seabury, Paul. (1973) *The United States in World Affairs.* New York: McGraw-Hill.

Seib, Gerald F. (1990) "Prodded by Quayle and Cheney, Bush Becomes Fervent Supporter of Strategic Defense Initiative," *Wall Street Journal*, February 23, p. A12.

———. (1989) "To a Surprising Extent, Bush Quietly Discards Many Reagan Stands," *Wall Street Journal*, April 20, p. A1.

———. (1988) "No Ideologue, Bush Is Likely to Be Pragmatic, Work with Congress," *Wall Street Journal*, November 10, pp. A1, A16.

Seib, Gerald F., and Tim Carrington. (1988) "Bush Attacks Dukakis on Defense, but Deficit Will Tie Either's Hands," *Wall Street Journal*, September 23, pp. 1, 28.

Semmel, Andrew K. (1983) "Evolving Patterns of U.S. Security Assistance 1950–1980," pp. 79–95 in Charles W. Kegley, Jr., and Eugene R. Wittkopf (eds.), *Perspectives on American Foreign Policy*. New York: St. Martin's.

Serfaty, Simon. (1978) "Brzezinski: Play It Again, Zbig," *Foreign Policy* 32 (Fall): 3–21.

Sewell, John W., and Stuart K. Tucker. (1988) *Growth, Jobs, and Exports in a Changing World Economy: Agenda 1988*. New Brunswick, N.J.: Transaction Books.

Sewell, John W., and the Staff of the Overseas Development Council. (1980) *The United States and World Development: Agenda 1980*. New York: Praeger.

Shapiro, Robert Y., and Harpreet Mahajan. (1986) "Gender Differences in Policy Preferences: A Summary of Trends from the 1960s to the 1980s," *Public Opinion Quarterly* 50 (Spring): 42–61.

Shapiro, Robert Y., and Benjamin I. Page. (1988) "Foreign Policy and the Rational Public," *Journal of Conflict Resolution* 32 (June): 211–247.

Sherry, Michael. (1977) *Preparing for the Next War*. New Haven, Conn.: Yale University Press.

Sherwin, Martin J. (1973) "The Atomic Bomb and the Origins of the Cold War," *American Historical Review* 78 (October): 945–968.

Sherwood, Elizabeth D. (1990) *Allies in Crisis: Meeting Global Challenges to Global Security*. New Haven, Conn.: Yale University Press.

Sigelman, Lee. (1979) "Rallying to the President's Support: A Reappraisal of Evidence," *Polity* 11 (Summer): 542–561.

Sigmund, Paul E. (1974a) "The 'Invisible Blockade' and the Overthrow of Allende," *Foreign Affairs* 52 (January): 322–340.

———. (1974b) "Chile: What Was the U.S. Role? Less than Charged," *Foreign Policy* 16 (Fall): 142–156.

Simon, Dennis M., and Charles W. Ostrom, Jr. (1988) "The Politics of Prestige: Popular Support and the Modern Presidency," *Presidential Studies Quarterly* 18 (Fall): 741–759.

Simon, Herbert A. (1985) "Human Nature in Politics: The Dialogue of Psychology with Political Science," *American Political Science Review* 79 (March): 293–304.

———. (1957a) *Administrative Behavior: A Study of Decision-Making Process in Administration Organizations*, 2nd ed. New York: Macmillan.

———. (1957b) *Models of Man*. New York: Wiley.

Simpson, Smith. (1967) *Anatomy of the State Department*. Boston: Houghton Mifflin.

Singer, J. David. (1991) "Peace in the Global System: Displacement, Interregnum, or Transformation?" pp. 56–84 in Charles W. Kegley, Jr. (ed), *The Long Postwar Peace*. New York: Harper-Collins.

Singer, J. David. (ed.) (1965) *Human Behavior and International Politics*. Chicago: Rand McNally.

Sivard, Ruth Leger. (1989) *World Military and Social Expenditures 1989*. Washington, D.C.: World Priorities.

Slovic, Paul, Baruch Fischhoff, and Sarah Lichtenstein. (1977) "Behavioral Decision Theory," *Annual Review of Psychology* 28: 1–39.

Smith, Michael Joseph. (1987) *Realist Thought from Weber to Kissinger*. Baton Rouge: Louisiana State University Press.

Smith, Steven S., and Christopher J. Deering. (1984) *Committees in Congress*. Washington, D.C.: CQ Press.

Smith, Tom W. (1985) "The Polls: America's Most Important Problems Part I: National and International," *Public Opinion Quarterly* 49 (Summer): 264-274.

———. (1984) "The Polls: Gender and Attitudes toward Violence," *Public Opinion Quarterly* 48 (Spring): 384–396.

Smoller, Fred. (1986) "The Six O'Clock Presidency: Patterns of Network News Coverage of the President," *Presidential Studies Quarterly* 16 (Winter): 31–49.

Smolowe, Jill. (1989) "There Goes the Bloc," *Time*, November 6, pp. 48–51.

Snyder, Mark. (1980) "The Many Me's of the Self-Monitor," *Psychology Today* 13 (March): 32–40ff.

Sobel, Richard (1989) "The Polls—A Report: Public Opinion about United States Intervention in El Salvador and Nicaragua," *Public Opinion Quarterly* 53 (Spring): 114–128.

Sofaer, Abraham D. (1987) "The ABM Treaty: Legal Analysis in the Political Cauldron," *Washington Quarterly* 10 (Autumn): 59–75.

Sorensen, Theodore C. (1987–1988) "The President and the Secretary of State," *Foreign Affairs* 66 (Winter): 231–248.

———. (1965) *Kennedy*. New York: Harper & Row.

———. (1963) *Decision-Making in the White House: The Olive Branch or the Arrows*. New York: Columbia University Press.

Soros, George. (1988) "After Black Monday," *Foreign Policy* 70 (Spring): 65–82.

Spanier, John. (1990) *Games Nations Play*, 7th ed. Washington, D.C.: CQ Press.

———. (1988) *American Foreign Policy since World War II*, 11th ed. Washington, D.C.: CQ Press.

———. (1975) *Games Nations Play*, 2nd ed. New York: Praeger.

Spero, Joan Edelman. (1990) *The Politics of International Economic Relations*, 4th ed. New York: St. Martin's.

———. (1988–1989) "Guiding Global Finance," *Foreign Policy* 73 (Winter): 114–134.

Spiegel, Steven L. (1985) *The Other Arab-Israeli Conflict*. Chicago: University of Chicago Press.

Spiers, Ronald I. (1989) "Washington Is Trashing the Foreign Service," *Washington Post National Weekly Edition*, July 31-August 26, pp. 23–24.

———. (1988) "The 'Budget Crunch' and the Foreign Service." Address during Foreign Service Day at the Department of State, May 6. U.S. Department of State, Bureau of Public Affairs, Current Policy no. 1073.

———. (1985a) "Managing the State Department, address before the Carnegie Endowment for International Peace and the American Foreign Service Association, United States Department of State, Bureau of Public Affairs, Current Policy No. 747, September 26.

———. (1985b) "Thinning the Soup," *Foreign Service Journal* 62 (March): 34–37.

Stagner, Ross. (1971) "Personality Dynamics and Social Conflict," pp. 98–109 in Clagett G. Smith (ed.), *Conflict Resolution: Contributions of the Behavioral Sciences*. Notre Dame, Ind.: University of Notre Dame Press.

Stanley, Harold W., and Richard G. Niemi. (1990) *Vital Statistics on American Politics*, 2nd ed. Washington, D.C.: CQ Press.

Starr, Harvey. (1984) *Henry Kissinger: Perceptions of International Politics*. Lexington: University Press of Kentucky.

Steeper, Frederick T., and Robert M. Teeter. (1976) "Comment on 'A Majority Party in Disarray,'" *American Political Science Review* 70 (September): 806–813.

Steigman, Andrew L. (1985) "From Surfeit to Shortage," *Foreign Service Journal* 62 (September): 32–34.

Steinbruner, John. (ed.). (1989) *Restructuring American Foreign Policy*. Washington, D.C.: Brookings Institution.

Stevens, Charles J. (1977) "The Use and Control of Executive Agreements: Recent Congressional Initiatives," *Orbis* 20 (Winter): 905–931.

Stevenson, Adlai E., and Alton Frye. (1989) "Trading with the Communists," *Foreign Affairs* 68 (Spring): 53–71.

Stimson, Henry L., and McGeorge Bundy. (1947) *On Active Service in Peace and War*. New York: Harper & Row.

Stoessinger, John G. (1985) *Crusaders and Pragmatists: Movers of Modern American Foreign Policy*. New York: Norton.

Stouffer, Samuel A., Edward A. Suchman, Leland C. DeVinney, Shirley A. Star, and Robin M. Williams, Jr. (1949) *The American Soldier*. Princeton, N.J.: Princeton University Press.

Strange, Susan. (1987) "The Persistent Myth of Lost Hegemony," *International Organization* 41 (Autumn): 551–574.

Struck, Myron. (1985) "A Bumper Crop of Plums: Political Appointments are Proliferators," *Washington Post National Weekly Edition*, May 20, p. 31.

Stuart, Douglas, and Harvey Starr. (1981–1982) "The 'Inherent Bad Faith Model' Reconsidered: Dulles, Kennedy, and Kissinger," *Political Psychology* 3 (Fall/Winter): 1–33.

Sullivan, Mark P. (1989) "Central American and U.S. Foreign Assistance: Issues for Congress," *CRS Issue Brief*, November 29. Washington, D.C.: Congressional Research Service.

Sullivan, William H. (1980) "Dateline Iran: The Road Not Taken," *Foreign Policy* 40 (Fall): 175–186.

Summers, Harry G., Jr. (1989) "A Bankrupt Military Strategy," *Atlantic Monthly* 263 (June): 34–40.

Sundquist, James L. (1976) "Congress and the President: Enemies or Partners?" pp. 583–618 in Henry Owen and Charles L. Schultze (eds.), *Setting National Priorities: The Next Ten Years*. Washington, D.C.: Brookings Institution.

Sussman, Barry. (1988) *What Americans Really Think: And Why Our Politicians Pay No Attention*. New York: Pantheon.

_____. (1985) "The 'Porcupine Theory': Explaining Contradictory Opinions," *Washington Post National Weekly Edition*, August 5, p. 37.

Szanton, Peter L. (1985) "OMB's Defense Cop-Out," *Foreign Policy* 58 (Spring): 99–114.

Talbott, Strobe. (1990a) "How to Avoid the Bush Folly," *Time*, February 12, p. 34.

_____. (1990b) "Rethinking the Red Menace," *Time*, January 1, pp. 66–72.

_____. (1989a) "Happy Campers, for a Change," *Time*, August 28, p. 24.

_____. (1989b) "Why Bush Should Sweat," *Time*, November 6, p. 59.

_____. (1984) *Deadly Gambits*. New York: Knopf.

_____. (1979) *Endgame*. New York: Harper & Row.

Taubman, Philip. (1984) "Secret Budgets Become a Public Issue," *Gainesville Sun*, September 30, p. B5.

_____. (1983) "Casey and His CIA on the Rebound," *New York Times Magazine*, January 16, pp. 20–21ff.

Taylor, Paul. (1988) "The GOP Has a Woman Problem," *Washington Post National Weekly Edition*, July 4–10, p. 9.

Tebbel, John, and Sarah Miles Watts. (1985) *The Press and the Presidency*. New York: Oxford University Press.

Theoharis, Athan. (1970) *The Yalta Myths*. Columbia: University of Missouri Press.

Thomas, Keith. (1988) "Just Say Yes," *New York Review of Books* 35 (November 24): 43–45.

Thompson, Kenneth W. (1960) *Political Realism and the Crisis of World Politics*. Princeton, N.J.: Princeton University Press.

Thompson, Randal Joy. (1990) "Mandates for AID Reform," *Foreign Service Journal* 67 (January): 34–36.

Thompson, William R. (1988) *On Global War: Historical-Structural Approaches to World Politics*. Columbia: University of South Carolina Press.

Thomson, James C., Jr. (1988) "How Could Vietnam Happen? An Autopsy," pp. 205–214 in Charles W. Kegley, Jr., and Eugene R. Wittkopf (eds.), *The Domestic Sources of Foreign Policy*. New York: St. Martin's.

_____. (1972) "On the Making of U.S. China Policy, 1961–69: A Study in Bureaucratic Politics," *China Quarterly* 50 (April/June): 220–243.

Thurow, Lester. (1985) "America, Europe, and Japan: A Time to Dismantle the World Economy," *The Economist* 297 (November 9): 21–26.

Thurow, Lester C., and Laura D'Andrea Tyson. (1987) "The Economic Black Hole," *Foreign Policy* 67 (Summer): 3–21.

Tillema, Herbert K. (1989) "Foreign Overt Military Intervention in the Nuclear Age," *Journal of Peace Research* 26 (May): 179–195.

_____. (1973) *Appeal to Force: American Military Intervention in the Era of Containment*. New York: Crowell.

Tillema, Herbert K., and John R. Van Wingen. (1982) "Law and Power in Military Intervention," *International Studies Quarterly* 26 (June): 220–250.

Tivnan, Edward. (1987) *The Lobby: Jewish Political Power and American Foreign Policy*. New York: Simon & Schuster.

Tolchin, Martin, and Susan Tolchin. (1988) *Buying into America: How Foreign Money Is Changing the Face of Our Nation*. New York: Times Books.

Toth, Robert C. (1989) "U.S. Shifts Nuclear Response Strategy," *Los Angeles Times*, July 23, p. A1.

Train, John. (1990) "America's Invulnerable Deterrent," *Wall Street Journal*, March 26, p. A8.

Treverton, Gregory F. (1990) "Intelligence: Welcome to the American Government," pp. 70–108 in Thomas E. Mann (ed.), *A Question of Balance: The President, the Congress, and Foreign Policy*. Washington, D.C.: Brookings Institution.

_____. (1987) *Covert Action: The Limits of Intervention in the Postwar World* New York: Basic Books.

Truman, David B. (1951) *The Governmental Process*. New York: Knopf.

Truman, Harry S. (1966) *Public Papers of the Presidents of the United States, Harry S Truman, 1952–53*. Washington, D.C.: Government Printing Office.

Tugwell, Rexford Guy. (1971) *Off Course: From Truman to Nixon*. New York: Praeger.

Tunander, Ola. (1989) "The Logic of Deterrence," *Journal of Peace Research* 26 (November): 353–365.

Turner, Robert F. (1988) "The Power of the Purse: Controlling National Security by Conditional Appropriations," *Atlantic Community Quarterly* 26 Spring): 79–96.

Turner, Stansfield. (1985) *Secrecy and Democracy: The CIA in Transition*. Boston: Houghton Mifflin.

Turner, Stansfield, and George Thibault. (1982) "Intelligence: The Right Rules," *Foreign Policy* 48 (Fall): 122–138.

Tyler, Patrick E. (1990) "Keeping the Threat Alive," *Washington Post National Weekly Edition*, February 19–25, p. 31.

Tyler, Patrick E., and David B. Ottaway. (1986) "Reagan's Secret Little Wars," *Washington Post National Weekly Edition*, March 31, pp. 6–7.

Ulam, Adam B. (1985) "Forty Years of Troubled Coexistence," *Foreign Affairs* 64 (Fall): 12–32.

———. (1983) *Dangerous Relations: The Soviet Union in World Politics, 1970–82*. New York: Oxford University Press.

U.S. Arms Control and Disarmament Agency. (1989) *World Military Expenditures and Arms Transfers 1988*. Washington, D.C.: Government Printing Office.

———. (1975) *World Military Expenditures and Arms Trade 1963–1973*. Washington, D.C.: Government Printing Office.

U.S. Bureau of the Census. (1989) *Statistical Abstract of the United States, 1989*. Washington, D.C.: Government Printing Office.

U.S. Department of Commerce. (1978) *Selected Trade and Economic Data of the Centrally Planned Economies*, December 1977. Washington, D.C.: Government Printing Office.

U.S. Department of State. (1985) *Atlas of NATO*. Washington, D.C.: Government Printing Office.

U.S. Departnent of State. (1983) "International Security and Development Program," Special Report No. 108, April 4. Washington, D.C.: Department of State

Uslaner, Eric M. (1986) "One Nation, Many Voices: Interest Groups in Foreign Policy Making," pp. 236–257 in Allan J. Cigler and Burdett A. Loomis (eds.), *Interest Group Politics*, 2nd ed. Washington, D.C.: CQ Press.

U.S. Office of Personnel Management. (1989) *Federal Civilian Workforce Statistics: Employment and Trends as of January 1989*. Washington, D.C.: U.S. Office of Personnel Management.

van den Haag, Ernest. (1985) "The Busyness of American Foreign Policy," *Foreign Affairs* 64 (Fall): 113–129.

Van Evera, Stephen. (1990) "The Case against Intervention," *Atlantic Monthly* 266 (July): 72–80.

Vasquez, John A. (1991) "The Deterrence Myth: Nuclear Weapons and the Prevention of Nuclear War," pp. 205–223 in Charles W. Kegley, Jr. (ed.), *The Long Postwar Peace*. New York: HarperCollins.

———. (1985) "Domestic Contention on Critical Foreign Policy Issues: The Case of the United States," *International Organization* 39 (Autumn): 606–643.

———. (1983) *The Power of Power Politics*. New Brunswick, N.J.: Rutgers University Press.

Vasquez, John A., and Richard W. Mansbach. (1983) "The Issue Cycle: Conceptualizing Long-Term Global Political Change," *International Organization* 37 (Spring): 257–280.

Verba, Sidney. (1969) "Assumptions of Rationality and Non-Rationality in Models of the International System," pp. 217–231 in James N. Rosenau (ed.), *International Politics and Foreign Policy*. New York: Free Press.

von Vorys, Karl. (1990) *American National Interest: Virtue and Power in Foreign Policy*. New York: Praeger.

Walker, Stephen G. (1977) "The Interface between Beliefs and Behavior: Henry Kissinger's Operational Code and the Vietnam War," *Journal of Conflict Resolution* 21 (March): 129–168.

Wallis, Allen. (1986) "U.S.-EC Relations and the International Trading System." Address before the Luxembourg Society for International Affairs, October 8. U.S. Department of State, Bureau of Public Affairs, Current Policy no. 889.

Waltz, Kenneth N. (1979) *Theory of International Politics*. Reading, Mass.: Addison-Wesley.

———. (1971) "Opinions and Crisis in American Foreign Policy," pp. 47–55 in Douglas M. Fox (ed.), *The Politics of U.S. Foreign Policy Making*. Pacific Palisades, Calif.: Goodyear.

———. (1967) *Foreign Policy and Democratic Politics*. Boston: Little, Brown.

———. (1964) "The Stability of a Bipolar World," *Daedalus* 93 (Summer): 881–909.

Warburg, Gerald Felix. (1989) *Conflict and Consensus: The Struggle between Congress and the President over Foreign Policymaking*. New York: Harper & Row.

Warnke, Paul. (1991) "Now More Than Ever: No First Use," pp. 55–65 in Charles W. Kegley, Jr., and Kenneth L. Schwab (eds.), *After the Cold War: Questioning the Morality of Nuclear Deterrence*. Boulder, Colo.: Westview Press.

———. (1988) "Foreign Policy Fake, Arms Control Poseur," *New York Times*, October 19, p. A35.

Warwick, Donald P. (1975) *A Theory of Public Bureaucracy: Politics, Personality, and Organization in the State Department*. Cambridge, Mass.: Harvard University Press.

Wayman, Frank Whelon (1985) "Arms Control and Strategic Arms Voting in the U.S. Senate," *Journal of Conflict Resolution* 29 (June): 225–251.

Weatherford, M. Stephen. (1988) "The International Economy as a Constraint on U.S. Macroeconomic Policymaking," *International Organization* 42 (Autumn): 605–637.

Weede, Erich. (1978) "U.S. Support for Foreign Governments, or Domestic Disorder and Imperial Intervention, 1958–1965," *Comparative Political Studies* 10 (January): 497–527.

Weeks, John, and Andrew Zimbalist. (1989) "The Failure of Intervention in Panama: Humiliation in the Backyard," *Third World Quarterly* 11 (January): 1–27.

Weinraub, Bernard. (1989) "On Bush and Cheney and Their Dual Approach to the Soviet Union," *New York Times*, September 1, p. B7.

Weisband, Edward. (1973) *The Ideology of American Foreign Policy: A Paradigm of Lockian Liberalism*. Beverly Hills, Calif.: Sage.

Weisman, Steven R. (1983) "The Influence of William Clark," *New York Times Magazine*, August 14, pp. 17–21ff.

Weissberg, Robert. (1976) *Public Opinion and Popular Government*. Englewood Cliffs, N.J.: Prentice-Hall.

West, William F., and Joseph Cooper. (1990) "Legislative Influence v. Presidential Dominance: Competing Models of Bureaucratic Control," *Political Science Quarterly* 104 (Winter): 581–606.

Westing, Arthur H. (ed.). (1986) *Global Resources and International Conflict: Environmental Factors in Strategic Policy and Action*. Oxford: Oxford University Press.

"White House Tapes and Minutes of the Cuban Missile Crises." (1985) *International Security* 10 (Summer): 164–203.

White, Theodore H. (1973) *The Making of the President, 1972*. New York: Atheneum.

Wicker, Tom. (1990) "Diplomacy Too Late in Latin America," *State* (Columbia, S.C.), January 12, p. A22.

Wilensky, Harold L. (1967) *Organizational Intelligence: Knowledge and Policy in Government and Industry*. New York: Basic Books.

Williams, William Appleman. (1980) *Empire as a Way of Life*. New York: Oxford University Press.

———. (1972) *The Tragedy of American Diplomacy*, 2nd ed. New York: Delta.

Winik, Jay. (1989) "Restoring Bipartisanship," *Washington Quarterly* 12 (Winter): 109–122.

———. (1985) "Toward a Post-NATO Europe," *Wall Street Journal*, August 27, p. 30.

Wittkopf, Eugene R. (1990) *Faces of Internationalism: Public Opinion and American Foreign Policy*. Durham, N.C.: Duke University Press.

———. (1973) "Foreign Aid and United Nations Votes," *American Political Science Review* 67 (September): 868–888.

Wittkopf, Eugene R., and Charles W. Kegley, Jr. (1990) "Our Imperiled Environment: Impediments to a Global Response," *National Forum* 70 (Winter): 32–35.

Wittkopf, Eugene R., and James M. McCormick. (1990a) "The Cold War Consensus: Did It Exist?" *Polity* 22 (Summer): 627–653.

———. (1990b) "The Domestic Politics of Contra Aid: Public Opinion, Congress, and the President." Paper presented at the conference on "Public Opinion and U.S. Foreign Policy: The Case of Contra Funding," the Woodrow Wilson School of Public and International Affairs, Princeton University, Princeton, N.J., May 4–5.

Wolfers, Arnold. (1962) *Discord and Collaboration*. Baltimore: Johns Hopkins University Press.

Woods, Alan. (1989) *Development and the National Interest: U.S. Economic Assistance into the 21st Century*. Washington, D.C.: Agency for International Development.

Woodward, Bob. (1987) *Veil: The Secret Wars of the CIA 1981–1987*. New York: Simon & Schuster.

Woodward, Bob, and Carl Bernstein. (1979) *The Final Days*. New York: Simon & Schuster.

Woodward, J. David. (1989) Review of George Bush (with Victor Gold), *Looking Forward*, in *Presidential Studies Quarterly* 19 (Summer): 640–641.

World Bank. (1990) "The Developing Countries and the Short-term Outlook for the Global Economy: An Addendum." International Economics Department, Development Economics, September 12.

World Development Report 1989. (1989) New York: Oxford University Press for the World Bank.

World Development Report 1988. (1988) New York: Oxford University Press for the World Bank.

World Development Report 1987. (1987) New York: Oxford University Press for the World Bank.

World Development Report 1985. (1985) New York: Oxford University Press for the World Bank.

World Resources 1988–89. (1988) New York: Basic Books.

Yalem, Ronald J. (1972) "Tripolarity and the International System," *Orbis* 15 (Winter): 1051–1063.

Yankelovich, Daniel, and Sidney Harman. (1988) *Starting with the People*. Boston: Houghton Mifflin.

Yarmolinsky, Adam. (1971) *The Military Establishment: Its Impact on American Society*: New York: Harper & Row.

———. (1970–1971) "The Military Establishment (Or How Political Problems Become Military Problems)," *Foreign Policy* 1 (Winter): 78–97.

Yearbook of International Organizations, 1987/88. (1987) *Vol 1: Organization Descriptions and Index*. Munich: K.G. Saur.

Yergin, Daniel. (1978) *Shattered Peace: The Origins of the Cold War and the National Security State*. Boston: Houghton Mifflin.

———. (1977) "Politics and Soviet-American Trade: The Three Questions," *Foreign Affairs* 55 (April): 517–538.

"Z" [Martin Malia]. (1990) "To the Stalin Mausoleum," *Daedalus* 119 (Winter): 295–344.

Zelikow, Philip D. (1987) "The United States and the Use of Force: A Historical Summary," pp. 31–81 in George K. Osborn, Asa A. Clark IV, Daniel J. Kaufman, and Douglas E. Lute (eds.), *Democracy, Strategy, and Vietnam*. Lexington, Mass.: Lexington Books.

Zimmerman, William. (1973) "Issue Area and Foreign Policy Process: A Research Note in Search of a General Theory," *American Political Science Review* 67 (December): 1204–1212.

A Chronology of Selected Diplomatic Events, 1945–1990

ROOSEVELT ADMINISTRATION

1945

United States rejects Soviet request for $6 billion reconstruction loan
Churchill, Roosevelt, and Stalin sign Yalta agreement
United States recognizes Soviet control of Outer Mongolia
United States approves transfer of Kurile Islands to Soviet Union
Romanian government turns pro-Soviet
Arab League Pact signed in Cairo
Last German V 2 rocket falls on Britain
Roosevelt dies; Vice President Truman succeeds to the presidency

TRUMAN ADMINISTRATION

1945

V-E Day (German surrender to Allied forces in Europe), May 8
Truman cancels Lend-Lease allocations and shipments to the Allies
Truman sends Harry Hopkins to Moscow to discuss postwar settlement
Allied Control Council for Germany establishes four-power occupation of Berlin and
    right to determine Germany's boundaries
San Francisco Conference writes United Nations (UN) Charter
U.S. Senate approves United Nations Charter by a vote of 80–2
Western nations recognize Polish government
Truman informs Stalin that American scientists have successfully detonated world's first
    atomic bomb
Churchill, Stalin, and Truman attend Potsdam Conference
United States drops atomic bomb on Hiroshima, August 6
Soviet Union declares war on Japan and sends troops into Manchuria
United States drops atomic bomb on Nagasaki, August 9
Chiang Kai-shek and Molotov sign Sino-Soviet friendship treaty
Soviet-Polish treaty recognizes Oder-Neisse line as Poland's western border
Ho Chi Minh declares independent Vietnam Republic
V-J Day (Japan surrenders to Allied forces), August 14
Council of Foreign Ministers meets in London
Iranian rebellion, supported by Soviet arms, erupts
Civil war continues in China
Nuremberg War Crimes Tribunal convenes in Germany
Big Three meet at Moscow Conference; Secretary of State James F. Byrnes agrees to
    recognize Romanian and Bulgarian satellite governments
Yugoslavia is declared a Federated People's Republic

1946

People's Republic of Albania proclaimed

Soviet Union protests British role in Greek civil war

George C. Marshall mediates armistice in Chinese civil war

Mao's Tse-tung communists and Chiang Kai-shek's Nationalists resume Chinese civil war

United States protests the continued presence of Soviet troops in Iran

United States leads UN involvement in Iranian crisis over Soviet protest

Churchill delivers militantly anti-Soviet Iron Curtain speech in Fulton, Missouri

Soviets withdraw troops from Iran

Council of Foreign Ministers convene Paris Peace Conference

General Lucius Clay stops reparations to Soviet zone of Germany

Baruch Plan to destroy atomic weapons and place control of nuclear energy in international hands rejected by Soviets

United States grants independence to the Philippines

United States joins the United Nations Educational, Scientific, and Cultural Organization (UNESCO)

Truman tells Congress China received $600 million since V-J Day, and aid will continue

United States protests Soviet economic exploitation of Hungary

Secretary of State Byrnes outlines U.S. policy for German war recovery in Stuttgart speech

United States backs anti-Soviet faction in Turkish Straits crisis

Nuremberg Tribunal sentences ten Nazis to death and others to life imprisonment

Japan's wartime leaders imprisoned or hanged following Tokyo trials

United States signs treaty of friendship and commerce with China

United States begins first peacetime atomic tests in Bikini Atoll

Iran crushes independence movement in Azerbaijan with U.S. aid

Yugoslavia shoots down U.S. aircraft

Soviets agree to troop exit from Trieste and arms inspection

Treaties at New York Foreign Ministers Conference confirm U.S. recognition of Soviet control in southeastern Europe

United States and Britain begin joint administration of their occupation zones in Germany

Bulgaria is declared a People's Republic

War breaks out in Vietnam

1947

United States charges violation of Yalta agreement following communist electoral victory in Poland

Britain and France sign a fifty-year Treaty of Alliance and Mutual Assistance at Dunkirk

United States abandons efforts to mediate between Chinese Nationalists and communists

Truman Doctrine pledges aid to Greece, Turkey, and others resisting communism

Big Four Foreign Ministers Conference in Moscow concludes without agreement

Hungarian ruling party smashed by communists

United Nations makes the United States trustee for Pacific islands

Secretary of State George C. Marshall announces European Recovery Program (Marshall Plan)

Under Soviet pressure, Poland and Hungary decline Marshall Plan assistance

George F. Kennan's "X" article proposing U.S. containment of Soviet communism, based on 1946 telegram sent from Moscow, published in *Foreign Affairs*

National Security Act creates Defense Department, National Security Council (NSC), and Central Intelligence Agency (CIA)

United States proposes Japanese peace treaty to make Japan a stronghold against communism in the Far East

Soviet Union charges that the United States threatens war

India proclaimed independent and partitioned into India and Pakistan

Marshall refers Korean independence question to UN General Assembly

Crisis erupts in Kashmir (which is claimed by both India and Pakistan)

General Agreement on Tariffs and Trade (GATT) treaty signed by twenty-three countries

Rio Pact for collective defense of Western Hemisphere commits the United States and Latin American republics to mutual assistance against aggression

Comintern revived by Soviet Union and greatly expanded as Cominform

Romania becomes a People's Republic following the abdication of King Michael

1948

United States announces European reconstruction will occur without Soviet collaboration

Mohandas Gandhi assassinated in India

Communist coup occurs in Czechoslovakia

Juan Perón retains Argentinean presidency over U.S. complaints

Brussels Treaty calls for cooperation among Belgium, France, Luxembourg, the Netherlands, and the United Kingdom

Soviet Union refuses to meet in Allied Control Council because of Western obstruction in Germany

Organization of European Economic Cooperation (OEEC) established to disburse Marshall Plan funds

Organization of American States (OAS) created to replace the Pan American Union

Israel declares independence, receives immediate U.S. recognition

War between Israel and the Arab League erupts

United States provides military aid to Chinese Nationalists

Vandenberg Resolution pledges U.S. support for Brussels Treaty and defense agreements in Europe

Soviet Union stops road and rail traffic between Berlin and the West; airlift begins

Yugoslavia's Marshal Tito breaks with Cominform and proclaims neutrality in East-West dispute

Rebellion in Malaya begins

Separate North and South Korean governments established

Truman elected president

Brussels Treaty powers, Canada, and the United States meet in Washington to create North Atlantic defense treaty

Universal Declaration of Human Rights adopted by UN General Assembly

1949

"Point Four" of Truman's inaugural address promises aid to developing countries

Council for Mutual Economic Assistance (Comecon) is initiated for Soviet assistance in Europe

Philippine insurgency led by Huk rebels

United States guided missile launched to record height of 250 miles

Israel admitted to the United Nations

Negotiating powers invite Denmark, Iceland, Italy, Norway, and Portugal to adhere to the North Atlantic Treaty

Soviet Union protests that prospective North Atlantic Treaty Organization (NATO) is contrary to UN Charter

NATO (first permanent U.S. alliance concluded in peacetime) formed with signing of North Atlantic Treaty

London Ten-Power Agreement creates the Council of Europe

Berlin blockade lifted; separate East and West German governments established

French install Bao Dai as head of Vietnamese puppet government

United States withdraws occupation forces from South Korea

Vietnamese state established with capital at Saigon

Soviet Union acquires atomic bomb

Nationalists flee mainland China to island of Formosa Taiwan

Joint Chiefs of Staff advise against U.S. occupation of Formosa

State Department issues China White Paper placing blame for communist takeover on Nationalists' corruption

Mao Tse-tung unifies mainland China and proclaims People's Republic of China

Soviet Union and its European satellites recognize People's Republic of China

Greek civil war ends in communist defeat

Mutual Defense Assistance Act pledges U.S. aid to countries vulnerable to communist pressure

Truman and Shah of Iran declare U.S.-Iranian solidarity

India recognizes Communist China

1950

Britain recognizes Communist China

Truman announces the United States will take no military measures to protect Formosa

Secretary of State Dean Acheson reaffirms "hands-off" policy for Formosa

United States announces intention to build hydrogen bomb

Soviet Union begins eight-month boycott of UN Security Council

Senator Joseph McCarthy claims State Department is riddled with communists and communist sympathizers

Far Eastern Economic Assistance bill assures continued aid to Formosa

Soviet Union and Communist China sign thirty-year Mutual Aid Pact

National Security Council issues Memorandum No. 68

United States, Britain, and France issue Tripartite Declaration promising protection of Israel's boundary lines

United States gives France military assistance to fight Vietnamese rebels

North Korean forces invade South Korea and capture Seoul; U.S. troops enter Korea with orders to defend Formosa and prevent Chiang's forces from attacking mainland China

Chiang Kai-shek and General Douglas MacArthur meet on Formosa

McCarren Act calling for severe domestic restrictions of communists passed by Congress over presidential veto

United States invades North Korea; South Korean troops cross thirty-eighth parallel

Greece and Turkey accept North Atlantic Council invitation to participate in Mediterranean defense planning

General Eisenhower named Supreme Allied Commander of Europe by North Atlantic Council

East German-Polish treaty ends dispute over border

Communist Chinese forces occupy Tibet

Tibet appeals to United Nations but China rejects UN appeal for cease-fire

Communist China enters Korean War

UN General Assembly passes the Uniting for Peace Resolution

1951

UN General Assembly accuses China of aggression in Korea

U.S. troops stationed in NATO countries

House Minority Leader Joseph W. Martin discloses MacArthur letter endorsing use of Chiang's troops to open second front on Chinese mainland

Truman recalls General MacArthur, who sought U.S. invasion of mainland China

Secretary of State Marshall tells Senate that Chinese Nationalists were beaten by communists due to lack of public support and "the character of government"

Treaty establishing European Coal and Steel Community (ECSC) signed

Mohammed Mossadegh appointed Prime Minister of Iran, nationalizes Anglo-Iranian Oil Company

United States and Philippines sign mutual security pact

McCarren's Internal Security subcommittee begins hearings on "subversive" influences on U.S. foreign policy

Truman proposes $307 million aid program to Nationalist China

ANZUS Pact signed by Australia, New Zealand, and the United States

Mutual Security Act pledges U.S. military assistance throughout the world

Korean truce line (thirty-eighth parallel) accepted at United Nations

1952

Franco-German crisis erupts over administration of Saar region

Soviet Union creates three-mile buffer zone on East German border

Greece and Turkey join NATO

United States doubles size of Military Assistance Advisory Group on Formosa

European Defense Community (EDC) treaty signed by Belgium, France, Italy, Luxembourg, The Netherlands, and West Germany

Cyprus begins fight for independence

Gamal Abdel Nasser emerges as leader following ouster of Egyptian monarchy

Britain successfully completes first atomic test

United States explodes first hydrogen bomb at Eniwetok Atoll

National Security Agency created by a classified presidential directive

Eisenhower elected president

Truman considers using atomic bomb on Moscow and Leningrad to prompt a Soviet agreement on Korea

Fulgencio Batista seizes power in Cuba

EISENHOWER ADMINISTRATION

1953

Eisenhower announces end of Formosa's neutralization, thereby unleashing Chiang Kai-shek to attack Chinese mainland

Secretary of State John Foster Dulles pledges to "roll back" the Iron Curtain and liberate Eastern Europe

Chinese Nationalists attack Communist Chinese mainland

Greece, Turkey, and Yugoslavia sign treaty of friendship

Stalin dies; power struggle erupts involving Malenkov, Molotov, and Khrushchev

Eisenhower administration proposes nuclear weapons to redress personnel gaps in European rearmament

Vietnamese rebels attack Laos

Soviet Union extends diplomatic recognition to East Germany

Soviet tanks crush riots in East Berlin

Korean armistice signed at Panmunjom

Congressional resolution supports "liberation" of Eastern Europe

Dulles threatens resumption of Korean War

Soviet Union announces possession of hydrogen bomb

Shah of Iran returns from abroad to claim throne after CIA-designed coup overthrows government of Prime Minister Mohammed Mossadegh

Pact of Madrid approves U.S. naval bases in Spain

United States and South Korea sign mutual defense treaty

Eisenhower proposes "atoms for peace" plan at United Nations

1954

Dulles proclaims policy of deterrence through massive retaliation

Big Four foreign ministers meet in Berlin; Soviets reject German unification

Inter-American Conference in Caracas passes anticommunist declaration

Soviet Union accelerates Third World aid program to gain influence

United States and Japan sign mutual defense agreement

U.S. creates Food for Peace Program

Dulles proposes Anglo-American military intervention in Vietnam

Geneva Conference on Korea and Indochina opens

Nasser becomes prime minister of Egypt

Dien Bien Phu falls to Vietnamese communists

France, Britain, and the United States reject Soviet bid to join NATO

CIA helps conservative military officers overthrow a reform-minded Guatemalan government

Geneva Accords partitions Vietnam and with U.S. support terminates French rule in Indochina

French National Assembly refuses to ratify treaty establishing the European Defense Community

Senator Joseph McCarthy attempts to prove communist infiltration of the U.S. Army in nationally televised hearings; Senate censures McCarthy

Algerian war for independence from France begins

Southeast Asia Treaty Organization (SEATO) created

Quemoy-Matsu crisis erupts; Dulles declares the United States is prepared to use atomic bomb on mainland China

Britain, Italy, Yugoslavia, and the United States sign a Memorandum of Understanding ending the Trieste dispute

Paris agreements signed; West Germany invited to join NATO and rearm

United States signs a mutual defense treaty with Nationalist Chinese on Formosa

1955

Soviet Union ends the state of war with Germany

Baghdad Pact between Iraq and Turkey signed

Eisenhower pledges U.S. forces will remain in Europe as long as necessary

Bandung Conference convenes the nonaligned countries of Asia and Africa

West Germany joins NATO

Soviet Union signs a treaty with the Pankow regime of the Soviet occupied zone of Germany, granting it the prerogatives of a state

Iran, Pakistan, and the United Kingdom join Baghdad Pact

Warsaw Pact formed by the Soviet Union, Albania, Bulgaria, Czechoslovakia, East Germany, Hungary, Poland, and Romania

Soviet Union evacuates occupation forces from Austria and signs Austrian State Treaty requiring Austrian neutrality

United States and Communist China hold ambassadorial-level talks in Geneva

Taiwan-straits crisis develops; Eisenhower pledges defense of Formosa and the Pescadores Islands

First conference on the peaceful uses of atomic energy convenes in Geneva

Ngo Dinh Diem announces suspension of elections in South Vietnam

U.S. military advisers sent to South Vietnam

1956

Soviet Premier Khrushchev consolidates power; attacks Stalin's policies at the Twentieth Communist Party Congress

Pravda announces the dissolution of Cominform

United States offers aid to rebellious East European countries

United States withdraws offer of assistance in Aswan Dam project, accuses Nasser of playing the Soviet Union against the West

Seventy nations, including the United States and the Soviet Union, create International Atomic Energy Agency

Nasser nationalizes Suez Canal

Israeli military attacks Egyptian troops in Sinai Peninsula

Britain and France intervene in Egypt by occupying Suez Canal area

Hungarian revolution suppressed by Soviet forces

Japan admitted to United Nations

Eisenhower reelected president

Britain, France, and Israel agree to cease-fire and withdrawal from Suez

1957

Eisenhower Doctrine pledges U.S. aid to Middle Eastern countries resisting communist takeovers

United States agrees to supply Britain with guided missiles

Treaties of Rome establishing the European Economic Community (EEC) and European Atomic Energy Community (Euratom) signed

United States resumes military support to Saudi Arabia in exchange for lease of Dhahran airfield

U.S. military aid supplied to Jordan's King Hussein

United States accedes to Baghdad Pact as an associate member

Britain tests hydrogen bomb

Syria expels U.S. embassy officials for allegedly plotting coup; United States expels Syrian ambassador in retaliation

Soviet Union develops intercontinental ballistic missile (ICBM) capability

United States builds Defense Early Warning System (DEW line) in Canada

UN General Assembly condemns Soviet intervention in Hungary

Soviet Union launches Sputnik I and II, first earth satellites

1958

United States launches its first space satellite, Explorer I

Mao Tse-tung announces "Great Leap Forward" to promote Chinese industrialization and agricultural production

Egypt and Syria form United Arab Republic with Nasser as president

United Nations convenes Law of the Sea Conference

Last U.S. ground troops leave Japan

Soviet Union announces a unilateral suspension of all nuclear arms tests

Vice President Nixon confronts hostile protesters on South American tour

European Parliamentary Assembly meets for the first time in Strasbourg

Khrushchev visits Beijing

Iraq's army takes power in bloody coup, allies with United Arab Republic

U.S. Marines land in Lebanon; Soviet Union protests intervention

U.S. nuclear submarine *Nautilus* navigates beneath the North Pole to link the Atlantic and Pacific oceans for first time

China bombards Quemoy; United States pledges defense of the island

Khrushchev refuses to back China in Formosan crisis

Soviet Union protests U.S. violation of its air space

Soviet Union offers United Arab Republic assistance to build Aswan Dam

Soviet Union announces desire to terminate the four-power agreement on the status of Berlin

Charles de Gaulle elected President of the French Republic

Batista overthrown in Cuba; Fidel Castro assumes power

1959

Anglo-Greek-Turkish agreement pledges independence for Cyprus

Dalai Lama flees Tibet during revolt

Iraq withdraws from Baghdad Pact

OAS members reiterate principle of nonintervention at Santiago Conference

Vice President Nixon and Soviet Premier Khrushchev hold "kitchen debate" in Moscow about the relative merits of their countries' systems

United States denounces Soviet activity in widening civil war in Laos

Central Treaty Organization (CENTO) formed to replace Baghdad Pact for Middle East defense

Khrushchev visits the United States for Camp David meetings

Khrushchev proposes total world disarmament to UN General Assembly

Members of European Free Trade Association ("The Seven") ratify treaty

Inter-American Development Bank formed

Antarctic Treaty prohibits any military use of the region

1960

United States and Japan sign Treaty of Mutual Cooperation and Security

France explodes nuclear device, becomes fourth nuclear power

Soviet Deputy Premier Anastas Mikoyan visits Cuba

Ten-nation UN Disarmament Committee begins negotiations in Geneva

U-2 spy plane piloted by Francis Gary Powers shot down over Soviet territory; Khrushchev cancels U.S. tour in response

Military coup in Turkey

Communist states withdraw from the UN disarmament negotiations in Geneva

China resumes shelling of Quemoy

United States denounces Soviet presence in Cuba

UN peace-keeping forces intervene to manage Congo crisis

U.S. Navy sent to Nicaragua and Guatemala to guard against Cuban threat

Soviet Union calls for ouster of UN Secretary General and substitution of "troika" system

Khrushchev disrupts twenty-fifth United Nations anniversary session by pounding his shoe on table

Kennedy elected president

United States develops submarine-launched ballistic missile (SLBM)

Organization of Petroleum Exporting Countries (OPEC) formed

United States and Canada join members of the OEEC to form the Organization for Economic Cooperation and Development (OECD)

1961

United States breaks relations with Cuba

KENNEDY ADMINISTRATION

Kennedy proposes Alliance for Progress

Patrice Lumumba is killed; Soviets threaten unilateral action in the Congo

Union of South Africa leaves British Commonwealth

United States calls SEATO to action in Laos

Soviet Union agrees to Laotian cease-fire and peace talks

Soviet Union launches first person, Major Yuri Gagarin, into space

UN General Assembly condemns *apartheid* in South Africa

Invasion of Cuba at the Bay of Pigs by CIA-trained exiles fails

First American astronaut, Alan Shepard, launched into space

Dominican Republic dictator Rafael Trujillo assassinated; CIA involvement alleged

Kennedy and Khrushchev confer at Vienna summit conference

Syria secedes from the United Arab Republic

Berlin Wall built by East Germany with Soviet help to separate East and West Berlin

United States mobilizes for second Berlin airlift

Congress passes Foreign Assistance Act

Peace Corps made permanent U.S. agency

United States and Soviet Union resume nuclear weapons testing

United States sends additional military advisers to Vietnam

Cuba is declared a socialist republic based on Marxist-Leninist principles

Albania and Soviet Union break diplomatic relations

India seizes Portuguese Goa

1962

Kennedy signs Trade Expansion Act

U.S. military presence in Vietnam expanded

OAS votes to expel Cuba

Indonesian insurgency erupts against Dutch rule

Soviet Union releases U-2 pilot Francis Gary Powers

United States sends 5,000 troops to Thailand during Laotian crisis

Laos agreement signed in Geneva

John Glenn becomes the first American to orbit the earth

Seventeen-nation disarmament conference convenes in Geneva

United States breaks diplomatic relations, suspends aid to Peru following coup

France recognizes Algerian independence

U-2 photographs reveal Soviet missile sites in Cuba

Pro-Nasser revolutionaries overthrow monarchy in Yemen

Sino-Indian border clash erupts

U.S. Navy blockades Cuba to prevent missile installation by Soviets

Kennedy and Khrushchev end war threat with Cuban missile agreement

1963

French President de Gaulle vetoes Britain's admission to the Common Market

United States thwarts effort to let Beijing replace Chinese Nationalist delegation at the
    United Nations

Ten thousand additional U.S. military personnel sent to Vietnam

Egypt, Syria, and Iraq discuss unity but fail to reach agreement

Organization of African Unity (OAU) Charter adopted in Addis Ababa

"Hot Line" agreement establishes direct communication link between White House and
    Kremlin

Kennedy speech at The American University urges end to Cold War

First Yaoundé Convention (between the European Economic Community and seventeen
    African countries) signed

Limited Nuclear Test Ban Treaty signed prohibiting nuclear tests in atmosphere, in outer
    space, and under water

China lays claim to Soviet-occupied territory

De Gaulle announces France will not sign Limited Test Ban Treaty

CIA backs assassination of South Vietnamese President Ngo Dinh Diem

Operation Big Lift airlifts 14,500 U.S. troops to Germany to demonstrate U.S. capability
    to reinforce NATO forces rapidly

Kennedy assassinated; Vice President Johnson succeeds to presidency

JOHNSON ADMINISTRATION

Military leaders oust Dominican Republic President Juan Bosch; rebellion erupts

Greek-Turkish armed conflict erupts in Cyprus

Kennedy Round of Multilateral Trade Negotiations begins

1964

France recognizes People's Republic of China

Panamanians riot over U.S. occupation of Canal Zone; United States and Panama break
    diplomatic relations

Soviet-Romanian rift develops

UN peace-keeping force (UNFICYP) enters Cyprus

Group of 77 formalized to pursue the objectives of Third World countries

OAS members impose trade sanctions on Cuba

Gulf of Tonkin Resolution gives Johnson congressional support to expand war in Vietnam

United Nations Conference on Trade and Development (UNCTAD) convenes in Geneva

Brezhnev replaces Khrushchev as Soviet leader

U.S. warplanes bomb Ho Chi Minh Trail in Laos

China explodes its first nuclear device

Insurgencies against Portuguese rule erupt in Angola and Mozambique

Johnson elected president

1965

United States escalates war by bombing North Vietnam and sending 125,000 additional combat troops to South Vietnam

United States launches world's first commercial telecommunications satellite, *Early Bird*

Kashmir crisis culminates in war between India and Pakistan

Soviet and East German authorities block land access to Berlin when West German Parliament holds session in West Berlin

United States intervenes in the Dominican Republic

Indonesian army crushes attempted coup, slaughters 500,000 people

Rhodesia issues unilateral declaration of independence; Britain imposes oil embargo on Rhodesia

1966

Indira Gandhi, Jawaharlal Nehru's daughter, becomes prime minister of India

Coups occur in Ghana, Nigeria, and Syria

France removes its armed forces from NATO military command

Civil war erupts in Uganda

International days of protest held against U.S. policy in Vietnam

United States begins bombing Hanoi-Haiphong area of North Vietnam

Johnson links U.S. action in Vietnam to Truman Doctrine

Chou En-lai visits Romania

European Economic Community establishes Common Agricultural Policy (CAP)

China tests its first guided missile

United States pledges at Manila Conference to continue Vietnam War until ''just peace'' reached

Unpiloted Surveyor I makes successful lunar landing

Chinese ''Cultural Revolution'' attempts to purge society of bourgeois elements

1967

United States and Soviet Union among over sixty nations that sign UN treaty governing exploration and use of outer space

United States deploys multiple warhead missiles (Soviet Union follows in 1968)

United States and Soviet Union increase commercial and cultural exchanges

Johnson and Vice President Nguyen Cao Ky of Vietnam confer at Guam

United States lends Bolivia military support against Cuban insurgency led by Ché Guevara

Arab-Israeli Six-Day War erupts

Suez Canal closed (until June 1975)

Treaty establishing a single executive for the European Community (EC) by replacing with one Commission and one Council the ECSC High Authority and the EEC and Euratom Commission enters into force

Association of South-East Asian Nations (ASEAN) created

Johnson and Soviet Premier Aleksey Kosygin meet for Glassboro summit

Biafra rebels against Nigerian rule, leading to bitter civil war

De Gaulle makes "Free Quebec" speech supporting French Canadian separatist movement during state visit to Canada

People's Republic of South Yemen proclaimed

King Hussein of Jordan visits Soviet Union

Ché Guevara killed in Bolivian ambush

1968

North Korea seizes U.S. intelligence ship *Pueblo* within or near its territorial waters

North Vietnamese and Vietcong forces launch Tet Offensive against U.S. and South Vietnamese troops; regarded a major setback for the United States

U.S. troops massacre Vietnamese civilians at My Lai

Johnson asks for peace settlement in Vietnam; announces he will not seek reelection

Martin Luther King, Jr., civil rights leader and winner of 1964 Nobel Peace Prize, assassinated

Vietnam peace talks begin in Paris

Communist party leaders in Czechoslovakia endorse policy of resisting Soviet pressure

Haiti charges the United States with bombing its capital

Nuclear Nonproliferation Treaty signed at the United Nations

Warsaw Pact troops invade Czechoslovakia to quell "Prague Spring"

U.S. ambassador to Guatemala killed by terrorists

Treaty prohibiting nuclear weapons in Latin America enters into force

Violent antiwar demonstrations occur during Democratic National Convention

Albania withdraws from Warsaw Pact

Peru nationalizes U.S. oil interests

Nixon elected president; promises "secret" plan to end Vietnam War

NATO denounces Soviet intervention in Czechoslovakia

Crew of *Pueblo* released by North Korea

NIXON ADMINISTRATION

1969

Nixon supports strategic arms talks; recommends deployment of antiballistic missiles (ABMs) to enhance U.S. bargaining position

Secret U.S. bombing of Cambodia begins

National Security Council study recommends U.S. support for white African regimes

Sino-Soviet border clashes erupt along Ussuri River and on Damansly Island

Nixon calls for "Vietnamization" of Southeast Asian war, announces troop reductions

French President de Gaulle resigns and is replaced by Georges Pompidou

El Salvador and Honduras engage in military clash

First phase (75,000 soldiers) of U.S. troop withdrawal from Vietnam begins

Nixon signals new line toward Beijing by allowing American tourists to bring home $100 worth of Chinese-made goods

Neil Armstrong becomes the first person to set foot on the moon

Second Yaoundé Convention signed
North Korea shoots down U.S. reconnaissance plane over Sea of Japan
Nixon Doctrine reduces U.S. commitment overseas and asks allies to share in the defense
    burden
North Vietnamese President Ho Chi Minh dies
Violence escalates between Protestants and Catholics in Northern Ireland
Nixon suspends Seventh Fleet's nineteen-year-long patrol of Taiwan Straits
First round of Strategic Arms Limitations Talks (SALT) talks held in Helsinki, Finland
Congress bars involvement of U.S. ground troops in Laos and Thailand

1970
Albania and People's Republic of China conclude trade agreement
First NATO communications satellite launched from Cape Kennedy
United States invades Cambodia
Student protests against Vietnam War result in four deaths by National Guard at Kent
    State University; 448 American universities close or go on strike
Senate repeals Gulf of Tonkin Resolution
United States offers cease-fire plan to end Arab-Israeli fighting
Soviet Union and West Germany sign friendship treaty affirming European borders as
    permanent
Nasser dies, Anwar Sadat becomes president of Egypt
Salvador Allende, a socialist, elected president of Chile
U.S. forces in Vietnam reduced to below 400,000
Treaty normalizing relations between Poland and West Germany signed in Warsaw

1971
Seabed Arms Control Treaty signed
Canada and People's Republic of China exchange diplomatic envoys
U.S.-China relations warm as China hosts U.S. table-tennis team
India-Pakistan war erupts following crisis in Bengal
Bengal, renamed Bangladesh, gains independence
The *New York Times* begins publication of the *Pentagon Papers*
National Security Advisor Henry Kissinger secretly visits China to arrange Nixon visit
Nixon inaugurates New Economic Policy (NEP), effectively suspending the 1944 Bret-
    ton Woods Agreement and convertibility of the U.S. dollar
United States and Soviet Union reach "accidents measures" agreement designed to
    reduce risk of nuclear war
People's Republic of China takes China's seat in the United Nations
Fighting in Indochina spreads to Laos and Cambodia
Four-Power Agreement on Berlin signed by World War II allies
United States conducts large-scale bombing of North Vietnam and Vietcong supply
    routes in Cambodia

1972
Britain, Denmark, and Ireland agree to join European Community by 1973
Nixon visits China, pledges normalization of relations in Shanghai Communiqué
Lon Nol takes control of Cambodian government
Britain assumes direct control of Northern Ireland
United States and Soviet Union sign Biological Weapons Convention

Nixon orders Haiphong Harbor mined and widens air war against Vietnam
United States returns Okinawa to Japan
Nixon becomes first American postwar president to visit Soviet Union
United States and Soviet Union sign interim SALT agreement and ABM Treaty
Watergate affair begins as burglars of Democratic National Headquarters in the Watergate
   complex are arrested
United States and North Vietnam resume Paris peace talks
Soviet Union purchases massive amounts of U.S. grain
Sadat expels all Soviet advisers and technicians from Egypt
Japan recognizes People's Republic of China and begins trade relations
Palestinian terrorists kill Israeli athletes and others in Munich Olympic Village
Philippine President Ferdinand Marcos declares martial law in response to alleged
   "communist rebellion"
Nixon reelected president
SALT II talks begin in Geneva
"Basic Treaty" signed by East and West Germany
Paris peace talks break down; United States resumes heavy bombing of North Vietnam
   on Christmas day

1973

Vietnam cease-fire signed in Paris provides for withdrawal of U.S. troops from Vietnam
   within sixty days
United States and China open liaison offices in each other's capitals
United States and Soviet Union sign agreement to prevent nuclear war
Conference on Security and Cooperation in Europe (CSCE) begins
Chile's socialist President Allende killed in military coup; CIA complicity alleged
Algiers summit of nonaligned nations begins
Juan Perón returns from exile, elected president of Argentina
East and West Germany establish diplomatic relations
Yom Kippur War erupts between Israel and its Arab adversaries
Arab members of OPEC impose oil embargo on Western supporters of Israel
Founding session of the Trilateral Commission is held in Tokyo
Talks on Mutual and Balanced Force Reductions (MBFR) in Europe begin
Congress passes War Powers Resolution over Nixon's veto
UN Conference on the Law of the Sea convenes with 157 participants
Tokyo Round of GATT trade negotiations begins
OPEC's six Persian Gulf members double the price of crude oil

1974

Military coup in Ethiopia places Marxist regime in power
Cuba sends troops to Yemen
Organization of Arab Petroleum Exporting Countries (OAPEC) lifts oil embargo
Military coup in Lisbon ends Portuguese rule in Guinea-Bissau and Mozambique
India explodes its first nuclear device
Group of 77 passes the Declaration on the Establishment of a New International Eco-
   nomic Order (NIEO)
Secretary of State Kissinger mediates Golan Heights cease-fire between Syria and Israel
United States and Soviet Union sign ABM Protocol Treaty on limitation of antiballistic
   systems and Threshold Test Ban Treaty limiting underground nuclear tests

Turkish-Greek conflict erupts when Turkey invades Cyprus following coup
Military regime in Greece resigns
Nixon resigns as Congress prepares impeachment; Vice President Ford becomes president

FORD ADMINISTRATION

Greece withdraws from NATO integrated command in protest over Turkish involvement in Cyprus
Ford pardons Nixon for any criminal offenses committed while in office; widespread domestic protest ensues
Hughes-Ryan amendment requires CIA to report covert operations to Congress
Jackson-Vanik amendment to U.S. Trade Act places restrictions on provisions for most-favored-nation status for the Soviet Union and other communist nations
Ford-Brezhnev meeting in Vladivostok results in agreement on principles to govern arms control
Arab League endorses Palestine Liberation Organization (PLO) as sole legitimate representative of the Palestinian people
United States suspends all military aid to Turkey following Turkish invasion of Cyprus

1975

U.S.-Soviet trade agreement nullified
Vietnam launches a full-scale invasion of Cambodia, its former ally
European Community and forty-six African, Caribbean, and Pacific (ACP) countries sign first Lomé Convention
United States lifts embargo on arms sales to Pakistan and India
Senate publishes report of CIA plots to assassinate foreign leaders
Civil war widens in Lebanon
Lon Nol regime in Cambodia falls to insurgents led by Pol Pot
Last U.S. troops leave Vietnam as Saigon falls to communist forces
Mayaguez seized by Cambodia; U.S. Marines killed in rescue operation
Civil war intensifies in Angola
U.S. and Soviet spacecrafts achieve linkup
Final act of the Conference on Security and Cooperation in Europe signed in Helsinki
UN General Assembly brands Zionism "racial discrimination" over strong U.S. and Israeli protests
Biological Weapons Convention enters into force
United States condemns Cuban intervention in Angola and elsewhere in Africa
Ford visits China, but Taiwan remains obstacle to improved relations
Egypt and Israel reach agreement providing for Israeli withdrawal from Sinai and creation of UN buffer zone

1976

Insurgents supported by Cuba win control in Angola
Group of 77 proposes an integrated Programme for Commodities and "Common Fund" at UNCTAD IV meetings in Nairobi
Isabel Perón ousted from power in Argentina and placed under arrest
Kissinger tours Africa; Rhodesian compromise introduced
U.S.-Soviet Underground Nuclear Test agreement signed

Syria sends 30,000 peace-keeping troops into Lebanon under auspices of Arab League
U.S. ambassador to Lebanon slain
Israeli commando raid at Entebbe Airport in Uganda rescues 103 hijacked passengers
Mao Tse-tung dies
Carter elected president

CARTER ADMINISTRATION

1977

Carter grants limited amnesty to Vietnam War draft evaders and military deserters
Carter pledges phased withdrawal of U.S. troops from South Korea
Argentina, Brazil, El Salvador, and Guatemala reject U.S. aid in reaction to attacks on
    their human rights practices
Angola invades Zaire
Soviet Union charges U.S. human rights stance constitutes interference in its internal
    affairs
Israeli prime minister Menachem Begin pledges never to negotiate over "liberated" ter-
    ritory
Spain holds first elections in thirty-eight years and legalizes Communist party
Carter cancels B-1 bomber, proposes development of cruise missile
U.S. resumes diplomatic representation in Cuba
Carter and Panamanian president sign Panama Canal treaties
Vietnam is admitted to the United Nations
United States and Soviet Union agree to adhere to existing SALT pact while SALT II
    negotiations continue
United States withdraws from International Labor Organization (ILO)
UN Security Council unanimously votes arms embargo against South Africa
Somalia breaks relations with Cuba, expels all Soviet advisers and renounces 1974
    friendship treaty with Moscow
Egyptian President Sadat visits Israel, other Arab states break relations with Egypt in pro-
    test

1978

Kampuchea (Cambodia) breaks relations with Vietnam after border clash
Ethiopian army, aided by Soviets and Cubans, captures Somali stronghold of Jijiga
Israeli armed forces invade southern Lebanon
Carter postpones production of neutron bomb
President Mohammed Daud of Afghanistan overthrown by procommunist forces
Sino-Japanese peace treaty signed
Camp David summit reaches framework for peace between Egypt and Israel
Vietnam withdraws request for U.S. war reparations; United States announces intention
    to establish diplomatic relations with Vietnam
United States and Soviet Union sign convention prohibiting hostile uses of environmen-
    tal modification techniques
Karol Cardinal Wojtyla of Poland becomes Pope John Paul II, furthers communications
    between Catholic Church and Eastern European leaders
China breaks negotiations with Vietnam
Shah of Iran orders military takeover to control protests against his regime
United States ends three-year Turkish arms embargo

Soviet Union announces testing of neutron bomb as well as decision not to put it into production
Carter administration establishes diplomatic relations with Beijing and renounces mutual defense treaty with Taiwan

1979

Deng Xiaoping becomes first top-ranking Chinese Communist leader to visit the United States
Kampuchea National United Front takes Phnom Penh and six other provinces with help of 100,000 Vietnamese troops
Shah leaves Iran; Ayatollah Khomeini returns triumphant from exile
Soviets deploy ten thousand troops in disputed islands north of Japan
China invades Vietnam in retaliation for its intervention in Kampuchea
Israeli Prime Minister Begin and Egyptian President Sadat sign a formal peace treaty in Washington
China allows 1950 Soviet friendship treaty to expire
United States cuts aid to Pakistan to deter Pakistan's acquisition of nuclear weapons
Tanzanian forces end Idi Amin's eight-year rule in Uganda
European Community launches European Monetary System
Europeans vote in first direct election of 410-member European Parliament
Carter and Soviet President Brezhnev sign SALT II agreement in Vienna
Vietnam joins Comecon
Nicaraguan dictator Antonio Somoza resigns and Sandinista rebels come to power
Central Treaty Organization dissolved
Treaty on exploitation of moon's riches agreed to by UN Committee on Peaceful Uses of Outer Space
Brezhnev offers unilateral withdrawal of twenty thousand troops and one thousand tanks from East Germany
Carter announces decision to deploy MX missile system
Iranian students seize hostages in U.S. embassy in Teheran
United States freezes Iranian assets
NATO agrees to deploy 572 U.S. cruise and medium-range missiles in Western Europe
Second Lomé Convention between the European Community and ACP countries signed
Soviet troops enter Afghanistan, install Babrak Karmal as prime minister
Islamic fundamentalists seize Grand Mosque in Mecca
Panama Canal Act returns Canal Zone to Panamanian jurisdiction, leaving canal under U.S. administration through 1999

1980

Carter imposes economic sanctions on the Soviet Union for its invasion of Afghanistan
United States announces sale of $280 million in defensive arms to Taiwan
United States and China complete process of normalizing relations
Senate tables SALT II treaty in light of Soviet invasion of Afghanistan
Carter Doctrine pledges U.S. defense of Persian Gulf oil fields
United States obtains access to military facilities in Oman, Kenya, and Somalia
UN Security Council Resolution 465 censures Israel
Rhodesia becomes independent, renamed Zimbabwe
Carter breaks diplomatic relations with Iran

U.S. military operation to rescue hostages in Iran aborted; Secretary of State Cyrus Vance resigns in protest

Marshal Tito of Yugoslavia dies

European Community foreign ministers agree to sanctions against Iran

United States leads boycott of Moscow Olympics over Soviet presence in Afghanistan

Israel annexes East Jerusalem

Presidential Directive 59 gives Soviet military targets priority over cities in U.S. strategic warplan

Polish Solidarity workers' strike wins right to form independent unions

Soviet Union threatens military intervention to end Polish liberalization

Iraq invades Iran in controversy over Shatt al Arab waterway

Boatlift brings 125,000 Cuban refugees to the United States

Reagan elected president

"Gang of Four" trial opens in China as criticisms of Mao Tse-tung mount

United States rejects Brezhnev proposal for nonintervention in Persian Gulf

1981

Greece becomes the tenth member of the European Community

The European currency unit (ECU) replaces the European unit of account (EUA)

REAGAN ADMINISTRATION

Fifty-two American hostages released by Iran after 444 days in captivity

United States announces international terrorism will replace human rights as foreign policy priority

United States halts aid to Nicaragua

President Reagan wounded in assassination attempt

Nonaligned nations call for withdrawal of Soviet troops from Kampuchea and Afghanistan

Zimbabwe announces diplomatic ties with Soviets

Rightist coup fails in Spain

United States sends military advisers to El Salvador

United States lifts Soviet grain embargo

Socialist candidate François Mitterand becomes president of France

Pope John Paul II wounded in assassination attempt

United States casts sole vote against a World Health Organization (WHO) proposal to limit sale of infant formula in Third World

Israeli jets destroy Iraq's nearly completed nuclear reactor

United States and China announce joint monitoring of Soviet missile development from China

Saudi Arabia proposes peace plan that names East Jerusalem as capital of independent Palestinian state

U.S. Navy jets shoot down two Libyan fighters over Mediterranean Sea

At UN, Secretary of State Alexander Haig berates Soviet's international behavior

China makes peace overture to Taiwan, is rebuffed

Egyptian President Sadat assassinated

Commonwealth nations decry the superpowers' slide from détente to confrontation

Twenty-two-nation Cancún summit on North-South relations convenes

Ninety-three nonaligned nations issue a report describing the United States as the only threat to world peace and prosperity

Reagan's remark that nuclear war could be limited to Europe unleashes storm of protests

Congress approves sale of airborne warning and control systems (AWACs) to Saudi Arabia

Polish government imposes martial law; United States retaliates with economic sanctions against Poland and the Soviet Union

1982

United States offers "zero-option" arms control proposal

Reagan announces United States will resume development of chemical weapons

Caribbean Basin Initiative announced

UN approves Law of the Sea Treaty, United States announces it will not sign

British Falkland Islands are captured by Argentine forces; Reagan pledges U.S. support for Great Britain

British land troops on the Falkland Islands, Argentine forces surrender

Nicaragua signs $166 million aid agreement with the Soviet Union

United States condemns alleged Soviet and Cuban-backed military buildup in Nicaragua

Brezhnev announces temporary freeze on deployment of Soviet SS-20 missiles

United States accuses Soviet Union of widespread use of chemical warfare agents

Morocco agrees to U.S. use of Moroccan air bases during emergencies in the Middle East

Spain becomes sixteenth member of NATO

Israel invades Lebanon and surrounds the PLO by laying seige to West Beirut

United States suspends comprehensive test ban negotiations

Japan announces plans to increase military spending

United States embargoes sale of equipment for natural gas pipeline between Siberia and Western Europe; European Community protests U.S. ban

Marines land in Lebanon as part of multinational peace-keeping force

United States assists Mexico with a multibillion dollar debt relief plan

Defense Department papers advocating a "winnable" nuclear war strategy cause outrage in Europe

Lebanese President Bashir Gemayel assassinated

Lebanese Christian forces massacre hundreds in Palestinian refugee camps

Polish government bans the Solidarity union; United States suspends Poland's most-favored-nation trade status in retaliation

Soviet President Leonid Brezhnev dies; Yuri Andropov becomes Communist party general secretary

Indira Gandhi asks the Soviet Union for assistance in building several nuclear power stations

1983

United States and Honduras hold joint war games in Central America

Reagan's Strategic Defense Initiative (SDI—"Star Wars") proposal seeks to render nuclear weapons "impotent and obsolete"

International Monetary Fund (IMF) lending capability increased substantially

Soviet Union proposes a nuclear free zone in Central Europe

Pope John Paul II meets with General Jaruzelski and Solidarity union leader Lech Walesa in Poland

Reagan endorses Central American peace efforts of the Contadora Group (Mexico, Colombia, Panama, and Venezuela)

United States and France assist Chad and the Sudan following Libyan attack on Chad

Philippine opposition leader Benigno Aquino assassinated on return to Manila from the United States
Soviet Union shoots down a Korean passenger plane after it strays into Soviet airspace
Truck-bomb attack in Beirut kills 241 U.S. military personnel
United States invades Grenada
Raul Alfonsin elected president of Argentina, ending eight years of military rule
PLO forces are evacuated from Lebanon to several Middle Eastern nations
Syria downs two U.S. jets during a U.S. raid on Syrian positions
West Germany deploys U.S. Pershing II missiles

1984

Rev. Jesse Jackson secures release of Navy pilot downed by Syria
Terrorists assassinate president of American University of Beirut
Pakistani scientist claims Pakistan can produce nuclear weapons
William Buckley, CIA station chief in Beirut, is kidnapped
U.S. Marines in Beirut withdraw to offshore ships
Soviet leader Andropov dies; Chernenko assumes power
CIA assists *contras* in mining the main Nicaraguan port
Reagan meets with Deng Xiaoping in China, signs agreements on economic and technological relations
Seven major industrialized countries issue a declaration on East-West relations and arms control at London summit
Soviet Union and several Soviet allies refuse to participate in the summer Olympic Games in Los Angeles
Indian army attacks Sikh holy shrine, killing Sikh leader Jarnail Bhindranwale and hundreds of others
Britain and China reach agreement on the future of Hong Kong
International banks agree to reschedule Mexico's debt obligations
Congress bans direct or indirect military aid to the *contras*
Prime Minister Indira Gandhi of India assassinated by Sikh bodyguards
Reagan is reelected

1985

United States launches first space shuttle for exclusively military purposes
PLO leader Yasser Arafat and Jordan's King Hussein agree on framework for peace
Soviet leader Chernenko dies; Gorbachev becomes Communist party general secretary
United States and Soviet Union begin comprehensive arms control negotiations
Eighty Asian and African countries convene in Bandung
Israel withdraws from Lebanon
Terry A. Anderson of the Associated Press is kidnapped in Beirut
Reagan visits Bitburg cemetery where Nazi soldiers are buried, provoking protests by Jewish leaders and others
Reagan announces the United States will continue to honor the unratified SALT II treaty
Gorbachev proposes a ban on nuclear weapons by 2000
Radio Marti begins broadcasts to Cuba; Castro breaks a U.S.-Cuba immigration pact and threatens to end his cooperation on hijackings in protest
Shi'ite Muslims hijack TWA airliner
South African President P.W. Botha declares state of emergency
Reagan approves shipment of arms to Iran

United States and China sign a nuclear cooperation agreement

Reagan and Gorbachev meet in Geneva to discuss arms control and the future of U.S.-Soviet relations

Palestinians hijack Italian cruise liner *Achille Lauro*

U.S. Navy fighter planes force Egyptian airliner carrying four fleeing Palestinian hijackers to land in Sicily

Yasser Arafat renounces terrorist acts outside Israeli-occupied territories

Reagan authorizes covert CIA assistance to *contras*

Ireland and Britain sign treaty giving Ireland role in Northern Ireland

Terrorists attack holiday travelers on the Israeli airline El Al at Rome and Vienna airports

1986

United States withdraws from UNESCO

Reagan authorizes arms shipments to Iran in an effort to win release of American hostages

Spain and Portugal join the European Community

U.S. space shuttle *Challenger* explodes seventy-four seconds after liftoff

President-for-life Haitian Jean-Claude Duvalier abdicates and flees

Philippine President Marcos flees to Hawaii, Corazon Aquino becomes new president

Senate approves treaty outlawing genocide thirty-seven years after it was first sent to the Senate by Truman

United States orders the Soviet Union to cut its UN staff in New York by a third

Reagan orders a military attack against Libya in retaliation for its alleged sponsorship of state terrorism

United States sends five hundred TOW precision-guided anti-tank missiles to Israel for shipment to Iran

OPEC nations condemn U.S. bombing of Libya but reject new oil embargo

Soviet nuclear reactor at Chernobyl explodes, emitting radiation over Western Europe

Kurt Waldheim, former UN secretary-general, accused of complicity in World War II atrocities as Nazi officer

United States condemns South Africa's attacks on border states

New Zealand withdraws from the ANZUS defense pact

World Court rules against United States in Nicaraguan case; United States ignores decision

South Korean students demonstrate against president Chun Doo Hwan

U.S. military joins Bolivia in war on international drug trafficking

Reagan administration reaffirms South African policy of "constructive engagement"; Bishop Desmond Tutu condemns the United States

East-West security pact grants signatories right to observe troop maneuvers in any European state

Summit of nonaligned nations held in Zimbabwe

GATT nations meet in Uruguay to plan new round of global trade negotiations

Reagan administration leaks "disinformation" about Libya to journalists; Assistant Secretary of State Bernard Kalb resigns in protest

Plane carrying arms to the *contras* as part of National Security Council supply operation shot down over Nicaragua; Eugene Hasenfus captured

Reagan and Gorbachev meet in Reykjavik, discuss strategic and intermediate-range nuclear weapons and the possible elimination of all nuclear forces

General Motors and IBM announce suspension of operations in South Africa

Northern Mariana Islands become U.S. commonwealth, ending status as UN trust territories administered by the United States

Saboteurs sink Icelandic whaling ship to protest Iceland's violation of international ban on whaling

Attorney General Edwin Meese reveals diversion of money from Iranian arms sales to the *contras*

United States exceeds SALT II treaty limits with deployment of B-52 bomber equipped to carry cruise missiles

Demonstrations by Chinese students calling for democratic reforms spread

United States and India reach tentative accord on export of supercomputer

Soviet Union ends internal exile of Soviet dissident and Nobel Peace Prize winner Andrei D. Sakharov

United States increases import duties on some European Community products in response to high Spanish tariffs on U.S. feed grains; EC pledges to retaliate

1987

Iran launches major offensive against Iraq

United States lifts ban on export of oil drilling equipment to Soviet Union

Reagan administration announces intention to sell $2.2 billion in military equipment to Egypt, Saudi Arabia, and Bahrain

Soviet Union resumes nuclear testing because of U.S. refusal to join its moratorium begun in August 1985

United States, Canada, Japan, and European Space Agency announce intention to operate jointly a space station in the mid-1990s

Brazil suspends interest payments on its foreign debt

Finance ministers of the leading industrial powers meeting at the Louvre in Paris agree to stabilize the U.S. dollar

Mexico signs agreement with its creditor banks for massive loan

Turkey suspends agreement with United States for leasing after Congress cuts military aid to Turkey

United States offers naval protection to Kuwaiti oil tankers

United States and Soviet Union agree to establish centers for information exchange on missile tests and military activities

United States reveals illegal exports to the Soviet Union by Japanese and Norwegian firm enabled the Soviet Union to develop quieter submarines

United States launches massive Central American military exercise with Honduras

USS Stark struck by missiles fired by an Iraqi fighter in the Persian Gulf

New Zealand Parliament bans nuclear-armed and nuclear-powered ships from New Zealand's ports

Afghan rebels reportedly down a Soviet transport plane with U.S. supplied Stinger missile

Reagan administration announces it will cut off all aid to Panama as opposition to government of Panamanian military ruler General Manuel Noriega grows

President Jayewardene of Sri Lanka and Prime Minister Rajiv Gandhi of India sign agreement to end rebellion of Sri Lankan Tamil minority

Reagan offers peace proposal to Nicaragua in cooperation with House Speaker Jim Wright

Western nations send minesweepers to Persian Gulf

Soviet Union confirms deployment of SS-24 missile, first to be launched from railroad cars

Defense Department approves testing of ground-based, space-based, and ground-launched components of SDI system

Costa Rican President Oscar Arias Sanchez awarded Nobel Peace Prize for his Central America peace efforts

Soviet Union agrees to repay all of its $245 million debt to the United Nations

U.S. stock market crashes; markets plummet worldwide

United States delays sale of high-technology equipment to China in retaliation for sale of Chinese Silkworm missiles to Iran

United States supplies Chad with Stinger missiles for its war with Libya

Spain announces it will not renew its bilateral defense agreement with the United States

UN Security Council condemns South African entry into Angola to combat Angolan and Cuban troops

Reagan and Gorbachev sign intermediate-range nuclear forces (INF) treaty during Washington summit

UN passes resolution ''strongly deploring'' Israel's reaction to Palestinian violence in the West Bank and Gaza strip

1988

United States and Canada sign free-trade agreement

Noriega indicted by federal grand juries in Florida on racketeering and drug trafficking charges

Nicaraguan President Daniel Ortega agrees to negotiate with the Nicaraguan resistance

United States announces intention to end special trade privileges granted Hong Kong, Singapore, South Korea, and Taiwan

Gorbachev announces Soviet Union will withdraw its troops from Afghanistan

India tests surface-to-surface missile

Secretary of State Shultz arrives in Jerusalem to revive Arab-Israeli peace prospects

United States announces Romania's loss of most-favored-nation trade status

United States sends 3,200 troops to Honduras amid charges of border crossings by Nicaraguan soldiers

Nicaragua and the *contras* agree to a truce and to reconvene peace talks

Finance ministers of the Group of Seven pledge to support the U.S. dollar

Pakistan tests surface-to-surface missile

The right-wing National Republican Alliance (ARENA) gains control of the legislative assembly in El Salvador

Reagan criticizes Soviet human rights practices during Moscow summit

Worldwide conference of acquired immune deficiency syndrome (AIDS) researchers held in Stockholm

Agreement to permit commercial mining of Antarctica signed by thirty-nine nations; strict environmental guidelines included

Tibet's exiled Dalai Lama proposes China grant Tibet autonomy but retain control of its external affairs

U.S. cruiser *Vincennes* shoots down an Iranian commercial jetliner over the Persian Gulf; all 290 aboard are killed

Saudi Arabia agrees to buy between $12 and $30 billion worth of military equipment from Britain

Iran and Iraq accept UN peace terms calling for a cease-fire

Polish police and protesters clash on occasion of the eighth anniversary of the founding of the Solidarity labor movement

Soviet and American scientists meet at Nevada test site for first joint nuclear test

North and South Korea open talks in Panmunjom in anticipation of joint session of their parliaments

Turkey opens its borders to thousands of Kurds fleeing Iraqi advance against Kurdish rebels amid claims Iraq used poisonous gas

United States releases funds to pay UN dues; authorizes payment of back debt

World Bank agrees to lend Argentina $1.25 billion without agreement between Argentina and the IMF for domestic restructuring program

Generals Augusto Pinochet in Chile and Alfredo Stoessner in Paraguay fall from power

Gorbachev becomes new Soviet president, confirms hold on power

United States and the Philippines agree to extend U.S. access to military facilities at Subic Bay and Clark Air Force Base

Bush elected president

United States denies visa to PLO leader Yasser Arafat seeking to address UN on Palestine; General Assembly deplores U.S. action and moves Palestine debate to Geneva

Soviet parliament, the Supreme Soviet, convenes in Moscow and approves sweeping constitutional changes

Gorbachev addresses UN, announces plan to sharply reduce Soviet military forces in Europe

Angola, Cuba, and South Africa sign agreement providing for Namibian independence and withdrawal of Cuban troops from Angola

International Court of Justice agrees to hear Nicaraguan suit against Honduras for harboring *contras*

India and Pakistan agree not to attack each other's nuclear power installations

1989

European Community bans some cattle imports; U.S. retaliates

U.S. fighters down two Libyan jets over Mediterranean Sea

BUSH ADMINISTRATION

North African common market, the Arab Maghred Union, created

Bush attends funeral of Japanese Emperor Hirohito

Conventional Forces in Europe (CFE) talks begin, replace unsuccessful Mutual and Balanced Force Reduction talks

International conference on the ozone layer convenes in London; European Community agrees to ban production of chlorofluorocarbons

Treasury Secretary Nicholas F. Brady announces Third World debt reduction plan

Ayatollah Khomeini calls on Muslims to execute Salman Rushdie, author of *The Satanic Verses*

Gorbachev rejects ''exporting revolution'' while on visit to Cuba

Israeli Prime Minister Yitzhak Shamir reveals plans during U.S. visit for elections in occupied territories as part of peace proposal

Brazilian President José Sarney reveals plan to develop and protect the Amazon region

Agreement reached in Warsaw to legalize Solidarity and open way to free elections in Poland for the first time in forty years

United States and Japan reach agreement on coproduction of FSX fighter plane

Hungary cuts down the barbed-wire fence separating it from Austria

United States denounces elections in Panama as fraud

Kenya calls for worldwide ban on trade in ivory to save the elephant from extinction

Gorbachev visits China in first Sino-Soviet summit in thirty years

Bush declares it is time to "move beyond the Cold War" and containment

India tests ballistic missile

Arab League meets to discuss Palestinian uprisings in Israeli-occupied territories and situation in Lebanon, calls for international conference on Palestine

United States opens way for retaliation by charging Brazil, India, and Japan engage in unfair trade practices

At fortieth anniversary NATO Summit in Brussels Bush presents plan for conventional force reductions in Europe

Chinese troops begin all-out assault on Tiananmen Square pro-democracy demonstrators, hundreds massacred

United States announces sanctions against China, including suspension of military sales

Negotiations on strategic and space weapons resume in Geneva

South Africa tests ballistic missile

Warsaw Pact communique declares "there are no universal models of socialism"

Japan announces $43 billion aid program

Gorbachev tells summit of Western industrial powers the Soviet Union seeks integration in the world economy

Austria applies for membership in the European Community

Agreement reached on reducing Mexican debt under the Brady Plan

Israeli commandos capture spiritual leader of Hezbollah militia, precipitate crisis involving Americans held hostage in Lebanon

Cuban and South Africa withdraw forces from Angola

Solidarity assumes power in Poland as the first noncommunist government in Eastern Europe

African heads of state meet in Zaire to discuss Angolan civil war

Bush proposes U.S. and Soviet reduction of chemical weapons stockpiles

Thousands of East Germans seek new lives in West Germany; use newly opened Hungarian borders as route to the West

Secretary of State James A. Baker and Soviet Foreign Minister Eduard Shevardnadze meet; Soviets offer to "delink" space-based defense from strategic arms talks

Vietnam's final troop withdrawal from Cambodia leads to heightened civil war and return of Khmer Rouge

Hungary's Communist party becomes the Hungarian Socialist Party; hardline party chief Karoly Grosz is ousted

Thousands demonstrate in Leipzig, East Germany, against East German government

Shevardnadze concedes Soviet radar installation at Krasnoyarsk violates 1972 AMB Treaty

Gorbachev declares the Brezhnev doctrine "dead," pledges not to interfere in Eastern Europe upheaval

United States and Soviet Union sponsor UN resolution calling for improved UN effectiveness in maintaining peace

UN Security Council approves UN Observer Force for Central America

East Germany opens its borders to the west; thousands cross the Berlin Wall unopposed

Iran-Iraq war ends

Bulgarian leader Todor Zhivkov is ousted after thirty-five years in power

Elections held in Namibia; South West African People's Organization (SWAPO) captures majority of seats in constituent assembly

Parliaments in Czechoslovakia and Hungary remove constitutional provisions guaranteeing Communist party a "leading role" in society

Philippine rebels attempt coup; United States supports Aquino government with military show of force

Gorbachev meets with Pope John Paul II at the Vatican

Bush and Gorbachev meet at Malta to discuss trade and arms reductions

Entire East German Politburo and Central Committee resign

Warsaw Pact discusses future of alliance; Bulgaria, Hungary, East Germany, Poland, and the Soviet Union condemn their own intervention in 1968 to crush Czechoslovakia's reform movement

French President Mitterrand warns West Germany not to pursue German unification in way that would upset the European balance of power

Lithuania abolishes the constitutional guarantee of Communist party supremacy

Iraq tests ballistic missile

European Community leaders announce support for the unification of Germany but maintain other European borders must remain intact

National security adviser Brent Scowcroft arrives in Beijing in a surprise visit; discloses earlier visit following the Tiananmen Square massacre

Cuban President Fidel Castro pledges to uphold socialism, fight global domination by United States alleged to have been made possible by the demise of communist rule in Eastern Europe

First noncommunist government in forty-one years assumes power in Czechoslovakia

Tibet's Dalai Lama accepts Nobel Peace Prize; remains committed to nonviolence in seeking end to China's forty-year occupation of Tibet

Presidents of Central American countries meet in regional peace summit, call for end to U.S. aid to *contras* and demobilization of rebels in El Salvador

War against narcotics traffickers and cocaine warlords escalates in Colombia

Noriega named chief of government; Panamanian assembly declares a "state of war" exists with the United States

Soviet Union and European Community sign ten-year trade agreement

Shevardnadze makes historic visit to NATO headquarters in Belgium

United States invades Panama

United States administration approves export of satellites expected to be launched by China, lifts restrictions on aid to companies doing business in China

Romanian soldiers and citizens overthrow government of Ceausescu, who is tried and executed

OAS, by a vote of 20–1, "deeply deplores" U.S. invasion of Panama

Soviet Congress of People's Deputies condemns 1939 Nazi-Soviet nonaggression pact and secret protocols dividing Europe into spheres of influence

1990

Noriega claims to be political prisoner, refuses to enter plea in Miami court on drug charges

Gorbachev ends objection to multiple political parties in the Soviet Union

Soviet Union military quells fighting between Soviet Armenians and Azerbaijanis

Government of Yugoslavia announces intention to end constitutionally guaranteed role of Communist party

Military government in Haiti declares a state of seige

Soviet Union announces willingness to withdraw all of its troops from Eastern Europe in exchange for U.S. and allied withdrawal from Western Europe

Bush calls in State of Union address for sharp cuts in U.S. and Soviet combat forces in Europe

Bulgarian communist government resigns

South Africa lifts ban on African National Congress and other anti-*apartheid* groups

Gorbachev signals acceptance of German unification

Bush calls for balancing economic and environmental issues at international conference on global warming

Baker makes unprecedented appearance before the International Affairs Committee of the Supreme Soviet

Bush reiterates support for Strategic Defense Initiate (SDI)

Hungary follows Poland to become second Eastern European nation to reestablish diplomatic ties with the Vatican

Nelson Mandela freed by South African government after twenty-seven years in prison

"Open skies" conferences between NATO and Warsaw Pact nations opens in Ottawa

U.S. and Soviet negotiators begin talks on normalizing trade

Violence breaks out in Soviet republic of Tadzhikistan

Agreement reached to unite Germany; two-stage process outlined

United States and Soviet Union agree to troop cuts in Europe

Secretary of Defense Dick Cheney pledges unequivocal U.S. support of South Korea

Bush meets in Cartagena, Colombia, with presidents of Bolivia, Colombia, and Peru to deal with drug trade

African National Congress announces willingness to meet with South African government to discuss end to three-decade guerrilla war against *apartheid*

Czechoslovakian President Vaclav Havel visits United States

Cheney announces plans to reduce U.S. troops in Asia

Violeta Barrios de Chamorro defects Sandinista President Ortega, ends decade of leftist rule in Nicaragua

United States promises to lift sanctions against Nicaragua and provide aid to new government

Soviet Union begins withdrawing troops from Czechoslovakia

U.S.-Japanese negotiations seek to reduce conflict over trade, other economic issues

Israel accepts U.S. proposal for involving Palestinians in preliminary peace talks with Israel

Haitian military ruler Lt. Gen. Posper Avril steps down; Ertha Pascal-Trouillot chosen as first women president

Israel blames U.S. for upsetting peace efforts with comments on status of Jerusalem

Lithuania declares independence from the Soviet Union

Soviet Union agrees to withdraw troops from Hungary

Gorbachev granted a more powerful Western-style presidency by Soviet Congress of People's Deputies

Fernando Collor de Mello becomes Brazil's first popularly elected president in twenty-nine years

Gorbachev warns Lithuania to end revolt

Libyan leader Qaddafi denies U.S. charge that Libya is making chemical weapons

OPEC ministers agree on oil production quotas

U.S. orders Nicaraguan *contras* to disband

East Germany holds first free elections; coalition favoring quick unification victorious

Namibia, Africa's last colony, becomes independent; ends seventy-five years of South African rule

Colombian presidential candidate Bernardo Jaramillo slain; Medellin drug cartel believed responsible

Cuba jams South Florida radio stations in battle over proposed U.S. TV Marti

Hungarians hold first free elections after forty-three years of Communist rule

Five arrested in London in alleged plot to smuggle U.S.-made nuclear weapons triggers to Iraq

Estonia's Communist party votes to split with Moscow

Iraq admits stockpiling nerve gas; threatens to use gas against Israel

Bomb believed set by Sikh radicals kills thirty-three in India during Hindu celebration

East Germany's first freely elected parliament declares the nation a democracy

Nepalese security forces attack pro-democracy demonstrators in Katmandu

Latvian Communist Party Congress refuses to declare the party independent of Moscow

China launches a U.S.-made telecommunications satellite with its own rocket

U.S. cancels trade mission to Iraq as Congress considers sanctions legislation

Libyan-backed Palestinian group headed by Abu Nidal releases three European hostages; France denies it paid Libya ransom of three warplanes for release of hostages

Bush administration rejects appeals to recognize Lithuania as independent nation

East German parliament embraces quick unification with West Germany

Bush promises "appropriate response" if Moscow imposes cuts in fuel supplies to Lithuania

U.S. announces it will not rejoin UNESCO

American hostage Robert Polhill is released by Shiite Moslem militants in Beirut after 1,182 days in captivity

U.S. delays sanctions on Soviet Union for its crackdown on Lithuania

Japan removed from list of countries with unfair trade barriers against American products

European Community adopts plan for political union by 1993

Poland seeks guarantees Germany will not reclaim former German land, now part of Poland

India, cited by U.S. for unfair trade practices, refuses to negotiate trade treaty under threat

President F.W. de Klerk and African National Congress leader Nelson Mandela begin historic talks on ending white-minority rule in South Africa

U.S. agrees to ease restrictions on high-technology exports to the Soviet Union

U.S. drops plans to upgrade battlefield nuclear weapons in Europe; Bush reaffirms role of nuclear weapons in Europe

U.S. "open skies" proposal stalls in East-West talks

Baltic states revive pre-World War II alliance and forge united front on separatist policies toward Soviet Union

Bush calls for volunteer crops to help build a democratic Eastern Europe

Communist rebels in the Philippines warn U.S. to "go home" as negotiations on future of U.S. bases begin

U.S. presidential commission urges "preemptive or retaliatory military strikes" in response to terrorism in the air

U.S. troops take over patrol of border between Panama and Colombia

Romanians vote in nation's first free elections in more than 50 years

U.S. renews most-favored-nation trade status for China

Bush and Gorbachev sign chemical weapons accord approve outlines of treaty to cut strategic weapons during Washington summit; sign chemical weapons accord

U.S. ships move toward African coast as rebel troops threaten Liberian capital

PLO leader Yasser Arafat denounces U.S. veto of UN resolution urging deployment of UN forces to Israeli-occupied territories

Bush signs U.S.-Soviet trade agreement that refuses Soviet request for most-favored-nation trade status

U.S. and Iran settle $600 million oil company claim

U.S. announces support of international fund to help developing nations end use of ozone-depleting chemicals

Gorbachev agrees to permit a reunited Germany to remain in NATO, pledges to remove 380,000 Soviet troops from East Germany within the next four years

U.S. breaks off dialogue with PLO in retaliation for guerrilla raid on Israel's coast

East and West Germany approve treaty to merge economies; Checkpoint Charlie on Berlin Wall removed

Mandela cheered at UN; criticizes U.S. aid to noncommunist guerrillas in Angola; defends use of violence to free South Africa from white-minority rule; asks for "material resources" from U.S. to end apartheid

U.S. and Japan agree to drastic measures to cut U.S. trade deficit with Japan

Lithuanian parliament agrees to 100-day moratorium on its declaration of independence; Soviets lift embargo of Lithuania

East and West Germany join economies

NATO foreign ministers agree to end rivalry with Warsaw Pact; U.S. pushes policy of "last resort" for use of nuclear weapons in Europe

Iraq threatens Kuwait with military attack to force compliance with OPEC oil production quotas

European companies agree to sell Brazil the technology to build an intercontinental ballistic missile

Albanians win right to flee their hard-line Communist homeland

Western leaders conclude economic summit with pledge to aid the Soviet economy if Soviet military spending and aid to Communist regimes is reduced

Polish legislature approves privatization of state enterprises

Gorbachev ends Communist party monopoly of the press

United States ends recognition of rebels fighting Vietnam-backed Cambodian government

Liberian rebels overrun most of Monrovia; U.S. military attache expelled by Liberian president

Iraqi troops pull back from Kuwaiti border in anticipation of talks over disputed lands, oil production

Cuba charges the U.S. with systematic campaign to destabilize Cuba

Foreign Ministers of the Association of South East Asian Nations (ASEAN) convene in Jakarta, announce steps to strengthen political and economic ties

Iraqi President Saddam Hussein reiterates military threats against OPEC nations pumping too much oil

Black Moslem rebels attempt coup in Trinidad, later free Prime Minister Arthur N. R. Robinson and surrender

Iraq invades Kuwait, overthrows Kuwaiti government

U.S. blocks all commerce with Iraq

Tamil militants massacre over a hundred people in Sri Lankan Mosques

Marines rescue sixty-two Americans from Liberia, secure U.S. embassy

Bush reportedly authorizes covert action to topple Iraqi President Saddam Hussein

UN Security Council orders worldwide embargo on trade with Iraq

African National Congress announces suspension of all armed actions against the white-minority government of South Africa

U.S. troops dispatched to Persian Gulf region; U.S. mobilizes multi-nation defense of Saudi Arabia that includes Arab military forces

Iraq refuses foreign nationals permission to leave Kuwait and Iraq

Pro-democracy political rally in Zambia calls for end to two-decade single-party rule

Soviet Union joins U.S. in backing UN Security Council resolution calling for enforcement of embargo of Iraq

U.S. expels Iraqi diplomats

Multinational African military force takes control of Liberian capital

Bush and Gorbachev meet in Helsinki summit spawned by Persian Gulf crisis

Cambodian factions agree to peace plan, UN supervision

World War II victors sign historic treaty giving sanction to German unification

Iraq threatens terrorist attacks on U.S. targets, raids diplomatic compounds in Kuwait

West Germany and Soviet Union sign landmark friendship treaty

IMF accelerates supply of funds to Third World nations harmed by oil price hikes

UN Security Council orders an air embargo against Iraq

East and West Germany unite

France gives asylum to Lebanese Christian strongman Michel Aoun

Israel blasts unanimous UN Security Council resolution condemning Israel for Palestinians' deaths

Gorbachev named winner of 1990 Nobel Peace Prize

United States announces plan to send up to 100,000 additional troops to Saudi Arabia; figure later revised to 200,000

Iraq releases French hostages

Congressional leaders caution Bush against Persian Gulf war

Israelis reject UN proposal for increased protection of Arabs under Israel occupation

Soviet Union and Germany sign nonaggression pact

Socialist leader Chandra Shekhar named new Indian prime minister

UN Convention Against Illicit Traffic in Narcotic Drugs and Psychotropic Substances takes effects, ends safe havens for drug lords

Emperor Akihoto ascends to Japan's throne as new monarch

Summit of thirty-four nation Conference on Security and Cooperation in Europe marks end of the Cold War; landmark treaty on Conventional Forces in Europe eliminates thousands of non-nuclear weapons

Iraq announces plans to send 250,000 additional troops to Kuwait

British Prime Minister Margaret Thatcher resigns, ends tenure as Europe's longest-serving prime minister in twentieth century

Bush charges Iraq with effort to acquire nuclear arms

John Major elected British prime minister

Bush promises Mexican President Carlos Salinas de Gortari to seek U.S.-Mexican free-trade agreement

UN Security Council authorizes use of force against Iraq

Bulgarian government falls, marks true end of communism in country

Bush announces diplomatic initiative to send Baker to Iraq

Iraq fires surface-to-surface missile in first test since invasion of Kuwait

Kohl's Christian Democrat and Christian Social Union coalition wins first free all-German elections since 1932

Iraq announces hostages are free to leave country

Bush visits Chile during Latin American trip in first U.S. presidential visit in thirty years

Uruguay Round of GATT trade negotiations collapses

President Hissene Habre of Chad overthrown by Idriss Deby; United States evacuates former Libyan prisoners from Chad

Oliver Tambom, president of the African National Congress, returns to South Africa after thirty-year exile

Lech Walesa elected in Poland's first popular presidential vote

United States announces forthcoming Soviety-American summit, grants credit for Soviet purchase of food

European Community plans move toward European currency, pledges aid to Soviet Union, eases sanctions on South Africa

Shevardnadze resigns as Soviet Foreign Minister, cites impending dictatorship

United States joins in unanimous UN Security Council resolution condemning Israel

Slovenia votes to secede from Yugoslavia

United States denounces military coup that topples democratically elected government of Suriname

Hundreds of Albanians flee to Greece

Index